Fodor's

GREEK
ISLANDS

3rd Edition

Fodor's Travel Publications   New York, Toronto, London, Sydney, Auckland

www.fodors.com

FODOR'S GREEK ISLANDS
Editor: Robert I. C. Fisher

Editorial Contributors: Alexia Amvrazi, Stephen Brewer, Elizabeth Carson, Jeffrey Carson, Angelike Contis, Natasha Giannousi, Donald Steven Olson, Kim Trathen, Adrian Vrettos

Production Editor: Evangelos Vasilakis
Maps & Illustrations: Mark Stroud and Henry Colomb, Moon Street Cartography; David Lindroth; Inc., William Wu;, *cartographers;* Bob Blake, Rebecca Baer, *map editors;* William Wu, *information graphics*
Design: Fabrizio La Rocca, *creative director;* Guido Caroti, *art director;* Tina Malaney, Nora Rosansky, Chie Ushio, *designers;* Melanie Marin, *associate director of photography*
Cover Photo: (Mykonos): Bill Heinsohn/Alamy
Production Manager: Angela L. McLean

3rd Edition

ISBN 978-0-307-92845-0

ISSN 1940-3291

SPECIAL SALES
This book is available at special discounts for bulk purchases for sales promotions or premiums. Special editions, including personalized covers, excerpts of existing books, and corporate imprints, can be created in large quantities for special needs. For more information, write to Special Markets/Premium Sales, 1745 Broadway, MD 3-2, New York, NY 10019, or e-mail specialmarkets@randomhouse.com.

AN IMPORTANT TIP & AN INVITATION
Although all prices, opening times, and other details in this book are based on information supplied to us at press time, changes occur all the time in the travel world, and Fodor's cannot accept responsibility for facts that become outdated or for inadvertent errors or omissions. So **always confirm information when it matters,** especially if you're making a detour to visit a specific place. Your experiences—positive and negative— matter to us. If we have missed or misstated something, **please write to us.** Share your opinion instantly through our online feedback center at fodors.com/contact-us.

PRINTED IN COLOMBIA

10 9 8 7 6 5 4 3 2 1

CONTENTS

Fodor's Features

ABOUT THIS BOOK

Our Ratings

At Fodor's, we spend considerable time choosing the best places in a destination so you don't have to. By default, anything we recommend in this book is worth visiting. But some sights, properties, and experiences are so great that we've recognized them with additional accolades. Orange **Fodor's Choice** stars indicate our top recommendations; black stars highlight places we deem **Highly Recommended;** and **Best Bets** call attention to top properties in various categories. Disagree with any of our choices? Care to nominate a new place? Visit our feedback center at ⊕ *www.fodors.com/feedback*.

Hotels

Hotels have private bath, phone, TV, and air-conditioning, and do not offer meals unless we specify that in the review. We always list facilities but not whether you'll be charged an extra fee to use them.

> For expanded hotel reviews, visit **Fodors.com**

Restaurants

Unless we state otherwise, restaurants are open for lunch and dinner daily. We mention dress only when there's a specific requirement and reservations only when they're essential or not accepted—it's always best to book ahead.

Credit Cards

We assume that restaurants and hotels accept credit cards. If not, we'll note it in the review.

Budget Well

Hotel and restaurant price categories from ¢ to $$$$ are defined in the opening pages of the respective chapters. For attractions, we always give standard adult admission fees; reductions are usually available for children, students, and senior citizens.

Listings		Hotels & Restaurants	Outdoors
★ Fodor's Choice	⊘ E-mail	🏨 Hotel	⛳ Golf
★ Highly recommended	🎟 Admission fee	🛏 Number of rooms	⛺ Camping
⊠ Physical address	⊙ Open/closed times	⚲ Facilities	**Other**
⊹ Directions or Map coordinates	Ⓜ Metro stations	⏍ Meal plans	☺ Family-friendly
⌂ Mailing address	⊟ No credit cards	✕ Restaurant	⇨ See also
☏ Telephone		⟁ Reservations	⊠ Branch address
⊟ Fax		⚲ Dress code	☞ Take note
⊕ On the Web		⚲ Smoking	

Experience
Greece

WHAT'S NEW

Giving Those "Worry Beads" A Workout

It doesn't take someone with a job on the Athens Stock Exchange to tell you that times are tough in the cradle of democracy—but don't be spooked by the headlines. No, the Acropolis isn't for sale, and yes, all the natural beauty and updated tourism and cultural sites are still open. Life goes on—in colorful Greek style—and having fun is of more national importance than ever.

With gloomy economic news a fixture on front pages, Greece faces a long period of reconstruction. But it is a proud country, with a glorious past and a long and winding road to restoring balance. So, just as Greeks cringe at making international headlines for all the wrong reasons, while witnessing their paychecks shrinking, they have fallen back on several survival mechanisms, with that timeless unit of Greek society—the family—coming to the rescue, thanks to hearth and home (with generations living together and vacations now at Aunt Athena's seaside villa). There's an expression in Greece: "Poverty requires you have a good time." Greeks are trying to keep their spirits up by doing just that—today, you'll delightfully discover, they will still await new travellers with a smile and a comforting glass of ouzo and a plate of *mezedes*. Greeks also know the secret of amusing themselves with little or no money. "They are," said one admirer, "the enchanters of themselves." You can see this in their timeless singing, dancing, and now, their political discussions.

Instead of visiting France, many Greeks will va-cay in Athens, home, since it opened two years ago, to the biggest "must see" spot in town: the New Acropolis Museum, with what's not in it generating as much interest as what is on display at the museum. For decades, Greece has demanded that the lion's share of the Parthenon Marbles be repatriated from the British Museum to Athens. From its inception, Greece made no secret that the new museum's raison d'etre would be creating a state-of-the-art home for the marble frieze sculptures that British diplomat Lord Elgin removed from the Acropolis in 1803. The gallery is ready. Will the fabled Marbles ever be returned? Stay tuned.

A Modern Greek Tragedy?

With a scary 329 billion euro debt hanging over the country, everybody has become an economist in today's Greece. Talk of IMF/EU/ECB (European Central Bank) loan terms, credit ratings agencies, VAT tax changes and price hikes have spilled from breakfast tables to the modern Greek agora of the street, the café, the evening news, and even sometimes the beach. While many people will be happy to offer their take on the situation with you—usually blaming politicians for mismanagement and corruption in lengthy critiques—others may prefer to avoid the unpleasant pink elephant in the room, instead waving a hand in exasperation.

But if no two solutions are the same, and the country teetered on default as this publication went to press (Fall 2011), everyone is feeling The Crisis' belt-tightening. Most families have been hit by 16.5% unemployment levels, with major cuts in salaries and benefits for the country's many public workers and pensions for the growing body of state pensioners, while new and unwelcome taxes churn out—it seems every week—for real estate owners, private sector employees, and even the struggling self-employed. In retrospect,

policies of the past thirty years look not only decadent but downright toxic—with the generous public handouts of successive governments, an inability to curb the expansive black market, poor tax collection, price hikes after the introduction of the euro, and the costly buildup to the Athens 2004 Olympic Games all taking their fair share of the blame.

In 2011, the Greeks are facing their third consecutive year of economic contraction and the future doesn't look too bright either. Widespread expectations of more austerity measures are leading to a further shrinkage of the economy, lower tax revenues, and the imposition of even more taxes to increase state revenue.

It is a vicious circle, many people fear, that hinders development and economic growth. One can almost begin to understand all the frustration and its ultimate outcome, the city riots.

Daily life is impacted in many ways: schools can't afford textbooks, hospitals are closing down, ministries are occupied by disgruntled workers, and the welfare state seems to be crumbling. Feeble economic prospects, higher rates of unemployment, deteriorating government services, and a lower standard of living are already leading to lower birth rates, emigration, and unrest.

Home Is Where the Heart Is

Having survived many rough times in the past, Greeks have turned to their tried-and-true survival mechanisms. For one, the family unit remains fiercely intact. Never has it made more sense to have three generations living in the same home or apartment building, swapping childcare for extra attention to cash-strapped pensioners.

Those who can't afford to go on summer holidays are welcome to stay at friends and family' summer houses by the sea. Many Greeks still have a strong connection to their home village—and never have hearty, healthy goodies from the countryside, such as fruit or olive oil, come in so handy.

In today's Greece, big purchases or long-term investments, such as buying a car or a house, or taking exotic trips abroad, are out.

Making the most of local bargains, gathering with friends at home or at inexpensive cafés/neighborhood taverns, and making the most of the country's abundant charming local scenery is in. The Greek islands and the beautiful mountainous regions of central Greece continue to attract locals, and foreign visitors alike.

This is good news for at least one sector of the Greek economy—tourism. While "for sale" signs are visible on businesses throughout the country and "for rent" signs dominate everywhere, a record number of 16.5 million foreign visitors were predicted by the Association of Greek Tourism Enterprises (SETE) for 2011, up over 10% from the previous years.

In an effort to welcome visitors from abroad, there are often slashed rates for accommodations and other major travel expenses (so don't hesitate to look for bargains and special offers when booking your stay), while the prices of a coffee and local travel expenses have not shown any downward movements.

Happily, you will find that the beauty of the country and the warm heart of the people remain intact despite the hardships.

WHAT'S WHERE

Numbers refer to chapters.

3 Athens. The capital has greeted the new millennium with new swaths of parkland, a sleek subway, and other spiffy and long-overdue municipal makeovers. But for 5 million Athenians and their 15 million annual visitors, it's still the tried-and-true pleasures that put the spin on urban life here: sitting in an endless parade of cafés, strolling the streets of the Plaka and other old neighborhoods, and, most of all, admiring the glorious remnants of one of the greatest civilizations the West ever produced, such as the Acropolis, the Agora, and the Theater of Herodes Atticus.

4 The Saronic Gulf Islands. When Athenians want a break, they often make a quick crossing to the idyllic islands of the Saronic Gulf. You're well advised to follow suit, and all the better if your island of choice is Hydra, where what's here (stone houses set above a gorgeously festive harbor) and what's not (cars) provide a relaxing retreat. Aegina is noted for its medieval Palaiachora (Old Town) and magnificent Temple of Aphaia; while Spetses has a time-burnished town hiding treasures like Bouboulina's House.

5 The Sporades. Island hopping the northern Sporades, strung from Mt. Pelion to the center of the Aegean, delivers quintessential Greek-island pleasures: boat journeys, pretty harbors, villages spilling down hillsides like giant sugar cubes, Byzantine monasteries, and silent paths, cobbled in the last millennium, where the tinkle of goat bells may be the only sound for miles. Weekenders don't make it far beyond Skiathos, but Skopelos has great beaches, and Skyros is washed by some of the clearest waters in Greece.

6 Corfu. Temperate, multihued Corfu—of emerald mountains; turquoise waters lapping rocky coves; ocher and pink buildings; shimmering silver olive leaves; puffed red, yellow, and orange parasails; scarlet roses, bougainvillea, lavender wisteria, and jacaranda spread over cottages—could have inspired impressionism. The island has a history equally as colorful, reflecting the commingling of Corinthians, Romans, Goths, Normans, Venetians, French, Russians, and British. First stop, of course, is Corfu town—looking for all the world like a stage set for a Verdi opera.

ALBANIA

Ioannina

6 Corfu Town

CORFU

PAXI

Preveza

KEFALLONIA

Adriatic Sea

Zakinthos

ZAKINTHOS

WHAT'S WHERE

7 The Cyclades. The ultimate Mediterranean archipelago, the Cyclades easily conjure up the magical words of "Greek islands." Santorini, with its picturesque caldera, is the most unapologetically romantic; Mykonos, with its sexy jet-set lifestyle, takes the prize for hedonism. Mountainous Folegandros, verdant Naxos, idyllic Sifnos, church-studded Tinos, and Antiparos—Tom Hanks' summer residence of preference—have their own distinct charms, and all center on ancient Delos, birthplace of Apollo.

8 Crete. Crete is the southernmost and largest island, and the claims to superlatives don't stop there. Here, too, are some of Greece's tallest mountains, its deepest gorge, many of its best beaches, and a wealth of man-made wonders—the copious remains of Minoans, Romans, Byzantines, Turks, and Venetians. The Palace of Knossos is the incomparable monument of ancient Minoan culture. If these charms don't cast a spell, the island's upland plateaus, remote seaside hamlets, and quiet mountain villages will.

9 Rhodes and the Dodecanese. Wrapped enticingly around the shores of Turkey, the Dodecanese ("Twelve Islands") are the easternmost holdings of Greece. Their key position in the sea-lanes of Asia Minor have attracted some notable visitors. St. John the Divine received his Revelations on Patmos, Hippocrates established a healing center on Kos, and the Crusader Knights of St. John lavished their wealth on palaces in Rhodes. The recent legacy of legions of vacationers on Rhodes and Kos is glitzy resort life, but on Symi, and some of the other isles, life seems to be unfazed by outsiders.

10 Northern Aegean Islands. Each of these green and gold islands is distinct: Though ravaged by fire, Chios retains an eerie beauty and fortified villages, old mansions, Byzantine monasteries, and stenciled-wall houses. Lesbos, Greece's third-largest island and birthplace of legendary artists and writers, is dense with gnarled olive groves and dappled with mineral springs. Lush, mountainous Samos, land of wine and honey, whispers of the classical wonders of antiquity.

Larissa

Volos

Elios

SK

Lamia

Galaxidi

Khalkis

Gulf of Corinth

Megara

Korinthos

Temple of Aphaia

Nafplion

Portocheli

HYDRA

Sparti

Kalamata

KITHIRA

MEDITERRANEAN SEA

GREEK ISLANDS PLANNER

Drive Defensively

You've probably considered all the pluses. Driving makes it easier to reach remote ruins, find the perfect slip of a beach, see the countryside.

Car rental fees are not exorbitant in Greece, on par with those in North America, and gasoline, while expensive by U.S. standards, is comparable to prices in Western Europe.

But are you really ready to tackle Greek roads? Greece has one of the highest accident rates in Europe, a dubious distinction shared with Ireland and Portugal, and after a few minutes on the road it's pretty easy to see why.

Accounting for the perils, not surprisingly, are bad roads (often narrow, poorly surfaced, and full of hairpin turns and blind corners) and bad, reckless drivers (who speed and are often aggressive behind the wheel).

In some places you can add stubborn, won't-get-out-of-the-road livestock and slowpoke farm vehicles to the watch-out-fors. You'll have more cautions to add to this list with each passing milepost. Be sure to heed them.

It's Greek to Me

Though it's a byword for incomprehensible ("It was all Greek to me," says Casca in Shakespeare's *Julius Caesar*), much of the difficulty of the Greek language lies in its different alphabet. Not all the 24 Greek letters have precise English equivalents, and there is usually more than one way to spell a Greek word in English. For instance, the letter delta sounds like the English letters "dh," and the sound of the letter gamma may be transliterated as a "g," "gh," or "y." Because of this the Greek for Holy Trinity might appear in English as Agia Triada, Aghia Triada, or Ayia Triada.

In most cities and tourist areas, all Greeks know at least one foreign language. It's best to use close-ended queries, however; if you ask, "Where is Galissas?" a possible answer will be "Down a ways to the left and then you turn right by the baker's house, his child lives in Chicago, where did you say you went to school?"If you only have 15 minutes to learn Greek, memorize the following: *yiá sou* (hello/good-bye, informal for one person); *yiá sas* (hello/good-bye, formal for one person and used for a group); *miláte angliká?* (do you speak English?); *den katalavéno* (I don't understand); *parakaló* (please/you're welcome); *signómi* (excuse me); *efharistó* (thank you); *ne* (yes); *óhee* (no); *pósso?* (How much?); *pou eéne . . . ?* (Where is . . . ?), . . . *ee twaléta?* (. . . the toilet?), . . . *to tahidromío?* (. . . the post office?), . . . *o stathmós?* (. . . the station?); *kali méra* (good morning), *kali spéra* (good evening); *kali níhta* (good night).

What to Pack

Outside Athens, Greek dress tends to be middle of the road—you won't see torn jeans or extremely expensive suits, though locals tend to dress up for nightclubs. In summer bring lightweight, casual clothing and good walking shoes. A light sweater or jacket, or a shawl, is a must for cool evenings. There's no need for rain gear in high summer, but don't forget sunglasses and a sun hat. Be prepared for cooler weather and some rain in spring and fall. Remember to dress conservatively when visiting churches or monasteries.

1

Don't Miss the Boat

Greece's extensive boat system—ranging from ferries to catamarans and hydrofoils, known as *iptamena delphinia* ("flying dolphins")—provides the best way to get to and from the Greek islands. Individual lines have Web sites (⇨ *Boat Travel sections in each regional chapter of this guide*), but in the absence of centralized listings it's difficult to compare schedules and prices. Travel agencies often sell tickets for just one line.

What to do? The GNTO office in Athens provides lists of sailings from Piraeus, along with Merchant Marine Ministry (⊕ *www.yen.gr*), the weekly newspaper Athens News, and the English edition of Kathimerini of the International Herald Tribune. Our Boat Travel chapter sections also detail scheduled sailings. Greek Travel Pages is a great Web portal (⊕ *www.gtp.gr*).

Buy tickets from a travel agency, from the local shipping agency office, online through travel Web sites (the most reliable is ⊕ *www.greekferries.gr*), or direct from ferry companies. Boat timetables change in winter and summer. Boats may be delayed by weather conditions, especially when the northern winds called *meltemia* hit in August, so stay flexible—one advantage of not buying a ticket in advance.

Greece's largest port is Piraeus, which lies 10 km (6 mi) south of downtown Athens. From Piraeus port, the quickest way to get into Athens, if you are traveling light, is to walk to the metro station and take a 25-minute ride on the electric train to Monastiraki, Thisseion, Omonia, or Syntagma. Be aware that Piraeus port is so vast that you may need to walk some distance or take a public bus, or even use a port minibus (gratis) from the port entrance. Every day dozens of vessels depart for the Saronic Gulf islands, the Cyclades, the Dodecanese, and Crete. Patras, on the Peloponnese, is the main port for ferries to Italy and to Corfu. Boats for the Sporades depart from Agios Konstantinos and Volos on the mainland.

When choosing a ferry, take into account the number of stops and the arrival time: sometimes a ferry that leaves an hour later gets you there faster! Catamarans and hydrofoils are pricier and you need to reserve in advance in summer but they cut travel time in half. Remember if the sea is choppy, sailings are often cancelled. The main line is Hellenic Seaways (☎ *210/419–9000* ⊕ *www. hellenicseaways.gr*).

When Less Is Not More . . .

Though Greece is becoming more liberal socially, old standards still prevail, especially among the middle-aged and elderly. Some Western habits can cause offense, and the big no-no's include:

Showing public displays of affection. Greeks hug, stroll arm and arm, kiss each cheek in greeting, but an amorous smooch or wandering hand will raise eyebrows in rural villages.

Baring it all. Nudity is common on Greek beaches, but it's a question of where you decide to drop trou—this is usually appropriate only at the far ends of a strand, away from the areas where families congregate. Topless sunbathing is permissible, especially on the more cosmopolitan islands, but again, discretion is advised.

Showing legs and arms. Appendages, especially female, should be well covered when entering monasteries and churches. An attendant will usually be waiting near the entrance to drape the underclad in cloaks or skirtlike garments. Women might want to bring along a wrap or large scarf for such occasions.

To decipher the complexity of Greek culture, read *Exploring the Greek Mosaic*, by Benjamin Broome (1996), for insights into Greece's social landscape still valuable today.

ISLAND FINDER

Not sure which Greek island is your kind of paradise? Use this chart to compare how each island measures up to your vacation dreams.

	Aegina	Hydra	Spetses	Corfu	Skiathos	Skopelos	Skyros	Crete
Tops for Hotels	○	●	◐	◐	●	◐	◐	●
Tops for Beauty	○	●	◐	●	●	●	●	●
Tops for Food	◐	●	○	◐	●	◐	◐	●
White-Cube Houses	○	○	○	○	○	○	○	○
Charming Harbors	○	●	●	◐	◐	●	●	●
Deserted Beaches	●	◐	○	○	○	●	◐	●
Beaches for Activities	●	○	◐	◐	●	◐	○	●
Gorgeous Beaches	●	○	◐	◐	◐	●	◐	●
Authentically Greek	○	●	◐	○	◐	●	●	●
Picturesque Villages	○	●	◐	◐	○	◐	●	●
Archaeological Sites	●	◐	○	○	○	○	○	●
Medieval and Byzantine Sites	◐	●	○	○	◐	◐	◐	●
Good for Families	●	○	◐	●	◐	●	◐	●
For Partygoers	○	◐	◐	◐	○	○		◐
Folkloric Shopping	○	●	◐	○	○	◐	●	●
Historic Homes/Museums	○	●	◐	◐	◐	◐	●	●
Crowds	○	●	◐	●	●	◐	○	●
Postcard Churches	◐	●	○	○	◐	●	◐	◐
For Romantics	○	●	◐	◐	○	●	●	○
Good Bus System	●	○	○	◐	◐	◐	◐	●
Good Walks	◐	●	○	○	◐	●	◐	◐
Natural Wonders	◐	●	○	○	○	◐	◐	◐
Blue Sea Vistas	●	◐	○	●	◐	●	●	●
For Culture Lovers	◐	●	◐	◐	○	◐	◐	◐

KEY: ○ few or none ◐ moderate ● noteworthy

Mykonos	Tinos	Naxos	Paros	Santorini	Folegandros	Sifnos	Rhodes	Symi	Kos	Patmos	Lesbos	Chios	Samos
●	◐	◐	◐	●	○	◐	◐	○	◐	◐	◐	◐	●
◐	●	●	◐	●	◐	◐	◐	●	◐	●	●	●	●
●	○	◐	◐	●	○	○	○	○	○	◐	●	●	◐
●	●	◐	◐	●	●	●	○	○	○	○	○	○	○
●	○	◐	◐	○	○	◐	○	●	○	○	○	○	●
◐	◐	●	●	○	◐	◐	◐	●	◐	●	◐	◐	◐
●	○	◐	◐	○	○	○	●	○	●	◐	◐	◐	●
●	◐	●	●	◐	◐	◐	◐	◐	◐	●	●	●	●
○	●	◐	◐	○	●	●	◐	●	○	●	●	●	●
●	●	●	◐	●	●	●	◐	◐	○	◐	◐	●	●
●	◐	●	◐	●	○	○	◐	○	◐	○	◐	◐	●
○	●	◐	●	◐	○	◐	◐	◐	○	●	●	●	●
◐	◐	●	●	○	○	◐	●	◐	●	◐	●	●	●
●	○	◐	●	◐	○	◐	◐	○	●	○	●	○	●
●	●	◐	◐	◐	○	○	◐	◐	◐	◐	○	◐	◐
◐	◐	●	◐	●	○	◐	●	◐	○	○	●	●	◐
●	●	◐	◐	●	○	◐	●	○	●	○	○	○	◐
●	●	●	●	◐	◐	◐	◐	●	◐	●	◐	●	●
●	◐	●	●	●	○	●	○	●	○	●	◐	●	●
●	◐	●	●	◐	◐	◐	●	○	●	◐	◐	◐	◐
○	◐	●	●	●	○	◐	◐	●	◐	●	●	●	●
○	●	●	◐	●	◐	◐	◐	●	◐	●	●	●	●
◐	●	●	◐	●	◐	◐	●	●	●	●	◐	◐	●
●	○	◐	●	◐	○	○	◐	○	◐	◐	●	●	●

GREECE TODAY

Eurozone in Trouble

With the largest public debt and one of the largest budget deficits in the EU, since 2009 Greece has been at the epicenter of global finance's attention. Today, being part of the EU, and of the Eurozone in particular, is proving more crucial for the future of the country than ever before. The good news is that, in May 2010, Eurozone countries agreed on a multi-billion-dollar aid package to help Greece fight its crippling debt and deficit burden.

Realizing that the fates of Greece and the rest of the Eurozone countries are closely intertwined, this much-needed support has also seen an EU task force arrive in Athens, with the aim of helping Greece overhaul its tax system, reduce its bloated public sector bureaucracy, and adhere to the austerity conditions of its bailout deal.

The EU is not alone in its rescue efforts; joined by the IMF and the ECB, they now form the so-called troika of foreign lenders. On a daily basis Greeks monitor the EU, European Central Bank, and IMF officials molding their fate more closely than their traditional future-revealing coffee grinds. In turn, global markets anxiously eye the small Mediterranean country, extrapolating from each movement there volumes regarding their fears of contagion and risks to the euro.

Since 2009 an increasingly stringent set of cuts and taxes have been implemented by the ruling Greek socialist government, which came to power after a surprise early election vowing to resolve the ever-deepening economic crisis and uneasy relationships with its neighbors. Socialist PASOK party head George Papandreou currently faces a behemoth task. With some delays in the implementation of measures and a level of social resistance

not to be ignored—as we went to press in Fall 2011 riots had once again broken out in Athens—things might take a turn for the worse before they get better. The fact remains that Greece faces a long way to economic recovery, even with the help of its Eurozone partners.

Refined Greek Tastes That Travel

Around long enough to be more than a trend. . . . Shoppers will delight at the boom in elegantly-packaged and increasingly eco-friendly Greek foodstuffs, wine, and cosmetics—and even furniture and fashion. Happily, many of these can be found not only at Greek supermarkets, pharmacies, and airport duty-free shops—but also, increasingly, in the United States, too. It may be a tradition with ancient roots (literally) but olive oil and olive products—staples of the Mediterranean diet—are being bottled by select estates throughout the country in gift packaging, with organic or specially flavored products making their way into homes around the world.

Pure olive-oil soap remains a firm favorite. In addition, regional cooperatives and family-run businesses alike have excelled in recent years in baking sweet and savory baked goods to die for, using olive oil as a key ingredient while updating Grandma's recipes.

Greek wine has made nothing short of a renaissance in the 1990s, and, according to some experts, the crisis will weed out those who just rode on the fad—establishing those with staying power—be it from Santorini, the Peloponnese's Nemea, or northern Greece. Several cosmetics companies have also made a name for themselves worldwide—with products drawing from Greece's abundant botanical offerings (mastic gum-infused skin-care lines

are absolutely to die for). Though harder to lug around on your flight, at least one ecologically and socially minded home furnishing company, Xanthi-based Coco-Mat, has made a name for itself with ecological mattresses in recent years, while the Greek ceramics trade is undergoing a big revival, with hand-painted salad bowls being coveted by design aficionados.

Greek fashion designers such as Angelos Bratis and Hara Lebessi are making a name for themselves internationally, while funky or more classical-style jewelry made in Greece is sold all over the world. Word-of-mouth, innovative ideas, and tasteful branding (think neutral hues, straw ribbons, and pure white) make these Hellenic luxury exports increasingly necessary for people around the world—which is great news for a Greece in economic crisis.

People

You don't have to be a sociologist to note some pretty stellar qualities of the Greek character. For one thing, even amidst these times of crisis, Greeks are warm-hearted, outgoing, assertive and generous, even to the tourists who besiege them—they will often offer a plate of cookies or a bottle of home-brewed *raki*, just to establish a level of comfort.

If you are late catching the boat from the island and can't find a taxi, they will willingly drive you to the port and refuse any mention of the word "tip." They are family-oriented, to say the least—it's still common for men and women to live with their parents until they marry.

Greek men might swagger around in what outwardly can seem to be a male-dominated society, but women run the home, often take a partnership role in family businesses, and—now that the Greek birthrate is one of the lowest in the EU, freeing women to pursue careers—are an increasing presence in the white-collar workplace.

As for children, Greeks spoil them rotten: among other privileges, kids can wander freely around restaurants, play safely in many squares, and stay up late (it's not unusual to see a family enjoying a round of ice cream around midnight).

Real Estate Opportunities

It's a good thing Greeks are optimistic by nature, as the economic news is not particularly sunny. However, even in times of economic fragility, there are still business opportunities for the taking.

It wasn't too long ago that a Greek village was, well, Greek. If there were any outsiders, they were transplants from the other side of the island. But now that EU membership has made it easier for residents of other countries to buy property in Greece, properties that have been in Greek families for generations are suddenly vacation getaways for Klaus and Gudrun and Colin and Priscilla.

It's common to hear grumbling that the foreigners are snapping up property that's the birthright of Greeks, but no one seems to be complaining about the new influx of cash the newcomers are pouring into local economies or even the rejuvenation of dying villages that had been fatally hurt by the massive urbanization wave of the past 50 years.

And what's best for prospective buyers, more than ever before, right now the price is right. Real estate selling and rent prices are falling in Greece at the moment, so this is the time to buy!

GREEK ISLANDS
TOP ATTRACTIONS

The Acropolis

(A) The great emblem of classical Greece has loomed above Athens (whose harbor of Piraeus is gateway to all the Greek islands) for 2,500 years. Even from afar, the sight of the Parthenon—the great marble temple that the 5th-century BC statesman Pericles conceived to crown the site—stirs strong feelings about the achievements and failings of Western civilization.

Corfu

(B) Three-quarters of a million visitors a year answer the call of the island that inspired the landscapes of Shakespeare's *The Tempest*. Historically, these admirers are in good company—Normans, Venetians, Turks, Napoléon Bonaparte, and the British have all occupied Corfu, leaving fortresses, seaside villas, and an unforgettable patina of cosmopolitan elegance.

Hydra

(C) This barren island, a hop and skip away from Athens, is home to one of Greece's most picturesque ports, immortalized in all its Hollywoodian splendor when Sophia Loren emerged from its waters in the 1960 film *Boy on a Dolphin*. Today, sophisticated travelers head here to enjoy the 19th-century merchant's mansions and the white-and-periwinkle cafés.

Knossos

(D) Crete will introduce you to the marvels of the Minoans, the first great European civilization that flourished around 1500 BC. First stop is Knossos, the massive palace complex of King Minos, then it's on to the nearby archaeological museum in Heraklion, where the playful frescoes that once lined the royal chambers show just how urbane these early forbearers were.

Mykonos

(E) Backpackers and jet-setters alike share the beautiful beaches and the Dionysian nightlife—this island is not called the St-Tropez of the Aegean without reason—but the old ways of life continue undisturbed in fishing ports and along mazelike town streets. Not only are the hotels and cafés picture-perfect, the famous windmills actually seem to be posing for your camera.

Old Rhodes Town

(F) The famed Colossus of Rhodes may have toppled, but the sturdy walls and palaces the Knights of St. John built in the wake of the Crusades have fared better. Protected as a UNESCO World Heritage Site, this remarkable medieval assemblage bespeaks of the vast wealth of the knights, who for all their might lost their fiefdom to the 300 Ottoman ships of Süleyman the Magnificent in 1522.

Patmos

(G) The relics, ornate icons, silver artifacts, and rich vestments on view at the medieval monastery of St. John the Theologian are among the great cultural treasures of the Orthodox church. The well-educated monks had the buildings decorated with fine sculptures and other artwork. Unfortunately, only men are allowed to visit.

Santorini

(H) One of the world's most picturesque islands cradles the sunken caldera of a volcano that last erupted around 1600 BC. To merely link the phenomenon to the Atlantis myth and the Minoan collapse misses the point—what matters is the ravishing sight of the multicolor cliffs rising 1,100 feet out of sparkling blue waters, a visual treat that makes the heart skip a beat or two especially at sunset.

QUINTESSENTIAL GREEK ISLANDS

The Greek Spirit

"Come back tomorrow night. We're always here at this time," is the gracious invitation that usually terminates the first meeting with your outgoing Greek hosts.

The Greeks are open, generous, affectionate, and above all, full of a frank, probing curiosity about you, the foreigner. They do not have a word for standoffishness, and their approach is direct: American? British? Where are you staying? Are you married or single? How much do you make? Thus, with the subtlety of an atomic icebreaker, the Greeks get to know you, and you get to know them.

In many villages there seems to always be at least one English-speaking person for whom it is a matter of national pride and honor to welcome you and, perhaps, insist on lending you his only mule to scale a particular mountain, then offer a tasty dinner meal.

This is the typically Greek, deeply moving hospitality, which money cannot buy and for which, of course, no money could be offered in payment.

Worry Beads

Chances are that your host—no doubt, luxuriantly moustached—will greet you as he counts the beads of what appears to be amber rosaries.

They are *komboloia* or "worry beads," a legacy from the Turks, and Greeks click them on land, on the sea, in the air to ward off that insupportable silence that threatens to reign whenever conversation lags. Shepherds do it, cops do it, merchants in their shops do it.

More aesthetic than thumb-twiddling, less expensive than smoking, this Queeg-like obsession indicates a tactile sensuousness, characteristic of a people who have produced some of the Western world's greatest sculpture.

If you want to get a sense of Greek culture and indulge in some of its plea-sures, start by familiarizing yourself with the rituals of daily life. These are a few highlights—things you can take part in with relative ease.

Siestas

When does Greece slow down? In Athens, it seems never. But head out to the coun-tryside villages, especially in the summer, and you can find another tradition, the siesta—the only time Greeks stop talking and really sleep, it seems.

Usually after lunch and until 4–5 pm, barmen drowse over their bars, waiters fall asleep in chairs, and all good Greeks drift off into slumber wherever they are, like the enchanted courtiers of Sleeping Beauty. Then, with a yawn, a sip of coffee, and a large glass of ice water, Greece goes back to the business of the day.

Folk Music and Dance

It's a rare traveler to Greece who does not encounter Greek song and folk dancing, sure to be vigorous, colorful, spontane-ous, and authentic. The dances are often rooted in history or religion, or both: the *zeimbekiko,* a man's solo dance, is performed with a pantherlike grace and an air of mystical awe, the dancer, with eyes riveted to the floor, repeatedly bend-ing down to run his hand piously across the ground. The music, played by bou-zoukis, large mandolins, is weighted with melancholy.

The most popular, however, are the *kal-amatianos* and *tsamikos.* The former is performed in a circle, the leader waving a handkerchief, swirling and lunging acro-batically. The latter, more martial in spirit, represents men going to battle, all to the sound of cries of *opa!*

IF YOU LIKE

Ancient Splendors

The sight greets you time and again in Greece—a line of solid, sun-bleached masonry silhouetted against a clear blue sky. If you're lucky, a cypress waves gently to one side. What makes the scene all the more fulfilling is the realization that a kindred spirit looked up and saw the same temple or theater some 2,000 or more years ago. Temples, theaters, statues, a stray Doric column or two, the fragment of a Corinthian capital: these traces of the ancients are thick on the ground in Greece, from the more than 3,000-year-old **Minoan Palace of Knossos** on the island of Crete to such relatively "new" monuments as the **Parthenon.** You can prepare yourself by reading up on mythology, history, and Greek architecture, but get used to the fact that coming upon these magnificent remnants of ancient civilizations is likely to send a chill up your spine every time you see them.

Temple of Aphaia, near Aegina Town, Aegina. The ancients knew where to build: on a looming hill stands this spectacularly extant ruin of a great temple, with nearly 25 Doric columns standing.

Delos, off Mykonos, the Cyclades. Birthplace of Apollo, Delos is the sacred center around which the 29 Cyclades islands form a rough circle (*kyklos* in Greek). Extensive ruins include the famous Avenue of the Lions, where five archaic beasts (Naxian work of the 7th century) are symbolical guardians of the sanctuary.

Temple of Hera in Heraion, Samos, Northeast Aegean. The tyrant Polycrates built this temple where the Samians worshipped their patron goddess, Hera. Pythagoras, Aesop, and Anthony and Cleopatra all visited.

Majestic Monasteries

A legacy of the great Byzantine era, and often aligned with great historic churches of the Greek Orthodox Church, the monasteries of Greece seem as spiritual and as peaceful as when the land was strode by St. John. A religious mystique hangs over many of these island retreats, infusing them with a sense of calm that you will appreciate even more when escaping from party-central towns like Mykonos or overcrowded beaches. The natural beauty and calm of many of these places, many visitors find, heal your body and soul, revitalizing you for the rest of your trip.

Monastery of St. John the Theologian, Patmos. On the hill overlooking Hora is this retreat built to commemorate St. John in the 11th century—not far away is the cave where he wrote the text of *Revelation,* near the Monastery of the Apocalypse.

Nea Moni, Chios, the Northern Aegean Islands. The island of Chios has an array of stunningly perched monasteries, including this one, whose interior blazes with color, marble slabs, and mosaics of Christ's life. Built by an 11th-century emperor, it has a rare octagonal Katholikon church.

Monastery of Taxiarchis Michael Panormitis, Symi, the Dodecanese. Dedicated to Symi's patron saint, the protector of sailors, this magnificently frescoed monastery—landmarked by its elaborate bell tower—makes a great day trip from Symi but why not make a night of it by booking one of its sixty guest rooms?

Evangelistria, Skiathos, the Sporades. Sitting on Skiathos's highest point, not far from the town of Lalaria, is this late-18th-century jewel, looming above a gorge and set with a magnificent church with three domes.

Natural Wonders

Some countries have serene pastures and unobtrusive lakes, environments beautiful in a subtle way. Not Greece. Its landscapes seem put on Earth to astound outright, and often the intertwined history and spiritual culture are equally powerful. This vibrant modern nation is a land of majestic mountains whose slopes housed the ancient gods long before they nestled Byzantine monasteries or ski resorts. The country's sapphire-rimmed islands served as a cradle of great civilizations before they became playgrounds for sailors and beach lovers. If there are no temples to the ancient gods on many of the mountains on the Greek islands, the looming summits that seem to reach into the heavens, impressive from any perspective, inspired the Greeks to worship natural forces. Many islands have ancient goat and donkey trails that are sublime hikes; prime walking months are April, May, and September, when temperatures are reasonable, wildflowers seem to cover every surface, and birds are on their migratory wing.

Samaria Gorge, Hania, Crete. From Omalos, a zigzag path descends steeply 2,500 feet into the tremendous Samaria gorge that splits the cliffs here for 13 km (8 mi) down to Ayia Roumeli on the Libyan Sea. Catch views of the Cretan *kri-kri* goat near the famous "Iron Gates" stone passageway.

The flooded caldera, Santorini, the Cyclades. What may be the most beautiful settlements in the Cyclades straddle the wondrous crescent of cliffs, striated in black, pink, brown, white, and pale green, rising 1,100 feet over the haunting, wine-color Aegean Sea.

The Most Beautiful Towns and Villages

Historic, simple, famous, nondescript, or perfectly preserved: almost any Greek village seems to possess that certain balance of charm and mystique that takes your breath away. The sight of mirage-like, white clusters of houses appearing alongside blue waters or tumbling down cliffs and hillsides is one of the top allures of any trip here. Villages are awash in cubical, whitewashed houses—often built atop one another along mazelike streets (designed to confound invaders). Add in distinctive architectural landmarks—a Byzantine cathedral, a Venetian 16th-century *kastro* (or fortress), and monasteries that seem sculpted of zabaglione custard—and these villages and towns often look like unframed paintings.

Rethymnon, Crete. A Venetian *fortessa* rests on a hill above this city, where cobblestone alleyways squirm their way through Turkish and Italianate houses. Bypass the newer parts of town to stroll through the Venetian harbor, packed solid with atmospheric cafés and shops.

Ia, Santorini, the Cyclades. Here is where you can find the cubical white houses you've dreamed of, and a sunset that is unsurpassed.

Hydra, the Saronic Gulf Islands. The chicoscenti steal away to this harbor beauty, set with crumbling 19th-century merchant's mansions, joyously festive waterside cafés, art galleries, and some Hollywood pixie dust (Sophia Loren filmed *Boy on a Dolphin* here).

Corfu town, Corfu. A little beauty of a city, Corfu town retains evocative traces of its Venetian, French, and British occupiers. It is a grand gateway to one of the greenest and perhaps prettiest islands in all Greece.

LIVING LIKE THE GODS: TOP HOTELS

The new, post-Olympic, EU Greece with its boutique hotels, luxury villas, sybaritic spas, and sophisticated nightlife overturns most of the Zorba-era conceptions of "Spartan" Greece. The days of the bare cottage, the creaky apartment, and the shabby motel have come and gone. Of course, many travelers still want hotels that deliver on the simple—or rather, simpler—life.

These chosen Greek getaways may lack worldly amenities but compensate with other luxuries—an abundance of sand and sea, perhaps, or stunning mountain views and other natural enhancements.

At these places, the greatest luxury is knowing you don't have to do anything except maybe notice how the water in the pool color-coordinates with the sky. But, today, Greece has also a much more stylish side, and not only in Mykonos and Santorini.

Some new Greek resort Xanadus would not only please the gods but might even make them blush a bit. Several such temples of hedonism, including the Elounda Mare and the Elounda Beach, are nestled on the Elounda peninsula on the coast of Crete. Others, such as the Princess on Skiathos, are set amid a flurry of resort action and nightlife.

At their skyward rates, you expect world-class service and accommodation, but the vibe also comes with an easygoing elegance that is distinctly Greek, plus amenities that set the gold standard. Satellite TV, Wi-Fi, gyms, bars, restaurants, lounges—all these are to be taken for granted at top resorts.

Some of the other amenities to expect include: your own villa or bungalow, swimming pool, and slip of beach or waterside terrace; a sumptuous marble bathroom with whirlpool, steam room, and/or sauna; a spa with treatment pools and a full range of services; tennis courts and golf courses; a full array of water sports like windsurfing, parasailing, snorkeling, and boating; and a helipad for those harried, overworked CEOs.

Although accommodations in Greece can vary from grand hotel to country house, all happily provide the quintessentially Greek quality of *filoxenia*, or welcome—easygoing, heartfelt hospitality.

Greek Chic

Aigialos, Santorini, the Cyclades. No need to venture out to view the jaw-dropping sunset over Santorini's caldera—a cluster of sumptuously restored 18th- to 19th-century village houses in Fira are the perfect perch.

Semeli, Mykonos. Traditional furnishings and elegant surroundings evoke the high Mykoniot style.

Marco Polo Mansion, Rhodes, the Dodecanese. Live like a pasha in a 15th-century Ottoman mansion fitted out with all the trappings—plush carpets, cushioned divans, and canopied beds.

Elounda Mare, Elounda, Eastern Crete. The first of the superluxe Greek resorts, this is Relais-&-Chateaux fabulous.

Tsitouras Hotel, Santorini, the Cyclades. Like stepping into the pages of *Architectural Digest*, this Firostefani redoubt has welcomed the likes of Nana Mouskouri and Jean-Paul Gaultier.

Corfu Palace, Corfu, Ionian Islands. Lush gardens, a sprawling pool, and a sea view from every room complement huge marble baths and elegant furnishings.

WHEN TO GO

The best time to visit Greece is late spring and early fall. In May and June the days are warm, even hot, but dry, and the seawater has been warmed by the sun. For sightseeing or hitting the beach, this is the time. Greece is relatively tourist free in spring, so if the beach and swimming aren't critical, April and early May are good; the local wildflowers are at their loveliest, too. Carnival, usually in February just before Lent, and Greek Easter are seasonal highlights. July and August (most locals vacation in August) are always busy—especially on the islands. If you visit during this peak, plan ahead and be prepared to fight the crowds. September and October are a good alternative to spring and early summer, especially in the cities where bars and cultural institutions reopen. Elsewhere, things begin to shut down in November. Transportation to the islands is limited in winter, and many hotels outside large cities are closed until April.

Climate

Greece has a typical Mediterranean climate: hot, dry summers and cool, wet winters. Chilliness and rain begin in November, the start of Greece's deceptive winters. Any given day may not be cold, and snow is uncommon in Athens and to the south except in the mountains. But the cold is persistent, and many places are not well heated. Spring and fall are perfect, with warm days and balmy evenings. In the south, a hot wind may blow across the Mediterranean from Africa. The average high and low temperatures for Athens and Heraklion and the average temperature for Thessaloniki are presented below.

Forecasts **National Observatory of Athens** ⊕ *www.noa.gr*. **Weather Channel Connection**

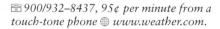 *900/932–8437, 95¢ per minute from a touch-tone phone* ⊕ *www.weather.com.*

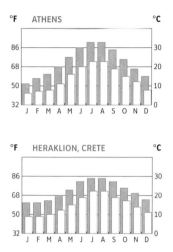

ISLAND-HOPPING: CYCLADES TO CRETE

There is no bad itinerary for the Greek islands. Whether you choose the Sporades, the Dodecanese, or any of those other getaways floating in the Aegean, the leading isles in Greece differ remarkably, and they are all beautiful. But the needle flies off the beauty-measuring gauge when it comes to the Cyclades. It might be possible to "see" any of these famous islands in a day: the "must-see" sights—monasteries or ancient temples—are often few. Still, it is best to take a slower pace and enjoy a sumptuous, idyllic, 14-day tour. Planning the details of this trip depends on your sense of inclusiveness, your restlessness, your energy, and your ability to accommodate changing boat schedules. Just be warned: the danger of sailing through the Cyclades is that you will never want to leave them. From these suggested landfalls, some of the most justly famous, you can set off to find other idyllic retreats on your own.

Days 1–2: Mykonos

Jewel of the Cyclades, this island manages to retain its seductive charm. Spend the first day and evening enjoying appealing Mykonos town, where a maze of beautiful streets is lined with shops, bars, restaurants, and discos; spend time on one of the splendid beaches; and, if you want to indulge in some hedonism, partake of the wild nightlife. The next morning take the local boat to nearby Delos for one of the great classical sites in the Aegean. Mykonos is one of the main transport hubs of the Greek islands, with many ferries, boats, and planes connecting to Athens and its port of Piraeus. ⇨ *Mykonos in Chapter 7.*

Days 3–4: Naxos

Sail south to Naxos—easily done in summer, harder in other seasons. Plan on arriving from Mykonos in the late afternoon or evening, and begin with a pre-dinner stroll around Naxos town, visiting the Portara (an ancient landmark), the castle, and other sights in the old quarter. The next morning, visit the Archaeological Museum; then drive through the island's mountainous center for spectacular views. Along the way, visit such sights as the Panayia Drosiani, a church near Moni noted for 7th-century frescoes; the marble-paved village of Apeiranthos; and the Temple of Demeter. If you have time, stop for a swim at one of the beaches facing Paros, say Mikri Vigla. ⇨ *Naxos in Chapter 7.*

Days 5–7: Paros

Go west, young man, to Paros, where the large spaces provide peace and quiet. Paros town has delights profane—buzzing bars—and sacred, such as the legendary Hundred Doors Church. But the highlight will be a meal in the impossibly pretty little fishing harbor of Naousa or, on a morning drive around the island, a visit to the lovely mountain village of Lefkes. Then spend an extra night of magic on the neighboring isle of Antiparos, where off-duty Hollywood celebs bliss out with all the white sands, pink bougainvillea, and blue seas. ⇨ *Paros in Chapter 7.*

Days 8–9: Folegandros

This smaller isle is not only beautiful but, rarer in these parts, authentic. It boasts one of the most stunning Chora towns; deliberately downplayed touristic development; several good beaches; quiet evenings; traditional local food; and respectful visitors. The high point, literally and figuratively, is the siting of the

main town—set on a towering cliff over the sea, its perch almost rivals that of Santorini. ⇨ *Folegandros in Chapter 7.*

Days 10–12: Santorini

Take a ferry from Folegandros south to the spectacle of all spectacles. Yes, in summer the crowds will remind you of the running of the bulls in Pamplona but even they won't stop you from gasping at the vistas, the seaside cliffs, and stunning Cycladic cubist architecture. Once you've settled in, have a sunset drink on a terrace overlooking the volcanic caldera. You can also find many view-providing watering holes in Fira, the capital, or Ia, Greece's most-photographed village. The next day, visit the Museum of Prehistoric Thera; then enjoy a third day just swimming one of the black-sand beaches at Kamari or Perissa. ⇨ *Santorini in Chapter 7.*

Days 13–14: Crete

Despite the attractions of sea and mountains, it is still the mystery surrounding Europe's first civilization and empire that draws many travelers to Crete. Like them, you can discover stunning testimony to the island's mysterious Minoan civilization, particularly at the legendary Palace of Knossos. Along these shores are blissful beaches as well as the enchanting Venetian-Turkish city of Hania.

BY PUBLIC TRANSPORTATION

■ High-speed catamarans have halved travel time between Piraeus and Santorini.

■ In summer, when ferries and boats run frequently, you should have little trouble moving from any of these islands to another.

■ All islands are served by air as well as by boat.

From Heraklion, Crete's main port, there are frequent flights and ferries back to Piraeus. Athens. and reality. ⇨ *Crete in Chapter 8.*

GREECE
THE GREAT BEACH QUEST

Computed by the acres of sun-tanned flesh exposed along 9,000 miles of shoreline, Greece's beaches are to Europeans what Florida's are to Americans. But there are so many SPFabulous beaches that choosing the right one is a task of almost Herculean proportions. To help you decide, here's a look at Greece's best—the most beautiful, the liveliest, the quietest, the most active, the best for kids, and others to suit every taste.

LIFE'S A BEACH

For us *xènos* (foreigners), Greek beaches are paradises around the corner—sandy playgrounds that live up to their promise of sun, sand, and azure seas. But from May through October, when seas are warm and sunshine can be taken for granted, the beach also becomes the center of Greek social life, an extension of the *platia* (square) or the *kafenion* (café). Let Americans seek out patches of sand as far from the crowds as possible; for the locals, the beach is another place to gather, gossip, catch up on local news, argue about politics, play a game of tavli, and keep an eye on the neighbors.

Happily, as the song says, the best things in life are free: all Greek beaches are freely accessible to the public—even if rented beach lounges line the sands, you can always find a place to plop down on a towel. And when night falls, the gear gets put away and the Versace sandals come out. At island hot-spots like Mykonos, Aegean style nightlife takes over. There, the dance-til-sunrise party scene ends with the promise that dawn will bring another flawless day on the beach.

LICENSE TO CHILL

But is every trip "a day at the beach"? No, not when the famed *meltemi*, the dry northwesterly winds, usually hit in August. These summer bummers can be both a curse and a blessing for beachgoers. Scorching temperatures drop when the winds pick up, but waters on north-facing beaches can become dangerous churns for swimmers and gusts kick sand into the faces of 90-pound weaklings and muscle men alike. Beachgoers in the know often make a beeline for south-facing strands, where the meltemi usually, but not always, packs a less powerful punch.

Lemonakia beach, Kokkari, Samos

SHORE TO PLEASE: GREECE'S BEST BEACHES

When Greece starts to sizzle, there's no better way to beat the heat than to hit the beach. So keep your cool and make a splash by savoring these top beaches— Greece has no greater liquid assets.

GOOD BEACHES FOR KIDS

Santa Maria, Paros, Cyclades Windsurfers love the winds here, and parents will welcome the warm, shallow waters and those beautiful dunes that are irresistible to the sandbox set.

Ayia Marina, Aegina, Saronic Gulf Shallow waters, paddle-boat rentals, and other amenities make this beach outside Aegina town especially popular with Athenian families.

Elafonisi, Crete Turquoise waters, pure-white sandbars, with a sea shallow enough to create a beautiful wading pool for youngsters. Young explorers love to wade across the "bathtub" to Elafonisi islet.

BEST PARTY BEACH SCENES

Super Paradise Beach and Paradise Beach, Mykonos, Cyclades Greece's celebrated party island lives up to its reputa-

Elafonisi, Crete

tion at a string of bars that line these soft sands, where an international crowd lingers until dawn.

Aegina town, Saronic Gulf Islands A party scene prevails at a parade of bars on the coast just outside of town, where a spectacular sunset kicks off a night of cocktails and notched-up music.

Skiathos town, Sporades For those who prefer drinking and dancing next to the sea, come evening the lively harbor front becomes a big party, one long row of hopping clubs and bars.

OUT-OF-THE-WAY BEACHES

Ayios Georgios, Rhodes, Dodecanese Shaded with heavenly scented cedars, this pristine strand is the loveliest beach on Rhodes and well worth the harrowing, four-wheel drive down a cypress-lined track.

Psili Amos, Patmos, Dodecanese A caïque ride or half-hour hike are the ways to reach the island's most beautiful stretch of sand.

Red Beach, Matala, Crete A beautiful hike from Matala allows you to plunge in the surf at this delightfully isolated strand. Nearby caves have sheltered everyone from prehistoric nomads to hippies.

Golden Beach, Paros

BEACHES WITH A PAST

Olous, Elounda Peninsula, Crete Strap on a snorkel mask, dive into the crystal clear waters, and regard the Roman settlement on the sandy seafloor—finds from this seafloor are on view at the nearby archaeological museum in Agios Nikolas.

Kommos Beach, Matala, Crete This mile-plus-long strand of golden sand is justifiably popular with sunbathers, who would be humbled to know ancient Minoans once inhabited this now-being-excavated spot.

PRIME SPOTS FOR WATER SPORTS

Chrissi Akti (Golden Beach), Paros, Cyclades The long stretch of golden sand is Greece's windsurfing capital, hosting the International Windsurfing World Cup every August.

Vai, Crete

Paradise Beach, Mykonos, Cyclades
Mykonos is considered to be the diving center of the Aegean, and Mykonos Diving Center is the place for serious instruction and rewarding dives.

Paleokastritsa, Corfu
This stretch of sand-rimmed coves and seaside grottoes rewards divers and snorkelers with crystal clear waters. Korfu Diving and other outfitters provide all the necessary equipment for underwater fun.

THE MOST BEAUTIFUL BEACHES
Plaka, Naxos, Cyclades
The most beautiful beach of all on an island of beautiful beaches is backed by sand dunes and bamboo groves, an exotic setting enhanced by a predictably spectacular sunset almost every evening.

Vai, Crete A grove of palm trees provides an MGM-worthy backdrop to a beach that even the ancients raved about.

Mavra Volia, Chios, Northern Islands A "wine-dark sea" washes the black volcanic shores of a cove nestled between sheltering cliffs—little wonder the hauntingly appealing place is aptly called "Black Pebbles."

Kolimbithres, Paros, Cyclades Smooth boulders whimsically shaped by the wind create a string of coves backed by golden sands. The calm, warm waters are ideal for swimming.

Myrtidiotissa, Corfu Sheer cliffs shelter soft sands backed by olive groves; Lawrence Durrell was not exaggerating when, in *Prospero's Cell*, he described this spot as "perhaps the loveliest beach in the world."

Lemonakia, Kokkari, Samos Beauty and the Beach describes this winner, with its perfect half-moon crescent magnificently framed by rocky promontories green with pine trees.

Paleokastritsa, Corfu

GOOD TO KNOW

WHAT SHOULD I WEAR?

Although on Mykonos you may encounter some of those multi-hundred-dollar designer straps of cloth that never come into contact with the water, for the most part Greek beach wear is decidedly casual and non-fussy. In addition to a swimming suit, you will want to bring the following: a tee-shirt or other cover-up for the strong sun; a hat; Jellies or other water-ready sandals for walking on hot sand and over pebbles; a pair of shorts or a cover-up to slip on for walks through a town or for a taverna meal. Remember, bathing suits are not acceptable street wear in many places in Greece. "No Nudity" signs are posted on many Greek beaches, especially those close to towns. Even if no sign is present, be discreet—find a spot removed from attired Greek beachgoers, many of whom find the notion of baring it all to be a distinctly foreign habit.

Skiathos

Boat in sunny waters at Elafonisi beach

Relaxing under parasol, beach on Skiathos island

HOW DO I GET THERE?

Many, but certainly not all, beaches on most resort islands are served by public buses running on a fairly limited schedule—drop off in the morning, pick up in the afternoon (tourist offices and major hotels can provide schedules). However, the only way to reach some beaches—including many of the prettiest and least crowded—is by car; parking is almost always free, though it can be scarce in high season. On Patmos and other islands another option is a caïque, a

BEACH TALK

- **Paralia** means "beach."

- **Amos** means "sand."

- **Thalassa** means "sea."

- **Petseta** means "towel."

- **Is the water warm?**
  To nero ineh zesto?

- **Pou tha noikiaso?**
  Where do I rent . . .

- **. . . an umbrella**
  obrella

- **. . . a beach lounge**
  xsaplosra

motor launch that usually leaves from the main port in the morning for remote beaches and returns in the afternoon; expect to pay about €15 for this pleasant mode of transport.

WHAT SHOULD I BRING?

Consider a towel and beach mat or blanket; a large bottle of water; plenty of sunscreen; and an umbrella for shade (these are not always available for rental). Your own snorkel gear is another option. Umbrella rentals, along with shade, are a rare commodity at many beaches and the sun can be fierce. You can usually buy one for about €10 in shops in beach towns.

WHAT SHOULD I EXPECT?

Activities and Rentals: In some of the major getaways—Kos, Paros, Mykonos, the north coast of Crete—you'll come upon every water sport under the sun, and sailboats, jet skis, and snorkeling and diving gear are often available from outfits operating out of large resorts. If your exertions in these places are going to be no more strenuous than lounging, you can usually rent a beach lounge and umbrella for about €12 a day.

Eating and Drinking: Some of the more popular beaches on resort islands are backed by tavernas and bars; these are usually casual, outdoor places that are open seasonally and serve sandwiches or such basic but delicious Greek grub as grilled octopus or lamb kebabs. At some beaches, a snack wagon (cantina) will dispense cold drinks, ice cream, and snacks. Many beaches, however, offer nothing in the line of food, so come prepared. Lunch at a beachside taverna is a Greek tradition, especially popular on Sunday. Expect to find yourself surrounded by families, many dressed in their Sunday best.

Facilities: Lifeguards are on duty at very few Greek beaches, and most beaches lack any kind of public facilities. A few have port-a-potties, but in many places beachside bars or tavernas fill the gap; out of courtesy order something if you use the facilities.

WHAT SHOULD I WATCH OUT FOR?

Grecian seas are gentle, with few hazards from undertows or strong waves which can strike the southern coast of Crete. Some underwater hazards to keep an eye out for are sharp rocks, sea urchins (*achinos*, which live on rocks and whose quills can inflict a sharp sting), and the now-rare jellyfish (*medusa*).

LOOK FOR THE BLUE FLAGS

The Blue Flags that fly above 425 Greek beaches mean they have met the standards set by the nonprofit Foundation for Environmental Education for water cleanliness, garbage disposal, overall safety, and other criteria. You will find a listing of Greece's Blue Flag beaches at ⊕ www.blueflag.org.

WATER WORLDS

Greece entertains its young visitors and their adult companions with a growing number of water parks. While none offer a particularly Greek experience, your kids won't mind—they'll love the pools, slides, and concessions. Two of Greece's largest and most popular are Aqua Paros Waterpark (Kolimbithres, Paros, Cyclades) and Acquaplus Waterpark (Hersonissos, Crete).

Local flags at Elafonisi beach, Crete

2

Cruising the Greek Islands

THE BEST SHIPS AND ITINERARIES

WORD OF MOUTH

"How can anyone pass up a cruise to Greece? Santorini, Mykonos, Crete, and Rhodes: these are the islands that launched a thousand trips! Even Poseidon, god of the waters, would have been jealous of the beautiful cruise ships now sailing the Aegean seas."

—WiseOwl

By Linda Coffman

Travelers have been sailing Greek waters ever since 3,500 B.C.C. (before Chris-Crafts). The good news is that today's visitor will have a much, much easier time of it than Odysseus, the world's first tourist and hero of Homer's *Odyssey*. Back in his day, exploring the Greek islands—1,425 geological jewels thickly scattered over the Aegean Sea like stepping-stones between East and West—was a fairly daunting assignment. Zeus would often set the schedule (during the idyllic days in midwinter the master of Mt. Olympus forbade the winds to blow during the mating season of the halcyon or kingfisher); waterlogged wooden craft could be tossed about in summer, when the *meltemi,* the north wind, would be a regular visitor to these waters; and pine-prow triremes often embarked with a scramble of 170 oarsmen, not all of them pulling in the right direction.

Now, in 2012, travelers can sail those same blue highways in effortless fashion. A flotilla of—often—spectacularly outfitted cruise ships helps banish many typical landlubbers' irritations: ferry schedules, hotel reservations, luggage porterage, to name a few. When you add in 21st-century allurements—pulling into Santorini after a deck-side luncheon created by the gastronomic wizardry at Nobu; a game of golf in Mykonos via your onboard 18-hole miniature-golf course; a renowned archaeologist illuminating the fascinating history of Rhodes, your next stop—you can see why a vacation aboard one of these gleaming white islands has become one of the most popular travel choices available.

Cruises have always had a magical quality, even without dramatic views of whitewashed Cycladic villages and ancient ruins anchored for eternity above a sheer drop *(for a rundown of the ABCs, see the Cruise Basics at the end of this chapter)*. Sailing into a harbor has a grand ceremonial feel lacking in air travel arrivals and Greece, the eastern Mediterranean's showcase, is an ideal cruise destination for travelers with limited time who wish to combine sightseeing with relaxation. This is especially true in spring and autumn, when milder Aegean and Ionian climates are better suited than the sweltering summer months to, for example, explore those hilltop ancient ruins.

Although cruises have historically attracted an older group of travelers, more and more young people and family groups are setting sail in Europe. With the peak season conveniently falling during school's summer hiatus, cruise lines have responded to multigenerational travel with expanded children's programs and discounted shore excursions for youngsters under age 12. Shore excursions have become more varied, too, often incorporating activities that families can enjoy together, such as bicycling and hiking. Cruise lines now offer more programs than ever before for adults as well, including pre- or post-cruise land tours as options, plus extensive onboard entertainment and learning programs. Some lines increasingly hire expert speakers to lead discussions based on local cultures.

Cruise ships may idyllically appear to be floating resorts, but keep in mind that if you decide you don't like your ship, you can't check out and move somewhere else. Whichever one you choose will be your home for seven days, or more in some cases. The chosen ship will determine the type of accommodations you'll enjoy, the kind of food you'll eat, the entertainment program, and even the destinations you'll visit. That is why the most important endeavor you can undertake when planning a cruise is evaluating the proposed itinerary, the cruise line, and the particular ship.

CHOOSING YOUR CRUISE

Which cruise is right for you depends on a number of factors, notably the size and style of ship you opt for, the itinerary you choose, and how much you're willing to spend.

DREAM ITINERARIES

Cruise ships typically follow one of two itinerary types in the eastern Mediterranean: round-trip loops that start and finish in the same port city, and one-way cruises that pick you up in one port and drop you off at another for the flight home. Itineraries are usually 7 to 10 days, though some lines offer longer sailings covering a larger geographic span. Some cruises concentrate on covering an area that includes the Greek islands, Turkish coast, Cyprus, Israel, and Egypt, while others reach from Gibraltar to the Ionian isles, the western Peloponnese, and Athens.

For an overview of Greece's top sights, choose an itinerary that includes port calls in Piraeus for a shore excursion to the Acropolis and other sights in Athens; Mykonos, a sparkling Cycladic isle with a warren of whitewashed passages, followed by neighboring Delos, with its Pompeii-like ruins; Santorini, a stunning harbor that's actually a partially submerged volcano; Rhodes, where the Knights of St. John built their first walled city before being forced to retreat to Malta; and Heraklion, Crete,

> **THE MED FROM STERN TO STERN**
>
> Many of today's most popular Greek islands cruises are actually part and parcel of larger itineraries that cover wider swaths of the Mediterranean, extending from Rome to Alexandria, but this has been the Greek way of seafaring for more than 3,000 years. In ancient time, the Aegean and the Mediterranean were propitious for coastal trade, and it was by sea that the Greek way was spread. Greek ships colonized the whole Mediterranean coast to such an extent that for a thousand years the Mediterranean was known as a veritable Greek lake.

where you'll be whisked through a medieval harbor to the reconstructed Bronze Age palace at Knossos. Port calls at Katakolon and Itea mean excursions to Olympia and the Temple of Apollo at Delphi. Some cruises call at Epidauros and Nafplion, offering an opportunity for visits to the ancient theater and the citadel of Mycenae, or at Monemvassia or Patmos, the island where St. John wrote the book of *Revelation*.

If you'd rather relax by the pool than trek through temples, opt for a cruise with more time at sea and fewer or shorter port calls. If you'd like time to explore each island destination, you'll want to choose a cruise where the ship spends the entire day in port and travels at night. Alternately, if the number of places you visit is more important than the time you spend in each one, book a cruise with a full itinerary and one or two port calls a day.

A cruise spares the planning headaches of solitary island-hopping and the inconvenience of carting luggage from one destination to the next, and, for budget-conscious travelers, cruises offer the advantage of controlled expenses. However, because one disadvantage is that port calls may be long enough only to allow time for a quick visit to one or two main attractions, cruises may be best for an overview, useful for planning a return trip to the more appealing island stops.

WHEN TO GO

When to go is as important as where to go. In July or August, the islands are crowded with Greek and foreign vacationers, so expect sights, beaches, and shops to be crowded. High temperatures could also limit time spent on deck. May, June, September, and October are the best months—warm enough for sunbathing and swimming, yet not so

CLOSE UP

Top Questions for Your Travel Agent

If you've decided to use a travel agent, ask yourself these 10 simple questions, and you'll be better prepared to help the agent do his or her job:

1. Who will be going on the cruise?

2. What can you afford to spend for the entire trip?

3. Where would you like to go?

4. How much vacation time do you have?

5. When can you get away?

6. What are your interests?

7. Do you prefer a casual or structured vacation?

8. What kind of accommodations do you want?

9. What are your dining preferences?

10. How will you get to the embarkation port?

uncomfortably hot as to make you regret the trek up Lindos. Cruising in the low seasons provides plenty of advantages besides discounted fares. Availability of ships and particular cabins is greater in the low and shoulder seasons, and the ports are almost completely free of tourists.

THE MAIN CRUISE LINES: AZAMARA TO WINDSTAR

Should it be posh or penny-pinching? Two weeks or seven days? Burgers by the pool aboard a Royal Caribbean megaship or SeaDream Yacht Club's intimate champagne-and-caviar beach barbecues? There are any number of questions you have to ask yourself when lining up your dream Greek islands cruise but deciding to opt for either a large or small ship may be the most important of them all.

Large cruise lines account for the vast majority of passengers sailing in Europe. These typically have both larger cruise ships and megaships in their fleets. Cruise ships have plentiful outdoor deck space, and many have a wraparound outdoor promenade deck that allows you to stroll or jog the ship's perimeter. In the newest vessels, traditional meets trendy, but for all their resort-style innovations, they still feature cruise ship classics—afternoon tea, complimentary room service, and lavish pampering. The smallest cruise ships carry 500 or fewer passengers, while larger vessels accommodate 1,500 passengers and offer a wide variety of diversions. Megaships boast even more amenities and amusements, and carry between 1,500 and 3,000 passengers—enough people to outnumber the residents of many Greek port towns.

Megaships are a good choice if you're looking for nonstop activity and lots of options; they're especially appealing for groups traveling together and families with kids of all ages. Experiences on these ships range from basic, comfortable vacations to white-glove luxury; from traditional cruises with formal nights, afternoon tea, and assigned dining places, to lively casual ships bustling with activity. All of them allow you the flex-ibility of seeing a variety of ports while still enjoying such cruise ameni-ties as spas, nightly entertainment, and fine dining. These ships tend to follow conventional itineraries and stop at the best-known, larger ports of call; because of their size they can't venture too close to shore, thus you won't see much scenery from the deck. If you prefer a gentler pace and a chance to get to know your shipmates, consider a smaller ship.

Classic or midsize ships, which are more popular with Europeans than with Americans, offer a range of amenities and comfortable accommo-dations but are not as flashy as the new megaships. Luxury ships are generally small to midsize and are distinguished by high staff-to-guest ratios, superior cuisine, few onboard charges, and much more space per passenger than you'll find on the mainstream lines' vessels.

SMALL SHIPS

Compact vessels bring you right up to the shoreline where big ships don't fit. Destinations, not casinos or spa treatments, are the focus of these cruises. You'll call into smaller ports, as well as the larger, better-known cities. Port lectures and cultural talks are the norm. But in com-parison with those on traditional cruise ships, cabins on these ships can be quite tiny and some bathrooms are no bigger than cubbyholes. Often, the dining room and the lounge are the only common public areas on these vessels. Some small ships, however, are luxurious yachtlike vessels with cushy cabins, comfy lounges and libraries, and hot tubs on deck. You won't find discos or movie theaters aboard, but what you trade for space and onboard diversions is a unique and detailed glimpse of ports that you're unlikely to forget.

Small-ship cruising can be pricey as costs are spread over a few dozen, rather than hundreds of, passengers. Fares tend to be quite inclusive (except for airfare), with few onboard charges, and, given the size of ship and style of cruise, fewer opportunities to spend money on board. Small ships typically offer the same kinds of early-booking and other discounts as the major cruise lines.

AZAMARA CLUB CRUISES

"The adventuresome (yet pampered) soul has met its match" is the catchy new slogan for this premium line launched by parent company Royal Caribbean in 2007. Named partly in honor of the star Acamar—the most-southerly bright star that can be viewed from the latitude of Greece—the firm has two vessels, built for now-defunct Renaissance Cruises, and refitted for the deluxe-cruise crowd. Designed to offer exotic destination-driven itineraries, Azamara offers a more intimate onboard experience while allowing access to the less-traveled ports of call experienced travelers want to visit. And the enrichment programs are some of the best on offer. Since its launch Azamara Club Cruises has added a number of more inclusive amenities to passengers' fares, with no charge for a specific brand of bottled water, soft drinks, spe-cialty coffees and teas; shuttle bus service to and from port communi-ties, where available; house wine served at lunches and dinners; and complimentary self-service laundry. Also included in the cruise fare are gratuities.

Itineraries and Ships. Sister-ships *Azamara Quest* and *Azamara Journey* (694 passengers each) both offer eastern Mediterranean cruises that include Greece and the Greek isles. On the *Azamara Quest* you can take a 7-night voyage that sails from Athens to Nafplion, Kos, Santorini, Rhodes, and Chania (Souda), Crete, then stops in Kusadasi, Turkey, before returning to Athens. For travelers with more time, *Azamara Quest* also offers an 11-night voyage from Athens that calls at Kusadasi (Ephesus), Turkey, before visiting Santorini, Mykonos, Katakolon, Corfu, Chania (Souda), Crete, Kotor, Montenegro, and Dubrovnik and Hvar, Croatia, before ending in Venice. Fares begin at $1,999 and $2,999, respectively (note that itineraries and rates quoted in this chapter are as of Fall 2011 and are subject to change). In addition, Azamara Journey offers 10- or 11-night "Holyland" cruises that sail round-trip from Athens and include Mykonos and Rhodes in Greece; Haifa and Ashdod in Israel; Alexandria in Egypt; and Kusadasi (Ephesus) in Turkey. Fares begin at $2,299.

> **HOW TO EARN YOUR SEA MAJOR**
>
> A distinguishing aspect of Azamara is a wide range of enrichment programs to accompany the destination-rich itineraries. Programs include guest speakers and experts on a wide variety of topics, including technology, cultural explorations, art, music, and design.

Your Shipmates. Azamara is designed to appeal to discerning travelers, primarily American couples of any age who appreciate a high level of service in an unstructured atmosphere. The ships are not family-oriented and do not have facilities or programs for children.

Food. Expect all the classic dinner favorites but with an upscale twist, such as gulf shrimp with cognac and garlic, or a filet mignon with black truffle sauce. Each ship offers two specialty restaurants: the Mediterranean-influenced Aqualina and the stylish steak-and-seafood restaurant Prime C. Passengers in Club Suite accommodations may dine in the specialty restaurants every night of the cruise at no charge; all other passengers pay a cover charge.

Fitness and Recreation. In addition to a well-equipped gym and an outdoor jogging track, Azamara's fitness program includes yoga at sunset, Pilates, and access to an onboard wellness consultant. Both ships offer a full menu of spa treatments, an outdoor spa relaxation lounge, and an aesthetics suite featuring the traditional Chinese healing art of acupuncture.

Contact: *1050 Caribbean Way, Miami, FL 33132 877/999–9553 www. azamaracruises.com.*

CELEBRITY CRUISES

Founded in 1989, Celebrity has gained a reputation for fine food and professional service. The cruise line has built premium, sophisticated ships and developed signature amenities, including a specialty coffee shop, a martini bar, large standard staterooms with generous storage, spas, and butler service for passengers booking the top suites. Although spacious accommodations in every category are a Celebrity standard, the addition of Concierge Class makes certain premium ocean-view and balcony staterooms almost the equivalent of suites in terms of amenities and service.

Itineraries and Ship. *Celebrity Equinox* (2,850 passengers) offers winning cruises on one of Celebrity Cruises' newest ships. Ten- and eleven-day "eastern Mediterranean" voyages travel round-trip from Rome and, depending on departure date, make stops in the Italian ports of Naples and Messina, Sicily, and Kusadasi (Ephesus) in Turkey, but spend a sizable chunk of time in Greek ports including Athens, Mykonos, Rhodes, Santorini, or Corfu. Rates for the itineraries, which have multiple sailings throughout the year, range from $899 to $1,949, depending on the date. Passengers aboard *Celebrity Equinox* enjoy a high-style, contemporary ship with multiple choices to dine and play, including the "Lawn Club"—a deck where you can picnic or practice putting on real grass.

Your Shipmates. Celebrity caters to American cruise passengers, primarily couples from their mid-thirties to mid-fifties. Many families enjoy cruising on Celebrity's fleet during summer months and holiday periods. Each vessel has a dedicated playroom and offers a four-tiered program of activities designed for children and teens aged 3 to 17, plus Toddler Time for parents and their children under age 3.

Food. Celebrity has made it a top priority to advance its already superior culinary program to the next level, including a choice of four specialty restaurants on *Celebrity Equinox*, for which reservations are required and there is an extra charge. Every ship in the fleet has a highly experienced team headed by executive chefs and food and beverage managers.

Fitness and Recreation. Celebrity's fitness centers and AquaSpa by Elemis are some of the most tranquil and nicely equipped at sea. State-of-the-art exercise equipment, a jogging track, and some fitness classes are available at no charge. Spa treatments include a variety of massages, body wraps, and facials. *Celebrity Equinox* has an Acupuncture at Sea program administered by a specialist in Asian medicine. Hair and nail services are offered in the salons.

Contact: 1050 Caribbean Way, Miami, FL 33132 305/539–6000 or 800/647–2251 www.celebrity.com.

COSTA CRUISES

Europe's number one cruise line combines a Continental experience, enticing itineraries, and the classical design and style of Italy with romantic nights at sea. Genoa-based Costa Crociere, parent company of Costa Cruise Lines, had been in the passenger business for almost

50 years when Carnival Corporation completed a buyout of the line in 2000 and began expanding the fleet with larger and more-dynamic ships. "Italian-style" cruising is a mixture of Mediterranean flair and American comfort. Beginning with a *buon viaggio* (bon voyage) celebration, the supercharged social staff works overtime to get everyone in the mood and encourages everyone to be a part of the action.

Itineraries and Ships. *Costa Deliziosa* (2,260 passengers), launched in 2010, is one of Costa Cruises' newest and largest ships with a little something to offer everyone, including a splendid selection of

> ### SHIP SHAPE
>
> Taking a cue from the ancient Romans, Costa places continuing emphasis on wellness and sybaritic pleasures. Spa treatments include a variety of massages, body wraps, and facials that can be scheduled à la carte or combined in packages to encompass an afternoon or the entire cruise. State-of-the-art exercise equipment in the terraced gym, a jogging track, and basic fitness classes for all levels of ability are available.

balcony cabins and multiple dining venues. Seven-day cruises sail from Savona or Rome (Civitavecchia), then steam south to Katakolon (Olympia), Greece, before visiting Athens and continuing on to Valletta, Malta, and Cagliari (on Sardinia), before concluding the cruises at their embarkation ports. *Costa Fascinosa* (3,000 passengers), launched in 2012, sails 7-day "Ancient Treasures" cruises from Venice that head to Bari in Italy before visiting Santorini, Katakolon, and Rhodes in Greece, and return to Venice via Dubrovnik, Croatia. *Costa Classica* (1,308 passengers), the line's smallest ship in the Mediterranean, sails 7-day cruises from Trieste, Italy, that call at Ancona, Italy, and then spend the majority of the week in Greece, with calls at Mykonos, Athens, and Corfu before visiting Dubrovnik, Croatia, on the way back to Trieste. Cruises are scheduled from April through November and fares range from $739 to $1,099, depending on ship and sailing date.

Your Shipmates. An international air prevails on board and announcements are often made in a variety of languages. On Mediterranean itineraries approximately 80% of passengers are Europeans, including many from Italy. Youth programs provide daily age-appropriate activities for children ages 3 to 17. Special counselors supervise activities and specific rooms are designed for children and teens, depending on the ship.

Food. Dining features regional Italian cuisines, a variety of pastas, chicken, beef, and seafood dishes, as well as authentic pizza. European chefs and culinary school graduates, who are members of Chaîne des Rôtisseurs, provide a dining experience that's notable for a delicious, properly prepared pasta course. Vegetarian and healthful diet choices are also offered. Alternative dining on newer ships is by reservation only in the upscale supper clubs, which serve regional Italian specialties. Costa chefs celebrate the cruising tradition of lavish midnight buffets.

Contact: ⌕ *200 S. Park Rd., Suite 200, Hollywood, FL 33021-8541* ☎ *954/266–5600 or 800/462–6782* ⊕ *www.costacruise.com.*

CRYSTAL CRUISES

Winner of accolades and hospitality-industry awards, Crystal Cruises offers the grandeur of the past with all the modern touches discerning passengers demand. Founded in 1990 and owned by Nippon Yusen Kaisha (NYK) in Japan, Crystal ships, unlike other luxury vessels, are large—carrying upward of 900 passengers. Superior service, a variety of dining options, spacious accommodations, and some of the highest ratios of space per passenger of any cruise ships make them distinctive. Beginning with ship designs based on the principles of feng shui, not even the smallest detail is overlooked to provide passengers with the best imaginable experience. Crystal stands out in their variety of enrichment and educational programs.

Itineraries and Ships. *Crystal Serenity* (1,080 passengers) and her smaller fleetmate *Crystal Symphony* (922 passengers) are stylish, uncrowded, and uncluttered, with clubby drawing rooms done in muted colors and warm woods, creating a refined environment. A West Coast laid-back vibe prevails, with sensational restaurants (the alternative choices are yours to enjoy at no extra cost). The design of smallish standard cabins for this level of luxury ship is disappointing, while public spaces are design-award worthy. *Crystal Serenity* sails several one-way 12-night itineraries that call on ports in Greece throughout the season. Embark in Athens and conclude in Venice with ports of call in Corfu, Mykonos, and Nafplion in Greece; Zadar, Croatia; and Kotor, Montenegro. Or begin your cruise in Venice and finish up in Istanbul, Turkey after visiting Mykonos, Corfu, and Athens, Greece, as well as Kotor, Montenegro, and Ravenna, Italy. Rates begin at $6,970 and $6,070 respectively.

Your Shipmates. Affluent, well-traveled couples, from their late thirties to retirees, are attracted by Crystal Cruises' destination-rich itineraries, onboard enrichment programs, and the ship's elegant ambience. Children are welcome aboard, but Crystal Cruises reserves the right to restrict the number of children under age 3 traveling with their parents and is unable to accommodate children younger than six months of age.

Food. The food alone is a good enough reason to book a cruise on Crystal ships. Dining in the main restaurants is an event starring Continental-inspired cuisine served by trained European waiters. Off-menu item requests are honored when possible. Casual poolside dining from the grills is offered on some evenings in a relaxed, no-reservations-required option. A variety of hot and cold hors d'oeuvres is served in bars and lounges every evening before dinner and again during the wee hours. Where service and the dishes really shine are in the complimentary specialty restaurants; both ships feature Asian-inspired and Italian specialty restaurants.

Fitness and Recreation. Large spas offer innovative pampering therapies, body wraps, and exotic Asian-inspired treatments. Fitness centers feature a range of exercise and weight-training equipment and workout areas for aerobics classes, plus complimentary yoga and Pilates instruction. In addition, golfers enjoy extensive shipboard facilities, including a driving range, practice cage, and putting green.

Contact: ⌖ *2049 Century Park E, Suite 1400, Los Angeles, CA 90067* ☎ *310/785–9300 or 800/722–0021* ⊕ *www.crystalcruises.com.*

> ## SEA AND CRUMPETS
>
> Not surprisingly, entertainment and authentic pubs have a decidedly English flavor aboard Cunard, as do some of the grand salons found on *Queen Elizabeth* and *Queen Victoria.* The double-height Queens Room is a loggia-style venue designed in the manner of the grand ballrooms found in large English country houses, such as Her Majesty's own Osborne House.

CUNARD LINE

One of the world's most-distinguished names in ocean travel since 1840, Cunard Line's history of transatlantic crossings and worldwide cruising is legendary for its comfortable British style. After a series of owners tried with little success to revive the company's flagging passenger shipping business in the era of jet travel, Carnival Corporation saved the day in 1998 with an infusion of ready cash and the know-how to turn the cruise line around. There is a decidedly British vibe to salons and pubs, while a wide variety of musical styles can be found for dancing and listening in the bars and lounges. Quality enrichment programs are presented by expert guest lecturers in their fields.

Itinerary and Ships. Traditional with contemporary accents, *Queen Victoria* (1,970 passengers), which premiered in 2008, features an extensive Cunardia museum exhibit, a two-deck library connected by a spiral staircase, posh entertainment venues, and shops inspired by London's Burlington and Royal Arcades. A whopping two-thirds of staterooms boast private balconies to catch the sea winds. Her "Greek Isles and Aegean Treasures" and "Ancient Wonders" itineraries are 12-night explorations that set sail respectively from Rome and Venice. "Greek Isles and Aegean Treasures" passengers visit such popular Greek ports as Athens, Santorini, Samos, and Zakinthos, while those aboard "Ancient Wonders" call at Athens, Santorini, Rhodes, and Corfu. Both itineraries journey to far-flung Istanbul, Turkey, and either Dubrovnik, Croatia, on the former, or Split, Croatia, on the latter. Fares begin at $1,391. Sister ship *Queen Elizabeth* (2,092 passengers), which launched in 2010, sails similarly named 12-night routes with her "Greek Isles and Aegean Treasures" and "Greek Isles and Ancient Wonders" cruises following near-identical itineraries. After embarking in Athens and stopping in Mykonos, Mytileni, Rhodes, Santorini, Olympia (Katakolon), and Corfu in Greece, as well as Istanbul and Kusadasi (Ephesus), Turkey, and Dubrovnik, Croatia, both journeys finish up in Venice, Italy. The "Greek Isles and Ancient Wonders"

Shore leave? Mykonos has plenty of delights in store for lucky cruise travelers.

itinerary also offers the same ports in the opposite direction, from Venice to Athens. Fares start at $2,196.

Your Shipmates. Discerning, well-traveled British and American couples from their late thirties to retirees are drawn to Cunard's traditional style. The availability of spacious accommodations and complimentary self-service laundry facilities make Cunard liners a good option for families, although there may be fewer children on board than you might expect. Kid-friendly features include a dedicated play area for children ages 1–6. Separate programs are reserved for older children ages 7–12 and teens. Toddlers are supervised by English nannies. Children ages 1–2 sail free (except for government fees).

Food. In the tradition of multiple-class ocean liners, dining room assignments are made according to the accommodation category booked: you get the luxury you pay for. Passengers in junior suites are assigned to single-seating Princess Grill, while the posh Queen's Grill serves passengers booked in the most lavish suites. All other passengers are assigned to the single-seating Britannia Club, or to one of two seatings in the dramatic Britannia Restaurant. Specialty restaurants require reservations and there is an additional charge.

Fitness and Recreation. Swimming pools, golf driving ranges, table tennis, a paddle tennis court, shuffleboard, and jogging tracks barely scratch the surface of onboard facilities dedicated to recreation. Top-quality fitness centers offer high-tech workout equipment, a separate weight room, and classes ranging from aerobics to healthful living workshops. The spas are top-shelf with a long menu of treatments and salon services for women and men.

Contact: ⊡ *24303 Town Center Dr, Valencia, CA 91355* ☎ *661/753–1000 or 800/728–6273* ⊕ *www.cunard.com.*

HOLLAND AMERICA LINE

Holland America Line has enjoyed a distinguished record of traditional cruises, world exploration, and transatlantic crossings since 1873—all facets of its history that are reflected in the fleet's multimillion dollar shipboard art and antiques collections. Noted for focusing on passenger comfort, Holland America Line cruises are classic in design and style. Although they may never be considered cutting edge, even with an infusion of younger adults and families on board, they remain refined without being stuffy or stodgy.

Itineraries and Ships. The *Prinsendam* (794 passengers) was launched in 1998 and refurbished with an array of Holland America Line signature goodies, including an exhilarating Crow's Nest observation lounge. A sample itinerary is the 16-day "Holy Land Explorer" cruise, which kicks off in Piraeus (Athens) and pulls into Greece's Corfu and Katakolon (Olympia), with other stops including Alexandria (Cairo) and Port Said in Egypt; Ashdod (Jerusalem) and Haifa in Israel; Korcula in Croatia; Brindisi in Italy; and Antalya, Marmaris, and Kusadasi (Ephesus) in Turkey before ending in Civitavecchia (Rome), Italy. Rates begin at $3,499. *Noordam* (1,918 passengers) is a more youthful and family-friendly ship, where an exquisite Waterford Crystal sculpture adorns the triple-deck atrium and reflects keep-your-sunglasses-on color schemes throughout; nearly 80% of rooms have a private balcony, although those next to the panoramic elevator are not as "private" as they seem. This ship sails a series of 10-day "Roman Empire" cruises, which begin and end in Rome (Civitavecchia) and stops in Greece's Corfu, Katakolon (Olympia), Santorini, and Athens while also calling at Dubrovnik in Croatia, Kusadasi (Ephesus), Turkey, and Messina in Sicily; rates begin at $1,499. Holland America Line's largest and most elegant ship, *Nieuw Amsterdam* (2,106 passengers), features a 12-night "Mediterranean Empires" sailing round-trip from Venice that calls on the Greek ports of Mykonos, Santorini, and Athens, while also including Split in Croatia; Kusadasi (Ephesus) in Turkey; and Kotor, Montenegro, for fares starting at $1,699.

Your Shipmates. No longer your grandparents' cruise line, today's Holland America attracts families and discerning couples, mostly from their late thirties on up. Comfortable retirees are often still in the majority, particularly on longer cruises; however, holidays and summer months are peak periods when you'll find more children in the mix. Group activities are planned for children ages 3–7 and 8–12 in Club HAL, Holland America Line's professionally staffed youth program. Club HAL After Hours offers late-night activities from 10 pm until midnight for an hourly fee. Teens aged 13–17 have their own lounge with activities.

Food. You have your choice of two assigned seatings or open seating for evening meals in the formal dining room. In the reservations-required, $20-per-person Pinnacle Grill alternative restaurant, fresh seafood and premium cuts of Sterling Silver beef are used to prepare creative specialty dishes. *Nieuw Amsterdam* adds even more dining choice with Italian and Asian alternative restaurants. Delicious onboard traditions are afternoon tea, a Dutch Chocolate Extravaganza, and Holland America Line's signature bread pudding.

Fitness and Recreation. Well-equipped and fully staffed fitness facilities contain state-of-the-art exercise equipment; basic fitness classes are available at no charge. There's a fee for personal training, and specialized classes such as yoga and Pilates. The Greenhouse Spa offers a variety of treatments. Ships have a jogging track, multiple swimming pools, and sports courts.

Contact: ⌂ *300 Elliott Ave. W, Seattle, WA 98119* ☎ *206/281–3535 or 877/932–4259* ⊕ *www.hollandamerica.com.*

MSC CRUISES

Since it began introducing graceful new designs to large ships in 2003, MSC Cruises has grown to be a formidable presence in European cruising. The extensive use of marble, brass, and wood in ships' interiors reflect the best of Italian styling and design. Clean lines and bold colors often set the modern sophisticated tone—no glitz, no clutter. Elegant simplicity is the standard of MSC's decor.

Itineraries and Ships. Often sailing with a Greece-heavy itinerary, the MSC *Musica* (2,550 passengers) is an extravaganza of curves and seductive colors, crowned by a vast red-and-gold La Scala theater. A highlight is a three-deck waterfall in the central foyer, where a piano is suspended on a transparent floor above a pool of water. Interiors are a blend of art deco and art nouveau themes, with some restaurants saddled with rather cartoony murals. Elsewhere, the elegant Cigar Bar and Giardino restaurant bring things down to Earth. A whopping 80% of staterooms have an ocean view and 65% have balconies. Decorated in jewel-tone colors, all are comfortable yet somewhat smaller than the average new-ship cabin. A typical cruise is the seven-night journey that starts in Venice, then calls on Greece's Katakolon (Olympia) and Santorini (the same day), Mykonos, Piraeus/Athens, and Corfu, plus Dubrovnik in Croatia and Bari in Italy. Rates start at $999 and up, depending on sailing date. MSC *Fantasia* (3,274 passengers), which entered service in 2008, is one of the line's newest and largest ships. With an emphasis on the authentic Italian designs for which MSC Cruises ships are known, interiors also incorporate touches of art deco and art nouveau stylings One of the cruises sailing to Greece includes a 10-night itinerary that begins in Genoa, Italy, and stops at Greece's Piraeus/Athens, Rhodes, Heraklion, and Zakynthos, with other ports including Izmir, Turkey, and Naples, Italy. Fares begin at $899.

Your Shipmates. On Mediterranean itineraries you will find a majority of Europeans, including Italians, and announcements are made in a number of languages. Most American passengers are couples in the 35- to 55-year-old range and family groups who prefer the international atmosphere prevalent on board. Children from ages 3–17 are welcome to participate in age-appropriate youth programs in groups for ages 3–8 and 9–12; the Teenage Club is for youths 13 years and older.

MAMMA MIA, SOPHIA!

Garnering plenty of headlines, the MSC *Musica* was launched in 2006 by silver-screen diva Sophia Loren and commentators noted that this curvaceous, sexy vessel was one Sophia of a ship.

Food. Dinner on MSC ships is a traditional seven-course event centered on authentic Italian fare. Menus list Mediterranean regional specialties and classic favorites prepared from scratch the old-fashioned way. "Healthy Choice" and vegetarian items are offered as well as tempting sugar-free desserts. Highlights include pizza and breads, freshly baked on board daily. The aptly named Gala midnight buffet is a retro food feature missing from most of today's cruises.

Fitness and Recreation. Up-to-date exercise equipment, a jogging track, and basic fitness classes for all levels are available. Spa treatments include a variety of massages, body wraps, and facials that can be scheduled à la carte or combined in packages to encompass an afternoon or the entire cruise.

Contact: 6750 N. Andrews Ave., Fort Lauderdale, FL 33309 800/666–9333 www.msccruises.com.

NORWEGIAN CRUISE LINE

A cruise industry innovator since its founding in 1966, Norwegian Cruise Line's "Freestyle" cruising style was born when Asian shipping giant Star Cruises acquired the Miami-based line. Confounded that Americans meekly conformed to rigid dining schedules and dress codes, the new owners set out to change the traditional formula by introducing a variety of dining options in a casual, free-flowing atmosphere. Now co-owned by Star Cruises and Apollo Management, a private equity company, NCL continues to be an industry innovator noted for top-quality, high-energy entertainment and an emphasis on fitness facilities and programs. NCL successfully combines action, activities, and a resort-casual atmosphere.

Itinerary and Ship. Purpose-built for NCL's revolutionary Freestyle cruising concept (eat when you want and where you want—or almost), the *Norwegian Jade* (2,402 passengers) has more than a dozen dining options. Decor showstoppers include the theater reminiscent of a European opera house, with lavish production shows and a full proscenium stage. Reflecting perhaps the somewhat gaudy painting of gemstones on the exterior of the ship's hull, a bevy of public spaces have some over-the-top gem-tone furnishings and carpets; other settings, including Cagney's Steakhouse, the Champagne & Wine Bar, and the Star Bar, are lush and, if not exactly understated, elegantly decorated. A popular itinerary is featured on the seven-day "Greek Isles" cruise, which sails every other week round-trip from Venice, and stops at Greece's

Mykonos, Santorini, Olympia (Katakolon), and Corfu; prices start at $759. On alternate weeks *Norwegian Jade* sails a seven-night itinerary from Venice that calls on Dubrovnik, Croatia; Athens (Piraeus), Greece; Izmir (Ephesus), Turkey; and Split, Croatia. The itineraries can be combined for a two-week cruise starting at $1,389.

Your Shipmates. NCL's mostly American cruise passengers are active couples ranging from their mid-thirties to mid-fifties. Longer cruises and more-exotic itineraries attract passengers in the over-55 age group. Many families enjoy cruising on NCL ships during summer months. For children and teens, each NCL vessel offers the "Kid's Crew" program of supervised entertainment for young cruisers ages 2–17. Younger children are split into three groups from age 2 to 5, 6 to 9, and 10 to 12; for 13- to 17-year-olds there are clubs where they can hang out in adult-free zones.

Food. Main dining rooms serve what is traditionally deemed Continental fare, although it's about what you would expect at a really good hotel banquet. Where NCL stands above the ordinary is in their specialty restaurants, especially the French-Mediterranean Le Bistro (on all ships), the Pan-Asian restaurants, and steak houses (on the newer ships). In addition, you will find pizza around the clock in the buffet and an Italian trattoria. Some, but not all, restaurants carry a cover charge or are priced à la carte and require reservations. An NCL staple, the late-night Chocoholic Buffet continues to be a favorite event.

Fitness and Recreation. Mandara Spa offers a long list of unique and exotic spa treatments fleet wide on NCL. State-of-the-art exercise equipment, jogging tracks, and basic fitness classes are available at no charge. There's a nominal fee for personal training, and specialized classes such as yoga and Pilates.

Contact: ⌂ *7665 Corporate Center Dr., Miami, FL 33126* ☎ *305/436–4000 or 800/327–7030* ⊕ *www.ncl.com.*

OCEANIA CRUISES

This distinctive cruise line was founded by cruise industry veterans with the know-how to satisfy the wants of inquisitive passengers by offering itineraries to interesting ports of call and upscale touches— all for fares much lower than you would expect. Oceania Cruises set sail in 2003 to carve a unique, almost "boutique" niche in the cruise industry by obtaining midsize "R-class" ships that formerly made up the popular Renaissance Cruises fleet. Intimate and cozy public room spaces reflect the importance of socializing on Oceania ships while varied, destination-rich itineraries are an important characteristic of the line.

Itineraries and Ships. *Nautica* and *Regatta* (684 passengers each) and their newer and larger fleetmates, *Marina* and *Riviera* (1,258 passengers each), strike some of the most sumptuous, elegant decor notes of any ships sailing—lobbies and public salons are dazzling with old-world gilt-famed paintings, glittery banisters, tapestried rugs, and enough wood paneling to line a hundred libraries—the effect is like a Vanderbilt yacht but magnified to the nth degree. A popular itinerary offered on the *Regatta* and *Riviera* is the 10-day "Pearls of the Aegean," which embarks in Venice and continues with Greece's Monemvassia, Delos, Santorini, Mykonos, Corfu, and Aghios Nikolaos (Crete), then continues on to Kusadasi (Ephesus) in Turkey, Kotor, Montenegro, and Dubrovik, Croatia, before ending up in Athens; rates begin at $3,299. Another itinerary aboard the *Riviera* is the 10-day "Greek Glory," which kicks off in Istanbul, Turkey, with a stop in Kusadasi (Ephesus), Turkey, and takes in Greece's Mytilini (Lesbos), Mykonos, Athens (Piraeus), Argostoli (Cephalonia), and Corfu, with other stops in Dubrovnik and Split, Croatia, before disembarkation in Venice, Italy; rates begin at $3,499.

> ### CROWD PLEASERS
>
> On Princess ships, personal choices regarding where and what to eat abound, but there's no getting around the fact that most are large and carry a great many passengers. Unless you opt for traditional assigned seating, you could experience a brief wait for a table in one of the open-seating dining rooms. Alternative restaurants are a staple. With a few breaks in service, Lido buffets on all ships are almost always open, and a pizzeria and grill offer casual daytime snack choices.

Your Shipmates. Oceania Cruises appeal to singles and couples from their late thirties to well-traveled retirees who have the time for and prefer longer cruises. Most are attracted to the casually sophisticated atmosphere, creative cuisine, and European service. Oceania Cruises are adult-oriented and not a good choice for most families, particularly those traveling with infants and toddlers. Teenagers with sophisticated tastes (and who don't mind the absence of a video arcade) would enjoy the emphasis on intriguing ports of call.

Food. Top cruise industry chefs ensure that the artistry of world-renowned master chef Jacques Pépin, who crafted five-star menus for Oceania, is carried out. The results are sure to please the most discriminating palate. Oceania simply serves some of the best food at sea, particularly impressive for a cruise line that charges far less than luxury rates. The main open-seating restaurant offers trendy French-Continental cuisine with an always-on-the-menu steak, seafood, or poultry choice and vegetarian option. Intimate specialty restaurants require reservations, but there is no additional charge.

Fitness and Recreation. Operated by Canyon Ranch, the spa, salon, and well-equipped fitness center are adequate for the number of passengers on board. In addition to individual body-toning machines and complimentary exercise classes, there is a walking/jogging track circling the top of the ships. Spa menus list massages, body wraps, and facials. Forward of the locker rooms on *Regatta* and *Nautica*, you'll find a large therapy pool and quiet deck for relaxation and sunning on padded wooden steamer chaises.

Contact: ⌂ *8300 N.W. 33rd St, Suite 308, Miami, FL 33122* ☎ *305/514–2300 or 800/531–5658* ⊕ *www.oceaniacruises.com.*

PRINCESS CRUISES

Princess Cruises may be best known for introducing cruise travel to millions of television viewers when its flagship became the setting for *The Love Boat* TV series in 1977. Since that heady time of small-screen stardom, the Princess fleet has grown both in the number and the size of ships. Although most are large in scale, Princess vessels manage to create the illusion of intimacy in understated yet lovely public rooms graced by impressive art collections. In today's changing times, Princess has introduced more flexibility; Personal Choice Cruising offers alternatives for open-seating dining and entertainment options as diverse as those found in resorts ashore. Welcome additions to Princess's roster of adult activities are ScholarShip@Sea Enrichment programs featuring guest lecturers, cooking classes, wine-tasting seminars, pottery workshops, and computer and digital photography classes.

Itineraries and Ships. *Crown Princess* (3,080 passengers) was built in 2006 and is one of the largest megaships prowling the Mediterranean. Typical of grand Princess ships, interiors feature soothing pastel tones with splashy glamour in the sweeping staircases and marble-floor atriums. Four pools, a disco, and Times Square–style LED screens draw the crowds, yet you can escape to your own seaside aerie: 80% of outside staterooms have balconies (although many are stepped, with a resultant loss in total privacy). A typical itinerary is the 12-day "Greek Isles" Venice-to-Rome cruise, which calls on Greece's Corfu, Katakolon (Olympia), Mykonos, Athens, Rhodes, and Santorini, along with other ports including Naples, Italy, and Turkey's Kusadasi; rates are from $2,290. From the opposite direction, *Crown Princess* sails from Rome-to-Venice and includes Greece's Santorini, Mykonos, Athens, Corfu, and Katakolon (Olympia), with stops in Monte Carlo, Monaco; Naples and Florence/Pisa (Livorno) in Italy; and Split in Croatia; rates start at $2,490. Fleetmates *Pacific Princess* (670 passengers) and *Ocean Princess* (710 passengers) feature Greece on their more-far-flung schedules. Intimate and refined, Princess's small-ship options appear positively tiny beside their megaship fleetmates. In reality, they are medium-size ships that offer real choice to Princess loyalists—a true alternative for passengers who prefer the clubby atmosphere of a smaller "boutique"-style ship, yet one that has big-ship features galore. *Pacific Princess* sails a 12-day "Holy Land" itinerary from Athens to Venice with a stop in Patmos in Greece, and *Ocean Princess* departs Dover in the United Kingdom for a 22-day "European Explorer Grand Adventure" voyage that calls on Atlantic and Western Mediterranean posts before visiting Cephalonia, (Argostoli), Itea, Aghios Nikolaos, and Santorini in Greece, and concluding in Athens. Rates begin at $3,040 and $4,597 respectively. *Ocean Princess* also sails a one-week Rome to Athens itinerary calling on Itea, Cephalonia, (Argostoli), Santorini, and Aghios Nikolaos in Greece, as well as Kusadasi (Ephesus), Turkey; rates begin at $1,349. A 14-day *Ocean Princess* cruise departs Rome for calls in Itea, Cephalonia, (Argostoli), Santorini, Aghios Nikolaos, Athens (Piraeus), Mykonos, Katakolon (Olympia), and Corfu in Greece, along with Kusadasi (Ephesus),

Turkey; Dubrovnik, Croatia; and Koper, Slovenia, before ending in Venice, Italy; rates start at $2,898.

Your Shipmates. Princess Cruises attract mostly American passengers ranging from their mid-thirties to mid-fifties. Longer cruises appeal to well-traveled retirees and couples who have the time. Families enjoy cruising together on the Princess fleet, particularly during summer months, when many children are on board. For young passengers aged 3 to 17, each Princess vessel has a playroom, teen center, and programs of supervised activities designed for different age groups. To afford parents independent time ashore, youth centers operate as usual during port days.

Food. Menus are varied and extensive in the main dining rooms, and the results are good to excellent considering how much work is going on in the galleys. Vegetarian and healthy lifestyle options are always on the menu, as well as steak, fish, or chicken. A special menu is offered for children. Possible options run from round-the-clock Lido buffets to specialty Italian and steak-house restaurants and Ultimate Balcony Dining, where a server is on duty and a photographer stops by to capture the romantic evening.

Fitness and Recreation. Spa and salon rituals include massages, body wraps, facials, and numerous hair and nail services, as well as a menu of special pampering treatments designed specifically for men, teens, and couples. Modern exercise equipment, a jogging track, and basic fitness classes are available at no charge. Grand-class ships have a resistance pool so you can get your "laps" in.

Contact: 24305 Town Center Dr., Santa Clarita, CA 91355-4999 ☎ 661/753-0000 or 800/774-6237 ⊕ www.princess.com.

REGENT SEVEN SEAS CRUISES

Regent Seven Seas Cruises (formerly Radisson Seven Seas Cruises) sails an elegant fleet of vessels that offer a nearly all-inclusive cruise experience in sumptuous, contemporary surroundings. The line's tried-and-true formula works; delightful ships feature exquisite service, generous staterooms with abundant amenities, a variety of dining options, and superior enrichment programs. Cruises are destination focused, and most sailings host guest lecturers—historians, anthropologists, naturalists, and diplomats. A real bonus is that unlimited shore excursions are included in the fare.

Itineraries and Ships. The world's first all-suite, all-balcony ship, the *Seven Seas Mariner* (700 passengers), is a jewel of the fleet, with a high-tech Constellation Theater and four soigné restaurants keeping the beat going. For pure pampering, the Canyon Ranch Spa Club can't be beat. A typical itinerary is featured on the seven-day "Hellenic Reflections" voyage, which starts in Istanbul, then sails for Greece's Kavaka, Mykonos, Rhodes, Santorini, and Heraklion, plus a stop in Kusadasi, Turkey, before completing the voyage in Athens; rates begin at $5,799. Other Greek-centric cruises include the 10-day "Treasures of Dalmatia "sailing from Istanbul to Venice with calls in Santorini, Athens, Olympia

(Katakolon), and Corfu in Greece, as well as Ephesus (Kusadasi), Turkey; Kotor, Montenegro; Dubrovnik, Croatia; and Urbino (Ancona), Italy; fares begin at $6,099.

Your Shipmates. Regent Seven Seas Cruises are inviting to active, affluent, well-traveled couples ranging from their late thirties to retirees who enjoy the ships' elegance and destination-rich itineraries. Longer cruises attract veteran passengers in the over-60 age group. Regent vessels are adult-oriented and do not have dedicated children's facilities. However, a "Club Mariner" youth program for children ages 5–9, 10–13, and 14–17 is offered on selected sailings.

Food. Menus may appear to include the usual cruise ship staples, but in the hands of Regent Seven Seas chefs, the results are some of the most outstanding meals at sea. Specialty dining varies within the fleet, but the newest ships have the edge with the sophisticated Signatures, which features the cuisine of Le Cordon Bleu of Paris, and Prime 7, offering menus inspired by either regional American favorites or nouveau international cuisine. In addition, Mediterranean-inspired bistro dinners are served in the venues that are the daytime-casual Lido buffet restaurants. Nice touch: wines are chosen to complement dinner menus.

Fitness and Recreation. Although gyms and exercise areas are well-equipped, Regent vessels are not large ships, so the facilities tend to be on the small side. Each ship has a jogging track, and the larger ones feature a variety of sports courts.

Contact: ⌂ *1000 Corporate Dr., Suite 500, Fort Lauderdale, FL 33334* ☎ *954/776–6123 or 877/505–5370* ⊕ *www.rssc.com.*

ROYAL CARIBBEAN INTERNATIONAL

Big, bigger, biggest! More than a decade ago, Royal Caribbean launched the first of the modern megasize cruise ships for passengers who enjoy traditional cruising with a touch of daring and whimsy tossed in. Expansive multideck atriums and the generous use of floor-to-ceiling glass windows give each RCI vessel a sense of spaciousness and style. A variety of lounges and high-energy stage shows draws passengers of all ages out to mingle and dance the night away. Production extravaganzas showcase singers and dancers in lavish costumes. The action is nonstop in casinos and dance clubs after dark, although daytime hours are filled with games and traditional cruise activities. Port "talks" tend to lean heavily on shopping recommendations and the sale of shore excursions. And then there are those famous rock-climbing walls.

Itineraries and Ships. *Splendour of the Seas* and *Grandeur of the Seas* (1,800 passengers each) are Royals noted for their acres of floor-to-ceiling windows that allow sunlight to flood in and offer wide sea vistas. A double-height dining room with sweeping staircase is a showstopper on both ships, but has competition with the two specialty restaurants added to *Splendour of the Seas* during a 2011 refurbishment. Smaller cabins can be a tight squeeze for more than two people. A popular itinerary, with a good helping of Greece, is the *Splendour of the Seas'* seven-night "Greek Isles and Turkey" cruise, which sails from Venice, then calls at Santorini, Kalakolon (Olympia), and Corfu, before returning to Venice via Kusadasi (Ephesus), Turkey and Bari, Italy; rates start at $999. Another *Splendour* 7-night Greek Isles option from Venice calls at Corfu, Mykonos, and Piraeus (Athens) in Greece; Dubrovnik, Croatia; and Bari, Italy, before returning to Venice; rates begin at $1,049. Also from Venice, sister-ship *Grandeur of the Seas* sails an 11-night "Greece and Turkey Cruise" that heads for Piraeus (Athens), Mykonos, and Santorini in Greece, as well as Kotor, Montenegro; Kusadasi (Ephesus) and Bodrum in Turkey; and Split, Croatia, before the return to Venice; rates start at $1,099.

> ## WHAT, NO FERRIS WHEEL?
>
> Royal Caribbean has pioneered such new and unheard-of features as rock-climbing walls, ice-skating rinks, bungee trampolines, and even the first self-leveling pool tables on a cruise ship. Exercise facilities vary by ship class but all Royal Caribbean ships have state-of-the-art exercise equipment and jogging tracks, and passengers can work out independently or participate in a variety of basic exercise classes. Spas are top-notch.

Your Shipmates. Royal Caribbean cruises have a broad appeal for active couples and singles, mostly in their thirties to fifties. Families are partial to the newer vessels that have larger staterooms, huge facilities for children and teens, and seemingly endless choices of activities and dining options. Supervised age-appropriate activities are designed for children ages 3 through 17. Children are assigned to the Adventure Ocean youth program by age. For infants and toddlers 6 to 36 months of age, interactive playgroup sessions are planned, while a teen center with a disco is an adult-free gathering spot that will satisfy even the pickiest teenagers. Pluses are "family-size" staterooms on most newer ships, but a drawback is the lack of self-service laundry facilities.

Food. Dining is an international experience with nightly changing themes and cuisines from around the world. Passenger preference for casual attire and a resortlike atmosphere has prompted the cruise line to add laid-back alternatives to the formal dining rooms in the Windjammer Café.

Fitness and Recreation. Can a surfing pool be next? Actually, yes, but not on their ships plying the Greek isles. Fabled for its range of top-of-the-line recreations, Royal Caribbean also delivers on the basics: most exercise classes, aimed at sweating off those extra calories, are included in the fare (although there's a fee for specialized spinning, yoga, and Pilates classes, as well as the services of a personal trainer). Spas have full spa-style menus and full services for pampering for adults and teens.

Contact: ⌂ *1050 Royal Caribbean Way, Miami, FL 33132–2096* ☎ *305/539–6000 or 800/327–6700* ⊕ *www.royalcaribbean.com.*

Remember that many cruises offer fascinating and customized tours of such fabled landmarks as the Palace of the Grand Masters in Rhodes.

SEABOURN CRUISE LINE

Seabourn was founded on the principle that dedication to personal service in elegant surroundings would appeal to sophisticated, independent-minded passengers whose lifestyles demand the best. Lovingly maintained since their introduction in 1987, the smaller megayachts and larger flagships are favorites with people who can take care of themselves, but would rather do so aboard a ship that caters to their individual preferences. Recognized as a leader in small-ship luxury cruising, you can expect complimentary wines and spirits, elegant amenities, and even the pleasure of mini-massages while lounging poolside. Guest appearances by luminaries in the arts and world affairs highlight the enrichment program. Wine tasting, trivia, and other quiet pursuits might be scheduled, but most passengers prefer to simply do what pleases them.

Itineraries and Ships. *Seabourn Pride* (208 passengers) had its maiden voyage in 1988 but received an extensive makeover in 2010. The ship's intimate scale is a nice plus, as is the generous passenger-to-space ratio. You'll never feel crowded. Exotic colors, warm woods, stupendous fabrics, and conversation-piece rooms have been traded in for a restaurant and entertainment lounge that would not upset a staid banker, but if you're looking for tranquility and oh-so-subtle decor, this ship delivers. It often sails the eastern Mediterranean, and one of its popular itineraries is the seven-day "Mediterranean Wonders" cruise, which kicks off in Rome and calls at Messina, Sicily and Crotone in Italy, then sails to Greece's Corfu and Mykonos, and completes a rare transit of the

Corinth Canal before the cruise ends in Piraeus (Athens); rates begin at $6,500. Larger, and with more dining and entertainment choices than the original trio of megayachts, *Seabourn Quest* (450 passengers) is the line's newest vessel and latest entry into the eastern Mediterranean with a seven-day Venice to Athens itinerary that makes stops in Koper, Slovenia, and Zadar and Dubrovnik in Croatia, before calling at Corfu, Greece, cruising the Ionian Sea, and visiting Mykonos, Greece; fares start at $7,800.

Your Shipmates. Seabourn's yachtlike vessels appeal to affluent couples of all ages who enjoy destination-rich itineraries, a subdued atmosphere, and exclusive service. Passengers tend to be 50-plus and retired couples who are accustomed to formality. Seabourn is adult-oriented and unable to accommodate children under one year of age.

Food. Exceptional cuisine created by celebrity chef-restaurateur Charlie Palmer is prepared "à la minute" and served in open-seating dining rooms. Creative menu offerings include foie gras, quail, and fresh seafood. Vegetarian dishes and meals low in cholesterol, salt, and fat are prepared with the same care and artful presentation. Wines are chosen to complement each day's luncheon and dinner menus and caviar is always available.

Fitness and Recreation. A full array of exercise equipment, free weights, and basic fitness classes are available in the small gym, while some specialized fitness sessions are offered for a fee. The water-sports marina is popular with active passengers who want to Jet Ski, windsurf, kayak, or swim in the integrated saltwater "pool" while anchored in calm waters.

Contact: ⌂ *300 Elliott Ave. W., Seattle, WA 98119* ☎ *800/929-9391* ⊕ *www.seabourn.com.*

SEADREAM YACHT CLUB

SeaDream yachts began sailing in 1984 and, after a couple of changes of ownership and a total renovation in 2002, they have evolved into the ultimate boutique ships—as they put it, "it's yachting, not cruising." Passengers enjoy an unstructured holiday at sea doing what pleases them, making it easy to imagine the diminutive vessels are really private yachts. The ambience is refined and elegantly casual. Fine dining and socializing with fellow passengers and the ships' captains and officers are preferred pastimes. Other than a tiny piano bar, a small casino, and movies in the main lounge, there is no roster of activities. A well-stocked library has books and movies for those who prefer quiet pursuits in the privacy of their staterooms.

Itineraries and Ships. *SeaDream I* and *SeaDream II* (each 112 passengers) are known for their gorgeously soigné decor, flawless service, and one-of-a-kind delights, such as the Balinese sun beds (so comfortable that passengers sometimes choose

ROW, ROW, ROW YOUR BOAT

The SeaDream water-sports marina is well used by active passengers who want to water-ski, kayak, windsurf, or take a Jet Ski for a whirl while anchored in calm waters.

to forsake their own quarters to spend the night on them) and beach-barbecue "splashes" replete with champagne and caviar. Although not huge ships, the public areas on board are quite spacious; the chic ambience conjures up a rich man's yacht, with tons of warm woods, brass accents, laid-back rattan chairs, and high-style deck awnings to shade you from the sun. Add in a richly hued entertainment lounge, an extensive library, and perfect-taste cabins with sleep-inducing mattresses, ultradeluxe bedding, and a shower big enough for two, and even Onassis would have approved. A popular cruise on *SeaDream I* is a 10-day voyage from Piraeus (Athens) to Istanbul, Turkey, with stops in Hydra, Santorini, and Lindos Island, before entering Turkish waters to call at Antalya and Bodrum, then returning to Patmos in Greece and swinging back to Kusadasi (Ephesus) and Kepez (Troy & Gallipoli) in Turkey and spending an overnight in Istanbul onboard; rates start at $11,900. A typical itinerary on *SeaDream II* is the seven-day round-trip Piraeus (Athens) cruise, with stops in Hydra, Galaxidi (Delphi), Katakolon, Gythion (Sparta), Elafonisos, and Santorini; rates begin at $8,900.

Your Shipmates. SeaDream yachts appeal to energetic, affluent travelers of all ages, as well as groups. Passengers tend to be couples from 45-year-olds and up to retirees who enjoy the unstructured informality, subdued ambience, and exclusive service. No children's facilities or organized activities are available.

Food. Every meal is prepared to order using the freshest seafood and prime cuts of beef. Menus include vegetarian alternatives and Asian wellness cuisine for the health-conscious. Cheeses, petits fours, and chocolate truffles are offered with after-dinner coffee, and desserts are to die for. All meals are open seating, either in the main restaurant or, weather permitting, alfresco in the canopied Topsider Restaurant daily for breakfast, lunch, and special dinners. Complimentary wines accompany each meal.

Fitness and Recreation. Small gyms on each ship are equipped with treadmills, elliptical machines, recumbent bikes, and free weights. A personal trainer is available. SeaDream's unique Asian Spa facilities are also on the small size, yet offer a full menu of individualized gentle pampering treatments including massages, facials, and body wraps utilizing Eastern techniques. Mountain bikes are available for use ashore.

Contact: ⌂ *601 Brickell Key Dr., Suite 1050, Miami, FL 33131* ☎ *305/631–6100 or 800/707–4911* ⊕ *www.seadreamyachtclub.com.*

SILVERSEA CRUISES

Intimate ships, paired with exclusive amenities and unparalleled hospitality, are the hallmarks of Silversea luxury cruises. Personalization is a Silversea maxim. Their ships offer more activities than other comparably sized luxury vessels, although you can also opt for quiet pursuits. Guest lecturers are featured on nearly every cruise; language, dance, and culinary lessons and excellent wine-appreciation sessions are always on the schedule of events. A multitiered show lounge is the setting for classical concerts, big-screen movies, and folkloric entertainers from ashore.

Itineraries and Ships. *Silver Cloud* and *Silver Wind* (296 passengers each) are yachtlike gems all about style, understatement, and personal choice. While simply not large enough for huge public spaces, room on board is more than adequate and functions as well as on their larger fleetmates. A typical *Silver Wind* itinerary is the 12-night "Athens, Greece, to Istanbul, Turkey" cruise, with stops at Greece's Heraklion, Crete; Alexandria and Port Said, Egypt; Beirut, Lebanon; Tarous, Syria; Larnaca, Cyprus; Antalya, Turkey; Rhodes, Greece; and a call at Kusadasi (Ephesus) before arriving in Istanbul; rates begin at $6,348. *Silver Spirit* (540 passengers), the new flagship of the Silversea fleet, cuts a beautiful picture, large enough for ocean grandeur, small enough for smaller-port charm. Clean, modern decor that defines public areas and lounges showcases large expanses of glass for sunshine and sea views, and that's a huge plus. Other signature touches include a stylish smoking lounge, totally no-charge laundry rooms, and butler service for all levels of accommodation. A popular itinerary is the seven-day "Athens to Istanbul" cruise, with ports of call including Turkey's Kusadasi and Greece's Aghios Nikolaos, Crete, Rhodes, Mykonos, and Santorini; rates start at $4,958.

Your Shipmates. Silversea Cruises appeals to sophisticated, affluent couples who enjoy the country club-like atmosphere, exquisite cuisine, and polished service. Although Silversea Cruises is adult-oriented and unable to accommodate children less than one year of age, occasionally there's a sprinkling of children on board. There are no dedicated children's facilities available.

Food. Dishes from the galleys of Silversea's master chefs are complemented by those of La Collection du Monde, created by Silversea's culinary partner, the world-class chefs of Relais & Châteaux. Special off-menu orders are prepared whenever possible, provided that the ingredients are available. Nightly alternative theme dinners in La Terrazza (by day, the buffet restaurant) feature regional specialties from the Mediterranean.

Fitness and Recreation. The rather small gyms are well equipped with cardiovascular and weight-training equipment, and fitness classes are held in the mirror-lined exercise rooms. South Pacific-inspired Mandara Spa offers numerous treatments including exotic-sounding massages, facials, and body wraps.

Contact: 110 E. Broward Blvd., Fort Lauderdale, FL 33301 954/522-2299 or 800/722-9955 www.silversea.com.

LOVE FOR SAIL

The Star Clippers ships rely on sail power while at sea unless conditions require the assistance of the engines; you can't help but appreciate the silence and harmony with the sea when the engines are turned off and the ship is under sail.

STAR CLIPPERS

Satisfy your inner pirate on Star Clippers' four- and five-masted sailing beauties—the world's largest barkentine and full-rigged sailing ships—which come filled with modern high-tech equipment as well as the amenities of private yachts. They were launched in 1991 as a new, spectacularly lovely tall-ship alternative for sophisticated travelers whose wants included adventure at sea, but not on board a conventional cruise ship. One of their most appealing attractions is that Star Clippers are not cruise ships in the ordinary sense with strict schedules and pages of activities. You are free to do what you please day and night, but many passengers enjoy the simplicity of socializing on deck.

Itineraries and Ship. *Star Clipper* (170 passengers) is a gorgeous four-master with brass fixtures, teak-and-mahogany paneling and rails, and antique prints and paintings of famous sailing vessels—the decor is a homage to the days of grand sailing ships. The library is vaguely Edwardian in style, replete with a belle epoque fireplace, while the main restaurant has surprisingly vast dimensions but is made cozy by warm red hues, panel detailing, and elegant French Provençal–style chairs. Guest cabins are yachtlike and can be compact, with stepladders to beds. Popular cruises are the seven-night "Greek Isles and Turkey" sailings, which head either north or south from Athens. Northbound voyages sail for Kusadasi (Ephesus), Turkey and return to Greek waters to explore Patmos, Amorgos, Mykonos, and Monemvassia. Southbound from Athens, ports include Rhodes, Santorini, and Hydra in Greece, and Bodrum and Dalyan River in Turkey. Fares for either itinerary begin at $2,075.

Your Shipmates. Star Clippers cruises appeal to active, upscale American and European couples from their thirties on up who enjoy sailing, but in a casually sophisticated atmosphere with modern conveniences. Many sailings are about fifty-fifty from North America and Europe, and announcements are made in several languages accordingly. This is not a cruise line for the physically challenged; there are no elevators, ramps, or staterooms/bathrooms with wheelchair accessibility. Star Clippers is adult-oriented and there are no dedicated youth facilities.

Food. Not noted for gourmet fare, the international cuisine is what you would expect from a trendy shoreside bistro, albeit an elegant one. Fresh fruits and fish are among the best choices from Star Clippers' galleys. Lunch buffets are quite a spread of seafood, salads, and grilled items.

Fitness and Recreation. Formal exercise sessions take a backseat to water sports, although aerobics classes and swimming are featured on all ships.

Contact: 760 NW 107th Ave., Suite 100, Miami, FL 33172 305/442-0550 or 800/442-0551 www.starclippers.com.

WINDSTAR CRUISES

Are they cruise ships with sails or sailing ships designed for cruises? Since 1986, the Windstar vessels have presented a conundrum. In actuality they are masted sailing yachts, pioneers in the upscale sailing niche. Often found in ports of call inaccessible to large traditional ships, Windstar ships seldom depend on wind alone to sail—their motors are necessary in order to maintain their schedules.

A SHORE THING

If a particular shore excursion is important to you, consider booking it when you book your cruise to avoid disappointment later. You can even book your spa and salon services precruise on some cruise lines' Web sites so you can have your pick of popular times, such as sea days or the afternoon before a formal night.

2

Itineraries and Ships. *Wind Spirit* and *Wind Star* (148 passengers each) are blue-and-cream-hue essays in Windstar style, with proportionately small public spaces replete with yachtlike touches of polished wood, columns wrapped in rope, and nautical artwork. Lots of time is spent on deck, which can get crowded; you can always escape to your cabin and watch DVDs with room-service popcorn. With its large windows and skylight, the main lounge is flooded with natural light. A popular itinerary for both ships is the seven-day "Istanbul to Athens" sailing (or the reverse, from Athens to Istanbul), which includes Bodrum and Kusadasi in Turkey and Greece's Rhodes, Santorini, Mykonos, and Athens; rates begin at $3,431.

Your Shipmates. Windstar Cruises appeals to upscale professional couples in their late thirties to sixties and on up to retirees who enjoy the unpretentious, yet casually sophisticated atmosphere, creative cuisine, and refined service. The unregimented atmosphere is adult-oriented; children, especially toddlers, are not encouraged. No dedicated children's facilities are available.

Food. Dining on Windstar ships is as casually elegant as the dress code. There's seldom a wait for a table in open-seating dining rooms where tables for two are plentiful. Whether meals are taken in the open and airy top-deck buffet with its floor-to-ceiling windows and adjacent tables outside, or in the formal dining room, dishes are as creative as the surroundings. In a nod to healthful dining, low-calorie and low-fat spa cuisine is available. A mid-cruise deck barbecue featuring grilled seafood and other favorites is fine dining in an elegantly casual alfresco setting. With afternoon tea and hot and cold hors d'oeuvres served several times during the afternoon and evening, no one goes hungry.

Fitness and Recreation. Windstar's massage and exercise facilities are quite small on *Wind Star* and *Wind Spirit,* as would be expected on ships that carry fewer than 150 passengers. Stern-mounted water-sports marinas are popular with active passengers who want to kayak, windsurf, and water-ski.

Contact: ⌂ *2101 4th Ave., Suite 210, Seattle, WA 98121* ☎ *206/292–9606 or 800/258–7245* ⊕ *www.windstarcruises.com.*

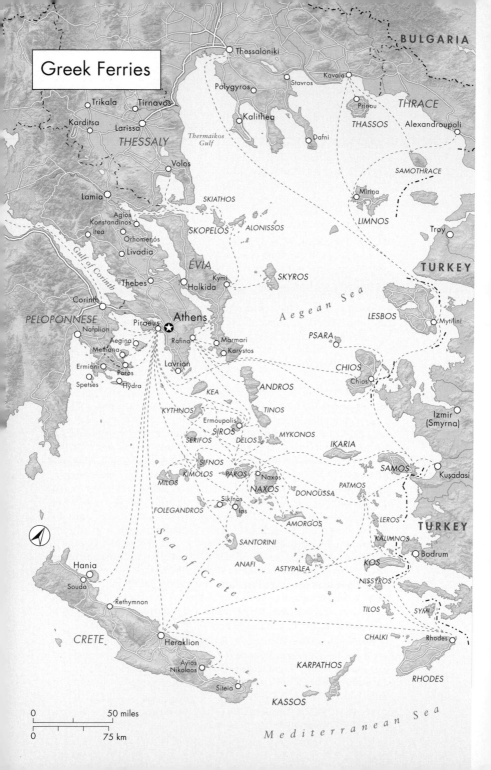

CRUISE BASICS

BOOKING YOUR CRUISE

According to the Cruise Line International Association (CLIA), cruisers plan their trips anytime from a year to a month in advance, with the majority planning four to six months ahead of time. It follows then that a four- to six-month window should give you the pick of sailing dates, ships, itineraries, cabins, and flights to the port city. You need more time if you're planning to sail on a small adventure vessel, as some of their more-popular itineraries can be fully booked six to eight months ahead of time. If you're looking for a standard itinerary and aren't choosy about the vessel or dates, you could wait for a last-minute discount, but industry experts warn that these are harder to find than they used to be now that cruising is so popular in Europe.

If you cruise regularly with the same line, it may be easiest to book directly with them, by phone or Web. Most cruises (nearly 75% according to CLIA) are, however, booked through a travel agent. Your best bet is a larger agency that specializes in cruises. They'll be able to sort through the myriad options for you, and often have the buying clout to purchase blocks of cabins at a discount. Cruise Lines International Association (⊕ *www.cruising.org*) lists recognized agents throughout the United States.

CRUISE COSTS

The average daily price for a cruise varies dramatically depending on when you sail, which ship and grade of cabin you choose, and when you book. At the bargain end, cruising remains one of the best travel deals around: a weeklong cruise on an older ship, for example, with an interior stateroom, in the off-season, can still be had at a basic fare of less than $100 per day (before airfare, taxes, and other costs); or about $150 per day in the high season. At the other end of the scale, a voyage on a luxury line such as Silversea Cruises or a small luxury yacht may cost more than four times as much as a cruise on a mainstream line such as Royal Caribbean. Cruises on smaller vessels tend to be pricier than trips on mainstream lines because there are fewer passengers to cover the fixed costs of the cruise.

When you sail will also affect your costs: published brochure rates are highest in July and August; you'll pay less, and have more space on ship and ashore, if you sail in May, June, or September.

Whenever you choose to sail, remember that the brochure price is the highest fare the line can charge for a given cruise. Most lines offer early-booking discounts. Although these vary tremendously, many

AND ONE LAST TIP

Although most other kinds of travel are booked over the Internet nowadays, for cruises, booking with a travel agent who specializes in cruises is still your best bet. Agents have built strong relationships with the lines, and have a much better chance of getting you the cabin you want, and possibly even a free upgrade.

lines will offer at least some discount if you book several months ahead of time, usually by the end of January for a summer cruise; this may require early payment as well. You may also find a discounted last-minute cruise if a ship hasn't filled all its cabins, but you won't get your pick of cabins or sailing dates, and you may find airfare is sky-high or unavailable. However, since most cruise lines will, if asked, refund the difference in fare if it drops after you've booked and before the final payment date, there's little advantage in last-minute booking. Some other deals to watch for are "kids sail free" specials, where children under 12 sail free in the same cabin as their parents; free upgrades rather than discounts; or discounted fares offered to frequent cruisers from their preferred cruise lines.

SOLO TRAVELERS

Solo travelers should be aware that single cabins are extremely rare or nonexistent on most ships; taking a double cabin for yourself can cost as much as twice the advertised per-person rates (which are based on two people sharing a room). Exceptions are found on some older ships belonging to European-based cruise lines. A few cruise lines will find roommates of the same sex for singles so that each can travel at the regular per-person, double-occupancy rate.

EXTRAS

Your cruise fare typically includes accommodation, onboard meals and snacks, and most onboard activities. It does not normally include airfare to the port city, shore excursions, tips, soft drinks, alcoholic drinks, or spa treatments. You may also be levied fees for port handling, security and fuel surcharges, as well as sales taxes, which will be added to your cruise fare when you book.

Athens

WORD OF MOUTH

"Is there still scaffolding at the Parthenon? It was there when we were there in 1992. When will they get it done?"

—twoflower

"I was 21 and living just outside Athens when they put the crane up in the middle of the Parthenon. And they just took it down this past year. I'm 53 now."

—paradiselost

WELCOME TO ATHENS

TOP REASONS TO GO

★ **The Acropolis:** An ancient beacon of bygone glory rising above Athens's smog, this iconic citadel represents everything the Athenians were and still aspire to be.

★ **Evzones on Syntagma Square:** Unmistakable in tasseled hats and pom-pom shoes, they act out a traditional changing of the guard that falls somewhere between discipline and comedy.

★ **The Ancient Agora and Monastiraki:** Socrates and Plato once discoursed—and scored excellent deals on figs—at the Agora, and today you can do the same at the nearby Monastiraki marketplace.

★ **Opa!:** Whether jamming to post-grunge in Gazi—Athens's Greenwich Village—or dirty dancing on the tables at live bouzoukia clubs, the Athenians party like no one else.

★ **Benaki Bounty:** Housed in a neoclassic mansion, the Benaki Museum—Greece's oldest private collection—has everything from ancient sculpture to modern art.

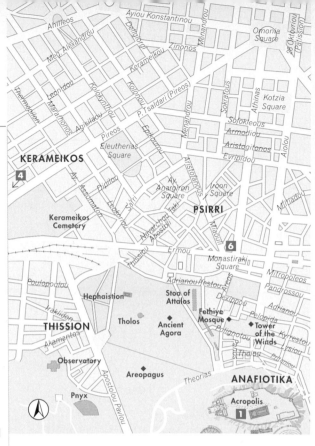

1 **Acropolis.** A survivor of war, time, and smog, this massive citadel and its magnificent buildings epitomize the glories of classical Greek civilization—its fabled relics and sculpture are now housed in the spectacular New Acropolis Museum.

2 **Plaka/Anafiotika.** This pretty neighborhood remains the last corner of 19th-century Athens, a quiet maze of streets dotted by Byzantine churches. Tiny Anafiotika, climbing up the Acropolis slope, looks like a whitewashed Cycladic village.

3 **Central Athens.** Ranging from ancient Athens's majestic Kerameikos cemetery to top people-watching cafés, this is a chaotic mix of 16th-century Byzantine churches and 1970s apartments. South lies Psirri, a district beating to the hedonistic pulse of Athenian clubbers.

4 **Gazi-Rouf.** A few decades ago, these neighborhoods were covered in soot from the gasworks that powered Athens. Today the Gazi foundry is an arts complex glowing crimson with colored lights, illuminating

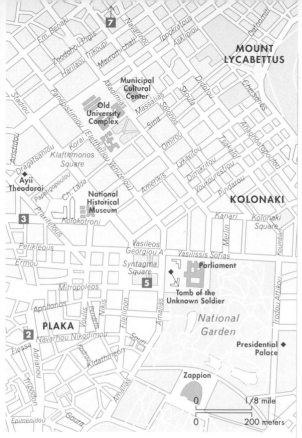

MOUNT LYCABETTUS

KOLONAKI

PLAKA

GETTING ORIENTED

Athens's main grid consists of three parallel streets—Stadiou, Eleftheriou Venizelou (widely called—and known—as Panepistimiou by natives), and Akadimias—that link two main squares, Syntagma and Omonia. But be sure to detour to the Central Food Market, the shops in Monastiraki and Psirri, and Gazi and Metaxourgeio, the emerging arts district. For if ancient glory still defines Athens internationally, the city also has a modern cachet as a chaotic, exhilarating, spontaneous metropolis. In the midst of a mass of concrete apartment blocks, you'll happily find Athens's Greek, Roman, and Byzantine landmarks are mercifully concentrated around the city center, whose hub stretches from the Acropolis in the southwest to Mt. Lycabettus in the northeast. You'll find you can walk from the Parthenon to many other sites and still find time to sip an icy frappé in a belle epoque café.

what has become the hottest downtown arts-and-entertainment district in Athens.

5 Syntagma Square. The heart of modern Athens, the streets radiating out from Syntagma Square are lined with government agencies, neoclassic mansions, Queen Amalia's National Garden, and the Temple of Olympian Zeus. Here, too, is the museum district, where star attractions include the Goulandris Collection of ancient Cycladic art and the Benaki Museum. To the east, at the foot of Mt. Lycabettus,

lies Kolonaki—a fashionable residential area loaded with see-and-be-seen cafés and restaurants.

6 Monastiraki. This area—adjacent to the ancient Agora—once housed the Turkish bazaar and baths and it retains that Near East feel. Go to the flea market here to revel in the bustle of an energizing marketplace.

7 Exarchia. In the northern reaches of the city, this somewhat run-down neighborhood is Student Central and home to the famed National Archaeological Museum.

Updated
by Natasha
Giannousi

It's no wonder that all roads lead to the fascinating and maddening metropolis of Athens. Lift your eyes 200 feet above the city to the Parthenon, its honey-color marble columns rising from a massive limestone base, and you behold architectural perfection that has not been surpassed in 2,500 years. But, today, this shrine of classical form dominates a 21st-century boomtown.

Athens is now home to 4.5 million souls, many of whom spend the day discussing the city's faults: the murky pollution cloud known as the *nefos,* the overcrowding, the traffic jams with their hellish din, and the characterless cement apartment blocks. Romantic travelers, nurtured on the truth and beauty of Keats's Grecian urn, are dismayed to find that much of Athens has succumbed to that red tubular glare that owes only its name, neon, to the Greeks. But if Athens is a difficult city to love, its concentration of culture makes it impossible to ignore.

To experience Athens—Athìna in Greek—fully is to understand the essence of Greece: ancient monuments surviving in a sea of cement, startling beauty amid the squalor, tradition juxtaposed with modernity—a smartly dressed lawyer chatting on her cell phone as she maneuvers around a priest in flowing robes heading for the sleek, space-age metro. Locals depend on humor and flexibility to deal with the chaos and lately, the raging economic crisis; you should do the same. The rewards are immense.

THE NEW ATHENS

Those rewards are even greater now thanks to the many splendid features created for the city's 2004 Olympics. In 2000, Athens opened its new metro, many of whose gleaming stations function as minimuseums, displaying ancient artifacts found on-site (the new trains have blissfully cut down the effects of Athens's notorious gridlock and pollution). About a decade ago, the city unveiled Eleftherios Venizelos International airport, high-tech and efficient (affectionately called by many locals El.Vel.). New infrastructure blessings include a tram line running from the city center to the south-coast beaches; an express train running to the airport and far-flung suburbs; and a beltway and the repaving and expansion of most of the city's potholed highways.

Within the city, beautification projects took priority. The most successful has been the completion of Athens's Archaeological Park, which links the capital's ancient sites in a pedestrian network. The stone-paved, tree-lined walkway allows you to stroll through the city center undisturbed by traffic from the Panathenaic stadium, home of the first modern Olympics in 1896, past the Temple of Olympian Zeus, the Acropolis, Filopappou hill, the ancient Greek and Roman agoras, Hadrian's Library, and Kerameikos, the city's ancient cemetery. Cars have also been banned or reduced in other streets in the historical center thanks to the introduction of odd/even plate-numbers traffic restrictions.

While various museums have received renovations, such as the National Archaeological Museum and the Benaki Museum, one new museum garnered headlines around the world when it opened in June 2009: the New Acropolis Museum, a spectacularly modern showcase for some of the most venerated ancient statues in the world. And the invigorating buzz that seized Athens pre-2004 has also helped newly transform entire neighborhoods like Gazi, Thission, Metaxourgeio, Rouf, and Psirri from industrial warehouse districts to hot spots of hip restaurants and happening nightclubs.

THE AGELESS CITY

Happily, you can still wander into less-touristy areas to discover pockets of timeless charm. Here, in the lovelier Athenian neighborhoods, you can delight in the pleasures of strolling. *Peripatos,* the Athenians call it, and it's as old as Aristotle, whose students learned as they roamed about in his Peripatetic school. This ancient practice survives in the modern custom of the evening *volta,* or stroll, taken along the pedestrianized Dionyssiou Areopagitou street skirting the base of the Acropolis.

Along your way, be sure to stop in a taverna to observe Athenians in their element. They are lively and expressive, their hands fiddling with worry beads or gesturing excitedly. Although often expansively friendly, they are aggressive and stubborn when they feel threatened, and they're also insatiably curious.

Amid the ancient treasures and the 19th-century delights of neighborhoods such as Anafiotika and Plaka, the pickax, pneumatic drill, and cement mixer have given birth to countless office buildings and modern apartments. Hardly a monument of importance attests to the city's history between the completion of the Temple of Olympian Zeus 19 centuries ago and the present day. That is the tragedy of Athens: the long vacuum in its history, the centuries of decay, neglect, and even oblivion. But within the last 150 years the Greeks have created a modern capital out of a village centered on a group of ruined marble columns. And since the late 1990s, inspired by the 2004 Olympics, they have gone far in transforming Athens into a sparkling modern metropolis that the ancients would strain to recognize but would heartily endorse.

PLANNER

WHEN TO GO

Athens often feels like a furnace in summer, due to the capital's lack of parks and millions of circulating cars. Mornings between 7 am and 9 am or evenings after 5 pm are often pleasant but temperatures can still hover in the 90s during heat waves. The capital is far more pleasant in spring and fall. The sunlight is bright but bearable, the air feels crisp and invigorating, and even the famously surly Athenians are friendlier. Winters are mild here, just as they are in all of Greece: it rains but rarely snows, so a light coat is all that is needed.

PLANNING YOUR TIME

Although still an agelessly beautiful city, the post-Olympic "European" Athens is burgeoning with energy, life, and wonders. And the only way you'll be able to see most of them is if you have a planned itinerary to guide you through this most challenging of cities.

IF YOU HAVE ONE DAY: ATHENS 101
Early in the morning, pay homage to Athens's most impressive legacy, the Acropolis. Then descend through Anafiotika, the closest thing you'll find to an island village. Explore the 19th-century quarter of Plaka, with its neoclassical houses, and stop for lunch at one of its many tavernas. Do a little bargaining with the merchants in the old Turkish bazaar around Monastiraki Square. Spend a couple of hours in the afternoon marveling at the stunning collection of antiquities in the National Archaeological Museum; then pass by Syntagma Square to watch the changing of the costumed Evzone guards in front of the Tomb of the Unknown Soldier. You can then window-shop or people-watch in the tony neighborhood of Kolonaki. Nearby, take the funicular up to Mt. Lycabettus for the sunset before enjoying a show at the Roman theater of Herod Atticus, followed by dinner in the newly revived district of Psirri.

IF YOU HAVE 3 DAYS
After a morning tour of the Acropolis, with a stop at the Acropolis Museum to view sculptures found on the site, pause on your descent at Areopagus, the site of the ancient supreme court; the view is excellent. Continue through Anafiotika and Plaka, making sure to stop at the Greek Folk Art Museum; the Roman Agora, with its Tower of the Winds, an enchanting water clock from the 1st century BC; and the Little Mitropolis church on the outskirts of the quarter. After a late lunch, detour to Hadrian's Arch and the Temple of Olympian Zeus, Athens's most important Roman monuments. In Syntagma Square, watch the changing of the Evzone guards, and then head to Kolonaki, followed by an ouzo on the slopes of Mt. Lycabettus at one of the cafés that grace the peak, with their splendid panorama of the Acropolis and the sea. Dine in a local taverna, perhaps in a neighborhood near the Panathenaic Stadium, which is lit at night. This Roman arena was reconstructed for the first modern Olympics in 1896.

On day two, visit the cradle of democracy, the fabled Ancient Agora, with Greece's best-preserved temple, the Hephaistion. Explore the Monastiraki area, including the tiny Byzantine chapel of Kapnikarea, which stands in the middle of the street. In Monastiraki you can snack on the city's best souvlaki but leave room for your night of nights: In the evening, splurge at stunning "new/old," hot/cool Kuzina, and then dance the *tsifteteli* (the Greek version of a belly dance) to Asia Minor blues in a rembetika club, or, if it's summer and you're the hardy sort, visit the coastal stretch toward the airport, where the irrepressible bars stay open until dawn.

On the third day, start early for the legendary National Archaeological Museum, crammed with many of ancient Greece's most spectacular sculptures, breaking for lunch in one of the city's mezedopolia (places that sell mezes). Swing through the city center, past the Old University complex, a vestige of King Otho's reign, to the Cycladic Museum in Kolonaki, with the curious figurines that inspired artists such as Modigliani and Picasso. Stroll through the lovely National Gardens, and have a coffee in the romantic setting of the historic cafés here. Complete the evening with a ballet performance or pop music show at Herod Atticus, a movie at a therina (open-air cinema), or, in winter, a concert at the Megaron Symphony Hall.

DISCOUNTS AND DEALS

Athens's best deal is the €12 ticket that allows one week's admission to all the sites and corresponding museums along the Unification of Archaeological Sites walkway. You can buy the ticket at any of the sites, which include the Acropolis, ancient Agora, Roman Agora, Temple of Olympian Zeus, Kerameikos, and Theater of Dionysus. Entrance is usually free every day for European Union students, half off for students from other countries, and about a third off for senior citizens.

EMERGENCIES

Call an ambulance in the event of an emergency but taxis are often faster. Most hotels will call a doctor or dentist for you. Dial 106 (in Greek), check the *Athens News* or the English-language *Kathimerini,* inserted in the *Herald Tribune,* or ask your hotel to find out which emergency hospitals are open.

Contacts Ambulance ☎ *166.* **Athens City Police** ✉ *Ayiou Konstantinou 14* ☎ *100, 210/3259050.* **Hellenic Coast Guard** ☎ *108* ⊕ *www.hdc.gr.* **Fire Service** ☎ *199* ⊕ *www.fireservice.gr.* **Tourist Police** ☎ *171.*

ENGLISH LANGUAGE PUBLICATIONS

English-language books, newspapers, and magazines are readily available in central Athens at international bookstores and kiosks in Kolonaki and Syntagma. Local English-language publications include the weekly *Athens News,* which offers a mix of politics, features, travel, and style articles; the English-language version of *Kathimerini,* sold as an insert with the daily *International Herald Tribune; Odyssey* magazine, a glossy bimonthly; and *Insider,* a lifestyle monthly magazine.

GETTING HERE AND AROUND

Many major sights, as well as hotels, cafés, and restaurants, are within a fairly small central area of Athens. It's easy to walk everywhere, though sidewalks are often obstructed by parked cars. Most far-flung sights, such as beaches, are reachable by metro, bus, and tram.

Check the Organization for Urban Public Transportation (OASA) Web site *(⇨ Bus and Tram Travel)* for English-language information on how to use public transport to get to sights around the city. OASA also answers questions about routes (usually only in Greek; call center: ☎ 185). The office, open weekdays 7:30–3, distributes maps of bus routes with street names in Greek; these are also distributed at the white ticket kiosks at many bus terminals.

The price of public transportation has risen steeply, but it is still less than that in other western European capitals. Riding during rush hours is definitely not recommended. Buses especially are air-conditioned and have space for luggage, but they can sometimes get extremely crowded.

Upon boarding, validate your ticket in the orange canceling machines at the front and back of buses and trolleys and in metro stations. Keep your tickets until you reach your destination, as inspectors occasionally pop up to check that they have been canceled and validated. They are strict about fining offenders, including tourists.

You can buy a day pass covering the metro, buses, trolleys, and trams for €4; a weekly pass for €25; or, at the beginning of each month, a monthly pass for €45.

MULTITRIP PASSES
If you are planning to take the bus, trolley, and metro several times in one day during your stay, buy a 24-hour ticket for all the urban network (€4) or a single ticket (€1.40) valid for all travel completed within 90 minutes. A pass also saves you the hassle of validating tickets numerous times.

Or opt for a weekly pass (€14), or a monthly pass, available at the beginning of the month from terminal kiosks and metro stations (€20 for unlimited bus, trolley, and tram travel; €45 with metro included, not including the transportation to and from the El. Venizelos airport). You need a passport-size photograph of yourself for the pass.

AIR TRAVEL
The opening of Athens's sleek Eleftherios Venizelos International Airport has made air travel around the country much more pleasant and efficient. Greece is so small that few in-country flights take more than an hour or cost more than €200 round-trip.

Aegean Airlines and Olympic Airways have regular flights between Athens, Thessaloniki, and most major cities and islands in Greece. *For further information, see Air Travel in the Travel Smart chapter.*

TO AND FROM ATHENS AIRPORT
The best way to get to the airport from downtown Athens is by metro or light-rail. Single tickets cost €8 and include transfers within 90 minutes of the ticket's initial validation to bus, trolley, or tram. Combined tickets for two (€14) and three (€20) passengers are also available; if you're making a stopover in Athens, opt for a round-trip ticket (€20), valid for trips to and from the airport made during a single 48-hour period. In Athens four reliable express buses connect the airport with the metro (Nomismatokopeio, Ethniki Amyna and Dafni station), Syntagma Square, Kifissos Bus Station, and Piraeus. Express buses leave the arrivals level of the airport every 15 minutes and operate 24 hours a day. Bus X95 will take you to Syntagma Square (Amalias Avenue);

Bus X96 takes the Vari–Koropi Road inland and links with the coastal road, passing through Voula, Glyfada, and Alimos; it then goes on to Piraeus (opposite Karaiskaki Square). Bus X97 goes to the Dafni metro stop, while X93 brings voyagers to the dusty Kifissos intercity bus station. The Attiki Odos and the expansion of the city's network of bus lanes have made travel times more predictable.

Bus tickets to and from the airport cost €5 and are valid on all forms of transportation in Athens for 24 hours from the time of validation. Purchase tickets (and get bus schedules) from the airport terminal, kiosks, metro stations, or even on the express buses. Taxis are readily available at the arrivals level of the Athens airport; it costs an average of €35 to get into downtown Athens. (If you fear you have been overcharged, insist on a receipt with the driver's details and contact the tourist police.) Limousine Service and Royal Prestige Limousine Service provide service; an evening surcharge of up to 50% often applies, and you should call in advance. Prices start at around €90–€100 for one-way transfer from the airport to a central hotel.

Limousines Limousine Service Travel ☎ *210/970–6416* ⊕ *www.limousine-service.gr.* **Royal Prestige Limousine Service** ☎ *210/988–3221* ☎☎ *210/983–0378* ⊕ *www.limousine-services.gr.*

BOAT AND FERRY TRAVEL
Boat travel in Greece is common and relatively inexpensive. Every weekend thousands of Athenians set off on one- and two-hour trips to islands like Aegina, Hydra, and Andros, while in summer ferries are weighed down with merrymakers on their way to Mykonos, Rhodes, and Santorini. Cruise ships, ferries, and hydrofoils from the Aegean and most other Greek islands dock and depart every day from Athens's main port, Piraeus, 10 km (6 mi) southwest of Athens. Ships for Corfu sail from ports nearer to it, such as Patras and Igoumenitsa. Connections from Piraeus to the main island groups are good, while connections from main islands to smaller ones within a group less so.

Travel agents and ship offices in Athens and Piraeus have details. Boat schedules are published in *Kathimerini*, inserted in the *International Herald Tribune*. Check also the useful travel Web site ⊕ *www.openseas. gr.* You can also call a daily Greek recording *(listed below)* for ferry departure times. Timetables change according to seasonal demand, and boats may be delayed by weather conditions, so your plans should be flexible. Buy your tickets at least two or three days in advance, especially if you are traveling in summer or taking a car. Reserve your return journey or continuation soon after you arrive. *For further information, see Boat Travel in the Travel Smart chapter.*

GETTING TO AND FROM PIRAEUS AND RAFINA HARBORS FROM ATHENS' CITY CENTER To get to and from Piraeus harbor, you can take the Green Line metro (Line 1) from central Athens directly to the station at the main port. The trip takes 25–30 minutes. A taxi takes longer because of traffic and costs around €15–€18. Athens's other main port is Rafina, which serves some of the closer Cyclades and Evia.

KTEL buses run every 30 minutes between the port and the Mavromateon terminal in central Athens, from about 5:30 am until 9:30 pm, and cost €2.40 *(⇨ Bus and Tram Travel)*. At Rafina, the buses leave from an area slightly uphill from the port. The trip takes about one hour.

Boat and Ferry Information Piraeus boat departures/arrivals ☎ *14541, 14944.* **Piraeus Port Authority** ✉ *Piraeus Port Authority, 10 Akti Miaouli, Piraeus* ☎ *210/455–0000 through 210/455–0100* ⊕ *www.olp.gr.* **Rafina KTEL Buses** ☎ *22940/23440* ⊕ *www.ktelattikis.gr.*

BUS AND TRAM TRAVEL

Athens and its suburbs are covered by a good network of buses, with express buses running between central Athens and major neighborhoods, including nearby beaches.

During the day, buses tend to run every 15–30 minutes, with reduced service at night and on weekends. Buses run from about 5 am to midnight.

Main bus stations are at Akadimias and Sina and at Kaningos Square. Bus and trolley tickets cost €1.20 if intending to use them only once. The slightly more expensive €1.40 ticket is valid for a duration of 90 minutes and can be used for all modes of public transport (including bus, trolley, tram, metro, and suburban trains). Remember to validate the ticket (insert it in the ticket machine on the platform or on the train or bus to get it stamped with the date) once when you begin your journey. Day passes for €4, weekly passes for €14, and monthly passes for all means of transport for €45 (€20 for buses, trolleys, and trams only) are sold at special booths at the main terminals.

Passes are not valid for travel to the airport or on the E22 Saronida Express.

Maps of bus routes (in Greek) are available at terminal booths or from EOT. The Web site of the Organization for Urban Public Transportation (OASA) has a helpful English-language section (⊕ www.oasa.gr). Orange-and-white KTEL buses provide efficient service throughout the Attica basin. Most buses to the east Attica coast, including those for Sounion (€5.70 for inland route and €6.30 on coastal road) and Marathon (€3.70), leave from the KTEL terminal in Pedion Areos.

A tram link between downtown Athens and the coastal suburbs features two main lines.

Line A runs from Syntagma to Glyfada; Line B traces the shoreline from Glyfada to the Peace & Friendship Stadium on the outskirts of Piraeus. Single tickets cost €1.40 and are sold at machines on the tram platforms.

Bus and Tram Information City tram ⊕ *www.tramsa.gr.* **KTEL Buses - Attica** ✉ *Aigyptou Sq. at corner of Mavromateon and Leoforos Alexandras near Pedion Areos park, Pedion Areos* ☎ *210/880–8082 departure info for Marathon and Sounion, 210/880–80117 departure info for Marathon and Sounion* ⊕ *www. ktelattikis.org.* **Organization for Urban Public Transportation** ✉ *Metsovou 15, Exarchia* ☎ *210/820–0999, 210/883–6076* ⊕ *www.oasa.gr.*

BUS TRAVEL TO AND FROM ATHENS

Travel around Greece by bus is inexpensive and usually comfortable (though a lot depends on your driver and the condition of the bus). The journey from Athens to Thessaloniki takes roughly the same time as the regular train, though the InterCity Express train covers the distance 1¼ hours faster.

To reach the Peloponnese, buses are speedier than trains, though a new high-speed rail to Corinth and beyond (to Kiato) is slowly changing this. Information and timetables are available at tourist information offices and metro stations.

Make reservations at least one day before your planned trip, earlier for holiday weekends.

Terminal A—aka Kifissos Station—is the arrival and departure point for bus lines that serve parts of northern Greece, including Thessaloniki, and the Peloponnese destinations of Epidavros, Mycenae, Nafplion, Olympia, and Corinth. Each destination has its own phone number; EOT offices distribute a list. Terminal B serves Evia, most of Thrace, and central Greece, including Delphi. EOT provides a phone list *(⇨ Visitor Information)*. Tickets for these buses are sold only at this terminal, so you should call to book seats well in advance in high season or holidays. To get to the city center from Terminal A, take Bus 051 to Omonia Square; from Terminal B, take Bus 024 downtown. To get to the stations, catch Bus 051 at Zinonos and Menandrou off Omonia Square (for Terminal A) and Bus 024 on Amalias in front of the National Garden (for Terminal B). International buses drop their passengers off on the street, usually in the Omonia or Syntagma Square areas or in Plateia Karaiskaki, Metaxourgeio.

Bus Station Information Terminal A - KTEL Kifissou ⊠ *Kifissou 100, Kolonos* ☎ *210/512–4910, 210/512–4911.* **Terminal B– KTEL Liossion** ⊠ *Liossion 260, Kato Patissia* ☎ *210/831–7096 for Delphi, 210/831–7173 for Livadia [Ossios Loukas via Distomo], 210/831–1434 for Trikala [Meteora], 210/831–7186 general information.*

CAR TRAVEL IN ATHENS

Driving in Athens is not recommended unless you have nerves of steel; it can be unpleasant and even unsafe. Traffic tends toward gridlock or heart-stopping speeding and parking in most parts of the city could qualify as an Olympic sport. Locals are quick to point out that it is fairly easy to get around the city with a combination of public transportation and taxis, so why not save car rentals for excursions out of town? In town, red traffic lights are frequently ignored, and motorists often pass other vehicles while driving on hills and while rounding corners. Driving is on the right, and although the vehicle on the right has the right-of-way, don't expect this to be obeyed.

The speed limit is 50 "kph" (31 "mph") in town. Seat belts are compulsory, as are helmets for motorcyclists, though many ignore the laws. In the downtown sectors of the city do not drive in the bus lanes marked by a yellow divider; if caught, you may be fined. Downtown parking spaces are hard to find, and the few downtown garages—including ones in vacant lots—are both expensive and perpetually full. You're better off leaving your car in the hotel garage and walking or taking a cab. Gas pumps and service stations are everywhere, but be aware that all-night stations are few and far between.

CAR TRAVEL OUTSIDE ATHENS

Greece's main highways to the north and the south link up in Athens; both are called Ethniki Dodos (National Road). Take the Attiki Odos, a beltway around Athens that also accesses Eleftherios Venizelos International Airport, to speed your travel time entering and exiting the city. The toll is €2.80 for cars, payable upon entering this privately owned highway. At the city limits, signs in English clearly mark the way to both Syntagma Square and Omonia Square in the city center. Leaving Athens, routes to the highways and Attiki Odos are well marked; signs usually name Lamia for points north, and Corinth or Patras for points southwest. From Athens to Thessaloniki, the distance is 515 km (319 mi); to Kalamata, 257 km (159 mi); to Corinth, 84 km (52 mi); to Patras, 218 km (135 mi); to Igoumenitsa, 472 km (293 mi).

Most car rental offices are around Syngrou and Syntagma Square in central Athens but note it can be cheaper to book from your home country; small-car rentals start at around €40/day. *For more information, see Car Rental in the Travel Smart chapter.*

METRO (SUBWAY) TRAVEL

The best magic carpet ride in town is the metro. Cars are not worth the stress and road rage and, happily, the metro is fast, cheap, and convenient; its three lines go to all the major spots in Athens. Line 1, or the Green Line, of the city's metro (subway) system, is often called the *elektrikos* (or the electrical train) and runs from Piraeus to the northern suburb of Kifissia, with several downtown stops. Downtown stations on Line 1 most handy to tourists include Victoria Square, near the National Archaeological Museum; Omonia Square; Monastiraki, in the old Turkish bazaar; and Thission, near the ancient Agora and the nightlife districts of Psirri and Thission.

In 2000, the city opened Lines 2 and 3 of the metro, many of whose gleaming gray marble–stations function as mini-museums, displaying ancient artifacts found on-site. These lines are safe and fast but cover limited territory, mostly downtown. Line 2, or the Red Line, cuts northwest across the city, starting from surburban Ayios Antonios and passing through such useful stops as Syntagma Square, opposite the Greek Parliament; Panepistimiou (near the Old University complex and the Numismatic Museum); Omonia Square; Metaxourgeio; the Stathmos Larissis stop next to Athens's Central train station, and Acropolis, at the foot of the famous site, finishing off at the south suburb of Ayios Dimitrios.

Line 3, or the Blue Line, runs from the suburb of Aegaleo through Kerameikos (the stop for bustling Gazi) and Monastiraki; some trains on this line go all the way to the airport, but they only pass about every half hour and require a special ticket. The stops of most interest for visitors are Evangelismos, near the Byzantine and Christian Museum, Hilton Hotel, and National Gallery of Art, and Megaron Mousikis, next to the U.S. Embassy and the concert hall. The fare is €1.40, except from tickets to the airport, which are €8. A 24-hour travel pass, valid for use on all forms of public transportation, is €4. You must validate all tickets at the machines in metro stations before you board. Trains run between 5:30 am and 1 am. Maps of the metro are available in stations.

There is no phone number for information about the system, so check the Web site (⊕ *www.amel.gr*).

TAXI TRAVEL

Most drivers in Athens speak basic English. Although you can find an empty taxi on the street, it's often faster to call out your destination to one carrying passengers; if the taxi is going in that direction, the driver will pick you up. Likewise, don't be alarmed if your driver picks up other passengers (although he should ask your permission first). Each passenger pays full fare for the distance he or she has traveled. Taxi rates are still affordable compared to fares in other European capitals, but prices are steadily climbing. Get an idea from your hotel how much the fare should be, and if there's trouble, ask to go to a police station (most disagreements don't ever get this far, however). Make sure the driver turns on the meter and that the rate listed in the lower corner is 1, the normal rate before midnight; after midnight, the rate listed is 2.

Taxi drivers know the major central hotels, but if your hotel is less well known, show the driver the address written in Greek and make note of the hotel's phone number and, if possible, a nearby landmark. If all else fails, the driver can call the hotel from his mobile phone or a kiosk. Athens has thousands of short side streets, and few taxi drivers have maps, although newer taxis have GPS installed. Neither tipping nor bargaining is generally practiced; if your driver has gone out of the way for you, a small gratuity (10% or less) is appreciated.

TAXI FARES The Athens taxi meter starts at €1.19, and, even if you join other passengers, you must add this amount to your final charge. The minimum fare is €3.16. The basic charge is €0.68 per kilometer (½ mi); this increases to €1.19 between midnight and 5 am or if you go outside city limits. There are surcharges for holidays (€1), trips to and from the airport (€3.40), and rides to (but not from) the port, train stations, and bus terminals (€0.95). There is also a €0.35 charge for each suitcase over 22 pounds, but drivers expect €0.35 for each bag anyway. Waiting time is €9.60 per hour. Radio taxis charge an additional €3 to €5 for the pickup.

Taxi Companies **Athens 1 Intertaxi** ☎ *210/921–2800* ⊕ *www.athens1. gr*. **Ermis taxi service** ☎ *210/411–5200, 801116300*. **Radio Taxi Hellas** ☎ *210/645–7000*, ⊕ *www.radiotaxihellas.gr*. **Parthenon Radio Taxi** ☎ *210/532–3300*.

TRAIN TRAVEL

The *Proastiakos* ("suburban"), a light-rail network offering travelers a direct link from Athens El. Venizelos airport to Corinth for €12, is introducing Athenians to the concept of commuting. The trains now serve the city's northern and eastern suburbs as well as western Attica. The Athens-to-Corinth fare is €9; lower fares apply for points in between. If you plan on taking the train while in Athens, call the Greek Railway Organization (OSE) to find out which station your train leaves from, and how to get there. Trains from the north and international trains arrive at, and depart from, Stathmos Larissis, which is connected to the metro. If you want to buy tickets ahead of time, it's easier to visit a downtown railway office. *For further information, see Train Travel in the Travel Smart chapter.*

Train Information Greek Railway Organization (OSE) ☎ *1110 customer support* ⊕ *www.trainose.gr.* **Proastiakos** ☎ *1110* ⊕ *www.trainose.gr.***Stathmos Larissis Train Station** ☎ *210/529–8821, 210/529–8841, 210/529–8829.*

SIGHTSEEING GUIDES

Major travel agencies can provide English-speaking guides to take you around Athens's major sights. The Union of Official Guides provides licensed guides for individual or group tours, starting at about €100, including taxes, for a four-hour tour of the Acropolis and its museum. Hire only guides licensed by the EOT—they have successfully completed a two-year state program.

Personal Guides Union of Certified Guides ✉ *Apollonos 9A, Plaka* ☎ *210/322–9705, 210/322–0090* ⊟ *210/323–9200* ⊕ *www.tourist-guides.gr.*

VISITOR INFORMATION

The main office of the Greek National Tourism Organization (GNTO; EOT in Greece) is at Tsoha 7, in the Ambelokipi district, not far from the Megaron Mousikis concert hall, in the heart of Athens. Their offices generally close around 2 pm. The Web site of the city of Athens (⊕ *www. cityofathens.gr*) has a small but growing section in English but also check out their more enticing new entry (⊕ *www.breathtakingathens. com*). The English-speaking tourist police can answer questions about transportation, steer you to an open pharmacy or doctor, and locate phone numbers of hotels and restaurants.

Contact InformationCity of Athens Web site. The official City of Athens visitors' Web site for useful and up-to-date info on Athenian life. ⊕ *www. breathtakingathens.com.* **Greek National Tourism Organization (EOT)** ✉ *Tsoha 7, near Megaron Mousikis, Ambelokipi* ☎ *210/870–7000* ⊕ *www.visitgreece. gr* ✉ *Eleftherios Venizelos International Airport, arrivals hall* ☎ *210/353–0445* ✉ *EOT Information desk, Dionysiou Areopageitou 10, Plaka* ☎ *210/3310392, 210/3310716.* **Tourist Police** ✉ *Veikou 43, 4th fl., Koukaki* ☎ *171, 1572 GNTO - Tourist Protection Line for consumer complaints.*

TOUR OPTIONS
EXCURSION DAY TRIPS BY BUS

Most travel agencies offer excursions at about the same prices, but CHAT is reputed to have the best service and guides. Common excursion tours include a half-day trip to the Temple of Poseidon at Sounion (€42); a half-day tour to the Isthmus and ancient Corinth (€57); a full-day tour to Delphi (€89); a two-day trip to Delphi (from €130); a three-day tour taking in Delphi and the monasteries of Meteora with half-board in first-class hotels (€299); a one-day tour to Nafplion, Mycenae, and Epidavros (from €89); a two-day tour to Mycenae, Nafplion, and Epidavros (from €130); and a four-day "classical" tour covering all major sights in the Peloponnese, as well as Delphi and Meteora (from €458). Most tours run two to three times a week, with reduced service in winter. It's best to reserve a few days in advance. *For a full list of agencies that offer tours—including CHAT—see our list of tour operators under Travel Agencies in Athens, below.*

SIGHTSEEING HOP-ON, HOP-OFF TOUR BUSES

The best way to get quickly acquainted with Athens is to opt for a ride on the "Athens City Sightseeing Bus," a typical tourist double-decker with open top floors, which stops at all the city's main sights. Those privately-owned buses run every 15 minutes and tickets cost €18. The full tour takes 90 minutes, but you can hop on and off as you please in one of the 18 stops (including Syntagma Square), all through the day. There is an audio guide in eight languages (⊕ *www.city-sightseeing.com*).

Other sightseeing bus options include multihour guided tours, most of which visit the Acropolis and National Archaeological Museum, plus other sites, and lunch in a Plaka taverna. Let's not forget the fun "Athens by Night" bus tours. Morning tours begin around 8:45. Reserve through most hotels or travel agencies (many of which are clustered around Filellinon and Nikis streets off Syntagma Square). These excursion tours run daily, year-round, and cost around €60. Book at least a day in advance and ask if you'll be picked up at your hotel or if you have to meet the bus.

CONTACT INFORMATION

Two top tour bus companies are:

CHAT Tours ⊠ *Xenofontos 9, Syntagma* ☎ *210/322–2886, 210/322–3137* ⊕ *www.chatours.gr.* **Key Tours** ⊠ *Kallirois 4* ☎ *210/923–3166* ⊕ *www. keytours.gr.*

TRAVEL AGENCIES IN ATHENS

Throughout Greece, travel agencies often stand in for official tourism offices, so don't be shy in availing yourself of their services. They also organize many bus sightseeing excursions in and out of the city.

Contact Information American Express Travel Services ⊠ *L. Mesogeion 318, Ag. Paraskevi* ☎ *210/659–0700* ⊕ *americanexpress.com.* **Amphitrion Travel** ⊠ *Meg. Alexandrou 7 & Karaiskaki, Argyroupoli* ☎ *210/900–6000* ⊕ *www. amphitrionholidays.com.* **Chat Tours** ⊠ *Xenofontos 9, Syntagma* ☎ *210/322– 2886* ⊕ *www.chatours.gr.* **Dolphin Hellas** ⊠ *Syngrou 16, Makriyianni* ☎ *210/922–7772, 210/923–2101* ⊕ *www.dolphin-hellas.gr.* **Key Tours** ⊠ *Kalirrois 4* ☎ *210/923–3166, 210/923–3266* ⊕ *www.keytours.gr.* **Magic Travel** ⊠ *Nikis 33, Syntagma Sq.* ☎ *210/323–7471* ⊕ *www.magic.gr.* **Pharos Travel** ⊠ *Triti Septemvriou 18, Patissia* ☎ *210/523–3403.* **Travel Plan** ⊠ *Christou Lada 3* ☎ *210/333–3300* ⊕ *www.travelplan.gr.*

EXPLORING ATHENS

Although Athens covers a huge area, the major landmarks of the ancient Greek, Roman, and Byzantine periods are close to the modern city center. You can easily walk from the Acropolis to many other key sites, taking time to browse in shops and relax in cafés and tavernas along the way. From many quarters of the city you can glimpse "the glory that was Greece" in the form of the Acropolis looming above the horizon, but only by actually climbing that rocky precipice can you feel the impact of the ancient settlement. The Acropolis and Filopappou, two craggy hills sitting side by side; the ancient Agora (marketplace); and Kerameikos, the first cemetery, form the core of ancient and Roman

Athens. Along the Unification of Archaeological Sites promenade, you can follow stone-paved, tree-lined walkways from site to site, undisturbed by traffic. Cars have also been banned or reduced in other streets in the historical center. In the National Archaeological Museum, vast numbers of artifacts illustrate the many millennia of Greek civilization; smaller museums such as the Goulandris Museum of Cycladic Art Museum and the Byzantine and Christian Museum illuminate the history of particular regions or periods.

Athens may seem like one huge city, but it is really a conglomeration of neighborhoods with distinctive characters. The Eastern influences that prevailed during the 400-year rule of the Ottoman Empire are still evident in Monastiraki, the bazaar area near the foot of the Acropolis. On the northern slope of the Acropolis, stroll through Plaka (if possible by moonlight), an area of tranquil streets lined with renovated mansions, to get the flavor of the 19th-century's gracious lifestyle. The narrow lanes of Anafiotika, a section of Plaka, thread past tiny churches and small, color-washed houses with wooden upper stories, recalling a Cycladic island village. In this maze of winding streets, vestiges of the older city are everywhere: crumbling stairways lined with festive tavernas; dank cellars filled with wine vats; occasionally a court or diminutive garden, enclosed within high walls and filled with magnolia trees and the flaming trumpet-shaped flowers of hibiscus bushes.

Formerly run-down old quarters, such as Thission, Gazi and Psirri, popular nightlife areas filled with bars and *mezedopoleia* (similar to tapas bars), are now in the process of gentrification, although they still retain much of their original charm, as does the colorful produce and meat market on Athinas. The area around Syntagma Square, the tourist hub, and Omonia Square, the commercial heart of the city about 1 km (½ mi) northwest, is distinctly European, having been designed by the court architects of King Otho, a Bavarian, in the 19th century. The chic shops and bistros of ritzy Kolonaki nestle at the foot of Mt. Lycabettus, Athens's highest hill (909 feet). Each of Athens's outlying suburbs has a distinctive character: in the north is wealthy, tree-lined Kifissia, once a summer resort for aristocratic Athenians, and in the south and southeast lie Glyfada, Voula, and Vouliagmeni, with their sandy beaches, seaside bars, and lively summer nightlife. Just beyond the city's southern fringes is Piraeus, a bustling port city of waterside fish tavernas and Saronic Gulf views.

COLD RELIEF

The center of modern Athens is small, stretching from the Acropolis in the southwest to Mt. Lycabettus in the northeast, crowned by the small white chapel of Ayios Georgios. The layout is simple: three parallel streets—Stadiou, Eleftheriou Venizelou (familiarly known as Panepistimiou), and Akadimias—link two main squares, Syntagma (Constitution) and Omonia (Concord). Try to detour off this beaten tourist track: seeing the Athenian butchers in the Central Market sleeping on their cold marble slabs during the heat of the afternoon siesta may give you more of a feel for the city than seeing scores of toppled columns.

THE ACROPOLIS AND ENVIRONS ΑΚΡΟΠΟΛΗ ΚΑΙ ΠΕΡΙΧΩΡΑ

Although Athens, together with its suburbs and port, sprawls across the plain for more than 150 square mi, most of its ancient monuments cluster around the Acropolis, which rises like a massive sentinel, white and beautiful, out of the center of the city. In mountainous Greece, most ancient towns were backed up by an acropolis, an easily defensible upper town (which is what the word means), but when spelled with a capital "A" it can only refer to antiquity's most splendid group of buildings—the Acropolis of Athens.

Towering over the modern metropolis of 4.5 million as it once stood over the ancient capital of 50,000, it has remained Athens's most spectacular attraction ever since its first settlement around 5000 BC. It had been a religious center long before Athens became a major city-state in the 6th century BC. It has been associated with Athena ever since the city's mythical founding, but virtually all of the city's other religious cults had temples or shrines here as well. As Athens became the dominant city-state in the 5th century BC, Pericles led the city in making the Acropolis the crowning symbol of Athenian power and successful democracy.

After the Acropolis all will at first seem to be an anticlimax. But there is much more that is still well worth seeing on the citadel's periphery, including the New Acropolis Museum, the neoclassic buildings lining Dionyssiou Areopagitou, the centuries-old Odeon of Herodes Atticus, and Filopappou, the pine-clad summit that has the city's best view of the Acropolis. Have your Nikon ready!

TOP ATTRACTIONS

Fodor's Choice
★

Acropolis. Towering over a modern city of 4.5 million inhabitants much as it stood over the ancient capital of 50,000, the Acropolis (literally "high town") continues to be Athens's most spectacular, photogenic, and visited attraction despite hundreds of years of renovations, bombings, and artistic lootings. The buildings, constructed under the direction of Pericles during the city's Golden Age in the 5th century BC, were designed to be as visually harmonious as they were enormous, and they stand today in a perfect balance of stubborn immortality and elegant fragmentation. *For an in-depth look at this emblem of the glories of classical Greek civilization, and the adjacent, headline-making New Acropolis Museum, see our photo-feature, "The Acropolis: Ascent to Glory" in this chapter.*

Filopappou. This summit includes **Lofos Mousson** (Hill of the Muses), whose peak offers the city's best view of the Parthenon, which appears almost at eye level. Also there is the **Monument of Filopappus,** depicting a Syrian prince who was such a generous benefactor that the people accepted him as a distinguished Athenian. The marble monument is a tomb decorated by a frieze showing Filopappus driving his chariot. In 294 BC a fort strategic to Athens's defense was built here, overlooking the road to the sea. On the hill of the **Pnyx** (meaning "crowded"), the all-male general assembly (Ecclesia) met during the time of Pericles. Originally, citizens of the Ecclesia faced the Acropolis while listening to speeches, but they tended to lose their concentration as they gazed upon the monuments, so the positions of the speaker and the audience

Continued on page 96

THE ACROPOLIS
ASCENT TO GLORY

One of the wonders of the world, the Acropolis symbolizes Greece's Golden Age. Its stunning centerpiece, the Parthenon, was commissioned in the 5th century BC by the great Athenian leader Pericles as part of an elaborate building program designed to epitomize the apex of an iconic culture. Thousands of years later, the Acropolis pulls the patriotic heartstrings of modern Greeks and lulls millions of annual visitors back to an ancient time.

You don't have to look far in Athens to encounter perfection. Towering above all—both physically and spiritually—is the Acropolis, the ancient city of upper Athens and womb of Western civilization. Raising your eyes to the crest of this *ieros vrachos* (sacred rock), the sight of the Parthenon will stop you in your tracks. The term Akropolis (to use the Greek spelling) means "High City," and today's traveler who climbs this table-like hill is paying tribute to the prime source of civilization as we know it.

A TITANIC TEMPLE

Described by the 19th-century French poet Alphonse de Lamartine as "the most perfect poem in stone," the Acropolis is a true testament to the Golden Age of Greece. While archaeological evidence has shown that the flat-top limestone outcrop, 512 feet high, attracted settlers as early as Neolithic times, most of its most imposing structures were built from 461 to 429 BC, when the intellectual and artistic life of Athens flowered under the influence of the Athenian statesman, Pericles. Even

in its bleached and silent state, the Parthenon—the Panathenaic temple that crowns the rise—has the power to stir the heart as few other ancient relics do.

PERICLES TO POLLUTION

Since the Periclean Age, the buildings of the Acropolis have been inflicted with the damages of war, as well as unscrupulous transformations into, at various times, a Florentine palace, an Islamic mosque, a Turkish harem, and a World War II sentry. Since then, a more insidious enemy—pollution—has emerged. The site is presently undergoing conservation measures as part of an ambitious rescue plan. Today, the Erechtheion temple has been completely restored, and work on the Parthenon, Temple of Athena Nike, and the Propylaea is due for completion by the end of 2010. A final phase, involving massive landscaping works, will last through 2020. Despite the ongoing restoration work, a visit to the Acropolis today can evoke the spirit of the ancient heroes and gods who were once worshiped here.

THE PARTHENON

PINNACLE OF THE PERICLEAN AGE

DEDICATED TO ATHENA

At the loftiest point of the Acropolis stands the Parthenon, the architectural masterpiece conceived by Pericles and executed between 447 and 438 BC by the brilliant sculptor Pheidias, who supervised the architects Iktinos and Kallikrates in its construction. It not only raised the bar in terms of sheer size, but also in the perfection of its proportions.

Dedicated to the goddess Athena (the name Parthenon comes from the Athena Parthenos, or the virgin Athena) and inaugurated at the Panathenaic Festival of 438 BC, the Parthenon served primarily as the treasury of the Delian League, an ancient alliance of cities formed to defeat the Persian incursion. In fact, the Parthenon was built as much to honor the city's power as to venerate Athena. Its foundations, laid after the victory at Marathon in 490 BC, were destroyed by the Persian army in 480–479 BC. In turn, the city-state of Athens banded together with Sparta to rout the Persians by 449 BC.

To proclaim its hegemony over all Greece, Athens envisioned a grand new Acropolis. After a 30-year building moratorium, the titanic-scale project of reconstructing the temple was initiated by Pericles around 448 BC.

490 BC
Foundation for Acropolis laid

447–438 BC
The Parthenon is constructed

420 BC
Temple of Athena Nike is completed

TIMELINE

EDIFICE REX: PERICLES

His name means "surrounded by glory." Some scholars consider this extraordinary, enigmatic Athenian general to be the architect of the destiny of Greece at its height, while others consider him a megalomaniac who bankrupted the coffers of an empire and an elitist who catered to the privileged few at the expense of the masses.

Indeed, Pericles (460–429 BC) plundered the treasury of the Athenian alliance for the Acropolis building program. One academic has even called the Periclean building program the largest embezzlement in human history.

MYTH IN MARBLE

But Pericles's masterstroke becomes more comprehensible when studied against the conundrum that was Athenian democracy.

In truth an aristocracy that was the watchdog of private property and public order, this political system financed athletic games and drama festivals; it constructed exquisite buildings. Its motto was not only to live, but to live well. Surrounded by barbarians, the Age of Pericles was the more striking for its high level of civilization, its qualities of proportion, reason, clarity, and harmony, all of which are epitomized nowhere else as beautifully as in the Parthenon.

To their credit, the Athenians rallied around Pericles' vision: the respect for the individualistic character of men and women could be revealed through art and architecture.

Even jaded Athenians, when overwhelmed by the city, feel renewed when they lift their eyes to this great monument.

TRICK OF THE TRADE

One of the Parthenon's features, or "refinements," is the way it uses meiosis (tapering of columns) and entasis (a slight swelling so that the column can hold the weight of the entablature), deviations from strict mathematics that breathed movement into the rigid marble. Architects knew that a straight line looks curved, and vice versa, so they cleverly built the temple with all the horizontal lines somewhat curved. The columns, it has been calculated, lean toward the center of the temple; if they were to continue into space, they would eventually converge to create a huge pyramid.

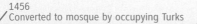

1456
Converted to mosque by occupying Turks

September 26, 1687
The Parthenon, used for gunpowder storage, explodes after being hit by a mortar shell

The Acropolis in Pericles's Time

RAISING A HUE

"Just my color—beige!" So proclaimed Elsie de Wolfe, celebrated decorator to J. Pierpont Morgan, when she first saw the Parthenon. As it turns out, the original Parthenon was anything but beige. Especially ornate, it had been covered with a tile roof, decorated with statuary and marble friezes, adorned with gilded wooden doors and ceilings, and walls and columns so brightly hued that the people protested, "We are adorning our city like a wanton woman" (Plutarch). The finishing touch was provided by the legendary sculptor Pheidias, who created some of the sculpted friezes—these were also brightly colored.

THE ERECHTHEION

PARTHENON

ATHENA PROMACHOS
Pheidias's colossal bronze statue of Athena Promachos, one of the largest of antiquity at 30' (9 m) high, could be seen from the sea. It was destroyed after being moved to Constantinople in 1203.

THE PROPYLAEA

TOURING THE ACROPOLIS

Most people take the metro to the Acropolis station, where the New Acropolis Museum opened in 2009. They then follow the pedestrianized street Dionyssiou Areopagitou, which traces the foothill of the Acropolis to its entrance at the Beulé Gate. Another entrance is along the rock's northern face via the Peripatos, a paved path from the Plaka district.

THE BEULÉ GATE

You enter the Acropolis complex through this late-Roman structure named for the French archaeologist Ernest Beulé, who discovered the gate in 1852. Made of marble fragments from the destroyed monument of Nikias on the south slope of the Acropolis, it has an inscription above the lintel dated 320 BC, dedicated by "Nikias son of Nikodemos of Xypete." Before Roman times, the entrance to the Acropolis was a steep processional ramp below the Temple of Athena Nike. This Sacred Way was used every fourth year for the Panathenaic procession, a spectacle that honored Athena's remarkable birth (she sprang from the head of her father, Zeus).

THE PROPYLAEA

This imposing structure was designed to instill the proper reverence in worshipers as they crossed from the temporal world into the spiritual world of the sanctuary, for this was the main function of the Acropolis. Conceived by Pericles, the Propylaea was the masterwork of the architect Mnesicles. Conceived to be the same size as the Parthenon, it was to have been the grandest secular building in Greece. Construction was suspended during the

TEMPLE OF
ATHENA NIKE

Peloponnesian War, and it was never finished. The structure shows the first use of both Doric and Ionic columns together, a style that can be called Attic. Six of the sturdier fluted Doric columns, made from Pendelic marble, correspond with the gateways of the portal. Processions with priests, chariots, and sacrificial animals entered via a marble ramp in the center (now protected by a wooden stairway), while ordinary visitors on foot entered via the side doors. The slender Ionic columns had elegant capitals, some of which have been restored along with a section of the famed paneled ceiling, originally decorated with gold eight-pointed stars on a blue background. Adjacent to the Pinakotheke, or art gallery (with paintings of scenes from Homer's epics and mythological tableaux), the south wing is a decorative portico. The view from the inner porch of the Propylaea is stunning: the Parthenon is suddenly revealed in its full glory, framed by the columns.

THE TEMPLE OF ATHENA NIKE

The 2nd-century traveler Pausanias referred to this fabled temple as the Temple of Nike Apteros, or Wingless Victory, for "in Athens they believe Victory will stay forever because she has no wings." Designed by Kallikrates, the mini-temple was built in 427–424 BC to celebrate peace with Persia. The bas-reliefs on the surrounding parapet depicting the Victories leading heifers to be sacrificed must have been of exceptional quality, judging from the section called "Nike Unfastening Her Sandal" in the New Acropolis Museum. In 1998, Greek archaeologists began dismantling the entire temple for conservation. After laser-cleaning the marble to remove generations of soot, the team will reconstruct the temple on its original site.

THE BEULÉ GATE

THE ERECHTHEION

If the Parthenon is the masterpiece of Doric architecture, the Erechtheion is undoubtedly the prime exemplar of the more graceful Ionic order. A considerably smaller structure than the Parthenon, it outmatches, for sheer refinement of design and execution, all other buildings of the Greco-Roman world.

For the populace, the much smaller temple—*not* the Parthenon—remained Athena's holiest shrine: legend has it that on this spot Poseidon plunged his trident into the rock, dramatically producing a spring of water, whereas Athena created a simple olive tree, whose fruit remains a main staple of Greek society. A panel of judges declared her the winner, and the city was named Athens. A gnarled olive tree still grows outside the Erechtheion's west wall, where Athena's once grew, and marks said to be from Poseidon's trident can be seen on a rock wedged in a hole near the north porch.

Completed in 406 BC, the Erechtheion was divided into two Ionic sanctuaries. The most delightful feature is the Caryatid Porch, supported on the heads of six strapping but shapely maidens (caryatids) wearing delicately draped Ionian garments, their folds perfectly aligned to resemble flutes on columns.

Now replaced by casts, the originals of the Erechtheion's famous Caryatid maidens are in the New Acropolis Museum.

PLANNING YOUR VISIT

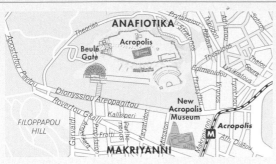

When exploring the Acropolis, keep the below pointers in mind. As the hill's stones are slippery and steep, it is best to wear rubber-soled shoes.

What Are the Best Times to Go? Such is the beauty of the Acropolis and the grandeur of the setting that a visit in all seasons and at all hours is rewarding. In general, the earlier you start out the better. In summer, by noon the heat is blistering and the reflection of the light thrown back by the rock and the marble ruins is almost blinding. An alternative, in summer, is to visit after 5 PM, when the light is best for taking photographs. In any season the ideal time might be the two hours before sunset, when occasionally the fabled violet light spreads from the crest of Mt. Hymettus (which the ancients called "violet-crowned") and gradually embraces the Acropolis. After dark the hill is spectacularly floodlighted, creating a scene visible from many parts of the capital. A moonlight visit—sometimes scheduled by the authorities during full moons in summer—is highly evocative. In winter, if there are clouds trailing across the mountains, and shafts of sun lighting up the marble columns, the setting takes on an even more dramatic quality.

How Long Does a Visit Usually Run? Depending on the crowds, the walk takes about three hours, plus several more spent in the New Acropolis Museum.

Are Tour Guides Available? The Union of Official Guides (Apollonos 9A, Syntagma, 210/322-9705, 210/322-0090) offers licensed guides for tours of archaeological sites within Athens. Another option is Amphitrion Holidays (Syngrou 7, Koukaki, 210/900-6000), which offers walking tours of the Acropolis. Guides will also help kids understand the site better.

What's the Handiest Place to Refuel? The Tourist Pavilion (Filoppapou Hill, 210/923-1665), a landscaped, tree-shaded spot soundtracked by chirping birds. It serves drinks, snacks, and a few hot dishes.

Dionysiou Areopagitou, Acropolis

☎ 210/321–4172 or 210/321-0219

🌐 www.culture.gr

🎫 Joint ticket for all Unification of Archaeological Sites €12. Good for five days—and for free admission—to the Ancient Agora, Theatre of Dionysus, Kerameikos cemetery, Temple of Olympian Zeus, and the Roman Forum.

🕐 Apr.–Oct., daily 8–6:30; Nov.–Mar., daily 8–3

Ⓜ Acropolis

DON'T FORGET:

■ If it's hot, remember to bring water, sunscreen, and a hat to protect yourself from the sun.

■ Get a free bilingual pamphlet guide (in English and Greek) at the entrance gate. It is packed with information, but staffers usually don't bother to give it out unless asked.

■ An elevator now ascends to the summit of the Acropolis, once inaccessible to people with disabilities.

■ All large bags, backpacks, and shopping bags will have to be checked in the site cloakroom.

Temple of Olympian Zeus

ACROPOLIS NOW: ATHENS'S NEWEST MUSEUM

Clambering up the Acropolis hill to view the Parthenon lets today's travelers witness, close-up, monuments of beauty and grace that have not been surpassed in two and a half millennia. But to fully pay homage to the glory that was Greece you must also head to the foot of the hill to explore the New Acropolis Museum. Opened in June 2009, this super-modern building seems a highly incongruous addition to historic Makriyanni, the district that lies at the southern end of the ancient Acropolis. But the glass-and-steel structure—designed by celebrated Swiss architect Bernard Tschumi—has won over most critics' reservations by the way it reaffirms the ever-old-but-always-new vitality of the ancient temple.

MODERN DRAMA

While the New Acropolis Museum respectfully nods to the ancient hill above it, it speaks—like I. M. Pei's glass pyramid at the Louvre—a contemporary architectural language. A subtle, light-embued blend of high-tech glass and timeless stone, it not only represents the latest in cutting-edge museum design but is seen, more importantly, as the perfect opportunity to showcase the Parthenon Marbles, which the government of Greece has long been fighting to repatriate from London's British Museum. In the five-level museum, every shade of marble is on display and bathed in abundant, UV-safe natural light. Regal glass walkways, very high ceilings, striking industrial accents, and panoramic views are all part of the experience. A second-floor restaurant, with its own eagle's-eye view of the Acropolis, has been an instant hit.

ANCIENT STONES

The ground-floor exhibit, "The Acropolis Slopes," features objects found in the sanctuaries around the Acropolis, with the next floor devoted to the Archaic period (650 BC–480 BC), with rows of precious statues mounted for 360-degree viewing. Perched on a wall balcony, the five Caryatids (or Korai)—the group of legendary female figures

✉ Dionysiou Areopagitou 15, Makriyianni, Acropolis, 11742
🌐 www.theacropolismuseum.gr
🎟 €5
🕐 Tues.–Sun., 8–8

who once supported the Acropolis's Erectheion building—symbolically leave a space for the sixth sister, who resides in London's British Museum.

At the topmost atrium level, you can watch a video on the Parthenon before entering the climactic Parthenon Gallery. Here, frieze pieces, metopes (sculpted panels), and pedimental sculptures are all laid out to follow the Parthenon's original blueprint. This is made easily apparent because the rectangular-shape gallery—whose floor-to-ceiling windows provide magnificent vistas of the temple—is tilted to align with the Parthenon itself.

GREAT MASTERPIECES

Pride of place goes to the Frieze of the Great Panathenaia, an extraordinary, 524-feet-long procession of 400 people, including maidens, magistrates, horsemen, and musicians, plus 200 animals, all parading in honor of the goddess Athena. To show ordinary mortals, at a time when almost all sculpture fea-

tured mythological or battle scenes, was lively and daring. Nearby are exhibited the incomparable metops, 92 of which depict scenes from three mythic battles: the Gigantomachy (between the Olympic gods and the giants), the Amazonmachy (between Athenian youths and Amazons), and the Centauromachy (between the Lapiths and the Centaurs). These battles were seen as inspiring symbols of the contest between the forces of civilization and barbarism, a potent message from the era that was the fountainhead of Western civilization.

TOP FIVE

1. The Frieze of the Great Panathenaia Procession
2. The Gigantomachy, Amazonmachy, and Centauromachy Metops
3. The Erechtheion's Caryatids
4. Nike Unfastening Her Sandal
5. The Moschophoros (Calf-Bearer)

HAS GREECE LOST ITS MARBLES?

Sleek, state-of-the-art, and sumptuous, the New Acropolis Museum has thrown down a gauntlet of sorts by challenging the venerable British claim that Greece has never provided a suitable home for the Parthenon treasures. Ever since the early 19th century, when Lord Elgin removed half of the Parthenon Marbles to England for "safekeeping," Greece has been fighting to have these masterworks of 5th-century BC art returned to their homeland. Now that Athens has created a magnificent new home for these sculptures, the debate has become even more heated.

Back in Pericles's day, the Parthenon was most famous for two colossal (now vanished) statues fashioned by Pheidias: a tall bronze statue of Athena inside the temple, and one of Athena the Champion (Promachos), which faced anyone climbing the great hill. Today, all attention is focused on the "missing" marbles—the statues from the temple frieze and pediments that were shipped to England by Lord Elgin between 1801 and 1805. At that time, during the rule of the Ottoman Empire, Elgin, as British ambassador in Constantinople, was given permission by the Sultan Selim III to remove stones with inscriptions from the Acropolis; he took this as permission to dismantle shiploads of sculptures.

Some historians say Elgin was neither ethical nor delicate in removing two-thirds of the famous Parthenon friezes and half the marbles, causing irreparable damage to both the marbles and the Parthenon by hacking or sawing the sculptures into pieces to extricate them. On the other side, many argue that the marbles would have been destroyed if left on site. About 50 of the best-preserved pieces of the Panathenaian procession, called the Parthenon Marbles by Greeks but known as the Elgin Marbles by others, are in the British Museum; some can be

> Dull is the eye that will not weep
> to see / Thy walls defaced, thy
> mouldering shrines removed / By
> British hands, which it had best
> behoved / To guard those relics
> ne'er to be restored.
>
> —From the poem "Childe Harolde's Pilgrimage" by the
> philhellene Lord Byron, published between 1812–18.

IN THIS CORNER: LORD ELGIN

The British nobleman and future diplomat Thomas Bruce, the seventh Earl of Elgin, became Britain's ambassador to the Ottoman Empire in 1799. His years in Constantinople were not happy: he suffered from what was very likely syphilis (the disease ate away his nose), and his wife soon took off with her personal escort. But Lord Elgin found purpose in "saving" priceless antiquities ignored by the ruling Turks and shipping them to Britain at enormous personal expense. Today, some consider him "a prince among thieves."

IN THIS CORNER: MELINA MERCOURI

She was so beloved as an actress and singer that people called her only by her first name. But behind the smoky eyes and husky voice that lit up the film *Never On Sunday* (1960) lay the heart of a fierce activist. As the country's first female culture minister, Melina led the fight to reclaim the Parthenon Marbles from Britain—"In the world over, the very name of our country is immediately associated with the Parthenon," she proclaimed. After she passed away, in 1994, a bust of her likeness was placed in the Dionysiou Areopagitou pedestrian walkway, in the shadow of the Acropolis.

seen in the Acropolis Museum, while a few remain on the temple itself.

GREECE VS. BRITAIN

The minuets of museum politics become fully apparent when one enters the top-floor Parthenon Gallery of the New Acropolis Museum. The Parthenon Marbles still in London are replaced here by replicas, instantly and provokingly apparent when their whiter tone is compared to the creamy stone hue of the original sculptures on view right alongside them. This gallery was designed—as Greek officials have made clear—to hold the Parthenon Marbles in their *entirety*. Their spirited long-term campaign aims to have them returned to Greece, to be appreciated in their original context, thanks to the spectacular New Acropolis Museum.

(Above): Scenes from the Parthenon Frieze (447- 432 BC) preserved at the British Museum in London; reconstruction of Parthenon interior, showing statue of Athena.

were reversed. The speaker's platform is still visible on the semicircular terrace; from here, Themistocles persuaded Athenians to fortify the city and Pericles argued for the construction of the Parthenon. Farther north is the **Hill of the Nymphs,** with a 19th-century observatory designed by Theophilos Hansen, responsible for many of the capital's grander edifices. He was so satisfied with his work, he had "servare intamina-tum" ("to remain intact") inscribed over the entrance. ✉ *Enter from Dionyssiou Areopagitou or Vasileos Pavlou, Acropolis* Ⓜ *Acropolis.*

Fodor's Choice **New Acropolis Museum.** Located at the foot of the Parthenon, and now
★ the repository of the greatest sculptural treasures of the Acropolis, this spectacular museum opened in 2009 to worldwide acclaim. *For an in-depth look, see our photo-feature, "The Acropolis: Ascent to Glory," in this chapter.*

★ **Odeon of Herodes Atticus.** Hauntingly beautiful, this ancient theater was built in AD 160 by the affluent Herodes Atticus in memory of his wife, Regilla. Known as the Irodion by Athenians, it is nestled Greek-style into the hillside, but with typically Roman arches in its three-story stage building and barrel-vaulted entrances. The circular orchestra has now become a semicircle, and the long-vanished cedar roof probably covered only the stage and dressing rooms, not the 34 rows of seats. The theater, which holds 5,000, was restored and reopened in 1955 for the Athens and Epidaurus Festival. To enter you must hold a ticket to one of the summer performances, which range from the Royal Ballet to ancient tragedies and Attic comedies usually performed in modern Greek. Con-tact the Elliniko Festival (Greek Festival) box office for ticket infor-mation. ✉ *Dionyssiou Areopagitou near intersection with Propylaion, Acropolis* ☎ *210/324–1807, 210/928–2900* ⊕ *www.greekfestival.gr* ☉ *Open only during performances* Ⓜ *Acropolis.*

Theater of Dionysus. It was on this spot in the 6th century BC that the Dionyssia festivals took place; a century later, dramas such as Sopho-cles's *Oedipus Rex* and Euripides's *Medea* were performed for the entire population of the city. Visible are foundations of a stage dating from about 330 BC, when it was built for 15,000 spectators as well as the assemblies formerly held on Pnyx. In the middle of the orchestra stood the altar to Dionysus. Most of the upper rows of seats have been destroyed, but the lower levels, with labeled chairs for priests and dig-nitaries, remain. The fantastic throne in the center was reserved for the priest of Dionysus: regal lions' paws adorn it, and the back is carved with reliefs of satyrs and griffins. On the hillside above the theater stand two columns, vestiges of the little temple erected in the 4th century BC by Thrasyllus the Choragus (the ancient counterpart of a modern impresario). ✉ *Dionyssiou Areopagitou across from Mitsaion street, Acropolis* ☎ *210/322–4625* 🎫 *€2; €12 joint ticket under the Unifica-tion of Archaeological Sites* ☉ *May–Oct., daily 8–7 (last entry 6:30); Nov.–Apr., daily 8:30–3* Ⓜ *Acropolis.*

WORTH NOTING

Fodor's Choice **Ilias Lalaounis Jewelry Museum.** Housing the creations of internationally
★ renowned artist-jeweler Ilias Lalaounis, this private foundation also operates as an international center for the study of decorative arts. The

CLOSE UP

Grand Promenade

One of the most popular features created in Athens for the 2004 Olympics was the Grand Promenade, a pedestrian walkway created to beautify some of the traffic-choked streets much favored by tourists. Part of the city's Archaeological Unification Project, the promenade connects fabled ancient sites along a landscaped walkway paved with gneiss cobblestones from Naxos island and marble slabs from Tinos island. It stretches through several neighborhoods but is often accessed near the Acropolis since its pedestrian ribbon includes the roads around its southern end.

Start out at the Acropolis metro stop, surface and walk north, and then left, to find Dionyssiou Areopagitou, the famed road running below the hill. You'll soon pass the New Acropolis Museum on your left and the Theater of Dionysus and Odeon of Herodes Atticus on your right. You can begin your climb here up to the Beulé Gate entrance to the Acropolis but, instead, take the marble walkway up Filopappou Hill—its summit flaunts Cinerama views of the Acropolis. Head back down to Apostolou Pavlou to find some of the best café real estate in the world: pull up a seat and enjoy a meal with the Acropolis looming above you.

Further up the road is the Thission metro station, the Agion Asomaton

Square, and Melidoni Street, which heads to the great ancient cemetery of Kerameikos. Here, Ermou Street connects with Piraeus Street, which leads to Technopolis and the Gazi district, Athens at its 21st-century hipster best.

The Grand Promenade provides easy pedestrian access to other major ancient sites, from the Temple of Hephaestus to the Ancient Agora. It also hurtles you through the centuries by depositing you in the buzzing neighborhoods of Makriyanni, Monastiraki, Thission, and Gazi with their brimming tavernas.

Speaking of which, keep the following restaurants and cafés in mind if you want to enjoy food-with-a-view, and not just any old view, but the Acropolis itself: Dionysos Zonars (built almost inside the archaeological site); Filistron mezedopoleio-restaurant (especially the rooftop on summer nights); Strofi restaurant (perfect for a summer post-performance dinner at the ancient Odeon of Herodes Atticus); Kuzina (for a wonderful view from its rooftop); and Orizontes (seen from another angle, this one from Lycabettus Hill). Last but not least, the café and restaurant of the New Acropolis Museum, with its huge glass windows and extensive verandas, is a definite must for spectacular photo ops of the ancient landmark.

3

---

fifty collections include 4,000 pieces inspired by subjects as diverse as the Treasure of Priam to the wildflowers of Greece; many of the works are eye-catching, especially the massive necklaces evoking the Minoan and Byzantine periods. Besides the well-made videos that explain jewelry making, craftspeople in the workshop demonstrate ancient and modern techniques, such as chain weaving and hammering. During the academic year the museum can arrange educational programs in English for groups of children. The founder also has several stores in Athens. The museum has a calendar of fascinating temporary exhibitions, usually focusing on the relation between Greek and jewelry. ⊠ *Kallisperi 12, at Karyatidon, Acropolis* ☎ *210/922–1044* 💷 *€5, free Wed. after 3* ⊙ *Tues.–Thurs., Fri.–Sat. 9–3, Wed. 9–9, Sun. 11–4* Ⓜ *Acropolis.*

PLAKA AND ANAFIOTIKA ΠΛΑΚΑ ΚΑΙ ΑΝΑΦΙΩΤΙΚΑ

Fanning north from the slopes of the Acropolis, picturesque Plaka is the last corner of 19th-century Athens. Set with Byzantine accents provided by churches, the Old Town district extends north to Ermou Street and eastward to the Leofóros Amalias. During the 1950s and '60s, the area became garish with neon as nightclubs moved in and residents moved out, but locals, architects, and academicians joined forces in the early 1980s to transform a decaying neighborhood. Noisy discos and tacky pensions were closed, streets were changed into pedestrian zones, and old buildings were well restored. At night merrymakers crowd the old tavernas, which feature traditional music and dancing; many have rooftops facing the Acropolis. If you keep off the main tourist shopping streets of Kidathineon and Adrianou, you will be amazed at how peaceful the area can be, even in summer, especially in beautiful Anafiotika. Set above Plaka and built on winding lanes that climb up the slopes of the Acropolis, its upper reaches resemble a tranquil village that seems airlifted in from an Aegean island.

TOP ATTRACTIONS

Fodor's Choice
★
😊

Anafiotika. Set in the shadow of the Acropolis and often compared to the whitewashed villages of rural Greek islands, the Anafiotika quarter is populated by many descendants of the Anafi stonemasons who arrived from that small island in the 19th century to work in the expanding capital. It remains an enchanting area of simple stone houses, many nestled right into the bedrock, most little changed over the years, others stunningly restored. Cascades of bougainvillea and pots of geraniums and marigolds enliven the balconies and rooftops, and the prevailing serenity is in blissful contrast to the cacophony of modern Athens. In classical times, this district was abandoned because the Delphic Oracle claimed it as sacred ground. The buildings here were constructed by masons from Anafi island, who came to find work in the rapidly expanding Athens of the 1840s and 1850s. They took over this area, whose rocky terrain was similar to Anafi's, hastily erecting homes overnight and taking advantage of an Ottoman law that decreed that if you could put up a structure between sunset and sunrise, the property was yours. Ethiopians, imported as slaves by the Turks during the Ottoman period, stayed on after independence and lived higher up, in caves, on the northern slopes of the Acropolis.

Today, the residents are seldom seen—only a line of washing hung out to dry, the lace curtains on the tiny houses, or the curl of smoke from a wood-burning fireplace indicate human presence. Perched on the bedrock of the Acropolis is **Ayios Georgios tou Vrachou** (St. George of the Rock), which marks the southeast edge of the district. One of the most beautiful churches of Athens, it is still in use today. **Ayios Simeon,** a neoclassic church built in 1847 by the settlers, marks the western boundary and contains a copy of a famous miracle-working icon from Anafi,

STEP-BY-STEP: A WALK THROUGH PLAKA

Take time to explore the side streets graced by old mansions under renovation by the Ministry of Culture. Begin your stroll at the ancient, jewel-like **Monument of Lysikrates**, one of the few remaining supports (334 BC) for tripods (vessels that served as prizes) awarded to the producer of the best play in the ancient Dionyssia festival. Take Herefondos to Plaka's central square, Filomoussou Eterias (or Kidathineon Square), a great place to people-watch.

Up Kidathineon Square is the small but worthy **Greek Folk Art Museum**, with a rich collection ranging from 1650 to the present, including works by the beloved native artist Theophilos Hatzimichalis. Across from the museum is the 11th- to 12th-century church of Sotira Tou Kottaki, in a tidy garden with a fountain that was the main source of water for the neighborhood until sometime after Turkish rule. Down the block and around the corner on Hatzimichali Aggelou is the **Center of Folk Art and Tradition**. Continue west to the end of that street, crossing Adrianou to Hill, then right on Epimarchou to the striking Church House (on the corner of Scholeiou), once a Turkish police post and home to Richard Church, who led Greek forces in the War of Independence.

At the top of Epimarchou is Ayios Nikolaos Rangavas, an 11th-century church built with fragments of ancient columns. The church marks the edge of the **Anafiotika** quarter, a village smack-dab in the middle of the metropolis: its main street, Stratonos, is lined with cottages, occasional murals painted on the stones, and a few shops. Wind your way through the narrow lanes off Stratonos, visiting the churches Ayios Georgios tou Vrachou, Ayios Simeon, and Metamorphosis Sotiros. Another interesting church is 8th-century Ayioi Anargyroi, at the top of Erechtheos. From the church, make your way to Theorias, which parallels the ancient *peripatos* (public roadway) that ran around the Acropolis. The collection at the **Kanellopoulos Museum** spans Athens's history; nearby on Panos you'll pass the Athens University Museum (Old University, otherwise known as the Kleanthis Residence), the city's first higher-learning institution. Walk down Panos to the **Roman Agora**, which includes the Tower of the Winds and the Fethiye Mosque. Nearby visit the engaging **Museum of Greek Popular Musical Instruments**, where recordings will take you back to the age of rembetika (Greek blues). Also next to the Agora is Athens' only remaining Turkish bathhouse, providing a glimpse into a daily social ritual of Ottoman times. On your way back to Syntagma Square, cut across Mitropoleos Square to the impressive 12th-century church of **Little Mitropolis**.

3

Our Lady of the Reeds. The **Church of the Metamorphosis Sotiros** (Transfiguration), a high-dome 14th-century stone chapel, has a rear grotto carved right into the Acropolis. For those with children, there is a small playground at Stratonos and Vironos. ⊠ *On northeast slope of Acropolis rock, Plaka* Ⓜ *Acropolis.*

★ **Greek Folk Art Museum.** Run by the Ministry of Culture, the museum focuses on folk art from 1650 to the present, with especially interesting embroideries, stone and wood carvings, Carnival costumes, and *Karaghiozis* (shadow player figures). In recent years, the museum has undergone an impressive expansion and now incorporates the beautiful 19th-century neoclassical Bath-House of the Winds in Kyrristou Street, a spectacularly vast mosque (now deconsecrated and given over to museum displays) located in Areos Street, and exhibitions at nearby 22 Panos Street, which handles the vast overflow of objects on view. Everyday tools—stamps for communion bread, spinning shuttles, raki flasks—attest to the imagination with which Greeks have traditionally embellished the most utilitarian objects. Don't miss the room of uniquely fanciful landscapes and historical portraits by beloved Greek folk painter Theophilos Hatzimichalis, from Mytilini. ⊠ *Main building:Kidathineon 17, Plaka* ☎ *210/322–9031* ⊕ *www.melt.gr, www.culture.gr* ▱ *€2, valid for each of the 4 buildings* ⊙ *Tues.–Sun. 9–2:30* Ⓜ *Acropolis.*

Kanellopoulos Museum. The stately Michaleas Mansion, built in 1884, now showcases the Kanellopoulos family collection. It spans Athens's history from the 3rd century BC to the 19th century, with an emphasis on Byzantine icons, jewelry, and Mycenaean and Geometric vases and bronzes. Note the painted ceiling gracing the first floor. ⊠ *Theorias 12 and Panos, Plaka* ☎ *210/324–4447, 210/321–2313* ⊕ *www. pakanellopoulosfoundation.org* ▱ *Free* ⊙ *Tues.–Sun. 8:30–2:30* Ⓜ *Monastiraki.*

NEED A BREAK?

Melina. If you're craving a good dessert combined with some Greek cinematic history, go to the lovely nearby café-bistrot Melina, dedicated to famous Greek actress-turned-politician, Melina Mercouri. The walls are loaded with memorabilia from her life and distinguished career. ⊠ *Lysiou 22, Plaka* ☎ *210/324–6501* ⊕ *www.melinacafe.gr.*

★ **Little Mitropolis.** This church snuggles up to the pompous **Mitropolis** (on the northern edge of Plaka), the ornate Cathedral of Athens. Also called Panayia Gorgoepikoos ("the virgin who answers prayers quickly"), the chapel dates to the 12th century; its most interesting features are its outer walls, covered with reliefs of animals and allegorical figures dating from the classical to the Byzantine period. Look for the ancient frieze with zodiac signs and a calendar of festivals in Attica. Most of the paintings inside were destroyed, but the famous 13th- to 14th-century Virgin, said to perform miracles, remains. If you would like to follow Greek custom and light an amber beeswax candle for yourself and someone you love, drop the price of the candle in the slot. ⊠ *Mitropolis Sq., Plaka* ⊙ *Hrs depend on services, but usually daily 8–1* Ⓜ *Syntagma.*

★ **Monument of Lysikrates.** Located on one of the ancient city's grandest avenues (which once linked the Theater of Dionysus with the Agora), this tempietto-like monument is a delightfully elegant jewel of the Corinthian style. It was originally built (335–334 BC) by a *choregos* (theatrical producer) as the support for the tripod (a three-footed vessel used as a prize) he won for sponsoring the best play at the nearby Theater of Dionysus. Six of the earliest Corinthian columns are arranged in a circle on a square base, topped by a marble dome from which rise acanthus leaves. In the 17th century the exceedingly picturesque monument was incorporated into a Capuchin monastery where Byron stayed while writing part of *Childe Harold*. The monument was once known as the Lantern of Diogenis because it was incorrectly believed to be where the famous orator practiced speaking with pebbles in his mouth in an effort to overcome his stutter. A fresh-looking dirt track at the monument's base is a section of the ancient street of the Tripods (now called Tripodon), where sponsors installed prizes awarded for various athletic or artistic competitions. ✉ *Lysikratous and Herefondos, Plaka* Ⓜ *Acropolis.*

★ **Roman Agora.** The city's commercial center from the 1st century BC to the 4th century AD, the Roman Market was a large rectangular courtyard with a peristyle that provided shade for the arcades of shops. Its most notable feature is the west entrance's Bazaar Gate, or **Gate of Athena Archegetis,** completed around AD 2; the inscription records that it was erected with funds from Julius Caesar and Augustus. Halfway up one solitary square pillar behind the gate's north side, an edict inscribed by Hadrian regulates the sale of oil, a reminder that this was the site of the annual bazaar where wheat, salt, and oil were sold. On the north side of the Roman Agora stands one of the few remains of the Turkish occupation, the **Fethiye (Victory) Mosque.** The eerily beautiful mosque was built in the late 15th century on the site of a Christian church to celebrate the Turkish conquest of Athens and to honor Mehmet II (the Conqueror). During the few months of Venetian rule in the 17th century, the mosque was converted to a Roman Catholic church; now used as a storehouse, it is closed to the public. Three steps in the right-hand corner of the porch lead to the base of the minaret, the rest of which no longer exists.

Tower of the Winds (Aerides). Surrounded by a cluster of old houses on the western slope of the Acropolis, the world-famous Tower of the Winds (Aerides), located inside the Roman Agora, is the most appealing and well preserved of the Roman monuments of Athens, keeping time since the 1st century BC. It was originally a sundial, water clock, and weather vane topped by a bronze Triton with a metal rod in his hand, which followed the direction of the wind. Its eight sides face the direction of the eight winds into which the compass was divided; expressive reliefs around the tower personify these eight winds, called *I Aerides* (the Windy Ones) by Athenians. Note the north wind, Boreas, blowing on a conch, and the beneficent west wind, Zephyros, scattering blossoms. ☎ *210/324–5220* 🎟 *€2; €12 joint ticket under the Unification of Archaeological Sites* ✉ *Pelopidas and Aiolou, Plaka* ☎ *210/324–5220* ⊕ *www.culture.gr* 🎟 *€2; €12 joint ticket for all Unification of Archaeological Sites* 🕐 *Daily 8:30–2:45* Ⓜ *Monastiraki.*

WORTH NOTING

Center of Folk Art and Tradition. Exhibits in the neoclassical family mansion of folklorist Angeliki Hatzimichali (1895–1965) include detailed costumes, ceramic plates from Skyros, handwoven fabrics and embroideries, and family portraits. ✉ *Hatzimichali Aggelikis 6, Plaka* ☎ *210/324–3972* 🎟 *Free* 🕐 *Sept.–July, Mon.–Sat. 9–1* Ⓜ *Syntagma.*

NEED A BREAK?
Vyzantino. Vyzantino is directly on Plaka's main square—great for a good, reasonably priced bite to eat in the center of all the action. Try the seafood pasta, the eggplant and cheese croquettes, or the stuffed oven chicken.

✉ *Kidathineon 18, Plaka* ☎ *210/322–7368* ⊕ *www.vyzantinorestaurant.gr.*

Glikis. Traditional-looking Glikis and its shady, far-from-the-madding-crowd courtyard are perfect for a Greek coffee or ouzo and a *mikri pikilia* (a small plate of appetizers, including cheese, sausage, olives, and dips). ✉ *Aggelou Geronta 2, Plaka* ☎ *210/322–3925* 🕙 *10 am–1:30 am.*

☯ **Museum of Greek Popular Musical Instruments.** An entertaining crash course in the development of Greek music, from regional *dimotika* (folk) to rembetika (blues), this museum has three floors of instruments. Headphones are available so you can appreciate the sounds made by such unusual delights as goatskin bagpipes and discern the differences in tone between the Pontian lyra and Cretan lyra, string instruments often featured on world-music compilations. The museum, which is housed in the historic Lassanis Mansion and has a pretty shaded courtyard, is home to the Fivos Anoyiannakis Center of Ethnomusicology. ✉ *Diogenous 1–3, Plaka* ☎ *210/325–0198* ⊕ *www.instruments-museum.gr* ☜ *Free* 🕙 *Tues., Thurs., Fri., Sat.–Sun. 10–2, Wed. noon–6* Ⓜ *Monastiraki.*

WATER GAMES

During Ottoman times, every neighborhood in Athens had a hammam, or public bathhouse, where men and women met to socialize among the steam rooms and take massages on marble platforms. If you want to see Athens' last remaining example, head to Kyrrestou 8. Sunlight streaming through holes cut on the domed roofs of the Bath House of the Winds and playing on the colorful tiled floors created a languorous atmosphere here. The pretty 15th-century building now functions as part of the Greek Folk Art Museum (☎ *210/324–4340*). Admission is €2 (including audio tour) and hours are Monday–Sunday 9–2:30.

THE ANCIENT AGORA, MONASTIRAKI, AND THISSION
ΑΡΧΑΙΑ ΑΓΟΡΑ, ΜΟΝΑΣΤΗΡΑΚΙ ΚΑΙ ΘΗΣΕΙΟ

The Times Square, Piccadilly Circus, and St. Basil's Square of ancient Athens, the Agora was once the focal point of urban life. All the principal urban roads and country highways traversed it; the procession of the great Panathenaea Festival, composed of chariots, magistrates, virgins, priests, and sacrificial animals, crossed it on the way to the Acropolis; the Assembly met here first, before moving to the Pnyx; it was where merchants squabbled over the price of olive oil; the forum where Socrates met with his students; and centuries later, where St. Paul went about his missionary task. Lying just under the citadel of the Acropolis, it was indeed the heart of the ancient city and a general meeting place, where news was exchanged and bargains transacted, alive with all the rumors and gossip of the marketplace. The Agora became important under Solon (6th century BC), founder of Athenian democracy; construction continued for almost a millennium. Today, the site's sprawling confusion of stones, slabs, and foundations is dominated by the best-preserved Doric temple in Greece, the Hephaistion, built during the 5th century BC, and the impressive reconstructed Stoa of Attalos II, which houses the Museum of the Agora Excavations.

You can still experience the sights and sounds of the marketplace in Monastiraki, the former Turkish bazaar area, which retains vestiges of the 400-year period when Greece was subject to the Ottoman Empire. On the opposite side of the Agora is another meeting place of sorts: Thission, a former red-light district. Although it has been one of the most sought-after residential neighborhoods since about 1990, Thission remains a vibrant nightlife district.

TOP ATTRACTIONS

FodorśChoice
★

Ancient Agora. The commercial hub of ancient Athens, the Agora was once lined with statues and expensive shops, the favorite strolling ground of fashionable Athenians as well as a mecca for merchants and students. The long colonnades offered shade in summer and protection from rain in winter to the throng of people who transacted the day-to-day business of the city, and, under their arches, Socrates discussed matters with Plato and Zeno expounded the philosophy of the Stoics (whose name comes from the six *stoa*, or colonnades of the Agora). Besides administrative buildings, it was surrounded by the schools, theaters, workshops, houses, stores, and market stalls of a thriving town. The foundations of some of the main buildings, which may be most easily distinguished include the circular Tholos, the principal seat of executive power in the city; the Mitroon, shrine to Rhea, the mother of gods, which included the vast state archives and registry office (*mitroon* is still used today to mean registry); the Bouleterion, where the council met; the Monument of Eponymous Heroes, the Agora's information center, where announcements such as the list of military recruits were hung; and the Sanctuary of the Twelve Gods, a shelter for refugees and the point from which all distances were measured.

The Agora's showpiece was the **Stoa of Attalos II,** where Socrates once lectured and incited the youth of Athens to adopt his progressive ideas on mortality and morality. Today the Museum of Agora Excavations, this two-story building was first designed as a retail complex and erected in the 2nd century BC by Attalos, a king of Pergamum. The reconstruction in 1953–56 used Pendelic marble and creamy limestone from the original structure. The colonnade, designed for promenades, is protected from the blistering sun and cooled by breezes. The most notable sculptures, of historical and mythological figures from the 3rd and 4th centuries BC, are at ground level outside the museum.

Take a walk around the site and speculate on the location of Simon the Cobbler's house and shop, which was a meeting place for Socrates and his pupils. The carefully landscaped grounds display a number of plants known in antiquity, such as almond, myrtle, and pomegranate. By standing in the center, you have a glorious view up to the Acropolis. **Ayii Apostoloi** is the only one of the Agora's nine churches to survive, saved because of its location and beauty.

On the low hill called Kolonos Agoraios in the Agora's northwest corner stands the best-preserved Doric temple in all Greece, the **Hephaistion,** sometimes called the Thission because of its friezes showing the exploits of Theseus. Like the other monuments, it is roped off, but you can walk around it to admire its preservation. A little older than the Parthenon, it is surrounded by 34 columns and is 104 feet in length, and was once filled with sculptures (the only remnant of which is the mutilated frieze, once brightly colored). It never quite makes the impact of the Parthenon, in large part due to the fact that it lacks a noble site and can never be seen from below, its sun-matured columns towering heavenward. The Hephaistion was originally dedicated to Hephaistos, god of metalworkers, and it is interesting to note that metal workshops still exist in this area near Ifestou. Behind the temple, paths cross the northwest slope past archaeological ruins half hidden in deep undergrowth. Here you can sit on a bench and contemplate the same scene that Englishman Edward Dodwell saw in the early 19th century, when he came to sketch antiquities. ⊠ *3 entrances: from Monastiraki on Adrianou; from Thission on Apostolou Pavlou; and descending from Acropolis on Ayios Apostoloi, Monastiraki* ☎ *210/321–0185* ⊕ *www.culture.gr* ⊠ *€4; €12 joint ticket for holders of the Acropolis (Unification of Archaeological Sites) ticket* ⊙ *May–Oct., daily 8–7 (last entrance 6:30); Nov.–Apr., daily 8:30–3; museum closes ½ hr before site* Ⓜ *Thiseio.*

IN AND AROUND THE AGORA

After browsing through the market stalls, enter the ancient Agora at the corner of Kinetou and Adrianou (the latter runs parallel to Ifestou). Be sure to visit the site's Museum of Agora Excavations, which offers a fascinating glimpse of everyday life in the ancient city. Exit at the site's opposite end onto Dionyssiou Areopagitou, crossing the boulevard to the Thission quarter, a lively area with neoclassic homes overlooking trendy cafés and home to the noted Melina Mercouri Cultural Center, where exhibits re-create the streets of Athens during different epochs.

★ **Melina Mercouri Cultural Center.** Named in honor of the famous *Never on Sunday* Greek actress who became a political figure in the 1980s, this center is installed in the former Poulopoulos hat factory built in 1886. Throughout the year the center has a calendar of temporary exhibitions, usually featuring contemporary Greek art. But the permanent collection includes some delightful surprises. Several rooms give a rare glimpse of Athens during the 19th century. You can walk through a reconstructed Athens street with facades of neoclassic homes that evoke the civilized elegance of the past, along with a pharmacy, printing press, dry goods store, *kafeneio* (coffeehouse), and dress shop, all painstakingly fitted out with authentic objects collected by the Greek Literary and Historical Archives. The other permanent exhibition showcases the puppets of the traditional Greek shadow theater, thanks to a vast collection amassed by the Haridimos performing family. ⊠ *Iraklidon 66a, at Thessalonikis, Thission* ☎ *210/345–2150* ⊠ *Free* ⊙ *Tues.–Sat. 9–1 and 5–9, Sun. 9–1* Ⓜ *Kerameikos.*

Thission. This neighborhood, easily accessible by metro and offering a lovely view of the Acropolis, has become one of the liveliest café and restaurant districts in Athens. The area has excellent *rakadika* and *ouzeri*—publike eateries that offer plates of appetizers to go with *raki*, a fiery spirit made from grape must; *rakomelo*, a mix of raki and honey heated to boiling point; the ever-appealing ouzo; as well as barrels of homemade wine. The main strip is the Nileos pedestrian zone across from the ancient Agora entrance, lined with cafés that are cozy in winter and have outdoor tables in summer. The rest of the neighborhood is quiet, an odd mix of mom-and-pop stores and dilapidated houses that are slowly being renovated; take a brief stroll along Akamantos (which becomes Galatias) around the intersections of Dimofontos or Aginoros, or down Iraklidon, to get a feel for the quarter's past. ⊠ *West of ancient Agora, Apostolou Pavlou, and Akamantos, Thission* Ⓜ *Thiseio.*

NEED A BREAK?

Athinaion Politeia. For a fancy coffee (think espresso mixed with sambuca), sweet crepes (such as banana and chocolate hazelnut), and impromptu lunches (thanks to a wide selection of salads and hot and cold dishes), stop at Athinaion Politeia, a restored neoclassical-style mansion and watch the crowds on Apostolou Pavlou. Thirtysomething hipsters hold court here, telling raucous stories that spill into laughter, making you feel like you're in the middle of the best party in town. ⊠ *Akamantos 1 and Apostolou Pavlou, Thission* ☎ *210/341-3795* ⊕ *www.athinaionpoliteia.gr.*

WORTH NOTING

Flea Market. Here is where the chaos, spirit, and charm of Athens turn into a feast for the senses. The Sunday-morning market has combined sight, sound, and scent into a strangely alluring little world where everything is for sale: 1950s-era scuba masks, old tea sets, antique sewing machines, old tobacco tins, gramophone needles, old matchboxes, army uniforms, and lacquered eggs. Haggle, no matter how low the price. ⊠ *Along Ifestou, Kynetou, and Adrianou, Monastiraki* Ⓜ *Monastiraki.*

Monastiraki Square. One of Athens's most popular meeting places, the square has recently been renovated and much of it now glitters thanks to a pavement of golden mosaic pieces. Look for the special glassed-in view revealing the ancient Iridanos riverbed. The square takes its name from the small **Panayia Pantanassa Church,** commonly called Monastiraki ("Little Monastery"). Recently renovated, the square itself is now covered with shiny golden mosaic pieces apart from a glassed-in view revealing the ancient Iridanos riverbed. It once flourished as an extensive convent, perhaps dating to the 10th century, which stretched from Athinas to Aiolou. The nuns took in poor people, who earned their keep weaving the thick textiles known as *abas.* The buildings were destroyed during excavations and the train (and later metro) line construction that started in 1896. The convent's basic basilica form, now recessed a few steps below street level, was altered through a poor restoration in 1911, when the bell tower was added.

Tzistarakis Mosque. The square's focal point, the 18th-century Tzistarakis Mosque, is now one of the four branches of the Greek Folk Art Museum. It now houses a beautifully designed ceramics collection, with the exhibits handsomely lighted and labeled. The mosque's creator Tzistarakis, a then newly appointed Turkish civil governor, knocked down a column from the Temple of Olympian Zeus to make lime for the mosque. Punished by the sultan for his audacity, he was also blamed by Athenians for an ensuing plague; it was believed the toppling of a column released epidemics and disasters from below Earth. The ticket here ensures entry to all four branches of the Greek Folk Art Museum. ⊠ *Areos 1, Monastiraki* ☎ *210/324–2066* ⊕ *www.melt. gr* 🎫*€2* ⊙ *Wed.–Mon.* *9–2:30* Ⓜ *Monastiraki* ⊠ *South of Ermou and Athinas junction, Monastiraki* Ⓜ *Monastiraki.*

█ NEED A
BREAK?

On Mitropoleos off Monastiraki Square are a handful of counter-front places selling souvlaki—grilled meat rolled in a pita with onions, *tzatziki* (yogurt-garlic dip), and tomatoes—the best bargain in Athens. Make sure you specify either a "souvlaki me pita" (sandwich) or a "souvlaki plate," an entire meal.

3

Thanassis. With the hands-down best kebab in town, Thanassi is always crowded with hungry Greeks who crave the specially spiced ground meat, along with a nicely oiled pita bread, onions, tomatos, and tzatziki. ⊠ *Mitropoleos 69, Monastiraki* ☎ *210/324–4705.*

FROM CENTRAL ATHENS TO NATIONAL ARCHAEOLOGICAL MUSEUM
ΑΘΗΝΑ (ΚΕΝΤΡΟ) ΠΡΟΣ ΕΘΝΙΚΟ ΑΡΧΑΙΟΛΟΓΙΚΟ ΜΟΥΣΕΙΟ

Downtown Athens is an unlikely combination of the squalid and the grand: the cavernous, chaotic Central Market, which replaced the bazaar in Monastiraki when it burned down in 1885, is 10 minutes from the elegant, neoclassic Old University complex. The surrounding area is filled with the remains of the 19th-century mansions that once made Athens world renowned as a charming city. Some of these are crumbling into the streets; others, like the exquisite mansion that has been converted into the Numismatic Museum (once the grand abode of Heinrich Schliemann, discoverer of Troy) have regained their lost loveliness. Such buildings rub shoulders with incense-scented, 12th-century Byzantine churches as well as some of the city's most hideous 1970s apartment blocks. The mix has become headier as artists and fashionistas have moved to the neighborhoods of Kerameikos, Metaxourgeio, and Gazi and transformed long-neglected warehouses into galleries, nightclubs, and ultrachic restaurants.

A good 10 blocks directly north of the Old University complex, the glory that was Athens continues at the city's legendary National Archaeological Museum. One of the most exciting collections of Greek antiquities in the world, this is a must-do for any travelers to Athens, nay, Greece. Here are the sensational finds made by Heinrich Schliemann, father of modern archaeology, in the course of his excavations of the royal tombs on the Homeric site of Mycenae in the 1870s. Here, too, are world-famous bronzes such as the *Jockey of Artemision* and a bronze of Poseidon throwing a trident (or is it Zeus hurling a thunderbolt?). An added treat is the neighborhood the museum presides over: Exarchia, a bohemian, free-spirited (though nowadays a bit rundown) district that is mentioned in hundreds of Greek folk songs and novels. The area evokes strong feelings in every Athenian for here, in 1973, the students

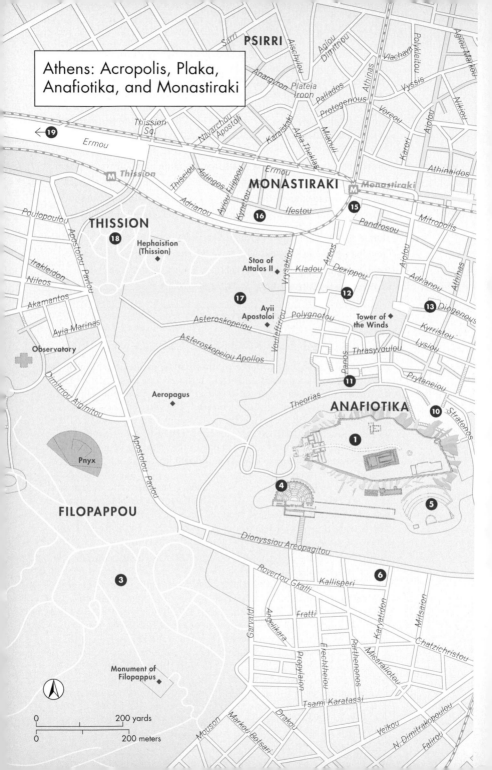

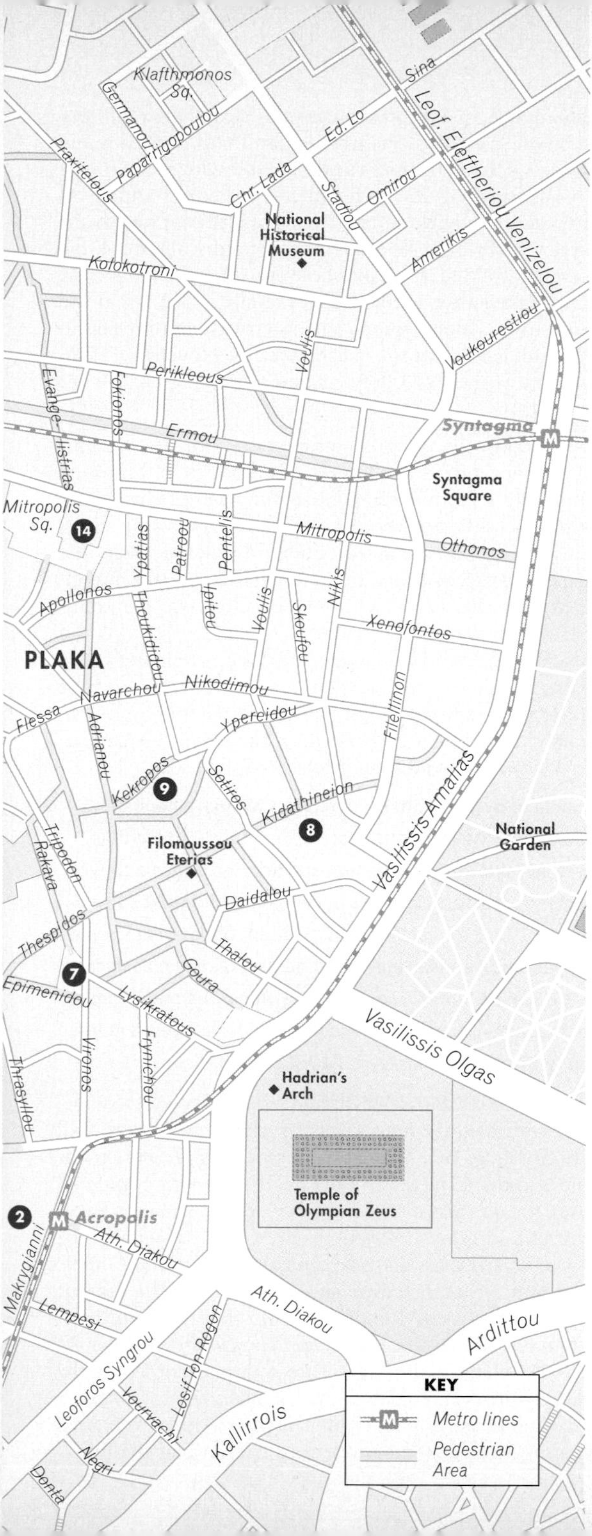
Klafthmonos Sq.
Germanou
Paparrigopoulou
Praxitelous
Chr. Lada
Ed. Lo
Sina
Leof. Eleftheriou Venizelou
Stadiou
Omirou
National Historical Museum
Amerikis
Kolokotroni
Voukourestiou
Voulis
Perikleous
Evange-listrias
Fokionos
Ermou
Syntagma
M
Syntagma Square
Mitropolis Sq.
14
Ypatias
Patroou
Pentelis
Mitropolis
Othonos
Apollonos
Ipitou
Thoukididou
Voulis
Skoufou
Nikis
Xenofontos
PLAKA
Navarchou
Nikodimou
Flessa
Adrianou
Ypereidou
Filellinon
Kekropos
9
Sotiros
Kidathineon
8
Vasilissis Amalias
National Garden
Tripodon
Rakava
Filomoussou Eterias
Daidalou
Thespidos
Thalou
7
Goura
Epimenidou
Lysikratous
Vasilissis Olgas
Thrasyllou
Vironos
Frynichou
Hadrian's Arch
Temple of Olympian Zeus
2
M
Acropolis
Ath. Diakou
Makrygianni
Lempesi
Ath. Diakou
Arditou
Leoforos Syngrou
Iosif Ton Rogon
Vourvachi
Kallirrois
Negri
Donta
KEY
Metro lines
Pedestrian Area

of Athens Polytechnic rose up in protest against Greece's hated military dictatorship. The colonels crushed the uprising and tanks killed many students, but the protests led to the junta's fall the following year. Today, students, intellectuals, and anarchists often fill its many cafés and tavernas, debating the latest in domestic and global affairs. Recent reverberations shook the area when rioting of an unprecedented scale shook the city center in December 2008 after clashes between the Athenian police and local youths, provoked after a police officer fatally shot 15-year-old Alexander Grigoropoulos. Today, things have pretty much returned to normal (though it is advisable not to visit the area on November 17th, the annual anniversary of the 1973 Polytechneion uprising).

TOP ATTRACTIONS

Central Market. The market runs along Athinas: on one side are open-air stalls selling fruit and vegetables at the best prices in town, although wily merchants may slip overripe items into your bag. At the corner of Armodiou, shops stock live poultry and countless varieties of olives. Across the street, in the huge covered market built in 1870, the surrealistic composition of suspended carcasses and shimmering fish on marble counters emits a pungent odor that is overwhelming on hot days. The shops at the north end of the market, to the right on Sofokleous, sell the best cheese, olives, halvah, bread, and cold cuts, including *pastourma* (spicy cured beef), available in Athens. Small restaurants serving *patsa*, or tripe soup, dot the market; these stay open until almost dawn and are popular stops with weary clubbers trying to ease their hangovers. ⊠ *Athinas, Central Market* ⊙ *Weekdays and Sat. morning* Ⓜ *Monastiraki.*

NEED A BREAK?

Krinos. For a true taste of bygone Athens, don't miss Krinos, an endearingly old-timey café that serves Athens's best *loukoumades*—irresistible, doughnutlike fritters sprinkled with cinnamon and drizzled with a honeyed syrup based on a Smyrna recipe. Krinos has been serving the treat since it opened its doors in the 1920s and also makes excellent *boughatsa* (cream pies), *rizogalo* (rice pudding), and kaymak-flavored ice cream, an eastern version of vanilla; it is closed Sunday. Squeeze into one of the many tables and enjoy your treat with the old gents and ladies who have been regulars for decades. ⊠ *Aiolou 87, Central Market* ☏ *210/321–6852.*

Kerameikos Cemetery. At the western edge of the Gazi district lies the wide, green expanse of Kerameikos, the main cemetery in ancient Athens until Sulla destroyed the city in 86 BC. The name is associated with the modern word "ceramic": in the 12th century BC the district was populated by potters who used the abundant clay from the languid Iridanos River to make funerary urns and grave decorations. From the 7th century BC onward, Kerameikos was the fashionable cemetery of ancient Athens. During succeeding ages cemeteries were superimposed on the ancient one until the latter was discovered in 1861. From the main entrance, you can still see remains of the **Makra Teixoi** (Long Walls of Themistocles), which ran to Piraeus, and the largest gate in the ancient world, the **Dipylon Gate,** where visitors entered Athens. The walls rise to 10 feet, a fraction of their original height (up to 45 feet). Here was also the **Sacred Gate,** used by pilgrims headed to the mysterious rites in Eleusis and by those who participated in the Panathenaic procession, which followed the Sacred Way. Between the two gates are the foundations of the **Pompeion,** the starting point of the Panathenaic procession. It is said the courtyard was large enough to fit the ship used in the procession. On the **Street of Tombs,** which branches off the Sacred Way, plots were reserved for affluent Athenians. A number of the distinctive *stelae* (funerary monuments) remain, including a replica of the marble relief of Dexilios, a knight who died in the war against Corinth (394 BC); he is shown on horseback preparing to spear a fallen foe. To the left of the site's entrance is the **Oberlaender Museum,** also known as the Kerameikos Museum, whose displays include sculpture, terra-cotta figures, and some striking red-and-black-figured pottery. The extensive grounds of Kerameikos are marshy in some spots; in spring, frogs exuberantly croak their mating songs near magnificent stands of lilies. ⊠ *Ermou 148, Gazi* ☎ *210/346–3552* 🖃 *€2 site and museum; €12 joint ticket for all Unification of Archaeological Sites* ⊙ *Daily 8:30–3* Ⓜ *Kerameikos.*

★ **Municipal Gallery of Athens.** One of Athens's oldest neoclassic buildings—an architectural jewel set in the rapidly-regaining-its-former-glory Metaxourgeio neighborhood—became the new home of the city's Municipal Art Collection in 2010. The former silk factory, designed in 1833 by Danish architect Hans Christian Hansen, now houses almost 3,000 important art works from leading 19th- and 20th-century Greek artists (most of the works were acquired during the '30s and '40s). The newly renovated building was inaugurated with a major showing of the Economou Collection (he's a well-known Greek businessman and art collector) and will continue hosting its municipal permanent collection as well as an evolving calendar of temporary exhibitions and events. ⊠ *Leonidou and Myllerou, Metaxourgeio* ☎ *210/520–2420* ⊕ *odysseus. culture.gr* 🖃 *Free* ⊙ *Tues.–Sat. 9–1 and 5–9, Sun. 10–2.*

Fodor's Choice
★ **National Archaeological Museum.** Many of the greatest achievements in ancient Greek sculpture and painting are housed here in the most important museum in Greece. Artistic highlights from every period of its ancient civilization, from Neolithic to Roman times, make this a treasure trove beyond compare. With a massive renovation completed, works that have languished in storage for decades are now on view, reorganized displays are accompanied by enriched English-language information, and the panoply of ancient Greek art appears more spectacular than ever.

While the classic culture that was the grandeur of the Greek world no longer exists—it died, for civilizations are mortal—it left indelible markers in all domains, most particularly in art, and many of its masterpieces are on show here. The museum's most celebrated display is the **Mycenaean Antiquities.** Here are the stunning gold treasures from Heinrich Schliemann's 1876 excavations of Mycenae's royal tombs: the funeral mask of a bearded king, once thought to be the image of Agamemnon but now believed to be much older, from about the 15th century BC; a splendid silver bull's-head libation cup; and the 15th-century BC Vaphio Goblets, masterworks in embossed gold. Mycenaeans were famed for their carving in miniature, and an exquisite example is the ivory statuette of two curvaceous mother goddesses, each with a child nestled on her lap.

Athens: Central Athens,
Syntagma Square,
Kolonaki and Exarchia

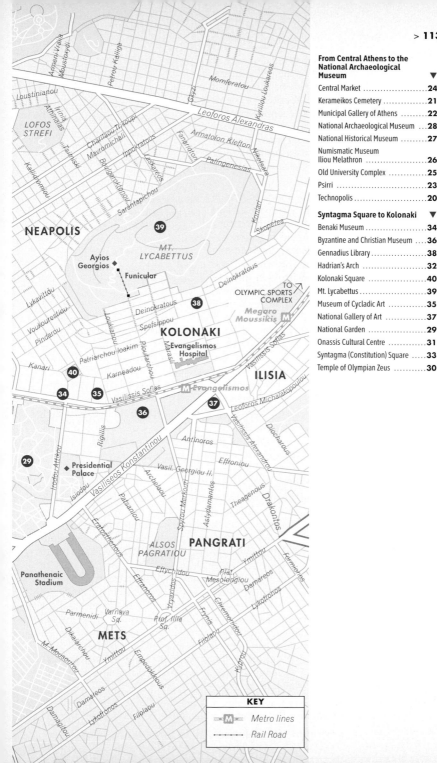

Withheld from the public since they were damaged in the 1999 earthquakes, but not to be missed, are the beautifully restored **frescoes from Santorini,** delightful murals depicting daily life in Minoan Santorini. Along with the treasures from Mycenae, these wall paintings are part of the museum's Prehistoric Collection.

Other stars of the museum include the works of Geometric and Archaic art (10th to 6th century BC), and kouroi and funerary stelae (8th to 5th century BC), among them the stelae of the warrior Aristion signed by Aristokles, and the unusual *Running Hoplite* (a hoplite was a Greek infantry soldier).

> ## SHOELESS IN ATHENS
>
> Some of the museum's most moving displays are those of funerary architecture: the spirited 2nd-century relief of a rearing stallion held by a black groom, which exemplifies the transition from classical to Hellenistic style, the latest period in the museum's holdings. Among the most famous sculptures in this collection is the humorous marble group of a nude *Aphrodite* getting ready to slap an advancing Pan with a sandal, while Eros floats overhead and grasps one of Pan's horns.

The collection of classical art (5th to 3rd century BC) contains some of the most renowned surviving ancient statues: the bareback *Jockey of Artemision,* a 2nd-century BC Hellenistic bronze salvaged from the sea; from the same excavation, the bronze *Artemision Poseidon* (some say Zeus), poised and ready to fling a trident (or thunderbolt?); and the *Varvakios Athena,* a half-size marble version of the gigantic gold-and-ivory cult statue that Pheidias erected in the Parthenon.

Light refreshments are served in a lower ground-floor café, which opens out to a patio and sculpture garden. During the summer months, concerts are often organized in the front garden (check the museum's Web site). ⊠ *28 Oktovriou (Patission) 44, Exarchia* ☎ *210/821–7717, 210/821–7724* ⊕ *www.namuseum.gr* ⌨ *€7* ☉ *Mon. 1:30–8, Tues.–Sun. 9:30–5:30* Ⓜ *Victoria, then 10-min walk.*

★ **National Historical Museum.** After making the rounds of the ancient sites, you might think that Greek history ground to a halt when the Byzantine Empire collapsed. A visit to this gem of a museum, housed in the spectacularly majestic Old Parliament mansion (used by parliamentarians from 1875 to 1932), will fill in the gaps, often vividly, as with Lazaros Koyevina's copy of Eugene Delacroix's *Massacre of Chios,* to name but one example. Paintings, costumes, and assorted artifacts from small arms to flags and ships' figureheads are arranged in a chronological display tracing Greek history from the mid-16th century and the Battle of Lepanto through World War II and the Battle of Crete. A small gift shop near the main entrance—framed by a very grand neoclassical portico of columns—has unusual souvenirs, like a deck of cards featuring Greece's revolutionary heroes. ⊠ *Stadiou 13, Syntagma Sq.* ☎ *210/323–7617* ⊕ *www.nhmuseum.gr* ⌨ *€3, free Sun.* ☉ *Tues.–Sat. 9–2, Sun. 10–3* Ⓜ *Syntagma.*

Fodor's Choice **Numismatic Museum Iliou Melathron.** Even those uninterested in coins
★ might want to visit this museum for a glimpse of the former home of

One of the hearts of the center city, Monastiraki Square is presided over by the 18th century Tzistarakis Mosque.

Heinrich Schliemann, who famously excavated Troy and Mycenae in the 19th century. Built by the Bavarian architect Ernst Ziller for the archaeologist's family and baptized the "Iliou Melanthron" (or Palace of Troy), it flaunts an imposing neo-Venetian facade. Inside are some spectacular rooms, including the vast and floridly decorated Hesperides Hall, ashimmer with colored marbles and neo-Pompeian wall paintings. Today, in this exquisite neoclassic mansion, seemingly haunted by the spirit of the great historian, you can see more than 600,000 coins; displays range from the archaeologist's own coin collection to 4th-century BC measures employed against forgers to coins grouped according to what they depict—animals, plants, myths, and famous buildings like the Lighthouse of Alexandria. Instead of trying to absorb everything, concentrate on a few cases—perhaps a pile of coins dug up on a Greek road, believed to be used by Alexander the Great to pay off local mercenaries. There is also a superb 4th-century BC *decadrachm* (a denomination of coin) with a lissome water goddess frolicking among dolphins (the designer signed the deity's headband). A silver *didrachm* (another denomination of coin) issued by the powerful Amphictyonic League after Philip II's death shows Demeter on one side and, on the other, a thoughtful Apollo sitting on the navel of the world. To relax, head to the museum's peaceful garden café—a cozy oasis just a few feet away from Panepistimiou Avenue's hustle and bustle. ✉ *Panepistimiou 12, Syntagma Sq.* ☎ *210/361–2190, 210/364–3774* ⊕ *www.nma.gr* 🖃*€3* ⊙ *Tues.–Sat. 8 am–8 pm, Sun. 8:30 am–3 pm, Mon. 1:30 pm–8 pm* Ⓜ *Syntagma or Panepistimiou.*

When Greece Worshipped Beauty

As visitors to the many treasure-filled galleries of the National Archaeological Museum will discover, Greek art did not spring in a blinding flash like Athena fully modeled from the brain of Zeus. The earliest ceramic cup in a Greek museum, said by legend to have been molded after the breast of Helen of Troy, is a libel on that siren's reputation: it is coarse, clumsy, and rough. But fast-forward a millennium or so and you arrive at the Golden Age, when Greek art forevermore set the standard for ideals of beauty, grace, and realism in Western art, when the Parthenon gave proof of an architectural genius unique in history. The time was the 5th century BC, about 2,000 years before the Italian Renaissance. Just as that glorious age flourished, thanks to Italian city-states, so did ancient Greece reach its apogee in its cities. And it was in Athens that Greek citizens realized they could reveal the free blossoming of the human being and respect the individualistic character of men and women through art and architecture. This affirmation was largely the work of one man, Pericles, the famous Athenian general and builder of the Parthenon. During his day, Greek artistic genius fed on a physical ideal—spectacularly represented in the culture with its hero worship of athletes—as it did on religion. Religion itself, far from being an abstraction, was an anthropomorphic reflection of a passion for physical beauty.

The inspiration, however, would not have sufficed to ensure the grandeur of Greek art had it not been served by a perfection of technique. Whoever created any object had to know to perfection every element of his model, whether it was a man or woman or god or goddess. Witness the marvels of the sculpture of the age, such as the *Delphi Charioteer,* the Parthenon frieze figures, or the *Venus de Milo.* Basically the cult of the god was the cult of beauty. The women of Sparta, desirous of having handsome children, adorned their bedchambers with statues of male and female beauties. Beauty contests are not an invention of modern times. The Greeks organized them as early as the 7th century BC, until Christianity came to frown on such practices.

In like form, architecture was also the reflection of the personality of this Greek world. Thus, when we note the buildings of the Acropolis, we note the Doric order is all mathematics; the Ionian, all poetry. The first expresses proud reserve, massive strength, and severe simplicity; the second, suppleness, sensitivity, and elegance. No matter what the order, the column was the binding force—the absolute incarnation of reason in form. Study the columns of the Parthenon and you quickly realize that the Greeks did not propose to represent reality with its clutter of details; their aim was to seize the essence of things and let its light shine forth.

But it would be false to conclude, as certain romantic spirits have done, that the Greeks were mere aesthetes, lost in ecstasy before abstract beauty and subordinating their lives to it. Quite the reverse: it was the art of living, which, for the Greeks, was the supreme art. A healthy utilitarian inclination combined with their worship of beauty to such an extent that art within their homes was not an idle ornament, but had a functional quality related to everyday life.

WORTH NOTING

Old University complex. In the sea of concrete that is central Athens, this imposing group of marble buildings conjures up an illusion of classical antiquity. The three dramatic buildings belonging to the University of Athens were designed by the Hansen brothers in the period after independence in the 19th century and are built of white Pendelic marble, with tall columns and decorative friezes. In the center is the **Senate House** of the university. To the right is the **Academy,** flanked by two slim columns topped by statues of Athena and Apollo; paid for by the Austro-Greek Baron Sina, it is a copy of the Parliament in Vienna. Frescoes in the reception hall depict the myth of Prometheus. At the left end of the complex is a griffin-flanked staircase leading to the **National Library,** containing more than 2 million Greek and foreign-language volumes and now undergoing the daunting task of modernization. The University complex, as well as Syntagma Square, often serves as the meeting point for protest groups before their marches through the city center, so don't be surprised if city traffic comes to a halt when marchers stride by (during certain times of the year, there are at least one or two marches a week, much to the chagrin of Athenians). ⊠ *Panepistimiou between Ippokratous and Sina, Central Athens* ☎ *210/368–9765 Senate, 210/366–4700 Academy, 210/360–8185 Library* ⊕ *www.nlg.gr* ☉ *Senate and Academy weekdays 9–2; library Sept.–July, Mon.–Thurs. 9–8, Fri. 9–2* Ⓜ *Panepistimiou.*

> ### POETRY 101 CLASSROOM
>
> Hermann Schliemann called his magnificent neoclassic house, designed for him by Ernst Ziller, the "Palace of Troy." Note the Pompeiian aesthetic in the ocher, terra-cotta, and blue touches; the mosaic floors inspired by Mycenae; and the dining-room ceiling painted with food scenes, under which Schliemann would recite the *Iliad* to guests.

3

NEED A BREAK?

Clemente VIII. One of the toniest pedestrian malls in Athens is Voukourestiou, where you will find the one of the hippest cafés in the city, Clemente VIII. With the best espresso and cappuccino (both hot and iced) in town and a fresh daily platter of sandwiches and sweets, this Italianate-style café (named after the 16th-century pope who gave his blessing to the then exotic coffee bean) is a favorite of the Armani-clad business lunch crowd. ⊠ *Voukourestiou 3, City Link, Kolonaki* ☎ *210/321–9340.*

Zonar's Café d'Athenes. Clemente VIII no longer basks in its glory alone, for 100 feet away sits Zonar's Café d'Athenes. After a heartbreaking closure and more than six years of renovation, this is back with a vengeance. Despite hefty prices, the sleek "moderne" decor of this very exclusive café triumphantly looks better than ever while the mouth-watering pastry corner attracts the attention of old and young alike. ⊠ *Panepistimiou and Voukourestiou, Attica department store, Kolonaki* ☎ *210/321–1158* ☉ *9 am–1am.*

Psirri. Similar to New York City's Tribeca, this district has been targeted by developers who have spurred a wave of renovations and a bevy of

For patriotic Greeks, the Changing of the Guard in front of the Tomb of the Unknown Soldier is always a heart-stirring ceremony.

new nightspots. At dusk, this quiet quarter becomes a whirl of theaters, clubs, and restaurants, dotted with dramatically lighted churches and lively squares. Defined by Ermou, Kerameikou, Athinas, Evripidou, Epikourou, and Pireos streets, Psirri has many buildings older than those in picturesque Plaka. If you're coming from Omonia Square, walk down Aiolou, a pedestrian zone with cafés and old shops as well as an interesting view of the Acropolis. Peek over the wrought-iron gates of the old houses on the narrow side streets between Ermou and Keramei-kou to see the pretty courtyards bordered by long, low buildings, whose many small rooms were rented out to different families. In the Square of the Heroes, revolutionary fighters once met to plot against the Ottoman occupation. Linger on into the evening if you want to dance on table-tops to live Greek music, sing along with a soulful accordion player, hear salsa in a Cuban club, or watch hoi polloi go by as you snack on updated or traditional *mezedes* (appetizers). ⊠ *Off Ermou, centered on Iroon and Ayion Anargiron Sqs., Psirri* ⊕ *www.psirri.gr* Ⓜ *Monastiraki.*

★ **Technopolis.** Gazi, the neighborhood surrounding this former 19th-century-foundry–turned–arts complex, takes its name from the toxic gas fumes that used to spew from the factory's smokestacks. Today Gazi is synonymous with the hippest restaurants, edgiest galleries, and trendiest nightclubs in town. The smokestacks now glow crimson with colored lights, anchoring a burgeoning stretch that runs from the central neighborhood of Kerameikos to the once-decrepit neighborhood of Rouf. The city of Athens bought the disused foundry in the late 1990s and helped convert it into Technopolis, a city of arts and culture. The transformation preserved all the original architecture and stonework, and includes six exhibition spaces and a large courtyard open to the public. The spaces regularly host shows on a range of topics—war photography, open-air jazz, comic-book art, rock and theater performances, rave nights, and parties. It is also the home of the biannual Athens Fashion Week. ⊠ *Pireos 100, Gazi* ☎ *210/346–1589* ⬛ *Free* ⊙ *9–9 during exhibitions* Ⓜ *Kerameikos.*

SYNTAGMA SQUARE TO KOLONAKI
ΠΛΑΤΕΙΑ ΣΥΝΤΑΓΜΑΤΟΣ ΠΡΟΣ ΚΟΛΩΝΑΚΙ

From the Tomb of the Unknown Soldier to Queen Amalia's National Garden, to the top of Mt. Lycabettus (three times the height of the Acropolis), this center-city sector is packed with marvels and wonders. Sooner or later, everyone passes through its heart, the spacious Syntagma Square (Constitution Square), which is surrounded by sights that span Athens's history from the days of the Roman emperors to King Otho's reign after the 1821 War of Independence. Some may have likened his palace (now the Parliament) to a barracks but they shouldn't complain: it was paid for by Otho's father, King Ludwig I of Bavaria, who luckily vetoed the plans for a royal residence atop the Acropolis itself, using one end of the Parthenon as the entrance and blowing up the rest. The palace was finished just in time for Otho to grant the constitution of 1843, which gave the name to the square. Neighboring Kolonaki—the chic shopping district and one of the most fashionable residential areas—occupies the lower slopes of Mt. Lycabettus. Besides visiting its several museums, you can spend time window-shopping and people-watching, since cafés are busy from early morning to dawn. Nursing a single coffee for hours remains not only socially acceptable—but a vital survival tactic in frequently stressful modern Greek life.

TOP ATTRACTIONS

Fodor's Choice ★ **Benaki Museum.** Just in time for the 2004 Olympics, Greece's oldest private museum received a spectacular face-lift with the addition of a hypermodern wing that looks like it was airlifted in from New York City. Located on the gentrifying Pireos Street, this construction is all the more striking when compared to the main museum, set in an imposing neoclassic mansion in the posh Kolonaki neighbourhood. Established in 1926 by an illustrious Athenian family, the Benaki was one of the first to place emphasis on Greece's later heritage at a time when many archaeologists were destroying Byzantine artifacts to access ancient objects. The permanent collection (more than 20,000 items are on display in 36 rooms, and that's only a sample of the holdings) moves chronologically from the ground floor upward, from prehistory to the formation of the modern Greek state. You might see anything from a 5,000-year-old hammered gold bowl to an austere Byzantine icon of the Virgin Mary to Lord Byron's pistols to the Nobel medals awarded to poets George Seferis and Odysseus Elytis. Some exhibits are just plain fun—the re-creation of a Kozani (Macedonian town) living room; a tableau of costumed mannequins; a Karaghiozi shadow puppet piloting a toy plane—all contrasted against the marble and crystal-chandelier grandeur of the Benaki home. The mansion that serves as the main building of the museum was designed by Anastassios Metaxas, the architect who helped restore the Panathenaic Stadium. The Benaki's gift shop, a destination in itself, tempts with exquisitely reproduced ceramics and jewelry. The second-floor café serves coffee and snacks, with a few daily specials, on a generous veranda overlooking the National Garden.

The eye-knocking new Benaki museum wing is located at 138 Pireos Street, one of the busiest and most industrially developed city axis. The minimalistic exterior is covered in smooth pink stone—a kind of beacon of modernity, clean lines, and creativity on the dusty, loud avenue. Inside, all is high-ceilinged atriums, walkway ascents, and multiple levels, a dramatic setting for the museum's temporary exhibitions (many of which are more avant-garde in character than the ones housed in the main building). Topping the complex off is a state-of-the-art amphitheater. Latest addition to the Benaki museum is the Islamic Art collection, which is housed in a beautifully restored neoclassical mansion behind the Kerameikos cemetery. ⊠ *Koumbari 1, Kolonaki* ☎ *210/367–1000* ⊕ *www. benaki.gr* 🖃 *€6, free Thurs.* ☉ *Mon., Wed., Fri., and Sat. 9–5, Thurs. 9 am–midnight, Sun. 9–3* Ⓜ *Syntagma or Evangelismos.*

Hadrian's Arch. One of the most important Roman monuments surviving in Athens, Hadrian's Arch has become, for many, one of the city's most iconic landmarks. This marble gateway, built in AD 131 with Corinthian details, was intended both to honor the Hellenophile emperor Hadrian and to separate the ancient and imperial sections of Athens. On the side facing the Acropolis an inscription reads "this is athens, the ancient city of theseus," but the side facing the Temple of Olympian Zeus proclaims "this is the city of hadrian and not of theseus." ⊠ *Vasilissis Amalias at Dionyssiou Areopagitou, National Garden* ⊕ *www. culture.gr* 🖃 *Free* ☉ *Daily* Ⓜ *Acropolis.*

Ⓒ
★
Fodor's Choice
★
Mt. Lycabettus. Myth claims that Athens's highest hill came into existence when Athena removed a piece of Mt. Pendeli, intending to boost the height of her temple on the Acropolis. While she was en route, a crone brought her bad tidings, and the flustered goddess dropped the rock in the middle of the city. Kids love the ride up the steeply inclined *teleferique* (funicular) to the summit (one ride every 30 minutes), crowned by whitewashed **Ayios Georgios** chapel with a bell tower donated by Queen Olga. On a clear day, you can see Aegina island, with or without the aid of coin-operated telescopes. Built into a cave on the side of the hill, near the spot where the I Prasini Tenta café used to be, is a small

---

FULL FRONTAL FASHION

Near the Parliament, you can watch the **Changing of the Evzones Guards** at the Tomb of the Unknown Soldier—in front of Parliament on a lower level—which takes place at intervals throughout the day. On Sunday the honor guard of tall young men don a dress costume—a short white and very heavy *foustanella* (kilt) with 400 neat pleats, one for each year of the Ottoman occupation, and red shoes with pom-poms—and still manage to look brawny rather than silly. A band accompanies them: they all arrive by 11:15 am in front of Parliament.

shrine to **Ayios Isidoros.** In 1859 students prayed here for those fighting against the Austrians, French, and Sardinians with whom King Otho had allied. From Mt. Lycabettus you can watch the sunset and then turn about to watch the moon rise over "violet-crowned" Hymettus as the lights of Athens blink on all over the city. Refreshments are available from the modest kiosk popular with concertgoers who flock to events at the hill's open-air theater during summer months. Diners should also note that Lycabettus is home to Orizontes Lykavittou, an excellent fish restaurant (by day this establishment also houses the relaxing Café Lycabettus). ⊠ *Base: 15-min walk northeast of Syntagma Sq.; funicular every 10 mins from corner of Ploutarchou and Aristippou (take Minibus 060 from Kanari or Kolonaki Sq.), Kolonaki* ☏ *210/721–0701 Funicular information, 210/721–0721 Funicular information* ⛟ *Funicular €6* ⊙ *Funicular daily 9 am–3 am.*

☾ **Museum of Cycladic Art.** Also known as the Nicholas P. Goulandris Founda-
Fodor'sChoice tion, and funded by one of Greece's richest families, this museum has an
★ outstanding collection of 350 Cycladic artifacts dating from the Bronze Age, including many of the enigmatic marble figurines whose slender shapes fascinated such artists as Picasso, Modigliani, and Brancusi. The main building is an imposing glass-and-steel design dating from 1985 and built to convey "the sense of austerity and the diffusion of refracted light that predominate in the Cycladic landscape," as the museum puts it. Along with Cycladic masterpieces, a wide array from other eras is also on view, ranging from the Bronze Age through the 6th century AD. The third floor is devoted to Cypriot art while the fourth floor showcases a fascinating exhibition on "scenes from daily life in antiquity." To handle the overflow, a new wing opened in 2005. A glass corridor connects the main building to the gorgeous 19th-century neoclassic Stathatos Mansion, where temporary exhibits are mounted. There is also a lovely sky-lit café in a courtyard centered around a Cycladic-inspired fountain, a charming art shop, and many children-oriented activities all year round. ⊠ *Neofitou Douka 4, Kolonaki* ☏ *210/722–8321 through 210/722–8323* ⊕ *www.cycladic.gr* ⛟ *€7* ⊙ *Mon., Wed., Fri., and Sat. 10–5, Thurs. 10–8, Sun. 11–5* Ⓜ *Evangelismos.*

★ **National Gallery of Art.** The permanent collections of Greek painting and sculpture of the 19th and 20th centuries (including the work of folk artist Theophilos) are always on display, but popular traveling exhibitions enliven the National Gallery of Art-Alexandros Soutsos museum. The exhibitions are usually major loan shows from around the world, such as an El Greco retrospective, Dutch 17th-century art, modern Spanish architecture, and an exhibit tracing the movements of art nouveau and modernism in early 20th-century Paris. ⊠ *Vasileos Konstantinou 50, Ilisia* ☏ *210/723–5857, 210/723–5937* ⊕ *www.nationalgallery.gr* ⛟ *€6.50* ⊙ *Mon., Thurs., Fri., Sat. 9 am–3 pm, Sun. 10–2, Wed. 3 pm–9 pm* Ⓜ *Evangelismos.*

☾ **National Garden.** When you can't take the city noise anymore, step into
★ this oasis completed in 1860 as part of King Otto and Queen Amalia's royal holdings. Here old men on the benches argue politics, police officers take their coffee breaks, runners count early-morning jog laps, and animal lovers feed the stray cats that roam among the more than 500

species of trees and plants, many labeled. At the east end is the neo-classic **Zappion Hall**, built in 1888 as an Olympic building (with funds from Greek benefactor Evangelos Zappas). Since then it has been used for major political and cultural events: it was here that Greece signed its accession to what was then the European Community. Next door, a leafy café and open-air cinema attract Athenians all year round. If you like walking, make the trek to the nearby Panathenaic Stadium, which was built on the very site of an ancient stadium for the revived Olympic Games in 1896. You can look at the stadium only from the outside, but there is an elevated dirt running track behind it (free entrance through a big gate on Archimidous street, which runs directly behind the stadium). The tree-lined track area and adjacent Ardittos hill constitute one of the most pleasant, quiet public spaces in the city—they also offer some stunning vantage points.

National Garden playgrounds, duck pond, and small zoo. Children appreciate the playgrounds, duck pond, and small zoo at the east end of the National Garden. ⊠ *East end of park, Amalias 1, National Garden* ☎ *210/721–5019, 210/725–5106* ☎ *210/323–7830* ⊕ *www.zappeion. gr* Ⓜ *Syntagma.*

NEED A BREAK?

Aeglí Zappiou. Visit the elegant Aeglí Zappiou, an excellent spot for a classic Greek coffee experience. Nestled among fountains and flowering trees next to the Zappion Exhibition Hall in the National Garden, it's an ideal spot to sample a fresh dessert or some haute cuisine, or watch a movie at the open-air Cine Aegli next door! Adjacent to this café is the noted Cibus restaurant, which offers a special *degustation* menu of modern Greek cuisine every Wednesday evening (reservations recommended). ⊠ *National Garden* ☎ *210/336–9300* ⊕ *www.aeglizappiou.gr.*

★ **Syntagma (Constitution) Square.** At the top of the city's main square stands the Greek **Parliament,** formerly King Otto's royal palace, completed in 1838 for the new monarchy. It seems a bit austere and heavy for a southern landscape, but it was proof of progress, the symbol of the new ruling power. The building's saving grace is the stone's magical change of color from off-white to gold to rosy mauve as the day progresses. Here you can watch the **Changing of the Evzone Guards** at the **Tomb of the Unknown Soldier**—in front of Parliament on a lower level—which takes place at intervals throughout the day. On a wall behind the Tomb of the Unknown Soldier, the bas-relief of a dying soldier is modeled after a sculpture on the Temple of Aphaia in Aegina; the text is from the funeral oration said to have been given by Pericles. In recent years the square has become the new frontline of mass protests against harsh austerity measures and the ongoing economic crisis in Greece, as well as the base for the citizen movement of the "Indignants."

Syntagma metro station. Pop into the gleaming Syntagma metro station to examine artfully displayed artifacts uncovered during subway excavations. A floor-to-ceiling cross section of earth behind glass shows finds in chronological layers, ranging from a skeleton in its ancient grave to traces of the 4th-century BC road to Mesogeia to an Ottoman

Try to catch the purple glow of sundown from atop Mt. Lycabettus, Athens's highest hill.

cistern. The 21st century arrived here in 2006 when the first public wireless network with free access to the Internet was set up in Syntagma Square. (Note that this station is the first one to shut its doors for security reasons when a demonstration takes place outside in Syntagma Square.) ⊠ *Upper end of Syntagma Sq.* ⊕ *www.ametro.gr* ⊙ *Daily 5 am–midnight* Ⓜ *Syntagma* ⊠ *Vasilissis Amalias and Vasilissis Sofias, Syntagma Sq.* Ⓜ *Syntagma.*

NEED A BREAK?

Café Voulis. On Voulis street, the tiny pedestrian road just behind Syntagma Square, you can stop for a swift espresso coffee break. Café Voulis has been voted one of the Top 10 espresso bars in the country, but its aficionados also swear by the fresh sandwiches and salads for an easy lunch break. It is also remarkably cool in summer. ⊠ *Voulis 17 and Ermou* ☏ *210/331–0676.*

Temple of Olympian Zeus. Begun in the 6th century BC, this gigantic temple was completed in AD 132 by Hadrian, who also commissioned a huge gold-and-ivory statue of Zeus for the inner chamber and another, only slightly smaller, of himself. Only 15 of the original Corinthian columns remain, but standing next to them may inspire a sense of awe at their bulk, which is softened by the graceful carving on the acanthus-leaf capitals. The clearly defined segments of a column blown down in 1852 give you an idea of the method used in its construction. The site is floodlighted on summer evenings, creating a majestic scene when you round the bend from Syngrou. On the outskirts of the site to the north are remains of Roman houses, the city walls, and a Roman bath. Hellenic "neopagans" also use the site for ceremonies. Hadrian's Arch lies just outside the enclosed archaological site. ✉ *Vasilissis Olgas 1, National Garden* ☎ *210/922–6330* 🎫 *€2; €12 joint ticket for all Unification of Archaeological Sites* ⊙ *Tues.–Sun. 8:30–3* Ⓜ *Acropolis.*

WORTH NOTING

★ **Byzantine and Christian Museum.** One of the few museums in Europe focusing exclusively on Byzantine art displays an outstanding collection of icons, mosaics, tapestries, and sculptural fragments (the latter provides an excellent introduction to Byzantine architecture). The permanent collection is divided in two main parts: the first is devoted to Byzantium (4th–15th century AD) and contains 1,200 artifacts while the second is entitled "From Byzantium to the Modern Era" and presents 1,500 artworks dating from the 15th to the 21st century. ✉ *Vasilissis Sofias 22, Kolonaki* ☎ *213/213–9572, 213/723–9511* ⊕ *www.byzantinemuseum.gr* 🎫 *€4* ⊙ *Tues.–Sun. 8:30–3* Ⓜ *Evangelismos.*

Gennadius Library. Book lovers who ascend the grand staircase into the hallowed aura of the Reading Room may have difficulty tearing themselves away from this superb collection of material on Greek subjects, from first editions of Greek classics to the papers of Nobel Laureate poets George Seferis and Odysseus Elytis. The library's collection includes Lord Byron's memorabilia (including a lock of his hair); Heinrich Schliemann's diaries, notebooks, and letters; impressionistic watercolors of Greece by Edward Lear; and the first edition printed in Greek of Homer's *Iliad* and *Odyssey*. The Gennadius is not a lending library (first-time users, usually scholars, must apply for a library card). ✉ *Souidias 61, Kolonaki* ☎ *210/721–0536* ⊕ *www.ascsa.edu.gr* ⊙ *Sept.–June, Mon.–Wed. and Fri. 9–5, Thurs. 9–8, Sat. 9–2; check with reception for special hours during July and Aug.* Ⓜ *Evangelismos.*

Kolonaki Square. To see and be seen, Athenians gather not on Kolonaki Square—hub of the chic Kolonaki district—but at the cafés on its periphery and along the Tsakalof and Milioni pedestrian zones. Clothespin-thin models, slick talk-show hosts, middle-aged executives, elegant pensioners, university students, and expatriate teen queens all congregate on the square (officially known as Filikis Eterias) for a coffee before work, a lunchtime gossip session, a drink after a hard day of shopping, or an afternoon of sipping iced cappuccinos while reading a stack of foreign newspapers and magazines purchased from the all-night kiosk.

British Council. On the lower side of Kolonaki Square are the headquarters of the British Council in Greece, which organizes a lively program of arts and cultural events, greatly helping to bring contemporary UK culture a little closer to home. ✉ *Kolonaki Sq. 17, Kolonaki* ☎ *210/369–2333* ⊕ *www.britishcouncil.org* ✉ *Intersection of Patriarchou Ioakeim and Kanari, Kolonaki* Ⓜ *Syntagma, then 10-min walk.*

NEED A BREAK?

Caffe Da Capo. Enjoy a cappuccino and an Italian dolce standing inside Caffe Da Capo or, if you have more time, try to find a table. This place is usually packed with young trendsetters and stern policy makers; people-watching is part of the pleasure. ✉ *Tsakalof 1, Kolonaki* ☎ *210/360-2497.*

WHERE TO EAT

THE SCENE

Doesn't anybody eat at home anymore? When you're on vacation, travelers don't have much choice in the matter, but these days—even in the throes of the current economic crisis—Athenians are going out to restaurants in record numbers. And it's easy for visitors to the capitol to become a part of the clatter, chatter, and song, especially at the city's neighborhood tavernas.

These Athenian landmarks were famous for their wicker chairs that inevitably pinched your bottom, checkered tablecloths covered with butcher paper, wobbly tables that needed coins under one leg, and wine drawn from the barrel and served in small metal carafes. Today, some of their clientele have moved up to a popular new restaurant hybrid: the "neo-taverna," which serves traditional fare in surroundings that are more stylish than the usual tavern decor of island posters and wooden figurines; most are located in the up-and-coming industrial-cum-arty districts of central Athens, such as Gazi and Metaxourgeio. At the same time, enduring in popularity are the traditional *magereika* ("cookeries"): humble, no-frills eateries where the food, usually displayed behind glass windows, is cooked Grandma's style—it's simple, honest, time-tested, filling comfort (note that some of the best, like Anthos at 10 Kolokotroni street and Doris at Praxitelous 30, are only open for lunch). Even local fast-food chain Goody's has been influenced by this style of cooking and offers a seasonal selection of dishes and salads that emulate home cooking.

Trends? Athens's got 'em. On the one hand, there is a marked return to Greek regional cooking, especially Cretan cuisine, widely regarded as one of the healthiest versions of the olive oil–rich Mediterranean diet. On the other hand, Athenians are increasingly eager to explore international flavors. With many groundbreaking chefs obsessed with modern nouveau cuisine, there was, for a while, a real danger of some loss of tradition. Since then, things have stabilized. What saved the day were Greek ingredients: fresh out of the garden and right off the boat, they inspired chefs to get reacquainted with their culinary roots. A whole constellation of hip, all-in-one bar-restaurants have emerged, revolving around star chefs and glitterati customers. Sleek interior designs, very late-night hours, dedicated DJs, and adjoining lounges full of beautiful people have become Athenian recipes for success.

RULES OF THE GAME

If you can't understand the menu, just go to the kitchen and point at what looks most appealing, especially in tavernas. In most cases, you don't need to ask—just walk to the kitchen (some places have food displayed in a glass case right at the kitchen's doorway), or point to your eye and then the kitchen; the truly ambitious can ask a question (Bo-*ro* na dtho tee *eh*-he-teh steen koo-*zee*-na?, or "May I see what's in the kitchen?"). When ordering fish, which is priced by the kilo, you often go to the kitchen to pick out your fish, which is then weighed and billed accordingly.

3

But some things remain eternal. Athenian dining is seasonal. In August, when residents scatter to the hills and seaside, many restaurants and tavernas close, with the hippest bar-restaurants reopening at choice seaside positions. And visitors remain shocked by how late Greeks dine. It's normal (even on a weekday) to show up for a meal at 9 or 10 and to leave long after midnight, only to head off for drinks. Hotel restaurants, Piraeus seafood places, and Plaka tavernas keep very late hours. Most places serve lunch from about noon to 4 (and sometimes as late as 6) and dinner from about 8 or 9 until at least midnight. When in Athens, don't hesitate to adopt this Zorbaesque lifestyle. Eat, drink, party, and enjoy life—knowing full well that, as a traveler, there can always be a siesta at your disposal the next day.

DINING, ATHENS STYLE

Taverna culture is all about sharing. People often order their own main meat, fish, or vegetable courses, but often share these, salads, and appetizers with the entire dinner party. It's a nice alternative to being stuck with just one choice. Vegetarians will find some of their best options in the appetizers, though they'd be wise to avoid grill restaurants, where fried potatoes may be their only option. Tipping is less strict than in many countries. There is a service charge on the bill, but it doesn't necessarily go to the staff, so Athenians often leave a tip of 10%. Feel free to request tap water in a pitcher (it's good in Athens) as opposed to bottled water, which may be brought automatically to your table without your request. As in most other cosmopolitan cities, dress varies from casual to fancy, according to the establishment. Although Athens is informal and none of the restaurants listed here requires a jacket or tie, locals make an effort to look their best when out on the town, so you may feel more comfortable dressing up a bit, especially at more-expensive places. After years of swallowing secondhand smoke, the scales are tilting in nonsmokers' favor. Smoking is no longer permitted inside bars and restaurants (though some still allow smoking in their outside areas). Some larger establishments, however, are allowed to have special smoking sections. It's best to check a restaurant's smoking policy by phone first. Children are welcome in most places, but it's best to check in advance for upscale establishments.

WHAT IT COSTS IN EUROS				
	¢	$	$$	$$$	$$$$
AT DINNER	under €10	€10–€20	€20–€30	€30–€40	over €40

Prices are for one main course at dinner, or for two mezedes (small dishes) at restaurants that serve only mezedes.

ACROPOLIS AND SOUTH ΑΚΡΟΠΟΛΗ ΚΑΙ ΝΟΤΙΑ

Use the coordinate (✛ B2) at the end of each listing to locate a site on the corresponding map.

BEST BETS FOR ATHENS DINING

In the shadow of Greece's most famous landmark, arty-chic neighborhoods such as Koukaki and Philopappou offer both historic views and classical-meets-urban ambience.

$$$$
CONTEMPORARY
★

✕**Edodi.** Bajazzo—the restaurant that introduced Athenians to haute cuisine—is no more, but when it closed in 1999, several top staffers decided to open an intimate, candlelit dining room (with fewer than 10 tables) in a neoclassic house. You have to ring the bell to be let in the cozy space. The menu still pays homage to the gastronomic splendor of Bajazzo but in a decidedly dramatic manner: instead of a printed menu, raw seasonal ingredients are brought to your table, chosen by you, then cooked to order according to your mood and tastes, which the waitstaff are quite skilled at gauging. Offerings are always changing, but the lobster with spicy Parmesan sauce and spinach al dente is a perennial favorite. Allow plenty of time for your dinner—here it is treated as a sacred ritual. Take advantage of the early bird (5 pm–8 pm) dinner prices. ✉ *Veikou 80, 1st floor, Koukaki* ☏ *210/921–3013* ⊕ *www.edodi.gr* ⌨ *Reservations essential* ☾ *Closed Sun. and July–Aug. No lunch* ✛ *D5.*

$$
GREEK

✕**Manimani.** Featuring inspired recipes—and many ingredients—from the southern Peloponnese's Mani region, Manimani strikes the perfect balance between sophistication and heartiness. Located in a converted neoclassic residence, the decor has the relaxed precision of an upscale home-decor catalog (a gauzy drape or rag rug here, a beautiful glass vase there), but the food and extensive regional wine list quickly take center stage. It's comfort food that sweetly screams "village"—from

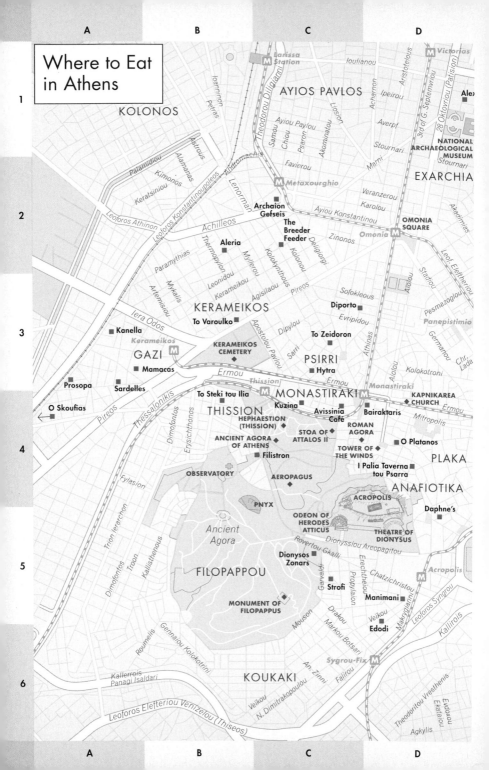

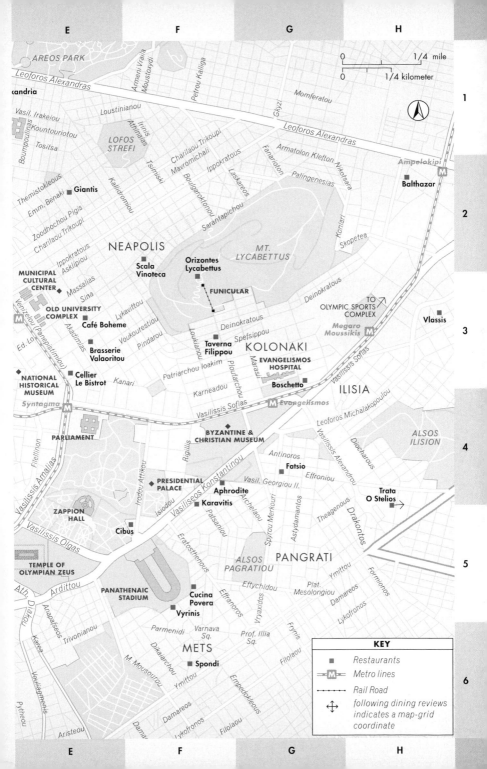

LANDING A SEAFOOD FEAST, GREEK STYLE

Enjoying the bounty of the seas that wash against Greek shores can be a fishy business. The waters have been over-fished for decades and much "Greek" fish served today is often frozen from other waters. Take heart, though. You can still feast on delicious fish in Greece—it's just a question of what you order, and where.

Patrons of fish restaurants are usually greeted with iced displays of the catch of the day. Proprietors will often spout some mumbo-jumbo about the fish being caught only an hour earlier—allow the shills some poetic license and go for the operative word here, *fresco*, fresh, as opposed to *katepsigmeno*, frozen.

The fish you choose will be sold by the portion, *merida*, and priced by the kilo. Expect to pay at least €55 a kilo for such popular fish as *xifia*, swordfish; *lavraki*, sea bass; *tsipoura*, sea bream; and *barbounia*, red mullet.

Yes, fish is expensive in Greece, but remember, that price is per kilo, and the portion you order may well weigh, and cost, less.

SEAFOOD BOUNTY

A wonderful place to cast your line for local color, along with getting a good look at the denizens of the Greek seas, is the Fish Market in the Athens Central Market at Athinas and Evripidou Streets, between Monastiraki and Omonia squares.

Vociferous vendors hose down iced piles of scales, shells, and tentacles while reeling in customers.

Can't accommodate a red mullet in your hotel room? Not to worry.

Yours truly can satisfy the appetite this most Athenian of institutions will no doubt trigger in one of the city's many fine fish restaurants.

WHAT'S WHAT IN THE SEA

These creatures make an appearance on many Greek menus, often as appetizers, *mezedes*, and you usually can't go wrong ordering any of them, in any variation.

Garides, shrimp, are often served deliciously as saganaki, baked with fresh tomatoes and feta cheese and brought to the table sizzling.

Sardelles, sardines, are grilled, fried, or eaten raw and marinated. *Papalina* are small sardines, and *atherina* are very small sardines.

Gavros, anchovies, are almost always fried and served with lemon and vinegar.

Kalamari, squid, are often fried. A far more satisfying treat is whole kalamari, grilled or stuffed with rice and herbs and baked. A tasty relative is the *soupia*, cuttlefish, usually baked in tomato sauce.

Htapodi, octopus, is grilled, marinated in vinegar and oil, or stewed with tomatoes and onions.

Mydia, mussels, are usually steamed, and are often taken out of their shells and served in risotto, seafood pasta, or salads.

OLD TIME FAVORITES
In addition to fresh fish, keep an eye out for these old standards. *Taramasalata*, fish roe salad, is a tasty spread, a poor man's caviar made from carp eggs,

blended with olive oil, lemon juice, and garlic.

Kakavia and *psarosoupa* are variations of fish soup, usually made from pieces of whatever fish is available, simmered in broth with vegetables, and always embellished with the special flourishes of the individual cook.

Cod, *bakaliaros*, is often served as *bakaliaros skordalia*, dipped in batter and deep fried.

WHERE TO CAST YOUR LINE FOR A SEAFOOD MEAL

Hytra. This fashionable bistro is famed for its fish soup garnished with sea urchin.

I Taverna tou Psarra. Brigitte Bardot and Laurence Olivier have dined here, perhaps on their celebrated octopus.

Orizontes. Atop Mt. Lycabettus, this is tops in taste, especially their sea bream with silver beet.

Sardelles. Sardines (*sardelles*) are the house specialty here, especially those "hot and spicy" in rock salt.

Trata O Stelios. The fish soup here is so good it might raise the dead.

To Varoulko. Octopus, crayfish, and other denizens of the deep find their way into magnificent creations, served with flair.

the *kayiana* omelet and citrus-flavor sausage to the regional noodles and rich salads. The chef adds delicate new fruity or spicy touches to dishes and embraces organic products at this spot just around the corner from the Acropolis metro. It's also open for lunch, which makes it the perfect pit stop after visiting the Acropolis and its museum. ⊠ *Falirou 10, Makriyianni* ☏ *210/921–8180* ⊕ *www.manimani.com.gr* ⌕ *Reservations essential* ☉ *Closed Mon. No dinner Sun.* ✛ *D5.*

$$ ✕ **Strofi.** Walls lined with autographed photos of actors from the nearby
GREEK Odeon of Herodes Atticus attest to Strofi's success with the after-theater
Fodor's Choice crowd that flocks to the Hellenic Festival. Despite the many tourists, the
★ recently renovated rooftop garden with dramatic views of the lighted Acropolis still attracts locals who have been coming here for decades. In fact, the amazing views come close to stealing the show, although the cuisine comes a very close second. Start with some mezedes, like a tangy *taramosalata* (fish roe dip) or velvety tzatziki, which perfectly complements the thinly sliced fried zucchini. Another good appetizer is *fava*, a puree of yellow split peas. For the main course, choose roast lamb with *hilopites* (thin egg noodles cut into small squares) and oregano, grilled chicken fillet, beef stew in a pot with cheese and potatoes, or the kid goat prepared with gruyere cheese and tomato. ⊠ *Rovertou Galli 25, Makriyianni* ☏ *210/921–4130* ⊕ *www.strofi.gr* ☉ *Closed Sun. No lunch* ✛ *C5.*

PLAKA ΠΛΑΚΑ

Use the coordinate (✛ B2) at the end of each listing to locate a site on the corresponding map.

Just northeast of the Acropolis, Plaka and Anafiotika delight in their traditional homes, winding alleys, and bustle of cafés and gift shops.

$$$$ ✕ **Daphne's.** Discreet service and refined Mediterranean and Greek
GREEK dishes (such as pork with celery and egg lemon sauce, fricassee of melt-
Fodor's Choice off-the-bone lamb with greens, beef with olives, rabbit in mavrodaphne
★ wine sauce and the traditional *moussaka*) help make Daphne's one of the most exclusive (and at times pricey) destinations in Plaka. The Pompeian frescoes on the walls, the fragments of an ancient Greek building in the garden, and the tasteful restoration of the neoclassic building in terra-cotta and ochre hues also contribute to a pleasant and romantic evening. ⊠ *Lysikratous 4, Plaka* ☏ *210/322–7991* ⊕ *www.daphnesrestaurant.gr* ✛ *D5.*

$$ ✕ **I Palia Taverna tou Psarra.** Founded way back in 1898, this is one of
SEAFOOD the few remaining Plaka tavernas serving reliably good food as well as having the obligatory mulberry-shaded terrace (with live music every day except Tuesday). The previous owners (the taverna is now run by a well-known family of Greek restaurateurs) claimed to have served Brigitte Bardot and Laurence Olivier, but it's the number of Greeks who come here that testifies to Psarra's appeal. Oil-oregano marinated octopus and *gavros* (a small fish) are good appetizers. Simple, tasty entrées include rooster in wine, *arnaki pilino* (lamb baked in clay pots), and pork chops with ouzo. Can't make up your mind? Try the *ouzokatastasi* ("ouzo situation"), a plate of tidbits to nibble while you decide.

✉ *Erechtheos 16, and Erotokritou 12, Plaka* ☎ *210/321–8733* ⊕ *www. psaras-taverna.gr* ✛ *D4.*

¢ ✕ **O Platanos.** Set on a picturesque pedestrianized square, this is one
GREEK of the oldest tavernas in Plaka (established 1932)—a welcome sight
Fodor'sChoice compared with the many overpriced tourist traps in the area. A district
★ landmark—it is set midway between the Tower of the Winds and the
Museum of Greek Popular Musical Instruments—it warms the eye with
its pink-hue house, nicely color-coordinated with the bougainvillea-
covered courtyard. Although the rooms here are cozily adorned with
old paintings and photos, most of the crowd opts to relax under the
courtyard's plane trees (which give the place its name). Platanos is
packed with locals, who flock here because the food is good Greek
home cooking and the waiters fast and polite. Don't miss the oven-
baked potatoes, lamp or veal casserole with spinach or eggplant, fresh
green beans in savory olive oil, fresh grilled fish, and the exceptionally
cheap but delicious barrel retsina. Open for lunch. ✉ *Diogenous 4,
Plaka* ☎ *210/322–0666* ⊟ *No credit cards* ☾ *Sun. in June–Aug. No
dinner Sun. year-round.* ✛ *D4.*

MONASTIRAKI AND THISSION ΜΟΝΑΣΤΗΡΑΚΙ ΚΑΙ ΘΗΣΕΙΟ

*Use the coordinate (✛ B2) at the end of each listing to locate a site on
the corresponding map.*

Northwest of Plaka, Monastiraki and Thission retain the gritty charm
of an Anatolian bazaar and magnetize the city's hard-core café and
bar crowd.

¢ ✕ **Bairaktaris.** Run by the same family for more than a century, this is an
GREEK almost legendary souvlaki eatery in Monastiraki Square. After admiring the painted wine barrels, the black-and-white stills of Greek film
stars, and the snapshots of politicians who have held lunches here, go
to the window case to view the day's *magirefta* (stove-top cooked dish,
usually made earlier)—maybe beef *kokkinisto* (stew with red sauce)
and *soutzoukakia* (oblong meatballs simmered in tomato sauce) spiked
with cloves. Or sit down and order the famed gyro or the kebab platter.
Bairaktaris is always packed, so don't be in a rush to be served. ✉ *Monastiraki Sq. 2, Monastiraki* ☎ *210/321–3036* ✛ *D4.*

$$$ ✕ **Dionysos Zonars.** Location, location, location used to be the catch-
INTERNATIONAL phrase that best summed up the raison d'être of this famously historic
Fodor'sChoice restaurant. It just happened to be the spot where movies were always
★ filmed (those window views!), political treaties were signed, and tourists
rested their feet after their heated Acropolis climbs. But a recent change
of management and renovation work have lifted this legendary high-end
restaurant up a notch. It now serves high-quality, traditional Greek and
international dishes with a creative twist, such as *arnaki ambelourgou*
(lamb wrapped in wine leaves, with melted cheese and vegetables) and
kritharoto me garides (Greek pasta in tomato sauce with shrimp). The
traditional syrupy *baklava* dessert is also exceptional. Extending all the
good vibes, the adjoining café now serves breakfast and stays open until
after midnight. ✉ *Robertou Galli 43, Makriyianni* ☎ *210/923–3182*
⊕ *www.dionysoszonars.gr* ✛ *C5.*

$$ ✕ **Filistron.** In warm weather it's worth stopping by this place just to
GREEK   have a drink and enjoy the delightful, painterly scene from the roof
garden—a sweeping view of the Acropolis and Mt. Lycabettus. In cooler
weather, take a seat in the sunny, cheerful dining room off a pedestrian
walkway and enjoy a traditional Greek coffee prepared on hot ashes
(*xovoli*) and homemade cookies. The long list of mezedes has classics
and more-unusual dishes: codfish croquettes with herb-and-garlic sauce;
pork with mushrooms in wine sauce; *sofrito* (a traditional omelet dish
from the island of Corfu), eggplant and meat rolls, grilled potatoes with
smoked cheese and scallions; and an array of regional cheeses, washed
down with a flowery white *hima* (barrel wine). The service is top-notch.
✉ *Apostolou Pavlou 23, Thission* ☎ *210/346–7554, 210/342–2897*
⊕ *www.filistron.com* ✍ *Reservations essential* ☾ *Open daily 12 pm–1
am* ☾ *Closed 1 wk in Aug.* ✚ *C4.*

$$$ ✕ **Kuzina.** Sleek, dazzlingly decorated, and moodily lit, this bistro
GREEK FUSION   attracts many style-conscious Athenians. But Kuzina isn't just a pretty
Fodor's Choice   face. The food—especially the inventive seafood and pasta dishes con-
★   cocted by chef Aris Tsanaklides—is among the best in Athens, standing
out on touristy Adrianou. Happily, the decor is almost as delicious as
the Sikomaida fig tart marinated in anise seed and ouzo. Past an outdoor table setting, the main room soars skyward, glittering with bird-
cage chandeliers and factory ducts, with a vast lemon yellow bar set
below a spotlighted wall lined with hundreds of wine bottles. The menu
showcases newfangled Greek as well as old faves; best bets include the
grilled and cured octopus with fennel shavings; the *melitzanosalata*
(smoky Greek roasted eggplant salad); the spaghettini with Myconian
cheese *ksinotiri*, croutons, cherry tomatoes, and garlic; and the pork
roasted in the oven for 12 hours, and seasoned with lime, pineapple,
and cucumber. Whether you sit outside on the street, in the spectacular
main dining room, or opt for a table on the roof (the *Tarazza* offers a
fantastic view of the Acropolis and tasty cocktails), finish your meal
off with a delicious dessert such as the strawberry soup with chocolate
mousse plus a stroll to the small but impressive art gallery, Porta, on the
second floor. Kuzina's Web site is a winner, too—take a look. Kuzina
is open for lunch with a separate set of dining options. ✉ *Adrianou 9,
Thission* ☎ *210/324–0133* ⊕ *www.kuzina.gr* ✚ *C4.*

$ ✕ **To Steki tou Ilia.** Athenians who love fresh-grilled lamb chops and
GREEK   thick-cut fried potatoes that could have come from *yiayia's* (Grandma's)
Fodor's Choice   very kitchen flock to this classic taverna (the original old-fashioned
★   hangout with gated garden at Eptahalkou and a more recent and more
modern-looking extension a bit farther down Thessalonikis street)
along a quiet pedestrianized street in Thission. It's a place to relax
with friends: split a giant plate of *paidakia* (lamb chops), fries, creamy
tzatziki, and fava bean spread. Even the bread is prepared the Greek
way: grilled and sprinkled with olive oil and oregano. The tables on
the street fill rapidly so arrive early to soak in the Greek island vibe.
Reservations accepted. ✉ *Eptachalkou 5 and Thessalonikis 7, Thission*
☎ *210/342–2407 Thessalonikis 7, 210/345–8052 Eptaxalkou 5* ▭ *No
credit cards* ☾ *Thessalonikis 7 closed Mon.; no lunch Tues.–Fri. Eptaxalkou 5 closed Sun. evening; no lunch Tues.–Fri.* ✚ *B4.*

CENTRAL ATHENS, PSIRRI, AND OMONIA SQUARE
AΘHNA (KENTPO), ΨYPPH KAI ΠΛATEIA OMONOIAΣ

Use the coordinate (⌖ B2) at the end of each listing to locate a site on the corresponding map.

Located north of Monastiraki, Omonia, the city's main square, is busy by day and seedy by night, but it bursts with cultural diversity and the kaleidoscopic Central Market. The former warehouse district of Psirri, which is between Omonia and Monastiraki, is party central for Athens.

$$
GREEK
Fodor's Choice
★

✕**Archaion Gefseis.** The epicurean owners of "Ancient Flavors" combed through texts and archaeological records in an effort to re-create foods eaten in antiquity—not to mention how they were eaten, with spoon and knife only. Dishes like pancetta seasoned with thyme, stuffed piglet (which must be specially ordered two days before), and squid cooked in its ink prove, if anything, the continuity between ancient and modern Greek cuisine. There's an undeniable kitsch factor in the setting: in a torch-lighted garden, waiters in flowing chitons serve diners reclining on couches. But Greeks and foreign visitors alike flock here to discover the culinary pleasures of the ancients, not to forget the divinely cool and leafy garden during the summer months. ⊠ *Kodratou 22, Karaiskaki Sq., Metaxourgeio* ☎ *210/523–9661* ⊕ *www.archeon.gr* ☽ *7 pm–1 am* ⌖ *C2.*

$
GREEK

✕**Avissinia Café.** Facing hoary and merchant-packed Abyssinia Square, this timeworn but exceptional eatery—the Greek version of a French bistro—is popular with locals who want home-cooked traditional food and endless servings of the excellent barrel wine and local ouzo. Diners love to nestle within the elegant glass-and-wood interior as they sample the mussels and rice pilaf, the wine-marinated octopus with pasta, the fresh garden salad, or any of the dips (including the spicy eggplant-and-garlic spread). Little wonder so many head here to relax after a day of shopping at the nearby flea market. Another plus: music is often in the air—on weekend afternoons, you can enjoy accordion music (and the waiters' impromptu piano accompaniment!). ⊠ *Abyssinia Sq., Kinetou 7, Psirri* ☎ *210/321–7047* ⊕ *www.avissinia.gr* ☽ *Tues.–Sat. 11–1, Sun. 11–7* ☽ *Closed Mon.* ⌖ *C4.*

$$$

✕**The Breeder Feeder.** You wouldn't think Athens is on the bleeding-edge of the restaurant scene but what can top this? This contemporary art space, housed in a mastefully converted old ice cream factory in the hot Metaxourgeio neighborhood, is now also an experimental, rotating restaurant, which invites different teams of chefs to cook for its eclectic crowd (in a concept not unlike the rotating exhibitions regularly held in the gallery's 1,000 feet of exhibition space). The compact 45-seater eaterie has been tastefully decorated with traditional Greek rugs and cushions, cleverly contrasting with the stark white furniture. Check the restaurant's blog, ⊕ *thebreederfeeder.blogspot.com,* for upcoming guest chef appearances and its "opening days" (usually Tuesdays, Thursdays, and Fridays). ⊠ *Iasonos 45, Metaxourgeio* ☎ *210/331–7527* ⊕ *www.thebreedersystem.com* ⌲ *Reservations essential* ⌖ *C2.*

$
GREEK

✕**Diporto.** It's the savvy local's treasured secret. Through the years, everyone in Omonia has come here for lunch—butchers from the Central Market, suit-clad businessmen and lawyers, artists, migrants, and even bejeweled ladies who lunch (and they're often sitting at the same tables when it gets crowded). Owner-chef Barba Mitsos keeps everyone happy with his handful of simple, delicious, and dirt-cheap homemade dishes. There's always an exceptional *horiatiki* (Greek salad), sometimes studded with fiery-hot green pepperoncini; other favorites are his buttery *gigantes* (large, buttery white beans cooked in tomato sauce), *vrasto* (boiled goat, pork, or beef with vegetables), and fried finger-size fish. Wine is drawn directly from the barrels lining the walls. As for decor, the feeling is authentic '50s Athens. There is no sign on the door: just walk down the staircase of this corner neoclassical building. ⊠ *Socratous 9, Platia Theatrou, Central Market* ☎ *210 3211463* ⊟ *No credit cards* ⊙ *No dinner* ✛ *C3.*

$$$$ ✕ **Hytra.** Don't let the understated bistro ambience fool you: this is one
SEAFOOD of the city's most fashionable eateries. Young Greek chef Nikos Karathanos has created an imaginative menu that has garnered many culinary awards and captured the attention of the international press. If you find it hard to choose, sample the range of culinary combinations—fish soup garnished with sea urchin, the classic lamb in egg-lemon sauce—with a tasting menu of 15 dishes. The wine list features an intriguing selection of vintages to accompany your meal. Every summer Hytra's faithful clientele pick up and move from the restaurant's postindustrial city setting (complete with painting on the walls from the Adam art gallery) to a different temporary home ever nearer to the sea; check the Web site for details of the latest venue of *Galazia Hytra*. In either case, don't miss the 3-course special degustation menu every Tuesday, Thursday, and Sunday at lunch with the special price of 40 euros per person. ⊠ *Navarhou Apostoli 7, Psirri* ☎ *210/331–6767* ⊕ *www.hytra.gr* ⌂ *Reservations essential* ⊙ *Closed Mon.; For winter location: June–Sept.* ✛ *C3.*

$$$$ ✕ **To Varoulko.** Not one to rest on his Michelin star, acclaimed chef
SEAFOOD Lefteris Lazarou is constantly trying to outdo himself, with magnificent
Fodor's Choice results. Rather than use the menu, give him an idea of what you like
★ and let him create your seafood dish from what he found that day at the market. Among his most fabulous compilations are octopus simmered in sweet red *mavrodafni* wine and served with mousse made from a sourdough pasta called *trahana*, crayfish dolmas wrapped in sorrel leaves, and red snapper with black truffle-and-eggplant mousse. Some dishes fuse traditional peasant fare like the Cretan *gamopilafo* ("wedding rice" flavored with boiled goat) with unusual flavors like bitter chocolate. The multilevel premises stand next to the Eridanus Hotel; in summer, dinner is served on a rooftop terrace with a wonderful Acropolis view. ⊠ *Pireos 80, Gazi* ☎ *210/522–8400* ⊕ *www.varoulko. gr* ⌂ *Reservations essential* ⊙ *Closed Sun.* ✛ *B3.*

$ ✕ **To Zeidoron.** This usually crowded, artsy Psirri hangout has decent
GREEK mezedes, but the real draw is its strategic location. Metal tables line the main pedestrian walkway, great for watching all the world go by and for enjoying the sight of the neighborhood's illuminated churches and alleys. For a quieter setting, opt for the peaceful backyard. Small dishes include hot feta sprinkled with red pepper, grilled green peppers stuffed with cheese, eggplant baked with tomato and pearl onions, shrimp with ouzo, and an impressive array of dips and spreads. The wines are

overpriced; opt for ouzo instead. ⊠ *Taki 10, at Ayion Anargiron, Psirri* ☎ *210/321–5368* ☾ *Closed Aug.* ✥ *C3.*

SYNTAGMA SQUARE AND KOLONAKI
ΣΥΝΤΑΓΜΑΤΟΣ ΚΑΙ ΚΟΛΩΝΑΚΙ

Use the coordinate (✥ B2) at the end of each listing to locate a site on the corresponding map.

Located east of Plaka, Kolonaki is an old-money neighborhood that's a haunt for politicians, expats, and high-maintenance ladies who lunch (and shop). Syntagma, a bustling central square between Parliament and Ermou Street, is also popular with tourists.

$$
MODERN GREEK

✕ **Brasserie Valaoritou.** This cosmopolitan-yet-homey brasserie draws a varied crowd, from high-flying businessmen to politicians to theater buffs, who come here to enjoy a delicious cappuccino or, at lunchtime, a generous and delicious salad, or a late dinner after an evening at the theatre. There is also a range of pasta dishes and traditional Greek fare like lemon-oregano chicken, lamb, and seafood. Also recommended are the rye-bread baguettes with smoked salmon. But save room for the fabulous desserts, especially the lemon pie and the amazing *galaktoboureko* (custard in phyllo) made with Camembert cheese instead of the traditional custard. ⊠ *Valaoritou 15, Kolonaki* ☎ *210/361–1993* ⊕ *www.brasserie.gr* ✥ *E3.*

$$
ECLECTIC
Fodor's Choice
★

✕ **Café Boheme.** Comfort food and splashy cocktails abound at this petite hangout situated on the cusp of Kolonaki and the city center. Opt for a huge wood table, a pillow-strewn nook, or a romantic table-for-two at this spot, which boasts live jazz, DJ parties, and acoustic guitar sessions by night. The international ownership is reflected in Mediterranean-meets-U.K. culinary fusions. Try the aromatic risotto with mint, beetroot, and walnuts or grilled seafood. And don't miss out on the mouthwatering desserts and cocktails dreamed up by Cassie. ⊠ *Omirou 36, Kolonaki* ☎ *210/360–8018* ⌲ *Reservations essential* ✥ *E3.*

$$$
MEDITERRANEAN

✕ **Cellier Le Bistrot.** On the same spot occupied by Apotsos, a historical ouzeri that was a fixture on the Athenian social scene for decades, Cellier Le Bistrot has introduced an upmarket eatery fashioned around wine. The bistro has one of the largest selections of by-the-glass wines (some 250 wines from all over the world) in the city, which you can sample with a light dish from the ever-changing menu: maybe fresh pasta, salad, or seafood. You can still bring your own wine though (at a charge of 5 euros per bottle). The decor is both timeless and contemporary, with earthy hues, leather banquettes, and mahogany surfaces. The service is as impeccable as the wine list, which is culled from the finest vintages from nearby Cellier, one of the city's top wineshops. The action begins here at 10 in the morning for coffee. ⊠ *Panepistimiou 10, inside the Apotsou arcade, Syntagma Sq.* ☎ *210/363–8525* ⊕ *www.cellier.gr* ✥ *E3.*

$$$
ECLECTIC

✕ **Cibus.** The lush Zappion Gardens have always been a tranquil green oasis for stressed-out Athenians, who head here to gaze at the distant views of the Parthenon and Temple of Olympian Zeus, or catch an open-air cinema showing, or chill out at the landmark café Aegli. Sharing the same premises as the café, this chic minimalist restaurant

If you're lucky, "dessert" will include a wonderful live performance of Greek folk music.

is luring both fashionables, businesspeople, and families. The food is Greek Fusion, expensive but unique (reservations essential for dinner). Top favorites include the salad with different tomato varieties from all over Greece, quinoa, sweet peas and Mytilini cheese sauce, or the Vineyard lamb with dried grapes, oven potatoes, feta cheese, and vine-leave sauce, and for dessert, the Guanaja chocolate with chocolate biscuits, strawberry jam and Mosxato (sweet Lemnian wine) ice cream. At night, many diners savor their drinks (and cigars) and listen to the latest grooves serenading the beautiful people at the neighboring Lallabai club. ✉ *Zappion Gardens, National Garden* ☎ *210/336–9364* ⊕ *www.aeglizappiou.gr* ⊹ *F5.*

$$$$
SEAFOOD

✕ **Orizontes Lycabettus.** Have a seat on the terrace atop Mt. Lycabettus: the Acropolis glitters below, and, beyond, Athens unfolds like a map out to the Saronic Gulf. It's tough to compete with such a view, although this mostly seafood restaurant has a decent kitchen and better than decent service. Best bets include the mille-feuille of smoked trout with small *mikromani* artichokes and fresh tartar sauce, and the red mullets *escabeche* with cherry tomatoes and thyme on a layer of summer vegetables. Some meat dishes, like the bull fillets peppered with fresh rucola and a dust of Parmesan, are also available. For dessert, try a modernized version of traditional *kataifi* rolls (shredded pastry filled with nuts and honey), with *bougatsa* cream and *kaimaki* ice cream. Remember that no road goes this high: the restaurant is reached by cable car (the ticket price of €6 is deductible from your restaurant bill). ✉ *Mt. Lycabettus, Kolonaki* ☎ *210/722–7065* ⊕ *www.orizonteslycabettus.gr* ⌖ *Reservations essential* ⊹ *F3.*

$$$ ✕ **Scala Vinoteca.** The latest brainchild of renowned Greek chef Christo-

MODERN GREEK foros Peskias, this urban wine-restaurant divides its menu into four main price ranges, with dishes priced at 7, 10, 12 and 17 euros—the result is a flexible and budget-friendly dining option. Delicious dishes include asparagus in Mastello (sweet Santorini wine) sauce, beef tartare with marinated swedes, ravioli with shrimp and crab in a bisque seafood sauce, or the lasagna bolognese with foie gras. More than 110 wine labels are on offer, while most of the wines are also served by the glass. The chic, downtown location is a hidden Athenian gem, an additional bonus being that the warm, wooden, minimalist interiors have been designed by New Benaki Museum architects Maria Kokkinou and Andreas Kourkoulas. ✉ *Sina 50 and Anagnostopoulou, Kolonaki* ☎ *210/361–0004* ⌘ *Reservations essential* ☉ *Closed Sun.* ✛ *F2.*

3

$$ ✕ **Taverna Filippou.** This unassuming urban taverna is hardly the sort

GREEK of place you'd expect to find in chic Kolonaki, yet its devotees (since 1932) have included cabinet ministers, diplomats, actresses, and film directors. The appeal is simple, well-prepared Greek classics, mostly *ladera* (vegetable or meat casseroles cooked in an olive-oil–and–tomato sauce), roast chicken, or fish baked in the oven with tomatoes, onions, and parsley. Everything's home-cooked, so the menu adapts to what's available fresh at the open-air produce market. In summer and on balmy spring or autumn evenings, choose a table on the pavement under the ivy; in winter, seating is in a cozy dining room a few steps below street level. ✉ *Xenokratous 19, Kolonaki* ☎ *210/721–6390* ☉ *Sun. and mid-Aug. No dinner Sat.* ✛ *F3.*

PANGRATI AND KAISARIANI ΠΑΓΚΡΑΤΙ ΚΑΙ ΚΑΙΣΑΡΙΑΝΗ

Use the coordinate (✛ B2) at the end of each listing to locate a site on the corresponding map.

Urbane without being snobby or expensive, Pangrati and Kaisariani are havens for academics, artists, and expats who bask in the homey warmth of these neighborhoods set in the southeastern quarter of the city.

$$ ✕ **Aphrodite.** This mezedopoleio's menu changes more often than the

GREEK faces of its regulars, a mix of locals, politicians, and intellectuals who have elevated this cozy neighborhood square into a city insider's alternative to Kolonaki. Sip the complimentary raki and crunch on bread sticks dipped in olive paste while deciding whether to order the day's special or a round of mezedes: roasted red peppers stuffed with goat cheese, mushrooms in lemon sauce, whole grilled squid, marinated anchovies, and a range of salads in season. Don't forget to taste Yiayia's (Grandma's) meatballs and *froutalia*, a special omelet recipe from the Cycladic island of Andros. In warm weather tables go out on the *platia* (square) under the shady trees; in winter, seating is in a split-level dining room with a casual island ambience. ✉ *Ptolemeon and Amynta 6, Proskopon Sq., Pangrati* ☎ *210/724–8822* ✛ *F4.*

$$ ✕ **Cucina Povera.** "Poor cuisine"? Nothing is of poor taste in this chic

GREEK eaterie, which has become so popular among gourmet urbanites that bookings are necessary for every day of the week, not just weekends. "Peasant food" has become highly fashionable throughout Europe's hippest restaurants, and here chef/co-owner Manos Zournatzis tours local markets daily and adapts his finds—cherry tomatoes from Santorini, shrimp from Symi, pork from Sparta, tuna from Sporades—to create authentic Greek fare, at once simple, tasty, and affordable. Wines are as important as food—bottles are on display everywhere in this small, pale-hued, simple space—and we should not be surprised: the other co-owner is sommelier Yiannis Kaimenakis and he has compiled a fabulous list of more than 200 mainly Greek labels. ✉ *Eforionos 13, Stadion, Pangrati* ☎ *210/756–6008* ⊕ *www.cucinapovera.gr* ⌨ *Reservations essential* ✣ *F5.*

$$
GREEK

✕ **Fatsio.** Don't be fooled by the Italian name: the food at this old-fashioned restaurant is all home-style Greek, albeit with an Eastern influence. Walk past the kitchen and point at what you want before taking a seat. Favorites include a "soufflé" that is actually a variation on baked macaroni-and-cheese, with pieces of ham and slices of beef and a topping of eggplant and tomato sauce. The flavorful pasta-based dish *pastitsio* (meat pie with macaroni and béchamel sauce) is another customer-favorite. Quick service and good value for the money are the reasons for Fatsio's enduring popularity (since 1948) among both elder Kolonaki residents and office workers seeking an alternative to fast food. ✉ *Effroniou 5–7, off Rizari, Pangrati* ☎ *210/725–0028* ⊙ *1 wk mid-Aug.* ✣ *G4.*

$$
GREEK

✕ **Karavitis.** The winter dining room maintains its prewar ambience ("since 1926") and is insulated with huge wine casks; in summer there is garden seating in a courtyard across the street (get there early so you don't end up at the noisy sidewalk tables). The classic Greek cuisine is well prepared, including pungent *tirokafteri* (a peppery cheese dip), *bekri mezes* (lamb chunks in zesty red sauce), lamb ribs (when in season), *stamnaki* (beef baked in a clay pot), and melt-in-the-mouth meatballs, the taverna's specialty. Regarded as this neighborhood favorite hangout, —Greek politicians are frequently seen to enjoy a meal here—is located near the Panathenaic Stadium. ✉ *Arktinou 35, at Pausaniou, Pangrati* ☎ *210/721–5155* ▭ *No credit cards* ⊙ *Closed 1 wk mid-Aug. No lunch Mon.–Sat.* ✣ *F4.*

$$$$
MODERN FRENCH
Fodor'sChoice
★

✕ **Spondi.** One of Athens's most intensely designed temples to great food, celebrated and awarded Spondi is a feast for both the eyes and the taste buds. One salon shimmers with arty Swarovski chandeliers, walls of hot pink and cool aubergine, and chic black leather couches; for less glamour opt for the white-linen vaulted room, a beige-on-beige sanctorum; or, in summer, chill in the vast, bougainvillea-draped courtyard. No matter where you sit, however, you'll be able to savor the transcendentally delicious creations of Arnaud Bignon and consultant chef Eric Frechon (of Paris's Hotel Bristol fame). Highlights of their French-inspired Mediterranean menu (which has been awarded two Michelin stars) include the candied foie gras with dates, lemon, and tonka nut, the scallops with grapefruit, quinoa, pepper mint, and red pepper, and the duck with cherry, rosemary, nougat, and turnip. Or you can try the five-course "Tomatoes and Melons" taster menu accompanied by wines. For dessert, try a plate of vanilla chocolate Grand Cru with Equador chocolate, coffee, and almond nougatine. You may wish to opt for a taxi ride out to Pangrati—but isn't one of the best meals in all of

Greece worth it? ⊠ *Pirronos 5, Varnava Sq., Pangrati* ☎ *210/756–4021* ⊕ *www.spondi.gr* ⌂ *Reservations essential* ⊘ *No lunch* ✛ *F6.*

$$ ✕ **Trata O Stelios.** The owner works directly with fishermen, guaranteeing that the freshest catch comes to the table. Just point to your preference and it will soon arrive in the way Greeks insist upon: grilled with exactitude, coated in the thinnest layer of olive oil to seal in juices, and accompanied by lots of lemon. The deep-fried calamari and buttered prawns are house specialties. Even those who scrunch up their nose at fish soup will be converted by this version of the dense yet delicate *kakkavia.* Stelios is also one of the few remaining places you can get real homemade taramosalata. Avoid the lively square during Sunday lunch unless you want to squeeze in with the entire city. Parking is available. ⊠ *Anagenisseos Sq. 7–9, off Ethnikis Antistaseos, Kaisariani* ☎ *210/729–1533* ⊘ *10 days at Orthodox Easter* ✛ *H5.*

SEAFOOD

$$ ✕ **Vyrinis.** Huge wine barrels line one wall—and white Christmas lights cover the other—in this always-busy neighborhood eatery located just behind the Panathenaic Stadium. In summer, couples and groups of all ages find refuge in its adjacent open-air garden and enjoy its mellow social effervescence. Choose grilled pork, rabbit in lemon sauce, lamb with fries, oven-cooked perch, or go for standard nibbles like fava, grilled cheese saganaki, or the tomato-based eggplant stew. With lots of students and staff from the nearby international schools, this tavern, run by the third generation of the same family, sees a lot of red house wine flowing with every meal. ⊠ *Archimidou 11, Pangrati* ☎ *210/701–2153* ⊘ *No dinner Sun.* ✛ *F5.*

GREEK

GAZI, KERAMEIKOS, AND ROUF
ΓΚΑΖΙ, ΚΕΡΑΜΕΙΚΟΣ ΚΑΙ ΡΟΥΦ

Use the coordinate (✛ B2) at the end of each listing to locate a site on the corresponding map.

West of Psirri, the greater Gazi district has turned into the city's hottest art, culture, and nightlife zone. The new Kerameikos metro station has also made it ultraconvenient.

$$ ✕ **Aleria.** Athenian trend watchers are so enthusiastic about the gritty-cool neighborhood of Metaxourgeio that they say it will soon be like Paris's boho-chic Marais district. Restaurants like the award-winning Aleria, a gem of neoclassic design and inventive Mediterranean cuisine, are one reason the area's star is rising. Try the vegetable tarte; the mushroom tagliatelle with truffle oil, estragon, and thyme; or the chicken wrapped in smoked pork, lentil salad, and smoked meat vinaigrette, or the five-course "Special Degustation" menu (35 euros per person). Stylish yet scrumptious, you'll undoubtedly agree. ⊠ *Meg. Alexandrou 57, Metaxourgeio* ☎ *210/522–2633* ⊕ *www.aleria.gr* ⌂ *Reservations essential* ⊘ *Closed Sun. No lunch* ✛ *B2.*

MEDITERRANEAN

$$ ✕ **Kanella.** Housed in a sleek, airy building with modern and traditional touches, this lively example of a neo-taverna is infused with Gazi's energy. The excellent home cooking includes the braised beef in tomato sauce with spaghetti; the simmered pork with mushrooms and mashed potatoes; the Cephalonia-style rooster in red sauce; the

MODERN GREEK

Greek Fast Food

Souvlaki is the original Greek fast food: spit-roasted or grilled meat, tomatoes, onions, and garlicky tzatziki wrapped in a pita to go. Greeks on the go have always eaten street food such as the endless variations of cheese pie, *koulouri* (sesame-covered bread rings), roasted chestnuts or ears of grilled corn, and palm-size paper bags of nuts. But modern lifestyles and the arrival of foreign pizza and burger chains have cultivated a taste for fast food—and spawned several local brands definitely worth checking out. **Goody's** serves burgers and spaghetti as well as some salads and sandwiches. Items like baguettes with grilled vegetables or seafood salads are seasonal additions to the menu. **Everest** is tops when it comes to

tost—oval-shaped toasted sandwich buns with any combination of fillings, from omelets and smoked turkey breast to fries, roasted red peppers, and various spreads. It also sells sweet and savory pies, ice cream, and desserts. Its main rival is **Grigoris**, a chain of sandwich and pie shops which also serves freshly-squeezed orange juice and wonderful cappuccino freddo. If you want to sit down while you eat your fast food, look for a **Flocafe Espresso Bar**, where you can find great iced espresso *freddo* coffee. Along with espresso, frappé, *filtrou* (drip), and cappuccino, they also serve a selection of pastries and sandwiches, including brioche with mozzarella and pesto.

cold lentil salad; and a tasty salad with boiled zucchini, sliced avocado, and grated graviera cheese. Wine comes in beautifully designed glass carafes. Warning: when the neutral-tone interior gets busy, it gets almost psychedelically loud. Thankfully, there are outside pavement tables in good weather. ⊠ *Konstantinoupoleos 70 and Evmolpidon, Gazi* ☎ *210/347–6320* ✛ *A3.*

$$$
MODERN GREEK
Fodor's Choice
★

✕ **Mamacas.** This whitewashed restaurant started the wave of "modern neo-tavernas," which offer new takes on traditional Greek food amid the chicness of minimalist decor (think cotton-canvas tablecloths and tin accessories). Mamacas, which means "the mommies" in Greek, was also the first restaurant to spark the rebirth of Gazi, the once-forlorn neighborhood around what was once a gas foundry. Since it opened in 1998, Mamacas has consistently offered fresh, delicious Greek and Mediterranean home cooking such as pork with prunes, tomatoes, and peppers stuffed with rice and raisins, and, when they make it, arguably the best walnut cake in town. After hours, the restaurant turns into a bar where well-known DJs regularly pick the tunes and draws a flashy crowd of miniskirted young women and open-shirted men who strike poses as if the whole world is looking. Since the long-awaited opening of the Kerameikos metro station just across the street, it's easier than ever to go to the restaurant that helped turn Gazi into the hottest spot in Athens. The eaterie's roof garden was recently renovated and now hosts some of the hottest summer parties in town. ⊠ *Persofonis 41, Gazi* ☎ *210/346–4984* ⊕ *www.mamacas.gr* ⌲ *Reservations essential* ✛ *A3.*

3

$$ **╳ O Skoufias.** This pretty taverna has some of the best food in town—
GREEK and at reasonable prices. Menus are the royal-blue lined notebooks
Fodor'sChoice used by Greek schoolchildren; the proprietors have handwritten the
★ Cretan-inspired offerings on the pages. Enjoy Skoufias's signature
honey-roasted pork shank, or Sfakian (i.e., from the town of Sfakia)
lamb with manouri cheese, which is so tender it just falls off the bone,
at one of the tables outside. Other excellent choices include braised beef
with eggplant puree (*hunikiar beyianti,* as it is called), wild-greens pie,
potato salad with orange peels and herbs, and syrupy *ravani* cake with
mastic-flavor *kaimaki* ice cream. On weekends O Skoufias is open for
both lunch and dinner. ⊠ *Vasileiou Megalou 50, Rouf* 🕾 *210/341–2252*
▤ *No credit cards* ✛ *A4.*

$$$ **╳ Prosopa.** Despite the regular influx of local celebrities, this modern,
GREEK FUSION industrial looking bar-restaurant near the train tracks has never lost its
Fodor'sChoice friendly, down-to-earth face (after all, *Prosopa* means "faces" in Greek).
★ Service is impeccable —expect to be treated "on the house" with a plate
of appetizers upon arrival, as well as with dessert and liqueurs upon
departure. Menu faves include shrimp wrapped in spaghetti with potato
and mango sauce, vegetable salad with hot goat cheese, pistachio, and
apple vinagrette, or the rump steak with espresso sauce and figs. Food
and wine are of exceptional quality, music is played at the right level,
the waiting staff is attentive and helpful: this hip eaterie is definitely
worth the short taxi ride to its slightly off-the-beaten-track location
(where it moved from its previous home in 2010). On Sunday only
lunch is served. ⊠ *Meg. Vasileiou 52 and Konstantinoupoleos 4, Rouf*
🕾 *210 341–3433* ⊕ *www.prosopa.gr* ⚱ *Reservations essential* ✛ *A3.*

$$ **╳ Sardelles.** If you love seafood and don't want to pay a fortune for it,
SEAFOOD don't miss this trendy and beautifully designed eatery near Mamacas.
Fodor'sChoice The simple lines of Greek island decor are evident in wooden *kafeneio*
★ (coffeehouse) tables and 1950s-style metal-frame garden chairs picked
up at auctions and painted dazzling white. Try the cod cutlets, the
grilled fish drizzled with mastic-flavor sauce, and the house specialty, the
sardines ("sardelles")—either the classic recipe or the "hot and spicy" in
rock salt. Also recommended are any of the house salads, especially the
mixed greens with goat cheese and pomegranate seeds and the potato-
and-zucchini salad with spearmint. Top it off with a free hot mastiha
drink and a slice of lemon or chocolate tart. In the summer the tables
extend out to the busy street bustling with nightlife. ⊠ *Persofonis 15,
Gazi* 🕾 *210/347–8050* ✛ *A3.*

ATHENS NORTH AND EAST ΑΘΗΝΑ, ΒΟΡΕΙΑ ΚΑΙ ΑΝΑΤΟΛΙΚΗ

*Use the coordinate (✛ B2) at the end of each listing to locate a site on
the corresponding map.*

$$ **╳ Alexandria.** Egyptian spice infuses Greek cuisine with an exotic, eclec-
GREEK FUSION tic, and dynamic menu at this popular restaurant, making for a spot
that Lawrence Durrell would truly relish. The choices include simple but
stunning fare such as a tomato salad with thick yogurt and caramelized
onions as well as a tender lamb cooked with dried plums and apricots
and veal with vegetables and couscous. If you're an adventurous foodie,

don't miss Alexandria's signature dish: tender, wine-simmered baby octopus on a creamy bed of fava. The wine list is extensive and well priced, the Om Ali dessert with warm chocolate and nuts is a dream come true, and the service is outstanding. The relaxing, clean-white interior design recalls the cosmopolitan flair of the Egyptian Greeks. ⊠ *Metsovou 13 and Rethymnou, behind Park Hotel, near Archaeological Museum, Exarchia* ☎ *210/821–0004* ▭ *No credit cards* ⊙ *Closed Sun.* ✛ *D1.*

$$$$
CONTEMPORARY
Fodor'sChoice
★

✕ **Balthazar.** With its airy neoclassic mansion and leafy minimalist courtyard—paved with original painted tiles, canopied by huge date palms, and illuminated by colored lanterns—Balthazar truly feels like a summer oasis in the middle of Athens. The crowd is fun and hip, moneyed, cosmopolitan, and beautiful, so you might wish to come for dinner, then stay to mingle and taste the cocktails (like the passion fruit martini) as the DJ picks up the beat. Chef Aris Kallipolitis keeps the quality and flavor high on the up-to-the-minute menu, with prices to match. Try any of the creative appetizers (especially the "trilogy" of marinated tuna, salmon, and shrimp), the tasty main dishes (such as the sea bream with cherry tomatoes and capers sauce, as well as the various risottos), and the homemade desserts, especially the Napoleon Pavlova with fresh strawberries or the various sorbets and ice creams. Though it's been around for a decade, the place has miraculously managed to remain as fresh and trendy today as when it first opened. ⊠ *Tsoha 27, at Vournazou, Ambelokipi* ☎ *210/644–1215* ⊕ *www.balthazar.gr* ⌔ *Reservations essential* ⊙ *No lunch* ✛ *H2.*

$$
MEDITERRANEAN

✕ **Giantes.** In a flower-filled courtyard—fashionably green and framed by wisteria and jasmine—you peruse Gigantes' menu, which, although it has a modern streak, reads like an ambitious culinary journey through the far reaches of Greece. Although a little pricier than the norm, this neo-taverna, which opened in 2000, now attracts intellectuals, students, lawyers, actors, and health buffs, partly because it is co-owned by two of Greece's foremost organic farmers. Almost everything is fresh and delicious, as the chef estimates that about 90% of the ingredients he uses are organic, including the house wine. Perennial favorites on the menu include the organic pork with orange sauce, the liver with caramelized onions, and the chicken with honey, raisins, and coriander. ⊠ *Valtetsiou 44, Exarchia* ☎ *210/330–1369* ⊙ *Mon. and 1st 2 wks in Aug.* ✛ *E2.*

$$
GREEK
Fodor'sChoice
★

✕ **Vlassis.** Relying on traditional recipes from Thrace, Roumeli, Thessaly, and the islands, the chefs here whip up what may be the best Greek home-style cooking in Athens. There's no menu in this modern Greek bistro with huge glass windows, adorned with authentic works of art by well-known Greek painters. Just start by picking from the tray of 20 or so small dishes brought to your table: they're all good, but best bets include the fried eggplant with yogurt and tomato, *lahanodolmades* (cabbage rolls), fried red mullets, *katsiki ladorigani* (goat with oil and oregano), and the octopus stifado, which is tender and sweet with lots of onions. For dessert, order the halvah or a huge slice of galaktoboureko. For your main course, just follow the waiter's lead. ⊠ *Maiandrou 15, Ilisia* ☎ *210/646–3060, 210/725-6335* ▭ *No credit cards* ⊙ *Closed Aug.–mid-Sept. No dinner Sun.* ✛ *H3.*

WHERE TO STAY

THE SCENE

Greeks pride themselves for their "philoxenia," or hospitality. Even in antiquity, many of them referred to Zeus as Xenios Zeus—the God in charge of protecting travelers. Today, Greek philoxenia is alive and well in the capital city, whether displayed in the kindness of strangers you ask for directions or in the thoroughness of your hotel receptionist's care. With 20% of the small country's GDP derived from tourism, philoxenia isn't optional.

The city is full of hotels, many of which were built in Greek tourism's heyday in the 1960s and 1970s. In the years prior to the 2004 Athens Olympic Games, financial incentives were provided to hoteliers to upgrade and renovate their facilities, to the effect that many hotels— such as the Athens Hilton—completely renovated themselves inside and out as they increased their range of services.

But if prices have increased since then, all kinds of accommodation are happily available at all price levels. In Athens you can find everything from boutique hotels dreamed up by prestigious designers and decorated by well-known artists to no-fuss youth hostels that for decades have served the backpacking crowds on their way to Mykonos and Santorini. Athens's budget hotels—once little better than dorms—now usually have air-conditioning and television, along with prettier public spaces. In the post-Olympics years, there was a notable increase in the number of good-quality, middle-rank family hotels. At the same time, the city's classic luxury hotels, such as the Grande Bretagne, have introduced modern perks like up-to-date spa therapies.

The most convenient hotels for travelers are in the heart of the city center. Some of the older hotels in Plaka and near Omonia Square are comfortable and clean, their charm inherent in their age. But along with charm may come leaking plumbing, sagging mattresses, or other lapses in the details—take a good look at the room before you register. The thick stone walls of neoclassic buildings keep them cool in summer, but few of the budget hotels have central heating, and it can be devilishly cold in winter.

PRICES

Along with higher quality have come higher hotel prices: room rates in Athens are not much less than in many European cities. Still, there are bargains to be had. It's also a good idea to bargain in person at smaller hotels, especially off-season. When negotiating a rate, bear in mind that the longer the stay, the lower the nightly rate, so it may be less expensive to spend six consecutive nights in Athens rather than staying for two or three nights at either end of your trip through Greece.

Bear in mind that usually hotels will charge extra for a view of the Acropolis, and that breakfast is usually not included in the price of the smaller budget hotels. It is sometimes best to book through an agent for better bulk rates (this can lead to cost savings of up to 20%). Often it is also worth checking the Web sites of the hotels for special seasonal offers or bargain packages. In the off-season months (October to April) it is possible to negotiate for, and achieve, better rates.

WHAT IT COSTS IN EUROS				
¢	$	$$	$$$	$$$$
FOR TWO PEOPLE	under €80	€80–€150	€150–€200	€200–€250	over €250

Hotel prices are for a standard double room in high season, including taxes.

For expanded hotel reviews, visit Fodors.com.

ACROPOLIS AND SOUTH ΑΚΡΟΠΟΛΗ ΚΑΙ ΠΡΟΣ ΤΑ ΝΟΤΙΑ

Use the coordinate (✢ B2) at the end of each listing to locate a site on the corresponding map.

Under Athens's iconic landmark, newly chic neighborhoods such as Koukaki and Philopappou offer both historic vibes and hipsterious ambience.

¢   **Acropolis Select.** For only €10 more than many basic budget options,
Fodor'sChoice   you get to stay in a slick-looking hotel with a lobby full of designer fur-
★   niture in the residential neighborhood of Koukaki, south of Filopappou Hill, a 15-minute walk from the Acropolis, so not quite in the center of things. **Pros:** comfortable rooms; friendly staff; located in a pretty, low-key neighborhood; great value for money. **Cons:** no free Wi-Fi; small elevator. ⊠ *Falirou 37–39, Koukaki* ☎ *210/921–1610* ⊕ *www.acropoliselect.gr* ⌫ *72 rooms* ⌂ *In-room: a/c, Internet. In-hotel: restaurant, bar, parking ✢ D5.*

$ **Art Gallery Pension.** A handsome house on a residential street, this pension is comfortably old-fashioned, with family paintings on the muted white walls, comfortable beds, hardwood floors, ceiling fans, and with balconies in many guest rooms that have views of Filopappou or the Acropolis—though the residential neighborhood (a 10-minute walk south of the Acropolis) lacks the charm of Plaka, it has many fewer tourists and the metro offers easy access to many of the city's sights. **Pros:** clean, comfy rooms; free Wi-Fi in every room; lounge with Acropolis view; located in a pretty and quiet neighborhood. **Cons:** basic rooms; small showers; no credit cards. ⊠ *Erechthiou 5, Koukaki* ☎ *210/923–8376, 210/923–1933* ⊕ *www.artgalleryhotel.gr* ⌫ *21 rooms* ⌂ *In-room: a/c, Wi-Fi. In-hotel: bar, business center* ▭ *No credit cards ✢ C5.*

$ **Hera Hotel.** Attention to elegant detail—the lobby's marble floors, wood paneling, and leather sofas—reigns at this boutique hotel, fully renovated for the Athens 2004 Olympic Games and perfectly located just across the street from Athens's new architectural gem, the New Acropolis Museum. **Pros:** unbeatable location; the Acropolis view from the dreamy roof garden; cleanliness and service; friendly staff; good value for money. **Cons:** smallish rooms; lofty restaurant prices. ⊠ *Falirou 9, Makriyianni* ☎ *210/322–5891* ⊕ *www.herahotel.gr* ⌫ *38 rooms, 3 suites* ⌂ *In-room: a/c, Wi-Fi. In-hotel: restaurant, bar, business center, parking* ⑩ *No meals ✢ D5.*

$$ **Herodion Hotel.** A good compromise between the area's budget venues and deluxe digs, this hospitable hotel is down the street from the Odeon of Herodes Atticus, where Athens Festival performances are held, and a few minutes from the Acropolis—service is friendlier and more efficient

BEST BETS FOR ATHENS LODGING

Fodor's Choice★

Acropolis Select, ₵, p. 146

Athens Hilton, $$$$, p. 154

Classical BabyGrand, $, p. 152

Electra Palace, $$$$, p. 150

Eridanus, $, p. 152

Grand Bretagne, $$$$, p. 153

King George Palace, $$$, p. 154

The New Hotel, $$, p. 154

O&B, $$$$, p. 152

Periscope, $, p. 154

Phidias Hotel, $, p. 152

Plaka Hotel, $, p. 150

Students and Travellers' Inn, ₵, p. 151

By Price

₵

Acropolis Select, p. 146

Students and Travellers' Inn, p. 151

$

Classical BabyGrand, p. 152

Eridanus, p. 152

Hera Hotel, p. 146

Periscope, p. 154

Plaka Hotel, p. 150

$$

Amalia Hotel, p. 153

Herodion Hotel, p. 146

The New Hotel, p. 154

$$$

King George Palace, p. 154

$$$$

Athens Hilton, p. 154

Electra Palace, p. 150

Grand Bretagne, p. 153

O&B, p. 152

here than at most other Plaka neighborhood hotels, while the marble in the renovated lobby lends a touch of grandeur. **Pros:** tastefully designed rooms; knowledgeable and polite staff; great Acropolis views from some rooms; wide choice at buffet breakfast. **Cons:** rooms a bit small; no free Wi-Fi. ⊠ *Rovertou Galli 4, Acropolis* ☎ *210/923–6832 through 210/923–6836* ⊕ *www.herodion.gr* ⤵ *86 rooms, 4 suites* ᐃ *In-room: a/c, Internet. In-hotel: restaurant, bar* ❖| *Breakfast* ✥ *D5.*

$$ ☷ **Ledra Marriott.** The Ledra's main calling cards are its high-performance staff, high style, and dining comfort: the lobby piano bar sits below a spectacular 1,000-crystal chandelier; Kona Kai, the Polynesian restaurant, offers excellent quality food and is popular with locals; and the Zephyros Café has a bountiful Sunday brunch. **Pros:** gorgeous modern-chic rooms; relaxed and jazzy atmosphere in bar; great Polynesian food in Kona Kai. **Cons:** Syngrou is an ugly and busy street; a long walk or short taxi ride to the city center (alternatively, use the hotel's shuttle van). ⊠ *Syngrou 115, Neos Kosmos* ☎ *210/930–0000* ⊕ *www.marriott. com* ⤵ *308 rooms, 6 suites* ᐃ *In-room: a/c, Internet, Wi-Fi. In-hotel: restaurant, bar, pool, gym, laundry facilities, business center, parking, some pets allowed* ✥ *C6.*

₵ ☷ **Marble House.** This popular and recently renovated guesthouse has a steady clientele—even in winter, when it has low monthly and weekly rates—thanks to guests who don't mind the fact that this spot is a little off the tourist circuit. **Pros:** good price; quiet neighborhood; friendly staff. **Cons:** nine euros extra for air-conditioned rooms; far from the main sights of Athens if you're not into walking. ⊠ *Anastassiou Zinni*

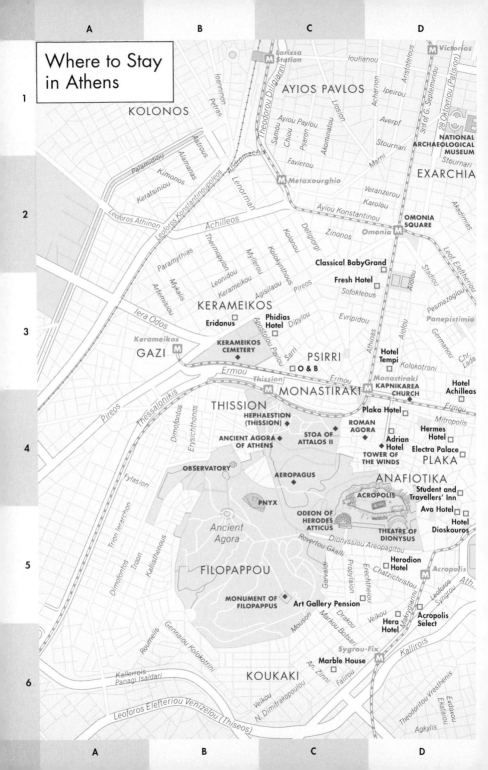

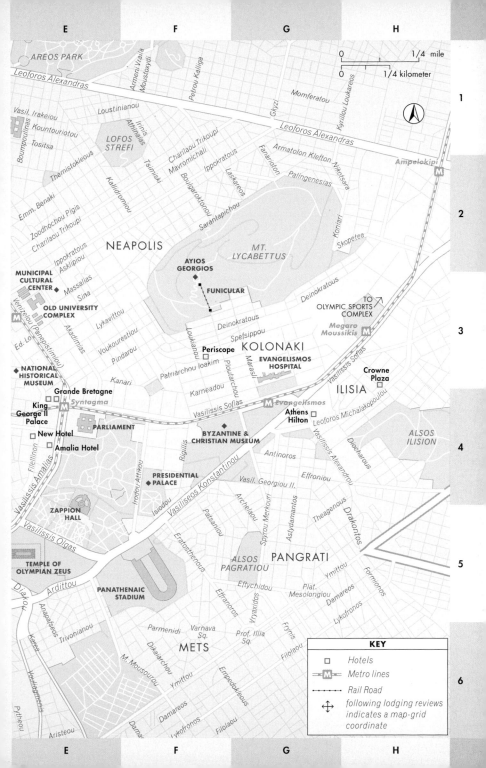

35, Koukaki ☎ *210/923–4058, 210/922–8294* ⊕ *www.marblehouse.gr* ➳ *16 rooms, 11 with bath* ⚐ *In-room: no a/c, Wi-Fi* ✢ *C6.*

PLAKA ΠΛΑΚΑ

For expanded hotel reviews, visit Fodors.com.

Use the coordinate (✢ B2) at the end of each listing to locate a site on the corresponding map.

Northeast of the Acropolis, Plaka and Anafiotika are Athens's old-world villages, replete with winding alleys and a bevy of cafés and shops.

$ 🏨 **Adrian Hotel.** This comfortable pension offers friendly service and an excellent location in the heart of Plaka—incurable romantics should ask for one of just three rooms looking toward the Acropolis; if you like being in the thick of things, enjoy your buffet breakfast (May–October) **Pros:** great central location; friendly staff; reasonably priced. **Cons:** Adrianou Street can be noisy during the summer months; some bathrooms need updating. ⊠ *Adrianou 74, Plaka* ☎ *210/325–0454* ⊕ *www. douros-hotels.com* ➳ *22 rooms* ⚐ *In-room: a/c, Wi-Fi* ✢ *D4.*

$$ 🏨 **AVA Hotel & Suites.** Set on a quiet sidestreet of the quaint Plaka district, this lovely small hotel is ideally located for all the major Athens attractions—fully renovated in 2010, it has quickly become a firm favorite among leisure and business travelers alike. **Pros:** spacious rooms; pleasant furnishings; impeccable service; amazing views. **Cons:** boutique establishment, so lacks huge array of amenities at the large hotel chains. ⊠ *Lyssicratous 9–11, Plaka* ☎ *210/325–9000* ⊕ *www.avahotel.gr* ➳ *16 rooms* ⚐ *In-room: a/c, Internet, Wi-Fi. In-hotel: restaurant, bar, laundry facilities, business center* ✢ *D5.*

$$$$ 🏨 **Electra Palace.** If you want simple elegance, excellent service, and a
Fodor's Choice   great location, this is the hotel for you—rooms from the fifth floor up
★   have a view of the Acropolis and in summer you can bask in the sunshine at the outdoor swimming pool as you take in the view of Athens's greatest monument or catch the sunset from the rooftop garden. **Pros:** gorgeous rooms; great location; outstanding service: early check-in available. **Cons:** pricey! ⊠ *Nikodimou 18–20, Plaka* ☎ *210/337–0000* ⊕ *www.electrahotels.gr* ➳ *135 rooms, 20 suites* ⚐ *In-room: a/c, Wi-Fi. In-hotel: restaurant, bar, pool, gym, parking* ⦿ *Breakfast* ✢ *D4.*

$ 🏨 **Hermes Hotel.** Athens's small, modestly priced establishments have generally relied on little more than convenient central locations to draw visitors but this is not quite the case at the Hermes; sunny guest rooms with brightly colored decorative details and marble bathrooms feel warm and welcoming. **Pros:** great staff; sleak, clean decor; central location. **Cons:** some smallish rooms, some without a balcony (check availability). ⊠ *Apollonos 19, Plaka* ☎ *210/323–5514* ⊕ *www.hermeshotel. gr* ➳ *45 rooms* ⚐ *In-room: a/c. In-hotel: bar, children's programs, business center* ⦿ *Breakfast* ✢ *D4.*

$ 🏨 **Plaka Hotel.** Comfortable, with deep-blue velvet curtains that match
Fodor's Choice   the upholstery on the wood-arm easy chairs, the guest rooms in this
★   charming, central hotel are a comfortable place to rest while in the heart of old Athens. **Pros:** excellent location; diligent staff; good breakfast and lounge areas. **Cons:** small and sometimes stuffy rooms; no pets

For food-with-a-view, the Plaka district is famed for its lovely garden restaurants with front-row seats to the Acropolis Hill.

allowed. ✉ *Kapnikareas 7 and Mitropoleos, Plaka* ☎ *210/322–2706, 210/322–2318* ⊕ *www.plakahotel.gr* ⤴ *67 rooms* ⅃ *In-room: a/c, Wi-Fi. In-hotel: restaurant, business center* ⦿ *Breakfast* ⊕ *D4.*

¢ ⛨ **Student and Travellers' Inn.** Not only is it cheap, this place is in the

Fodor's Choice pricey Plaka—even better is the fact that wood floors and large windows

★ make this spotless hostel (with an array of private rooms) cheerful and homey. **Pros:** champagne neighborhood; beer rates. **Cons:** noisy; some shared bathrooms; minimal privacy; no visitors. ✉ *Kidathineon 16, Plaka* ☎ *210/324–4808* ⊕ *www.studenttravellersinn.com* ⤴ *35 rooms, 14 with bath* ⅃ *In-room: a/c, no TV. In-hotel: bar, business center, parking* ⊕ *D4.*

MONASTIRAKI, PSIRRI, AND THISSION
ΜΟΝΑΣΤΗΡΑΚΙ, ΨΥΡΡΗ ΚΑΙ ΘΗΣΕΙΟ

For expanded hotel reviews, visit Fodors.com.

Use the coordinate (⊕ B2) at the end of each listing to locate a site on the corresponding map.

Northwest of Plaka, Monastiraki and Thission conjure up the gritty charm of an Anatolian bazaar and yet attract the city cognoscenti to hard-core cafés and bars.

¢ ⛨ **Hotel Tempi.** It's all about location for this bare-bones budget hotel just a short, pleasant stroll from Plaka, the Roman Agora, and Psirri's nightlife. **Pros:** friendly staff; nice roof terrace; central location. **Cons:** smallish, basic rooms; hostel-like vibe. ✉ *Aiolou 29, Monasti-*

raki ☎ *210/321–3175* ⊕ *www.tempihotel.gr* ⤳ *24 rooms, 12 with bath* & *In-room: a/c. In-hotel: business center* ⊹ *D3.*

$$$$ 🖵 **O&B.** Once called Ochre & Brown, this elegant boutique hotel with a
Fodor'sChoice   sleek design and an outstanding restaurant-bar was recently expanded
★   to 22 rooms and 5 suites, each a little haven of urban cool, thanks
to flat-screen TVs, personal stereo/DVD systems, Molton Brown bath
products, high-drama color schemes, black minimalistic headboards,
and soft white Egyptian cotton sheets. **Pros:** beautiful rooms; excellent
food; personalized service; informed and multilingual staff; relaxed and
stylish atmosphere. **Cons:** all rooms but the penthouse have limited
views. ⊠ *Leokoriou 7, Psirri* ☎ *210/331–2950* ⊕ *www.oandbhotel.com*
⤳ *22 rooms, 5 suites* & *In-room: a/c, Wi-Fi. In-hotel: restaurant, bar,
parking* ❘⊙❘ *Breakfast* ⊹ *C3.*

$ 🖵 **Phidias Hotel.** Stay here and you'll have the impression that Athens is
Fodor'sChoice   all fun and not a car-packed, frantic metropolis—simply put, there's no
★   better spot to stay, location-wise, on Athens's most beautiful pedestrian
walkway. **Pros:** ideal location; inexpensive; quiet; proximity to train/
shopping; pets okay; those gentle prices. **Cons:** public and private spaces
could use a makeover; sometimes the nearby Thission partying is loud;
parking difficult. ⊠ *Apostolou Pavlou 39, Thission* ☎ *210/345–9511*
⊕ *www.phidias.gr* ⤳ *15 rooms* & *In-room: a/c. In-hotel: business center, some pets allowed* ⊹ *C3.*

CENTRAL ATHENS, GAZI, AND OMONIA SQUARE
ΑΘΗΝΑ (ΚΕΝΤΡΟ), ΓΑΖΙ ΚΑΙ ΠΛΑΤΕΙΑ ΟΜΟΝΟΙΑΣ

For expanded hotel reviews, visit Fodors.com.

*Use the coordinate (⊹ B2) at the end of each listing to locate a site on
the corresponding map.*

Located north of Monastiraki, Omonia, the city's main square, roars
by day and is seedy by night, but offers multicultural excitement and
that foodie fave, the Central Market. The former warehouse districts
of Psirri and Gazi, a short walking distance from Omonia, are "party
central" for many Athenians.

$ 🖵 **Classical BabyGrand.** Fun yet posh, this dream pad for the young
Fodor'sChoice   and the young-at-heart is a crazy/cool boutique art hotel (just note the
★   vintage convertible parked in the lobby)—though its locale is slightly
sketchy if you're not fond of inner-city grit, it is also strategic: City
Hall, Omonia, and the Central Market are all close by. **Pros:** beautiful
rooms; great staff; excellent in-house food; good amenities; room rates
have dipped. **Cons:** many rooms have poor views; neighborhood is a
little rundown. ⊠ *Athinas 65 and Lykourgou, Omonia Sq.* ☎ *210/325–
0900* ⊕ *www.classicalhotels.com* ⤳ *76 rooms, 11 suites* & *In-room: a/c,
Wi-Fi. In-hotel: restaurant* ⊹ *D2.*

$ 🖵 **Eridanus.** Dazzling modern art, a sparkling staircase, luscious beds, top-
Fodor'sChoice   line bath products, and interiors that are cool/hot 21st century, thanks to
★   a dramatic, white minimalistic lobby, and some high-style marble bathrooms—this lovely hotel on the edge of the rising-star neighborhood of
Gazi has it all. **Pros:** beautifully designed and comfortable rooms; lush
bedding and sheets; Hermès bath products; knowledgeable staff. **Cons:**

transitioning neighborhood looks a bit pockmarked in places. ⊠ *Pireos 78, Gazi* ☎ *210/520–5360* ⊕ *www.eridanus.gr* ⊰*38 rooms, 3 suites* ⟐ *In-room: a/c, Internet. In-hotel: restaurant, bar, gym, parking* ✛ *B3.*

$ ⛩ **Fresh Hotel.** Reveling in minimalist glam, this attractive boutique hotel has relaxing and expertly decorated rooms, a plugged-in staff, and two restaurants that feature nouvelle-Mediterranean cuisine—no matter that the nabe is slightly dodgy at night this is really an excellent central location with easy access to many major attractions (the Athens Central Market, Monastiraki Square, and Omonia Square are nearby). **Pros:** Air Lounge Bar restaurant has great food and atmosphere; central location; relaxing rooms; plugged-in staff. **Cons:** surrounding neighborhood is a bit unattractive and dodgy at night. ⊠ *Sofokleous 26, Omonia Sq.* ☎ *210/524–8511* ⊕ *www.freshhotel.gr* ⊰*133 rooms* ⟐ *In-room: a/c, Internet. In-hotel: restaurant, pool, gym, parking* ✛ *D3.*

SYNTAGMA SQUARE AND KOLONAKI
ΠΛΑΤΕΙΑ ΣΥΝΤΑΓΜΑΤΟΣ ΚΑΙ ΚΟΛΩΝΑΚΙ

For expanded hotel reviews, visit Fodors.com.

Use the coordinate (✛ B2) at the end of each listing to locate a site on the corresponding map.

Located east of Plaka, Kolonaki is a posherie favored by politicians, expats, and the ladies who lunch. Syntagma, on the other hand, is a busy central square, near Parliament, that is a fave with tourists and locals alike.

$$ ⛩ **Amalia Hotel.** The central location and competitive prices are the main attractions here for most visitors—while located right on one of Athens's biggest, busiest streets, directly across from Parliament, double-glazed windows (fortunately) and a view to the pretty National Garden keep things peaceful inside. **Pros:** perfect central location; easy access to transport, to Plaka and the pretty National Garden. **Cons:** on a busy thoroughfare, Internet in rooms for a fee. ⊠ *Amalias 10, Syntagma Sq.* ☎ *210/323–7300* ⊕ *www.amalia.gr* ⊰*98 rooms, 1 suite* ⟐ *In-room: a/c, Internet. In-hotel: restaurant, bar, parking, some pets allowed* ✛ *E4.*

$$$$ ⛩ **Grande Bretagne.** With a guest list that includes more than a century's
Fodor'sChoice worth of royals, rock stars, and heads of state, the landmark Grande
★ Bretagne remains the most exclusive hotel in Athens but as you marvel at one of the most eye-knocking views of the Acropolis from the terrace restaurant, or rest on custom-made silk ottomans in the lobby, or call your personal butler 24 hours a day from your room, you may very well think it is the very best. **Pros:** all-out luxury; beautiful rooms; excellent café, spa and pool lounge; central location. **Cons:** pricey, no free Wi-Fi. ⊠ *Vasileos Georgiou A'1 at Syntagma Sq., Syntagma Sq.* ☎ *210/333–0000, 210/331–5555 through 210/331–5559 reservations* ⊕ *www.grandebretagne.gr* ⊰*321 rooms, 56 suites* ⟐ *In-room: a/c, Internet. In-hotel: restaurant, bar, pool, gym, spa, parking* ✛ *E4.*

$ ⛩ **Hotel Achilleas.** This hotel combines modern amenities with the friendly, personal service that comes from being family-run—and a price at the lower end of its category. **Pros:** excellent location; reasonable price; free use of Internet in the lobby. **Cons:** blah breakfasts;

somewhat basic rooms. ✉ *Lekka 21, Syntagma Sq.* ☎ *210/322–5826* ⊕ *www.achilleashotel.gr* ⬏ *34 rooms* ♿ *In-room: a/c, Internet. In-hotel: bar, parking* ❙◯❙ *Breakfast* ✛ *D4.*

¢ 📺 **Hotel Dioskouros.** The real draws of this students' and independent travelers' favorite over similarly cheap, downtown hostel-type accomodations are its central but quiet location at Plaka's edge, and its shaded garden, where you can relax with a beer at the end of the day. **Pros:** central location; cheap price; some rooms have small fridges. **Cons:** tiny rooms; thin walls; breakfast is just jam, butter and bread with coffee. ✉ *Pittakou 6, Plaka* ☎ *210/324–8165* ⊕ *www.hostelworld.com* ⬏ *18 rooms without bath* ♿ *In-room: a/c, no TV* ❙◯❙ *Breakfast* ✛ *D5.*

$$$ 📺 **King George Palace.** One of the most historic and luxurious hotels in
Fodor's Choice Athens, this is where Madonna and Woody Allen stayed while visiting
★ Athens (in the same Royal Penthouse suite, but not at the same time!) **Pros:** beautiful design; high-luxe, opulent rooms; attentive service; outstanding food; 24-hour business center. **Cons:** slow elevators; thin walls in rooms. ✉ *Vasileos Georgiou A' 3, Syntagma Sq.* ☎ *210/322–2210* ⊕ *www.classicalhotels.com* ⬏ *78 rooms, 25 suites* ♿ *In-room: a/c, Internet. In-hotel: restaurant, bar, spa, parking* ✛ *E4.*

$$ 📺 **The New Hotel.** Four years in the making, the completion of the New
Fodor's Choice Hotel has been heralded as an aesthetic triumph in the inner city's ever-
★ changing landscape, thanks to the fact that this five-star, cutting-edge boutique hotel (inaugurated September 2011) is part of the chain of Yes! hotels that has been masterminded by the celebrated modern art collector Dakis Ioannou. **Pros:** that "Dakis" touch; brand new, sleek design; helpful staff; free Wi-Fi in public areas; sumptuous breakfasts; central location. **Cons:** pricey pay-per-view TV. ✉ *Filellinon 16, Syntagma Sq.* ☎ *210/628–4800* ⊕ *www.yeshotels.gr* ⬏ *79 rooms and suites* ♿ *In-room: a/c, Wi-Fi. In-hotel: restaurant, bar, gym, laundry facilities, business center, parking* ✛ *E4.*

$ 📺 **Periscope.** This sleek concept hotel combines minimalist urban-chic
Fodor's Choice design, amenity-filled rooms, and exceptional service for a truly relax-
★ ing experience—business travelers and urbane globe-trotters love the efficient service, spotless rooms, and the old-money, chic neighborhood of Kolonaki. **Pros:** great locale; eatery created by award-winning chef; great breakfast; outstanding service. **Cons:** rooms are a bit on the small side and have limited views; only suites have balconies. ✉ *Haritos 22, Kolonaki* ☎ *210/729–7200* ⊕ *www.periscope.gr* ⬏ *17 rooms, 4 suites* ♿ *In-room: a/c, Wi-Fi. In-hotel: bar, business center* ✛ *F3.*

ATHENS NORTH AND EAST ΑΘΗΝΑ, ΒΟΡΕΙΑ ΚΑΙ ΑΝΑΤΟΛΙΚΗ

For expanded hotel reviews, visit Fodors.com.

Use the coordinate (✛ B2) at the end of each listing to locate a site on the corresponding map

$$$$ 📺 **Athens Hilton.** While the impressive Hilton hotel is one of the city's
Fodor's Choice venerable architectural landmarks, it also reflects the trend sweeping
★ through most of Athens's high-end properties, whose recent revamps have left them with modern, clean-lined, and minimal design. **Pros:** outstanding service; beautiful rooms; great Acropolis and city view

The landmark Grande Bretagne Hotel is widely considered Athens's best.

One of the new breed of boutique hotels, the Classical Baby Grand Hotel is way-cool.

from rooftop; orgasmically good food; excellent buffet breakfast. **Cons:** very expensive; have to pay for entrance to the pool and day access to spa or gym, unless you are staying in one of the suites; extra charge for Internet access for most room deals. ✉ *Vasilissis Sofias 46, Ilisia* ☎ *210/728–1000, 210/728–1100 reservations* ⊕ *www.athens.hilton. com* ⇆ *498 rooms, 19 suites* ⚭ *In-room: Internet. In-hotel: restaurant, bar, pool, gym, parking* ✛ *G4.*

$ 🏨 **Crowne Plaza.** Located on the site of the city's former Holiday Inn (it opened its doors in mid-2008), this may be the most technology-friendly Athens hotel. **Pros:** new infrastructure; small outdoor swimming pool (closes at 7 pm); spacious rooms and bathrooms; 30-min free daily Internet access in the lobby per room. **Cons:** costly breakfast; high rates for relatively slow Wi-Fi access; a bit off-center. ✉ *50 Michalakopoulou Ave., Ilisia* ☎ *210/727–8000* ⊕ *www.cpathens.com* ⇆ *186 rooms, 7 suites* ⚭ *In-room: a/c, Wi-Fi. In-hotel: restaurant, bar, pool, gym, spa, business center, parking* ✛ *H3.*

NIGHTLIFE AND THE ARTS

From ancient Greek tragedies in quarried amphitheaters to the chicest dance clubs, Athens rocks at night. Several of the former industrial districts are enjoying a renaissance, and large spaces have filled up with galleries, restaurants, and theaters—providing one-stop shopping for an evening's entertainment. The Greek weekly *Athinorama* covers current performances, gallery openings, and films, as do the English-language newspapers *Athens News* (published Friday), and *Kathimerini,* inserted in the *International Herald Tribune* (available Monday through Saturday). The monthly English-language magazine *Insider* has features and listings on entertainment in Athens, with a focus on the arts. *Odyssey,* a glossy bimonthly magazine, also publishes an annual summer guide in late June, sold at newsstands around Athens with the season's top performances and exhibitions. You can also "tune in" to the regular English reports on municipal station Athens International Web Radio for what's happening around town; click for Athens International Radio on their Web site (⊕ www.athina984.gr).

NIGHTLIFE

Athens's heady nightlife starts late. Most bars and clubs don't get hopping until midnight and they stay open at the very least until 3 am. Drinks are rather steep (about €9–€15), but generous. Often there is a cover charge on weekends at the most popular clubs, which also have bouncers. In summer many major downtown bars and clubs close their in-town location and move to the seaside. Ask your hotel for recommendations and summer closings. For a uniquely Greek evening, visit a club featuring rembetika music, a type of blues, or the popular *bouzoukia* (clubs with live bouzouki, a stringed instrument, music). Few clubs take credit cards for drinks.

BARS

Fodor's Choice ★ **Aliarman.** Hidden in one of the tiny backstreets of the popular district of Gazi is this cozy treasure. The converted workers' house has a fairy-tale vibe, with impressive floor mosaics, floral frescoes, and atmospheric lighting. Colorful cocktails include the apple martini, strawberry daiquiri, mai tai, and you can also grab a bite to eat. ⊠ *Sofroniou 2, Gazi* ☏ *210/342–6322.*

Balthazar. Athenians of all ages come to escape the summer heat at this stylish, upscale bar-restaurant in a neoclassic house with a lush garden courtyard and subdued music. Advance bookings are highly recommended for the restaurant section. ⊠ *Tsoha 27, Ambelokipi* ☏ *210/644–1215, 210/641–2300* ⊕ *www.balthazar.gr.*

★ **Baraonda.** Beautiful people, breakneck music, and a VIP vibe have made this club-restaurant a perennial city favorite all year-round. The food here is also top-line and there's a beautiful garden when you need a breather. Reservations are highly recommended for both the club and the restaurant. ⊠ *Tsoha 43, Ambelokipi* ☏ *210/644–4308 Restaurant, 210/6445–8406 Club* ⊕ *www.baraonda.gr.*

Mad Club. Dance to '80s pop and all eras of rock at this fun and popular club in the hot Gazi district. ⊠ *Persefonis 53, Gazi* ☏ *210/346–2007* ⊕ *www.mad-club.gr.*

Fodor's Choice ★ **To Parko Eleftherias.** With low-key music and a romantic setting, Parko is located in the greenery next to the Megaron Mousikis concert hall and is a summer favorite for snacks, food and drink, day and night. ⊠ *Eleftherias Park, Ilisia* ☏ *210/722–3784* ⊕ *www.toparko.gr.*

Sodade. This gay-friendly bar-club-lounge attracts a standing-room-only crowd every weekend. The draw is the great music, the joyous vibe, and the very fact that it's in Gazi, the hottest place in central Athens. ⊠ *Triptolemou 10, Gazi* ☏ *210/346–8657.*

Stavlos. All ages feel comfortable at the bar in what used to be the Royal Stables. Sit in the courtyard or in the brick-wall restaurant for a snack like Cretan *kaltsounia* (similar to a calzone), or dance in the long bar. Stavlos often hosts art and jewelry exhibits, film screenings, miniconcerts, and other "happenings," as the Greeks call them, throughout the week. ⊠ *Irakleidon 10, Thission* ☏ *210/345–2502, 210/346–7206* ⊕ *www.stavlos.gr.*

BOUZOUKIA

Many tourists think Greek social life centers on large clubs where live bouzouki music plays while patrons smash up the plates. Platesmashing is now prohibited, but plates of flowers (at high prices) are sold for scattering over the performer or your companions when they take to the dance floor. Upscale bouzoukia clubs line the middle section of Pireos Avenue and stretch out to the south coast, where top entertainers command top prices. Be aware that bouzoukia food is overpriced and often second-rate. There is a per-person minimum (around €40) or a prix-fixe menu; a bottle of whiskey may cost around €150. For those who choose to stand at the bar, a drink runs about €15 to €20 at a good bouzoukia place.

Fever. One of Athens's most popular bouzoukia clubs showcases the most popular singers of the day, including the Yiannis Parios, Sakis Rouvas, and Stamatis Gonidis. It's open Friday and Saturday, from September to June. ⊠ *Syngrou Ave. and Lagoumitzi 25, Neos Kosmos* ☏ *210/921–7333.*

★ **Iera Odos.** Local pop and bouzouki stars regularly appear at this popular nightspot delivering all the joyous frenzy expected of a Greek-style night out. The place (open Thursday to Sunday) is packed on weekends as Athenians flock there to sing along with popular and traditional Greek music hits as well as some international tunes. ⊠ *Iera Odos 18–20, Gazi* ☏ *210/342–8272* ⊕ *www.ieraodos.gr.*

Rex Music Theatre. Over-the-top is the way to describe a performance at Rex Music Theater—it's a laser-light show, multicostume-change extravaganza, with headlining pop and bouzouki stars. Programs and performances change every six months or so, so do check out the local press for the most current listings. ⊠ *Panepistimiou 48, Central Athens* ☏ *210/381–4591, 211/850–1100.*

CLUBS

Nightclubs in Greece migrate with the seasons. From October through May, they're in vast, throbbing venues in central Athens and the northern suburbs; from June through September, many relocate to luxurious digs on the south coast. The same spaces are used from year to year, but owners and names tend to bounce around. Before heading out, check local listings or talk to your concierge. Most clubs charge a cover at the door and employ bouncers, aptly called "face-control" by Greeks because they tend to let only the "lookers" in. One way to avoid both of these, since partying doesn't get going until after 1 am, is to make an earlier dinner reservation at one of the many clubs that have restaurants as well.

Fodor's Choice
★ **Akrotiri Lounge.** Luxurious Akrotiri has as much of a reputation for chef Michalis Ntounetas' excellent Mediterranean cuisine as it does for the open-air sushi bar, runway-beautiful clientele, sea views, famous DJ's, and poolside dance floor. ⊠ *Vasileos Georgiou B5, Ayios Kosmas, Kalamaki* ☏ *210/985–9147* ⊕ *www.akrotirilounge.gr.*

★ **Bios.** Cool architects and graphic designers, arty students and intellectuals, revolutionaries and experimental philosophers: they all hang out in the cavernous basement of this Bauhaus building in the Kerameikos neighborhood, part of the greater Gazi district. Expect to hear the best electronica music in town. In summer, relish the view of the Acropolis from the postmodern, neon-lighted roof terrace. A handful of "multi-space" imitators have emerged, offering offbeat film/video and music events in painfully hip industrial spaces—but Bios remains the standard. ⊠ *Pireos 84, Gazi* ☏ *210/342–5335* ⊕ *www.bios.gr.*

Fodor's Choice
★ **Booze Cooperativa.** Laptops, coffee mugs, and chess sets cover the long wooden tables in this central Athens joint by day. By night, chatty partygoers squeeze—booze in hand—into any spot they can find at this 20-year-old bar. It often feels like a laid-back party, as DJs navigate through rock, pop, and dance tunes and the multitasking bar hosts art exhibits, dance performances, and theater. Wood details and wax art-

works give a warm feel to the high-ceilinged space. ✉ *Kolokotroni 57, Syntagma Sq.* ☎ *210/324–0944* ⊕ *www.boozecooperativa.com.*

Central Gold. From September to May, Athens's hippest people make an appearance at this designer-styled minimalist club/restaurant to groove to dance music ranging from R&B to Greek pop hits while nibbling on sushi prepared by Michelin-star awarded chef Nikos Skliras and languidly sipping fancy cocktails. From May to September, Central is closed in town; it reopens on the coast as Island, in an atmospheric space in the sunny suburb of Varkiza, about a 45-minute drive away from the city center. ✉ *Kolonaki Sq. 14, Kolonaki* ☎ *210/724–5938* ⊕ *www.islandclubrestaurant.gr* ✉ *On Km 27 of Athens-Sounio avenue, Varkiza* ☎ *210/965–3563* ⊕ *www.islandclubrestaurant.gr.*

Venti. This successful Psirri club-restaurant is also now open in summer, one of the few in the city center to do so. Its open-air style comes complete with a canopy of olive and palm trees while the crowd dances to a furious beat of Greek pop music. ✉ *Lepeniotou 20, Psirri* ☎ *210/325–4504* ⊕ *www.venti.gr.*

Fodor's Choice
★

W Night Club. A change in the name for Venue, this landmark Athenian club reopened its doors in 2009 with a stunning three-stage space decorated with silver touches, luscious sofas, private rooms, and tons of Swarovski crystals. The best DJs, happiest dancers, and most party-loving Athenians still flock to the W Night Club to party until the early morning hours. In the summer, the W club moves to Glyfada, right by the beach—you can find it at the Second Marina (Diadochou Pavlou street), on site of the ex-Cataralla club. ✉ *Pireos 130, Gazi* ☎ *6972/700712.*

REMBETIKA

The Greek equivalent of the urban blues, rembetika music is rooted in the traditions of Asia Minor and was brought to Greece by refugees from Smyrna in the 1920s. It filtered up from the lowest economic levels to become one of the most enduring genres of Greek popular music, still enthralling club goers today. At these thriving clubs, you can catch a glimpse of Greek social life and even join the dances (but remember, it's considered extremely rude to interrupt a solo dance). The two most common dances are the *zeimbekiko,* in which the man improvises in circular movements that become ever more complicated, and the belly-dancelike *tsifteteli.* Most of the clubs are closed in summer; call in advance. Drink prices range from €10 to €15, a bottle of whiskey from €70 to €100, and the food is often expensive and unexceptional; it's wisest to order a fruit platter or a bottle of wine.

Anifori. This friendly, popular club is housed in the neighborhood's old primary school and has been proudly hosting both rembetika and *dimotika* (Greek folk music) performers for more than a century. It's open Friday through Sunday nights. ✉ *Vasileos Georgiou A' 47, Pasalimani, Piraeus* ☎ *210/411–5819.*

Boemissa. Usually crowded and pleasantly raucous, the recently renovated Boemissa attracts many young people who quickly start gyrating in various forms of the *tsifteteli.* Doors are open Friday and Saturday (closed during the summer months). ⊠ *Solomou 19, Exarchia* ☎ *210/384–3836, 210/333–8803.*

Fodor's Choice ★ **Kapnikarea.** The ideal refreshing lunchtime spot to relax after shopping on busy Ermou Street, Kapnikarea is named after the sunken Byzantine church that's next to it. Take in live rembetika music as you sip ouzo and savor traditional specialties and ethnic dishes inspired from owner Dimitris's world travels. ⊠ *Hristopoulou 2 and Ermou 57* ☎ *210/322–7394.*

★ **Stoa Athanaton.** "Arcade of the Immortals" has been around since 1930, housed in a converted warehouse in the meat-market area. Not much has changed since then. The music is enhanced by an infectious, devil-may-care mood and the enthusiastic participation of the audience, especially during the best-of-rembetika afternoons (3:30–7:30). The small dance floor is always jammed. Food here is delicious and reasonably priced, but liquor is expensive. Make reservations for evening performances, when the orchestra is led by old-time rembetika greats. This landmark is closed Sunday and in summer. ⊠ *Sofokleous 19, Central Market* ☎ *210/321–4362, 210/321–0342.*

Fodor's Choice ★ **Taximi.** At one time or other, most of Greece's greatest rembetika musicians have played at this old-time live venue housed in an elegant neoclassic building (closed in summer); many of their black-and-white portraits and photos are on the smoke-stained walls. Not to be missed: the *Smyrnaika* music night every Tuesday, with old rembetika songs from Asia Minor. ⊠ *Isavron 29, at Harilaou Trikoupi, Exarchia* ☎ *210/363–9919.*

TAVERNAS WITH MUSIC

Klimataria. In the evenings, a rembetika band plays sing-along favorites much appreciated by the largely Greek crowd. The price of the old-style Greek entertainment at this century-old taverna is surprisingly reasonable. Meanwhile, the food is displayed on big trays which allows you to choose the dish of your choice with help from owners Mario and Pericles (who is also a noted rembetika singer). Klimataria is also open for lunch. ⊠ *2 Theatrou Sq.* ☎ *210/321–6629* ⊕ *www.klimataria.gr.*

Neos Rigas. At this traditional music taverna you can get a taste of folk dances and costumes from throughout Greece. At the end of the night the music turns more "Eastern," and everybody is invited to show off their own dance moves. The price of this slice of old-style Greek entertainment is surprisingly reasonable. ⊠ *Adrianou and Hatzimihali 13, Plaka* ☎ *210/324–0830* ⊕ *www.newrigas.gr.*

★ **Stamatopoulos PaliaTaverna.** This taverna has everything: good food, barrel wine, an acoustic band with three guitars, and bouzouki troupes playing old Athenian songs in an 1882 house. In summer the show moves to the garden. Whatever the season, Greeks will often get up and dance, beckoning you to join them (don't be shy). Live music starts at

The biggest cultural ticket of the year, the Athens and Epidavros Festival brings summertime performances of top troupes to venues around the city.

about 8:30 and goes on until 1 am. ⊠ *Lysiou 26, Plaka* ☏ *210/322–8722, 210/321–8549* ⊕ *www.stamatopoulostavern.gr.*

THE ARTS

Athens's energetic year-round performing arts scene kicks into a higher gear from June through September, when numerous stunning outdoor theaters host everything from classical Greek drama (in both Greek and English), opera, symphony, and ballet, to rock, pop, and hip-hop concerts. In general, dress for summer performances is fairly casual, though the city's glitterati get decked out for events such as a world premiere opera at the Odeon of Herodes Atticus. From October through May, when the arts move indoors, the Megaron Mousikis/Athens Concert Hall is the biggest venue. Athenians consider the Megaron a place to see and be seen, and dress up accordingly. Performances at outdoor summer venues, stadiums, and the Megaron tend to be priced between €25 to €120 for tickets, depending on the location of seats and popularity of performers.

CONCERTS, DANCE, AND OPERA

Two Athens 2004 Olympic venues located about 20–30 minutes from the city center by taxi or public transportation host the biggest concerts. Madonna, Jennifer Lopez, and U2 have performed at the open-air Athens Olympic Sports Complex (OAKA), while Brazilian star Caetano Veloso and the international *West Side Story* troop have appeared inside the Badminton Theater. It's easiest to buy tickets through ticket vendors like Ticket House (⊠ *Panepistimiou 42* ☏ *210/360–8366*), at Public music shop (✉ *Karageorgi Servias 1, Syntagma Sq.*), or by phone/online (☎ *211/108–6000* ⊕ *www.ticketnet.gr*).

In summer, the city center is covered with posters for a host of big-act rock/pop/alternative festivals. Sting, Metallica, and Peter Gabriel have performed at the Terravibe (⊕ *www.terravibe.gr*) and Rockwave (⊕ *www.rockwavefestival.gr*) festivals. Note that both events take place far out of town, in Malakassa, on Km 37 of the Athens-Lamia National Highway (☎ *210/882–0426*). The Eject Festival, which brings together pop, rock and electronica bands, usually takes place every July in one of the Olympic venues in Faliro (⊕ www.detoxevents.gr).

Athens Olympic Sports Complex (OAKA). Big acts fill the main Athens 2004 Games arena with music—as many as 75,000 people jammed the place when U2 appeared during their 2010 "360" tour. ✉ *OAKA complex, off Kifissias avenue 37, Maroussi* ☎ *210/683–4060* ⊕ *www.oaka.com.gr.*

★ **Dora Stratou Theater.** The country's leading folk-dance company performs exhilarating and sublime Greek folk dances (from all regions), as well as from Cyprus, in eye-catching authentic costumes in programs that change every two weeks. Performances are held Tuesday through Sunday from the end of May through September. Show times are at 9:30 pm, with shows on Saturday and Sunday at 8:15 pm. Tickets cost €15 and they can be purchased at the box office before the show (each performance lasts 90 minutes, with no intermission). ✉ *Arakinthou and Voutie, Filopappou* ☎ *210/921–4650 theater, 210/324–4395 troupe's office* ⊕ *www.grdance.org.*

★ **Megaron Mousikis/Athens Concert Hall.** World-class Greek and international artists take the stage at the Megaron Mousikis to perform in concerts and opera from September through June. Information and tickets are available weekdays 9–5 and Saturday 10–4. Prices range from €15 to €160; there's a substantial discount for students and those 8 to 18 years old. Tickets go on sale a few weeks in advance, and many events sell out within hours. On the first day of sales, tickets can be purchased by cash or credit card only in person at the Athens Concert Hall. From the second day on, remaining tickets may be purchased by phone, in person from the downtown box office (weekdays 10–4), and online. ✉ *Vasilissis Sofias and Kokkali, Ilisia* ☎ *210/728–2333* ⊕ *www.megaron.gr.*

★ **Onassis Cultural Centre.** Athens' impressive new cultural space, the Onassis Cultural Centre, hosts events from across the whole spectrum of the arts, from theater, dance, and music to the written word. Its construction has been exclusively funded by the Onassis Foundation, in memory of the legendary Greek tycoon, and the architecturally noteworthy building now occupies an entire block along one of Athens's main busy thoroughfares. Inside the airy rectangular shell, contructed in a design composed of white marble bands (which reflect the sun by day) and encompassing the lit interiors at night, the interior is home to two amphitheaters, a bar, a restaurant, and exhibition spaces that occupy more than 18,000 square meters and can be seen bustling with activity from October to June. The emphasis here is on contemporary artistic expression—to that effect, an ongoing calendar of exhibitions and art programs showcase and assist contemporary Greek artists. ⊠ *107–109 Syngrou Ave.* ☏ *210/900–5800* ⊕ *www.sgt.gr.*

FESTIVALS

★ **The Athens and Epidavros Festival.** The city's primary artistic event (formerly known as the Hellenic Festival) runs from June through August at a dozen venues, including the ancient Odeon of Herodes Atticus. The festival has showcased performers such as Norah Jones, Dame Kiri Te Kanawa, Luciano Pavarotti, and Diana Ross; such dance troupes as the Royal London Ballet, the Joaquin Cortes Ballet, and Maurice Béjart; symphony orchestras; and local groups performing ancient Greek drama. Usually a major world premiere is staged during the festival. Starting in 2006, creative director Yiorgos Loukos rejuvenated the festival, adding more youthful venues and bringing a wider gamut of performances, including world musicians, modern dance, and multimedia artists. The Odeon theater makes a delightful backdrop, with the floodlighted Acropolis looming behind the audience and the Roman arches behind the performers. The upper-level seats have no cushions, so bring something to sit on, and wear low shoes, since the marble steps are steep. For viewing most performances, the *Gamma* zone is the best seat choice. Tickets go on sale two to three weeks before performances but sell out quickly for popular shows; they are available from the festival box office and major bookshops in Athens (for a full list, check the Web site). Prices range from €20 to as high as €120 for the big names; student and youth discounts are available. ⊠ *Odeon of Herodes Atticus, Dionyssiou Areopagitou, Acropolis* ☏ *210/928–2900 General Information* ⊕ *www.greekfestival.gr* ⊠ *Festival box office, Panepistimiou 39, Syntagma Sq.* ☏ *210/928–2900 General information, 210/928–2952 box office, 210/327–2000 telephone bookings* ⊕ *www.greekfestival.gr.*

★ **Lycabettus Theater.** The specialty of this theater (capacity: 5,000), set on a pinnacle of Mt. Lycabettus, is popular concerts; past performers have included Bryan Ferry, Marianne Faithful, Thievery Corporation, and Cesaria Evora. Since buses travel only as far as the bottom of the hill, and taxi drivers often won't drive to the top, buy a one-way ticket on the funicular and walk about 10 minutes to the theater. Check local listings for scheduled concerts during the summer months. ⊠ *At top of Mt. Lycabettus, Kolonaki* ☏ *210/322–7200, 210/727–2233, 210/722–7209 theater box office.*

Vyronas Festival. Performances by well-known Greek musician Dimitris Mitropanos, international acts such as the Beijing Opera and Kruder & Dorfmeister, and ancient Greek theater classics are staged in an old quarry, now known as the Theatro Vrahon. The festival begins in mid-August and lasts until the end of September every year; most performances start around 9:30 pm. Buy tickets (€20–€1,540) at the theater before the show, or at any of the chain of Metropolis music stores, or online (⊕ *www.ticketservices.gr, www.i-ticket.gr*). ⊠ *Tatoulon (where Trolley 11 ends), Vyrona* ☏ *210/762–6438, 210/760–9340* ⊕ *www.festivalbyrona.gr.*

Fodor's Choice

3

FILM

Films are shown in original-language versions with Greek subtitles (except for major animated films), a definite boon for foreigners. Downtown theaters have the most advanced technology and most comfortable seats. Tickets run about €9. Check the *Athens News* or *Kathimerini* in the *International Herald Tribune* for programs, schedules, and addresses and phone numbers of theaters, including outdoor theaters. Unless old cinema theaters have air-conditioning, they close from June through September, making way for *therina* (open-air theaters), an enchanting, uniquely Greek entertainment that offers instant escapism under a starry sky; about 55 now operate in the greater Athens area.

Attikon Cinemax Class. With its old-fashioned red-velvet and gold-trim embellishments, huge crystal chandelier, wide screen, enormous seats, and central location, this is the best theater in all of Athens. It screens world premieres and classic rereleases. ✉ *Stadiou 19, Syntagma Sq.* ☎ *210/322–8821* ⊕ *www.cinemaxshop.gr.*

★ **Cine Paris.** Kitschy posters of old Greek movies are for sale in the lobby of this rooftop-garden movie theater. It's close to many hotels and tavernas, on Plaka's main walkway, and now boasts Dolby Digital sound. It is open from May to October. ✉ *Kidathineon 22, Plaka* ☎ *210/322–2071, 210/324–8057* ⊕ *www.cineparis.gr.*

Fodor'sChoice **Cine Thisio.** Films at this open-air theater, the oldest in Athens (1935),
★ compete with a view of the Acropolis. It's on the Unification of Archaeological Sites walkway and conveniently boasts tables among the seating. The owners offer homemade sour cherry juice or *tsipoures (dorado)* accompanied with fish-roe, a Messolonghi delicacy from the town. ✉ *Apostolou Pavlou 7, Thission* ☎ *210/342–0864, 210/347–0980* ⊕ *www.cine-thisio.gr.*

MOONLIGHT SERENADES

Many years, on the night of the full moon in August (believed to be the brightest moon of the year), the Ministry of Culture holds an August Moon Festival in Athens and other sites around the country. In the past, venues including the Acropolis, Roman Agora, and the Odeon of Herodes Atticus have been open for free, with performances of opera, Greek dance, and classical music amid the ancient columns by moonlight. Check the ministry's site (⊕ *www.culture.gr*) and local English-language publications to see if you're lucky enough to be there on a year when this must-see is happening.

SHOPPING

For serious retail therapy, most natives head to the shopping streets that branch off central Syntagma and Kolonaki squares. Syntagma is the starting point for popular Ermou, a pedestrian zone where large, international brands like Zara, Sephora, H & M, Massimo Dutti, Mothercare, Replay, Benetton, and Marks & Spencer's have edged out small, independent retailers. You'll find local shops on streets parallel and perpendicular to Ermou: Mitropoleos, Voulis, Nikis, Perikleous, and Praxitelous among them. Poke around here for real bargains, like strings of freshwater pearls, loose semiprecious stones, or made-to-fit hats. Much ritzier is the Kolonaki quarter, with boutiques and designer shops on fashionable streets like Anagnostopoulou, Tsakalof, Skoufa, Solonos, and Kanari. Voukourestiou, the link between Kolonaki and Syntagma, is where you'll find Louis Vuitton, Ralph Lauren, and similar brands. In Monastiraki, coppersmiths have their shops on Ifestou. You can pick up copper wine jugs, candlesticks, cookware, and more for next to nothing. The flea market centered on Pandrossou and Ifestou operates on Sunday mornings and has practically everything, from secondhand guitars to Russian vodka. Keep one rule in mind: always bargain!

ANTIQUES AND ICONS

Antiques are in vogue now, so the prices of these items have soared. Shops on Pandrossou sell small antiques and icons, but keep in mind that many of these might be fakes. You must have government permission to export genuine objects from the ancient Greek, Roman, or Byzantine periods.

★ **Elliniko Spiti.** Art restorer Dimitris Koutelieris is inspired by his home island of Naxos. He salvages most of his materials from houses under restoration, then fashions them into picture frames, little wooden boats, small chairs, and other decorative objects. In his hands objects like cabin doors or window shutters gain a magical second life. ⊠ *Kekropos 14, Plaka* ☎ *210/323–5924.*

Fodor'sChoice **Martinos.** Antiques collectors should head here to look for items such
★ as exquisite dowry chests, old swords, precious fabrics, and Venetian glass. You will certainly discover something you like in the four floors of this renovated antique shop that has been an Athens landmark over the past 100 years. ⊠ *Pandrossou 50, Monastiraki* ☎ *210/321–3110* ⊕ *www.martinosart.gr* ⊠ *Pindarou 24, Kolonaki* ☎ *210/360–9449* ⊕ *www.martinosart.gr.*

CLOTHING

Greece is known for its well-made shoes (most shops are clustered around the Ermou pedestrian zone and in Kolonaki), its furs (Mitropoleos near Syntagma), its jewelry (Voukourestiou and Panepistimiou), and its durable leather items (Pandrossou in Monastiraki). In Plaka shops you can find sandals (currently making a fashionable comeback), fishermen's caps—always a good present—and the hand-knit sweaters worn by fishermen; across the United States these have surfaced at triple the Athens price.

★ **Me Me Me.** Whether you're shopping around for a new cocktail dress or for funky accessories, this is the place to head for trendsetting creations by emerging Greek designers such as Katerina Alexandraki, Grace, Enoe Me, Two in a Gondola, and Studio Fiori. ⊠ *Haritos 19, Kolonaki* ☎ *210/722–4890.*

Occhi Concept Store. Art and the latest clothes, jewelry, and accessories by progressive Greek designers are displayed side-by-side in this gallery-style shop (which recently moved here from its old location down the street). ⊠ *Sarri 28, Psirri* ☎ *210/321–3298* ⊕ *www.occhi.biz.*

Fodor's Choice ★ **Pantelis Melissinos.** Pantelis follows on the steps of his father Stavros, a poetic figure, gentle soul, and longtime fixture of the Monastiraki scene, as well as artist shoemaker, whose shop was once visited by the Beatles and Jackie O. Pantelis also writes poetry but his main claim to fame remains the handmade sandals that continue to delight countless tourists and celebrities. ⊠ *Ayias Theklas 2, Monastiraki* ☎ *210/321–9247* ⊕ *www.melissinos-art.com.*

Parthenis. Fashion designer Dimitris Parthenis opened his first boutique in 1970. Today his daughter Orsalia Parthenis continues the family tradition of creating urban chic fashion with a Bohemian hint. Natural fibers, such as wool, silk, and cotton are used to create relaxed, body-hugging silhouettes. There is a children's line and a wedding collection, too. ⊠ *Dimokritou 20 and Tsakalof, Kolonaki* ☎ *210/363–3158* ⊕ *www.orsalia-parthenis.gr.*

Fodor's Choice ★ **Whitebox Praxitelous.** This is an avant-garde collective of creative Greek independent designers and artists, specializing in handmade jewelry, handbags, shoes, clothes, and decorative objects. Their creations can be found in a postindustrial loft show-room/gallery with an impressive black-and-white tile floor. Many of the accessories are one-of-a-kind, limited editions. ⊠ *Praxitelous 26, 5th fl.* ☎ *210/323–2343.*

GIFTS

Discover touristy treasures in the numerous souvenir shops along the streets of Plaka and Monastiraki—in particular, look for them in the Monastiraki flea market and the shops along Adrianou Street, behind the Monastiraki train station.

Fodor's Choice ★ **Benaki Museum Gift Shop.** The airy museum shop has excellent copies of Greek icons, jewelry, and folk art—at fair prices. You will also find embroideries, ceramics, stationery, art books, small reliefs, and sculpture pieces. The museum annex on Piraeus Street has its own shop with an interesting collection of modern Greek jewelry. ⊠ *Koumbari 1, at Vasilissis Sofias, Kolonaki* ☎ *210/362–7367* ⊕ *www.benaki.gr.*

Fodor's Choice ★ **Diplous Pelekys.** A large variety of handwoven articles, genuine folk art, ceramics from all over Greece, and traditional and modern jewelry all on show here make excellent, and affordable, gifts. The cozy and tasteful shop is run by third-generation weavers and is the oldest folk art shop in Athens (established 1925). ⊠ *Voulis 7 and Kolokotroni 3, inside Bolani Arcade, Syntagma Sq.* ☎ *210/322–3783* ⊕ *www.diplouspelekys.gr.*

Katerina Folk Art. Greeks can spend hours heatedly playing *tavli* (backgammon). To take home a game set of your own, look closely for this hole-in-the-wall souvenir shop, which sells tavli and chessboards and glass beads in all sizes and designs. ⊠ *Ifestou 21, Monastiraki* ☎ *210/321–5694.*

Fodor's Choice ★ **Kombologadiko.** From pinhead-size "evil eyes" to 2-inch-diameter wood, sugar cane, or shell beads, you'll find a dizzying selection of beads here to string your own *komboloi* (worry beads). You'll admire the variety of this unique Greek version of a rosary, which can be made

Continued on page 171

GREEK BY DESIGN

Shopping is now considered an Olympic sport in Greece. Many get the urge to splurge in the chic shops of Mykonos, Rhodes, and Crete, the islands that launched a thousand gifts. But if you really want to bag the best in Greek style, Athens is where to get the goods.

The Greeks had a word for it: *tropos.* Style. You would expect nothing less from the folks who gave us the Venus de Milo, the Doric column, and the lyre-back chair. To say that they have had a long tradition as artisans and craftsmen is, of course, an understatement. Even back in ancient Rome, Greece was the word. The Romans may have engineered the stone vault and perfected the toilet, but when it came to style and culture, they were perfectly content to knock off Grecian dress, sculpture, décor, and architecture, then considered the height of fashion. Fast-forward 2,500 years and little has changed. Many works of modern art were conceived as an Aegean paean, including the statues of Brancusi and Le Corbusier's minimalistic skyscrapers—both art-

ists were deeply influenced by ancient Cycladic art. Today, the goddess dress struts the runways of Michael Kors and Valentino while Homer has made the leap to Hollywood in such box-office blockbusters as *300* and *Troy.*

Speaking of which, those ancient Trojans may have once tut-tutted about Greeks bearing gifts but would have second thoughts these days. Aunt Ethel has now traded in those plastic souvenir models of the Parthenon for a new Athenian bounty: pieces of Byzantine-style gold jewelry; hand-woven bedspreads from Hydra; strands of amber *komboloi* worry beads; and reproductions of red-figure ceramic vases. These are gifts you cannot resist and will be forever be glad you didn't.

(above) Byzantine design jewelry

BEARING GIFTS?

Seeing some of the glories of Aegean craftsmanship is probably one of the reasons you've come to Greece. The eggshell-thin pottery Minoans were fashioning more than 3,500 years ago, Byzantine jewelry and icons, colorful rugs that were woven in front of the fire as part of a dowry, not to mention all those bits of ancient masonry—these comprise a magnificent legacy of arts and crafts.

LEATHER SANDALS

Ancient Greek women with means and a sense of style wore sandals with straps that wrapped around the ankles—what today's fashion mags call "strappy sandals," proof that some classics are always in vogue. The most legendary maker is Athens's very own Stavros Melissinos, whose creations were once sported by the Beatles and Sophia Loren. He has been crafting sandals for more than 50 years.

TAVLÍ BOARDS

No matter where you are in Greece, follow the sound of clicking dice and you'll probably find yourself in a kafenion. There, enthusiasts will be huddled over Greece's favorite game, a close cousin to backgammon. Tavlí boards are sold everywhere in Greece, but the most magnificent board you'll ever see is not for sale—a marble square inlaid with gold and ivory, crafted sometime before 1500 BC for the amusement of Minoan kings and now on display at the archaeological museum in Heraklion, Crete.

WORRY BEADS

Feeling fidgety? Partake of a Greek custom and fiddle with your worry beads, or komboloi. The amber or coral beads are loosely strung on a long strand and look like prayer beads, yet they have no religious significance. Even so, on a stressful day the relaxing effect can seem like divine intervention. Particularly potent are beads painted with the "evil eye."

ICONS

Icon painting flourished in Greece as the Renaissance took hold of Western Europe, and panels of saints and other heavenly creatures are among the country's greatest artistic treasures. Some, like many of those in the 799 churches on the island of Tinos, are said to possess miraculous healing powers, attracting thousands of cure-seeking believers each year. Icons attract art buyers too, but if you can easily afford one, it's almost certainly a modern reproduction.

JEWELRY

Greece's long gold- and silver-smithing tradition thrives in workshops on Rhodes and Corfu and in such mainland towns and villages as Ioannina and Stemnitsa. Many artisans turn to the past for inspiration—Bronze Age cruciform figures, gold necklaces from the Hellenistic period dangling with pomegranates, Byzantine-style pendants—while others tap out distinctly modern creations using age-old techniques.

WEAVING

Even goddesses spent their idle hours weaving (remember Arachne, so proud of her skills at the loom that Athena turned her into a spider?). From the mountains of Arcadia to such worldly enclaves as Mykonos, mortals sit behind handlooms to clack out folkloric rugs, bedspreads, and tablecloths.

BARGAINING FOR BEGINNERS

In Greece there is often the "first price" and the "last price." Bargaining is still par for the course (except in the fanciest stores). And if you're planning a shopping day, leave those Versace shoes at home—shopkeepers often decide on a price after sizing up the prospective buyer's income bracket.

CERAMICS

Ancient Greek pottery was a black-and-red medium: the Spartans and Corinthians painted glossy black figures on a reddish-orange background; later ceramists switched the effect with stunning results, reddish-hued figures on a black background. Artisans still create both, and potters on Crete and elsewhere in Greece throw huge terracotta storage jars, pithoi, that are appealing, if no longer practical, additions to any household.

ATHENS: PASSPORT TO STYLE

If you want to find the finest in Greek craftsmanship, head to the shops of Athens. Greece may not have always been a land of great artists, but these top offerings will remind you that it has always been a place for great artistry.

Baba (✉ Ifestou 30, Monastiraki) is Backgammon Central—get a great tavlí board here.

Center of Hellenic Tradition (✉ Mitropoleous 59, Monastiraki) is a mecca for old Greek folk crafts, with regional ceramics, weavings, and antique sheep bells all making for evocative room accents.

Kombologadiko (✉ 6 Koumbari, Kolonaki) was praised by Vogue a few years ago for its chic take on old traditional komboloi worry beads, having remade this previously for-men-only item into high-fashion necklaces.

Lalaounis (✉ Panepistimiou 6, Syntagma Square), Athens's most famous jeweler, allows jet-setters and collectors to "go for the gold" with necklaces, bracelets, headpieces, and rings inspired by ancient pieces.

Lykeio Ellinidon (✉ Dimokritou 7a, Kolonaki) is famed for its resident weavers who copy folkloric motifs at two on-site looms.

Stavros Melissinos (✉ Ayias Theklas 2, Monastiraki), Athens's most famous sandal-maker, boasts a clientele that has included Jackie Onassis and Gary Cooper.

A. Patnkiadou (✉ 58 Pandroussou, Plaka) has fashionistas raving about jewelry that incorporates ancient coins and Byzantine jewels.

Pylarinos (✉ Panepistimious 18, Syntagma Square) is known for its selection of ancient coins and vintage engravings—pick up a 19th-century view of the Acropolis here.

Riza (✉ Voukourestiou 35, Kolonaki) is tops for Greek Island accents like traditional brass candlesticks.

Tanagrea (✉ Voulis 26 and Mitropoleous 15, Syntagma Square) is one of Athens's oldest gift shops and is famed for its hand-painted ceramic pomegranates, symbol of good fortune.

Thiamis (✉ Asklipiou 71, Syntagma Square) gives a new take on an old art form with hand-painted icons.

Shop-til-you-droppers love the Monastiraki district.

from traditional amber, but also from coral root, camel bone, semi-precious stones, and many more materials. ⊠ *Amerikis 9, Kolonaki* ☎ *212/700–0500* ⊕ *www.kombologadiko.gr.*

Fodor'sChoice **Korres.** Natural beauty products blended in traditional recipes using
★ Greek herbs and flowers have graced the bathroom shelves of celebrities like Rihanna and Angelina Jolie but in Athens they are available at most pharmacies for regular-folk prices. For the largest selection of basil-lemon shower gel, coriander body lotion, olive-stone face scrub, and wild-rose eye cream, go to the original Korres pharmacy (behind the Panathenaic Stadium). Not surprisingly, Korres also maintains a traditional laboratory for herbal preparations such as tinctures, oils, capsules, and teas. ⊠ *Eratosthenous 8 and Ivikou, Pangrati* ☎ *210/722–2744* ⊕ *www.korres.com.*

★ **Mastiha Shop.** Medical research lauding the healing properties of gum mastic, a resin from trees only found on the Greek island of Chios, has spawned a range of exciting wellness products, from chewing gum and cookies to liqueurs and cosmetics. ⊠ *Panepistimiou 6 and Kriezotou, Syntagma Sq.* ☎ *210/363–2750.*

Fodor'sChoice **Tanagrea.** Hand-painted ceramic pomegranates—a symbol of fertility
★ and good fortune—are one of the most popular items in one of the city's oldest gift shops. ⊠ *Petraki 3 (entrance from Ermou 11), Syntagma Sq.* ☎ *210/321–6783.*

Thiamis. Iconographer Aristides Makos creates beautiful hand-painted, gold-leaf icons on wood and stone. His slightly cluttered shop also sells beautiful handmade model ships and made-to-order items. ⊠ *Asklipiou 71, Kolonaki* ☎ *210/363–7993* ⊕ *www.thiamis.com.*

HANDICRAFTS

Fodor'sChoice **Center of Hellenic Tradition.** The center is an outlet for quality handi-
★ crafts—ceramics, weavings, sheep bells, wood carvings, prints, and old paintings. Take a break from shopping in the center's quiet and quaint I Oraia Ellas café, to enjoy a salad or mezedes in clear view of the Parthenon. Upstairs is an art gallery hosting temporary exhibitions of Greek art. ⊠ *Mitropoleos 59 and Pandrossou 36, Monastiraki* ☎ *210/321–3023, 210/321–3842 café.*

JEWELRY

Prices are much lower for gold and silver in Greece than in many Western countries, and the jewelry is of high quality. Many shops in Plaka carry original pieces available at a good price if you bargain hard enough (a prerequisite). For those with more-expensive tastes, the Voukourestiou pedestrian mall off Syntagma Square has a number of the city's leading jewelry shops.

Fodor'sChoice **Elena Votsi.** Elena Votsi designed jewelry for Gucci and Ralph Lauren
★ before opening her own boutiques, where she sells exquisite, larger than life creations in coral, amethyst, aquamarine, and turquoise. In 2003 she designed the Athens 2004 Olympic Games gold medal and in 2009 her handmade 18-karat gold ring with diamonds won a Couture Design Award in the "Best-to-Couture" category in Las Vegas. Brava! ⊠ *Xanthou 7, Kolonaki* ☎ *210/360–0936* ⊕ *www.elenavotsi.com.*

★ **Lalaounis.** This world-famous Greek jewelry house experiments with its designs, taking ideas from nature, biology, African art, and ancient Greek pieces—the last are sometimes so close to the original that they're mistaken for museum artifacts. The pieces are mainly in gold, some in silver—look out for the decorative objects inspired by ancient Greek houseware. The famed tradition here started with Ilias Lalaounis (also founder of the Lalaounis Jewelry Museum) and is now proudly continued by his four daughters and grandchildren. ⊠ *Panepistimiou 6 and Voukourestiou, Syntagma Sq.* 🕾 *210/361–1371* ⊠ *Papadiamandi 7, Kifissia* 🕾 *210/623–9000.*

ARE YOU GIFTED?

An inexpensive but unusual gift is a string of *komboloi* (worry beads) in plastic, wood, or stone. You can pick them up very cheaply in Monastiraki or look in antiques shops for more-expensive versions, with amber, silver, or black onyx beads. Another popular gift option is *matia*, the good-luck charms (usually turquoise) that ward off the evil eye. Reasonably priced natural sponges also make good presents. Look for those that are unbleached, since the lighter ones tend to fall apart quickly.

Museum of Cycladic Art Shop. Exceptional modern versions of ancient jewelry designs are available in the gift shop of this museum, where you can also find museum replicas and inspired ceramics. ⊠ *Neofitou Douka 4, Kolonaki* 🕾 *210/722–8321* ⊕ *www.cycladic.gr.*

★ **Sagiannos Gallery.** For five generations, the Sagiannos family's creations have adorned the fingers, necks, and ears of stylish Athenian matrons. The tradition continues in this shop/gallery, but with more-modern, one-of-a-kind pieces inspired by ordinary objects like bar codes and buttons. The contemporary space often hosts the work of young and progressive Greek designers and offers many pieces at affordable prices. ⊠ *Makriyianni 3, Makriyianni* 🕾 *210/924–7323.*

★ **Zolotas.** Since 1895, this jeweler, Lalaounis's main competitor in the status sweepstakes, is noted for its superb museum copies in gold and also its exquisite *objets d'art.* ⊠ *Panepistimiou 10* 🕾 *210/360–1272* ⊕ *www. zolotas.gr* ⊠ *Stadiou 9, Syntagma Sq.* 🕾 *210/322–1212.*

MUSIC
Metropolis. Take your pick of a huge selection of all-Greek music, from rembetika to the latest Greek club hits. This is the flagship store of the most influential Greek music chain. ⊠ *Panepistimiou 54, Omonia Sq.* 🕾 *210/380–1179* ⊕ *www.metropolis.gr.*

The Saronic Gulf Islands

WORD OF MOUTH

"When you go to Aegina, be sure to go to the Temple of Aphaia ruin at the top of the mountain. It is fantastic. . . . Also stop at one of the waterfront tavernas. We met Costa, barbequing octopi with a dousing of his 'special sauce.' He told us to watch for world-wide introduction of 'Costa's Own' soon!"

—grasshopper

WELCOME TO
THE SARONIC GULF ISLANDS

TOP REASONS TO GO

★ **Handsome Hydra:** The place for the jet-setter who appreciates walking more than showing off new wheels, Hydra offers both tranquillity and sociability— a bustling main town and abundant walking trails. What's here (stone houses set above a welcoming harbor) and what's not (cars) provide a relaxing retreat.

★ **Ship-Shape Spetses:** A fine jumping-off point for the Peloponnesian shore, cosmopolitan Spetses is famed for its Spetsiot seafaring tradition—not surprisingly, the Old Town harbor is car-free and picture-perfect.

★ **Ancient Aegina:** Not far from this vast island's medieval Paliachora—with nearly 20 churches—is the Temple of Aphaia, one of Greece's best-preserved Archaic sites. Aegina's isle is the closest Saronic island to Athens's port of Piraeus.

★ **Pistachio Perfection:** You can already taste them—salty, sweet, mellow—and the best pistachio nuts anywhere may come from Aegina.

1 Aegina. The largest of Saronic islands, Aegina is a land of contrasts—from its crowded beach towns to its isolated, rugged mountain peaks, scattered ruins, and forgotten monasteries. Take in the main town's famous fish market, visit the pre-Hellenic Temple of Aphaia, then explore the ghost town of Paliachora, still spirit-warm thanks to its 20 chapels.

2 Hydra. Noted for its 19th-century *archontika* (mansions), its crescent-shape waterfront, and fashionable boutiques, Hydra has been catnip for decades for writers and artists—visit the isle's galleries or bring along your easel and let your own creative juices flow. For Hydriot splendor in excelsis, visit the 1780 Lazaros Koundouriotis Mansion or buy a glittering jewel or two at Elena Votsi's harbor-front jewelry shop.

Thisvi

Gulf of Corinth

Perakhora

Korinthos

Sofikon

Nafplion

Portochelion
Kosta
Spetses
SPETSES **3**
SPETSOPOULA

GETTING ORIENTED

4

Bounded on three sides by sea, Atikí (Attica) has an indented, sun-gilded coastline fringed with innumerable sandy beaches and rocky inlets. Just to the south of Athens, straddling the gulf between its bustling port of Piraeus and the Peloponnese, are the Saronic Gulf islands, the aristocracy of the Greek isles. Set with coves and natural harbors ideal for seafaring, the islands of Aegina, Hydra, and Spetses are enveloped in a patrician aura that is the combined result of history and their more recent cachet as the playgrounds of wealthy Athenians. Owing to their proximity and beauty, they can get swamped with vacationers during the summer, yet they retain their distinct cultural traditions, perhaps best appreciated out of season.

3 Spetses. The island, with regular boat service to pine-lined beaches, is perfect for beach hopping. It's also top contender for the most dining and nightlife offerings of the Saronic isles. As for sights, Bouboulina Museum in the main town offers fascinating details about the island's storied history.

Updated
by Natasha
Giannousi

Only have a few days in Greece but need to taste island life? One of the Saronic isles offers the perfect solution. Called the "offshore islands" by day-tripping Athenians, they are treasured for their proximity to the burly city. Just south of hectic Piraeus, Aegina still feels like another world. Heading southward you'll find chic and cosmopolitan Hydra, a fitting stage for one of Sophia Loren's first forays into Hollywood. Finally, there is splendid Spetses, anchored off mainland Kosta—a playground prized by carefree vacationing Greeks.

The Saronic Gulf islands, whose ancient city-states rivaled Athens, are now virtually a part of the capital. Aegina, one of the most-visited islands in Greece because of its proximity to the capital city, is 30 minutes from Piraeus by hydrofoil, while Spetses, the most "remote" and the greenest of the Saronic islands, is 90 minutes away. South of the Argolid, the peninsula that divides the Saronic Gulf from the gulf of Argolis, rests Hydra, poor in beaches but rich in charm.

Aegina's pretty country villas have drawn shipping executives, who often commute daily from the island to their offices in Piraeus. Here pine forests mix with groves of pistachio trees, a product for which Aegina is justly famous. Water taxis buzz to Poros, more like an islet, from the Peloponnese, carrying weary locals eager to relax on its beaches and linger in the island cafés. The island's rustic clay-tile roofs have a cinematic beauty that has inspired poets, writers, and musicians who have lived here. Hydra and Spetses are farther south and both ban automobiles. Hydra's stately mansions, restaurants, and boutiques cater to the sophisticated traveler. Spetses has both broad forests and regal, neoclassic buildings. Rather than being spoiled by tourism, all four islands have managed to preserve their laid-back attitude, well suited to the hedonistic lifestyle of weekend pleasure-seekers arriving by yacht and hydrofoil.

PLANNER

WHEN TO GO

The weather on the islands tends to be the same as in Athens, though the heat can feel more intense on the arid peaks of Aegina and Hydra. The island breeze—felt on all the Saronic isles, particularly later in the day—makes these vacation destinations more refreshing than the mainland on summer evenings (and in winter, more bitter, due to the colder humidity). Due to the risk of summer fires, do not wander into forested areas in the hot-weather months. Check the forecast before heading to Aegina, Hydra, or Spetses at any time of year—bad weather in the off-season or strong August winds (*meltemi*) may strand you on the island you only intended to visit briefly.

PLANNING YOUR TIME

The Saronic isles make fabulous day trips, though an overnight stay—or hop to a second isle—is recommended. To ease into the pace of island life probably requires at least two days per island. However, it's doable to visit all the islands within a week, or even four days. A day trip is best spent at any of the island's main-port towns (Aegina—the closest to Piraeus, with the most regular traffic to and fro—is a good choice if your time is very limited). All of the Saronic islands have bathing places close to the main ports, so you can squeeze a dip in, too, though it's doing Spetses's greatest beaches an injustice if you rush your swimming there. In three days you can explore most of Hydra or Spetses, or really get to know Aegina. However, if you wish to visit more than one island, you can start with a day or two on the beaches of Spetses before setting sail for another destination. Island-hopping on your agenda? First, check your budget: a three-island trek will hit your wallet harder than choosing two islands and exploring them in depth. If funds aren't an issue, try starting in Spetses and working your way north to Aegina. (Note that from October through April there are fewer daily boats and hydrofoils between the islands, so check the whole route in advance with a travel agent or boat company.) Our recommended itinerary: Devote the first two days to Spetses's small main town and beautiful beaches. In the next two, wander Hydra's port town, and if you're ambitious (and in shape), hike to a monastery. Then give Aegina its day's due. One no-sweat tip to keep in mind: In July and August visit Saronic island archaeological sites like the Temple of Aphaia as early in the day as possible. There is little shade at such sites, and the midday heat can be withering. And, of course, an early start may help you avoid crowds.

GETTING HERE AND AROUND

A car is only truly useful on Aegina, as cars are prohibited on the islands of Hydra and (except by special permit) Spetses. Renting scooters, mopeds, and bicycles is popular with tourists on Aegina and Spetses. But extreme caution is advised: the equipment may not be in good condition, roads can be narrow and treacherous, and many drivers scorn your safety. Wear a helmet. If braving the road isn't part of your plan, never fear: on Aegina, there is regular bus service between towns and beaches. But on Hydra, you can famously travel only by water

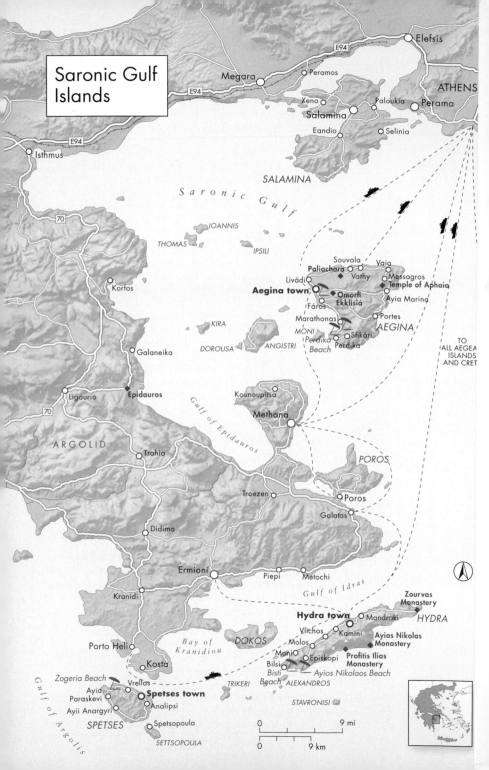

Saronic Gulf Islands

Elefsis

E94

Megara

Peramos

ATHENS

Isthmus

E94

Xeno

Paloukia

Perama

Salamina

Selinia

Eandio

70

SALAMINA

S a r o n i c   G u l f

IOANNIS

THOMAS

IPSILI

Souvala

Vaia

Paliachara

Vathy

Messagros

Korfos

Livádi

Aegina town

Omorfi

Temple of Aphaia

Fáros

Ekklisiá

Ayia Marina

KIRA

Marathonas

Portes

Galaneika

MONI

AEGINA

DOROUSA

ANGISTRI

Perdika

Sfikári

Beach

Perdika

Kounoupitsa

TO
ALL AEGEAN
ISLANDS
AND CRETE

Epidauros

Gulf of Epidauros

Methana

Ligourio

70

POROS

ARGOLID

Trahia

Troezen

Poros

Didima

Galatas

Ermioni

Piepi

Metochi

Kranidi

Gulf of Idras

Zourvas
Monastery

Porto Heli

DOKOS

Hydra town

Mandraki

HYDRA

*Bay of
Kranidiou*

Vlichos

Kamini

Kosta

Molos

Ayios Nikolas
Monastery

Zogeria Beach

Vrellas

Moni

Episkopi

Profitis Ilias
Monastery

Ayia
Paraskevi

Bilsi

Ayios Nikolaos Beach

Bisti

Ayii Anargyri

Analipsi

Spetses town

Beach

ALEXANDROS

TRIKERI

Gulf of Argolis

SPETSES

Spetsopoula

STAVRONISI

SETTSOPOULA

0   9 mi

0   9 km

taxi, mule, bike, or donkey—no cars or buses allowed! On Spetses, get around by buggy, scooter, boat, and two buses. But, as with any personal transportation in Greece, it's best to confirm prices first, so you don't get taken for a different kind of ride.

BOAT AND FERRY TRAVEL

The islands of Poros and Spetses are so close to the Peloponnese mainland that you can drive there, park, and ferry across the channel in any of a number of *caïques* (price negotiable) at the ports, but to get to them from Athens or to visit the other Saronic Gulf islands, you must take to the sea in a ferry. You can get a weekly boat schedule from the Greek National Tourism Organization (GNTO or EOT ⊕ *www.gnto.gr*).

Hellenic Seaways Ferries, ANES Ferries, and Nova Ferries carry you and your car from the main port in Piraeus (Gate E8, about a thousand feet from the train station, beyond Karaiskaki Square, to Aegina (1 hour) or you alone—no cars allowed—to Hydra (3 hours, 15 minutes) and Spetses (4 hours, 25 minutes).

There are approximately a half dozen departures per day, and boat fares range from about €9.50 per person for Aegina to €13.30 for Poros. Car rates are usually three to four times the passenger rate (but remember that no cars are allowed in Hydra or Spetses, which are serviced only by Flying Dolphin or catamaran). Ferries are the leisurely and least-expensive way to travel; however, most people prefer the speedier Hellenic Seaways and the ANES Ferries (for Aegina) hydrofoils (faster than the catamarans; no cars allowed) that also depart from Piraeus, at Gate E8 or E9. You can get to Aegina in 40 minutes (€14), to Hydra in 90 minutes (€21.50), and to Spetses (€35) in just under two hours. There are about a half dozen departures daily to each island, but make reservations ahead of time—boats fill quickly. You can get detailed info about ferries' departures on the Web site (⊕ *www.ferries.gr*). You can also reserve through a travel agent.

What about boats and ferries between the various Saronic Gulf islands? Hellenic Seaways' Flying Dolphins travel regularly, year-round, from Piraeus to Hydra and Spetses (and back again). There are about five such daily rounds from October to April, more the rest of the year. In summer, Hellenic Seaways has a daily boat between Aegina, Angistri, Poros, and Methana. But plan your Argo-Saronic island hopping carefully in the off-season. During that time, boats between the islands are much less frequent, and you may have to do a ferry–and–Flying Dolphin or catamaran combination. In addition, on certain days and seasons, remember you cannot hydrofoil or catamaran your way from one Saronic isle to the next but will have to backtrack to the main port at Piraeus to catch another boat.

Boat Contacts ANES Ferries ✉ *Ioulias Katsa 6, Aegina town* ☎ *210/422–5625 in Piraeus, 22970/25625 in Aegina* ⊕ *www.anes.gr.* **Hellenic Seaways** ✉ *6 Astiggos, Karaiskaki Sq., Piraeus* ☎ *210/419–9000 Ticket information, 210/419–9100 Central office* ⊕ *www.hellenicseaways.gr.* **Nova Ferries** ✉ *L. Dimokratias 1, Aegina town* ☎ *22970/24200 in Aegina, 210/4126528 in Piraeus* ⊕ *www. novaferries.gr.*

BUS TRAVEL

To get around while in Aegina, use the KTEL buses that leave from the main bus station on Ethneyersias Square (⊠ *Platia Ethneyersias* ☎ *22970/22787)*, just left of the main port; purchase tickets here, not on the bus. Routes stop at many spots, including Ayia Marina and Perdika; a popular destination is the Temple of Aphaia, with nearly hourly departures in summer (€2.50). Service on the island becomes infrequent from late October to early May.

CAR TRAVEL

On Aegina, there is a good network of mostly narrow rural roads (two lanes at best). Drivers should be prepared for occasional abrupt turns; major towns and sites are well marked. Karagiannis Klimis Travel, on Aegina, rents both cars and motorcycles. Cars are not allowed on Hydra; homeowners and special-permission permits only for cars on Spetses.

What about the "auto ban"? Unlike on Hydra, cars are not banned outright on Spetses; residents are permitted to ferry their autos to the island. In some rare cases, for medical or professional reasons, it's possible for nonresidents to get a car permit from the port authority (☎ *22980/72245)*, but it must be obtained at least two days prior to arrival. In fact, the presence of cars seems to be getting more pronounced every year, despite the wishes of many inhabitants.

Car Contacts Karagiannis Klimis Travel ⊠ *Kanari 2, Aegina town* ☎ *22970/25664, 22970/28780* ✎ *nklimi@otenet.gr.*

RESTAURANTS

The cuisine of the Saronic islands resembles that of Athens, Attica, and the Peloponnese. Local ingredients predominate, with fresh fish perhaps the greatest (and most expensive) delicacy. Since much of Attica's vegetation used to support herds of grazing sheep and the omnivorous goat, the meat of both animals is also a staple in many country tavernas. Although it is becoming increasingly difficult to find the traditional Greek taverna with large stewpots full of the day's hot meal, or big *tapsi* (pans) of *pastitsio* (layers of pasta, meat, and cheese laced with cinnamon) or *papoutsakia* (eggplant slices filled with minced meat), market towns still harbor the occasional rustic haunt, offering tasty, inexpensive meals. Always ask to see the *kouzina* (kitchen) to look at the day's offerings, or even peer inside the pots. When it comes to regional cuisine on the Saronic islands fresh fish and seafood courses dominate. Informal dress is appropriate at all but the very fanciest of restaurants, and unless noted, reservations are not necessary.

DINING AND LODGING PRICES IN EUROS				
¢	$	$$	$$$	$$$$
Restaurants	under €10	€11–€15	€16–€20	€21–€25	over €25
Hotels	under €80	€81–€120	€121–€160	€161–€200	over €200

Restaurant prices are for one main course at dinner, or for two mezedes (small dishes). Hotel prices are for a standard double room in high season, including taxes. Inquire when booking whether meal plans (which can entail higher rates) are mandatory.

HOTELS

Accommodations on the Saronic Gulf islands range from elegant 19th-century mansions—usually labeled as "traditional settlements"—and boutique-style hotels to spare rental rooms overlooking a noisy water-front. Rented rooms can be less expensive than hotels, and an easy option for fly-by-the-seaters: just follow signs, or solicitors who show up when boats come in. (And note that it's okay to check out the room before committing.) From June to September, book far in advance. Off-season (October–April), you'll have fewer hotels to choose from, as many close during the colder months. Souvala and Ayia Marina are suitable lodging alternatives to Aegina's main town, but on the other islands, if you'd like choices when it comes to eating and nightlife, make sure to stay in the main ports. If you want to plan a great off-season trip with minimum hassle, putting your itinerary in the hands of a professional is your best bet. On Aegina we recommend Karagiannis Travel (⊠ *Kanari 2, Aegina town* ☎ *22970/25664* ⊕ *www.aegina-travel.com*). Also note that during certain times of the year (most notably summer) you may get better deals on weekdays than on Athenian-heavy weekends. Remember to ask at small hotels if solar water heaters are used in summer; if so, find out when it's best to bathe—otherwise you may be forced to choose between taking a freezing cold shower or not bathing at all.

VISITOR INFORMATION

There are few main official tourist offices for the Saronic Gulf islands. The closest you'll come is the Aegina Municipality agency (*see Visitor Information, below, on Aegina*). There are also Tourist Police offices listed for each island. The main starting point is the Greek National Tourism Organization Web site (⊕ *www.gnto.gr*). Keep in mind that in lieu of official agencies, there are an array of private travel agencies, and these offer myriad services, tickets, car rentals, and guided tours. Top agencies include CHAT and Key Tours (*see addresses listed in Tour Options, below*). These travel agencies are usually based in offices near the island's harbor port.

TOUR OPTIONS

Most agencies run tour excursions at about the same prices, but CHAT and Key Tours have the best service and guides. A full-day cruise from Piraeus, with either CHAT or Key Tours, visits Aegina, Poros, and Hydra, and costs around €98 (including buffet lunch on the ship).

If you're traveling in a group, consider pushing off in your own vessel to see these isles by water. Six people can rent a sailboat, complete with skipper, from Vernicos Yachts (☎ *210/989–6000* ⊕ *www.vernicos. com*). At about €100 a head per night (excluding fuel) for a week, it's less expensive than staying in some hotels, and you won't have to contend with the oft-postponed ferries. Sailors at various Saronic ports offer to ferry folks to isolated beaches—just remember to agree on a price beforehand and arrange a time for your return so you're not stranded!

Contacts CHAT ⊠ *Xenofontos 9, Syntagma, Athens* ☎ *210/322–2886, 210/323–0827.* **Key Tours** ⊠ *Kallirois 4, Athens* ☎ *210/923–3166, 210/923–3266* ✎ *keytours@otenet.gr* ⊕ *www.keytours.gr.*

AEGINA ΑΙΓΙΝΑ

30 km (19 mi) south to Aegina town from Athens's port of Piraeus.

The eastern side of Aegina is rugged and sparsely inhabited today, except for Ayia Marina, a former fishing hamlet now studded with hotels. The western side of the island, where Aegina town lies, is more fertile and less mountainous than the east; fields are blessed with grapes, olives, figs, almonds, and, above all, the treasured pistachio trees. Idyllic seascapes, quaint backstreets, and a number of beautiful courtyard gardens make Aegina town attractive.

GETTING HERE AND AROUND

BOAT TRAVEL Aegina is so close to the port of Piraeus that many Athenians live on the island and commute (from central Athens reach Piraeus station by taking the green metro Line 1; the trip takes 25–30 minutes and the ticket costs €1.20). Ferry companies carry you and your car from the main port in Piraeus (Gate E8, which is about 1,300 feet from the train station) to Aegina in little more than an hour's time for about €10. More frequent departures are scheduled for the catamarans and Flying Dolphins for passengers (no cars) departing from Gate E8 or E9, at a cost of about €14. These take you to the island about half an hour faster (but usually do not offer connecting services to other Saronic isles; you have to backtrack to Piraeus to hydrofoil to another island). Two well-known companies that offer boat service to Aegina are Hellenic Seaways and Aegean Flying Dolphins.

BUS TRAVEL To get around while in Aegina, use the KTEL buses that leave from the main bus station on Ethneyersias Square (⊠ *Platia Ethneyersias* ☎ *22970/22787*), just left of the main port; purchase tickets here, not on the bus. Routes stop at many spots, including Ayia Marina and Perdika; a popular destination is the Temple of Aphaia, with nearly hourly departures in summer (€2.5). Service on the island becomes infrequent from late October to early May.

Visitor Information Aegina Municipality ⊠ *Town hall, Xristou Lada 1, Aegina town* ☎ *22973/20015, 15516 Aegina info line* ⊕ *www.aegina.gr.* **Aegina Tourist Police** ⊠ *Leonardou Lada 12, Aegina town* ☎ *22970/22100.* **Greek National Tourism Organization** ⊕ *www.visitgreece.gr.*

EXPLORING

Although it may seem hard to imagine, by the Archaic period (7th to 6th century BC), Aegina was a mighty maritime power. It introduced the first silver coinage (marked with a tortoise) and established colonies in the Mediterranean. By the 6th century BC, Egina—to use its alternative spelling—had become a major art center, known in particular for its bronze foundries (worked by such sculptors as Kallon, Onatas, and Anaxagoras) and its ceramics, which were exported throughout the Mediterranean. Testimony to its great glory is the Temple of Aphaia, one of the most extant of the great Greek temples and famed for its spectacular array of Doric columns.

As it turns out, this powerful island, lying so close off the coast of Attica, could not fail to come into conflict with Athens. As Athens's imperial ambitions grew, Aegina became a thorn in its side. In 458 BC Athens laid siege to the city, eventually conquering the island. In 455 BC the islanders were forced to migrate from the island, and Aegina never again regained its former power.

From the 13th to the 19th century, Aegina ping-ponged between nations. A personal fiefdom of Venice and Spain after 1204, it was fully claimed by Venice in 1451. Less than a century later, in 1537, it was devastated and captured by the pirate Barbarossa and repopulated with Albanians. Morosini recaptured Aegina for Venice in 1654, but Italian dominance was short-lived: the island was ceded to Turkey in 1718. Its Greek roots were brushed off in the early 19th century, when it experienced a rebirth as an important base in the 1821 War of Independence, briefly holding the fledgling Greek nation's government (1826–28). The first modern Greek coins were minted here. At this time many people from the Peloponnese, plus refugees from Chios and Psara, emigrated to Aegina, and many of the present-day inhabitants are descended from them.

AEGINA TOWN ΑΙΓΙΝΑ ΠΟΛΗ

84 km (52 mi) southwest of Piraeus.

As you approach from the sea, your first view of Aegina town takes in the sweep of the harbor, punctuated by the tiny white chapel of Ayios Nikolaos. A large population of fishermen adds character to the many waterfront café-taverna hybrids serving ouzo and beer with pieces of grilled octopus, home-cured olives, and other *mezedes* (appetizers). Much of the ancient city lies under the modern, although the world-famous ancient Temple of Aphaia looms over the entire island from its hilltop perch. Although some unattractive contemporary buildings (and some less well-preserved older ones) mar the harborscape, a number of well-preserved neoclassic buildings and village houses are found on the backstreets. It takes between 60 and 90 minutes for ferries from Piraeus to dock at Souvala, a sleepy fishing village on the island's northern coast, or at the main port in Aegina town. Hydrofoils reach Aegina town in 40 minutes.

Aegina Archaeological Museum. This small but choice collection was the first to be established in Greece (1829). Finds from the famed Temple of Aphaia and excavations throughout the island, including early- and middle–Bronze Age pottery, are on display. Among the Archaic and classical works of art are the distinctive Ram Jug, depicting Odysseus and his crew fleeing the Cyclops, and a 5th-century BC sphinx, a votive monument with the head of a woman and a body that is half-eagle, half-lion. Aegina was one of the best schools of pottery and sculpture in antiquity and the exhibits here prove it. Just above the Archaeological Museum is the ancient site of the **Acropolis of Aegina**, the island's religious and political center. The settlement was first established in the Copper Age, and was renamed Kolona, or "column," in the Venetian era, after the only remaining pillar of the Temple of Apollo that once stood there. While in great disarray—11 successive cities once stood here—it remains a true treat for those into archaeology. Examine ruins and walls dating back to 1600–1300 BC, as well as Byzantine-era buildings. ⊠ *Harbor front, 350 ft from ferry dock, Aegina town* ☎ *22970/22248* 🖾 *€3* ☉ *Tues.–Sun. 8:30–3.*

Ayia Marina. The small, somewhat-overrun port of Ayia Marina has many hotels, cafés, restaurants, and a family-friendly beach with shallow waters. On the opposite side of the Ayia Marina harbor, you'll find small bays with deeper waters, ideal for diving. Ayia Marina is easily accessible by regular KTEL bus service from Aegina town (about 25-min drive). ⊠ *13 km (8 mi) east of Aegina town, via small paved road below Temple of Aphaia.*

NEED A BREAK?

Agora (*market*). Having a bite to eat at the *psaragora* (fish market) is a must in Aegina town. A small dish of grilled octopus at the World War II–era Taverna Agora is perfect with an ouzo—if you aren't averse to the smell of raw fish wafting over. Fishermen gather midafternoon and early evening in the pedestrianized street, worrying their beads while seated beside glistening octopus hung up to dry—as close to a scene from the film *Zorba the Greek* as you are likely to see in modern Greece. ⊠ *Covered fish market on Panayi Irioti, Aegina town* ☎ *22970/27308.*

Markelon Tower. During the negotiations for Greece during the War of Independence, Ioannis Kapodistrias, the first president of the country, conducted meetings in the Markelon Tower, dating back to the late 17th century. Today, the pink- and ochre-hued tower occasionally houses cultural events and exhibitions. ⊠ *Town center, Aegina town.*

Fodor's Choice ★ **Paliachora (*Old Town*).** The haunting remains of Aegina's medieval Paliachora (Old Town), built in the 9th century by islanders whose seaside town was the constant prey of pirates, are set on the rocky, barren hill above the monastery. Capital of the island until 1826, Paliachora has the romantic aura of a mysterious ghost town, a miniature Mistras that still has more than 30 churches (out of the original 365). They are mostly from the 13th century, and a number of them have been restored and are still in use. They sit amid the ruins of the community's houses abandoned by the inhabitants in the early 19th century. Episkopi (often closed), Ayios Giorgios, and Metamorphosi have lovely but faded (by dampness) frescoes. The frescoes of the church of Ayioi Anargyroi are especially fascinating because they are of pagan subjects, such as the mother goddess Gaia on horseback and Alexander the Great. The view from the castle on top of the hill to the beach of Souvala, on the other side of the island, is impressive. The massive Ayios Nektarios Monastery, 1 km (½ mi) west of Paliachora, is one of the largest in the Balkans. The memory of its saint is celebrated every year on his nameday, November 9th. ⊠ *7 km (4½ mi) south of Aegina town center* ☎ *22970/53802 Ayios Nectarios Monastery.*

🔆 **Perdika.** Follow the lead of the locals and visiting Athenians, and, for
Fodor's Choice an excursion, take a bus (a 25-minute ride from Ethneyersias Square)
★ to the pretty port village of Perdika to unwind and eat lunch at a seaside taverna. Places to eat in Perdika have multiplied over the years but are still low-key and have a strong island flavor, transporting you light-years away from the bustle of much of modern Greece. Try O Nontas, the first fish taverna after the bus station, for a meal on the canopied terrace overlooking the little bay, the sailing boats and the islet of Moni. Antonis, the famous fish tavern, draws big-name Athenians year-round. Across the bay, and only a short walk away, stands the sole modern building of a camera obscura. Inside, the cylindrical chamber allows the light to enter and projects an inverted image of the landscape outside—a technique that is now thought to have been used by many celebrated artists, including Leonardo and Vermeer. It is definitely worth a visit. ⊠ *9 km (5½ mi) south of Aegina town.*

Fodor's Choice **Temple of Aphaia.** One of the great glories of ancient Greek art, the
★ Temple of Aphaia is among the most extant examples of classical Doric architecture. Once adorned with an exquisite group of pedimental sculptures (now in the Munich Glyptothek) it still proudly bears 25 of its original 32 columns, which were either left standing or have been reconstructed. The structure is perched on a pine-clad promontory, offering superb views of Athens and Piraeus across the water—with binoculars you can see both the Parthenon and the Temple of Poseidon at Sounion. The saying goes that the ancient Greeks built the Temple of Aphaia in Aegina, the Parthenon in Athens, and the Temple of Poseidon at Sounion as the tips of a perfect equidistant triangle (called Antiquity's Perfect Triangle). This site has been occupied by many sanctuaries to Aphaia; the ruins visible today are those of the temple built in the early 5th century BC. Aphaia was apparently a pre-Hellenic deity, whose worship eventually converged with that of Athena.

You can visit the museum for no extra fee. The exhibit has a reconstructed section of the pediment of the temple, many fragments from the once brilliantly colored temple interior and the votive tablet (560 BC) on which is written that the temple is dedicated to the goddess Aphaia. From Aegina town, catch the KTEL bus for Ayia Marina on Ethneyersias Square, the main Aegina town bus station; ask the driver to let you off at the temple. A gift and snack bar across the road is a comfortable place to have a drink and wait for the return bus to Aegina town or for the bus bound for Ayia Marina and its pebbled beach. ⊠ *15 km (9 mi) east of Aegina town, Ayia Marina* ☎ *22970/32398* ⊕ *www.culture.*

4

An often overlooked wonder of ancient Greece, Aegina's Temple of Aphaia boasts more than 25 of its original 32 columns and spectacularly perches atop a promontory.

gr ⌂ *€4* ⊙ *Temple: Apr.–Nov., daily 8–8; Dec.–Mar., daily 8:15–3; museum: Tues.–Sun. 8:30–2:15.*

BEACHES

Kolona beach. Aegina town's beaches, notably the pine-surrounded Kolona beach, are pleasant enough with their shallow waters—and crowds. ⌂ *Near Kolona site.*

Marathonas beach. There's a good swimming spot at the sandy Marathonas A beach on the west side of the island, with sun beds and umbrellas available for hire and the Ammos and Ostria restaurants set right on the beach. Beyond the village lies another nice beach, Marathonas B. ⌂ *6 km [4 mi] south of Aegina town* ☎ *22970/28160 Ammos, 22970/27677 Ostria.*

Souvala. The sandy and pebbled beach of Souvala is one the nicest on the island and is famous for its therapeutic hot and cold springs. Located close to the Souvala village, it offers umbrellas, sun beds, and the Banio Banio beach bar. Elsewhere along the coastline here are many other spots where you can sunbathe and swim off the rocks. ⌂ *10 km [6 mi] north-east of Aegina town* ☎ *22970/54140* ⊕ *www.baniobanio.gr.*

WHERE TO EAT

$

GREEK

Fodor's Choice

★

✕ **Antonis.** Seafood is the word at this famed taverna run by Antonis and his sons. The octopus grilled in front of the establishment lures bathers and other visitors who tuck into options ranging from teeny fried smelt to enormous lobsters. People-watching is as much of a draw as the food, since the tables afford a view of all the comings and goings of the harbor's small boats as well as some sleek yachts. Other than splurging on the bouillabaisse here (expect to pay around €50 euros per kilo for sole, mullet, grouper—you name it), most dishes here, such as the veal and onions or "vegetables in the oven (*briam*)" rarely exceed more than €10. ✉ *Waterfront, Perdika* ☎ 22970/61443.

$$ ✕ **Kyriakakis.** This taverna is the old-
GREEK est and the most established one in Ayia Marina. In fact it has been here since 1950, when Kyriakos Haldaios brought out a gas stove and started frying fish and fries under the pine trees for local sunbathers. Today, the seafront taverna is owned by his grandson, also named Kyriakos, and offers traditional Greek specialties, like *moussaka,* the famous dish of layered eggplant and ground meat, and plenty of fresh fish, especially gilthead and sea bass. In the summer these are served in the spacious veranda overlooking the crystal blue waters. ✉ *Ayia Marina* ☎ 22970/32165 ⊕ *www.kyriakakis-aegina.gr.*

$$ ✕ **Vatzoulias.** Ask a local to name the best restaurant in Aegina, and the
GREEK response is invariably Vatzoulias. In summer the garden is a pleasant
Fodor's Choice oasis, scented with jasmine and honeysuckle; in winter, nestle inside
★ the cozy dining room. Eggplant in garlic sauce, and zucchini croquettes are can't-go-wrong starters. Continue with taverna classics such as veal in red sauce; thick, juicy grilled pork chops; or *pastitsio,* oven-baked pasta with minced meat enlivened with cinnamon and a wonderfully fluffy béchamel. In winter try the hare stew. A 10-minute walk from Aegina town center gets you to this rustic taverna where only dinner is served, please note, only three evenings a week. ✉ *Aphaias 75, Ayioi Asomatoi, Aegina town* ☎ 22970/22711 🍴 *Reservations essential* ▤ *No credit cards* ☾ *Closed Mon., Tues., Thurs., and Fri.*

WHERE TO STAY
For expanded hotel reviews, visit Fodors.com.

¢ 🏨 **Aeginitiko Archontiko.** Staying at this small pension within a neoclas-
Fodor's Choice sic house from the 1700s feels like a crash course in Greek history:
★ it's easy to imagine what living in Aegina in 1827 was like, when it became the first capital of the newborn nation and shipping minister Admiral Kountouriotis lived in this house; or later, at the beginning of the 1920s, when poet Kostas Varnalis resided here for two years and was visited by author Nikos Kazantzakis; and, today, when the historical roots of the terracotta-hue house come alive in the breathtaking murals of rooms on the first floor and in select antique furniture carefully placed in the public salons, the shady internal garden, and in the guest rooms. **Pros:** homey feeling; historic mansion; bright, feelgood colors; central location in town. **Cons:** no sea view; bathrooms look a bit tired and could do with a makeover. ✉ *Ayiou Nikolaou,*

BEACH BUMMED?

If Aegina's beaches don't wow you, climb aboard one of the many daily boats from Aegina's harbor to the smaller nearby isle of **Angistri**. Without cars, but with food, drink, and small coves to swim in, Angistri has a relaxed, out-of-the-way feel, and more than its share of lovely beaches. A closer alternative is the tiny Moni Island, which can be reached in less than 10 minutes from the fishing village of Perdika.

4

Thomaidou & Liakou 1, Aegina town ☎ *22970/24968* ⊕ *www.
aeginitikoarchontiko.gr* ⤳ *10 rooms* 🔥 *In-room: a/c* ❀ *Breakfast.*

¢ ☷ **Hotel Apollo.** Take advantage of this hotel's beautiful hillside location over a beach by relaxing on the restaurant terrace or renting a boat to water-ski in the clear blue waters; not surprisingly, guest rooms at this white, block-shaped hotel, built in a typical '70s style, all have balconies and sea views. **Pros:** panoramic views of the Saronic Gulf; pool with saltwater; crystal seawater. **Cons:** room decor is on the spartan side; rocky beach. ⊠ *Ayia Marina beach, Ayia Marina* ☎ *22970/32271, 210/323–4292 winter in Athens* ⊕ *www.apollohotel.gr* ⤳ *107 rooms* 🔥 *In-room: a/c. In-hotel: restaurant, pool, tennis court, business center* ⊙ *Closed Nov.–Mar.* ❀ *Breakfast.*

$ ☷ **Rastoni.** Quiet and secluded, this boutique hotel's peaceful quality is
Fodor's Choice heightened by the landscaped Mediterranean garden, which has pista-
★ chio trees, wood pergolas and benches, and rattan armchairs where you can curl up with a book or just spend the day staring out at sea. **Pros:** oh, those private verandas with panoramic views!; beautiful 4-poster beds; fabulous Mediterranean garden. **Cons:** few hotel facilities. ⊠ *Dimitriou Petriti 31, Aegina town* ☎ *22970/27039* ⊕ *www.rastoni.gr* ⤳ *11 studios* 🔥 *In-room: a/c, kitchen* ❀ *Breakfast.*

FESTIVALS

Panayia Chrysoleontissa. On the Assumption of the Virgin Mary, August 15th—the biggest holiday of the Catholic summer throughout Europe— a celebration is held at Panayia Chrysoleontissa, a mountain monastery built between 1403 and 1614. ⊠ *6 km [4 mi] east of Aegina town.*

Ayios Sostis. On September 6th and 7th, the feast of the martyr Sozon is observed with a two-day *paniyiri* (saint's day festival), celebrated at Ayios Sostis. ⊠ *9 km [5½ mi] south of Aegina town, Perdika.*

NIGHTLIFE

Aqua Loca. An Aegina mainstay since 1996, beach bar Aqua Loca promises delicious cocktails (ask for the house special), relaxing music, and magical sunsets. Consider nibbling on a *poikilia mezedon,* an hors d'oeuvre assortment, served until 7 pm. ⊠ *1½ km [1 mi] north of Aegina town, on road toward Perdika, on the Ayios Vasileios beach, Ayios Vasileios* ☎ *22970/28500.*

Avli. The ever-popular Avli serves delicious appetizers in a small courtyard, crowned by an impressively tall palm tree, that goes from café-bistro by day to bar (playing Latin rhythms) by night. Free Wi-Fi is available. ⊠ *Panayi Irioti 17, Aegina town* ☎ *22970/26438.*

Fodor's Choice **Inn on the Beach.** On the outskirts of Aegina town, the multileveled Inn
★ on the Beach draws an early crowd with its sunset seafront cocktails and chill-out music, before notching up the music to a beach-party tempo. ⊠ *1 km [½ mi] north of center, Aegina town* ☎ *22970/25116* ⊕ *www.innonthebeach.gr.*

SHOPPING

Aegina's famous pistachios, much coveted by Greeks, can be bought from stands along the town harbor. They make welcome snacks and gifts. A treat found at some of the Aegean town bakeries behind

Be at the regal Ayios Nekarios Monastery on November 9 to see the saint's day celebration, when the streets are covered with carpets and strewn with flowers.

the harbor is *amigdalota,* rich almond cookies sprinkled with orange flower water and powdered sugar. If you want to have a picnic lunch on the island or on the ferryboat while en route to another Saronic island, check out the luscious fruit displayed on several boats in the center of the harbor.

Animal Respect. Cheap secondhand items from lamps to undergarments can be found at the Animal Respect charity shop. Run by the nonprofit organization *Animal Protection Aegina-Angistri* that cares for stray animals on the islands, the shop also sells fashionable pet accessories. ⊠ *Panayi Irioti 73, behind town hall, Aegina town* ☎ *22970/27049* ⏰ *10–1:30.*

Ceramics Art Workshop. Martha Kottaki is a talented example of the new generation of Aegina potters, creating useful and elegant household items such as colorful salad bowls and country-chic fruit platters. ⊠ *33 Spyrou Rodi, Aegina town* ☎ *22970 shop, 22970 workshop.*

Eginaaigina. Naif paintings by local artists, monochromatic ceramics, and minimalist sculptures can be found in this petite yet refined art gallery. ⊠ *23 Aiakou str., Aegina town* ☎ *22970/23967* ⏰ *10:30–1:30, 6:30–9:30.*

Fistiki. Flip-flops, shoes, bikinis, jewelry, papier-mâché figures, dangling Turkish charms, and kitchenware form the rainbow of items available at Fistiki. The shop's small entrance opens into a maze of boxy rooms filled with everything you could possibly need to stay stylish on your trip. ⊠ *Panayi Irioti 15, Aegina town* ☎ *22970/28327.*

HYDRA ΥΔΡΑ

139 km (86 mi) south of Aegina town port.

As the full length of Hydra stretches before you when you round the easternmost finger of the northern Peloponnese, your first reaction might not, in fact, be a joyful one. Gray, mountainous, and barren, Idra (to use its alternative spelling) has the gaunt look of a saintly figure in a Byzantine icon. But as the island's curved harbor—one of the most picturesque in all of Greece—comes into view, delight will no doubt take over. Because of the nearly round harbor, the town is only visible from a perpendicular angle, a quirk in the island's geography that often saved the island from attack, since passing ships completely missed the port. Although there are traces of an ancient settlement, the island was sparsely inhabited until the Ottoman period. Hydra took part in the Greek War of Independence, begun in 1821, and by the early 19th century the island had developed an impressive merchant fleet, creating a surge in wealth and exposing traders to foreign cultures. Their trade routes stretched from the mainland to Asia Minor and even America.

In the middle of the 20th century the island became a haven for artists and writers like Arthur Miller, Canadian singer-songwriter Leonard Cohen, and the Norwegian novelist Axel Jensen. In the early 1960s, an Italian starlet named Sophia Loren emerged from Hydra's harbor waters in the Hollywood flick *Boy on a Dolphin*. The site of an annex of Athens's Fine Arts School, today Hydra remains a favorite haunt of new and established artists.

The arrival of world-famous contemporary art collector Dakis Ioannou (who set up an exhibition space at the island's former Slaughterhouse in 2009 for his Deste Foundation) means that Hydra is now a magnet for today's chic art crowd. Every summer, the opening night of the Slaughterhouse is one of the art world's most coveted invitations; modern art lovers flock here to catch a glimpse of the most avantgarde artworks, refreshed by the fresh Hydriot breeze. In summer there are ongoing art exhibitions in many venues around the island, from the town's schools (where curator Dimitris Antonitsis organizes his annual collaborative Hydra School Projects) to the Melina Merkouri exhibition space right by the Hydra harbor, opposite the hydrofoils' dock.The Hydra Workshop is a waterfront art space that puts together an annual exhibition inspired by the collection of London-based art patron Pauline Karpidas.

GETTING HERE AND AROUND

BOAT TRAVEL It takes about 90 minutes to get to Hydra by Flying Dolphin hydrofoil or catamaran. These depart from Gate E8 or E9 in the port of Piraeus. There are eight departures per day, during high season. Scheduled itineraries become scarcer during the winter months. The price of the ticket starts at €25.50 for economy class. The price of the ticket starts at €25.50 for economy class. The journey takes about two hours but can be longer, as stops are often made along the way on Poros. You can get detailed information about departures on the Web sites ⊕ *www.hellenicseaways.gr* or *www.ferries.gr*. Currently the only company that travels to Hydra is Hellenic Seaways. Due to high-season demand, it is best to make reservations for boat tickets on weekends.

MULE TRAVEL Famously, cars are not allowed on Hydra—and that means there are no public buses either! When you arrive, mule tenders in the port will rent you one of their fleet to carry your baggage—or better yet, you—to your hotel, for around €10 (make sure to agree on a price before you leave). Other modes of transportation include water taxis and bikes for rent—hotel concierges can give you information.

Visitor Information Greek National Tourism Organization ⊕ *www. visitgreece.gr.* **Hydra Municipality** ✉ *Town hall, Hydra* ☏ *22980/53003, 22980/52210* ⊕ *www.hydra.gov.gr.* **Hydra Police** ✉ *Port, Hydra town* ☏ *22980/52205*

EXPLORING

Although there are many reasons that Hydra may become endeared to you, not the least of them is the fact that all motor traffic is banned from the island (except for several rather noisy garbage trucks). After the racket of inner Athens and ear-splitting assaults on the eardrums by motorbikes in Aegina and Spetses, Hydra's blissful tranquillity, especially off-season, is a cause for rejoicing.

HYDRA TOWN ΥΔΡΑ ΠΟΛΗ

146 km (91 mi) south of Aegina.

Even though Hydra's beautiful harbor is flush with bars and boutiques, Hydra town seems as fresh and innocent as when it was "discovered." The two- and three-story gray and white houses with red tile roofs, many built from 1770 to 1821, climb the steep slopes around Hydra town harbor. The noble port and houses have been rescued and placed on the Council of Europe's list of protected monuments, with strict ordinances regulating construction and renovation. Although Hydra has a landmass twice the size of Spetses, only a fraction is habitable, and after a day or so on the island, faces begin to look familiar—and not just because you saw them in last month's *Vanity Fair*.

All motor traffic is banned from the island (except for several rather noisy garbage trucks). When you arrive by boat, mule tenders in the port will rent you one of their fleet to carry your baggage—or better yet, you—to your hotel, for around €10. ■TIP➜ Make sure to agree on a price before you leave. Mule transport is the time-honored and most practical mode of transport up to the crest; you may see mules patiently hauling anything from armchairs and building materials to cases of beer.

Church of the Dormition. Founded in 1643 as a monastery, the Church of the Dormition has since been dissolved and the monks' cells are now used to house municipal offices and the small **ecclesiastical museum Ayios Makarios Notaras.** The church's most noticeable feature is an ornate, triple-tier bell tower made of Tinos marble, likely carved in the early 19th century by traveling artisans. There's also an exquisite marble iconostasis. ⊠ *Along central section of harbor front, Hydra town* ☎ *22980/54071 museum* ⬚ *Church: donations accepted; museum: €2* ⊙ *Church: daily 10–2 and 5–8; museum: Mar.–Oct., Tues.–Sun.10–2.*

Hydra Historical Archives and Museum. Housed in an impressive mansion, this collection of historical artifacts and paintings has exhibits that date back to the 18th century. Heirlooms from the Balkan wars as well as from World War I and II are exhibited in the ground floor lobby. A small first-floor room contains figureheads from ships that fought in the 1821 War of Independence. There are old pistols and navigation aids, as well as portraits of the island's heroes and a section devoted to traditional local costume, including the dark *karamani,* pantaloons worn by Hydriot men. There are also temporary Greek-art exhibits showcased from time to time. ⊠ *On east end of harbor, Hydra town* ☎ *22980/52355* ⊕ *www.iamy.gr* ⬚ *€5* ⊙ *Daily 9–4 and 7:30–9:30.*

Kamini. A small fishing hamlet built around a shallow inlet, Kamini has much of Hydra town's charm but none of its bustle—except on Orthodox Good Friday, when the entire island gathers here to follow the funerary procession of Christ. On a clear day, the Peloponnese coast is plainly visible across the water, and spectacular at sunset. Take the 20-minute stroll from Hydra town west; a paved coastal track gives way to a staggered, white path lined with fish tavernas; Kamini's small beach also has restaurants nearby, which you can spot arriving by boat or sea taxi. ⊠ *1 km (½ mi) west of Hydra town.*

★ **Lazaros Koundouriotis Mansion.** Impressed by the architecture they saw abroad, shipowners incorporated many of the foreign influences into their *archontika,* old, gray-stone mansions facing the harbor. The forbidding, fortresslike exteriors are deliberately austere, the combined result of the steeply angled terrain and the need for buildings to blend into the gray landscape. One of the finest examples of this Hydriot architecture is the Lazaros Koundouriotis Mansion, built in 1780 and beautifully restored in the 1990s as a branch of Greece's National Historical Museum. The interior is lavish, with hand-painted ceiling borders, gilt moldings, marquetry, and floors of black-and-white marble tiles. Some rooms have pieces that belonged to the Koundouriotis family, who played an important role in the War of Independence; other rooms have exhibits of costumes, jewelry, wood carvings, and pottery from the National Museum of Folk History. The basement level has three rooms full of paintings by Periklis Vyzantinos and his son, friends of the Koundouriotis family ⊠ *On a graded slope over port, on west headland, Hydra town* ☎ *22980/52421* ⊕ *www.nhmuseum. gr* ⬚ *€4* ⊙ *Mar.–Oct., Tues.–Sun.10–2, 5:30–8:30.*

★ **Slaughterhouse/DESTE Foundation Project Space.** Internationally renowned modern art collector Dakis Ioannou acquired this former Hydra slaughterhouse, located a leisurely 10-min walk from the town (towards Mandraki), in 2009 to host artistic events and projects organized by his budding Deste Foundation. Surprisingly, this is not what a chic and modern art gallery is supposed to look like: housed in an unassuming small building on a cliff by the sea, it is not difficult to miss if you don't actively look for it. But perhaps that is exactly the point that Ioannou wanted to make with the Slaughterhouse, which has already acquired a leading role in Hydra's cultural life. Starting with the 2009 multimedia project "Blood of Two" by Matthew Barney and Elizabeth Peyton (which paid homage to the space's morbid past) and the collaboration of Doug Aitken with actress Chloë Sevigny in the video installation "Black Mirror," every summer the space is now assigned to a different artist who is invited to stage a site-specific exhibition. ⊠ *10-min walk along the port, towards Mandraki, Hydra town* ☎ *No phone in Hydra* ⊕ *www.deste.gr* ⊠ *Free* ⊘ *Wed.–Mon., 11–1 and 7–10.*

Vlichos. From Kamini, the coastal track continues to Vlichos, another pretty village with tavernas, a historic bridge, and a gray-pebbled beach on a bay. It's a 5-minute water-taxi ride from the Hydra town port or a 40-minute walk (25 minutes past Kamini). ⊠ *6 km (4 mi) west of Hydra town.*

OFF THE
BEATEN
PATH

Hydra's monasteries. If you're staying for more than a day, you have time to explore Hydra's monasteries. Hire a mule (the donkey rank is located just outside the Alpha Bank in the western corner of Hydra's harbor; be sure to check prices with the muleteers first, as these can soar to more than €70 for some routes) for the ascent up Mt. Klimaki, where you can visit the **Profitis Ilias Monastery** (about two hours on foot from Hydra town) and view the embroidery work of an inhabitant of the nearby nunnery of **Ayia Efpraxia.** Experienced hikers might be tempted to set off for the **Zourvas Monastery** at Hydra's tip. It's a long and difficult hike, but compensation comes in the form of spectacular views and a secluded cove for a refreshing dip. An alternative: hire a water taxi to Zourvas.

The convent of **Ayios Nikolaos Monastery** is to the southeast of Hydra town, after you pass between the monasteries of Ayios Triadas and Ayias Matronis (the latter can be visited). Stop here for a drink and a sweet (a donation is appropriate), and to see the beautiful 16th-century icons and frescoes in the sanctuary. When hiking, wear sturdy walking shoes, and in summer start out early in the morning—even when traveling by mule—to minimize exposure to the midday sun. Your reward: stunning vistas over the island (resplendent with wildflowers and herbs in spring), the western and eastern coasts, and nearby islets on the way to area monasteries. ☎ *22980/53690 Water taxi info* ⌒ *Donkey rank on the western corner of the harbor, water taxis also in front of Alpha Bank.*

BEACHES

Hydronetta. At Hydronetta beach bar the gray crags have been blasted and laid with cement to form sundecks. Sunbathing, view gazing, and socializing at the beach bar may take priority over swimming, but old-timers can attest to the fact that diving off the rocks into the deep water is truly exhilarating. If in need of a snack, try a hearty club sandwich or the Mediterranean salad. ⊠ *Western edge of harbor, Hydra town.*

Southern Coast. Boats ferry bathers from Hydra town harbor near the Mitropolis church to pebble beaches on the island's southern coast, including **Bisti** and **Ayios Nikolaos,** where there are sun beds and umbrellas at a charge (starting at €3). The latter is located on the back side of the island, facing the Aegean Sea, and is the largest organized beach on the island. Large boats heading to and from here have set fees posted for particular other beaches on the island; water taxis, whose rates you should negotiate in advance, start at €12.

WHERE TO EAT

$$$

MEDITERRANEAN

Fodor'sChoice

★

✕ **Castello Bar and Restaurant.** Set right on Kamini beach, this fully reno-vated 18th-century fortress is now a popular bar-restaurant. Its mul-tilevel café serves breakfast, coffee, drinks, and snacks and is the ideal spot for enjoying Hydra sunsets. Just a leisurely 15-minute-walk from the port (or 5 minutes by mule or 1 minute by water taxi), the reward is some of the most fortifying dining on the island. Chef Nikos Baxeva-nis's casual but tasty menu includes tagliatelle with vegetable and chevre cheese, *cod frites* (a more refined version of English fish-and-chips), and stuffed burgers. You can come in early and have breakfast or you can try the best apple martini on the island later. Hiring a sun bed for the day right in front of Castello will set you back €5. ⊠ *Kamini beach, Hydra town* ☎ *22980/54101* ⊕ *www.castellohydra.gr* ⌂ *Reservations essential* ⊘ *Closed Dec.–Feb.*

$$

MEDITERRANEAN

Fodor'sChoice

★

✕ **Enalion.** The charming young duo of new owners—Yiannis and Panos—have imbued this beach taverna next to Vlichos beach with energy and attentive service. The recently renovated all-white (with cool blue undertones) surroundings contrast gloriously with the injec-tion of color from the surrounding pink bougainvillea. The traditional taverna fare includes favorite Greek dishes like fried tomato balls, beetroot salad, fried calamari, and stuffed tomatoes and peppers. All go perfectly with a glass of house wine and the accompanying relaxing tunes. ⊠ *2½ km (1½ mi) west of Hydra town, 100 ft from beach, Vli-chos* ☎ *22980/53455* ⊕ *www.enalion-hydra.gr* ⊘ *Closed Dec.–Mar.*

$$$$

GREEK

Fodor'sChoice

★

✕ **Kodylenia's.** Fantasy: a whitewashed fisherman's cottage on a prom-ontory overlooking the little harbor of Kaminia, with a veranda ter-race charmingly set with folkloric pennants and communal tables—the perfect perch to catch some sublime sunsets. Reality: Kodylenia's, an irresistibly alluring (if a little pricey) place that has enraptured town folk and off-duty billionaires alike. Talk a look at the Web site's slide show to see what all the fuss is about (get set for a 2-minute Greek vacation). When there, peek into the kitchen below the terrace to see what's cooking: a whole fish may be char grilling and, when available, order *kritamos* (rock samphire, a vegetation which grows on the island's rocky coast), the urchin salad, or share an order of

Hydra is a shore thing—who needs a beach when you have waters as electric-blue as this?

fresh caught grilled squid in tomato sauce. The views are delicious and so are the *kolokythokeftedes*, fried zucchini balls. ⊠ *1 km (½ mi) west of Hydra town, on headland above harbor, Kaminia* ☎ *22980/53520* ⊕ *www.hydra-kodylenia.gr* ▭ *No credit cards* ⊗ *Closed Nov.–Mar.*

$$
GREEK
Fodor's Choice
★
✕**Kyria Sofia-Leonidas.** "By reservation only" is the 11th commandment here, one that is strictly followed: no reservations means this tiny taverna stays closed. That is one scenario they never have to worry about, as the oldest restaurant on Hydra remains wildly popular. Sporting bright green, original woodwork inside and, outside, a terrace with half a dozen tables (quickly snapped up by those in the know), this place is owned by Leonidas, who lived in New York for many years and is more than happy to share his culinary stories as he serves your meal (his partner Panayiota is cooking in the little kitchen that's open to the dining room). Don't miss out on the small cheese pies with cinnamon, the eggplant salad, the roasted goat, or the fresh salads. ⊠ *Miaouli 60, past Miranda hotel, Kala Pigadia, Hydra town* ☎ *22980/53097* ◿ *Reservations essential* ▭ *No credit cards* ⊗ *Closed mid-Jan.–mid-Mar. No lunch (except big parties).*

$$$$
MEDITERRANEAN
✕**Omilos.** The spot where Aristotle Onassis and Maria Callas once danced is now a vision in minimalist island white, reopened in 2007 by one of Enalion's owners. Tables nestle in the small, high-ceiling Hydra Nautical Club and wind around the deck outside, which affords an exquisite sea view. The setting is romantic at this pricey gourmet bar restaurant offering an extensive salad menu and tempting starters such as Greek caviar with fava bean mash and caramelized onions. Try the extremely moist grilled salmon with wild rice and vegetables or select from six different sauces for your grilled meats. After dinner,

Continued on page 200

EAT LIKE A GREEK

Hailed for its healthfulness, heartiness, and eclectic spicing, Greek cuisine remains one of the country's greatest gifts to visitors. From gyros to galaktoboureko, moussaka to myzthira, and soutzoukakia to snails, food in Greece is rich, exotic, and revelatory.

To really enjoy communal meals of fresh fish, mama's casseroles, flavorful salads, house wine, and great conversation, keep two ground rules in mind.

ORDER LIKE A NATIVE

Go for *tis oras* (grilled fish and meat "of the hour") or *piato tis imeras* (or "plate of the day," often stews, casseroles, and pastas). Remember that fish is always expensive, but avoid frozen selections and go for the freshest variety by asking the waitstaff what the day's catch is (you can often inspect it in the kitchen). Note that waiters in Greece tend to be impatient—so don't waffle while you're ordering.

DINE LIKE A FAMILY

Greeks share big plates of food, often piling bites of *mezedes*, salads, and main dishes on small dishes. It's okay to stick your fork into communal platters but not in each other's personal dishes (unless you're family or dear friends).

(top) lunching alfresco; (bottom) Kadalee with cinnamon

GRECIAN BOUNTY

Can't understand the menu? Just point!

Greece is a country of serious eaters, which is why there are so many different kinds of eateries here. Here is a list of types to seek out.

Estiatorio: You'll often find fine tablecloths, carefully placed silverware, candles, and multipage menus at an *estiatorio*, or restaurant; menus range from traditional to nouvelle.

Oinomageirio: Now enjoying a retro resurgence, these simple eateries were often packed with blue-collar workers filling up on casseroles and listening to *rembetika*, Greece's version of the blues.

Taverna: This is vintage Greece—family-style eateries noted for great spreads of grilled meat *tis oras* (of the hour), thick-cut fried potatoes, dips, salads, and wine—all shared around a big table and with a soundtrack of *bouzouki* music.

Psarotaverna: Every bit like a regular taverna, except the star of the menu is fresh fish. Remember that fish usually comes whole; if you want it filleted, ask *"Mporo na exo fileto?"* Typical fish varieties include *barbounia* (red mullet), *perka* (perch), *sardella* (sardine), *bakaliaros* (cod), *lavraki* (sea bass), and *tsipoura* (sea bream).

Mezedopoleia: In this Greek version of tapas bars, you can graze on a limited menu of dips, salads, and hot

and cold mezedes. Wildly popular with the pre-nightclub crowd.

Ouzeri and Rakadiko: *Ouzo* and the Cretan firewater *raki* (also known as *tsikoudia*) are the main attractions here, but there's always a generous plate of hot or cold mezedes to go with the spirits. A mix of old-timers and young scenesters make for great people-watching.

Kafeneio (café): Coffee rules here—but the food menu is usually limited to sandwiches, crepes, *tiropites* (cheese pies), and *spanakopites* (spinach pies).

Zacharoplasteio (patisserie): Most dessert shops are "to go," but some old-style spots have a small klatch of tables to enjoy coffee and that fresh slice of *galaktoboureko* (custard in phyllo dough).

FOR THOSE ON THE GO

Greeks are increasingly eating on the run, since they're working longer (right through the afternoon siesta that used to be a mainstay) and happy that eateries have adapted to this lifestyle change. *Psitopoleia* (grill shops) have the most popular takeaway food: the wrapped-in-pita *souvlaki* (pork, lamb, or chicken chunks), *gyros* (slow-roasted slabs of pork and lamb, or chicken), or *kebabs* (spiced, grilled ground meat). Tzatziki, onions, tomatoes, and fried potatoes are also tucked into the pita. Toasted sandwiches and tasty hot dogs are other satisfying options.

Gyros: a take-away treat

ON THE GREEK TABLE

Mezedes Μεζέδες **(appetizers):** Eaten either as a first course or as full meals, they can be hot (pickled octopus, chickpea fritters, dolmades, fried squid) or cold (dips like *tzatziki*; *taramosalata*, puree of salted mullet roe and potato; or the spicy whipped feta called *htipiti*). Start with two or three, then keep ordering to your heart's content.

Salata Σαλάτα **(salad):** No one skips salads here since the vegetables burst with flavor, texture, and aroma. The most popular is the *horiatiki*, or what the rest of the world calls a "Greek salad"—this country-style salad has tomato, onion, cucumber, feta, and Kalamata olives. Other popular combos include *maroulosalata* (lettuce tossed with fresh dill and fennel) and the Cretan *dakos* (bread rusks topped with minced tomato, feta, and onion).

Kyrios Piato Κύριο Πιάτο **(main course):** Main dishes were once served family-style, like mezedes, but the plates are now offered as single servings at many restaurants. Some places serve the dishes as they are ready while more Westernized eateries bring all the plates out together. Order all your food at the same time, but be sure to tell the waiter if you want your main dishes to come after the salads and mezedes. Most grilled meat dishes come with a side of thick-cut fried potatoes, while seafood and casseroles such as *moussaka* are served alone. *Horta*, or boiled greens, drenched in lemon, are the ideal side for grilled or fried fish.

Epidorpio Επιδόρπιο **(dessert):** Most restaurants give diners who have finished their meals a free plate of fresh seasonal fruit or some homemade *halva* (a cinnamony semolina pudding-cake with raisins).

Krassi Κρασί **(wine):** Greeks almost always have wine with a meal, usually sharing a carafe or two of *hima* (barrel or house wine) with friends. Bitter resinated wine, or *retsina*, has become less common in restaurants. Instead, the choice is often a dry Greek white wine that goes well with seafood or poultry.

Psomi Ψωμί **(bread):** Bread, often pita-fashion, always comes with a meal and usually costs 1 to 2 euros—a *kouver* (cover) charge—regardless of whether you eat it.

Nero Νερό **(water):** If you ask for water, waitstaff will usually bring you a big bottle of it—and charge you, of course. If you simply want tap water (free and safe to drink) ask for a *kanata*—or a pitcher.

Tzatziki (cucumber in yogurt)

Horiatiki (Greek salad)

Sardines with rice, potatoes, and salad

Moussaka

Galaktoboureko (custard-filled phyllo pastry)

LIKE MAMA USED TO MAKE

Nearly all Greek restaurants have the same homey dishes that have graced family dinner tables here for years. However, some of these dishes are hardly ever ordered by locals, who prefer to eat them at home—most Greeks just avoid moussaka and pastitsio unless they're made fresh that day. So if you order the following foods at restaurants, make sure to ask if they're fresh ("*tis imeras*").

■ **DOLMADES**—grape leaves stuffed with rice and herbs

■ **KOTOPOULO LEMONATO** —whole chicken roasted with thickly sliced potatoes, lemon, and oregano

■ **MOUSSAKA**—a casserole of eggplant and spiced beef topped with béchamel

■ **PASTITSIO**—tube-shaped pasta baked with spiced beef, béchamel, and cheese

Best bet: Grape leaves

■ **PSARI PLAKI**—whole fish baked with tomato, onions, garlic, and olive oil

■ **SOUPA AVGOLEMONO**— an egg-lemon soup with a chicken stock base

4

IN FOCUS EAT LIKE A GREEK

COFFEE CULTURE

Greek coffee: tiny but strong

A *kafeneio* coffeehouse

Greeks go out for coffee not because of caffeine addiction but because they like to spend at least two hours mulling the world with their friends. *Kafeneia*, or old-style coffeehouses, are usually full of courtly old men playing backgammon and sipping tiny but strong cups of *elliniko* (Greek coffee). Modern cafés (*kafeterias*) are more chic, packed with frappé-loving office workers, freddo-swilling college students, and arty hipsters nursing espressos. Order your coffee *sketos* (without sugar), *metrios* (medium sweet), or *glykos* (sweet).

■ **Frappé**—a frothy blend of instant coffee (always Nescafé), cold water, sugar, and evaporated milk

■ **Elliniko**—the strong traditional coffee made from Brazilian beans ground into a fine powder

Frappé

■ **Freddo**—an iced cappuccino or espresso

■ **Nes**—instant coffee, often served with froth

the owners will treat you to a glass of limoncello, or you can try the strawberry daquiri and mojito at the lively bar. ✉ *Hydra port, on the way to Hydronetta* ☎ *22980/ 53800* ⊕ *www.omilos-hydra.com* ⚏ *Reservations essential* ⊙ *Closed Mon.–Thurs. Oct.–Apr.*

$$$
GREEK
★

✕ **To Geitoniko.** Christina and her husband, Manolis, cook home-style Greek dishes in a typical old Hydriot house with stone floors and wooden ceilings, where time seems to have been standing still since the '50s. Try the octopus *stifado* (stew) with pearl onions; cuttlefish in wine sauce; beef with

quince; or eggplant stuffed with ground meat. Grilled meats and fresh fish, including the island's own calamari, are also available. Scrumptious desserts include baklava and two types of halvah. It's a good idea to arrive before 9 pm for dinner; there are only 20 tables under the open-air vine-covered pergola upstairs, and they fill up quick. ✉ *Spiliou Harami, opposite Pension Antonis, Hydra town* ☎ *22980/53615* ▭ *No credit cards* ⊙ *Closed Dec.–Feb.*

WHERE TO STAY

$$$
★

▦ **Bratsera Hotel.** An 1860 sponge factory was transformed into this charming character hotel (doors made out of old packing crates still bearing the "Piraeus sponge" stamp, etc.) **Pros:** helpful staff; regular clientele returns year after year; the relaxing-by-the-pool experience. **Cons:** some basic, tired rooms; some small dark bathrooms; hard beds. ✉ *On left leaving port, Hydra town* ☎ *22980/53971, 22980/52794 restaurant* ⊕ *www.bratserahotel.com* ⇌ *17 rooms, 8 suites* ⚏ *In-room: a/c, Wi-Fi. In-hotel: restaurant, bar, pool, laundry facilities, business center* ⊙ *Closed mid-Oct.–Mar.* ⦿ *Breakfast.*

$$$
▦ **Four Seasons Hotel.** No, this is not one of the famous chain's hotels but a tiny (6-room) hotel inspired by the magical colors of the four seasons (the Sun Suite is the cream of the crop) sweetly set in an atmospheric, fully-renovated 150-year-old stone mansion in Vlichos (a 35-minute walk from the port or 5 minutes via water taxi or boat), right next to the pebbled Plakes beach. **Pros:** alluring interiors; next to the beach; homey feeling. **Cons:** challenging distance from town; pricey. ✉ *Vlichos beach, Vlichos* ☎ *22980/53698* ⊕ *www.fourseasonshydra.gr* ⇌ *6 suites* ⚏ *In-room: a/c, kitchen, Internet, Wi-Fi. In-hotel: restaurant* ⊙ *Closed Nov.–late Mar.* ⦿ *Breakfast.*

$$$
▦ **Hotel Hydra.** Situated in an idyllic setting, this boutique establishment of eight relaxing, modern, and beautifully decorated guest rooms features suites with panoramic views of the port and separate living and bedroom areas (as well as a small kitchenette). **Pros:** looks more like small apartment studios rather than rooms; great views; friendly hostess; clean beach towel provided daily. **Cons:** climbing about 150

stairs to get to the hotel from port means that hiring a mule might be necessary if you are carrying a lot of luggage; a bit expensive; not all rooms have panoramic views of the harbor, so make sure you ask in advance if that is what you want. ✉ *Petrou Voulgari 8(close to the Lazaros Koundouriotis mansion), Hydra town* ☎ *22980/53420* ⊕ *www.hydrahotel.gr* ⇆ *6 suites* ⬠ *In-room: a/c, kitchen, Wi-Fi. In-hotel: bar, laundry facilities* ☾ *Closed Nov.–late Mar.* ❍| *Breakfast.*

$$$ ⛵ **Hotel Leto Hydra.** Right in the middle of Hydra town, this small upscale hotel has a sparkling new renovation inside with an elegant "old Greece" touch provided by an array of antique Hydriot rugs, mirrors, and lanterns—and some modern artworks by well-known Greek painters (Papanikolaou and Akrithakis to name two) thrown in to liven things up. **Pros:** the distinguished feel of an old mansion; spacious, shady rooms; marble bathrooms. **Cons:** a bit pricey; no views and no significant outside spaces; might be difficult to find on your own (ask for directions at the harbor port). ✉ *Town center, Hydra town* ☎ *22980/53385* ⊕ *www.letohydra.gr* ⇆ *30* ⬠ *In-room: a/c, Wi-Fi. In-hotel: gym, laundry facilities, business center* ☾ *Closed Nov.–mid-Mar.* ❍| *Breakfast.*

$ ⛵ **Miranda Hotel.** Antique-lovers might feel right at home among the
★ 18th- and 19th-century furniture and decor (Oriental rugs, wooden chests, nautical engravings, ceilings painted in detailed Venetian motifs) decorating this traditional Hydriot home, built around 1810 for a Captain Danavasis and now classified by the Ministry of Culture as a national monument—for a change of pace they can head to the main salon, whose walls are hung with giant black and white photographs, or go outside to a garden lush with pink and red blossoms. **Pros:** peaceful garden; precious artworks on display. **Cons:** somewhat dated and smallish bathrooms; thin doors do not provide enough sound insulation. ✉ *Miaouli, 2 blocks inland from port center, Hydra town* ☎ *22980/52230* ⊕ *www.mirandahotel.gr* ⇆ *12 rooms, 2 suites* ⬠ *In-room: a/c, Wi-Fi* ☾ *Closed Nov.–Feb.* ❍| *Breakfast.*

$$ ⛵ **Orloff Boutique Hotel.** Commissioned in 1796 by Catherine the Great
Fodor'sChoice for her lover Count Orloff, who came to Greece with a Russian fleet
★ to try to dislodge the Turks, this *archontiko* mansion retains its splendor, with antiques in the public (and some private) rooms carefully chosen—curvaceous walnut sofas, chairs, dining sets, and highboys; old paintings and lithographs; and gilt mirrors—and beautifully offset by thick white walls and cornflower-blue window wells. **Pros:** homey feeling; friendly owners; refurbished bathrooms; lovely decor. **Cons:** a bit noisy air-conditioning; no balconies. ✉ *Rafalia 9 and Votsi, 350 ft from port, Hydra town* ☎ *22980/52564* ⊕ *www.orloff.gr* ⇆ *5 rooms, 4 suites* ⬠ *In-room: a/c, a/c in bedroom only (for rentals only), Wi-Fi. In-hotel: bar, business center* ☾ *Closed Nov.–late Mar.* ❍| *Breakfast.*

FESTIVALS

Municipal Events. Status as a weekend destination has made Hydra a popular venue for all sorts of events, from international puppet festivals and art exhibitions to sailing events and regattas. Exhibitions, concerts, and performances are usually held June–August; details are available from the municipality. The International Rembetika music festival takes place here in October. Plus the new and ever-growing contemporary art scene here is sure to to be highlighted with happenings that will draw an international crowd. ⊠ *Main street, Hydra town* ☎ *22980/52210, 22980/53003* ⊕ *www.hydra.gov.gr.*

Fodor's Choice   **Miaoulia.** The island celebrates its crucial role in the War of Indepen-
★   dence with the Miaoulia, which takes place the last weekend of June. At around 10 o' clock on Saturday night, Hydra's small port goes dark and a journey into history commences as the day's festivities culminate in a reenactment of the night Admiral Miaoulis loaded a vessel with explosives and sent it upwind to the Turkish fleet back in 1821. Naturally, the model enemy's ship goes down in flames. Fireworks, music, traditional dancing, and sports competitions all accompany the burning of the fleet, a glorious part of Hydra's Naval Week.

NIGHTLIFE

Amalour. On the ground floor of an early-19th-century mansion, Amalour attracts a thirtysomething crowd who sip expertly made cocktails (especially the exquisite daquiris) and listen to ethnic, jazz, soul, and funk music. ⊠ *Tombazi St., behind port, Hydra town* ☎ *22980/29680* ⊕ *www.amalour.com.*

Hydronetta. The minuscule Hydronetta bar restaurant has an enchanting view from its perch above the harbor. Embraced by rocks and surrounded by water, it is jam-packed during the day and it is *the* place to enjoy a glass of chilled beer or fruity long drink at sunset. Hydronetta's trademark is its "Full Moon" parties, fun-filled events under Hydra's starlit skies. ⊠ *West of Hydra town, on the way to Kamini, past the Canons* ☎ *22980/54160.*

Fodor's Choice   **The Pirate Bar.** Café-bar Pirate has been a fixture of the island's nightlife
★   since the late 1970s. It got a face-lift, added some mainstream dance hits to its rock music–only playlist, and remains popular and raucous. The spot is actually open all day with delicious home-cooked dishes (burgers, salads, and lemon pies) but it is at night that the fun really takes off, often with the help of one of the popular house drinks, such as the fruity Tropical Sun. ⊠ *South end of harbor, Hydra town* ☎ *22980/52711.*

Spilia. Tucked into the seaside rocks just below the Hydronetta bar, Spilia provides a nice escape from the midday sun and is a popular nocturnal haunt, too. It offers both coffee and drinks; the daquiris are excellent. ☎ *22980/54166* ⊕ *www.spiliacafe.com.*

SHOPPING

Elena Votsi. Worth a visit, the stylish store of local jewelry designer Elena Votsi showcases her exquisite handmade pieces—more works of art than accessories. Her designs sell well in Europe and New York. ⊠ *Ikonomou 3, Hydra town* ☎ *22980/52637* ⊕ *www.elenavotsi.com.*

Speak Out. This boutique is so hip the owners run a way-cool art and fashion blog (⊕ *speakouthydra.blogspot.com*). ⊠ *Hydra harbor* ☎ *22980/52099.*

Have mule, will travel—keep in mind that Hydra, blessedly, is a carless universe.

Spoiled!. Hydra's trendoisie head to Spoiled! for a top selection of glamorous evening togs in the latest fashion. ✉ *Tombazi St., Hydra town* ☎ *22980/52363* ⊕ *www.spoiled-shop.gr.*

SPETSES ΣΠΕΤΣΕΣ

24 km (15 mi) southwest of Hydra town port.

Spetses shows evidence of continuous habitation through all of antiquity. From the 16th century, settlers came over from the mainland and, as on Hydra, they soon began to look to the sea, building their own boats. They became master sailors, successful merchants, and, later, in the Napoleonic Wars, skilled blockade runners, earning fortunes that they poured into building larger boats and grander houses. With the outbreak of the War of Independence in 1821, the Spetsiots dedicated their best ships and brave men (and women) to the cause.

GETTING HERE AND AROUND

BOAT TRAVEL Hellenic Seaways' Flying Dolphins hydrofoils and catamarans travel regularly, year-round, from Piraeus (Gate E8 or E9) to Spetses (usually stopping at Poros and Hydra as well). There are half a dozen such daily rounds from April to October, and fewer the rest of the year. You can get to Spetses (€35 economy class) in just under two hours. Make reservations ahead of time—boats fill quickly. You can get detailed info about ferries' departures on the Web sites ⊕ *www.hellenicseaways.gr* or *www. ferries.gr.* Other boat companies that connect with the island include Hellenic Seaways. The island of Spetses is so close to the Peloponnese mainland that you also can drive to the small port of Costa (200 km

[124 mi] drive from Athens), park you car, and ferry across the channel in any of a number of caïques (price at around €5 per person, but you have to wait for the boat to fill up before it leaves for the 20-minute crossing) or water taxi (price negotiable; expect to pay around €30 in total for a 5-minute crossing). For more information on the crossings, contact the Spetses Port Authority (☎ 22980/72245). For water taxi information, call ☎ 22980/72072.

BUS TRAVEL Only homeowners are usually allowed to bring cars on the island. Visitors must hire bikes, scooters, mopeds, water taxis, or use one of the two high-season-only (Easter–May; June–September) municipal buses: one bus line goes from Ayios Mamas beach to Ayii Anaryiri, the other, with nearly hourly departures during the day, from Poseidonion Grand Hotel to Ligoneri and Vrellos beach. Tickets range from €1 to €3. Cars can be brought on the island if a special permit is granted. For bus schedule information you can contact the two bus drivers directly on their mobile phones (for Ayios Mamas and Ayoi Anargyroi, call Anargyros Kotzias at ☎ 6944/802536; for Ligoneri and Vrellos, call Konstantinos Mouratis at ☎ 6978/949722). It is worth going on one of the buses if only for taking in the scenic route.

Visitor Information Greek National Tourism Organization ⊕ *www. visitgreece.gr.* **Spetses Municipality** ✉ *Town hall, Spetses* ☎ *22980/72255, 22983/20010 info line (8:00–3:00)* ⊕ *www.spetses.gr.* **Spetses Police** ✉ *Hatziyianni-Mexi, near museum, Spetses town* ☎ *22980/73744, 22980/73100.*

EXPLORING

In the years leading up to the revolution, Hydra's great rival and ally was the island of Spetses. Lying at the entrance to the Argolic Gulf, off the mainland, Spetses was known even in antiquity for its hospitable soil and verdant pine tree–covered slopes. The pines on the island today, however, were planted by a Spetsiot philanthropist dedicated to restoring the beauty stripped by the shipbuilding industry in the 18th and 19th centuries. There are far fewer trees than there were in antiquity, but the island is still well watered, and the many prosperous Athenians who have made Spetses their second home compete to have the prettiest gardens and terraces. Today's visitor can enjoy spotting this verdant beauty all over the island.

SPETSES TOWN ΣΠΕΤΣΕΣ ΠΟΛΗ

91 km (56 mi) southwest of Hydra.

By most visitors' standards, Spetses town is small—no larger than most city neighborhoods—yet it's divided into districts. Kastelli, the oldest quarter, extends toward Profitis Ilias and is marked by the 18th-century Ayia Triada church, the town's highest point. The area along the coast to the north is known as Kounoupitsa, a residential district of pretty cottages and gardens with pebble mosaics in mostly nautical motifs. A water-taxi ride here from Kosta, across the channel on the mainland, takes about 15 minutes.

Analipsi. Walk along the coast to Analipsi, the old fisherman's village. At Easter, instead of setting off fireworks at midnight to celebrate the resurrection, local tradition dictates that a boat is set afire and put out to sea. Excavations here unearthed pottery shards and coins from the 7th century. ⊠ *1 km (½ mi) south of Spetses town.*

Fodor's Choice ★ **Anargyrios and Korgialenios School.** Known as the inspiration for the school in John Fowles's *The Magus*, this institution was established in 1927 as an English-style boarding school for the children of Greece's Anglophilic upper class. Up until 2010, tourism management students studied amid the elegant amphitheaters, black-and-white-tile floors, and huge windows. Today, the tourism students have relocated to Piraeus, the buildings are let for private seminars and events, but visitors can still take a peek (free) inside the school and stroll around the fabulous gardens throughout the year. ⊠ *½ km (¼ mi) west of Dapia, Spetses town* ☎ *22980/74306* ⊕ *www.akss.gr.*

Ayios Mamas. The town's stone promontory is the site of the little 19th-century church, Ayios Mamas—take your photos from a distance as the church is privately owned and often locked. ⊠ *Above harbor, Spetses town.*

Ayios Nikolaos. On the headland sits Ayios Nikolaos, the current cathedral of Spetses, and a former fortified abbey. Its lacy white-marble bell tower recalls that of Hydra's port monastery. It was here that the islanders first raised their flag of independence. ⊠ *On road southeast of waterfront, Spetses town* ☎ *22980/72423.*

Fodor's Choice ★ **Bouboulina Museum.** In front of a small park is Bouboulina's House, now a museum, where you can take a 45-minute guided tour (available in English) and learn about this interesting heroine's life. Laskarina Bouboulina was the bravest of all Spetsiot revolutionaries, the daughter of a Hydriot sea captain, and the wife—then widow—of two more sea captains. Left with a considerable inheritance and nine children, she dedicated herself to increasing her already substantial fleet and fortune. On her flagship, the *Agamemnon,* the largest in the Greek fleet, she sailed into war against the Ottomans at the head of the Spetsiot ships. Her fiery temper led to her death in a family feud many years later. It's worth visiting the mansion, which has been run by her fourth-generation grandson for the past 14 years, just for the architectural details, like the carved-wood Florentine ceiling in the main salon. Tour times (in groups of up of 35 visitors) are posted on the museum Web site, in front of the museum, and in announcement boards at the port of Dapia. The museum closes for maintentance during the winter. ⊠ *Behind Dapia, Spetses town* ☎ *22980/72416* ⊕ *www.bouboulinamuseum-spetses.gr* 🎫 *€6* ☉ *Late Mar.–Oct., daily 9:45–2:15 and 3:45–8:15.*

Dapia. Ships dock at the modern harbor, Dapia, in Spetses town. This is where the island's seafaring chieftains met in the 1820s to plot their revolt against the Ottoman Turks. A protective jetty is still fortified with cannons dating from the War of Independence. Today, the town's waterfront strip is packed with cafés; and the navy-blue-and-white color scheme adopted by Dapia's merchants hints of former maritime glory. The harbormaster's offices, to the right as you face the sea, occupy

4

a building designed in the simple two-story, center-hall architecture typical of the period and this place.

Palio Limani (*Old Harbor*). Spetses actually has two harbors; the Palio Limani, also known as Baltiza, slumbers in obscurity. As you stroll the waterfront, you might imagine it as it was in its 18th- and 19th-century heyday: the walls of the mansions resounding with the noise of shipbuilding and the streets humming with discreet whisperings of revolution and piracy. Today, the wood keels in the few remaining boatyards are the backdrop for cosmopolitan bars, cafés, and restaurants; the sailing boats linger lazily in the bay. Walk up the hill to the ochre-hued chapel of Panayia Armada for unforgettable sunset views. ⊠ *Waterfront, 1½ km (1 mi) southeast of Dapia, Spetses town.*

Poseidonion Grand Hotel. This waterfront 1914 landmark was the scene of glamorous Athenian society parties and balls in the era between the two world wars, and was once the largest resort in the Balkans and southeastern Europe. The hotel was the brainchild of Sotirios Anargyros, a visionary benefactor who was responsible for much of Spetses' development. It reopened in the summer of 2009, after extensive renovations to recapture its former glory, and has quickly regained its position as a Spetsiot landmark (*see our hotel review, below*). ⊠ *West side of Dapia, Spetses town* ☎ *22980/74553* ⊕ *www.poseidonion.com.*

Spetses Museum. A fine late-18th-century impressive *archontiko*, built in a style that might be termed Turko-Venetian, contains Spetses's municipal museum. It holds articles from the period of Spetses's greatness during the War of Independence, including the bones of the town's heroine, Bouboulina, and a revolutionary flag. A small collection of ancient artifacts is mostly ceramics and coins. Also on show are representative pieces of furniture and household items from the period of the Greek revolution. ⊠ *Archontiko Hatziyianni-Mexi, 600 ft south of harbor, Spetses town* ☎ *22980/72994* ⊒ *€3* ⊙ *Tues.–Sun. 8:30–2:30.*

BEACHES

Water taxis at Dapia make scheduled runs to the most popular outlying beaches but can also be hired for trips to more remote coves. The rides can be pricey, ranging from €7 to go from Dapia to the Old Port, up to €30 to the Ayia Paraskevi beach, and €60 for a tour of the island—but the experience is unique. There are currently seven water taxis serving Spetses.

Ayia Marina. Favored by fashionable Greek socialites, the mostly sandy beach at Ayia Marina is the home of the elegant Paradise Beach Bar, tavernas, and many water sport activities. You can hire a horse-drawn buggy from town to arrive in style. ⊠ *2 km [1 mi] southeast of Spetses town* ☎ *22980/72195 for Paradise Beach Bar.*

Ayia Paraskevi. Pine trees, a canteen, sun beds and umbrellas line Ayia Paraskevi, a sheltered and popular beach with a mostly sandy shore. Look for the cubic Ayia Paraskevi chapel at the back—it has given its name to the bay. Many locals consider this beach the most beautiful on the island; it can be reached either via road or with a caïque. ⊠ *8 km [5 mi] west of Spetses town.*

Spetses is studded with extravagant mansions, such as this one, built for Sotirios Anargyros, owner of the famed Poseidonion Grand Hotel.

Fodor's Choice
★

Kaiki. Trendy Kaiki beach is a triangular patch of sand beach that draws a young crowd with its beach volleyball courts, water sport activities (about €40 for 20 min of Jet Ski), and bars, including the Restaurant Kaiki, the hippest one on the island. It will cost you about €10 to rent a huge umbrella, two sun beds, two beach towels, and a bottle of water for a lovely and relaxing day on the beach. ⊠ *1 km [½ mi] southeast of Spetses town center, opposite Anargyrios and Korgialenios School* ☎ *22980/74507 for Kaiki Beach Bar Restaurant.*

Zogeria. A pine-edged cove with deep sapphire waters, Zogeria has a gorgeous natural setting that more than makes up for the lack of amenities—there's just a tiny church and the modest Loula taverna, where you can taste a killer chicken stew in tomato sauce. On a clear day you can see all the way to Nafplio. ⊠ *7½ km [4¾ mi] west of Spetses town* ☎ *22980/7599 for Taverna Loula.*

WHERE TO EAT

$$
GREEK

✕ **Exedra.** Called Sioras or Giorgos by locals (all three names are on the sign), this traditional waterside taverna lets you ogle mooring yachts while digging into a well-prepared and thoroughly Greek meal (not to mention reasonably priced as well). Mussels saganaki and a dish called Argo, shrimp and lobster baked with feta, are among the specialties, and if you've been stalking the elusive *gouronopoulo kokkinisto* (suckling pig slow-cooked in tomato sauce), your hunt can end here. This is also the ultimate place in Spetses to try fish *á la Spetsiota,* the local specialty of the broiled fish-and-tomato casserole. ⊠ *At edge of Old Harbor (Palio Limani), Spetses town* ☎ 22980/73497 ☉ *Closed Nov.–Feb.*

$$$$
MEDITERRANEAN
Fodor'sChoice
★

✕ **Liotrivi Restaurant.** A former olive-oil mill dating back to the 1800s, this fashionable bar-restaurant by the pier offers gourmand Mediterranean dishes, such as fresh ravioli stuffed with lobster, crab salad and *mayiatiko à la spetsiota,* a variation of the local specialty made with yellowtail fish. In summer, you can enjoy the live Latin music from the beachfront tables. At sunset, the candlelit tables and the boats moored nearby create a dreamlike experience. Later the place turns into a popular hangout. ⊠ *Old Harbor (Dapia), Spetses town* ☎ *22980/72269* ⟡ *Reservations essential* ⊗ *Closed Nov.–Mar.*

$$$
SEAFOOD
★

✕ **Patralis.** Sit on a seaside veranda and savor seafood mezedes and fresh fish right from the sea for affordable prices in a sometimes-overpriced island. As the very friendly waiters will tell you, the house specialties are the fish soup, *astakomakaronada* (lobster with spaghetti), and a kind of paella with mussels, shrimp, and crayfish. *Magirefta* (oven-baked dishes) include stuffed aubergines; oven-baked lamb; and roast scarpine fish with tomato and garlic. Expect to pay around €50 per kilo for the fresh grilled fish (compared to €60 in other fish tavernas). The chef makes a mean baked apple for dessert but remember that mini-portions of baklava, karydopita, and spoon sweets with yogurt are on the house. ⊠ *Kounoupitsa, near Spetses Hotel, Spetses town* ☎ *22980/72134* ⊕ *www.patralis.gr* ⊗ *Closed Nov. and Dec.*

WHERE TO STAY

For expanded hotel reviews, visit Fodors.com.

$$$

🛏 **Archontiko Economou.** Captain Mihail Economou's heirs have converted his 1851 stone mansion into a beautiful seaside spot, perfect for romantic getaways, with the atmosphere heightened by the pebbled gardens, home to a small, pretty swimming pool and a handful of live tortoises. **Pros:** relaxing atmosphere; car transport to the port; lovely renovation. **Cons:** some noise coming from the main street; 10 min walk from the harbor (and another 10 min walk from the old harbor); somewhat pricey. ⊠ *Harbor road, near town hall, Spetses town* ☎ *22980/73400* ⊕ *www.economouspetses.gr* ⟿ *6 rooms, 2 suites* ⟐ *In-room: a/c, kitchen, Wi-Fi. In-hotel: pool, laundry facilities* ⦿ *Breakfast.*

$
★

🛏 **Niriides Hotel.** With cheerful exteriors surrounded by myriad flowers, these four-bed apartments a short walk from the main harbor are a good value, especially in the off-season—the interiors, too, will charm guests with their old-fashion wood shutters and beds with wrought-iron frames, just the right accents to set off the cool white, minimalist interiors. **Pros:** quiet side street; hospitable owners; open all year; nice breakfast served in pretty, cool courtyard; rates negotiable. **Cons:** bathrooms a bit on the small side; not a hotel really, but more of a bed-and-breakfast. ⊠ *Near square with clock tower, Dapia, Spetses town* ☎ *22980/73392* ⊕ *www.niriides-spetses.gr* ⟿ *7 apartments* ⟐ *In-room: a/c, kitchen, Internet, Wi-Fi. In-hotel: laundry facilities* ⦿ *Breakfast.*

$$$
Fodor'sChoice
★

🛏 **Poseidonion Grand Hotel.** Set with fin-de-siècle cupolas, imposing mansard roof, and elegant neoclassical facade, this landmark mansion was acclaimed as the Saronic Gulf's own Hotel Negrescu in 1914—like that Nice landmark, this hotel was built to attract the cosmopolitan

Ayia Marina beach is one of the sizzling reasons why people love Spetses.

ocean-liner set and, today, after reopening its doors in 2009 after an extensive five-year refurbishment, the Poseidonion has been hailed as the most elegant hotel in all the Greek islands. **Pros:** an unforgettable experience, say many; deluxe and tasteful renovation; beautiful landmark building; impeccable service; simple but elegant guest rooms with high ceilings; good value for money. **Cons:** historic patina suffers a bit amidst modern decor; free Wi-Fi only in lobby not in rooms. ⊠ *Dapia, Spetses town* ☎ *22980/74553* ⊕ *www.poseidonion.com* ↗ *55 rooms* ⌂ *In-room: a/c, Internet. In-hotel: restaurant, bar, pool, spa, laundry facilities, business center* ❙◎❙ *Breakfast.*

FESTIVAL

Armata—War of Independence Naval Battle. Thousands flock in from all over Greece to attend the Armata celebrations, in what is probably the most glorious weekend on the island's calendar. Spetses mounts an enormous harbor-front reenactment of a War of Independence naval battle during the second week of September, complete with costumed fighters and burning ships. Book your hotel well in advance if you wish to see this popular event, popularly known as the Armata. There are also concerts and exhibitions the week leading up to it.

NIGHTLIFE

For the newest "in" bars, ask your hotel or just stroll down to the Old Harbor, which has the highest concentration of clubs.

BBack. Surviving many years and with ever bigger dimensions, including a seaside patio, is BBack (ex Figaro). International rhythms play earlier in the evening; late at night, it's packed with writhing bodies, and when the music switches to Greek at midnight, as the Greeks say, *ginete hamos*—chaos reigns, and so do high heels! ⊠ *Old Harbor, Spetses town* ☎ *22980/72849.*

Stavento Club. Popular for more than a decade, Stavento allows you to enjoy your drink by the club's veranda, taking in the view of the Old Harbor, before going back inside to resume a night of dancing to popular Greek and international hits. ⊠ *Dapia, on the waterfront, Spetses town* ☎ *22980/75245* ⊕ *www.staventoclub.com.*

SPORTS
The lack of cars and the predominantly level roads make Spetses ideal for bicycling. One good trip is along the coastal road that circles the island, going from the main town to Ayia Paraskevi beach.

Ilias Rent-A-Bike. Head here to rent well-maintained bikes (about €7 per day), motorbikes, and equipment. ⊠ *Ayia Marina Rd., by Analipsis Sq., Spetses town* ☎ *6973/86407.*

The Sporades

SKIATHOS, SKOPELOS, AND SKYROS

WORD OF MOUTH

"Of the Sporades, Skopelos is beautiful, forested, and rugged—it is the *Mamma Mia!* island. Skiathos is the most busy, packed, and touristy of the lot. Then there is Skyros—desolate, barren, and magical, it is very unspoiled, although there are yoga retreats and writing workshops galore (hello, yuppies!)."

—djuna

WELCOME TO THE SPORADES

TOP REASONS TO GO

★ **Sun-and-Fun Skiathos:** Thousands of international sunseekers head here to enjoy famous beaches and then work on their neon tans in the buzzing nightclubs.

★ **Skyros's Style:** Set against a dramatic rock, the main town of Skyros is a showstopper of Cycladic houses colorfully set with folk wood carvings and embroideries.

★ **Sylvan Skopelos:** Not far from the verdant forests lie 40 picturesque monasteries and Skopelos town, looking like a Sporades Positano.

★ **Golden Sands:** The beaches are best on Skiathos, the star location being Koukounaries, whose luscious sands are famous throughout Greece.

★ **"Forever England":** The grave of Edwardian poet Rupert Brooke draws pilgrims to Vouno on Skyros.

1 **Skiathos.** The 3,900 residents are eclipsed by the 50,000 visitors who come here each year for clear blue waters and scores of beaches, including the world-famous Koukounaries. Close to the mainland, this island has some of the aura of the Pelion peninsula, with red-roof villages and picturesque hills. Beauty spots include the monastery of Evangelistria and Lalaria beach. Skopelos draws a lot of artists for its scenic villages and spiritual energy.

2 **Skopelos.** Second largest of the Sporades, this island is lushly forested and more prized by ecologists than funseekers. The steep streets of Skopelos town need mountain-goat negotiating skills, but the charming alleys are irresistible, as are the island's monasteries, the famous cheese pies, and the traditional kalivia farmhouses around Panormos bay.

PSATHOURA

GIOURA

PIPERI

PELAGOS

A e g e a n S e a

SKANTZOURA

S P O R A D E S

SKYROS

Atsitsa

3

Skyros Town

SKYROPOULA

Linaria

Vouno

ERINIA

VALAXA

SARAKINA

GETTING ORIENTED

This small cluster of islands off the coast of central Greece is just a short hop from the mainland and, consequently, often overrun in high season. Obviously, the Cyclades aren't the only Greek islands that serve up a cup of culture and a gallon of hedonism to travelers looking for that perfect tan. Each of the Sporades is very individual in character. Due east of tourism oriented Skiathos are eco-blessed Skopelos and folk-craft-famous Skyros.

5

3 **Skyros.** Located at the virtual center of the Aegean Sea, this Sporades Shangri-la is the southernmost of the island group. The top half is covered with pine forests and is home to Skyros town, a Cycladic cubic masterpiece, which climbs a spectacular rock peak and is a tangle of lanes, whitewashed houses, and Byzantine churches. The arid southern half has the site of the grave of the noted Edwardian poet Rupert Brooke at Vouno.

THE SPORADES'S BEST BEACHES

BEACHY KEEN

You'll hit a Beach Blanket Bingo at any of the famous blonde beaches of the Sporades. With their crystal clear waters, they make an excellent retreat for those seeking super-relaxing holidays under the sun thanks to their big plus: unlike the Cyclades, most are not affected by strong *meltemia* winds.

Most beaches offer a wide range of facilities and services, from rental sun beds and umbrellas to windsurfing, snorkeling, and canoeing equipment for hire or organized water sports.

Restaurants, tavernas, and coffee shops are usually on the beach or nearby.

For those wishing for something more secluded and idyllic, a journey by boat to small nearby islets is an unforgettable experience.

The variety of scenic landscapes in the Sporades can satisfy even the most demanding visitor, as its beautiful beaches suit all tastes: golden sandy beaches, verdurous sceneries, or pebbled beaches surrounded by rocky coves. Happily, each offers perfect settings if you want to get into a real sunny daze, and if you prefer to avoid the glare, there are usually umbrellas and sun beds for rent. Apart from enjoying the sea, nature lovers will want to visit the unique pine forest that borders Skiathos's famous Koukounaries beach, behind which sits the Strofilia Lake, a biotope that is home to rare bird species. History buffs will enjoy Skopelos's Panormos, which still retains remnants of ancient settlements in the area.

SKIATHOS: KOUKOUNARIES

Though Koukounaries (12 km [8 mi] west of Skiathos town) has been much touted as Greece's best beach, photos displaying it must either have been taken a long time ago or on a brilliant, deserted spring day. All summer it is so packed with umbrellas, beach chairs, and blistering tourists that you can hardly see the sand. The multitudes can be part of the fun, however: think of this as an international Greek island beach party. Water activities abound, with waterskiing, sailing, paddleboats, and banana-boat rides all available. Have your Nikon ready to snap the beach's beautiful pine forest and adjacent Strofilia Lake bird preserve. Light lunches and refreshments are served at the beach bar.

SKYROS: KALAMITSA

If you want to be far away from the crowds, Kalamitsa is an ideal spot. The beach is situated at the northern coast of the island, 9 km (6 mi) from the capital. A large pebbled beach with crystal waters, this is an ideal place to enjoy sea, sun, and swimming, as it is not very busy even in August. Chill out here and you'll realize that the Sporades can be a state of mind.

SKYROS: AGHIOS PETROS

Located in Atsitsa town (around 18 km [11 mi] north of Chora) is Aghios Petros, a beautiful bay characterized by its white sand dunes lying concealed amid lush tree-covered hills.

Tall rock formations line most of the bay and cedar trees growing over the rocks add to an ambience of calm.

Part sand, part pebble beach, Aghios Petros—named after the chapel of Saint Peter standing above it—retains a peacefulness that draws sun-loving nature lovers and kayak fans alike.

If you are chilling out for the entire day, bring water and a snack along.

SKOPELOS: PANORMOS BEACH

The cove of Panormos (situated 15 km [9 mi] southwest of Chora) is one of the most beautiful in Skopelos.

Panormos's beach has pebbles but there are also parts covered with sand.

Very popular, it boasts a wide range of facilities such as sun beds, umbrellas, and sea sports. Visitors who wish for an idyllic, secluded spot to relax in privacy should try the bigger of the two islands inside the protected cove of Panormos.

Dassia has dense vegetation and a beautiful beach, pines that reach up to the sea, and deep blue-colored water but can only be approached with small boats from the cove of Panormos.

Updated
by Alexia
Amvrazi

Little mentioned in mythology or history, the Sporades confidently rely on their great natural beauty and cultural history to attract visitors. Some locals poetically claim them to be the handful of colored pebbles the gods were left with after creating the world, and as an afterthought, they flung them over the northwestern Aegean.

Bustling with tourists, Skiathos sits closest to the mainland; it has a pretty harbor area and the noisiest nightlife, international restaurants and pubs, and resort hotels. Due east is Skopelos, covered with dense, fragrant pines, where you can visit scenic villages, hundreds of churches, and lush beaches. The least contemporary of the islands, it is the most naturally beautiful and has a fascinating old hill town.

Then there is traditional Skyros. Some visitors return year after year to this mythical isle, southeast of the other islands, for its quiet fishing villages, expansive beaches, and stunning cubist rabbit warren of a town that seems to spill down a hill. As a current citadel of Greek defense, Skyros also has the bonus of an airport.

Like emerald beads scattered on sapphire satin, the aptly named Sporades ("scattered ones") are resplendent with pines, ripe fruit, and olive trees. The lush countryside, marked with sloping slate roofs and wooden balconies, reflects the aura of the neighboring, hauntingly beautiful Pelion peninsula, to which the islands were once attached. Only on Skyros, farther out in the Aegean, will you see a windswept, treeless landscape with steep cobbled slopes, or the cubist architecture of the Cyclades. Sitting by itself, Skyros is neither geographically nor historically related to the other Sporades.

The Sporades have changed hands constantly throughout history, and wars, plunder, and earthquakes have eliminated all but the strongest ancient walls. A few castles and monasteries remain, but these islands are now geared more for having fun than for sightseeing. Skiathos is the most touristy, in certain periods, to the point of overkill, while less-developed Skopelos has fewer (but purer) beaches and a far less contrived nightlife, but has a main town that is said to be the most beautiful in the Sporades. Late to attract tourists, Skyros is the least traveled of the Sporades (probably because it is harder to reach). It's also the quirkiest, with well-preserved traditions.

Quintessential Greek-island delights beckon on all three islands: sun, sand, and surf, along with starlit dinners. Almost all restaurants have outside seating, often under cooling trees, where you can watch the passing classically Greek, ubiquitous dramas of daily life: lovers arm-in-arm, stealing a kiss; children running free through village squares; sizzling arguments that end in friendship; fishermen cleaning their bright yellow nets and exchanging banter as they work. Relax and immerse yourself in the blue-and-green watercolor of it all.

PLANNER

WHEN TO GO

Winter is least desirable, as the weather turns cold and rainy; most hotels, rooms, and restaurants are closed, and ferry service is minimal. If you do go from November through April, book in advance and leave nothing to chance. The same advice applies to July and August peak season, when everything is open but overcrowded, except on Skyros. The meltemi, the brisk northerly summer wind of the Aegean, keeps things cooler than on the mainland even on the hottest days. Late spring and early summer are ideal, as most hotels are open, crowds have not arrived, the air is warm, and the roadsides and fields of flowers are incredible; September is also mild.

If you want to catch one of the Sporades' famous religious and cultural festivals on your visit, keep the following dates in mind. The lively Carnival (February) traditions of Skopelos, although not as exotic as those of Skyros, parody the expulsion of the once-terrifying Barbary pirates. August 15 is the day of the Panayia (Festival of the Virgin), celebrated on Skyros at Magazia beach and on Skopelos in the main town; cultural events there continue to late August. Skiathos hosts several cultural events in summer, including a dance festival in July. Feast days? Skiathos: July 26, for St. Paraskevi; Skopelos: February 25, for St. Riginosi.

PLANNING YOUR TIME

Inveterate island hoppers might spend one night on each island, although your trip might be more comfortable if you plant yourself on one. There are regular cruises that travel around the Sporades in three to four days, but as each of the three are so very varied, it's worth spending at least two days on each. That noted, you can get around Skiathos and Skopelos in a total of two days, since there are daily ferry connections between them and they are relatively near each other. Traveling between these islands and Skyros, however, requires advance planning, since ferries and flights to Skyros are much less frequent. Also, make sure that you are arriving and leaving from the correct harbor; some islands, such as Skopelos, have more than one from which to depart. Five days can be just enough for touching each island in summer; off-season you need more days to accommodate the ferry schedule.

How to choose if you're only visiting one of the Sporades? If you're the can't-sit-still type and think crowds add to the fun, Skiathos is your island. By day you can take in the beautiful, thronged beaches and Evangelistria Monastery or the fortress-turned-cultural-center, and at night stroll the port to find the most hopping nightclub. Day people with a historical bent should explore Skopelos's many monasteries and churches and its 18th-century Folk Art Museum. Skyros should be at the top of your list if you're a handicraft collector, as the island's furniture and pottery are admired throughout the country and can be bought and sent abroad at several shops.

GETTING HERE AND AROUND

Regular air shuttles and boat service have brought the scattered Sporades isles closer together. The islands are connected by ferry and sometimes hydrofoil, although some are infrequently scheduled, especially November to April. (You can always jump on a caïque and island hop.) Flying Dolphin hydrofoils and flight timetables are available from travel agents; for regular ferries, consult the Greek National Tourism Organization (EOT or GNTO), in Athens. It's a good idea to rent a car to get a real feel for the islands, but using public transport or a scooter can be perfectly suitable for those with less adventurous tendencies—also a lot of hotels now provide shuttle services in and out of town. Car rentals cost €40–€70 per day, while scooters cost €18–€30 (with insurance). If you rent a scooter, be extra cautious: some of those for hire are in poor condition. The locals are not used to the heavy summer traffic on their narrow roads, and accidents provide the island clinics with 80% of their summer business. Taxis are unmetered so be sure to negotiate your fare in advance. Bus service is available throughout the Sporades, although some islands' buses run more frequently than others. Caïques leave from the main ports for the most popular beaches, and interisland excursions are made between Skiathos and Skopelos. You can also head to the harbor and look around for a caïque (haggle over the price) or a sailboat with skipper to hire and tour around the islands; they are generally the preferred way to get around by day. For popular routes, captains have signs of their destinations and departure times posted. On Skyros, check with Skyros Travel (⇨ *Tour Options below*) for caïque tours.

AIR TRAVEL

During the summer Olympic Air flies two or three times a week—or even daily—depending on the period, to Skiathos from Athens International Airport at varying times. The trip takes 45 minutes; the fare is €78 (economy) one way. It is highly recommended that you book your ticket as early as possible.

In summer there are also weekly flights from Athens and Thessaloniki to Skyros Airport. From Athens the flight takes 40 minutes and the one-way fare is €60 (economy). From Thessaloniki the flight takes 40 minutes and the one-way fare is €82 (economy).

Skiathos Airport handles direct charter flights from many European cities.

CARRIERS **Olympic Airways** ☏ *80180/10101 within Greece, 210/355–0500 in Athens* ⊕ *www.olympicair.com.*

Airports Athens International Airport ✉ *Spata* ☏ *210/353–0000.* **Skiathos Airport** ✉ *1 km [½ mi] northeast of Skiathos town* ☏ *24270/29100, 24270/29101.* **Skyros Airport** ✉ *11 km [7 mi] northwest of Skyros town* ☏ *22220/91607.*

BOAT AND FERRY TRAVEL

Ferry travel to Skiathos and Skopelos requires that you drive or take a bus to Agios Konstantinos, located a two and a half hours north of Athens; if arriving from central or northern Greece, however, you may wish to board a ferry at the big port of Volos. Altogether, there are at least three to four ferries per day (regular, or the fast Flying Dolphin hydrofoils) in summer from Agios Konstantinos to Skiathos and Skopelos, fewer in winter. There are also some ferries from Volos and Thessaloniki. For all ferries, it's best to call a travel agency (Vlaikos Travel for Volos and Agios Konstantinos) ahead of time to check schedules and prices, which change seasonally. Tickets are available from several travel agents on the dock. The fast ferry from Agios Konstantinos costs €35 to Skiathos and takes one and a half to two hours; the fare is higher to continue on to Skopelos (€40–€47.50, depending on the port of Skopelos you want to travel to). The regular ferry takes two to two and a half hours and costs €27–€34 to continue on to Skopelos.

Getting to Skyros is equally tricky. You must drive or take a bus to Kimi—on the giant Sporades island of Evia—and then catch one of the two daily ferries, or the weekly hydrofoil, to Skyros. You can buy ferry tickets at the Kimi dock when you get off the bus; the trip to Skyros takes two hours and costs €10. Should you choose to book your return when you get to Skyros, note that Skyros Travel (⇨ *Tour Options)* has a virtual monopoly on hydrofoil tickets.

Regular ferries connect Skiathos and Skopelos. From Skopelos to Skyros there are two ferries weekly and the ticket price is €21. The once-per-week Flying Dolphin hydrofoil that travels from Kimi, on the large nearby island of Evia, to all the Sporades is by far the quicker, more reliable way to travel between the islands. Because schedules change frequently, check the times listed outside travel agencies in each of the port towns; the agents sell tickets. Connecting through Kimi is the easiest way to get between Skyros and the other islands (the alternative is to fly through Athens).

Boat Information Flying Dolphin ☏ *21041/99000* ⊕ *www.hellenicseaways. gr.* **Port Authority** ☏ *22350/31759 in Agios Konstantinos, 22220/22606 in Kimi, 24270/22017 in Skiathos town, 24240/22180 in Skopelos town, 22220/91475 in Skyros town.* **Vlaikos Travel** ☏ *24240/65220.*

BUS TRAVEL

From central Athens, buses leave every hour to Agios Konstantinos, the main port for the Sporades (except Skyros), cost €15.70 and take about 2½ hours. Buses from Athens to Kimi, on Evia Island (the only port where boats depart for Skyros), cost €15.30, and take two and a half hours. For those connecting to Agios Konstantinos from Halkidha, on Evia Island, the bus costs €8 and takes one and a half hours. Check the **KTEL** (⊕ *www.ktel.org*) site for schedules. *For information on connecting with the big port connection of Volos (via train for the most part), see Getting Here for Skiathos town below.* Buses on Skiathos leave Skiathos town to make the beach run as far as Koukounaries every 30 minutes from early morning until 11:30 pm. Buses on Skopelos run six times a day from Skopelos town to Glossa and Loutraki, stopping at the beaches. Skyros buses carry ferry passengers between Linaria and Horio, stopping in Molos in summer.

Bus Information Athens to Agios Konstantinos ☎ *210/831–7147 in Athens.* **Athens to Skyros** ☎ *210/8317163 in Athens.* **KTEL bus station** ☎ *22210/20400 in Halkidha.*

CAR TRAVEL

To get to Skiathos and Skopelos by car you must drive to the port of Agios Konstantinos (Agios) and from there take the ferry. The drive to Agios from Athens takes about two hours. For high-season travel you might have to reserve a place on the car ferry a day ahead. For Skyros you must leave from the port of Kimi on the big Sporades island of Evia. From Athens, take the Athens–Lamia National Road to Skala Oropou and make the 30-minute ferry crossing to Eretria on Evia (every half hour in the daytime). No reservations are needed. Because it is so close to the mainland, you can skip the ferry system and drive directly to Evia over a short land bridge connecting Agios Minas on the mainland with Halkidha. From Athens, about 80 km (50 mi) away, take the National Road 1 to the Schimatari exit, and then follow the signs to Halkidha. Beware that weekend crowds can slow traffic across the bridge.

If you want to rent wheels, keep the following suggestions in mind. It's a good idea to rent a car (ideally a four-wheel drive) in order to explore more fully for a day or more, and then use the bus or a scooter thereafter. Car rentals usually cost €40–€70 per day, while scooters cost about €18–€30. Four-wheel drives, cars, scooters, and motorbikes can be rented everywhere. Check with the travel agencies for rental information.

CAR RENTAL INFORMATION **Alamo/National** ⊠ *Paralia Skopelou, Skopelos* ☎ *24240/23033.*

Avis ⊠ *Skiathos town, Port of Skiathos–Seafront* ☎ ⊕ *www.avis.gr.*

Martina's ⊠ *Maheras, Skyros town* ☎ *22220/92022* ⊕ *www.web-greece.gr/rentacar/martinas/.*

TAXI TRAVEL

You will find "Piatsa" taxi ranks next to all the harbor ports and airports, and taxis will be lined up even late at night if there is a boat or flight coming in. On the other hand, your hotel can usually arrange a taxi for you, but if you need one in the wee hours of the morning make sure you book it in advance. The prices on the islands are not cheap (compared to Athens or Thessaloniki), and can be as much as €10 to €15 for a 10-minute drive. As for general taxi fares, it is always good to check with your hotel about prices beforehand. The best way to get around is by renting a car, but be warned: in the busy summer months, parking is hard to come by in the main towns and villages.

TAXI INFORMATION

Mr. G. Stamoulos ✉ *Taxi Rank, next to the Port, Skopelos town* ☎ *24240/33023.*

Mr. Kourgenis ✉ *Skyros* ☎ *697/2894088.*

Mr. Pergamalis ✉ *Skyros* ☎ *697/3665480.*

Mr. Traxanas ✉ *Skyros* ☎ *697/8361325.*

Mr. Z. Stamoulis ✉ *Glossa, Skopelos* ☎ *24240/33044.*

Skiathos Piatsa (Taxi Rank) ✉ *Port of Skiathos* ☎ *24270/24461.*

RESTAURANTS

In the Sporades, most tavernas are opened from midday until just past midnight, and welcome guests to stay as long as they like. Unless you are looking for a gourmet experience you can't go wrong with a salad and fish, or a home-cooked moussaka. Be sure to ask the waiter what fresh fish they serve and what are the dishes of the day, and don't hesitate to go inside and see the food for yourself before ordering. As with everywhere in Greece, the *hima* (homemade) house wine is usually good enough, sometimes excellent; the waiter will not mind if you order a taste before deciding.

As for your food, traditional recipes such as *mageirefta* (home-cooked) dishes based on local meat and vegetables, and a variety of fresh fish, reign supreme in the Sporades, but the rendition you taste can be a hit-and-miss experience—that is, if you are looking for truly succulent, fresh, and authentic food with an imaginative twist. To better your chance, dining where the locals dine is always a good idea, as is exploring past the harbor fronts and seeking out smaller tavernas often hidden along the side streets and catering to the neighborhood locals. Look for local specialties such as the *Skopelitiki tiropita*, or cheese pie (a spiral of tubed filo pastry filled with creamy white feta and fried to a crispy texture), or the fluffy *avgato* yellow plums in a light syrup that can be savored as a dressing for fresh yogurt or on a small plate as *glyko koutaliou* (spoon sweet).

DINING AND LODGING PRICES IN EUROS					
	¢	$	$$	$$$	$$$$
Restaurants	under €8	€8–€11	€11–€15	€15–€20	over €20
Hotels	under €60	€60–€90	€90–€120	€120–€160	over €160

Restaurant prices are for one main course at dinner, or for two mezedes (small dishes). Hotel prices are for a standard double room in high season, including taxes. Inquire when booking whether meal plans (which can entail higher rates) are mandatory.

HOTELS

Accommodations reflect the pace of tourism on each particular island: Skopelos has a fair number of hotels, Skiathos a huge number, but there are far fewer on Skyros. Most hotels close from October or November to April or May. Reservations are a good idea, though you may learn about rooms in pensions and private homes when you arrive at the airport or ferry landing. The best bet, especially for those on a budget, is to rent a converted room in a private house—look for the Greek National Tourism Organization (EOT or GNTO) license displayed in windows. Owners meet incoming ferries to tout their location, offer rooms, and negotiate the price. In Skyros most people take lodgings in town or along the beach at Magazia and Molos: you must choose between being near the sea or the town's bars and eateries. Accommodations are basic, and not generally equipped with television sets. Always negotiate rates off-season.

VISITOR INFORMATION

There are few main official tourist offices for the Sporades. The closest you'll come is the Skiathos Municipality agency *(see Visitor Information, below, on Skiathos)*. In lieu of official agencies, however, there are an array of private travel agencies, and these offer a myriad of services, tickets, car rentals, and guided tours. *Here below are the most popular travel agencies in the Sporades.*

Tour Information **CCL Tours** ⊠ *New port, Skiathos* ☎ *24270/22385, 24270/21384* 🖶 *24270/21136.*

Madro Travel. Because of owners Mahi and George Drossou's inviting personalities and impressively extensive knowledge of the island, this is the kind of travel agency most people wish existed on *every* island. Both with deep roots in Skopelos' own history, these two charismatic travel agents can offer quality suggestions for what to do—or avoid doing—during your time here. Local boat trips, ferry and hydrofoil tickets, exciting drives, and on-target tips on sites, restaurants, and memorable walks can be found at Madro, while their son Vaggelis can offer insights into the island's nightlife and more youth-oriented excursions. ⊠ *Old Harbor (next to Platanos Jazz Club), Skopelos town* ☎ *24240/22145* 🖶 *24240/22941* ⊕ *www.madrotravel.com.*

Skyros Travel ⊠ *Agora, Skyros town* ☎ *22220/91123, 22220/91600* 🖶 *22220/92123* ⊕ *www.skyrostravel.com.*

SKIATHOS ΣΚΙΑΘΟΣ

Part sacred (scores of churches), part profane (active nightlife), the hilly, wooded island of Skiathos is the closest of the Sporades to the Pelion peninsula. It covers an area of only 42 square km (16 square mi), but it has some 70 beaches and sandy coves. A jet-set island 25 years ago, today it teems with European—mostly British—tourists on package deals promising sun, sea, and late-night revelry. Higher prices and a bit of Mykonos's attitude are part of the deal, too.

GETTING HERE AND AROUND

AIR TRAVEL   From Athens, Olympic Air and Aegean Airlines have daily flights to Skiathos, with one evening flight to and one morning return. Flights take just over half an hour (€78.60 economy, one way). Olympic Air ramps up service during summer months to three flights a day. The island airport (☎ *24270/29100 or 24270/29101*) is located 1 km (½

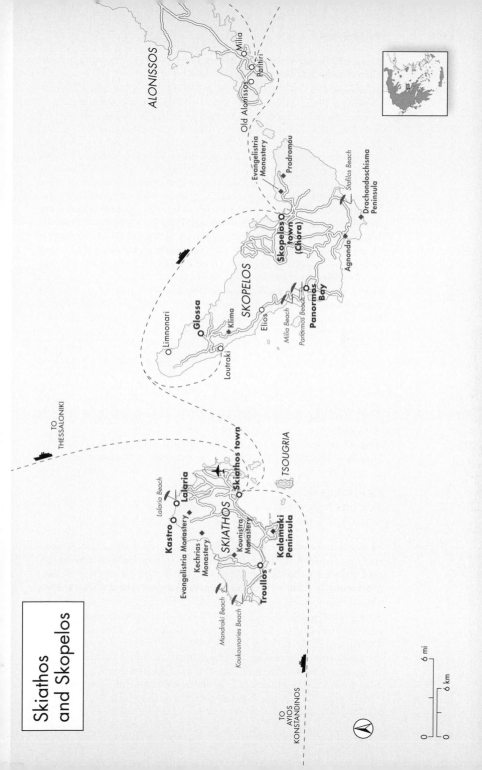

Skiathos and Skopelos

ALONISSOS

Milia
Patitiri
Old Alonissos

Evangelistria Monastery
Prodromou

Staflos Beach
Drachondoschisma Peninsula

Skopelos town (Chóra)
Agnonda

Limnonari

Glossa

SKOPELOS

Klima

Elios
Milia Beach
Panormos Bay
Panormos Beach

Loutraki

TO THESSALONIKI

Skiathos town

TSOUGRIA

Lalaria Beach
Lalaria
Kastro

SKIATHOS

Evangelistria Monastery
Kechrias Monastery

Kounistra Monastery

Kalamaki Peninsula

Troullos

Mandraki Beach
Koukounaries Beach

TO AYIOS KONSTANDINOS

0   6 mi

0   6 km

mi) northeast of Skiathos town; buses to town are very infrequent so plan on jumping in a taxi to get to your hotel.

BOAT TRAVEL If you wish to travel to Skiathos by boat, take a bus (€18, leaving every hour) from Athens to the port of Agios Konstantinos (a two- to three-hour bus ride from Athens) or a bus to the mainland port of Volos; buses connect Volos to Athens every couple of hours, and the trip takes 2½ hours and the Greek National Railway also has a train connecting Volos to Athens. From both Agios Konstantinos and Volos ferries or (in high season) hydrofoils head to Skiathos. The hydrofoil route between Agios Konstantinos and Skiathos runs twice a day; the trip is 1½ to 2 hrs (€35). The normal ferry takes 2 to 2½ hours and costs €27. To connect with Skopelos, use the regular ferry service departing from Skiathos; the quicker Flying Dolphin hydrofoils get you to Skopelos in 45 minutes and to Skyros in about two hours. There is also a daily hydrofoil to Thessaloniki as well as weekly ferry service to Santorini (13 hours). There are only a couple of boats that connect Skiathos with Skyros weekly so it is advisable only if you have plenty of time at your disposal or you are well organized, whereas there is a regular ferry service connecting Skiathos with neighboring Skopelos (which does not have an airport). For schedule information, see ⊕ *www.hellenicseaways.gr* and ⊕ *www.gtp.gr*. The regional Port Authority has information on boat schedules (☎ 24270/22017).

BUS TRAVEL The main bus route on Skiathos connects Skiathos town with the famed beach at Koukounaries (Maratha), a 30-minute ride. With half-hour departures in high season, the route has 20 other stops, mostly along the southern coast of the island. Fares are €1.50 to €3, with service from 7:30 am to 1 am in high season. The main taxi stand is near the ferry pier.

Visitor Information **Greek National Tourism Organization (GNTO or EOT)** ✉ *Tsoha 7, Athens* ☎ *210/8707000* ⊕ *www.visitgreece.gr.* **Skiathos Municipality** ✉ *Nikotsara 12, Skiathos town* ☎ *24270/22022* ⊕ *www.n-skiathos.gr.*

EXPLORING

In winter most of the island's 5,000 or so inhabitants live in its main city, Skiathos town, built after the War of Independence on the site of the colony founded in the 8th century BC by the Euboean city-state of Chalkis. Like Skopelos and Alonissos, Skiathos was on good terms with the Athenians, prized by the Macedonians, and treated gently by the Romans. Saracen and Slav raids left it virtually deserted during the early Middle Ages, but it started to prosper during the later Byzantine years.

When the Crusaders deposed their fellow Christians from the throne of Constantinople in 1204, Skiathos and the other Sporades became the fief of the Ghisi, knights of Venice. One of their first acts was to fortify the hills on the islet separating the two bays of Skiathos harbor. Now connected to the shore, this former islet, the Bourtzi, still has a few stout walls and buttresses shaded by some graceful pine trees.

SKIATHOS TOWN
ΣΚΙΑΘΟΣ (ΠΟΛΗ)

2½ hrs from Agios Konstantinos. Though the harbor is picturesque from a distance—especially from a ferry docking at sunset, when a violet-orange light casts a soft glow and the lights on the hills behind the quay start twinkling like faint stars—Skiathos town close-up has few buildings of any distinction. Many traditional houses were burned by the Germans in 1944, and postwar development has pushed up cement apartments between the pleasant, squat, red-roof older houses. Magenta bougainvillea, sweet jasmine, and the casual charm of brightly painted balconies and shutters camouflage most of the eyesores as you wander through the narrow lanes and climb up the steep steps that serve as streets. Activity centers on the waterfront or on Papadiamantis, the main drag, with banks, travel agents, telephones, post offices, police and tourist police stations, plus myriad cafés, fast-food joints, postcard stands, tacky souvenir shops, tasteful jewelry stores, and car- and bike-rental establishments. Shops, bars, and restaurants line the cobbled side streets, where you can also spot the occasional modest hotel and rooms-to-rent signs. The east side of the port (more commonly known as the new port), where the larger boats and Flying Dolphin hydrofoils dock, is not as interesting. The little church and clock tower of Ayios Nikolaos watch over it from a hill reached by steps so steep they're almost perpendicular to the earth.

Bourtzi. A lovely physical feature of Skiathos harbor—standing on a small, piney peninsula that divides the main port—the Bourtzi was a fortress built in 1207 by the Venetian Gyzi brothers to protect Skiathos from pirate attacks. Not much remains of the original building, also called "the castle of St. George," yet the cultural center here hosts wonderful events every summer, particularly in July and August, when art and antiquities exhibitions and open-air performances entertain tourists and locals alike. It's well worth taking in the view of the harbor from the tranquil, refreshing spots found here; west of the waterfront you'll see the fishing port where caïques come and go. The sidewalk is increasingly filled with cafés and *ouzeris* (ouzo bars) and, at the far end of the port beginning at the square and set around the 1846 church of Trion Hierarchon, more elegant restaurants spread out under awnings. There is also a café-bar at the Bourtzi itself. ⊠ *End of causeway extending from port, .*

Papadiamantis Museum. The House of Papadiamantis is a tribute to one of Greece's finest writers, Alexandros Papadiamantis (1851–1911), lauded by some as "the Greek Dostoyevsky." His native Skiathos played a prominent role in his essays, short stories, and novels, as did plots strongly inspired by the human condition, war, pirate invasions, the

On Skiathos, the coast is always clear.

Greek Orthodox faith, captivity, and simple rural life. Several of his novels have been translated into English, including the internationally acclaimed *The Murderess*. The exhibits here deal with the author's daily life, ranging from his furniture and personal belongings to vintage photographs. ⊠ *Right off Papadiamantis at fork, Skiathos town* ☎ *24270/23843* ▣ *€2* ⊙ *July and Aug., daily 9:30–1:30 and 5–8:30; Sept.–June, daily 9:30–1:30 and 5–8:30.*

BEACHES

Skiathos is known for its beaches, but as has happened so many times before throughout Greece, unchecked popularity has a way of spoiling special places. Since the arrival of mainly English expatriates in the early 1960s, the beautiful, piney 14-km (9-mi) stretch of coast running south of the town to the famed, gold-sand Koukounaries beach has by today become an almost continuous array of villas, hotels, and tavernas. One beach succeeds another, and in summer the asphalted coastal road carries a constant torrent of cars, buses, motorbikes, and pedestrians buzzing from beach to beach like frenzied bees sampling pollen-laden flowers. To access most beaches, you must take little, usually unpaved, lanes down to the sea. Along this coast, the beaches, **Megali Ammos, Vassilias, Achladia, Tzaneria, Vromolimnos,** and **Platania,** all offer water sports, umbrellas, lounge chairs, and plenty of company.

WHERE TO EAT

$$
INTERNATIONAL

✕ **Amphiliki.** Set on a balcony overlooking Siferi bay, this restaurant, open throughout the day, pairs an inviting ozonic breeze with one of the most sprawling views in town. The menu is focused on fresh local fish, and the latest additions to the menu are an entrée of fresh tuna fillet sautéed with onion and lemon and "Chef" mussels cooked in a mustard and feta sauce. Owner Christos takes pride in the organic vegetables he serves, which are all sourced from his own garden. Leave space for the featherlight traditional *ekmek* (custard cake) with mastic ice cream or try the restaurant's cheesecake if you prefer a more Western dessert. ⊠ *Opposite health center, Skiathos town* ☎ *24270/22839* ⊕ *www.amfiliki. gr* ⚞ *Reservations essential* ☰ *No credit cards* ⊘ *Closed Oct.–May.*

$$ — MODERN GREEK

✕ **Don Quijote Tapas Bar Restaurant.** The tapas bar, a rare type of restaurant to find not only on Skiathos but in the country overall, will provide you with a pleasant change of flavor and scene. Its colorful selection of hot and cold tapas includes classic Spanish eats such as paella and *jamon* (Spanish crude ham) as well as Greek-inspired appetizers, to be savored with a local or Spanish wine, or a refreshing mojito. The Catalan *cream* (a Spanish version of crème brûlée) or the chocolate soufflé make for two sweet finales. A friendly waitstaff is happy to advise you on dishes as you take in the expansive harbor view, intoxicated by the lively atmosphere—but not the noise—of the main town below. ⊠ *East harbor 37002, Skiathos town* ☎ *24270/21600* ⚞ *Reservations essential* ⊘ *Closed Nov.–Apr.*

$ — SEAFOOD

✕ **Ta Psarädika.** You can't get any closer to the fish market than this family-run taverna, and the fresh seafood dishes (served grilled or fried) prove it. Sit outside facing the sea and sip an icy ouzo while sampling a variety of *mezedes* (appetizers), or if you prefer a heartier meal, try some of the finny creatures: mussels steamed in wine, or the taverna's specialty of fresh swordfish with a rosemary, garlic, raisin and honey sauce, or a seafood pasta with tomato sauce. ⊠ *Far end of old port, Skiathos town* ☎ *24270/23412* ⊘ *Closed Oct.–Mar.*

$$ — INTERNATIONAL

✕ **The Windmill.** Escape the buzz of Skopelos town by climbing up the hill above Ayios Nikolaos to dine at this well-restored 1880s mill–turned–unpretentiously elegant restaurant. Run by Scottish Karen McCann, the Windmill offers the town's most awesome views of the moonlit harbor accompanied by a gourmet rendition of British pub dishes with a breezy Mediterranean and Southeast Asian twist. Start with the calamari with Parmesan crumb, chili, and ginger dip, then sample the popular chargrilled fillet of beef (with a choice of sauces such as peppercorn or mushroom and bacon) before ending with a rich dessert. The Windmill has a little balcony that seats two, which places diners at the highest spot above the town; if you'd like to dine at new heights, book this coveted perch way in advance. ⊠ *Above clock tower, Kotroni, Skiathos town*

☎ *24270/24550* ⊕ *www.skiathoswindmill.gr* ⚖ *Reservations essential* ⊗ *Closed mid-Oct.–mid-May. No lunch.*

WHERE TO STAY

For expanded hotel reviews, visit Fodors.com.

$$$ ☷ **Bourtzi Boutique Hotel.** Run by brothers Dimitris and Stanis, this stylish, contemporary hotel has received beaming reviews for its efficient staff and relaxing, luxurious ambience—the simple yet elegant exterior doesn't divulge the far sparklier plushness of the lobby and or the cream-and-gold bar, which is a popular hot spot for chic socializing over cocktails and snacks while watching the world go by on the main street. **Pros:** a great option for travellers seeking a more sophisticated stay; elevator and ramps. **Cons:** no rooms that accommodate large families. ⊠ *Moraitou 8, Skiathos town* ☎ *24270/21304* ⊕ *www.hotelbourtzi.gr* ⬙ *38* ⚲ *In-room: a/c, Wi-Fi. In-hotel: bar, pool* ⥋ *Breakfast.*

¢ ☷ **Mouria Hotel and Taverna.** Located in the heart of the main town and
★ a quality choice for budget travelers, Mouria first opened in 1830 as a delightful market and taverna—as you'll realize if you ask for a room overlooking the white bougainvillea-framed courtyard, where acclaimed author Papadiamantis once sat to write. **Pros:** very cozy and friendly; affordable. **Cons:** rooms overlooking Papadiamantis Street can be noisy during high season. ⊠ *Behind National Bank, Papadiamadis St., Skiathos town* ☎ *24270/23069* ⬙ *12 rooms* ⚲ *In-room: a/c. In-hotel: restaurant* ⊗ *Closed Oct–May* ⥋ *No meals.*

$ ☷ **Villa Ariadni.** Uniquely located near the beautiful lake of Aghios Georgios and a beach—while being only a 15-minute walk from the main town—Villa Ariadni offers simply furnished, newly renovated island-style studios and apartments (for up to six guests), all of which overlook the sea or lake. **Pros:** self-sufficiency; disability-friendly. **Cons:** no breakfast or restaurant. ⊠ *Aghios Georgios, Skiathos town* ☎ *24270/22931* ⊕ *www.ariadnivilla.gr* ⬙ *11 rooms* ⚲ *In-room: a/c, kitchen, Wi-Fi. In-hotel: parking, some pets allowed.*

NIGHTLIFE

Skiathos is filled with night owls, and for good reason. Bars for all tastes line main and side streets, from pubs run by Brits to quintessential Greek bouzouki joints in beach tavernas. Most of the nightlife in Skiathos town is centered along the waterfront and on Papadiamantis, Politechniou, and Evangelistrias streets.

CINEMAS **Cinema Attikon.** To enjoy the silver screen under the summer stars spend a few hours at Attikon Cinema, which screens three different films per week and two English language films per night (with a regular tribute to *Mamma Mia*), from 9 pm on. ⊠ *Papadiamanti street, Skiathos town* ☎ *24270/22352.*

MUSIC AND NIGHTCLUBS **Bourtzi Café.** For a real change of pace take a gentle stroll to a lesser-known café/bar at the tip of the Bourtzi fortress' promontory. Here, like the locals, you can enjoy an affordable seaside drink away from the madding crowds. ⊠ *Bourtzi, Skiathos town.*

De Facto Bar. Popular among the gay crowd and located behind the main church of Treis Ierarches, this cozy bar plays golden oldies and classic rock and serves an impressive choice of beers. ✉ *Skiathos town* ☏ *24270/22121.*

Kahlua. For late-night action along a row of hopping clubs, head to Kahlua, which has indoor and outdoor dancing and is open in summer until at least 3 am. ✉ *Tasos Antonaros [new port], Skiathos town* ☏ *24270/23205* ☉ *Closed Sept.–June.*

Kentavros Bar. The popular Kentavros Bar entertains a young professional crowd with rhythm and blues, funk, soul, and classic rock starting at 9:30 pm. ✉ *Papadiamantis Square, Skiathos town* ☏ *24270/22980* ☉ *Closed Oct.–Apr.*

Slip Inn. Slip Inn is liked for its good coffee during the day while at night it transforms into a funky lounge where passion-fruit margaritas are best enjoyed resting on one elbow, Dionysian style, on multicolor floor cushions. ✉ *Old port, Antoniou Riga bay, Skiathos town* ☏ *24270/21006* ☉ *Closed Oct.–Apr.*

SPORTS AND THE OUTDOORS

SAILING **Active Yachts.** For multiday charters with or without crew, contact Active Yachts, which also rents out motorboats by the day. ✉ *Portside, Skiathos town* ☏ *30/6972245391* ⊕ *activeyachts.gr* ☉ *Closed Oct.–Apr.*

SCUBA DIVING **Dolphin Diving Center.** Popular beaches often have diving-equipment rental and instructors on hand. Skiathos is the only Sporades island with scuba-diving schools. The first in operation, Dolphin Diving Center offers single or multiple dives, as well as full-certification programs. ✉ *Porto Nostos beach [off bus stop 12], Skiathos town* ☏ *24270/21599* 🖷 *24270/22525* ⊕ *www.ddiving.gr* ☉ *Closed Nov.–Apr.*

SHOPPING

ANTIQUES AND CRAFTS **Galerie Varsakis.** Kilims, embroideries, jewelry, icons, and hundreds of antiques from around the world are available here, all set off by proprietor Charalambos Varsaki's impressive surrealistic paintings and prints. Also noteworthy is his collection of guns and swords dating to 1780–1820 and used in the Greek War of Independence. ✉ *Trion Hierarchon 2, Skiathos town* ☏ *24270/22255.*

JEWELRY **Phaedra.** Celebrating jewelry making with an artsy twist, Phaedra showcases silver and gold pieces that are part of collections by noteworthy Greek designers. ✉ *Papadiamanti 23, Skiathos town* ☏ *24279/21233.*

Simos. Jewelry in 14-karat and 18-karat yellow and white gold, and more recently in silver, are Simos specialties, from simple designs to classical Greece-inspired baubles encrusted with precious stones. ✉ *Papadiamanti street 29, Skiathos town* ☏ *24270/23232.*

KALAMAKI PENINSULA ΚΑΛΑΜΑΚΙ (ΧΕΡΣΟΝΗΣΟΣ)

6 km (4 mi) south of Skiathos town.

The less-developed area on the south coast of Skiathos is the Kalamaki peninsula, where the British built their first villas. Some are available for rent in summer, many above tiny, unfrequented coves. Access here is by boat only, so you can usually find your own private beach. Motor launches run at regular intervals to the most popular beaches from Skiathos town, and you can always hire a boat for a private journey.

WHERE TO STAY

For expanded hotel reviews, visit Fodors.com.

$$$$ Fodor'sChoice ★ **Skiathos Princess.** Understated glamour and polished island chic rule at Skiathos Princess, which stretches over the whole of Ayia Paraskevi beach—as expected, it offers all the expected amenities of an exclusive luxury resort (guest rooms that look lifted from a glossy magazine, an absolute "wow" of a pool area, three restaurants) with polite, professional service to match. **Pros:** lullingly luxurious; wonderful views; airport shuttle. **Cons:** pricey (but worth it). ✉ *8 km (5 mi) from Skiathos town, Agia Paraskevi* ☎ *24270/49731* 🌐 *www.skiathosprincess.com* *131 rooms, 25 suites, 2 apartments* *In-room: Wi-Fi. In-hotel: restaurant, bar, pool, gym, spa, laundry facilities, parking* ⊗ *Closed Nov.–Apr.* *Multiple meal plans.*

TROULLOS ΤΡΟΥΛΛΟΣ

4 km (2½ mi) west of Kalamaki peninsula, 8 km (5 mi) west of Skiathos town.

On the coast road west of Kalamaki peninsula lies Troullos bay, a resort area. Continue west and you come to Koukounaries beach—famous, beautiful, and overcrowded.

Kounistra Monastery. The dirt road north of Troullos leads to beaches and to the small, now deserted, Kounistra Monastery. It was built in 1655 on the spot where a monk discovered an icon of the Virgin miraculously dangling from a pine tree. The icon spends most of the year in the church of Trion Hierarchon, in town, but on November 20 the townspeople parade it to its former home for the celebration of the Presentation of the Virgin the following day. You can enter the deserted monastery church any time, though its interior has been blackened by fire and its 18th-century frescoes are difficult to see. ✉ *4 km [2½ mi] north of Troullos .*

BEACHES

Fodor'sChoice ★ **Koukounaries.** If what you are looking for is the ideal combination of a scenic landscape with facilities like water sports, nice refreshments and light meals, and sun beds and umbrellas, then the world-renowned, picture perfect beach of Koukounaries is the place for you. Some call it "Golden Coast," after its fine, sparkling golden sand, but in high season, when boatloads of tourists land there you'll be lucky to find a free patch to sit on. This beautiful beach owes its name to the interesting surrounding forest of umbrella pines, which are almost watered by the waves. Enjoy a leisurely stroll behind the beach to Strofilia Lake, an impressive biotope where rare species of birds find shelter. ⊠ *4 km [2½ mi] northwest of Troullos, 12 km [8 mi] west of Skiathos town.*

Mandraki. A good 25 minutes walk from the road, the sandy beach of Mandraki offers a sense of peace and privacy. Sometimes called Xerxes's harbor, this is where the notorious Persian king stopped on his way to ultimate defeat at the battles of Artemisium and Salamis. The reefs opposite are the site of a monument Xerxes allegedly erected as a warning to ships, the first such marker known in history. ⊠ *5 km [3 mi] northwest of Troullos Bay, 12 km [7½ mi] west of Skiathos town, Troullos.*

WHERE TO EAT AND STAY

For expanded hotel reviews, visit Fodors.com.

$$$$
MEDITERRANEAN
Fodor's Choice
★

✕ **Elia's.** Located at the Mandraki Village boutique hotel but popular among nonguests, Elia's has received rave reviews from some of Greece's leading food critics and keeps visitors coming back for more. White, deep red, and shocking magenta are the theme colors at this airy, colonial-style restaurant with high-backed, material-covered chairs, soft, radiant lighting, and a sophisticated allure. The French chef combines mainly seasonal, local ingredients with creative, contemporary Franco-Mediterranean flair and few will be able to resist the aubergine and goat's cheese mille-feuille with pear, the octopus carpaccio, the fisherman's pasta with prawns and shellfish, or the homemade crème brûlée—the only such dessert you'll find on Skiathos is divine. ⊠ *Koukounaries, Troullos* ☎ *24270/493014.*

$
SEAFOOD

✕ **Taverna Troullos.** Tables line the beach practically up to the water's edge at this friendly taverna set right on the beach. The taverna is one of the few places in the area offering seaside a lunch or dinner, but be prepared for slow service during peak times. ⊠ *Waterfront, Troullos Bay, Troullos* ☎ *24270/49255* ⊕ *www.troulos.gr* ☉ *Closed Nov.–Mar.*

$$$$
★

⌂ **Aegean Suites.** In a league of its own on Skiathos, this luxurious boutique hotel pampers eclectic and demanding guests ages 18 and up in what resembles a Mediterranean grand villa. **Pros:** outstanding service; as-luxurious-as-it-gets amenities (champagne bar, yacht cruises, helicopter transfer, and dinners served in your balcony Jacuzzi). **Cons:** no elevator, a real problem when one climbs from the lobby 100 steps to the highest suite. ⊠ *Megali Ammos beach, Troullos* ☜ *Winter address: Santikmos Hotels & Resorts, Agios Konstantinos 40, Aethrio Centre, Office A40, Maroussi, Athens* ☎ *24270/24069* ⊕ *www.aegeansuites. com* ⋗ *20 suites* ঙ *In-room: a/c, Wi-Fi. In-hotel: restaurant, bar, pool* ☉ *Closed Nov.–Apr.* ⦿ *Breakfast.*

$$
☾
Fodor's Choice
★

⌂ **Mandraki Village.** Lovingly renovated by well-known architect Dimitris Tsitsos in 2007 and transformed into a top-class boutique hotel, Mandraki Village offers a gratifyingly familial holiday ambience in a setting of easy luxury and designer charm. **Pros:** three tempting restaurants, including top-rated Elia's; out-and-out gorgeous, some designers would say; high sophistication factor; in-house spa and beauty treatments. **Cons:** leaving. ⊠ *Koukounaries, Troullos* ☎ *24270/493014* ⊕ *www.mandraki-skiathos.gr* ⋗ *38 rooms* ঙ *In-room: a/c.*

5

Lalaria: Now *this* is why you came to Greece!

$ ⊞ **Troullos Bay.** A great place to stay if you desire a restful stay by the sea, this hotel was completely renovated in 2009 in a clean, minimalist, and modern style, with guest rooms that look out to the pretty beach. **Pros:** affordable; great location. **Cons:** a little too sedate for some tastes. ⊠ *Troullos, Troullos Bay* ☎ *24270/49390, 24270/49391* ↩ *43 rooms* ⚲ *In-room: a/c. In-hotel: restaurant, bar, pool* ☉ *Closed Nov.–Apr.* ⏍ *No meals.*

KASTRO ΚΑΣΤΡΟ

13 km (8 mi) northeast of Troullos, 9 km (5½ mi) northeast of Skiathos town.

Also known as the Old Town, Kastro perches on a forbidding promontory high above the water, accessible only by steps. Skiathians founded this former capital in the 16th century when they fled from the pirates and the turmoil on the coast to the security of this remote cliff—staying until 1829. Its landward side was additionally protected by a moat and drawbridge, and inside the stout walls they erected 300 houses and 22 churches, of which only 2 remain. The little Church of the Nativity has some icons and must have heard many prayers for deliverance from the sieges that left the Skiathians close to starvation.

You can drive or take a taxi or bus to within 325 feet of the Old Town, or wear comfortable shoes for a walk that's mostly uphill. Better, take the downhill walk back to Skiathos town; the trek takes about three hours and goes through orchards, fields, and forests on the well-marked paths of the interior.

Kechrias monastery. Four kilometers (2½ mi) southwest of Kastro is the deserted Kechrias monastery, an 18th-century church embellished with frescoes and surrounded by olive and pine trees. Be warned: the road to Kechrias from Skiathos town and to the beach below is tough going; stick to a four-wheel-drive vehicle.

LALARIA ΛΑΛΑΡΙΑ

Fodor's Choice
★
2 km (1 mi) east of Kastro, 7 km (4½ mi) north of Skiathos town.

The much-photographed, lovely Lalaria beach, on the north coast, is flanked by a majestic, arched limestone promontory. The polished limestone and marble add extra sparkle to the already shimmering Aegean. There's no lodging here, and you can only reach Lalaria by taking a boat from the old port in Skiathos town, where taxi and tourist boats are readily available. In the same area lie **Skoteini (Dark) cave, Galazia (Azure) cave,** and **Halkini (Copper) cave.** If taking a tour boat, you can stop for an hour or two here to swim and frolic. Bring along a flashlight to turn the water inside these grottoes an incandescent blue.

★ **Evangelistria.** The island's best-known and most beautiful monastery, Evangelistria, sits on Skiathos's highest point and was dedicated in the late 18th century to the Annunciation of the Virgin by the monks of Mt. Athos. It encouraged education and gave a base to revolutionaries, who pledged an oath to freedom and first hoisted the flag of Greece here in 1807. Looming above a gorge, and surrounded by fragrant pines and cypresses, the monastery has a high wall that once kept pirates out; today it encloses a ruined refectory kitchen, the cells, a small museum library, and a magnificent church with three domes. A gift shop sells the monastery's own Alypiakos wine, olive oil, locally made preserves, and Orthodox icons. It's near to Lalaria, and about a 10-minute drive, or an hour's walk, from Skiathos town. ⊠ *2 km (1 mi) south of Lalaria, 5 km (3 mi) north of Skiathos town, Lalaria* ☎ *No phone* ⊠ *Donations accepted* ⊙ *Daily 9–7.*

SKOPELOS ΣΚΟΠΕΛΟΣ

This triangular island's name means "a sharp rock" or "a reef"—a fitting description for the terrain on its northern shore. It's an hour away from Skiathos by hydrofoil and is the second largest of the Sporades. Most of its 122 square km (47 square mi), up to its highest peak on Mt. Delfi, are covered with dense pine forests, olive groves, and orchards. On the south coast, villages overlook the shores, and pines line the pebbly beaches, casting jade shadows on turquoise water.

Legend has it that Skopelos was settled by Peparethos and Staphylos, colonists from Minoan Crete, said to be the sons of Dionysus and Ariadne, King Minos's daughter. They brought with them the lore of the grape and the olive. The island was called Peparethos until Hellenistic times, and its most popular beach still bears the name Stafilos. In the 1930s a tomb believed to be Staphylos's was unearthed, filled with weapons and golden treasures (now in the Volos museum on the Pelion peninsula).

The Byzantines were exiled here, and the Venetians ruled for 300 years, until 1204. In times past, Skopelos was known for its wine, but today its plums and almonds are eaten rather than drunk, and incorporated into the simple cuisine. Many artists and photographers have settled on the island and throughout summer are part of an extensive cultural program. Little by little, Skopelos is cementing an image as a green and artsy island, still unspoiled by success.

GETTING HERE AND AROUND

AIR TRAVEL   There is no airport on Skopelos but you can take an Athens–Skiathos Olympic Airlines flight mid-June to mid-September, then taxi to Skiathos town port, and from there take a hydrofoil to Skopelos.

BY BOAT   To travel from the mainland by boat, take a ferry or hydrofoil from the ports of Agios Konstantinos (if arriving from Athens, a three-hour bus ride) or Volos (if arriving from central and northern Greece). There are two to three hydrofoils from either port in high season. The hydrofoil connecting Volos with Skopelos takes 2½ hours (€40); the hydrofoil connecting Agios Konstantinos with Skopelos takes 2 to 2½ hours (€40–€48, depending on the port you are traveling to). GA Ferries (⊕ *gaferries.gr*) has a morning ferry departing from Agios Konstantinos to Skopelos on a 3½ hr trip (€35). There are also ferry (90 minutes) and hydrofoil (45 minutes) connections with neighboring Skiathos, two with hydrofoil taking 30–50 minutes (€10–€16 depending on which port) and two ferries taking 1 hour (€9.50). Skopelos has two main ports: Skopelos town and, at the northwestern end of the island, Loutraki (near the town of Glossa). For schedule information, see ⊕ *www.hellenicseaways.gr* and *www.gtp.gr*.

BY BUS   The main bus station on Skopelos is located in front of a large church at a junction for Agiou Riginou and Loutraki. The last stop on the island-wide route is Glossa (€3.50, 1 hour), with stops along the way including Panormos and Elios.

Visitor Information Greek National Tourism Organization (GNTO or EOT)
✉ *Tsoha 7, Athens* ☎ 210/8707000 ⊕ *www.visitgreece.gr* **Skopelos Municipality** ✉ *Waterfront, Skopelos town* ☎ 24240/22205 ⊕ *www.skopelosweb.gr.*

EXPLORING

Although this is the most populated island of the Sporades, with two major towns, Skopelos remains peaceful and absorbs tourists into its life rather than giving itself up to their sun-and-fun desires. It's not surprising that ecologists claim it's the greenest island in the region.

SKOPELOS TOWN ΣΚΟΠΕΛΟΣ (ΠΟΛΗ)

3 hrs from Agios Konstantinos, ½ hr from Skiathos town.

Pretty Skopelos town, the administrative center of the Sporades, overlooks a bay on the north coast. On a steep hill below, scant vestiges of the ancient acropolis and medieval castle remain. The town works hard to stay charming—building permits are difficult to obtain, signs must be in native style, pebbles are embedded into the walkways.

Three- and four-story houses rise virtually straight up the hillside, reached by flagstone steps. The whitewashed houses look prosperous (18th-century Skopelos society was highly cultured and influential) and cared for, their facades enlivened by brightly painted or brown timber balconies, doors, and shutters. Flamboyant vines and potted plants complete the picture. Interspersed among the red-tile roofs are several with traditional gray fish-scale slate—too heavy and expensive to be used much nowadays.

Off the waterfront, prepare for a breath-snatching climb up the almost perpendicular steps in Skopelos town, starting at the seawall. You will encounter many churches as you go—the island has more than 300. The uppermost, located near the castle and said to be situated on the ruins of the ancient temple of Minerva, is the 11th-century Ayios Athanasios with a typically whitewashed exterior and an interior that includes 17th-century Byzantine murals. At the stairs' summit you're standing within the walls of the 13th-century castle erected by the Venetian Ghisi lords who held all the Sporades as their fief. It in turn rests on polygonal masonry of the 5th century BC, as this was the site of one of the island's three ancient acropoli. Once you've admired the view and the stamina of the old women negotiating the steps like mountain goats, wind your way back down the seawall steps by any route you choose. Wherever you turn, you may spy a church; Skopelos claims some 360, of which 123 are in the town proper. Curiously, most of them seem to be locked, but the exteriors are striking—some incorporating ancient artifacts, Byzantine plates or early Christian elements, and slate-capped domes. To gain a unique perspective on Skopelos town take one of the walking tours offered by Heather Parsons (⊕ *www.skopelos-walks.com*).

Agnonda. Used as an alternative port by hydrophoils and ferryboats during bad weather, Agnonda has numerous tavernas along its pebbled beach. It is named after a local boy who returned here victorious from Olympia in 569 BC brandishing the victor's wreath. ⊠ *5 km (3 mi) south of Skopelos town, Skopelos town.*

Evangelistria Monastery. Perched on Palouki Mountain and overlooking the sea and Skopelos' Chora, the impressive Evangelistria Monastery was founded in 1676 and completely rebuilt in 1712 by Ioannis Grammatikos, who believed he was saved from execution by an 11th-century icon of the Virgin. It contains no frescoes but has an intricately carved iconostasis and the miraculous icon. ⊠ *On mountainside opposite Skopelos town, 1½ km (1 mi) to northeast* ☎ *24240/23230* ☑ *Free* ⊙ *Daily 9–1 and 3–5.*

★ **Folk Art Museum.** For an impression of the interior of how an upper class Skopelan house looked 200 years ago, visit the Folk Art Museum, an 18th-century mansion (1795) with hand-carved period furniture, decorative items, paintings and embroideries. Don't miss the display of the elaborately sewn wedding dress in the bridal chamber. ⊠ *Hatzistamati, Skopelos town* ☎ *24240/23494* ☑ *€3* ⊙ *June–Sept., Mon.–Sat., 10 am–noon and 5 pm–10 pm, Sun. 7 pm–10 pm; Oct.–May, weekdays 9 am–3 pm.*

The Ayia Varvara monastery is just one of the 40 medieval beauties set on Skopelos. Some are open to visitors: wear suitable dress (no bare arms or skirts).

★ **Prodromou** (*Forerunner*). Dedicated to St. John the Baptist, Prodromou now operates as a convent. Besides being unusual in design, its church contains some outstanding 14th-century triptychs, an enamel tile floor, and an iconostasis spanning four centuries (half carved in the 14th century, half in the 18th century). The nuns sell elaborate woven and embroidered handiwork. Opening days and hours vary. ⊠ *2½ km (1½ mi) east of Skopelos town, Skopelos town.*

★ **Vakratsa.** Skopelos was once a hub for a well-travelled, politically influential, and highly cultured society and a fascinating peek into that world is offered by a visit to this 19th-century mansion. Furnishings, precious icons, and quotidian antiques made locally as well as from around the world make this a fine showcase of the life and traditions of a local family of high standing, namely that of Andigoni Vakratsa. She, along with her father, was a doctor who offered free medical services to the poor. Head upstairs to view the living room (used only for very special occasions) where you can admire a traditional island engagement dress with its 4,000-pleat skirt. ⊠ *A short walk up from Ambrosia sweet shop, Skopelos town* ☎ 🖥 *€3* ⊙ *Daily, 10–2 and 7–10.*

BEACHES

Stafilos beach. The cool, crystal waters at Stafilos are calm, and pines grow down to the azure waterfront. Scattered farms and two tavernas, small houses with rooms for rent, and one or two pleasant hotels line the road to the seaside, where you will find a simple canteen serving snacks, refreshments (and even mohitos at sunset), and a lifeguard stand. Nearby, prehistoric walls, a watchtower, and an unplundered grave suggest that this was the site of an important prehistoric settlement. ✉ *8 km [5 mi] southeast of Skopelos town.*

WHERE TO EAT

$$
GREEK

✕ **Klimataria.** The blackfish *stifado* (stew) with onions is so delicious here you may find yourself doing the quintessentially Greek *papara*—sponging the plate clean with a piece of bread. Patrons come to Klimataria for flavorsome local specialties such as the pork cooked in a sauce of red wine, honey, and prunes (the sweet and sour fruit was once the island's star export), succulent fresh fish, and a pleasant view of the moonlit sea. ✉ *Waterfront, Skopelos town* ☎ *24240/22273* ⊘ *Closed mid-Oct.–mid-Dec.*

$$
MEDITERRANEAN
Fodor's Choice
★

✕ **Molos.** A favorite amongst the cluster of tavernas near the far end at the old port, Molos serves quality *magirefta* (dishes cooked ahead in the oven), a broad choice of pasta dishes with fresh seafood, local goat cooked in a rich tomato sauce, stuffed courgette flowers (a Skopelos specialty) and fluffy *taramosalata* fish roe dip. Although most of the courses here are traditional Greek, chef/owner Panayiotis knows how to add his signature style, and his charisma extends to musical talents that he sometimes shares with clients in live performances. ✉ *Waterfront, Skopelos town* ☎ *24240/22551* ⊘ *Closed Nov.–Mar.*

$$
EUROPEAN
★

✕ **Perivoli.** The chef/owner of *To Perivoli* (garden) prides himself in the fact that the restaurant's menu has not changed at all in the last 20 years—the return of patrons year after year is living proof of its success. Indeed, the food and wine, charmingly served on a patio beside an herb and flower garden, is colorful and inventive enough to suit all tastes. Start with a salad with purslane, goat's cheese, and black sesame or the filo pouches stuffed with mushrooms and smoky metsovone cheese and then opt for the tender lamb cutlet with yogurt-mint sauce and wild rice. Leave room for the local specialty of *amygdalopitta* (almond cake) with ice cream. ✉ *Off Platanos Sq. close to waterfront, Skopelos town* ☎ *24240/23758* ⌁ *Reservations essential* ⊘ *Closed Oct.–May. No lunch.*

$
GREEK
★

✕ **Ta Kymata.** Spirited brothers Andreas, Riginos, and Christophoros enthusiastically run the seafront taverna that has belonged to their family since 1896, serving a gratifying lunch and dinner menu based on traditional Skopelos recipes. Try their wonderful summery salad of lettuce, sweet corn, artichokes, sundried tomatoes, capers, and kefalotyri cheese; for a main course choose the lamb cooked with plums or the delicious *pepperonata* stew. The signature dish is *Tis Maharas*, an intense, pungent, yet surprisingly light dish of vegetables and cheeses with a creamy sauce, dedicated to the brothers' grandmother, who's name *Mahi* means "battle" and whose physical strength and towering

---

MAMMA MIA!

The 2008 movie *Mamma Mia!* used a lot of Skopelos as its dreamy setting, something many locals take great pride in; sadly, a lot of these once-pure spots are now tainted by tourism. Film locations included the tiny Kastani bay—where they constructed Meryl Streep's taverna and then dismantled it after the film—Milia beach, and the breathtaking (literally) hilltop Ayios Ioannis monastery overlooking Glossa.

5

Forget all those worries back home with one delicious dinner on the town square in Skopelos town.

height was said to ensure there was never any trouble at the taverna. ⊠ *North end of the harbor, Skopelos town* ☎ *24240/22381* ⊟ *No credit cards.*

WHERE TO STAY

For expanded reviews, visit Fodors.com.

¢ ⊡ **Pension Sotos.** This cozy, restored, old Skopelete house on the waterfront is inexpensive and casual, with tiny rooms looking onto one of the hotel's two courtyard terraces. **Pros:** low prices. **Cons:** no breakfast. ⊠ *Waterfront, Skopelos town* ☎ *24240/22549* ↝ *12 rooms* ⚿ *In-room: no a/c* ⊟ *No credit cards* ⦿ *No meals.*

$$$ ⊡ **Skopelos Village.** A chic, contemporary take on traditional Greek island ☾ charm defines the design of the hotel, which is themed on breezy peace-★ fulness, understated luxury, and the comfort of a delightful villa. **Pros:** wonderful area; great views; steps away from the beach. **Cons:** relatively high prices; a 15-minute walk from the town center. ⊠ *1 km (½ mi) west of center, Skopelos town* ☎ *24240/23011, 24240/22517* ⊕ *www. skopelosvillage.gr* ↝ *35 suites* ⚿ *In-room: a/c, kitchen, Wi-Fi. In-hotel: restaurant, bar, pool, tennis court* ☉ *Closed Nov.–Apr.* ⦿ *No meals.*

¢ ⊡ **Thea Home.** A wonderful choice for budget travelers, the very clean, **Fodor's Choice** cozy, graceful, and family-run Kali Thea studios and maisonettes are ★ a short walk from the harbor and offer a beautiful vista of the town from Thea's large terrace (where guests can use free Wi-Fi and have a homemade snack or light meal). **Pros:** every image on the absolutely gorgeous slide show at this hotel's Web site is a "pro"! **Cons:** nearest beach 3 miles away. ⊠ *10 min walk up from harbor, Skopelos town*

☎ *24240/22859* 🖷 *24240/23556* ⊕ *www.skopelosweb.gr/theahome* 🛏 *13 ⚘ In-room: a/c. In-hotel: bar.*

NIGHTLIFE

Nightlife on Skopelos is more relaxed than it is on Skiathos. There's a smattering of cozy bars playing music of all kinds, and each summer at least one nightclub operates (look for advertisements). The *kefi* (good mood) is to be found at the western end of the waterfront, where a string of bar-nightclubs come to life after midnight. Take an evening *volta* (stroll); most bars have tables outside, so you really can't miss them.

MUSIC CLUBS **Anatoli.** At Anatoli, a converted barn perched at the highest point of the town by the old *kastro*, tap into a truly Greek vein with proprietor Giorgo Xithari. Sometimes accompanied by local musicians and friends, he strums up a storm on his bouzouki and sings *rembetika*, traditional Greek acoustic blues. With an ouzo or two, the atmosphere can get heady, and soon you may discover new dancing talents inspired by old classics. ✉ *Old kastro, Skopelos town* ☎ *24240/22851* ⊕ *www. anatolixintaris.gr.*

★ **Anemos.** Without a doubt the best cocktail bar on the island, laid-back and casual Anemos serves impeccably mixed cocktails; try the fragrantly sophisticated Paris Martini or ask the barman to create one of his inspired concoctions to suit—or perfectly alter—your mood, as you enjoy the DJ's eclectic mix of cool grooves on the large stone terrace. The place opens at 9 am for coffee and snacks. ✉ *Skopelos harbor front, Skopelos town* ☎ *24240/23564* ⊕ *www.skopelosweb.gr/anemosbar.*

Mercurius. Perched just above the waterfront, Mercurius is ideal for a leisurely breakfast or invigorating sunset drinks with a stunning view and a soundtrack of world music. ✉ *5-min walk up from the harbor, Skopelos town* ☎ *24240/24593.*

SHOPPING

FOOD SPECIALTIES **Kyria Leni.** Skopelos is well known for its almonds and plums, and at this dignified, classic store you will find a grand variety of delectable, locally sourced, and homemade goods to savor. Don't miss out on the fluffy *avgato* prunes in syrup, an island specialty best eaten as a *glyko koutaliou* (eaten with a spoon and often accompanied by strong Greek coffee to contrast its sweetness). ✉ *Waterfront, Skopelos town* ☎ *24240/33688, 24240/33115* ⊕ *www.kyraleni-skopelos.com.*

LOCAL CRAFTS **Archipelago.** Head here for modern ceramics and crafts, great jewelry, handbags, and a wonderful selection of pricey antiques. Operating since 1973, it's the oldest craft shop on the island. ✉ *Waterfront, Skopelos town* ☎ *24240/23127.*

★ **Armoloi.** For 35 years Armoloi has been creating exquisite ceramic crockery, inspired Greek-style jewelry, and colorful decor items. The shop is also a wonderful spot for buying traditional-style pottery, handmade leather handbags, and crafts by artists from around the country. ✉ *Waterfront, Skopelos town* ☎ *24240/22707.*

SPORTS AND THE OUTDOORS

Fodor's Choice ★ **Aegeo Sailing.** A wonderful way to explore Skopelos by sea is to hop onto "Captain" Vasilis' sailing boat, which seats up to 10 people, and travel where the winds will take you. The skipper's knowledge of the island, its waters and whimsical winds, as well as about surrounding islets and islands such as the gorgeous Alonissos wildlife preserve, offers a fantastic break from land-leg reality. Customers are shown sailing tricks, stunning out-of-the-way beaches, delectable cuisine in the form of a fish lunch in Alonissos' miniharbor of Steni Vala, and if they're lucky, dolphins. In other words: a great way to relax, open your eyes and nostrils to the pure open sea, and learn a thing or two. Make sure you book your place in advance for a da -trip (you can even charter the boat for a longer sojourn) on the sea. ⊠ *Waterfront, Skopelos town* 📞 *30231/0953773* ⊕ *www.aegeo-sailing.gr.*

PANORMOS BAY ΟΡΜΟΣ ΠΑΝΟΡΜΟΥ

6 km (4 mi) west of Skopelos town, 4 km (2½ mi) northwest of Agnonda.

Due northwest of Agnonda is Panormos Bay, the smallest of the ancient towns of Peparethos, founded in the 8th century BC by colonists from Chalkis. A few well-concealed walls are visible among the pinewoods on the acropolis above the bay. With its long beach and its sheltered inner cove ideal for yachts, this is fast becoming a holiday village, although so far it retains its quiet charm. Inland, the interior of Skopelos is green and lush, and not far from Panormos Bay traditional farmhouses called *kalivia* stand in plum orchards. Some are occupied; others have been turned into overnight stops or are used only for feast-day celebrations. Look for the outdoor ovens, which baked the fresh plums when Skopelos was turning out prunes galore. This rural area is charming, but the lack of signposts makes it easy to get lost, so pay attention.

BEACHES

Fodor's Choice ★ **Milia.** Skopelos's longest beach, Milia is considered by many to be its best. Though still secluded, the bay is up and coming—parasols and recliners are lined halfway across the beach and there's a large taverna serving average food, thankfully ensconced by pine trees. No matter: Milia is breathtaking, thanks to its white sands, clear turquoise waters, and vibrant green trees. If you'd like to live up this aquatic romance, locate the owner of one of the villas for rent that are set right on the beach—well-tended, they are but a few short strides from the water's edge. ⊠ *2 km (1 mi) north of Panormos Bay.*

WHERE TO STAY

For expanded reviews, visit Fodors.com.

$ 🏨**Afrodite.** Less than five minutes walk from beautiful Panormos Bay and ten minutes from Adrina beach stands this friendly, relaxing B-grade hotel—surrounded by lush mountains and with a good enough view of the sea, it offers a coveted sense of getting away from it all, yet is also located near enough to all the essentials one may want on a laid-back holiday: a lovely beach, where a handful of quality tavernas can be found, and two minimarkets. **Pros:** friendly; well situated. **Cons:** no Wi-Fi in rooms. ⊠ *Panormos Bay* ☎ *24240/23150* 🖹 *24240/23152* ⊕ *www.afroditehotel.gr* ⤵ *30* ᗕ *In-room: a/c. In-hotel: pool, parking.*

$ 🖬 **Delphi Apartments.** The garden filled with magnolia, cherry, plum, pear, and lemon trees, with lovely white oleander and herb bushes that frame the pool and patio, is one good reason to stay here; the well-spaced, clean, and self-sufficient apartments and maisonettes are another. **Pros:** great location thanks to backdrop of beautiful pine forest; just a few minutes walk to beach. **Cons:** rooms are pretty basic. ⊠ *Elios, Panormos Bay* ☎ *33301/33788–33172* ⊕ *www.hoteldelphi. net* ⤵ *40 apartments, 7 maisonettes* ᗕ *In-room: a/c, kitchen. In-hotel: restaurant, pool.*

Loutraki. Loutraki is the tiny port village where the ferries and hydrofoils stop to and from Skiathos, and it is not very charming. Around 300 yards from the port are the remains of the Acropolis of Selinous, the island's third ancient city. Unfortunately, everything lies buried except the walls.

EN
ROUTE

5

GLOSSA ΓΛΩΣΣΑ

38 km (23 mi) northwest of Skopelos town, 24 km (14 mi) northwest of Panormos Bay, 3 km (1½ mi) northwest of Klima.

Delightful Glossa is the island's second-largest settlement, where white-washed, red-roof houses are clustered on the steep hillside above the harbor of Loutraki. Venetian towers and traces of Turkish influence remain; the center is closed to traffic. This is a place to relax, dine, and enjoy the quieter beaches. Just to the east, have a look at Ayios Ioan-nis monastery, dramatically perched above a pretty beach. There's no need to tackle the series of extremely steep steps to the monastery, as it is not open to visitors.

WHERE TO EAT

$$$
MODERN GREEK
Fodor'sChoice
★

✕ **Restaurant Agnanti.** Located in the picturesque village of Glossa, this long-established landmark today entices with its playful and innovative take on classic Greek dishes. Instead of resting assured that the restaurant's awe-inspiring panoramic vista of the Aegean Sea is enough to please customers, owner Nikos Stamatakis and his chef father Stamatis keep upping the bar of the menu's wow factor, thanks to their vine leaf-wrapped chicken dressed in a rich lemon geranium sauce (a play on the traditional dolma), or the creamy moussaka which is blended with tuna instead of minced beef. ⊠ *Next to Glossa community, Louki, Glossa* ☎ *24240/33306* ⊕ *www.skopelosweb.gr* ⊘ *Closed Nov.–Apr.*

Meryl Streep's most unforgettable star turn in *Mamma Mia!* was filmed with Glossa's church of Ayios Ioannis as her beautiful backdrop.

SKYROS ΣΚΥΡΟΣ

Even among these unique isles, Skyros stands out. Its rugged terrain looks like a Dodecanese island, and its spectacularly sited main town—occupied on and off for the last 3,300 years and haunted by mythical ghosts—looks Cycladic. It has military bases, and an airport with periodic connections to Athens, yet it remains the most difficult ferry connection in the Sporades. With nothing between it and Lesbos, off the coast of Turkey, its nearest neighbor is the town of Kimi, on the east coast of Evia.

Surprisingly beguiling, this southernmost of the Sporades is the largest (209 square km [81 square mi]). A narrow, flat isthmus connects Skyros's two almost-equal parts, whose names reflect their characters—*Meri* or *Imero* ("tame") for the north, and *Vouno* (literally, "mountain," meaning tough or stony) for the south. The heavily populated north is virtually all farmland and forests. The southern half of the island is forbidding, barren, and mountainous, with Mt. Kochilas its highest peak (2,598 feet). Its western coast is outlined with coves and deep bays dotted with a series of islets.

Until Greece won independence in 1831, the population of Skyros squeezed sardine-fashion into the area under the castle on the inland face of the rock. Not a single house was visible from the sea. Though the islanders could survey any movement in the Aegean for miles, they kept a low profile, living in dread of the pirates based at Treis Boukes bay on Vouno.

GETTING HERE AND AROUND

BY AIR   From Athens, Sky Express offers three flights each week (Thursday and Friday at 8:10 am and Sunday at 12:10 departure times) throughout the year; each takes 40 minutes and costs €60. The airport is on the opposite side of the island from Skyros town but a shuttle bus always meets the plane; tickets on the shuttle run €2 to €6.

BY BOAT   To take a ferry, you must take buses from Athens to Evia (the largest of the Sporades islands, *and one that is not covered in this chapter*), where you can find boats run by the Skyros Shipping Company (⊕ *www.sne.gr*) departing for Skyros from the main port of Kimi; these usually cost €9 and take 2½ hours. On summer weekends, there are early afternoon and early evening departures; from Skyros to Kimi, early morning and midafternoon departures. On weekdays, there is only one departure. This ferry company helpfully sells bus tickets connecting with Athens (buses leave Athens's Terminal B four times daily; the ride can be as long as four hours so be sure to catch a bus that allows enough time to prevent your arriving in Kimi—actually you need to hop on a connecting bus from there to the Paralia Kimi port harborage to catch the ferry—just as the boat is heading out the harbor. All boats dock at Linaria, far from Skyros town. A shuttle bus, however, always meets the boat; bus tickets run €2 to €3. Taxis are another option but settle the fee before setting out. There are only a couple of boats that connect Skyros with Skiathos weekly so it is only advisable if you have plenty of time at your disposal.

Visitor Information Contacts Greek National Tourism Organization (GNTO or EOT) ⊠ *Tsoha 7, Athens* ☎ *210/8707000* ⊕ *www.visitgreece.gr.* **Skyros official Web site** ⊕ *www.skyros.gr.*

EXPLORING

Strangely enough, although Skyros is adrift in the Aegean, the Skyrians have not had a seafaring tradition, and have looked to the land for their living. Their isolation has brought about notable cultural differences from the other Greek islands, such as pre-Christian Carnival rituals. Today there are more than 300 churches on the island, many of them private and owned by local families. An almost-extinct breed of pony resides on Skyros, and exceptional crafts—carpentry, pottery, embroidery—are practiced by dedicated artisans whose creations include unique furniture and decorative linens. There are no luxury accommodations or swank restaurants: this idiosyncratic island makes no provisions for mass tourism, but if you've a taste for the offbeat, you may feel right at home.

SKYROS TOWN ΣΚΥΡΟΣ (ΧΩΡΙΟ)

Fodor's Choice ★   *1 hr, 40 mins from Kimi to Linaria by boat, 30 mins from Linaria by car.*
As you drive south from the airport, past brown, desolate outcroppings with only an occasional goat as a sign of life, Skyros town suddenly looms around a bend. It resembles a breathtaking imaginary painting by Monet, Cézanne, or El Greco: blazing white, cubist, dense, and otherworldly, clinging, precariously it seems, to the precipitous rock

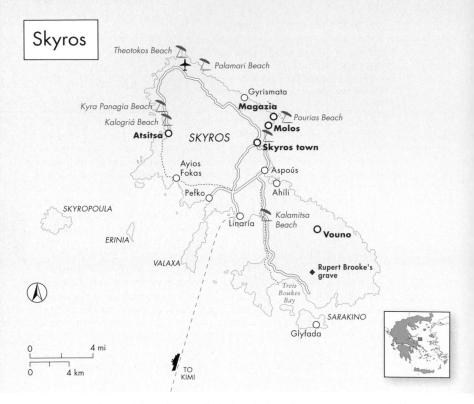

Theotokos Beach

Palamari Beach

Gyrismata

Magazia

Kyra Panagia Beach

Kalogriá Beach

Atsitsa

SKYROS

Pourias Beach

Molos

Skyros town

Ayios
Fokas

Aspoús

Pefko

Ahíli

SKYROPOULA

Linariá

Kalamitsa
Beach

ERINIA

Vouno

VALAXA

Rupert Brooke's
grave

Treis
Boukes
Bay

SARAKINO

Glyfada

0   4 mi

0   4 km

TO
KIMI

beneath it and topped gloriously by a fortress-monastery. This town more closely resembles a village in the Cyclades than any other you'll find in the Sporades.

Called *Horio, Hora,* and *Chora* ("town") by the locals, Skyros town is home to 90% of the island's 3,000 inhabitants. The impression as you get closer is of stark, simple buildings creeping up the hillside, with a tangle of labyrinthine lanes steeply winding up, down, and around the tiny houses, Byzantine churches, and big squares. As you stroll down from the ruins and churches of the kastro area, or explore the alleyways off the main drag, try to peek discreetly into the houses. Skyrians are house-proud and often leave their windows and doors open to show off. In fact, since the houses all have the same exteriors, the only way for families to distinguish themselves has been through interior design. Walls and conical mantelpieces are richly decorated with European- and Asian-style porcelain, copper cooking utensils, wood carvings, and embroideries. Wealthy families originally obtained much of the porcelain from the pirates in exchange for grain and food, and its possession was a measure of social standing. Then enterprising potters started making exact copies, along with the traditional local ware, leading to the unique Skyrian style of pottery. The furniture is equally beautiful, and often miniature in order to conserve interior space.

Farther up the hill, the summit is crowned with three tiny cube-like churches with blue and pink interiors, and the ruined Venetian cistern, once used as a dungeon. From there you have a spectacular view of the town and surrounding hills. The roofs are flat, the older ones covered with a dark gray shale that has splendid insulating properties. The house walls and roofs are interconnected, forming a pattern that from above looks like a magnified form of cuneiform writing. Here and there the shieldlike roof of a church stands out from the cubist composition of white houses that fills the hillside—with not an inch to spare.

> **BILLY GOAT'S BLUFF**
>
> **Apokries.** The Apokries, pre-Lenten Carnival revelry, on Skyros relates to pre-Christian fertility rites and is famous throughout Greece. Young men dressed as old men, maidens, or "Europeans" roam the streets teasing and tormenting onlookers with ribald songs and clanging bells. The "old men" wear elaborate shepherd's outfits, with masks made of baby-goat hides and belts dangling with as many as 40 sheep bells.

Most commercial activity takes place in or near the agora (the market street), familiarly known as Sisifos, as in the myth, because of its frustrating steepness. Found here are the town's pharmacies, travel agencies, shops with wonderful Skyrian pottery, and an extraordinary number of tiny bars and tavernas but few boutiques and even less kitsch. In the summer heat, all shops and restaurants close from 2 pm to 6 pm, but the town comes alive at night.

Archaeological Museum. This tiny archaeological museum (on the way to Magazia beach as you begin to descend from the town) contains few but rare finds, mostly from graves dating from Neolithic to Roman times. Weapons, pottery, and jewelry are exhibited. ⊠ *Rupert Brooke Square, Skyros town* ☎ *22220/91327* ⊕ *www.skopelos.net/sporades/skyros.htm* 🎫 *€3* ⊙ *Tues.–Sun. 8:30–3.*

Episkopi Church. Take the vaulted passageway from St. George's Monastery courtyard to the ruined church of Episkopi, the former seat of the bishop of Skyros, built in 895 on the ruins of a temple of Athena. This was the center of Skyros's religious life from 1453 to 1837. You can continue up to the summit from here. ⊠ *Above St. George's Monastery, Skyros town.*

Fodor's Choice ★ **Faltaits Historical and Folklore Museum.** This museum showcases an outstanding collection of Skyrian decorative arts. Built after Greek Independence by a wealthy family (who still owns the museum), the house is one of the most impressive in Skyros town. Just as well, as it is nearly overflowing with rare books, costumes, photographs, paintings, ceramics, local embroideries, Greek statues, and other heirlooms. Of particular note are the embroideries, which are famed for their flamboyant colors and vivacious renderings of mermaids, *hoopoes* (the Skyrians' favorite bird), and mythical human figures whose clothes and limbs sprout flowers. Top treasure among the museum's historical documents is a handwritten copy of the Proclamation of the Greek Revolution against the Ottoman Empire. The informative guided tour is well worth

Skyros is famed for its woodworking traditions, so be sure to visit one of its workshops and bring a little bit of Greece back home with you.

the extra euros. ⊠ *Rupert Brooke Square, Skyros town* ☎ *22220/91150* ☎ *€2, tour €5* ⊙ *Daily 10–2 and 6–9.*

Fodor's Choice **Monastery of St. George.** The best way to get an idea of the town and its
★ history is to follow the sinuous cobbled lanes past the mansions of the Old Town to the kastro, the highest point, and the 10th-century fortified Monastery of St. George, which stands on the site of the ancient acropolis and Bronze Age settlement. Little remains of the legendary fortress of King Lykomedes, portrayed in Skyros's two most colorful myths, though lower down on the north and southwest face of the rock are the so-called Pelasgian bastions of immense rectangular fitted blocks, dated to the classical period or later. A white marble lion, which may be left over from the Venetian occupation, is in the wall above the entrance to the monastery. This classical symbol is a reminder of when Skyros was under Athenian dominion and heavily populated with Athenian settlers to keep it that way. This part of the castle was built on ancient foundations (look right) during the early Byzantine era and reinforced in the 14th century by the Venetians.

The monastery itself was founded in 962 and radically rebuilt in 1600. Today it is inhabited by a sole monk. Unfortunately, the once splendid frescoes of the Monastery of St. George are now mostly covered by layers of whitewash, but look for the charming St. George and startled dragon outside to the left of the church door. Within, the ornate iconostasis is considered a masterpiece. The icon of St. George on the right is said to have been brought by settlers from Constantinople, who came in waves during the iconoclast controversy of the 9th century. The icon has a black face and is familiarly known as Ayios Georgis o Arapis ("the Negro"); the Skyrians view him as the patron saint not only of their island but of lovers as well. ⊠ *1 km (½ mi) above waterfront, Skyros town.*

★ **Rupert Brooke Memorial Statue.** It'd be hard to miss the classical bronze statue, "To Brooke," an honorary tribute to the heroic Edwardian-era English poet Rupert Brooke. Every street seems to lead either to it or to the kastro, and the statue stands alone with a 180-degree view of the sea behind it. In 1915, aged 28, Brooke was on his way to the Dardanelles to fight in World War I when he died of septicemia in a French hospital ship off Skyros. Brooke was a socialist, but he became something of a paragon for war leaders such as Winston Churchill. ⊠ *Rupert Brooke Square, Skyros town.*

> **MYTHIC SKYROS**
>
> In the legends of The *Iliad*, before the Trojan War, Theseus, the deposed hero-king of Athens, sought refuge in his ancestral estate on Skyros. King Lykomedes, afraid of the power and prestige of Theseus, took him up to the acropolis one evening, pretending to show him the island, and pushed him over the cliff—an ignominious end. In ancient times, Timon of Athens unearthed what he said were Theseus's bones and sword, and placed them in the Theseion—more commonly called the Temple of Hephaistion—in Athens, in what must be one of the earliest recorded archaeological investigations.

WHERE TO EAT AND STAY

$$$

SEAFOOD

✕ **Margetis Taverna.** A vest-pocket taverna wedged in among shops on the main drag of the agora, Margetis is known locally as the best place for fish on the island. It's popular, so get here early (8–8:30 pm). Though fish and lobster are always pricey, they are worth it here, as is the roast pork loin, lamb, or goat chops. Try the flavorful barrel wine, sit outside under the big tree, and watch the folks walk by. ⊠ *Agora, Skyros town* ☎ *22220/91311* ▭ *No credit cards* ⊙ *No lunch.*

$$$

Fodor's Choice

★

⌂ **Nefeli.** This superb little hotel is decorated in Cycladic white and soft green trim, with a dazzling seawater pool and elegant bar terrace. **Pros:** chock-full of delicious goodies, including impressive wine and cigar menus; a library of more than a thousand books; a telescope by the pool; karaoke nights. **Cons:** on the pricey side; preferred mode of accommodation in Skyros town is to book rooms in traditional houses, not hotels, but this one is a winner. ⊠ *Plageiá, Skyros town* ☎ *22220/91964, 22220/92060* ✑ *info@skyros-nefeli.gr* ⊕ *www.skyros-nefeli.gr* ⪪ *4 apartments, 7 studios, 8 rooms, 2 suites* ♴ *In-room: a/c, kitchen. In-hotel: restaurant, bar, pool, children's programs, laundry facilities, parking.*

$$$

GREEK

★

✕ **Papous Ki'Ego.** "My Grandfather and I," as the name translates in English, serves terrific Greek cuisine in an eclectic dining room decorated with hanging spoons, bottles of wine and ouzo, and whole heads of garlic. The proud grandson suggests that diners order a selection of mezedes and share with others at the table. The best include fried pumpkins with yogurt, tzatziki, zucchini croquettes, and meatballs doused with ouzo and served flambé. If you want a single dish, the baby goat served as a casserole tastes delicious. ⊠ *Agora, Skyros town* ☎ *22220/93200* ⊙ *Closed Nov. and Dec. No lunch.*

NIGHTLIFE

Skyros town's bars are seasonal affairs, offering loud music in summer.

Calypso. Jazz and blues are the standards at Calypso, the oldest bar-club. ⊠ *Agora, Skyros town.*

Posto. Modern Greek and foreign hits entertain a laid-back, youthful crowd here. ⊠ *Agora, Skyros town* ☎ *22220/92092.*

Rodon. Takis, the owner, is also the DJ here, and he loves spinning the best tunes in town. ⊠ *Agora, Skyros town.*

Skyropoula. Down the steps from the Archaeological Museum towards Magazia beach you'll find one of the most "happening" clubs in town—head here to party modern-Greek style until the early hours. ⊠ *Skyros town.*

SHOPPING

Want to buy something really unusual for a shoe lover? Check out the multi-thong *trohadia,* worn with pantaloons by Skyrian men as part of their traditional costume. Just as unique, elaborate Skyrian pottery and furniture are famous around the country. The pottery is both utilitarian and decorative, and the distinctive wooden furniture is easily recognizable by its traditionally carved style. Although you will see it all over town, the best places to shop are all on the agora. Skyrian furniture can be shipped anywhere. Don't try to shop between 1 and 6 pm, as all stores close for siesta.

CLOTHING **Argo Shop.** You can find the conversation-stopping *trohadia* footwear at the Argo Shop, which specializes in high-quality imitations of ceramics from the Faltaits Museum. ⊠ *Off Rupert Brooke Sq., Skyros town* ☎ .

FURNITURE **Lefteris Avgoklouris.** The workshop of Lefteris Avgoklouris, a carpenter with flair, is open to visitors. Ask around to find other master carpenters and craftspeople who make original Skyrian furniture, famous around Greece for its intricate technique, and other artistic handicrafts. This store also ships furniture abroad. ⊠ *About 100 yards from Rupert Brooke Sq. on right side of road heading down hill, Skyros town* ☎ *22220/91106* ⊕ *augoklouris.weebly.com.*

POTTERY **Srgastiri.** This is by far the best workshop/store selling beautiful and highly decorative Skyrian handmade ceramics and imports. ⊠ *Agora, Skyros town* ☎ *22220/91559, 22220/91887.*

MAGAZIA AND MOLOS ΜΑΓΑΖΙΑ ΚΑΙ ΜΩΛΟΣ

1 km (½ mi) northeast of Skyros town.

Coastal expansions of the main town, these two resort areas are the places to stay if you love to swim. Magazia, where the residents of Horio used to have their storehouses and wine presses, and Molos, a bit farther north, where the small fishing fleet anchors, are both growing fast. You can sunbathe, explore the isolated coastline, and stop at sea caves for a swim. Nearby are rooms to rent and tavernas serving the day's catch and local wine. From here, Skyros town is 15 minutes away, along the steps that lead past the archaeological museum to Rupert Brooke Square.

Panayia (*Festival of the Virgin*). On the major Greek Orthodox celebration of August 15 (Dormition of the Virgin) children gather at Magazia beach to race on the island's domesticated small ponies, similar to Shetland ponies.

BEACHES

From **Molos** to **Magazia** is a long, sandy beach.

Palamari beach. North of Molos, past low hills, fertile fields, and the odd farmhouse, a dirt road leads to the historical beach at Palamari, where ruins from a Neolithic fortress and settlement were discovered. Palamari has cool, crystal waters and offers a sense of privacy.

Pourias beach. A short walk south of Magazia, Pourias offers good snorkeling, and nearby on the cape is a small treasure: a sea cave turned into a chapel.

WHERE TO STAY

For expanded reviews, visit Fodors.com.

$ ⊞ **Perigiali.** Unlike other options in this area, Perigiali has many of the comforts of home and a few that home may be lacking—like private terraces and a pretty, lush garden with plenty of shade, where you can relax over breakfast or drinks in summer. **Pros:** next to Magazia beach; relatively cheap. **Cons:** no parking but free community parking a two-minute walk away. ⊠ *On beachfront at foot of Skyros town, Magazia* ☎ *22220/91889, 22220/92075* ⊕ *www.perigiali.com* ↵ *11 rooms* ⌂ *In-room: a/c, kitchen. In-hotel: restaurant, bar, pool.*

$ ⊞ **Skiros Palace.** With a big pool and a gorgeous, isolated beach, this is a water lover's dream. **Pros:** great location; great views. **Cons:** somewhat overpriced given the decor and space. ⊠ *North of Molos, Girismata, Kambos* ☎ *22220/91994, 22220/92212* ⊕ *www.skiros-palace.gr* ↵ *80 rooms* ⌂ *In-room: a/c. In-hotel: restaurant, pool* ☉ *Closed Oct.–May* ⦿| *Breakfast.*

NIGHTLIFE

Skiropoula. For late-night dancing, the best club is Skiropoula. Music is Western at first and later on, Greek. A laser lighting system illuminates the rocks of the acropolis after the sun has gone down. The club can be reached from Rupert Brooke Square by descending the steps past the archaeological museum. ⊠ *On beach before Magazia, Magazia* ☎ *No phone* ☉ *Closed Oct.–Apr.*

> ### THE WAY THE WIND BLOWS
>
> As of this writing, government and conservationists are locked in battle over putting a 100-turbine wind farm in the island's barren southeast. While the government sees it as a means to increase the country's sustainable energy sources, conservationists say it could be the death knell for the rare Skyrian horses and bird species that live there.

5

DID YOU KNOW?

Many of the remarkable cliff-face churches of Greece were originally caves colonized by ascetic hermits. This tiny example is the Ayios Nikolaos church near Pouria.

ATSITSA ΑΤΣΙΤΣΑ

14 km (9 mi) west of Molos.

On the northwest coast, pine forests grow down the rocky shore at Atsitsa. The beaches north of town—Kalogriá and Kyra Panayia—are sheltered from the strong northern winds called the *meltemi*.

Ayios Fokas. The road south from Atsitsa deteriorates into a rutted track, nerve-wracking even for experienced motorbike riders. If you're feeling fit and the weather's good, however, consider the challenging 6 km (4-mile) trek around the headland to Ayios Fokas. There are three lovely white-pebbled beaches and a small taverna where Kyria Kali serves her husband's just-caught fish with her own vegetables, homemade cheese, and bread. She also rents out a couple of very basic rooms without electricity or plumbing. ⊠ *5 km [3 mi] south of Atsitsa.*

Ayios Panteleimon. On July 27, the chapel of Ayios Panteleimon holds a festival in honor of its patron saint. ⊠ *On dirt road south of Atsitsa.*

Skyros Centre. Skyros Centre, founded in 1978, was the first major center in Europe for holistic vacations. Participants come to Atsitsa for a two-week session, staying in straw huts or in the main building, in a peaceful environment surrounded by pines and facing the sea. Studies and courses include windsurfing, creative writing with well-known authors, art, tai chi, yoga, massage, dance, drama, and sound healing. Courses also take place in Skyros town, where participants live in villagers' traditional houses. Skyros Centre's courses are highly reputed. Contact the London office well in advance of leaving for Greece. ⊠ *Atsitsa coast.* ⌖ *Prince of Wales Rd. 92, London, England* ☎ *207/267–4424, 207/284–3065* ⊕ *www.skyros.co.uk.*

BEACHES

★ **Aghios Petros beach.** North of Atsitsa, in the direction of the Chora, is this wonderful white sand and pebble beach, surrounded by lush greenery and serenely back-dropped, on the hill above it, by the little chapel of Aghios Petros. ⊠ *Atsitsa.*

Linaria. All boats and hydrofoils to Skyros dock at the tiny port of Linaria because the northeast coast is either straight, sandy beach, or steep cliffs. A bus to Skyros town meets arrivals. To get to the otherwise inaccessible sea caves of Pentekáli and Diatryptí, you can take a caïque from here. This dusty area offers scenes of fishermen tending their bright yellow nets and not much more. ⊠ *18 km [11 mi] southeast of Atsitsa, 10 km [6 mi] south of Skyros town, Atsitsa.*

EN ROUTE

VOUNO ΒΟΥΝΟ

Via Loutro, 5 km (3 mi) northwest of Linaria; access to southern territory starts at Ahilli, 4 km (2½ mi) south of Skyros town and 25 km (15½ mi) from Atsitsa.

In the mountainous southern half of Skyros, a passable dirt road heads south at the eastern end of the isthmus, from Aspous to Ahilli. The little bay of Ahilli (from where legendary Achilles set sail with Odysseus) is a yacht marina. Some beautiful, practically untouched beaches and sea caves are well worth the trip for hard-core explorers.

Thorny bushes warped into weird shapes, oleander, and rivulets running between sharp rocks make up the landscape; only goats and Skyrian ponies can survive this desolate environment. Many scholars consider the beautifully proportioned, diminutive horses to be the same breed as the horses sculpted on the Parthenon frieze. They are, alas, an endangered species, and only about 100 survive.

Rupert Brooke's grave. Pilgrims to Rupert Brooke's grave should follow the wide dirt road through the Vouno wilderness down toward the shore. As you reach the valley, you can catch sight of the grave in an olive grove on your left. He was buried the same night he died on Skyros, and his marble grave was immortalized with his prescient words, "If I should die think only this of me:/ That there's some corner of a foreign field/ That is forever England." Restored by the British Royal Navy in 1961, the grave site is surrounded by a stout wrought-iron and cement railing. You also can arrange for a visit by taxi or caïque in Skyros town.

BEACHES

Kalamitsa. The windy beach of Kalamitsa is 4 km (2½ mi) along the road south from Ahilli, and popular with windsurfers for obvious reasons. It is known for its clean waters. There are three tavernas at this old harbor.

Corfu

WORD OF MOUTH

"I loved Corfu . . . it's quite different from Greece's dry islands. It is lush with greenery and olive trees . . . and also it has such a varied history (various empires owned it at one time or another) that you can go into Corfu town, sit under a Venetian-style arcade, eat Greek food, and hear a discussion about a game of cricket."

—elaine

WELCOME TO CORFU

TOP REASONS TO GO

★ **Corfu Town:** Recognized by UNESCO as a World Heritage Site, this sophisticated little gem of a city glows with a profusion of picturesque reminders of its Venetian, French, and British past.

★ **Some Enchanted Islet:** As they savor the famous view of Pontikonisi, from the patio of a Starbucks in suburban Kanoni, how many of today's visitors know that tiny "Mouse Island" was thought by the ancients to be Odysseus's ship turned to stone by Poseidon?

★ **Mon Repos:** Owned by the Greek royal family before they were deposed, the elegant neoclassic villa of Mon Repos, with its enchanting seaside gardens and secret beach, was originally built as a love gift from a British lord high commissioner to his wife.

★ **Homer's City of the Phaeacians:** Once extolled by Odysseus, Paleokastritsa remains a swimmable, sunable spectacle of grottoes, cliffs, white sand, and turquoise waters.

1 Corfu Town. Along the east coast mid-island, Corfu town occupies a small peninsula anchored at its eastern tip by the massive Old Fortress and to the north by the New Fortress. Between the two is the gorgeous and lively Paleopolis (Old Town) crammed with Venetian and English Georgian houses, arcaded streets, narrow alleyways, and tiny squares, the entire urban ensemble buffered by the leafy Esplanade, built as a parade grounds by the British and now used as a popular public park.

2 South Corfu. Just south of Corfu town is a region that royals and their high-ranking officials once called home. Mon Repos, with its gorgeous seaside gardens, was the summer residence of the British lord high commissioners, later taken over by the Greek royal family, and was the birthplace of Prince Philip, Queen Elizabeth II's husband. Another 16 km (10 mi) south is Gastouri, site of the Achilleion, a late-19th-century Teutonic extravaganza built for Empress Elizabeth of Austria. To remind yourself you're really in Greece, head to Kanoni and take in the famed vista of the chapel-crowned Mouse Island.

3 West-Central Corfu. Corfu town is great for a day or three of sightseeing but you really need to head into the interior and along the western and northeastern coastlines to discover the natural beauty and charms of Corfu. Many head to Paleokastritsa, on the west side of the island, where you'll discover one of Greece's best beaches; rent a boat to visit the nearby caves.

GETTING ORIENTED

Scattered along the western coast of Greece the Ionian islands derive their name from the Ionian Greeks, their first colonizers. The proximity of these isles to Italy and their sheltered position on the East–West trade routes tempted many an occupier to the main island jewel, Corfu. Never subjected to Turkish rule, the Corfiots were greatly influenced by the urban life-styles of Venetian settlers as well as the orderly formality of the 19th-century British protectorate. With its fairy-tale setting, Corfu (Kerkyra in Greek) basks in the clear blue-green waters of the Ionian Sea at the mouth of the Adriatic. The island is connected by numerous ferries with Brindisi in Italy and Igoumenitsa and Patras on the Greek mainland. For many European travelers, Corfu is the gateway to Greece.

6

Updated
by Hilary P.
Paipeti

Temperate, multihued Corfu—of emerald mountains; turquoise waters lapping rocky coves; ocher and pink buildings; shimmering silver olive leaves; puffed red, yellow, and
orange parasails; scarlet roses, bougainvillea, and lavender wisteria and jacaranda spread over cottages—could
have inspired impressionism.

Kerkyra (Corfu) is certainly the lushest, and quite possibly, the loveliest
of all Greek islands. Breathlessly blue waters lap rocky, pine-rimmed
coves, and plants like bougainvillea, wisteria, and sweet-smelling jasmine spread over the countryside. Homer's "well-watered gardens"
and "beautiful and rich land" were Odysseus's last stop on his journey
home. Corfu is also said to be the inspiration for Prospero's island in
Shakespeare's *The Tempest*. This northernmost of the major Ionian
islands has, through the centuries, inspired other artists, as well as
conquerors, royalty, and, of course, tourists.

Today more than a million—mainly British—tourists visit every year, and
in summer crowd the evocative capital city of Corfu town (population
40,000). As a result, the town has a number of stylish restaurants and
hotels and a sophisticated European ambience. The interior of Corfu,
however, remains largely unspoiled, and the island has absorbed many
layers of architectural history, offering an alluring mix of neoclassic villas; Venetian palazzo; pastel-painted hill towns; old farmhouses; and
fancy classy, city-size resorts. You'll find all this, plus ancient olive groves,
pine-covered cliffs, and heart-stoppingly beautiful vistas of sea and sky.
Corfu remains an enchanting mixture of simplicity and sophistication.

The classical remains have suffered from the island's tempestuous
history and also from earthquakes; architecture from the centuries
of Venetian, French, and British rule is most evident, leaving Corfu
and especially Corfu town with a pleasant combination of contrasting
design elements. And although it was bombed during the Italian and
Nazi occupation in World War II, the town of Corfu remains one of
the most charming in all of Greece.

PLANNER

WHEN TO GO

Corfu enjoys a temperate climate, with a relatively long rainy season that lasts from late fall through early spring. Winter showers bring spring flowers, and the countryside goes into floral overdrive starting in April, when the air is perfumed with the heady fragrance of orange blossoms and jasmine and wildflowers carpet the hillsides. In May, the weather clears and starts to get warm enough for swimming. July and August are the hottest months and can also be humid. September is gloriously warm and dry, with warm evenings and the occasional cool breeze. Swimming is often possible through mid-October. Late September through late October are good for hiking and exploring the countryside, as is the spring.

PLANNING YOUR TIME

Corfu is often explored in a day—many people pass through quickly as part of a cruise of the Greek islands. Two days allows enough time to visit Corfu town and its nearby and most famous sites. With four days you can spend time exploring the island's other historic sites and natural attractions along both coasts. Six days allows you time to get a closer look at the museums, churches, and forts and perhaps even take a day trip to Albania. Because Corfu is small, it's easy to make day trips to outlying villages and return to accommodations in or near Corfu town. Alternatively, you could spend a night at the hilltop Pelekas or farther north at the seaside Paleokastritsa. To really get off the beaten path, take the coast road northeast from Corfu town and around Daphnila bay to Agni and from there into the most mountainous part of the island, or head west from Corfu town into the mountains and ancient olive groves to stay near Ano Korakiana, home to Etrusco, the best restaurant on Corfu, and many would say Greece itself. If you're planning a visit to the northwest, avoid the tatty beach towns of Sidari and Roda: both have been ruined by overdevelopment and neither beach is particularly clean or inviting.

As for Corfu town, where should you start upon your arrival? Catch your breath by first relaxing with a coffee or a gelato in Corfu town's shaded Liston arcade, then stroll the narrow lanes of the pedestrians-only quarter. For an overview of the immediate area, and a quick tour of Mon Repos palace, hop on the little tourist train that runs from May to September. Corfu town has a different feel at night, so book a table at one of its famed tavernas to savor Corfu's unique cuisine.

GETTING HERE AND AROUND

You don't need or want a car in Corfu town, which is compact and easily walkable. Buses run to the island's main towns and beaches, but if you want to visit some of Corfu's loveliest and most inaccessible places, all of them within an hour of Corfu town, you'll need a car. Corfu's gentle climate and rolling hills make it ideal motorbike country. You can rent cars and motorbikes at the airport or near the harbor in Corfu town. If you plan to visit only a few of the major towns, the inexpensive local bus system will do. Taxis can be hired for day trips from Corfu town.

AIR TRAVEL

Olympic Air and Aegean Airlines both have two or three flights a day from Athens to Corfu town. Fares change constantly, but the hour-long flight starts at about €180 round-trip from Athens. In the United Kingdom, easyJet has regularly scheduled flights to Corfu from Manchester, Bristol, and London's Gatwick. Monarch flies from Luton three times a week, and Jet2.com operates services from Leeds-Bradford, Newcastle, and East Midlands airports.

Carriers Aegean Airlines. ☎ *210/998–8350, 210/998–8300 in Athens* ⊕ *www. aegeanairlines.gr.* **easyJet** ☎ *No phone* ⊕ *www.easyjet.com.* **Jet2.com** ☎ *No phone* ⊕ *www.jet2.com.* **Monarch Airlines** ☎ *No phone* ⊕ *www.monarch.co.uk.* **Olympic Airlines** ☎ *26610/38694* ⊕ *www.olympicairlines.com.*

AIRPORTS Corfu Airport is northwest of Kanoni, 3 km (2 mi) south of Corfu town. A taxi from the airport to the town center costs around €10; there is no airport bus. Taxi rates are on display in the arrivals hall.

Corfu Airport ☎ *26610/39040.*

BUS TRAVEL

KTEL buses leave Athens Terminal A for Corfu town (11 hours, €45 one-way, plus ferry fares), via Patras and the ferry or overland, three or four times a day. Bus services run from Corfu town to the main towns and villages on the island; schedules and prices can change seasonally and yearly. There are two bus lines. The Green KTEL buses leave for distant towns from the Corfu town terminal near the New Port. Blue suburban buses (with stops including Kanoni and Gastouri) leave from in and around San Rocco Square. Get timetables at both bus depots and in the English-language news magazine the *Corfiot*. Tickets—farthest rides are around €4—can be bought at the depots or on the bus.

Bus Information Corfu Surburban (Blue) buses ✉ *San Rocco Sq., Corfu town* ☎ *26610/31595.***Corfu KTEL (Green) buses** ✉ *Ioanni Theotoki St., Corfu town* ☎ *26610/28928* ✉ *Terminal A, Kifissou 100, Athens* ☎ *210/512–9443.*

BOAT AND FERRY TRAVEL

There are no ferries from Athens/Piraeus to Corfu town. From the Greek mainland, ferries operated by Anek, Endeavor Lines, Blue Star lines, and Minoan sail to Corfu town from the port cities of Igoumenitsa and Patras, and from the island of Paxos. In winter, during severe weather conditions, the ferries from Igoumenitsa may stop running. In addition, many ferries arrive in Corfu hailing from Brindisi, in southern Italy—a frequent and traditional way travelers hop from Italy to Greece.

From Brindisi, Endeavor Lines offers six sailings a week to Corfu (about 8 hours, €60). Other ferries depart from Ancona, Bari, and Venice, but with most of them you must change ferries in Patras or Igoumenitsa to reach Corfu. A local ferry service operated by Kerkyra-Igoumenitsa-Paxos Consortium runs between Igoumenitsa and Corfu town several times a day.

The ferries (and cruise ships) dock at the New Port, in the northwest part of Corfu town; from the ferry terminal you can easily walk into town or take a cab to your hotel. You can buy ferry tickets at the ports, or book in advance through the ferry lines or travel agents. For the most up-to-date information on boat schedules (which change regularly and seasonally), call the port authority in the city of departure or check the Greek ferry information Web site.

Ferries from Patras to Corfu town (six to seven hours) generally leave around 11 pm or midnight. The one-way fare from Patras is about €33 per person, €90 per car, and €50 to €80 per person for a cabin. One-way tickets for the ferry between Igoumenitsa and Corfu town (1¼ to two hours) are about €10 per person and €40 per car.

Hydrofoils operated by Petrakis Lines and Cruises zip between Corfu and Paxos between one and three times daily. The company also runs a twice-daily hydrofoil service to Saranda in Albania. Please note that the information in our boat and ferry office listings on the next page lists the ferry office's main headquarters; to buy your tickets locally in Patras, Igoumenitsa, or Corfu, go to a local travel agent in the town or at the port.

Boat Information Endeavour Lines ⊠ *Poseidonos Ave. 35, Moschato* ☎ *210/940–5222* ⊕ *www.endeavour-lines.com.* **ANEK Lines** ⊠ *Akti Kondili 22, Piraeus, Corfu* ☎ *210/419–7400* ⊕ *www.anek.gr.* **Argostoli Port Authority** ☎ *26710/22200.* **Blue Star Ferries** ⊠ *Syngrou Ave. 123–125, Athens, Corfu* ☎ *210/891–9000* ⊕ *www.bluestarferries.com.* **Corfu Port Authority** ☎ *26610/32655.* **Greek ferry info** ⊕ *www.greekferries.gr.* **Igoumenitsa Port Authority** ☎ *26650/22235.* **Kerkyra-Igoumenitsa-Paxi Consortium** ⊠ *Agion Apostolon St., Igoumenitsa, Corfu* ☎ *26500/26280.* **Minoan Lines** ⊠ *25th August 17, Iraklio, Corfu* ☎ *2810/399800* ⊕ *www.minoan.gr.* **Patras Port Authority** ☎ *2610/341024.* **Petrakis Lines and Cruises** ⊠ *Ethnikis Antistaseos 4, Corfu town, Corfu* ☎ *26610/38690.*

CAR TRAVEL

The best route from Athens is the National Road via Corinth to Igoumenitsa (472 km [274 mi]), where you take the ferry to Corfu. As on all Greek islands, exercise caution with regard to steep, winding roads, and fellow drivers equally unfamiliar with the terrain. Corfu town has several car-rental agencies, most of them clustered around the port, ranging from international chains to local agencies offering cheap deals. Depending on the season, prices can range from €35 a day to €230 a week for a compact, all insurance included. Chains have a bigger selection, but the locals will usually give a cheaper price. Don't be afraid to bargain, especially if you want to rent a car for several days. You can generally make arrangements to pick up your car at the airport. A 50cc motorbike can be rented for about €25 a day or €100 a week, or a 125cc motorbike for about €30 a day and €110 a week, but you can bargain, especially if you want it for longer. Helmets are provided only on request; make certain you wear one. Check the lights, brakes, and other mechanics before you accept a machine. In Corfu town, try Easy Rider.

Car Information Ansa International Rent a Car ⊠ *Eleftheriou Venizelou 20, New Port, Corfu town* ☎ *26610/40390.* **Easy Rider** ⊠ *Eleftheriou Venizelou 50, New Port, Corfu town* ☎ *26610/43026.* **Ocean Car Hire** ⊠ *Gouvia Marina, Gouvia, Corfu town* ☎ *26610/44017* ⊕ *www.oceancar.gr.* **Reliable Rent-a-Car** ⊠ *Donzelot 5, Corfu town* ☎ *26610/35740.* **Top Cars** ⊠ *Donzelot 25, Corfu town* ☎ *26610/35237* ⊕ *www.carrentalcorfu.com.*

TAXI TRAVEL

Taxis rates are reasonable—when adhered to. If you want to hire a cab on an hourly or daily basis, negotiate the price before you travel. In Corfu town, taxis wait at San Rocco Square, the Esplanade, the airport, the Old Port Square, and the New Port. Many drivers speak English. Of course, long-distance trips on the island will pack a hefty price tag.

Taxi Information Corfu Taxis ☏ *26610/33811, 26610/30383, 26610/39911.*

RESTAURANTS

Traditionally, Corfiots tend to eat their main meal at midday, with simpler food in the evening. Though meat is eaten much more frequently these days, meals at home feature casseroles bulked out with lots of vegetables, such as the winter favorite *fassoulada,* a thick bean soup. Unless they cater for the local lunchtime trade, tavernas tend not to serve these home-style dishes, but prefer generic Greek dishes like *moussaka* and *stifado* (beef or rabbit cooked in a spicy sauce with small onions), plus the great Sunday-lunch and holiday dishes of the island, *pastitsada* (beef or rooster in a spicy tomato sauce served with pasta) and *sofrito* (beef casseroled with garlic and parsley), or the third great dish of Corfiot cooking, *bourdetto* (fish cooked in paprika, sometimes curry-hot). In the island's resorts, tavernas will also offer grills (such as pork chops and steaks), plus omelets and (invariably frozen) pizzas. Your main courses should be preceded by a variety of dips and small salads, and perhaps some *keftedes* (meatballs), which you all share.

Corfiot restaurants usually take the form of *psistaria*, or grillrooms, where all the meat is cooked on charcoal. Most of these places also run a takeaway service, so you'll eat in the company of neighborhood families waiting in line for souvlaki, whole spit-roasted chicken, or lamb chops. The most economical choice here is pita, a wrap enclosing meat, french fries, salad, *tzatziki* and sauce. Desserts are not a strong suit on Corfu, although many love *karidopitta*—walnut cake drenched in syrup. Locals head to a *zacharoplasteio* (patisserie) for a creamy cake, some baklava or *galaktoboureko* (custard pie). In summer, the last port of call is the *gelato-poleio* (ice-cream parlor). Corfu produces wines mainly from skopelitiko and kakotrigis grapes, all drinkable and many excellent. Most tavernas have their own house wine, served in carafes or jugs, and usually this is a good choice. Bottled water can be bought everywhere—Corfu's salty tap water is *not* one of its pleasures.*Kali oreksi*! (Bon appetit!)

DINING AND LODGING PRICES IN EUROS				
	¢	$	$$	$$$	$$$$
Restaurants	under €8	€8–€11	€12–€15	€16–€20	over €20
Hotels	under €60	€60–€90	€91–€120	€121–€160	over €160

Restaurant prices are for one main course at dinner, or for two mezedes (small dishes). Hotel prices are for a standard double room in high season, including taxes. Inquire when booking whether meal plans (which can entail higher rates) are mandatory.

HOTELS

Corfu has bed-and-breakfast hotels in renovated Venetian town houses, sleek resorts with children's programs and spas, and, outside Corfu town, simple rooms and studio apartments that can be rented out on the spot. The explosion of tourism in recent years has led to prepaid, low-price package tours, and the largest hotels often cater to groups. The availability of charter flights from the United Kingdom and other European cities means there's a steady flow of tourists from spring through fall. These masses can get rowdy and overwhelm otherwise pleasant surroundings, mainly in towns along the island's southeast and northwest coast. Budget accommodation is scarce, though rooms can sometimes be found in towns and villages. Many British companies offer villas for rent—some luxurious, others more basic—by the week or month. Corfu is popular from Easter (when the island is crammed with Greek tourists) through September, and reservations are strongly recommended during that period. Many hotels and restaurants are closed from the end of October to Easter.

VISITOR INFORMATION

The monthly English news magazine the *Corfiot*, written mostly by and for ex-pats, contains articles of Corfu interest as well as information on places to visit. It's available at foreign press newsstands.

Greek National Tourism Organization (GNTO or EOT). ✉ *Alikes, Potamou, Corfu town* ☎ *26610/20733, 26610/37639* ⊕ *www.visitgreece.gr.*

TOUR OPTIONS

From May through September, local travel agencies run half-day tours of Corfu's Old Town, and tour buses go daily to all the sights on the island; All-Ways Travel is reliable. Charitos Travel has more than 50 tours of the island and can create custom tours for groups of five or more. International Tours arranges hiking, mountain biking, horseback riding, jeep trips, and other excursions around the island. Ionian Cruises offers boat trips to other islands in the Ionian group and even to Albania. Aperghi Travel is an expert on hiking holidays and is a designated agent for accommodation and ground arrangements along the Corfu Trail (⊕ *www.thecorfutrail.com*), a top-to-bottom-of-the-island hike that offers lovely sections easily worth an hour or two.

TOUR INFORMATION **All-Ways Travel** ✉ *G. Theotoki Sq. 34, San Rocco, Corfu town* ☎ *26610/33955* ⊕ *www.allwaystravel.gr.* **Aperghi Travel** ✉ *Dimokratias Ave & Polyla 1, Corfu town* ☎ *26610/48713* ⊕ *www.travelling.gr/aperghi.* **Charitos Travel** ✉ *National Paleokastritsa Highway 66, Corfu town, Corfu* ☎ *26610/44611* ⊕ *www. charitostravel.gr.* **International Tours** ✉ *Eleftheriou Venizelou 38, Corfu town* ☎ *26610/39007, 26610/38107* ⊕ *www.intertourscorfu.com.* **Ionian Cruises** ✉ *Ethnikis Antistaseos 4, Corfu town* ☎ *26610/31649* ⊕ *www.ionian-cruises.com.*

CORFU TOWN ΠΟΛΗ ΤΗΣ ΚΕΡΚΥΡΑΣ

34 km (21 mi) west of Igoumenitsa, 41 km (26 mi) north of Lefkimmi.

Corfu town today is a vivid tapestry of cultures—a sophisticated weave, where charm, history, and natural beauty blend. Located about midway along the island's east coast, this spectacularly lively capital is the cultural heart of Corfu and has a remarkable historic center that UNESCO designated as a World Heritage Site in 2007. All ships and planes dock or land near Corfu town, which occupies a small peninsula jutting into the Ionian Sea.

Whether arriving by ferry from the mainland of Greece or Italy, from another island, or directly by plane, catch your breath by first relaxing with a coffee or a gelato in Corfu town's shaded Liston arcade, then stroll the narrow lanes of its pedestrians-only quarter. For an overview of the immediate area, and a quick tour of Mon Repos palace, hop on the little tourist train that runs from May to September. Corfu town has a different feel at night, so book a table at one of its famed tavernas to savor the island's unique cuisine.

The best way to get around Corfu town is on foot. The town is small enough so that you can easily walk to every sight. There are local buses, but they do not thread their way into the streets (many now car-free) of the historic center. If you are arriving by ferry (⇨ *see Getting Around near the front of this chapter*) or plane, it's best to take a taxi to your hotel. Expect to pay about €10 from the airport or ferry terminal to a hotel in Corfu town. To hire a taxi, call Radiotaxi Corfu (☎ *26610/33811*).

EXPLORING

Though beguilingly Greek, much of Corfu's Old Town displays the architectural styles of its conquerors—molto of Italy's Venice, a soupçon of France, and more than a tad of England; it may remind you of Venice or Bath. Many visitors will want to invest in the multi-attraction ticket (€8), available at any of the sights, which includes admission to the Archaeological Museum, the Museum of Asian Art, the Byzantine Museum, and the Old Fortress.

TOP ATTRACTIONS

Archaeological Museum. Examine finds from ongoing island excavations; most come from Kanoni, the site of Corfu's ancient capital. The star attraction is a giant bas-relief of snake-coiffed Medusa, depicted as her head was cut off by the hero Perseus—at which moment her two sons, Pegasus and Chrysaor, emerged from her body. The 56-foot-long sculpture once adorned the pediment of the 6th-century BC Temple of Artemis at Kanoni and is one of the largest and best-preserved pieces of Archaic sculpture in Greece. ⊠ *Vraila 1, off Leoforos Dimokratias, past Corfu Palace hotel, Corfu town* ☎ *26610/30680* 🎟 *€3* ☾ *Tues.– Sun. 8:30–3.*

★ **Byzantine Museum.** Panagia Antivouniotissa, an ornate church dating from the late 15th century, houses an outstanding collection of Byzantine religious art. More than 50 icons from the 13th to the 17th century hang on the walls. Look for works by the celebrated icon painters Tzanes and Damaskinos; they are perhaps the best-known artists of the Cretan style of icon painting, with unusually muscular, active depictions of saints. Their paintings more closely resemble Renaissance art—another Venetian legacy—than traditional, flat orthodox

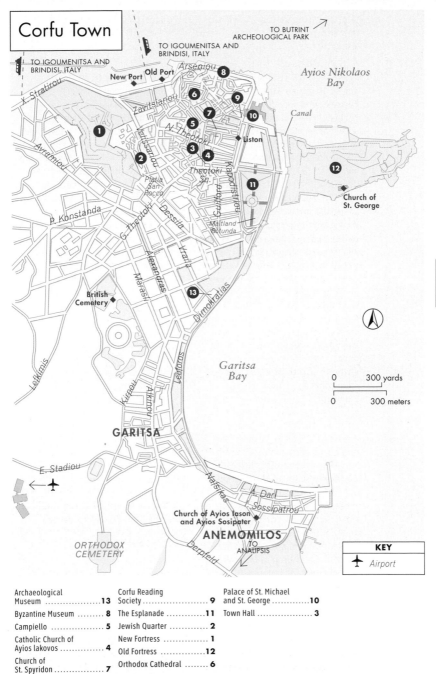

Corfu Town

TO IGOUMENITSA AND
BRINDISI, ITALY

TO IGOUMENITSA AND
BRINDISI, ITALY

TO BUTRINT
ARCHEOLOGICAL PARK

New Port   Old Port

Arseniou

*Ayios Nikolaos
Bay*

X. Stratirou

Avramiou

Zavitsianou

Velissariou

N. Theotoki

Liston

Canal

Theotoki
Sq.

Platia
San
Rocco

P. Konstanda

G. Theotoki

Dessila

Alexandras

Marasli

Vraila

Kapodistriou

Polilla

*Maitland
Rotunda*

British
Cemetery

12

Church of
St. George

Dimokratias

*Garitsa
Bay*

Lefkimis

Kirpou

Aikinou

Leoforos

GARITSA

E. Stadiou

ORTHODOX
CEMETERY

Narsikas

A. Dari

Sossipatrou

Church of Ayios Iason
and Ayios Sosipater

ANEMOMILOS

TO
ANALIPSIS

Derpfeld

0   300 yards

0   300 meters

6

CORFU TOWN: A STEP-BY-STEP WALK

Arriving by ferry from Igoumenitsa on mainland Greece, Venice, or Albania, you dock at the **New Port**, a 5- to 10-minute walk to the **New Fortress**, an impressive hilltop citadel built in the 16th and 17th centuries. Running along the eastern flank of the fortress is Velissariou Street, one of Corfu town's main streets and the name of a neighborhood that forms the western boundary of the historical center (also known as the Old Town or Historic Center). Wedged in this neighborhood is the former **Jewish Quarter**, with its 300-year-old synagogue. Walk up Velissariou and turn left at the top on Voulgareos Street. Soon the way plunges into the Historic Center; a short distance on, deviate right into Dimarchiou Square, anchored by the impressive 17th-century Venetian **Town Hall**, built originally as a theater. Adjacent is the neoclassic **Catholic Church of Agios Iakovos**, more commonly known as the Cathedral of San Giacomo. Retrace your steps to Voulgareos, then walk north on Mihail Theotoki Street, cross over a wide main street, and continue opposite on Filarmonikis Street; you'll be passing through the **Campiello**, a fascinating labyrinth of narrow winding streets filled with shops and restaurants. Continuing along Filarmonikis until you come to Agios Spyridonos Street; turn right and follow this narrow, shop-lined street to the **Church of St. Spyridon**, dedicated to the island's patron saint. Continue on Agios Spyridonos Street until you come to Kapodistriou Street, where you turn right. A left turn at the next junction brings you to the famed **Liston**, an arcaded building built by the French and one of the busiest spots in Corfu town.

Just beyond is the town's largest public park, with the **Esplanade** (also known as the Spianada) running down its center. Walking south along the Esplanade you'll pass a Victorian bandstand, an early-19th-century rotunda, and, at the southern end, a statue of Ioannis Kapodistrias, a Corfu resident who became the first president of modern Greece. At the northern end of the Esplanade you'll see the colonnaded facade of the very British-looking **Palace of St. Michael and St. George**, today home to the **Museum of Asian Art**. Find a table at one of the cafés in the Liston or lining the northwest corner of the Esplanade and relax over a coffee, a drink, or a gelato. Then head east across the Esplanade toward the impossible-to-miss **Old Fortress**; a **Statue of Count Schulenburg**, hero of the 1716 battle against the Turks, stands in front of the bridge leading into the fort. If, after exploring the Old Fortress, you're in the mood for museums, you have two choices. Heading south along the road that follows the curve of Garitsa Bay, you'll find, just beyond the Corfu Palace Hotel and up a side street, the **Archaeological Museum**. If you follow the sea road north from the Old Fortress, you'll come to the lovely **Byzantine Museum**. Both museums are signposted from the road.

icons. ⊠ *3rd Parados Arseniou St., Corfu town* ☎ *26610/38313* 🖃 *€2* ⊗ *Tues.–Sun. 8:30–3.*

Fodor's Choice
★
Campiello. This medieval quarter, part of a UNESCO-designated World Heritage Site, is an atmospheric labyrinth of narrow, winding streets, steep stairways, and secretive little squares. Laundry lines connect balconied Venetian palazzi engraved with the original occupant's coat of arms to neoclassic 19th-century buildings constructed by the British. Small cobbled squares with central wells and watched over by old churches add to the quiet, mysterious, and utterly charming urban space. If you enter, you're almost sure to get lost, but the area is small enough so that eventually you'll come out on one of Corfu town's major streets, or on the sea wall. ⊠ *West of the Esplanade, northeast of New Fortress, Corfu town* .

Fodor's Choice
★
Church of St. Spyridon. Built in 1596, this church is the tallest on the island, thanks to its distinctive red-dome bell tower, and is filled with silver treasures. The patron saint's remains—smuggled here after the fall of Constantinople—are contained in a silver reliquary in a small chapel; devout Corfiots visit to kiss the reliquary and pray to the saint. The silver casket is carried in procession through the town four times a year. Spyridon was not a Corfiot but a shepherd from Cyprus, who became a bishop before his death in AD 350. His miracles are said to have saved the island four times: once from famine, twice from the plague, and once from the hated Turks. During World War II, a bomb fell on this holiest place on the island but didn't explode. Maybe these events explain why it seems every other man on Corfu is named Spiros. If you keep the church tower in sight you can wander as you wish without getting lost around this fascinating section of town. Agios Spyridonos, the street in front of the church, is crammed with shops selling religious trinkets and souvenirs. ⊠ *Agios Spyridonos, Corfu town* ☎ *No phone.*

Fodor's Choice
★
Corfu Reading Society. The oldest cultural institution in modern Greece, the Corfu Reading Society was founded in 1836. The building, filled with books and archives relating to the Ionian islands, stands opposite the High Commissioner's Palace and has an impressive exterior staircase leading up to a loggia. Inside is a book-lover's delight, with 19th-century decor that is evocative testimony to the "English age" that gave Corfu so much of its character. ⊠ *Kapodistriou, Corfu town* ☎ *26610/39528* 🖃 *Free* ⊗ *Mon. and Fri. 5:45–7:45, Tues.–Thurs. 9:30–1:45, Sat. 9:30–1:45.*

Fodor's Choice
★
The Esplanade. Central to the life of the town, this huge, open parade ground and park just west of the Old Fortress is, many say, the most beautiful *spianada* (esplanade) in Greece. It is bordered on the west by a street lined with Venetian and English Georgian houses and a famous arcaded building called the **Liston,** built by the French under Napoleon and meant to resemble the Rue du Rivoli in Paris. Cafés spill out onto the passing scene, and Corfiot celebrations, games, and concerts take place here; at night, lovers promenade and children play in this festive public space. Sunday cricket matches, a holdover from British rule, are sometimes played on the northern half of the Esplanade, which was once a Venetian firing range. Standing in the center

6

is an ornate **Victorian bandstand** and, just south of it, the **Maitland Rotunda,** a circular Ionic memorial built in honor of Sir Thomas Maitland, the not-much-loved first British lord high commissioner who was appointed in 1814 when the island became a protectorate of Britain. At the southernmost tip of the Esplanade a **statue of Ioannis Kapodistrias,** a Corfu resident and the first president of modern Greece, looks out over Garitsa bay. Kapodistrias was also, unfortunately, the first Greek president to be assassinated, in 1831. ⊠ *Between Old Fortress and Old Town, Corfu town.*

New Fortress. Built in 1577–78 by the Venetians, the New Fortress was constructed to strengthen town defenses—only three decades after the construction of Venetian fortifications on the "Old" Fortress. The French and the British subsequently expanded the complex to protect Corfu town from a possible Turkish invasion. You can wander through the maze of tunnels and fortifications; the dry moat is the site of the town's fish-and-vegetable marketplace. A classic British citadel stands at its heart. At the top, there is an exhibition center. ⊠ *Solomou on promontory overlooking New Port, Corfu town* ☎ *No phone* ☒ *€2* ☉ *June–Oct., daily 9am–9:30pm.*

★ **Old Fortress.** Corfu's entire population once lived within the walls of the Old Fortress, or Citadel, built by the Venetians in 1546 on the site of a Byzantine castle. Separated from the rest of the town by a moat, the fort is on a promontory mentioned by Thucydides. Its two heights, or *korypha* ("peaks"), gave the island its name. Standing on the peaks, you have a gorgeous view west over the town and east to the mountainous coast of Albania. A statue of Count Schulenburg, an Austrian mercenary who became a local hero in 1716 when he helped to defeat the invading Turks, stands at the fort's entrance; just inside, there is an exhibition that tells Schulenburg's story. Most of the old Venetian fortifications inside the fortress were destroyed by the British, who replaced them with their own structures. The most notable of these is the **Church of St. George,** built to look like an ancient Doric temple. Near it, overlooking Garitsa bay, there is a shaded café where you can sit and enjoy the splendid view. ⊠ *On eastern point of Corfu town peninsula, Corfu town* ☎ *26610/48310* ☒ *€4* ☉ *Mon.–Sat. 8–8, Sun. 8–3.*

Fodor's Choice **Palace of St. Michael and St. George (Museum of Asian Art).** It may seem a bit
★   incongruous to admire Ming pottery in an ornate British colonial palace as the Ionian Sea shimmers outside the windows. But this elegant, colonnaded, 19th-century Regency structure houses the **Museum of Asian Art,** a notable collection of Asian porcelains, Japanese *ukiyo-e* prints, Indian sculpture, and Tibetan temple art. The building was constructed as a residence for the lord high commissioner and headquarters for the order of St. Michael and St. George; it was abandoned after the British left in 1864 and renovated about a hundred years later by the British ambassador to Greece. After visiting the galleries, stop at the Art Café in the shady courtyard behind the palace, where you may have trouble tearing yourself away from the fairy-tale view of the lush islet of Vido and the mountainous coast of Albania. ⊠ *Palaia Anaktora, at north end of Esplanade, Corfu town* ☎ *26610/30443* ☒ *€3* ☉ *Tues.–Sun. 8:30–3.*

WORTH NOTING

Catholic Church of Agios Iakovos. Built in 1588 and consecrated 50 years later, this elegant cathedral was erected to provide a grand place of worship for Corfu town's Catholic occupiers. If you use the Italian name, San Giacomo, locals will know it. When it was bombed by the Nazis in 1943, the cathedral's original neoclassic facade of pediments, friezes, and columns was practically destroyed; only the bell tower remained intact. It's now been restored. ⊠ *Dimarcheiou Sq. next to Town Hall, Corfu town* ☎ *No phone.*

Church of Agios Iason and Agios Sosipater. The suburb of Anemomilos is crowned by the ruins of the Paleopolis church and by the 11th-century Church of Agios Iason and Agios Sosipater. It was named after two of St. Paul's disciples, St. Jason and St. Sosipater, who brought Christianity to the island in the 1st century. The frescoes are faded, but the icons are beautiful, and the exterior is dramatic among the unspoiled greenery. This is one of only two Byzantine churches on the island; the other is in the northern coastal village of Agios Markos. ⊠ *Anemomilos at south end of Garitsa bay, Corfu town* ☎ *No phone.*

Orthodox Cathedral. This small, icon-rich cathedral was built in 1577. It is dedicated to St. Theodora, the island's second saint. Her headless body lies in a silver coffin by the altar; it was brought to Corfu at the same time as St. Spyridon's remains. Steps lead down to the harbor from here. ⊠ *Southwest corner of Campiello, east of St. Spyridon, Corfu town* ☎ *26610/39409.*

Statue of Count Schulenburg. The hero of the siege of 1716, an Austrian mercenary, is immortalized in this statue. The siege was the Turks' last (and failed) attempt to conquer Corfu. His story is documented in a special exhibition inside the Old Fortress. ⊠ *Beside entrance to Old Fortress, Corfu town.*

Tomb of Menekrates. Part of an ancient necropolis, this site held funerary items that are now exhibited in the Archaeological Museum. ⊠ *South around Garitsa bay, to right of obelisk dedicated to Sir Howard Douglas, Corfu town.*

Town Hall. The 17th-century Town Hall (now the offices of the Mayor) was originally built as a Venetian loggia and converted in 1720 into Greece's first modern theater. A second story was added by the British before it became a grand town hall early in the 20th century. Note the sculpted portraits of Venetian dignitaries over the entrance—one is actually a lion, the symbol of Venice. ⊠ *Dimarcheiou Sq., Corfu town* ☎ *26610/40401* 🎟 *Free* ⊙ *Weekdays 9–1.*

WHERE TO EAT

$$

GREEK

✕ **Aegli.** Both local and international dishes are on the menu of this long-established and casually elegant restaurant in the Liston arcade. Start with a plate of steamed mussels, then move on to hearty Corfiot classics such as spicy *bourdetto* (fish stewed in tomato sauce with lots of hot red pepper), or the more-unusual *arnaki kleftiko* (lamb cooked as the *kleftes*, War of Independence fighters, liked it), with onions, olives, mustard, and feta cheese. Tables in front overlook the nonstop parade on the Esplanade. Aegli keeps late hours, serving drinks and sweets from midnight until 2 am. ⊠ *Kapodistriou 23, Liston, Corfu town* ☏ *26610/31949.*

$ ✕ **Bellisimio.** Contrary to its Italian-sounding name, this is a traditional,
GREEK family-run Greek taverna where owner Stavros invites you into the
★ kitchen to look at what's fresh and available that day. The food here
is excellent and reasonably priced, and the location, in a little square
tucked off North Theotoki, adds to the cozy ambience. This is a great
place to get a vegetarian meal, and two or three starters will fill you up.
The spicy baked feta, fried zucchini, and spinach pie are all worth try-
ing. Traditional favorites such as *briam* (a mixture of eggplant, zucchini,
and potatoes in olive oil and tomato sauce) are expertly prepared. Only
Corfiot wine is sold, in order to keep prices affordable. ⊠ *Lemonia Sq.
off N. Theotoki, Corfu town* ☏ *26610/41112* ✆ *Closed Nov.–Easter.
No lunch Sun.*

$$ ✕ **En Plo.** This appealing café/restaurant sits on the edge of a wave-
GREEK lapped jetty in the little waterfront Faliraki area just north of the Old
★ Fortress. Come here for a snack, a salad, a couple of *mezedes* (appe-
tizers), or something more substantial, like a mixed-seafood platter.
The menu is small, the food good, and the atmosphere wonderful.
⊠ *On waterfront just north of Old Fortress, Faliraki, Corfu town*
☏ *26610/81813* ✆ *Closed Jan. and Feb.*

$$$$ ✕ **Etrusco.** While this is in the hamlet of Kato Korakiana, just outside
GREEK Dassia (about five miles north of Corfu town), some foodies would
Fodor's Choice drive there from Athens itself: this is considered one of the best restau-
★ rants in Greece. If not, it is certainly one of the most inventive, so be
sure to book both a table and a taxi *now.* Run by the Italian-Corfiot
Botrini family, this showcases their passion for marrying Greek and
Italian cuisine using flawless technique and a big blast of "molecular"
creativity. You know dinner will be a marvel with the starter of canapés,
each positioned over their place of origin on a cute ceramic map of the
Mediterranean. Then the delights of chef Ettore Botrini begin. You may
want to make a dinner just of the appetizers: sea urchin soup, salmon
cubes with green apple sorbet, octopus carpaccio, feta cheese "snow,"
or shrimp risotto with Peruvian bitter cocoa powder. One winning
main course was the slow-cooked pork belly with Granny Smith apple
puree. Prepared by Ettore's wife, the desserts are ecstasy: will it be the
chocolate soufflé with salty caramel sauce, the goat cheese ice cream
with tomato marmalade and lemon sherbet, or the orange soufflé with
chocolate crust? Rounding out the experience is the cozy and modern
decor, with the best tables—often booked solid with chic and wealthy
Corfiots—set out in a charmingly antique courtyard. ⊠ *Kato Korakiana, 1 km (½ mi) west of Dassia, Kato Korakiana* ☏ *26610/93342*
⊕ *www.etrusco.gr* ⚹ *Reservations essential* ✆ *No lunch.*

$$ ✕ **Fish Taverna Roula.** Choose from what you see—bream, snapper, squid,
SEAFOOD sole, mullet, sardines, and whatever else is fresh that day; when the fish
★ runs out, Roula stops serving. Sit on the waterfront terrace and watch
the boats heading in and out of the bay marina. It's a bit difficult to find;
pass the Kontokali Bay Hotel, then go left at every junction, keeping
your eyes open for the sign to Roula.⊠ *Kontokali bay, 6 km (4 mi) north
of Corfu town* ☏ *26610/91832* ⚹ *Reservations essential.*

6

$ ✕ **Gerekos.** One of the island's most famous seafood tavernas, Gerekos's
SEAFOOD   raw materials are supplied daily by the family's own fishing boats. The
menu varies according to the catch and the season, but the friendly
staff will guide your choice. For a light meze, opt for a table on the
terrace and try the whitefish *me ladi* (cooked in olive oil, garlic, and
pepper) with a salad and some crisp white wine. Too bad this place is
located on a dusty resort street with cars going past by diners' toes.
⊠ *Kontokali bay, 6 km (4 mi) north of Corfu town* ☎ *26610/91281*
⌁ *Reservations essential.*

$$ ✕ **Rex.** A friendly Corfiot restaurant in a 19th-century town house, Rex
GREEK   has been a favorite for nearly 100 years, and with good reason. Classic
Fodor'sChoice   local specialties such as a hearty and meaty *pastitsada* (layers of beef
★   and pasta, called *macaronia* in Greek, cooked in a rich and spicy tomato
sauce and topped off with béchamel sauce), *stifado* (meat stewed with
sweet onions, white wine, garlic, cinnamon, and spices), and *stamna*
(lamb baked with potatoes, rice, beans, and cheese) are reliably deli-
cious. Dishes such as rabbit stewed with fresh figs and chicken with
kumquats are successful twists on the regional fare. Look on the menu
for the "specials of the day," which might include some other unusual
dishes. Outside tables are perfect for people-watching. ⊠ *Kapodistriou
66, 1 street west of Liston, Corfu town* ☎ *26610/39649.*

$–$$ ✕ **Rouvas.** "Where do the locals eat?" One frequent answer—that is, if
GREEK   by "locals" you are referring to discerning executives and lawyers—is
Rouvas. Found near San Rocco Square and located in the center of Corfu
town's commercial district, it caters (lunchtime only) to natives who savor
the chef's tasty yet filling traditional dishes, such as fried fish with garlic
sauce, the superb Pastitsio (baked minced meat and pasta layered with
bechamel), or the rabbit Stifado (stewed with onions, tomato, and spices),
plus a seasonal dish of the day—Briam, a delicious meld of summer vegetables cooked in oil, is a favorite. ⊠ *Stamatis Desyllas 13, Corfu town*
☎ *26610/31182* ▭ *No credit cards* ☉ *No dinner.*

$$ ✕ **To Dimarcheio.** At the "town hall," menu items like marinated salmon
ECLECTIC   with fennel and veal carpaccio reflect the chef's classic French training.
★   But ask the waiter what else is in the kitchen, and he may reel off a list
of hearty village favorites that includes a rich *soffritto* (veal cooked in
a sauce of vinegar, parsley, and plenty of garlic), pastitsada, and pork
stewed with celery, leeks, and wine. In June you can sit beneath a jaca-
randa tree's electric-blue flowers and watch the comings and goings
around the Town Hall in Dimarcheiou Square. Reservations are recom-
mended on weekends. ⊠ *Dimarcheiou Sq., behind Town Hall, Corfu
town* ☎ *26610/39031.*

$$ ✕ **Venetian Well.** The scene is as delicious as the food in this wonderfully
GREEK   romantic restaurant set around a 17th-century well on the most beau-
Fodor'sChoice   tiful little square in the Old Town. Walls here are ablaze with yellow
★   flame, pomegrante-hued clouds, and ruby incense, all of which create
an eye-knocking surround. Sit at one of the ironwork tables or perhaps
relax on the one of the sofas and cuddle with one of the pillows worthy
of a pasha. As for the sophisticated menu, it comprises Greek and international specialties. Creative entrées include tomato dumplings; grilled
octopus with parsley pesto; or crepes with prosciutto, cheddar cheese,

and vanilla sauce. The service is deft and unobtrusive. Kremasti Square is difficult to find, so be sure to get very specific directions from your hotel. ⊠ *Kremasti Sq. across from Church of the Panagia, Corfu town* ☎ *26610/44761* ⚖ *Reservations essential* ⊙ *No lunch Sun.*

WHERE TO STAY

For expanded reviews, visit Fodors.com.

$$$ ⊡ **Cavalieri Hotel.** If you want a breathtaking view of the Old Fortress
Fodor's Choice and the sea, ask for a room on the fourth or fifth floor, with a num-
★ ber ending in 2, 3, or 4. **Pros:** fabulous location; great views; recently renovated rooms. **Cons:** service can be a bit brusque. ⊠ *Kapodistriou 4, Corfu town* ☎ *26610/39041* ⊕ *www.cavalieri-hotel.com* ⤴ *50 rooms* ⚐ *In-room: a/c, Wi-Fi. In-hotel: restaurant, bar.*

$$$$ ⊡ **Corfu Imperial Grecotel Exclusive Resort.** One of the most sumptuous
Fodor's Choice resorts on Corfu, the Imperial complex juts into Kommeno bay atop a
★ 14-acre peninsula—inside are stunningly luxurious rooms, bungalows, and villas (several with private pools) all featuring gilded Venetian-style headboards, painted wall murals, shimmering lights, and the best in interior volupté, while outside await the hotel's "exterior" decoration: a world of pools, lawns, and bay vistas that is an enchanting universe unto itself. **Pros:** beautifully maintained; excellent swimming; fine dining; a world unto itself. **Cons:** so large you may feel anonymous; not in Corfu town; you won't want to leave. ⊠ *Kommeno bay, 10 km (6 mi) north of Corfu town* ☎ *26610/88400* ⊕ *www.grecotel. com* ⤴ *184 rooms, 119 bungalows, 8 suites, 21 villas* ⚐ *In-room: a/c, Wi-Fi. In-hotel: restaurant, bar, pool, tennis court, spa, beach, water sports, children's programs* ⊙ *Closed Nov.–Apr.*

$$$$ ⊡ **Corfu Palace.** Built in 1950 as the island's first resort hotel—and these
★ days showing it—the Corfu Palace is a grande dame in back need of a face-lift, although this stolidly built landmark still provides the requisite grace notes inside: guest rooms have a spaciousness from an earlier age and they are all sweetly decorated with old-fashioned Louis XIV–style furniture. **Pros:** very friendly service; great breakfast buffet; wonderful outdoor pool; close to town center. **Cons:** decor is showing its age. ⊠ *Leoforos Dimokratias 2, Corfu town* ☎ *26610/39485* ⊕ *www. corfupalace.com* ⤴ *108 rooms, 11 suites* ⚐ *In-room: a/c. In-hotel: restaurant, bar, pool, spa* ⦿| *Breakfast.*

$$$ ⊡ **Hotel Bella Venezia.** This elegant two-story Venetian town house in the center of town has been used as a hotel since the 1800s, and now that it's just been renovated—the lobby is newly aglitter with sofas covered in rather harsh metallic-hued brocades—it's one of the nicest small hotels in town. **Pros:** friendly service; newly renovated rooms; modern bathrooms; lovely garden setting for breakfast. **Cons:** some rooms are narrow and a bit cramped; views are urban rather than maritime; renovation rather generic and cold. ⊠ *Zambelli 4, behind Cavalieri Hotel, Corfu town* ☎ *26610/20707, 26610/44290* ⊕ *www. bellaveneziahotel.com* ⤴ *30 rooms, 1 suite* ⚐ *In-room: a/c, Internet. In-hotel: bar* ⦿| *Breakfast.*

$ ⊡ **Hotel Hermes.** The old, no-frills Hermes was always popular with backpackers, but now that this hardworking hotel has been completely renovated, it will have more appeal for budget travelers in general. **Pros:**

6

newly renovated rooms; affordable rates; helpful staff. **Cons:** the road outside carries heavy traffic early morning; breakfast is not included in the price. ⊠ *G. Markora 14, Corfu town* ☎ *26610/39268* ⊕ *www. hermes-hotel.gr* ⤳ *25 rooms* ♻ *In-room: a/c.*

$$$$ 🏨 **Kontokali Bay Resort and Spa.** Built the same year as the super-luxurious
★ Corfu Imperial, this hotel-bungalow complex opened its doors in 1971 with a cleaner, more-modern look to it and—especially in the outdoor estate here, which includes a fantastic beach—a more-relaxed glam factor. **Pros:** great new spa; lovely grounds; beach access; contemporary decor. **Cons:** not in Corfu town; large and somewhat anonymous. ⊠ *Kontokali bay, 6 km (4 mi) north of Corfu town* ☎ *26610/90500 through 26610/90509, 26610/99000 through 26610/99002* ⊕ *www. kontokalibay.com* ⤳ *170 rooms, 89 bungalows* ♻ *In-room: a/c, Wi-Fi. In-hotel: restaurant, bar, pool, spa, beach, children's programs, business center* ⊙ *Closed mid-Oct.–Easter* ⦿ *Breakfast.*

$$$–$$$$ 🏨 **Siorra Vittoria Boutique Hotel.** Right in the heart of Corfu's historic
Fodor's Choice center and a minute's walk away from the Liston, this grand man-
★ sion—originally built in 1823 for the aristocratic Metaxas clan—has been converted to a hotel that still preserves its lovely Venetian style (note such time-burnished elements as the chequerboard tiled floor and original staircase) while adding some new delights: the personalized service is the nearest you'll find in Corfu to a B&B. **Pros:** exquisite accommodation with a real flavor of old Corfu; close to all the town's best facilities, yet tranquil; open all year. **Cons:** some rooms are small; most rooms lack balconies; not suitable for young children. ⊠ *Stefanou Padova 36, Corfu town* ☎ *26610/36300* ⊕ *www.siorravittoria.com* ⤳ *9 rooms* ♻ *In-room: a/c. In-hotel: Internet* ⦿ *Breakfast*

NIGHTLIFE AND THE ARTS

Corfu town is a late-night, café-crowded, club-happy city. During the summer months, the Greeks dine very late, often at 10 pm. The nightly volta, a pre- or post-dinner promenade along the Esplanade and the Liston starts at about 9 pm. Couples stroll, families gather, kids play, and the cafés and restaurants fill up. The club and disco scene heats up much later, around midnight. Party Central lies about 2 km (1 mi) north of the town center, near the New Port, on Ethnikis Antistaseos (also known as "Bar Street"). This is where you'll find a string of plushy lounge-bars (many with outdoor pools) and discos that really don't start swinging until after midnight. Clubs on Corfu come and go like tourists, with many featuring incredibly loud sound systems that throb with the latest Euro-pop and dance hits. Most clubs have a cover charge, which includes the first drink.

BARS AND **Amaze Bar.** For sunsets with your ouzo and mezedes, or a late-night
CLUBS cocktail with a view of the illuminated Old Fortress, try Amaze Bar on the water. ⊠ *Faliraki, north of Old Fortress, Corfu town, Corfu* ☎ *26610/22386.*

★ **Cavalieri Hotel.** The rooftop bar at the Cavalieri Hotel is hard to beat for views. Hotel guests happily mingle with locals as the scene slowly enlivens from a mellow, early-evening cocktail crowd to a more-energetic partylike atmosphere. ⊠ *Kapodistriou 4, Corfu town* ☎ *26610/39041.*

★ **Ekati.** At Ekati crowds are sophisticated, older, and largely native. No matter: the volume of live music is high enough to make dancing, not talking, the main matter of business at this chichi club, where excessive baubles and Paris designer labels are much in evidence. Ekati is at the end of the disco strip. ☎ *No phone.*

Internet Cafe Netoikos. Have a coffee or a drink from the bar while you do business online from 10 am to midnight every day. It also has Wi-Fi, and offers printing and scanning services. ✉ *Kalokeretou 12–14, Corfu town* ☎ *26610/47479.*

> ## A MUSICAL TRADITION
>
> Corfu has a rich musical tradition, partly the result of the Italian, French, and British influences evident throughout the island. The town's numerous marching bands take part in all official ceremonies, even religious observances. Throughout summer on Sunday you can catch the local philharmonic in concert on the Esplanade in Corfu town.

Libro d'Oro. Hip but relaxed Libro d'Oro has cane chairs out on the cobblestones and a good view of decked-out promenade strollers. ✉ *Liston, south end, Corfu town* ☎ *26610/27279.*

FILM **Finikas.** Corfu town's Finikas is said to be the oldest outdoor cinema in Greece. It shows undubbed international movies in a pretty courtyard from June to September. In summer, shows generally start at 9 pm and 11 pm; selections change every two to three weeks. ✉ *Akadimias, Corfu town* ☎ *No phone.*

Orpheus. All year-round, you can watch movies at the indoor Orpheus. ✉ *Aspioti, Corfu town* ☎ *26610/39769.*

SHOPPING

Corfu town has myriad tiny shops, and half of them seem to be selling jewelry. Designer boutiques, shoe shops, and accessory stores can be found in every nook and cranny of the town. The major tourist shopping streets are Nikiphorou Theotoki (designer boutiques, jewelry) and Agios Spyridonos (local souvenirs). The local fish-and-vegetable market is open Monday through Saturday from very early in the morning until about noon. For traditional goods, head for the narrow streets of the Campiello, where olive wood, lace, jewelry, and wineshops abound. For perishable products such as liqueurs and candies, you may do better checking out the supermarkets than buying in the Old Town. Most of the shops listed here are in the Campiello and are open May to October, from 8 am until late (whenever the last tourist leaves); they're generally closed during winter. Stores in outlying shopping areas tend to close Monday, Wednesday, and Saturday afternoons at 2:30 pm, and all day Sunday.

Nikos Sculpture and Jewellery. Corfu-born Nikos Michalopoulos creates original gold and silver jewelry and sculptures in cast bronze; they're expensive, but worth it. ✉ *Paleologou 50, Corfu town* ☎ *26610/31107* ⊕ *www.nikosjewellery.gr* ✉ *N. Theotoki 54, Corfu town* ☎ *26610/32009.*

6

Fantasy island: Legend has it that Pontikonisi—here pictured behind Vlacherena Monastery—is really Odysseus's ship turned to stone by an enraged Poseidon.

★ **Terracotta.** Contemporary Greek jewelry, ceramics, small sculptures, and one-of-a-kind art and craft objects are sold in this small, appealing shop. ☒ *Filamonikas 20, off N. Theotoki, Corfu town* ☎ *26610/45260.*

★ **Stella.** This shop sells religious icons, ceramics, religious icons, stone sculptures, and dolls in traditional costume, all handmade and sourced from Greece. ☒ *Kapodistriou 62, Corfu town* ☎ *26610/24012.*

SOUTH CORFU NOTIA KEPKYPA

Outside Corfu town, near the suburb of Kanoni, are several of Corfu's most unforgettable sights, including the lovely view of the island of Pontikonisi. The nearby palace and grounds of Mon Repos were once owned by Greece's royal family and are open to the public as a museum. A few villages south of Benitses, and some on the island's southern tip, are usually overrun with raucous package-tour groups. Avoid them unless you seek a binge-drinking, late-night, party-people scene and beaches chockablock with shrieking crowds and tanning bodies. If you're looking for more-solitary nature in the south, take a trip to Lake Korission.

KANONI KANONI

5 km (3 mi) south of Corfu town.

★ The suburb of Kanoni was once one of the world's great beauty spots, made famous by countless pictures. Today the landscape has been engulfed by development and a Starbucks has laid claim to the best spot to take in the legendary and still-lovely view, which looks out over two beautiful islets. If you truly want to commune with nature, visit the lush and lovely seaside gardens surrounding the country palace of Mon Repos.

Kanoni's famed vistas encompass the open sea separated by a long, narrow causeway lining the lagoon of Halikiopoulou, with the intensely green slopes of Mt. Agia Deka as a backdrop. A shorter breakwater leads to the white convent of Moni Vlahernes on a tiny islet—one of the most picturesque islets in all Greece and the one pictured on nearly all postcards of Mouse Island. However, it is the tiny island beyond that islet—the one in the middle of the lake with the tall cypresses—that is **Pontikonisi,** or Mouse Island, a rock rising dramatically from the clear water and topped by a tiny 13th-century chapel (not much close up). Legend has it that the island is really Odysseus's ship, which an enraged Poseidon turned to stone: the reason why Homer's much-traveled hero was shipwrecked on Phaeacia (Corfu) in *The Odyssey.* June to August a little motorboat runs out to Pontikonisi every 20 minutes. Keep in mind, though, that while the view *of* the islets has sold a thousand postcards, the view *from* the islets (looking back at Corfu) is that of a hilly landscape built up with resort hotels and summer homes and of the adjacent airport, where planes take off directly over the churches.

GETTING HERE

The local blue bus (line 2) offers frequent daily service (every half-hour Monday through Saturday, hourly on Sunday) to Kanoni from Plateia San Rocco in Corfu town; the fare is about €1.50. A taxi to Kanoni costs approximately €12. The islet of Pontikonissi can be reached by a short boat trip from the dock at Vlaherena, 2 km (about a mile) below Kanoni and costs €5 round-trip. The best way to reach Mon Repos from Corfu town is by walking; it takes about 15 minutes and you follow the seafront most of the way.

EXPLORING

Corfu Holiday Palace. Corfu's only casino is in the sleek and curving hotel, Corfu Holiday Palace. The nearly 5,500 square feet of gaming space is open daily 4 pm–5 am. The hotel has been completely renovated and has views of Mouse Island. ⊠ *Nausica St., Kanoni, Kanoni* ☎ *26610/36540* ⊕ *www.corfuholidaypalace.gr.*

Fodor's Choice
★

Mon Repos. The former royal palace of Mon Repos is surrounded by gorgeous English-style gardens that lend magic to an idyllic setting. The compact neoclassic palace (really a villa) was built in 1831 by Sir Frederic Adam for his wife, and it was later the summer residence of the British lord high commissioners; the architect, Sir George Whitmore, also designed the Palace of St. Michael and St. George in Corfu town. After Greece won independence from Britain in 1864, Mon Repos was used as a summer palace for the royal family of Greece. Queen Elizabeth II's husband, Prince Philip, was born here in 1921 (he was a royal prince of Greece and Denmark; the Corfiots, who have no love of royalty, call him "the penniless Greek who married a queen"). Today, the villa is a museum dedicated to the area's archaeological history. After touring the palace, wander around the extensive grounds (entrance is free, so

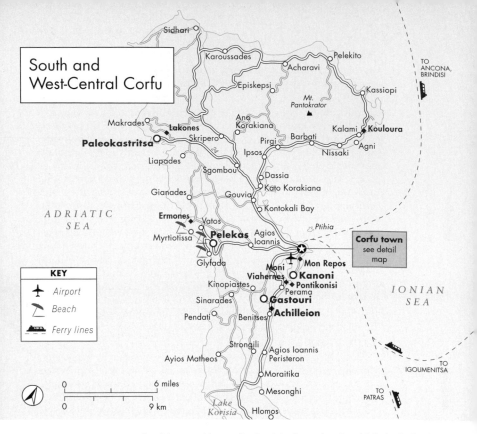

South and West-Central Corfu

TO ANCONA, BRINDISI

Sidhari
Karoussades
Acharavi
Pelekito
Episkepsi
Kassiopi
Mt. Pantokrator
Makrades
Lakones
Ano Korakiana
Kalami **Kouloura**
Paleokastritsa
Skripero
Pirgi
Barbati
Agni
Liapades
Ipsos
Nissaki
Sgombou
Dassia
Gianades
Kato Korakiana
Gouvia
Kontokali Bay

ADRIATIC SEA

Ermones
Vatos
Ptihia
Myrtiotissa
Pelekas
Agios Ioannis

Corfu town
see detail map

Glyfada
Moni
Mon Repos
Viahernes
Kanoni
Kinopiastes
Pontikonisi
Perama
Sinarades
Gastouri
Pendati
Benitses
Achilleion

IONIAN SEA

Strongili
Ayios Matheos
Agios Ioannis Peristeron
Moraitika

TO IGOUMENITSA

Mesonghi
TO PATRAS
Lake Korisia
Hlomos

KEY
✈ Airport
Beach
Ferry lines

0 ——— 6 miles
0 ——— 9 km

you can do this even if you don't visit the palace), which include the elusive remains of a Doric temple from the 7th and 6th centuries BC and the small but beautiful beach that was once used exclusively by the Greek royal family and is now open to the public. Bring your suit and join the locals on the long pier jutting out into the crystal-clear waters of the Ionian Sea. ✛ *1 km (½ mi) south of Old Fortress, following oceanfront walk* ☎ *26610/41369* 🎫 *€3, gardens free* 🕐 *Tues.–Fri. 8:30–7, Sat.–Sun. 8:30–3.*

THE ACHILLEION AND GASTOURI ΑΧΙΛΛΕΙΟΝ ΚΑΙ ΓΑΣΤΟΥΡΙ

19 km (12 mi) southwest of Corfu town.

GETTING HERE

The local blue bus (line No. 10) departs daily from Plateia San Rocco in Corfu town for Gastouri and the Achilleion, departing Monday through Saturday at 8 am, 10, noon, 2 pm, 5, and 8; Sunday at 9 am, 1 pm, 5, and 7 (schedules can change; check with ticket window at Plateia San Rocco). Return times are approximately 15 minutes after arrival times; round-trip fare is €3—buy your return ticket at the same time as your outgoing one. A taxi costs about €20 (ask the driver for an approximate fare before entering taxi).

EXPLORING

The village of Gastouri, overrun in summer by tour buses and day-trippers, is the site of the Achilleion.

Fodor's Choice ★ **Achilleion.** This Teutonic palace, built in the late 19th century for Empress Elizabeth of Austria, is perhaps the most popular tourist attraction in Corfu and remains a monument of 19th-century historicism. The empress used the place as a retreat to escape court life and to ease her heartbreak over husband Franz Josef's numerous affairs and her son Archduke Rudolph's mysterious murder or suicide at Mayerling in 1889. Elizabeth named the palace after her favorite hero, Achilles, whom she inexplicably identified with Rudolph. After Elizabeth was assassinated in 1898, Kaiser Wilhelm II bought the villa and lived in it until the outbreak of World War I, during which time the Achilleion was used by French and Serbian troops as a military hospital. After the armistice, the Greek government received it as a spoil of war.

Today it's a museum, but not a terribly inspiring one. The interior is a series of rather ungainly, uninteresting rooms done in various styles (a pseudo-Byzantine chapel, a pseudo-Pompeian room, a pseudo-Renaissance dining hall), with a smattering of period furniture scattered about; the vulgar fresco called *Achilles in His Chariot,* on the ceiling of the entrance hall, tells you all you need to know about the empress's taste in pseudo-classical art. More appealing is the terrace, laid out like an Ionic peristyle with a number of 19th-century statues, the best of which is *The Dying Achilles.* The gardens, surrounded by olive groves and with a distant view of the sea, are pretty but, all in all, the whole place looks a bit vacuous and forlorn. For a Web site on the estate, go to the Wikipedia entry (the easiest way to access it) and then hit the link to the Achilleion site. ⊠ *Main street, The Achilleion,* ☎ *26610/56210* ⊠€6 ☉ *Apr.–Oct., daily 8–7; Nov.–Mar., daily 8:30–3:30.*

WHERE TO EAT AND STAY

For expanded reviews, visit Fodors.com.

$$$$ GREEK Fodor's Choice ★ ✕**Taverna Tripa.** This famous (and heavily touristed) taverna in the charming hilltop village of Kinopiastes has been in business since 1936 and has had more than its share of famous visitors (snapshots of everyone from Anthony Quinn to Jimmy Carter and Jane Fonda are tacked up on the back wall). Today it's owned and operated by Spiros and Rena, the grandchildren of the original owner. The fixed-price menu (€35) begins with a choice of tasty mezedes (small appetizers) followed by juicy spit-roasted lamb or beef baked in parchment and, finally, a selection of seasonal fruit and desserts, all of it washed down by unlimited quantities of the house wine or other drinks. Eventually the live music begins and local dancers perform Greek dances in the courtyard; patrons are encouraged to join in. ⊠ *2 km (1 mi) northwest of Gastouri, Kinopiastes* ☎ *26610/56333* ⊕ *www.tripas.gr* ⚓ *Reservations essential* ☉ *No lunch.*

$$$$ Fodor's Choice ★ ▨ **Costa Blu Hotel.** Occupying a spectacular position on a hillside directly above the sea, the Costa Blu's accommodation is all in spacious and luxuriously furnished suites, so that it's more like staying in your own villa than a hotel—and the more so thanks to paths among the beautifully

6

Built by the tragic Empress Elizabeth of Austria, the Achilleion is a spectacular estate adorned with neoclassical statues of ancient heroes and idyllic gardens.

landscaped grounds that invite you for a stroll, the combination of bright flowers and the sleek building style imparting a distinctly Mediterranean atmosphere which many of Corfu's hotels lack. **ros:** wonderful accommodation and location; all suites have sea view; proximity to Benitses and its yacht marina. **Cons:** no cooking facilities in rooms; the road nearby can be busy. ⊠ *Benitses (2 km/1.6 mi south of Gastouri), Gastouri* ☎ *26610/72672* ⊕ *www.holidays-corfu.com marbella. gr* ⊅ *48 suites* ⅙ *In-room: a/c. In-hotel: restaurant, pool, gym, spa, business center* ⊘ *Closed Nov.–Apr.* ⊚ *some meals*

WEST-CENTRAL CORFU
ΔΥΤΙΚΗ-ΚΕΝΤΡΙΚΗ ΚΕΡΚΥΡΑ

Hairpin bends take you through orange and olive groves, over the mountainous spine of the island to the sandy beaches, rugged bays, and promontories of the west-central coast. The road descends to the sea, where two headlands near Paleokastritsa, 130 feet high and covered with trees and boulders, form a pair of natural harbors. The beaches on this western side of Corfu are lovely, but some of them, notably around Pelekas, have stronger surf and higher waves than the more-sheltered beaches on the east side of the island. The lush and fertile Ropa valley, Corfu's agricultural heartland, lies between the sandy beaches of the west-central coast near Ermones and the dramatic mountains and hilltop villages of the northwest.

PELEKAS ΠΕΛΕΚΑΣ

11 km (7 mi) northwest of Gastouri, 13 km (8 mi) west of Corfu town.

Inland from the coast at Glyfada (see Glyfada beach, below) is Pelekas, an attractive hilltop village that overflows with tourists because of its much-touted lookout point, called **Kaiser's Throne**, a rocky hilltop with spectacular views of the entire island and sea beyond. German Kaiser Wilhelm II enjoyed the sunset here when not relaxing at Achilleion Palace.

Ermones. On the coast north of Pelekas lies the resort town of Ermones, with pebbly sand beaches, heavily wooded cliffs, and a backdrop of green mountains. The Ropa River flows into the Ionian Sea here. ⊠ *8 km [5 mi] north of Pelekas .*

GETTING HERE

The local blue bus (line No. 11) has a regular all-day service from San Rocco Square for Pelekas, starting at 7, with the last bus at 10. In high season, the green KTEL bus has six daily departures for Glyfada, the most convenient being 9 and 11 am, from the bus terminal on Avramiou near the New Port. A taxi from Corfu town to the Kaiser's Throne costs about €11 and will save you about 20 minutes travel time.

BEACHES

Glyfada. The large, golden beaches at Glyfada are the most famous on the island. Though the sands are inevitably packed with sunbathers, it remains one of the hottest hot spots in Corfu. Sun beds, umbrellas, and water-sports equipment is available for rent and there are several tourist resorts. ⊠ *2 km [1 mi] south of Pelekas.*

Myrtiotissa. The isolated Myrtiotissa beach, between sheer cliffs, is known for its good snorkeling—and its nude sunbathing. Backed by olive and cypress trees, this sandy stretch was called by Lawrence Durrell in *Prospero's Cell* (with debatable overenthusiasm) "perhaps the loveliest beach in the world." ⊠ *3 km [2 mi] north of Pelekas.*

Pelekas. The beach at Pelekas has soft, golden sand and clear water but is developed and tends to be crowded. The huge Aquis Pelekas Beach Hotel resort complex rises up behind it, and Pelekas village is popular with summer tourists. Depending on time of year and demand, there is sometimes a free shuttle service between Pelekas Village and the beach (which is a long and steep walk otherwise).

WHERE TO EAT AND STAY

For expanded reviews, visit Fodors.com.

$$ ✕ **Jimmy's.** Only fresh ingredients and pure local olive oil are used at
GREEK this family-run restaurant serving traditional Greek food. Try *tsigareli,* a combination of green vegetables and spices, or some of Jimmy's own Corfiot meat dishes. There's a nice selection of vegetarian dishes and sweets. The place opens early in the morning for breakfast and stays open all day. ⊠ *Pelekas, Pelekas* ☎ *26610/94284* ☉ *Closed Nov.–May.*

$$ 🏨 **Levant Hotel.** Located at the top of Pelekas hill, next to the Kaiser's Throne lookout point, this small, inn-like hotel offers balconied guest rooms with breathtaking views (and sunsets) across silver-green olive groves to the shimmering Ionian Sea. **Pros:** great views, personable

service, in-house restaurant with terrace. **Cons:** the immediate vicinity often heaves with tour groups. ⊠ *Pelekas, near Kaiser's Throne, Pelekas* ☎ *26610/94230, 26610/94335* ⊕ *www.levanthotel.com* ⌇ *25 rooms, 1 suite* ₺ *In-room: a/c. In-hotel: restaurant, bar, pool* ⑩ *Breakfast.*

$$$$ 🔆 **Pelecas Country Club.** Some say this small, luxury hotel can be a bit Fodor'sChoice   snobbish, others insist that it lets you experience true Corfiot tradition, ★   thanks to its unique setting: the old family mansion of Nikos Veli-anitis—lovingly set amid 50 acres of olive and cypress trees—whose antiques-laden rooms form the core of this idyllic retreat. **Pros:** lovely rooms and flower gardens. **Cons:** if unempathetic to fine manners and old-world style, this place will not be for you. ⊠ *Kerkyra–Pelekas Rd., Pelekas* ☎ *26610/52239, 26610/52917* ⊕ *www.country-club.gr* ⌇ *7 studios, 4 suites* ₺ *In-room: a/c, kitchen. In-hotel: bar, pool, tennis court* ⊟ *No credit cards* ⑩ *Breakfast.*

PALEOKASTRITSA ΠΑΛΑΙΟΚΑΣΤΡΙΤΣΑ

Fodor'sChoice   *21 km (13 mi) north of Pelekas, 25 km (16 mi) northwest of Corfu* ★   *town.*

To quote one recent traveler: "I'd rather go to Paleokastritsa than to Heaven." Considered by many to be the site of Homer's city of the Phaeacians, this truly spectacular territory of grottoes, cliffs, and turquoise waters has a big rock named Kolovri, which the ancient Greeks said resembled the ship that brought Ulysses home. The jaw-dropping natural beauty of Paleo, as Corfiots call it, has brought hotels, tavernas, bars, and shops to the hillsides above the bays, and the beaches swarm with hordes of people on day trips from Corfu town. You can explore the idyllic coves in peace with a pedal boat or small motorboat rented at the crowded main beach. There are also boat operators that go around to the prettiest surrounding beaches; ask the skipper to let you off at a beach that appeals to you and to pick you up on a subsequent trip. Many visitors also enjoy a trip on the "Yellow Submarine," a glass-bottomed boat which also runs night excursions (reservations are recommended).

In the Paleokastritsa region, one of the most famous natural beauty spots is found off the Main Road: the Canal d'Amour, an amazing "canal" formed by towering layers of rock erosion. Unfortunately, one has to run the gauntlet of Sidari, a township packed with notorious discos and bars. The splendor of the rock formations may be worth it, their legend even more so: a person who swims the entire length of the canal may meet his or her life love at the end of the river bed. On the rocks lining the canal, look for the La Grotta bar, built grotto-like into the rocks of a tiny cove. A mini-Acapulco, the high cliffs here tempt local youths to dive into the turquoise waters—great entertainment as you sip your cold beer or cocktail.

GETTING HERE

Depending on the day and the season, the green KTEL bus has four to six daily departures for Paleokastritsa from the Corfu town's bus terminal on Avramiou near the New Port (the daily 9 am departure is the

Barely changed from the days of Homer, the Paleokastritsa region of Corfu is one of the most achingly beautiful landscapes in Greece.

fastest and most convenient). The trip takes about 45 minutes. A taxi from Corfu town to Paleokastritsa costs about €40.

EXPLORING

Paleokastritsa Monastery. Paleokastritsa Monastery, a 17th-century structure, is built on the site of an earlier monastery, among terraced gardens overlooking the Ionian Sea. Its treasure is a 12th-century icon of the Virgin Mary, and there's a small museum with some other early icons. Note the Tree of Life motif on the ceiling. Be sure to visit the inner courtyard (go through the church), built on the edge of the cliff and looking down a precipitous cliff to the placid green coves and coastline to the south. There's a small gift shop on the premises. ⊠ *On northern headland, Paleokastritsa* ☎ *No phone* 🖃 *Donations accepted* ☉ *Daily 7–1 and 3–8.*

Lakones. The village of Lakones, built on the steep mountain behind the Paleokastritsa Monastery, looks rather forbidding, but tourists flock there for the view. Kaiser Wilhelm was among many famous people who would make the ascent to enjoy the magnificent panorama of Paleokastritsa's coves from the cafés at Bella Vista, just beyond the village. From nearby Krini you can climb up to the ruins of the 13th-century **Angelokastro**, a fortress built by a despot of Epirus during his brief rule over Corfu. On many occasions during the medieval period the fort sheltered Corfiots from attack by Turkish invaders. Look for the chapel and caves, which served as sanctuaries and hiding places. ⊠ *5 km (3 mi) northeast of Paleokastritsa.*

WHERE TO EAT AND STAY

For expanded reviews, visit Fodors.com.

$$ ✕ **Taverna Limeri.** This taverna, which sits in the V formed by the two
GREEK   streets in the village of Kora Korakiana, is where locals come to dine
★   on wonderfully prepared local dishes. It's a good place to order several
small plates and share the tastes Litsa cooks up in the kitchen. Try the
gigantes (giant beans in red sauce), pork croquettes in cranberry sauce,
the meatballs, the grilled pork souvlaki, or the steak with mushroom
sauce. Ask for the daily specials not on the printed menu; you won't
be disappointed. The superb red house wine is a blend of Cabernet
and Merlot. On summer weekends, it is best to make a table reserva-
tion. ✉ *Kato Korakiana, 1 km (½ mi) west of Dassia, Paleokastritsa*
☎ *26610/97576* ⊘ *No lunch.*

$$$$ ✕ **Vrahos** (*The Rock*). The view from this rather expensive restaurant
GREEK   overlooking the cliff-enclosed bay in Paleokastritsa will make you want
to linger. The menu offers a bit of everything; the lobster and spaghetti
is delicious but ridiculously overpriced at €38, so you may want to
content yourself with a nice Greek salad or moussaka instead. ✉ *Paleo-
kastritsa, north end of beach, Paleokastritsa* ☎ *26630/41233* ⊘ *Closed
Nov.–Easter.*

$$$$ ⊡ **Akrotiri Beach Hotel.** Few hotels in Corfu are so superbly positioned
Fodor'sChoice   to take in its natural splendor the way the Akrotiri is, which lords
★   it over a paradisical little peninsula. **Pros:** the location could not be
bettered. **Cons:** the reception area looks a bit tired. ⬧ *Box 28, Paleo-
kastritsa, Corfu, Greece* ☎ *26630/41237* ⊕ *www.akrotiri-beach.com*
⤷ *127 rooms* ⚐ *In-room: a/c. In-hotel: restaurant, bar, pool, tennis
court, beach, water sports* ⊘ *Closed Nov.–Apr.* ⦿ *Breakfast.*

$$ ⊡ **Casa Lucia.** There are far grander places to stay on Corfu, but few
Fodor'sChoice   with as much quiet, unpretentious charm as Casa Lucia, where the
★   stone buildings of an old olive press have been converted into guest
cottages and smaller studios. **Pros:** rural retreat; cozy charm; family-
friendly atmosphere. **Cons:** fairly basic bathrooms in studios. ✉ *Corfu–
Paleokastritsa Rd., 13 km (8 mi) northwest of Corfu town, Sgombou*
☎ *26610/91419* ⊕ *www.casa-lucia-corfu.com* ⤷ *9 cottages* ⚐ *In-room:
no a/c, no TV. In-hotel: pool.*

The Cyclades

TINOS, MYKONOS, DELOS, NAXOS, PAROS,
SANTORINI, AND FOLEGANDROS

WORD OF MOUTH

"We pleasantly spent a half day on the ferry to Santorini and
enjoyed the views of the caldara upon our approach. Once you
arrive, it's not at Fira but the port of Athinios. You climb off the ferry
and into a bus that will take you to Fira. From there, it's another
bus to Ia. I wasn't expecting this much travel, so be forewarned!"
—elissaAAM

WELCOME TO THE CYCLADES

TOP REASONS TO GO

★ **Atlantis Refound?:** Volcanic, spectacular Santorini is possibly the last remnant of the "lost continent"—the living here is as high as the towns' cliff-top perches.

★ **Ariadne's Island:** Mythic haunt of the ancient Minoan princess, Naxos is the largest of the Cyclades and is noted for its 16th-century Venetian homes.

★ **Lively, Liberated Mykonos:** The rich arrive by yacht, the middle class by plane, the backpackers by boat—but everyone is out to enjoy the golden sands and Dionysian nightlife.

★ **Cubism, Cycladic Style:** The smiling island of Sifnos is studded with miragelike white clusters of houses that tumble down hillsides like so many cubist sculptures.

★ **Tantalizing Antiparos:** Hiding within the shadow of its mother island of Paros, this long-forgotten jewel has been discovered by Hollywood high-rollers like Tom Hanks and Brad Pitt.

1 Mykonos. Party Central because of its nonstop nightlife, the chief village of Mykonos, called Mykonos town, is the Cyclades' best preserved—a maze of flat-stone streets lined with white houses and flower-filled balconies. A short boat ride away is hallowed Delos, sacred to Apollo.

2 Tinos. Among the most beautiful of the Cyclades, Tinos's charms remain largely unheralded but include the "Greek Lourdes"—the Panayia Evangelistria church—1,000 traditional stone dovecotes, and idyllic villages like Pirgos.

3 Naxos. Presided over by the historic castle of Naxos town, largely the creation of the Venetian dukes of the archipelago, Naxos has a landscape graced with time-stained villages like Sangri, Chalki, and Apeiranthos, many with Venetian-era towers.

4 Paros. West of Naxos and known for its fine beaches and fishing villages, as well as the pretty town of Naousa, Paros often takes the summer overflow crowd from Mykonos. Today, crowds head here for Paros town and its Hundred Doors Church and undeveloped beaches.

5 Santorini. Once the vast crater of a volcano, Santorini's spectacular bay is ringed by black-and-red cliffs, which rise up a thousand feet over the sea. The main towns of Fira and Ia cling inside the rim in dazzling white contrast to the somber cliffs. South lies the "Greek Pompeii" that is ancient Akrotiri.

6 Folegandros. Tides of travelers have yet to discover this stark island, which makes it all the more alluring to Cyclades lovers, particularly those who prize its stunning cliff scenery.

Korissia
Kea
KEA

Merihas

KYTHNOS

Livadi
SERIFOS

Adamas
MILOS

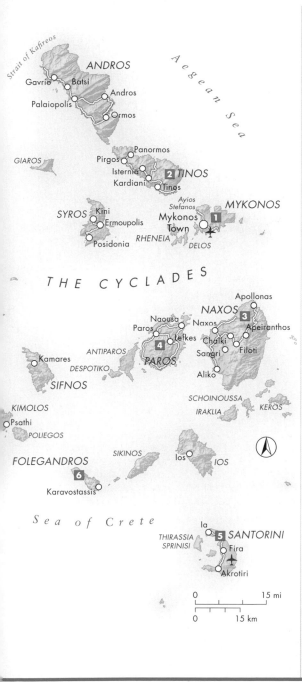

GETTING ORIENTED

With their magnificent fusion of sunlight, stone, and sparking aqua sea, the Cyclades are the islands that launched a thousand trips. Set in the heart of the Grecian Mediterranean, these nearly 2,000 islands and islets are scattered like a ring (Cyclades is the Greek word for "circling ones") around the sacred isle of Delos, birthplace of the god Apollo. All the top spots—Santorini, Naxos, Paros, Mykonos, Tinos, and Folegandros—are beloved for their postcard-perfect olive groves, stark whitewashed cubist houses, and bays of lapis lazuli. Gateways to this Aegean archipelago include the airports on Mykonos and Santorini and the harbors of Paros and Naxos.

THE CYCLADES'S BEST BEACHES

The Cyclades shimmer with beaches; every island has a dozen, two dozen, three dozen. They may be a few meters of packed earth, a long stretch of yellow sand, tiny black stones, marble pebbles, or smooth slate. But they are all washed by waters that are Aegean blue — the most unforgettable color in the world.

The Cyclades has a seemingly endless and diverse array of beautiful beaches, each curved like a water-nymph's hip. No one is really sure how many beaches there are. Is 10 feet of sand a beach? It is, if you know it is there. On some, the prevailing wind is northerly; beaches facing south or protected by northern promontories are, as the Greeks say, smooth as olive oil, while beaches facing north tend to turbulence (vice versa when the wind changes). More than 30 beaches here display the EU blue flags (awarded for pristine conditions), so it is little wonder Europeans flock here for the salubrious, pellucid waters their homelands lack.

GOOD TO KNOW

The beaches do not have restrooms per se, but their taverns all do.

Beach chairs and umbrellas cost plenty—usually €5–€7.

Submerged rocks may have spiny urchins on them. Jellyfish, a plague 25 years ago, have mostly vanished (watch out for the long, transparent tentacles) and soothing lotions can be purchased everywhere.

Although more and more of these beaches have access roads, even paved ones, there are plenty with only a perilously winding dirt road leading near them.

THE CYCLADES'S BEST BEACHES

There are so many wonderful beaches on the Cyclades we can't just pick out three or four to focus on but offer instead a generous selection.

MYKONOS

Mykonos's most famous beach is Super Paradise; although this is a beautiful stretch of sand with calm water, what makes it so famous is the all-night nightlife. The beach is nearly all taken up with umbrellas and chaise longues, and the back of the beach is lined with bars and clubs. Once gay, it is now mixed and swinging. For a quieter scene, opt for Mykonos's longest beach, Elia, parts of which are nude (although the difference between nude and not can be minuscule!)

NAXOS

Some consider Naxian beaches the best in the Cyclades. The western coast, facing pretty Paros across the strait, is basically a sand beach, broken by rocky promontories, that stretches for miles. Ayios Prokopios, 5 km (3 mi) from Chora, is noted for its little lagoon with waterfowl; families love it here. For a beach idyll, head all the way out to Kastraki; it is really a series of sandy inlets where aquatic hues change throughout the day.

PAROS

The most popular beaches on Paros are the ones across the bay from Parikia—Marcello and Krios—which are connected, and are gentle and sandy (get there by boat or walk a half hour).

Across the bay from Naousa (use the boat), Kolymbithres is famous for its tortuous rocks; a Mycenaean fortress tops the hill behind it. Further out, Monastiri beach has been discovered but the nearby eco-park ensures checked development.

The longest stretch of sand on Paros is aptly named Chrysi Akti, or Golden beach. The world windsurfing championships are held here in August, and umbrellas do not choke it, as so often elsewhere.

On Antiparos, also ringed with beaches, a 10-minute walk from town leads you to Apandima, protected by two islets.

SANTORINI

While the two "black" beaches of Santorini—Kamari and Perissa, separated by the mountain topped with Ancient Thera—are world-famous, the black stones lining them heat up and can become too hot to walk on, so rubber beach shoes are advisable.

These beaches face south and, on the clearest days, Crete is almost visible.

Updated by
Jeffrey and
Elizabeth
Carson

If the words "Greek Islands" suggest blazing sun and sea, bare rock and mountains, olive trees and vineyards, white rustic architecture and ancient ruins, fresh fish and fruity oils, the Cyclades are your isles of quintessential plenty, the ultimate Mediterranean archipelago.

"The islands with their drinkable blue volcanoes," wrote Odysseus Elytis, winner of the Nobel Prize for poetry, musing on Santorini. The major stars in this constellation of islands in the central Aegean Sea—Tinos, Mykonos, Naxos, Paros, and Santorini—remain the archetypes of the islands of Greece. No matter which of these islands you head for it always seems, at least in summer, that Zeus's sky is faultlessly azure, Poseidon's sea warm, and Dionysus's nightlife swinging (especially in Mykonos's clubs). The prevailing wind is the northern *vorias*; called *meltemi* in summer, it cools the always-sunny weather. In a blazing fusion of sunlight, stone, and aqua sparkle, the Cyclades offer both culture and hedonism: ancient sites, Byzantine castles and museums, lively nightlife, shopping, dining, and beaches plain and fancy.

Each island in the Cyclades differs significantly from its neighbors, so approach your exploration according to what sort of experience you seek. The most popular islands are Santorini, with its fantastic volcanic scenery and dramatic cliff-side towns of Fira and Ia, and Mykonos, a barren island that insinuates a sexy jet-set lifestyle, flaunts some of Greece's most famous beaches, has a perfectly preserved main town, and courts celebrities. These two islands have the fanciest accommodations. Naxos has the best mountain scenery and the longest, least-developed beaches. Tinos, the least visited and most scenic of the Cyclades, is the place to explore mountain villages, hundreds of churches, and fancifully decorated dovecotes.

These arid, mountainous islands are the peaks of a deep, submerged plateau; their composition is rocky, with few trees. They are volcanic in origin, and Santorini, southernmost of the group, actually sits on the rim of an ancient drowned volcano that exploded about 1600 BC. The dead texture of its rock is a great contrast to the living, warm limestone of most Greek islands. Santorini's basic geological colors—black, pink, brown, white, pale green—are not in themselves beautiful; as you arrive by boat, little shows above the cliff tops but a string of white villages—like teeth on the vast lower jaw of some giant monster. Still, the island was once called Kállisti, "Loveliest," and today, appreciative visitors seek its mixture of vaulted cliff-side architecture, European elegance, and stunning sunsets.

INFORMATION, PLEASE

The Cyclades remain among the most popular tourist destinations in Europe so it is all the more surprising to learn that most islands do not have an official government tourist agency. This role is often filled by private companies and they are noted as such under each island heading.

A more-idyllic rhythm prevails on many of the other Cyclades (and, of course, off-season in Santorini). Tinos has stayed authentically Greek, since its heavy tourism is largely owing to its miracle-working icon, not to its beautiful villages. In the town of Mykonos, the whitewashed houses huddle together against the meltemi winds, and backpackers rub elbows with millionaires in the mazelike white-marble streets. The island's sophistication level is high, the beaches fine, and the shopping varied and upscale. It's also the jumping-off place for a mandatory visit to tiny, deserted Delos. Apollo's windswept birth islet, still watched over by a row of marble lions, was once the religious and commercial center of the eastern Mediterranean.

Naxos, greenest of the Cyclades, makes cheese and wine, raises livestock, and produces potatoes, olives, and fruit. For centuries a Venetian stronghold, it has a shrinking aristocratic Roman Catholic population, Venetian houses and fortifications, and Cycladic and Mycenaean sites. Paros, a hub of the ferry system, has reasonable prices and is a good base for trips to other islands. It's also good for lazing on white-sand beaches and for visiting fishing villages. Of course, throughout the Cyclades, there are countless classical sites, monasteries, churches, and villages to be explored. The best reason to visit them may be the beauty of the walk, the impressiveness of the location, and the hospitality you will likely find off the beaten track.

Despite depredations, automobiles have brought life back to Cycladic villages. Many shuttered houses are being authentically restored, and much traditional architecture can still be found in Ia on Santorini and Apeiranthos on Naxos—villages that are part of any deep experience of the islands. In the countryside, many of the sites and buildings are often or permanently closed, though the fencing around sites may have fallen, and monks and nuns may let you in if you are polite and decently dressed—the gods may still be out there.

PLANNER

WHEN TO GO
The experience of the Cyclades is radically different summer and winter. In summer all services are operating on overload, the beaches are crowded, the clubs noisy, the restaurants packed, and the scene swinging.

Walkers, nature lovers, and devotees of classical and Byzantine Greece would do better to come in spring and fall, ideally in late April–June or September–October, when temperatures are lower and tourists are fewer. But off-season travel means less-frequent boat service; in fact, there is sometimes no service at all between November and mid-March, when stormy weather can make the seas too rough for sailing. In winter, many shops, hotels, and restaurants are closed, and the open cafés are full of locals recuperating from summer's intensities. The villages can feel shuttered and the nightlife zilch. Cultural organizations, film clubs, concerts of island music, and religious festivals become more important. The temperature will often seem colder than the thermometer indicates: if it is in the low 50s, cloudy, drizzling, and windy, you will feel chilled and want to stay indoors, and Greece is at her best outdoors.

> **BEEP BEEP**
>
> When your feet prove less than bionic, it may be time to rent wheels. Many people opt for scooters, but be careful—island hospitals are frequently filled with people with serious-looking injuries from scooter travels. ATVs overturn easily, bikes slide, and cars need to be parked; many places now rent Smart Cars for about €50 a day: these two-seaters are way cool for getting around.

PLANNING YOUR TIME

The Cyclades are more for lazing around than for book-nosed tourism. Start with the livelier islands (Mykonos, Santorini), add one or two of the larger islands (Naxos, Paros), and finish up with an untouristy one like Folegandros. While it is true that feverish partying can overwhelm the young in summer, in other seasons the temptations are fewer, gentler, and more profound. If you move fast, you will see little, and the beauty is in the general impression of sea, sky, mountain, and village, and in the details that catch your eye: an ancient column used as a building block, an octopus hung to dry in the sun, a wedding or baptism in a small church you are stopping into (welcome, stranger), a shepherd's mountain hut with a flagstone roof—they are endless. There are important sites such as Delos's ruins, but just enjoying the island rhythms often proves as soul-satisfying.

GETTING HERE AND AROUND

Transportation to the islands is constantly improving. Five of the Cyclades have airports, and the flight is short. But if you want to understand where you are, you really should travel by boat—after all, these are islands in the fabled Aegean, inhabited 5,000 years before Homer. But remember that boat schedules depend on Poseidon's weather whims, and also on the tippling gods of holidays, when they adjust. If you come for Easter, better buy tickets to and from in advance.

GETTING TO THE CYCLADES: BOAT VERSUS PLANE

To get to the Cyclades, you either fly or take a boat. Flights are short and convenient, but if you want to understand what it means to be in the Aegean archipelago, and why an island has a special feeling, take the boat. Flights are three times the price of the slower boats. But if you fly into Athens in time to make a flight connection, and don't want to visit the big city, it may be worth it. Seats are booked (sometimes overbooked) much in advance, and even in winter you need reservations. Single flights are much easier to get (even last-minute, owing to cancellations). High-rollers can also hire a helicopter for €4,000, and you would be surprised how many travelers do this. Note that airplanes are often canceled owing to rough weather; the islands have small airports, and crosswinds (but not the prevailing north winds, which are fine, however strong) ground planes. For flight schedules check the main Web sites (⊕ *www.olympicair.com,* ⊕ *www.aegeanair.com*).

AIR TRAVEL

Schedules change seasonally and are often revised; reservations are always a good idea. There are no airports on Tinos or Folegandros. Olympic Airways has four flights daily to Mykonos. The Olympic Airways offices in Mykonos are at the port and at the airport. Olympic Airways has three flights daily between Athens and Naxos airport. Olympic also offers four daily flights to the Paros Airport from Athens and five daily flights to Santorini Airport from Athens, more in peak season. Aegean Airlines has five daily flights to Mykonos and four to Santorini in summer, but their schedules are often subject to change. Some European countries now have charter flights to Mykonos.

Contacts Aegean Airlines ☎ *210/626–1700* ⊕ *www.aegeanair.com.* **Olympic Airways** ⊠ *Port, Mykonos town* ☎ *22890/22490, 22890/22495* ⊕ *www.olympicair.com*⊠, *Ayia Athanassiou, Santorini, Fira* ☎ *22860/22493, 22860/22793.***Airports Mykonos Airport** ⊠ *4 km [2½ mi] southeast of Mykonos town* ☎ *22890/22327.***Naxos Airport** ⊠ *1 km [½ mi] south of Naxos town* ☎ *22850/23969.* **Paros Airport** ⊠ *Near Alyki village, 9 km [5½ mi] south of Paros town ,* ☎ *22840/91257.* **Santorini Airport** ⊠ *On east coast, 8 km [5 mi] from Fira, Monolithos* ☎ *22860/31525.*

BIKE AND QUAD TRAVEL

All the major islands have car- and bike-rental agencies at the ports and in the business districts. Motorbikes and scooters start in summer at about €10 a day, including third-party liability coverage. Don't wear shorts or sandals, insist on the helmet (which the law requires), and get a phone number, in case of breakdown. Quads feel safer, but overturn easily; Greeks call them *gourounia* (piggies).

CAR TRAVEL

To take cars on ferries you must make reservations. Though there is bus service on the large and mountainous islands of Andros and Naxos, it is much more convenient to travel by car. Although islanders tend to acknowledge rules, many roads on the islands are poorly maintained, and tourists sometimes lapse into vacation inattentiveness. Drive with caution, especially at night, when you may well be sharing the roads with motorists returning from an evening of drinking. In 2004 motor accidents killed 40 people on little Mykonos.

All the major islands have car- and bike-rental agencies at the ports and in the business districts. Car rentals in summer cost about €50 per day, with unlimited mileage and third-party liability insurance. Full insurance costs about €8 a day more. Four-wheeled semi-bikes (quads), that look—but are not—safer than bikes, are also available everywhere. Choose a dealer that offers 24-hour service and a change of vehicle in case of a breakdown. Most will take you from and to your plane or boat. Beware: all too many travelers end up in Athenian hospitals owing to poor roads, slipshod maintenance, careless drivers, and excessive partying.

BOAT AND FERRY TRAVEL

There must be three times as many boats connecting Athens with the Cyclades as there were a decade ago. Most boats leave from Athens's port of Piraeus and also from Rafina; a few leave from Lavrio. The big boats are more stable, and islanders consider the various Blue Star Ferries as their main connection to the mainland. Remember that some fast boats are small, and can roll uncomfortably in high seas. Also, high-speeds have little or no deck space; you are closed in. Some older boats have no seat numbers, but usually these are the least crowded. The Blue Star will give you a seat number for a small extra fee, and the fast boats have reserved seats only. In summer, reserved seats must be secured in advance.

At Easter and around August 15, seats are hard to come by, and boat schedules alter for the holidays. Boats run much less frequently in winter, and many fast boats don't run at all. Complaints are often heard about scheduling or overcrowding, but don't listen to them. Yes, everything is unpleasantly crowded in August—but reservations are secure.

Off-season you don't need reservations, and you can purchase tickets at offices on the dock in Piraeus. Boats can be canceled owing to gales, and then schedules go haywire and hundreds of people and cars have to fight for new tickets (in effect, the boat agencies never cancel boats; the harbor police decide, according to international regulations).

The Greek boats in general are efficient, stable, fast, and comfortable. The new no-smoking law seems to be effective, and in summer they are all air-conditioned.

For schedules (not too far in advance, please), check ⊕ *www.openseas. gr.* You can get daily schedules from the Piraeus Port Authority (☎ *210/451–1311 or 210/415–1321*) and the Rafina Port Authority (☎ *22940/22300*). *Kaló taxídi* (bon voyage)!

Boat and Ferry Information Piraeus boat departures/arrivals ☎ *14541, 14944.* **Piraeus Port Authority** ✉ *Piraeus Port Authority, 10 Akti Miaouli, Piraeus* ☎ *210/455–0000 through 210/455–0100* ⊕ *www.olp.gr.* **Rafina KTEL Buses** ☎ *22940/23440* ⊕ *www.ktelattikis.gr.*

BUS TRAVEL

For information about Bus Travel consult the Getting Here and Around sections listed under each island.

CAR TRAVEL

To take cars on ferries you must make reservations. Though there is bus service on the large and mountainous islands of Andros and Naxos, it is much more convenient to travel by car. Although islanders tend to acknowledge rules, many roads on the islands are poorly maintained, and tourists sometimes lapse into vacation inattentiveness. Drive with caution, especially at night, when you may well be sharing the roads with motorists returning from an evening of drinking. In 2004 motor accidents killed 40 people on little Mykonos.

All the major islands have car- and bike-rental agencies at the ports and in the business districts. Car rentals in summer cost about €50 per day, with unlimited mileage and third-party liability insurance. Full insurance costs about €8 a day more. Four-wheeled semi-bikes (quads), that look—but are not—safer than bikes, are also available everywhere. Choose a dealer that offers 24-hour service and a change of vehicle in case of a breakdown. Most will take you from and to your plane or boat. Beware: all too many travelers end up in Athenian hospitals owing to poor roads, slipshod maintenance, careless drivers, and excessive partying.

HIKING

The Cyclades are justly famous for their hiking. Ancient goat and donkey trails go everywhere—through fields, over mountains, along untrodden coasts. Since tourists crowd beaches, clubs, and town promenades, walking is uncrowded even in July and August. Prime walking months, though, are April and May, when temperatures are reasonable, wildflowers seem to cover every surface, and birds migrate. October is also excellent for hiking—plus, olive groves provide their own sort of spectacle when dozens of gatherers spread their cloths.

RESTAURANTS

Eating is a lively social activity in the Cyclades, and the friendliness of most taverna owners compensates for the lack of formal service. Unless you order intermittently, the food comes all at once. Restaurant schedules on the Cyclades vary; some places close for lunch, most close for siesta, and all are open late. Reservations are not required unless otherwise noted, and casual dress is the rule. However, luxury restaurants are a different kettle of fish in some respects.

Greek food, like English or indeed American, used to have a bad international reputation, and you can certainly find bad food in Greece. This is often a result of restaurants' trying to adapt to the tastes and wallets of the throngs of tourists. For example: When a tourist asks for less of the islands' culinary gem—fruity, expensive olive oil—in a dish, the essence is lost. Greece produces top-quality tomatoes, lamb chops, melons, olive oil, and farmer's cheese. When Greeks go out to eat, they expect good, simple food culled from these elements, as should you. A few things to watch out for: "fresh" fish on the menu when the weather has been stormy; store-bought eggplant salad; frozen potatoes. Pay attention, and you will dine with much pleasure.

Dishes are often wonderfully redolent of garlic and olive oil; as an alternative, order grilled seafood or meat—grilled octopus with ouzo is a treat. A typical island lunch is fresh fried calamari with a salad of tomatoes, peppers, onions, feta, and olives. Lamb on a skewer and keftedes (spicy meatballs) are also favorites. Of course, nouvelle Greek has made great strides since it was first introduced a decade ago at the luxury hotels of the Cyclades. At the finer hotels, and at certain outstanding restaurants, you can now enjoy tasting the collision of centuries-old traditional dishes with newer-than-now-nouvelle spices and preparations. There are just so many times one can eat lamb-on-a-skewer, so go ahead and enjoy some big blow-outs at top restaurants—if you have a chubby wallet, that is.

The volcanic soil of Santorini is hospitable to the grape, and Greeks love the Santorini wines. Greek wines have tripled in quality in the last decade. Santorini and Paros now proudly produce officially recognized "origin" wines, which are sought throughout Greece. Barrel or farmer's wine is common, and except in late summer when it starts to taste a bit off, it's often good. Try to be on Santorini on July 20 for the celebration of St. Elias's name day, when a traditional pea-and-onion soup is served, followed by walnut and honey desserts and folk dancing.

DINING AND LODGING PRICES IN EUROS				
	¢	$	$$	$$$	$$$$
Restaurants	under €8	€8–€11	€11–€15	€15–€20	over €20
Hotels	under €60	€60–€90	€90–€120	€120–€160	over €160

Note that luxury hotel and restaurant prices in Santorini and Mykonos are more comparable to the Athens price chart. Restaurant prices are for one main course at dinner, or for two mezedes (small dishes). Hotel prices are for a standard double room in high season, including taxes. Inquire when booking whether meal plans (which can entail higher rates) are mandatory.

HOTELS

Overall, the quality of accommodations in the Cyclades is high, whether they be tiny pensions, private houses, or luxury hotels. The best rooms and service (and noticeably higher prices) are on Mykonos and Santorini, where luxury resort hotels are mushrooming and now rank among the world's favorites. Wherever you stay in the Cyclades, make a room with a view and a balcony a priority. If you're not interested in staying at luxury hotels and unless you're traveling at the very height of the season (July 15–August 30), you're unlikely to need advance reservations on some islands. Sometimes the easiest way to find something, in fact, is to head for a tourist office and describe your needs and price range. That noted, the higher the price, the more popular the island, the more the hotel will want to observe the proprieties: for top-drawer resorts, reserve in advance. And remember: few hotels have elevators, and even Santorini's best often have breathlessly picturesque cliff-side staircases and no porters.

SHOPPING

Mykonos, with Santorini taking a close second, is the best island in the Cyclades for shopping. You can buy anything from Greek folk items to Italian designer clothes, cowboy boots, and leather jackets from the United States. Although island prices are better than in the expensive shopping districts of Athens, there are many tourist traps in the resort towns, with high-pressure sales tactics and inflated prices for inferior goods. The Greeks have a word for naive American shoppers—Americanaki. It's a good sign if the owner of a shop selling traditional crafts or art lives on the island and is not a hot shot Athenian over for the summer to make a quick buck. Each island has a unique pottery style that reflects its individuality. Santorini potters like the bright shades of the setting sun, though the best pottery island is Paros. Island specialties are icons hand-painted after Byzantine originals; weavings and embroideries; local wines; and gold worked in ancient and Byzantine designs. Don't be surprised when the stores close between 2 and 5:30 in the afternoon and reopen in the evenings; even on the chic islands everybody takes a siesta.

VISITOR INFORMATION

For information about each island's tourist office (or travel agency) please consult the Visitor Information section listed under each island. General brochures and information about the Cyclades are also available through the Web site and offices of the Greek National Tourism Organization (*GNTO; EOT in Greece* ⊕ *www.gnto.gr*).

MYKONOS AND DELOS ΜΥΚΟΝΟΣ ΚΑΙ ΔΗΛΟΣ

177 km (95 nautical mi) southeast of Piraeus harbor in Athens.

From backpackers to the superrich, from day-trippers to yachties, from gays to celebrities (who head here by helicopter), Mykonos has become one of the most popular of the Aegean islands. Today's scene is a weird but attractive cocktail of tradition, beauty, and glitz, but travelers from all over the world have long been drawn to this dry, rugged island—at 16 km (10 mi) by 11 km (7 mi), one of the smaller Cyclades—thanks to its many stretches of sandy beach, its thatched windmills, and its picturesque port town. One thing is certain: Mykonos knows how to maintain its attractiveness, how to develop it, and how to sell it. Complain as you will that it is touristy, noisy, and overdeveloped, you'll be back.

In the 1950s a few tourists began trickling into Mykonos on their way to see the ancient marvels on the nearby islet of Delos, the sacred isle. For almost 1,000 years Delos was the religious and political center of the Aegean and host every four years to the Delian games, the region's greatest festival. The population of Delos actually reached 20,000 at the peak of its commercial period, and throughout antiquity Mykonos, eclipsed by its holy neighbor, depended on this proximity for income (it has been memorably described as Delos's "bordello"), as it partly does today. Anyone interested in antiquity should plan to spend at least one morning on Delos, which has some of the most striking sights preserved from antiquity, including the beautiful avenue of the Lions or the startling, enormous stone phalli in the Sanctuary of Dionysus.

GETTING HERE AND AROUND

AIR TRAVEL Mykonos is super-popular—luckily, it is easy to get there. It is totally jammed in season, in part thanks to five to ten daily flights from Athens in summer (there are almost as many in winter). For scheduled flights to and from Athens airport, check ⊕ *www.greeka.com* or *www.aia.gr*. Aegean Airlines and Olympic Airlines both go; it's a 45-minute flight.

BOAT TRAVEL Happily, Mykonos is also well served by boat, and the trip takes from 2½ to 5 hours depending on your route, the boat, and Poseidon's weather ways. There are 8 or more boats a day. For Easter and August

Continued on page 300

MYKONOS
AFTER DARK

Mykonos is unique and highly charged, thanks in large part to its fabled nightlife—the sexy young, the glittery rich, the relentless discos, all on a small, barren, starkly beautiful island. As Mykonos's summer life slides from one activity to another, the island's night clubs take on a starring role in the unfolding pageant.

Once you head out of your hotel, you'll either be right in town—where you can hop from venue to venue—or at one of the nightlife beaches, where you are likely to stay until dawn flexes her rosy fingers. The nightlife moods vary according to club, town or beach, price, hour (yes, there is nightlife before midnight), and chance passersby. And once the clubs are in heat, the action spills onto the street. Some say that after midnight, Mykonos is all nightlife—this throbbing beat is the background to Jeffrey Siger's popular mystery, *Murder in Mykonos.*

If Mykonos town is small the nightlife remains huge. The action starts along the main market street (which begins at the central taxi stand), then circles through the village, with bars, clubs, and pubs scattered along the way and down the narrow side streets. Young lovers do the rounds to get a bit of an idea of prices, music, and atmosphere. Many begin their nightlife prowl by heading toward the Little Venice quarter

and the tiny strip of cafés and bars that are located where Matogianni meets Enoplon Dynameon. This is the place to see and be seen—sort of Mykonos's equivalent to the square outside Capri's glamorous Hotel Quisisana. Celebrities, athletes, rich Athenians of all ages, and hipsters pack into the area for much of the night. And if it seems empty at midnight, just come back again at 2. Be and look paparazzi-ready.

And check your inhibitions at the door. This is the most famous summer gay-life destination east of Minorca, and the ladies sometimes complain that the good-looking guys are not checking them out, cute as they are. But the gay scene is not cordoned off here (you may even see a late-night gay wedding, "bridesmaids" and all). Because the gay clubs are often the funkiest, they attract many straights looking for a hyper-lively vibe. The truth is that many of Mykonos's most beloved night spots started out as gay hangouts but then became so chic everyone packed in. Opa!

(left) Alefkandra, Little Venice, (right) Notio Aigaio

People clubbing in the Scandinavian Bar and Disco

To discover the most exciting nightlife on Mykonos, start out with this Hot List.

Located under the Town Hall and next to Nikos' tavern, the **Thalami Bar** (✉ Town Hall, Mykonos town, no phone) gets going long after midnight. When other venues close, their owners come here for Greek music and dancing!

Coffee Cat (✉ *Plateia Agias Kyriakis* ☎ *22890/79796*) seems to have its foot in the door in Mykonos nightlife. The music is hot, half the customers are gay, and the prices standard. Though not large, it has a vast outside seating area for easy people-watching. Owner Marina, who likes to make sure her customers are having a good time, offers drag shows, live music, and even an art gallery for local artists.

W (✉ Old Harbor, Mykonos town, ☎ 22890/28999), formerly Remezzo, is right on the harbor, and blasts away all night. Its space is big and its dancers enthusiastic.

Wading into straight territory, **Mykonos Bar** (✉ *Little Venice* ☎ *22890/23529*) should be called Mykonos Disco: the music's so loud the speakers crack, but the dancers dig the frenzy.

Not a minute's walk from Mykonos Bar is **Caprice** (✉ *Little Venice* ☎ *22890/23541*) where the dancers are mostly young Greeks. The blasting music is dance-drive, the space small, and the prices high.

Not everyone wants to boogie the night away. And **Astra** (✉ *Tria Pigadia* ☎ *22890/24767* ⊕ *astra. org.gr*), since 1986, has an exclusive, somewhat more-mature elegance. The clientele is more upscale, and the drinks are expensive. Keith Richards shows up regularly. Owners Babis and Omiros are standing by to make sure

Young people dancing by the full moon party, Tropicana Club, Paradise Beach

you're enjoying yourself. The music is jazz/fusion, danceable, and not unbearably loud. Fashion shows and theme nights give variety.

In for some clubbing? **Space** (✉ *Lakka* ☎ *22890/24100* ⊕ *www.spacemykonos.com*) is big, its strobes blinding, its bass teeth-chattering, its dancers young.

If you want something up-to-date, refined, and not so adolescent go to Michalis's and Cartsten's **Jackie O** (✉ *Waterfront* ☎ *22890/79167* ⊕ *www. jackieomykonos.com*), since 2008 the most fashionable nightspot in Mykonos town—and not just for gays.

It is decorated all in white, and overlooks the water.

Babylon (✉ *Waterfront* ☎ *22890/25152*), next door to Jackie O, is its newest rival; Stratos and Jose have had bars on Mykonos for years. This one, with its electronic feel, is a real hit.

So many places! Damianos Griparis's **Galleraki** (✉ *Little Venice* ☎ *22890/27118*) is one of the best cocktail bars in town; it's so close to the water you get sprayed when a boat passes.

THOSE FAMOUS PARTY BEACHES
For raucous all-night dissipation, nothing beats those three fabled beaches: **Paranga, Paradise,** and **Super Paradise.**
Cava Paradiso (✉ *Paradiso Beach* ☎ *22890/26124* ⊕ *www.cavoparadiso.gr*), the famous megaclub on the rocks above Paradise Beach, is most popular. It cranks up at 4 AM. The beach clubs all close after dawn, and you don't have to change out of your bikini or Speedo until you stagger back to your hotel to sleep.

15 book early. In summer, reservations are a good idea; off-season, there is no problem; cars always need them. The boats usually pull in at the huge new dock area—it could serve a Mediterranean city (and is served by the Mykonos Port Authority (☎ *22940/22218*)—and from there you must take a bus or taxi, or get your hotel to pick you up (better hotels do this, and often charge you for it).

BUS TRAVEL In Mykonos town the Ayios Loukas bus station (☎ *22890/23360*) in the Fabrica quarter at the south end of town has buses to Ornos, Agios Ioánnis, Platys Yialos, Psarou, Paradise beach, the airport, and Kalamopodi. Another station near the Archaeological Museum is for Ayios Stefanos, Tourlos, Ano Mera, Elia, Kalafatis, and Kalo Livadi. Schedules are posted (hotel concierges also should have this info); fares run from €2 to €10. Regular taxis line up at Mavro Square (☎ *22890/23700*), while scooter-taxis greet new arrivals at the harbor; use them to get to your Mykonos town hotel, usually hidden away on a pedestrian (and scooter-only) street. Meters are not used on Mykonos; instead, standard fares for each destination are posted on a notice bulletin board; note there are only 13 regular cabs here even in August!

TOUR TRAVEL Windmills Travel takes a group every morning for a day tour of Delos (€35). The company also has half-day guided tours of the Mykonos beach towns, with a stop in Ano Mera for the Panayia Tourliani Monastery (€20). Windmills also provides excursions to nearby Tinos (€40–€50); arranges private tours of Delos and Mykonos and off-road jeep trips (€50); charters yachts; and, in fact, handles all tourist services. John van Lerberghe's office, the Mykonos Accommodations Center, is small, but he can plan your trip from soup to nuts.

Visitor Information and Tour/Travel Agencies Mykonos Accommodation Center ⊠ *In picturesque old building, up steep staircase, Enoplon Dynameon 10, Mykonos town* ☎ *22890/23160* 🖷 *22890/24137* ⊕ *mykonos-accommodation.com.* **Tourist police** ⊠ *Mykonos town harbor, near departure point for Delos, Mykonos* ☎ *22890/22482.* **Windmills Travel** ⊠ *Fabrica, Mykonos* ☎ *22890/26555, 22890/23877* ✎ *info@windmills-travel.com* ⊕ *www.windmillstravel.com.*

EXPLORING

Today, the natives of Mykonos seem to have been able to happily fit cosmopolitan New Yorkers, Londoners, and Athenians gracefully into their way of life. You may see, for example, an old island woman leading a donkey laden with vegetables through the town's narrow streets, greeting the suntanned vacationers walking by. The truth is, Mykonians regard a good tourist season the way a fisherman inspects a calm morning's catch; for many, the money earned in July and August will support them for the rest of the year. Not long ago Mykonians had to rely on what they could scratch out of the island's arid land for sustenance, and some remember suffering from starvation under Axis occupation during World War II. How things have changed.

MYKONOS TOWN ΜΥΚΟΝΟΣ (ΧΩΡΑ)

Although the fishing boats still go out in good weather, Mykonos largely makes its living from tourism these days. The summer crowds have turned one of the poorest islands in Greece into one of the richest. Old Mykonians complain that their young, who have inherited stores where their grandfathers once sold eggs or wine, get so much rent that they have lost ambition, and in summer sit around pool bars at night with their friends, and hang out in Athens in winter when island life is less scintillating.

Put firmly on the map by Jackie O in the 1960s, Mykonos town—called Hora by the locals—remains the Saint-Tropez of the Greek islands. The scenery is memorable, with its whitewashed streets, Little Venice, the Kato Myli ridge of windmills, and Kastro, the town's medieval quarter. Its cubical two- or three-story houses and churches, with their red or blue doors and domes and wooden balconies, have been long celebrated as some of the best examples of classic Cycladic architecture. Luckily, the Greek Archaeological Service decided to preserve the town, even when the Mykonians would have preferred to rebuild, and so the Old Town has been impressively preserved. Pink oleander, scarlet hibiscus, and trailing green pepper trees form a contrast amid the dazzling whiteness, whose frequent renewal with whitewash is required by law.

Any visitor who has the pleasure of getting lost in its narrow streets (made all the narrower by the many outdoor stone staircases, which maximize housing space in the crowded village) will appreciate how its confusing layout was designed to foil pirates—if it was designed at all. After Mykonos fell under Turkish rule in 1537, the Ottomans allowed the islanders to arm their vessels against pirates, which had a contradictory effect: many of them found that raiding other islands was more profitable than tilling arid land. At the height of Aegean piracy, Mykonos was the principal headquarters of the corsair fleets—the place where pirates met their fellows, found willing women, and filled out their crews. Eventually the illicit activity evolved into a legitimate and thriving trade network.

Morning on Mykonos town's main quay is busy with deliveries, visitors for the Delos boats, lazy breakfasters, and street cleaners dealing with the previous night's mess. In late morning the cruise-boat people arrive, and the shops are all open. In early afternoon, shaded outdoor tavernas are full of diners eating salads (Mykonos's produce is mostly imported); music is absent or kept low. In mid- and late afternoon, the town feels sleepy, since so many people are at the beach, on excursions, or sleeping in their air-conditioned rooms; even some tourist shops close for siesta. By sunset, people have come back from the beach, having taken their showers and rested. At night, the atmosphere in Mykonos ramps up. The cruise-boat people are mostly gone, coughing three-wheelers make no deliveries in the narrow streets, and everyone is dressed sexy for summer and starting to shimmy with the scene. Many shops stay open past midnight, the restaurants fill up, and the bars and discos make ice cubes as fast as they can.

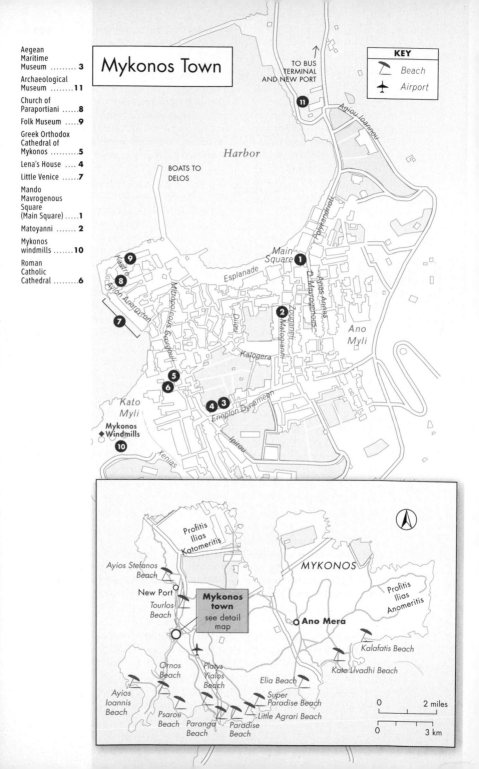

Mykonos Town

Aegean Maritime Museum 3

Archaeological Museum 11

Church of Paraportiani 8

Folk Museum 9

Greek Orthodox Cathedral of Mykonos 5

Lena's House 4

Little Venice 7

Mando Mavrogenous Square (Main Square) 1

Matoyanni 2

Mykonos windmills 10

Roman Catholic Cathedral 6

KEY

Beach

Airport

TO BUS TERMINAL AND NEW PORT

Agiou Ioannou

Harbor

BOATS TO DELOS

Main Square

Esplanade

Kastro

Ayion Anargyron

Mitropoleos Georgouli

Dilou

Kalogera

Matoyanni

Zouganeli

D. Mavrogenous

Ayias Annas

Enoplon Dynameon

Ipirou

Xenias

Kato Myli

Mykonos Windmills

Ano Myli

Profitis Ilias Katomeritis

Ayios Stefanos Beach

New Port

Tourlos Beach

Mykonos town
see detail map

MYKONOS

Ano Mera

Profitis Ilias Anomeritis

Kalafatis Beach

Kato Livadhi Beach

Ornos Beach

Platys Yialos Beach

Elia Beach

Super Paradise Beach

Ayios Ioannis Beach

Psarou Beach

Paranga Beach

Paradise Beach

Little Agrari Beach

0   2 miles

0   3 km

Ready to dive in? Begin your tour of Mykonos town (Hora) by starting out at its heart: Mando Mavrogenous Square.

TOP ATTRACTIONS

Aegean Maritime Museum. The charming Aegean Maritime Museum contains a collection of model ships, navigational instruments, old maps, prints, coins, and nautical memorabilia. The backyard garden displays some old anchors and ship wheels and a reconstructed 1890 lighthouse, once lighted by oil. ⊠ *Enoplon Dynameon, Mykonos town* ☎ *22890/22700* 🖅 *€3* ☉ *Daily 10:30–1 and 6:30–9.*

Archaeological Museum. Before setting out on the mandatory boat excursion to the isle of Delos, check out the Archaeological Museum, set at the northern edge of town. It affords insight into the intriguing history of its ancient shrines. The museum houses Delian funerary sculptures, many with scenes of mourning; most were moved to Rhenea when the Athenians cleansed Delos in the 6th century, during the sixth year of the Peloponnesian war, and, under instruction from the Delphic Oracle, the entire island was purged of all dead bodies. The most significant work from Mykonos is a 7th-century BC *pithos* (storage jar), showing the Greeks in the Trojan horse and the sack of the city. ⊠ *Ayios Stefanos, between boat dock and town, Mykonos town* ☎ *22890/22325* 🖅 *€3* ☉ *Wed.–Mon. 8:30–2:30.*

Fodor's Choice ★ **Church of Paraportiani** (*Our Lady of the Postern Gate*). Mykonians claim that exactly 365 churches and chapels dot their landscape, one for each day of the year. The most famous of these is the Church of Paraportiani. The sloping, whitewashed conglomeration of four chapels, mixing Byzantine and vernacular idioms, looks fantastic. It is solid and ultimately sober, and its position on a promontory facing the sea sets off the unique architecture. ⊠ *Ayion Anargyron, near folk museum, Mykonos town.*

Folk Museum. Housed in an 18th-century house, this museum exhibits a bedroom furnished and decorated in the fashion of that period. On display are looms and lace-making devices, Cycladic costumes, old photographs, and Mykoniot musical instruments that are still played at festivals. ⊠ *South of boat dock, Mykonos town* ☎ *22890/22591, 22890/22748* 🖅 *Free* ☉ *Mon.–Sat. 4–8, Sun. 5:30–8.*

Greek Orthodox Cathedral of Mykonos. This cathedral is noted for its number of old icons of the post-Byzantine period. ⊠ *On square that meets both Ayion Anargyron and Odos Mitropolis, Mykonos town.*

★ **Lena's House.** Take a peek into Lena's House, an accurate restoration of a middle-class Mykonos house from the 19th century. ⊠ *Enoplon Dynameon, Mykonos town* ☎ *22890/22591* 🖅 *Free* ☉ *Apr.–Oct., daily 7pm–9pm.*

THE PRANCE OF THE PELICAN

By the time morning's open-air fish market picks up steam in Mykonos town, Petros the Pelican—the town mascot—preens and cadges eats. In the 1950s a group of migrating pelicans passed over Mykonos, leaving behind a single exhausted bird; Vassilis the fisherman nursed it back to health, and locals say that the pelican in the harbor is the original Petros (though there are several).

7

★ **Little Venice.** Many of the early ship's captains built distinguished houses directly on the sea here, with wooden balconies overlooking the water. Today this neighborhood, at the southwest end of the port, is called Little Venice. This area, architecturally unique and one of the most attractive in all the islands, is so called because its handsome houses, which once belonged to shipowners and aristocrats, rise from the edge of the sea, and their elaborate buttressed wooden balconies hang over the water—these are no Venetian marble palazzi reflected in still canals. Many of these fine old houses are now elegant bars specializing in sunset drinks, or cabarets, or shops, and crowds head to the cafés and clubs, many found a block inland from Little Venice. These are sometimes soundproofed. ⊠ *Mitropoleos Georgouli, Mykonos town.*

Mando Mavrogenous Square. Mando Mavrogenous Square (sometimes called Taxi Square). Pride of place goes to a bust of Mando Mavrogenous, the island heroine, standing on a pedestal. In the 1821 War of Independence, the Mykonians, known for their seafaring skills, volunteered an armada of 24 ships, and in 1822, when the Ottomans landed a force on the island, Mando and her soldiers forced them back to their ships. After independence, a scandalous love affair caused the heroine's exile to Paros, where she died. An aristocratic beauty who becomes a great revolutionary war leader and then dies for love may seem unbelievably Hollywoodish, but it is true.

Matoyanni. The main shopping street, Matoyanni, is lined with jewelry stores, clothing boutiques, chic cafés, and candy shops. Owing to the many cruise ships that disgorge thousands of shoppers daily in season—some unload 3,000 jostling tourists—the rents here rival 5th Avenue's, and the more-interesting shops have skedaddled to less-prominent side streets. ⊠ *Perpendicular to harbor, Mykonos town.*

★ **Mykonos windmills.** Across the water from Little Venice, set on a high hill, are the famous Mykonos windmills, echoes of a time when wind power was used to grind the island's grain. The area from Little Venice to the windmills is called **Alefkandra,** which means "whitening": women once hung their laundry here. A little farther toward the windmills the bars chockablock on shore-side decks are barely above sea level, and when the north wind is up (often) surf splashes the tables. Farther on, the shore spreads into an unprepossessing beach, and tables are placed on sand or pebbles. After dinner (there are plenty of little tavernas here), the bars turn up their music, and knowing the beat thumps into the night, older tourists seek solace elsewhere.

WORTH NOTING

Mykonos Agricultural Museum. This museum displays a 16th-century windmill, traditional outdoor oven, waterwheel, dovecote, and more. ⊠ *Petassos, at top of Mykonos town* ☎ *22890/22591* ⌑ *Free* ☾ *June–Sept., daily 4–6 pm.*

Public Art Gallery. Located on Mando Mavrogenous Square, the Public Art Gallery often hosts changing exhibitions. ⊠ *Matoyanni, Mykonos town* ☎ *22890/27190.*

Roman Catholic Cathedral. Next to the Greek Orthodox Cathedral is the Roman Catholic Cathedral, the Virgin of St. Rosary, from the Venetian period. The name and coat of arms of the Ghisi family, which took over Mykonos in 1207, are inscribed in the entrance hall. ⊠ *On square that meets both Ayion Anargyron and Odos Mitropolis, Mykonos town.*

WHERE TO EAT

$$$$ ✕ **Avra.** Nikos Iliopoulos' Avra restaurant recently moved to a spacious, shady garden in the center of town. The hospitable service, Greek-Mediterranean menu, and quiet ambience make it the perfect place to go with friends, which is why locals eat here. A good starter would be fried feta in pastry topped with sesame seeds, grapes, and rose petal jelly. For a main dish, try the stuffed lamb (it is not on the menu, but usually available). Then again, you could always have tortilla shells filled with veal, pork, or chicken. For dessert, the orange pie is famous. To find it, look for the sign for the cross street off Matogianni. ⊠ *Kalogera 27, Mykonos town* ☎ *22890/22298.*

$$$ ✕ **Ithaki.** Ornos, a lovely family beach, attracts Mykonians, and Lefteris
GREEK Sikiniotis's beach taverna is where they eat, winter and summer, lunch and supper. The big lures here are the homey atmosphere, and Aegean cuisine freshly prepared. The numerous starters include round zucchini stuffed with seafood and rice, or fava with caper sauce. Continue with egg pasta with baby shrimp, dill, and carrots in an ouzo-cream sauce, or grilled octopus with chickpeas. The featured dessert is carrot cake, made by Lefteris's English wife Sharon, although few can resist the homemade ice cream. There is also a Thai menu and bakery. ⊠ *Ornos beach, Mykonos town* ☎ *22890/24546* ⊕ *www.ithakirestaurant.com.*

$$ ✕ **Kounelas.** This long-established fresh-fish taverna is where many fish-
GREEK ermen themselves eat, for solid, no-frills food. The menu depends on the weather—low winds mean lots of fish. Note: even in simple places such as Kounelas, fresh fish can be expensive. ⊠ *Off port near Delos boats, Mykonos town* ☎ *22890/28220.*

$$ ✕ **Lotus.** For more than 30 years, Giorgos and Elsa Cambanis have lov-
GREEK ingly run this tiny restaurant. Elsa is the cook, so compliment her on the fine starter, the mushroom "Lotos" with cream and cheese. The roast leg of lamb with oregano, lemon, and wine is succulent, and the moussaka is almost too good to be traditional. For dessert, have *pralina*, which resembles tiramisu. It's open year-round for dinner only: the porch is covered with bougainvillea in summer, and there's a fireplace in winter. ⊠ *Metoyanni 47, Mykonos town* ☎ *22890/22881* ⊗ *No lunch.*

$$$$ ✕ **La Maison de Catherine.** This hidden restaurant's Greek cuisine with a
GREEK Gallic touch is worth the search through the Dilou quarter of Mykonos.
Fodor's Choice Outdoor tables are on a narrow street, while the lovely interior features
★ Cycladic arches and whitewash with a faded 16th-century tapestry from Constantinople. Fine food keeps people coming, despite the prices, for such delights as the zuchini flowers stuffed with rice, mint, and pinenuts,

7

CLOSE UP

Mykonos's Sandtastic Beaches

Swimming in quiet Aegean bays with clean blue water enclosed by rugged hills cannot be overpraised—so it is little wonder some of Greece's finest strands of sand are found on Mykonos. Mostly protected from the prevailing north winds, they can be conveniently grouped. In general the beaches charge €5 for an umbrella and chaise longue. **Mykonos town's little beach** attracts local children or townies who just want a quick dip. All the others require transportation. The following beaches progress in a line along Mykonos's southern coast; from Mykonos town, Ornos beach is about 10 minutes, Kalafati less than an hour.

Ayios Stefanos, about a 45-minute walk north from Mykonos town, has water sports, restaurants, and umbrellas and lounge chairs for rent; kids love it, and you can watch the yachts and enormous cruise ships. The south coast's many beaches include three for families. **Ornos** has always been most popular with Mykonians, who like its relaxed atmosphere for a family swim and for beachside dining. There are several good restaurants, two fine hotels above the bay, and several cheaper ones lower down, and chairs and umbrellas for rent. In calm weather, boats start here for the other southern beaches, so that they are all connected (45 minutes to Elia), and you can beach hop easily. **Psarou** is trendy these days, and Nammos restaurant, which dominates the beach, is among Mykonos's most fashionable. Even in August you'll see empty sun chairs: wealthy Athenians with villas here, who rate this beach most highly, rent them for the season, so you can't. Nearby **Platys Yialos** (Broad beach), a long stretch of fine sand popular with families, is so chockablock with restaurants and umbrellas that it feels crowded even when it is not.

The young and sexy crowd heads to the next three beaches—all three were once mostly nude, and now are mostly dressed (if you consider a one-inch bit of stretched fabric dressed). All three keep a little undeveloped bit to the right as you enter, and nudists go here. All are lined with all-night bars and all-day cafés, and the public bus shows up into the wee hours. **Paranga** used be a secret, but it is all the rage now, and has a popular taverna and a dance-to-dawn club, Salty.

Paradise, twice as long as Paranga, is probably Mykonos's most famous beach for sexy straights, and it still attracts the young and lovely, who boogie here until dawn. The Tropicana Club takes up much of the beach; the Sunrise Club is appropriately named; Paradise Club is just as throbbing; and Cavo Paradise, not right on the beach, is Greece's most famous outdoor nightspot for the young. At the end of a precipitous road, **Super Paradise,** whose night scene is also throbbing, was once Mykonos's notorious gay beach but gaysters no longer dominate. Super Paradise beach bar closes blearily at 9 am. The rocky path between Paradise and Super Paradise, an hour's rough walk, was once a sexual no-man's land, but it is no longer.

Little Agrari and **Long Elia** are less developed, more nude, and quieter, though they too have not escaped the voyeur's wandering eye. At the easternmost end of the south shores is beautiful **Kalafatis,** known for package tours, and between Elia and Kalafatis there's remote **Kalo Livadhi**.

or the mussels in light cream sauce, white wine, and red peppercorns, or the chateaubriand with grilled vegetables. Finish with the apple tartine with Calvados cream. Divine! ⊠ *Ayios Gerasimos, Dilou, Mykonos town* ☎ *22890/22169* ⚱ *Reservations essential.*

$$$$ ✗ **Nammos.** This beach restaurant has become the in spot for well-to-do
MEDITERRANEAN Athenians and for Mykonians who want to strut a bit on fashion-
★ able Psarou beach. All open-air, white wood, stone, bamboo, and palm trees, it serves up Mediterranean fusion cuisine (their words) and is especially popular for a late lunch. For appetizer try *louza* (Mykonian sun-dried pork fillet), or eggplant mille-feuille with feta and shrimp. Sea sounds will tempt you to order fresh fish or sushi, or dive into the great seared tuna tartare with white sauce or the homemade pasta with sea urchins. A non-svelte dessert is the chunky chocolate crème "guanajo" with blackberries and praline. ⊠ *Psarou beach, Mykonos town* ☎ *22890/22440* ⊕ *www.nammos.gr.*

$$$$ ✗ **Sea Satin Market–Caprice.** If the wind is up, the waves sing at this
SEAFOOD magical spot, set on a far tip of land below the famous windmills of
★ Mykonos. The preferred place for Greek shipowners, Sea Satin Market sprawls out onto a seaside terrace and even onto the sand of the beach bordering Little Venice. When it comes to fish, prices vary according to weight. Shellfish is a specialty, and everything is beautifully presented. In summer, live music and dancing add to the liveliness. ⊠ *On seaside under windmills, Mykonos town* ☎ *22890/24676.*

$$$$ ✗ **Tagoo.** High Mykonian style can be yours at the eatery of this noted
GREEK hotel. It is a creation of Spondi, Athens' popular two-star restaurant.
★ The haute cuisine is served up in either an all-white room or at outdoor tables, with Mykonos bay on one side and an infinity pool on the other. Start with slow-cooked octopus with fava pureé, caper chutney, and orange-infused oil. Fine entrées include rolled sea bass with basmati rice, coconut milk, and melon, and also veal medallions in sundried tomato crust. Fish is always fresh and delicately prepared. To top things off, try the chocolate sable with homemade coffee ice cream and caramel. The sommelier helps with the large selection of wines. The restaurant is open May through October. ⊠ *Hotel Cavo Tagoo (12 min by foot north of Mykonos town on sea road), Mykonos town* ☎ *22890/20100* ⊕ *www.cavotagoo.gr/gastronomy.html* ⚱ *Reservations essential* ☽ *Closed Nov.–Apr.*

WHERE TO STAY

For expanded reviews, visit Fodors.com.

$$$$ ⊞ **Belvedere.** You may not have to go to Greece once you view the
★ "movie" presentation on this hotel's Web site—it is almost as relaxing, blue-and-white, and high style as this hotel (but not quite)—but lovers of style, who want to be with-it, and like to see what they are paying for, will want to make sure they book here, just to savor Matsuhita Mykonos—an outpost of famed sushi chef Nobu—along with the club-like atmosphere, convenient location, the view over Mykonos town, and all the magically decorated guest rooms. **Pros:** this is Mykonos's most "in" hotel. **Cons:** you can pay plenty for a small room with no view. ⊠ *School of Fine Arts district, Mykonos town* ☎ *22890/25122* ⊕ *www.belviderehotel.com* ⤶ *35 rooms, 8 suites* ☖ *In-room: a/c,*

7

Wi-Fi. In-hotel: restaurant, bar, pool, spa ⊙ *Breakfast.*

$$$$
Fodor's Choice
★

⊞ **Cavo Tagoo.** Many consider this to be the top hotel in Mykonos for luxuriousness, service, and comfort—it climbs the hill over the bay in sensuous white curves, with natural projecting rock and an island-aqueous feel, thanks to two public pools (one a 38-foot-long infinity) and many private pools, which lend it all a lovely "barefoot chic" feeling. **Pros:** modulated luxury; beautiful view; alluring Mykonos style; ladies love the fancy spa. **Cons:** a 12-minute walk to town, that shark tank. ✉ *Follow coast road, north of Old Port, Mykonos town* ☎ *22890/20100* ⊕ *www.cavotagoo.gr* ↵ *51 rooms, 18 suites, 11 villas* ⅍ *In-room: a/c, Wi-Fi. In-hotel: restaurant, bar, pool, spa* ⊘ *Closed Nov.–Apr.* ⊙ *Breakfast.*

WORD OF MOUTH

"Tagoo: we absolutely loved it. The owner and her husband were amazing. They helped so much with restaurants, picking us up at the port, rental cars, etc. By the time we left, we felt like family. The pool was wonderful and the bar was fun with lots of interesting people to talk to. They seem to get lots of repeat clients, too. It was a walk into town, though— maybe 10 to 15 minutes. Downhill going and uphill coming back, which was a bit tiring." —Leslie28

$$$$
★

⊞ **Deliades.** If you like comfort, large rooms, friendly service, a sea view, and quiet, Deliades is exactly for you—away from the fray, the Deliades ("Delian nymphs") is a welcome escape from the Mykonos beat, thanks especially to the capacious, airy guest rooms (many with beautiful wood beams and 19th-century-style lamps) which all have sea views and terraces, the stark white of the hotel architecture gracefully softened with accents in muted sand and sea shades. **Pros:** Ornos bay sea views; large rooms and baths; relaxed atmosphere. **Cons:** if you want to stay in the thick of the Mykonos scene, this isn't for you. ✉ *Far end of Ornos beach, follow road up 30 yards, Ornos, Mykonos* ☎ *22890/79430, 22890/79470* ⊕ *www.deliades.com* ↵ *30 rooms* ⅍ *In-room: a/c, Wi-Fi. In-hotel: restaurant, bar, pool* ⊘ *Closed Nov.–Mar.* ⊙ *Breakfast.*

$$$$

⊞ **Hotel Mykonos Adonis.** Set on the edge of town not far from Little Venice and overlooking the sea, this is not only Mykonos's friendliest hotel but is also both convenient and nicely out of the fray: the result is that the clientele, many of them artists and writers, return year after year to let owners Michalis and Roz Apostolou (he's Mykonian, she's American) take care of them. **Pros:** convenient to the scene, but not swamped by it. **Cons:** on a street with traffic. ✉ *Chora, Mykonos town* ☎ *22890/23433* ⊕ *www.mykonosadonis.gr* ↵ *12 rooms, 12 suites* ⅍ *In-room: a/c.* ⊘ *Closed Nov.–Mar.* ⊙ *Breakfast.*

$$$$

⊞ **Kivotos Clubhotel.** Spyros Michopoulos's deluxe hotel is architecturally ambitious and stylishly arrayed around an impressive pool, with the main floor done up in a richly decorative island style, with statues in niches and mosaic work, and unexpected little courtyards with bright flowers. **Pros:** exquisite design; quiet ambience. **Cons:** isolated; some rooms are small and lack views; those high room rates. ✉ *Ornos bay, Mykonos town* ✛ *2 km (1 mi) from Mykonos town* ☎ *22890/24094*

DID YOU KNOW?

For the best overview of Little Venice—Mykonos town's most beautiful district—walk through the Alefkandra quarter and head to the famous hilltop windmills of Kata Myli.

VERANDA

⊕ *www.kivotosclubhotel.gr* ⤴*35 rooms, 5 suites* ↺ *In-room: a/c, Wi-Fi. In-hotel: restaurant, bar, pool* ⊙ *Closed Nov.–Mar.* ⦿ *Breakfast.*

$$$$ ⊡ **Mykonos Grace.** A boutique hotel that deftly combines traditional architectural elements and sleek modern design, this option comes with an aquatic feel—small, charming, luxurious, and set above the beach of Aghios Stefanos, the Mykonos Grace has a truly impressive setting, replete with an encompassing view of Mykonos's harbor. **Pros:** impressive vistas; intimate atmosphere. **Cons:** not walking distance from town. ⊠ *Aghios Stefanos, Mykonos town* ☎ *22890/20000* ⊕ *www. mykonosgrace.com* ⤴*26 rooms, 5 suites* ↺ *In-room: a/c, Wi-Fi. In-hotel: restaurant, pool, spa* ⊙ *Closed Nov.–Mar.* ⦿ *Breakfast.*

$$$ ⊡ **Omiros.** If you are looking for an inexpensive, attractive, convenient, slightly out-of-town accommodation on a hill overlooking the bay, do try this spot—perfect for younger travellers who want beauty, convenience, friendliness, and a low price. **Pros:** good value for the money; simple and friendly. **Cons:** the walk back is uphill. ⊠ *Chora, Mykonos town* ☎ *22890/23328* ⊕ *www.omirosmykonos.com* ⤴*10 rooms, 2 apartments* ↺ *In-room: a/c.*

$$ ⊡ **Philippi.** Of the inexpensive hotels scattered throughout town, this is the most attractive, in large part because guest rooms have balconies that overlook the hotel gardens—and owner Christos Kontizas is a passionate gardener. **Pros:** very inexpensive; central. **Cons:** if you want to get away from it all, go elsewhere; no transfers. ⊠ *Kalogera 25, Mykonos town* ☎ *22890/22294* ✉ *info@philippihotel.com* ⤴*13 rooms* ↺ *In-room: a/c, Wi-Fi* ⊙ *Closed Nov.–Mar.*

$$$$ ⊡ **Semeli.** A carved-marble entrance doorway leads to an old stately home that has been expanded into an elegant hotel in the high Mykoniot style—named after a Greek nymph, this quiet and convenient. **Pros:** lounge areas are very inviting. **Cons:** guest rooms could be larger; stiff room rates. ⊠ *Below ring road, Mykonos town* ☎ *22890/27466, 22890/27471* ⊕ *www.semelihotel.gr* ⤴*53 rooms, 3 suites* ↺ *In-room: a/c, Wi-Fi. In-hotel: restaurant, bar, pool* ⦿ *Breakfast.*

$$$$ ⊡ **Villa Konstantin.** This complex of small apartments and studios is set on a hill near the town overlooking the bay and because the owners themselves live here, they go to lengths to make it attractive and friendly, as their many returning customers attest. **Pros:** inexpensive for what you get, which is a lot. **Cons:** walking distance from town, but very uphill on return, so not really. ⊠ *Aghios Vassilios, Mykonos town* ☎ *22890/26204* ⊕ *www.villakonstantin-mykonos.gr* ⤴*19 apartments* ↺ *In-room: a/c, kitchen. In-hotel: pool* ⊙ *Closed Nov.–Mar.*

NIGHTLIFE

Whether it's bouzouki music, break beat, or techno, Mykonos's nightlife beats to an obsessive rhythm until undetermined hours—little wonder Europe's gilded youth comes here *just* to enjoy the night scene. After midnight, they often head to the techno bars along the Paradise and Super Paradise beaches. Some of Little Venice's nightclubs become gay in more than one sense of the word, while in the Kastro, convivial bars welcome all for tequila-*sambukas* at sunset. What is "the" place of the moment? The scene is ever-changing and you'll need to track the buzz once you arrive. *To find the latest and greatest Hot List check out our special photo-feature, "Mykonos After Dark" in this chapter.* Along with those hipsterious spots, many other places tempt one to vibe the night away. Here are some popular options.

Kastro Bar. Kostas Karatzas's long-standing Kastro Bar, with heavy beamed ceilings and island furnishings, creates an intimate environment for enjoying the evening sunset over the bay to classical music. ✉ *Little Venice, Mykonos town* ☎ *22890/23072* ⊕ *www.kastrobar.com.*

Montparnasse. This lively spot hangs paintings by local artists; its superb sunset view precedes nights of live cabaret and musicals. ✉ *Ayion Anargyron 24, Little Venice, Mykonos town* ☎ *22890/23719* ⊕ *www. thepianobar.com.*

Rhapsody. Rubbing elbows with Montparnasse is Rhapsody, open all year for Greek dancing. ✉ *Little Venice, Mykonos town* ☎ *22890/23412.*

Skandinavian Bar. Toward the end of Mykonos town's main market street is the Skandinavian Bar, which spreads over two buildings, two floors (one for pub chats, one for dancing), and an outside seating area. Their music ranges from classic rock to pop dance; backpackers go there. ✉ *K. Georgouli St., Mykonos town* ☎ *22890/22669* ⊕ *www.angelfire.com/ trek/ellada/skandi.html.*

SPORTS AND THE OUTDOORS

DIVING **Mykonos Diving Center.** This popular resource has a variety of scuba courses and excursions at 30 locations. ✉ *Paradise, Mykonos* ☎ *22890/ 24808* ⊕ *www.dive.gr.*

WATER SPORTS The windy northern beaches on Ornos bay are best for water sports; you can rent surfboards and take lessons. There's windsurfing and waterskiing at Ayios Stefanos, Platys Yialos, and Ornos.

Aphrodite Beach Hotel. This hotel is known for its water sports facilities. ✉ *Kalafati beach, Mykonos town* ☎ *28890/72345* 🏠.

SHOPPING

FASHION **Galatis.** Designer Yiannis Galatis has outfitted such famous women as Elizabeth Taylor, Ingrid Bergman, and Jackie Onassis. He will probably greet you personally and show you some of his costumes and hostess gowns. His memoirs capture the old days on Mykonos, when Jackie O. was a customer. His new art gallery is adjacent. ✉ *Mando Mavrogenous Sq., opposite Lalaounis, Mykonos town* ☎ *22890/22255.*

Parthenis. Opened by Dimitris Parthenis in 1978, Parthenis now features designs by his daughter Orsalia, all showcased in a large Mykonian-style building on the up side of Alefkandra Square in Little Venice. The collection of cotton and silk garments (mostly in neutral colors) is very popular for their soft draping and clinging wrap effect. ✉ *Alefkandra Sq., Mykonos town* ☎ *22890/23080* ⊕ *www.orsalia-parthenis.gr.*

★ **Salachas.** A small shop, Salachas is filled with linen and cotton garments of all Greek materials and manufacture. Grandfather Joseph Salachas was a tailor in the 1960s, and once made clothes for Christian Dior and various celebrities. Today, his grandchildren keep up the tradition. ✉ *58 K. Georgeouli St., Mykonos town* ☎ *22890/22710.*

7

<table>
<tr><td>FINE AND
DECORA-
TIVE ART</td><td>

Anna Gelou. Anna Gelou's eponymous shop, started by her mother 50 years ago, carries authentic copies of traditional handmade embroideries, all using white Greek cotton, in clothing, tablecloths, curtains, and such. ⊠ *Ayion Anargyron 16, Little Venice, Mykonos town* ☎ *22890/26825.*

Nikoletta. Mykonos used to be a weaver's island, where 500 looms clacked away. Only Nikoletta remains, where Nikoletta Xidakis sells her skirts, shawls, and bedspreads made of local wool, as she has for 50 years. ⊠ *Little Venice, Mykonos town* ☎ *22890/27503.*

</td></tr>
</table>

JEWELRY   **Ilias Lalaounis.** This store is known internationally for fine jewelry based
★   on ancient Greek and other designs, reinterpreted for the modern woman. With many of their earrings and necklaces as lovingly worked as art pieces, the shop is as elegant as a museum. New collections are introduced every year. Stop by at the right hour and you'll get a glass of fine wine. The salespeople all live here and know everything about their island. ⊠ *Polykandrioti 14, near taxis, Mykonos town* ☎ *22890/22444* ✍ *lalaounismaykonos@lalaounis.gr.*

Precious Tree. Petros Labroulis' tiny shop is aglitter in gems elegantly set here and in its workshop in Athens; in its fabulous creativity, it hardly resembles Mykonos's mainline shops. ⊠ *Dilou 2, Mykonos town* ☎ *22890/24685* ✍ *precioustree@gmail.com.*

ANO MERA ΑΝΩ ΜΕΡΑ

8 km (5 mi) east of Mykonos town.

Monastery of the Panayia Tourliani. Monastery buffs should head to Ano Mera, a village in the central part of the island, where the Monastery of the Panayia Tourliani, founded in 1580 and dedicated to the protectress of Mykonos, stands in the central square. Its massive baroque iconostasis (altar screen), made in 1775 by Florentine artists, has small icons carefully placed amid the wooden structure's painted green, red, and gold-leaf flowers. At the top are carved figures of the apostles and large icons depicting New Testament scenes. The hanging incense holders with silver molded dragons holding red eggs in their mouths show an Eastern influence. In the hall of the monastery, an interesting **museum** displays embroideries, liturgical vestments, and wood carvings. A good taverna is across the street. The monastery's big festival—hundreds attend—is on August 15. ⊠ *On central square, Ano Mera* ☎ *22890/71249* ⊗ *By appointment only; call in advance.*

DELOS ΔΗΛΟΣ

GETTING HERE

BOAT TRAVEL   Most visitors arrive from Mykonos on one of the excursions helpfully organized by tour companies whose offices (☎ 22890/22259) are located at the west end of the harbor in Mykonos town (tour boats also leave from Tinos, Paros, and Naxos). These boats usually leave around 8:30 am every day except Monday (when Delos isle is closed) and any day when the sea is too rough, which can be surprisingly often. There are usually three to four departures from each end but the last

DID YOU KNOW?

While much of Mykonos is given over to worldly pleasures, the island is also home to several functioning monasteries, including Panagia Tourliani, seen here.

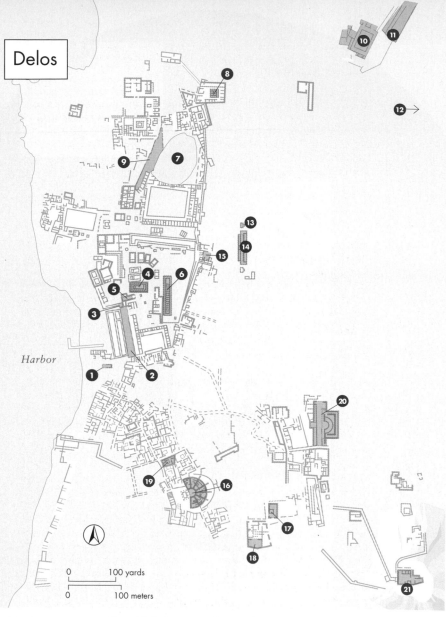

Delos

departure is always at 3 pm. Caïque boats (€12) also link Delos with Platys Yialos and Ornos beaches on Mykonos but these excursions only give you about three hours on the sacred isle.

EXPLORING

Fodor's Choice ★

Delos. Arrive at the mythical, magical, and magnificent site of Delos and you might wonder how this barren islet, which has virtually no natural resources, became the religious and political center of the Aegean. One answer is that Dhílos—to use the Modern Greek transliteration—provided the safest anchorage for vessels sailing between the mainland and the shores of Asia; another answer is that it had no other use. A third is provided if you climb Mt. Kynthos to see that the isle is shielded on three sides by other islands. Indeed, this is how the Cyclades—the word means "circling ones"—got their name: they circle around the sacred island.

Delos's amazing saga begins back in the times of myth:

Zeus fell in love with gentle Leto, the Titaness, who became pregnant. When Hera discovered this infidelity, she forbade Mother Earth to give Leto refuge and ordered the Python to pursue her. Finally Poseidon, taking pity on her, anchored the poor floating island of Delos with four diamond columns to give her a place to rest. Leto gave birth first to the virgin huntress Artemis on Rhenea and then, clasping a sacred palm on a slope of Delos's Mt. Kynthos, to Apollo, god of music and light.

By 1000 BC the Ionians, who inhabited the Cyclades, had made Delos their religious capital. Homeric Hymn 3 tells of the cult of Apollo in the 7th century BC. One can imagine the elegant Ionians, whose central festival was here, enjoying the choruses of temple girls—"Delian korai, who serve the Far-Shooter"—singing and dancing their hymn and displaying their graceful tunics and jewelry. But a difficult period began for the Delians when Athens rose to power and assumed Ionian leadership. In 543 BC an oracle at Delphi conveniently decreed that the Athenians purify the island by removing all the graves to Rhenea, a dictate designed to alienate the Delians from their past.

After the defeat of the Persians in 478 BC, the Athenians organized the Delian League, with its treasury and headquarters at Delos (in 454 BC the funds were transferred to the Acropolis in Athens). Delos had its most prosperous period in late Hellenistic and Roman times, when it was declared a free port and quickly became the financial center of the Mediterranean, the focal point of trade, where 10,000 slaves were sold daily. Foreigners from as far as Rome, Syria, and Egypt lived in this cosmopolitan port, in complete tolerance of one another's religious beliefs, and each group built its various shrines. But in 88 BC Mithridates, the king of Pontus, in a revolt against Roman rule, ordered an attack on the unfortified island. The entire population of 20,000 was killed or sold into slavery. Delos never fully recovered, and later Roman attempts to revive the island failed because of pirate raids. After a second attack in 69 BC, Delos was gradually abandoned.

In 1872, the French School of Archaeology began excavating on Delos—a massive project, considering that much of the island's 4 square km (1½ square mi) is covered in ruins. The work continues today. Delos remains dry and shadeless; off-season, the snack bar is often closed;

most guards leave on the last boat to Mykonos in the early afternoon. But if on the way to Mykonos you see dolphins leaping (it often happens), you'll know Apollo is about and approves.

On the left from the harbor is the **Agora of the Competialists** (circa 150 BC), members of Roman guilds, mostly freedmen and slaves from Sicily who worked for Italian traders. They worshipped the *Lares Competales*, the Roman "crossroads" gods; in Greek they were known as Hermaistai, after the god Hermes, protector of merchants and the crossroads. The **Sacred Way,** east of the agora, was the route, during the holy Delian festival, of the procession to the Sanctuary of Apollo. The **Propylaea,** at the end of the Sacred Way, were once a monumental white marble gateway with three portals framed by four Doric columns. Beyond the Propylaea is the Sanctuary of Apollo; though little remains today, when the Propylaea were built in the mid-2nd century BC, the sanctuary was crowded with altars, statues, and temples—three of them to Apollo. Inside the sanctuary and to the right is the **House of the Naxians,** a 7th- to 6th-century BC structure with a central colonnade. Dedications to Apollo were stored in this shrine. Outside the north wall a massive rectangular **pedestal** once supported a colossal statue of Apollo (one of the hands is in Delos's Archaeological Museum, and a piece of a foot is in the British Museum). Near the pedestal a bronze palm tree was erected in 417 BC by the Athenians to commemorate the palm tree under which Leto gave birth. According to Plutarch, the palm tree toppled in a storm and brought the statue of Apollo down with it. Odysseus in *The Odyssey* compares the Phaeacian princess Nausicaa to the palm he saw on Delos, when the island was wetter.

Southeast of the Sanctuary of Apollo are the ruins of the **Sanctuary of the Bulls,** an extremely long and narrow structure built, it is thought, to display a trireme, an ancient boat with three banks of oars, dedicated to Apollo by a Hellenistic leader thankful for a naval victory. Maritime symbols were found in the decorative relief of the main halls, and the head and shoulders of a pair of bulls were part of the design of an interior entrance. A short distance north of the Sanctuary of the Bulls is an oval indentation in the earth where the **Sacred Lake** once sparkled. It is surrounded by a stone wall that reveals the original periphery. According to islanders, the lake was fed by the river Inopos from its source high on Mt. Kynthos until 1925, when the water stopped flowing and the lake dried up. Along the shores are two ancient **palaestras,** buildings for physical exercise and debate. One of the most evocative sights of Delos is the 164-foot-long **avenue of the Lions.** These are replicas; the originals are in the museum. The five Naxian marble beasts crouch on their haunches, their forelegs stiffly upright, vigilant guardians of the Sacred Lake. They are the survivors of a line of at least nine lions, erected in the second half of the 7th century BC by the Naxians. One, removed in the 17th century, now guards the Arsenal of Venice (though with a later head). Northeast of the palaestras is the **gymnasium,** a square courtyard nearly 131 feet long on each side. "Gym" means naked in Greek, and here men and boys stayed in shape (and, in those heavily Platonic days, eyed each other). The long, narrow structure farther northeast is the **stadium,** the site of the athletic events of the Delian Games. East of the stadium site, by the seashore, are the remains of a **synagogue built by Phoenician Jews** in the 2nd century BC. A road south from the gymnasium leads to the **tourist pavilion,** which has a meager restaurant and bar. The **Archaeological Museum** is also on the road south of the gymnasium; it contains most of the antiquities found in excavations on

> ### LOOK, DON'T TOUCH
>
> If you put on a mask and flippers for a swim in Delos's pellucid water, remember that the site guards will check you, as the offshore waters here are gleaming with shards of Delos's past.

the island: monumental statues of young men and women, stelae, reliefs, masks, and ancient jewelry. Immediately to the right of the museum is a small **Sanctuary of Dionysus,** erected about 300 BC; outside it is one of the more-boggling sights of ancient Greece: several monuments dedicated to Apollo by the winners of the choral competitions of the Delian festivals, each decorated with a huge phallus, emblematic of the orgiastic rites that took place during the Dionysian festivals. Around the base of one of them is carved a lighthearted representation of a bride being carried to her new husband's home. A marble phallic bird, symbol of the body's immortality, also adorns this corner of the sanctuary. Beyond the path that leads to the southern part of the island is the **ancient theater,** built in the early 3rd century BC in the elegant residential quarter inhabited by Roman bankers and Egyptian and Phoenician merchants. Their one- and two-story houses were typically built around a central courtyard, sometimes with columns on all sides. Floor mosaics of snakes, panthers, birds, dolphins, and Dionysus channeled rainwater into cisterns below; the best-preserved can be seen in the **House of the Dolphins,** the **House of the Masks,** and the **House of the Trident.** A dirt path leads east to the base of Mt. Kynthos, where there are remains from many **Middle Eastern shrines,** including the **Sanctuary of the Syrian Gods,** built in 100 BC. A flight of steps goes up 368 feet to the summit of **Mt. Kynthos** (after which all Cynthias are named), on whose slope Apollo was born. ⊠ *Delos island and historic site, take a small passenger boat from Mykonos town, Delos* ☎ *22890/22259* ⊕ *www.culture.gr* ✉ *€7* ☉ *Apr.–Oct., Tues.–Sun. 8:30–3.*

TINOS ΤΗΝΟΣ

160 km (85 nautical mi) southeast of Piraeus harbor in Athens.

Tinos (or, as archaeologists spell it, Tenos) is among the most beautiful and most fascinating of the major Cyclades. The third largest of the island group after Naxos and Andros, with an area of 195 square km (121 square mi), it is inhabited by nearly 10,000 people, many of whom still live the traditional life of farmers or craftspeople. Its long, mountainous spine, rearing between Andros and Mykonos, makes it seem forbidding, and in a way it is. It is not popular among tourists for a few reasons: the main village, Tinos town (Chora), lacks charm; the beaches are undeveloped; there is no airport; and the prevailing north winds are the Aegean's fiercest (passing mariners used to sacrifice a calf to Poseidon, ancient Tinos's chief deity, in hopes of avoiding shipwreck).

As if posing for your camera, the ancient sculpted beasts of the Avenue of the Lions are Delos's most unforgettable photo op. They are copies; the originals are in Delos's museum.

On the other hand, Tinos is dotted with possibly the loveliest villages in the Cyclades.

GETTING HERE AND AROUND

BOAT TRAVEL   In high season many boats stop at Tinos, since it is on the Mykonos line, and consequently Tinos becomes crowded with travelers. But Tinos, owing to the famous church, is also hugely popular with Greeks who arrive on Friday night and leave in time to get to work on Monday. The boats vary from big ferries to fast passengers-only boats, and it takes four to five hours, depending mostly on route and weather. For August weekends, reservations are recommended. For Easter and August 15 they are absolutely necessary, and the boats will be packed (the many cars in transit don't help). Especially notice, as your boat rounds the point into the harbor, the high peak of Exambourgos with its acropolis and Venetian fort. For these holidays, boat schedules do change; information much in advance is not trustworthy. To check weather, you can call the Tinos Port Authority (☎ 22830/22348), where English is sometimes spoken. For good online information, go to ⊕ *www.openseas.gr*. Tinos has daily connections with Andros, Mykonos, and Paros, less often with Naxos. Returning boats go either to Piraeus or to Rafina. When buying tickets at the quay-side agencies, remember that not every office handles every boat, so check at more than one. The Tinos Port Authority (☎ 22830/22348) isn't as helpful as it should be. For any queries or recommendations contact Sharon Turner of Windmills Travel; a longtime Tinian resident, she knows. There is a lot of information at ⊕ *www.greeka.com*.

Continued on page 325

Myth Behavin'

✳

GREECE'S GODS AND HEROES

Superheroes, sex, adventure: it's no wonder Greek myths have reverberated throughout Western civilization. Today, as you wander ancient Greece's most sacred sites—such as Delos, island birthplace of the sun god Apollo—these ageless tales will come alive to thrill and perhaps haunt you.

Whether you are looking at 5th-century BC pedimental sculptures in Olympia or ancient red-figure vase paintings in Athens, whether you are reading the epics of Homer or the tragedies of Euripides, you are in the presence of the Greek mythopoetic mind. Peopled with emblems of hope, fear, yearning, and personifications of melting beauty or of petrifying ugliness, these ancient myths helped early Greeks make sense of a chaotic, primitive universe that yielded no secrets.

Frightened by the murder and mayhem that surrounded them, the Greeks set up gods in whom power, wisdom, and eternal youth could not perish. These gods lived, under the rule of Zeus, on Mount Olympus. Their rivalries and intrigues were a primeval, superhuman version of *Dynasty* and *Dallas*. These astounding collections of stories not only pervaded all ancient Greek society but have influenced the course of Western civilization: How could we imagine our culture—from Homer's *Iliad* to Joyce's *Ulysses* —without them?

Apollo, the sun god

ZEUS
Latin Name: Jupiter
God of: Sky, Supreme God
Attribute: Scepter, Thunder
Roving Eye: Zeus was the ruler of Mount Olympus but often went AWOL pursuing love affairs down on earth with nymphs and beautiful ladies; his children were legion, including Hercules.

HERA
Latin Name: Juno
Goddess of: Sky, Marriage
Attribute: Peacock
His Cheating Heart: Hera married her brother Zeus, wound up having a 300-year honeymoon with him on Samos, and was repaid for her fidelity to marriage by the many love affairs of her hubby.

APHRODITE
Latin Name: Venus
Goddess of: Love, Beauty
Attribute: Dove
And the Winner Is: Born out of the foam rising off of Cyprus, she was given the Golden Apple by Paris in the famous beauty contest between her, Athena, and Hera, and bestowed the love of Helen on him as thanks.

ATHENA
Latin Name: Minerva
Goddess of: Wisdom
Attribute: Owl, Olive
Top Billing: The goddess of reason, she gave the olive tree to the Greeks; her uncle was Poseidon, and the Parthenon in Athens was built in her honor.

APOLLO
Latin Name: Phoebus
God of: Sun, Music, and Poetry
Attribute: Bow, Lyre
Confirmed Bachelor: Born at Delos, his main temple was at Delphi; his love affairs included Cassandra, to whom he gave the gift of prophecy; Calliope, with whom he had Orpheus; and Daphne, who, fleeing from his embrace, changed into a tree.

ARTEMIS
Latin Name: Diana
Goddess of: Chastity, Moon
Attribute: Stag
Early Feminist: Sister of Apollo, she enjoyed living in the forest with her court, frowned on marriage, and, most notoriously, had men torn apart by her hounds if they peeked at her bathing.

YE GODS!

WHO'S WHO IN GREEK MYTHOLOGY

The twelve chief gods formed the elite of Olympus. Each represented one of the forces of nature and also a human characteristic. They also had attributes by which they can often be identified. The Romans, influenced by the arts and letters of Greece, largely identified their own gods with those of Greece, with the result that Greek gods have Latin names as well. Here are the divine I.D.s of the Olympians.

DEMETER
Latin Name: Ceres
Goddess of: Earth, Fecundity
Attribute: Sheaf, Sickle
Most Dramatic Moment: After her daughter Persephone was kidnapped by Zeus, Demeter decided to make all plants of the earth wither and die.

HERMES
Latin Name: Mercury
God of: Trade, Eloquence
Attribute: Wings
Messenger Service: Father of Pan, Hermes was known as a luck-bringer, harbinger of dreams, and the messenger of Olympus; he was also worshipped as the god of commerce and music.

POSEIDON
Latin Name: Neptune
God of: Sea, Earthquakes
Attribute: Trident
Water Boy: To win the affection of Athenians, Poseidon and Athena were both charged with giving them the most useful gift, with his invention of the bubbling spring losing out to Athena's creation of the olive.

ARES
Latin Name: Mars
God of: Tumult, War
Attribute: Spear, Helmet
Antisocial: The most famous male progeny of Zeus and Hera, he was an irritable man; considering his violent temper, few temples were erected in his honor in Greece.

HESTIA
Latin Name: Vesta
Goddess of: Hearth, Domestic Values
Attribute: Eternal Fire
Hausfrau: A famous virgin, she was charged with maintaining the eternal flame atop Olympus; the Vestal Virgins of ancient Romans followed in her footsteps.

HEPHAESTOS
Latin Name: Vulcan
God of: Fire, Industry
Attribute: Hammer, Anvil
Pumping Iron: The best-preserved Doric style temple in Athens, the Hephaestaion, was erected to this god in the ancient agora marketplace; today, ironmongers still have shops in the district there.

Poseidon

⟫ IN GODS WE TRUST ⟪

To the ancient Greeks, mythology was more than a matter of literature, art, philosophy, and ethics. For them, the whole countryside teemed with spirits and powers. Besides the loftier Olympian gods there were spirits of mountain, sea, trees, and stream—oreads, nereids, dryads, and naiads. The ancients preferred to personify natural phenomena than to depict them realistically.

Nymphs, for example, were primarily personifications of nature—oak trees, pools, sea waves, caves, peaks, isles. Monsters did the same; Scylla, who ate six of Odysseus' men, was the symbolic personification of a shipwrecking cliff in the Straits of Messina. In the darkness of the night (or of the mind), the ancients' ancestral fears and perverse desires became embodied in a world of brutal minotaurs, evil chimeras, mischievous sphinxes, terrifying centaurs, and ferocious Furies. To combat them, people looked to the gods, promoters of peace and justice at home, success in trade and war, and fertility.

⟫ TOGA PARTY ⟪

Was all human life doomed to disaster and woe? Zeus, many believed, had two jars—one of good fortune and one of ill—which he dipped into when making his decisions. To most people he distributed portions fairly equally—but Zeus himself often fell prey to pride and envy, and the latter often got this chronic double-dater into trouble. No matter that he had seven wives: He was a very "Your honey or your wife" philanderer, and his endless seductions provided innumerable scandals.

One notable case was Leda, queen to King Tyndareus of Sparta. Zeus saw her shapely naked limbs, seduced her by assuming the form of a swan, and she then gave birth to two eggs, one of which hatched with the Dioscuri, Castor and Pollux, the other with Clytemnestra and Helen of Troy, women of serious trouble. Clytemnestra married Agamemnon, king of Mycenae, and Helen married Menelaos,

king of Sparta. The Trojan War followed and the rest is history (or something like history). The whole story, embracing fantasy, politics, and cult has been retold endlessly in poems from Homer to Yeats and images from Leonardo to Gustave Moreau's surrealist paintings. The ancient myths turn out to be as modern as today.

⟫ GREEK LIGHTNING ⟪

Today, historians point to tribal origin-heroes and local cult figures of the ancient Near East as influencing the earliest Greek myths, first professed in the preliterate second millennium BC. Capturing primeval energies from the past that are still in us, these stories provide the backstory to great sites like Delos, the legendary birthplace of the god Apollo. The ancients believed that the sun crossed the sky in Apollo's chariot. Other gods were considered the cause of many phenomena. What caused earthquakes? Poseidon with his trident. Who used lighting bolts as weapons? Zeus. Who invented fire? Prometheus brought it down from Olympus. How did pain and sickness come into the world? Through the curiosity of Pandora (that other Eve). Before long, in the non-factual, gravity-free world of the ancient Greek imagination, the deeds of the gods became moralistic parables about man. Is gold the best thing of all? Consider Midas. Would it be a good thing to fly? Icarus did not find it so. Would you like to be married to Helen of Troy, or to Jason, the winner of the Golden Fleece? Consult Menelaus and Medea. How wonderful to be the supremely powerful and popular ruler of a fabulously great city! Not for Oedipus. Without some understanding of the ancient myths, half the meaning of Greece will elude you.

HERCULES

THE FIRST ACTION HERO

Greece's most popular mythological personage was probably Heracles, a hero who became a god, and had to work hard to do it. This paragon of masculinity was so admired by the Romans that they vulgarized him as Hercules, and modern entrepreneurs have capitalized on his popularity in silly sandal epics and sillier Saturday morning cartoons. His name means "glory of Hera," although the goddess hated him because he was the son of Zeus and the Theban princess Alcmene. The Incredible Bulk proved his strength and courage while still in the cradle, and his sexual prowess when he impregnated King Thespius' fifty daughters in as many nights. But the twelve labors are his most famous achievement. To expiate the mad murder of his wife and his three children, he was ordered to:

1. Slay the Nemean Lion
2. Kill the Lernaean Hydra
3. Capture the Ceryneian Hind
4. Trap the Erymanthian Boar
5. Flush the Augean stables of manure
6. Kill the obnoxious Stymphalian Birds
7. Capture the Cretan Bull, a Minoan story
8. Steal the man-eating Mares of Diomedes
9. Abscond with the Amazon Hippolyta's girdle
10. Obtain six-armed Geryon's Cattle
11. Fetch the Golden Apples of the Hesperides, which bestowed immortality
12. Capture three-headed Cerberus, watchdog of Hades

In other words, he had to rid the world of primitive terrors and primeval horrors. Today, some revisionist Hellenistic historians considered him to be a historical king of Argos or Tiryns and his main stomping ground was the Argolid, basically the northern and southern Peloponnese. Travelers can today still trace his journeys through the region, including Lerna (near the modern village of Myli), not far from Nafplion, where the big guy battled the Hydra, now seen by some historians as a symbol for the malarial mosquitoes that once ravaged the area. Herc pops up in the myths of many other heroes, including Jason, who stole the Golden Fleece; Perseus, who killed Medusa; and Theseus, who established Athens' dominance. And his constellation is part of the regularly whirling Zodiac that is the mythological dome over all our actions and today's astrology.

Hercules fighting with the centaur Nessus, sculpted by Giambologna

BUS TRAVEL On Tinos, buses (☎ *22830/22440*) run several times daily from the quay of Chora (Tinos town) to nearly all the many villages in Tinos, including Kionia (15 minutes) and Panormos (1 hour); in summer buses are added for beaches. Prices range from €2 to €5 and service stops around 7 pm. The bus station is near the new dock.

Visitor Information and Travel/Tour Agencies Windmills Travel. Sharon Turner at Windmills Travel runs daily guided bus tours of the island for €15, specialty tours by jeep, and unguided Delos–Mykonos trips (€25). ✉ *Above outer dock, behind playground, Chora* ☎☎ *22830/23398* ⊕ *www.windmillstravel.com.*

EXPLORING

Whether travelers head to Tinos or not, a visit here is essential for Greeks: its great Church of Panayia Evangelistria is the Greek Lourdes, a holy place of pilgrimage and miraculous cures; 799 other churches adorn the countryside. Encroaching development here is to accommodate those in search of their religious elixir and not, as on the other islands, the beach-and-bar crowd.

Tinos's magnificently rustic villages are, for some welcome reason, not being abandoned. The dark arcades of Arnados, the vine-shaded sea views of Isternia; the gleaming marble squares of Pirgos: these, finally, are what make Tinos unique. A map, available at kiosks or rental agencies, will make touring these villages by car or bike somewhat less confusing, as there are nearly 50 of them. Or download a good map at ⊕ *www.tinos.gr/eng.* Note that of all the major islands, Tinos is the least developed for sports—the strong winds discourage water sports, and sports outfitters come and go.

TINOS TOWN ΤΗΝΟΣ (ΧΩΡΑ)

14 km (9 mi) northwest of Mykonos town.

Civilization on Tinos is a millennium older than Tinos town, or Chora, founded in the 5th century BC. On weekends and during festivals, Chora is thronged with Greeks attending church, and restaurants and hotels cater to them. As the well-known story goes, in 1822, a year after the War of Independence began (Tinos was the first of the islands to join in), the Virgin sent the nun Pelagia a dream about a buried icon of the Annunciation. On January 30, 1823, such an icon was unearthed amid the foundations of a Byzantine church, and it started to heal people immediately.

Archaeological Museum. On the main street, near the church, is the small Archaeological Museum; its collection includes a sundial by Andronicus of Cyrrhus, who in the 1st century BC also designed Athens's Tower of the Winds. Here, too, are Tinos's famous huge, red storage vases, from the 8th century BC. ✉ *Megalohari, Tinos town* ☎ *22830/22670* 🎟 *€4* ⊙ *Tues.–Fri. 8–2.*

Cultural Center. The Cultural Center, in the large and splendid neoclassic building at the south end of the quay, has a full schedule of traveling exhibitions, a permanent exhibition of the sculptures of Iannoulis Chalepas, and a café. (⇨ *Pirgos, below).* ☎ *22830/29070* ⊕ *www.itip.gr* 🎟 *€3* ⊙ *Wed.–Mon. 10–2 and 7–9.*

Cape Firi Mithi
Cape Skali
Cape Ahinos
Panormos Bay
Panormos Bay
Rochari Beach
Pirgos
Kolymbithra Beach
Cape Halara
Kolimbithra Wetland
Cape Anganistis
TO ANDROS
Aspros Gialos Beach
Ormos Isternion
Isternia
Aetofolia
Kalloni
Kardianí
Komi
Agapi
Livada Beach
Loutra
Volakas
Livada
Cape Ayios Petros
Kambos
Exobourgo
Xynara
Mesi
Potamia
Ayios Romanou Beach
Kionia Beach
Kechrovouni
Arnados
Dio Horia
Lychnaftia Beach
Cape Vorni
Birdemiaros
Triandaros
Kionia
Ayios Nikolaos
Sanctuary of Poseidon & Amfitrite
Tinos town (Chora)
Cape Ayios Ioannis
Ayios Foka Beach
Ayios Sosti Beach

0   2 mi
0   2 km

TO SIROS
TO MYKONOS

Markos Velalopoulos's Ouzeri. Just 1½ km (¾ mi) from Chora you'll see a copse of pines shading a small parking lot, from which a path leads down to Stavros (Holy Cross) chapel; right on the water is the unmarked Markos Velalopoulos's Ouzeri, which serves *strophia* (raki), ouzo, and traditional snacks such as fried cheese or figs with sesame. This is Tinos's most romantic spot to watch the sunset. It is also good for swimming. Note that the sunken breakwater along the coastal road in front of the *ouzeri* (casual bar) is ancient. ⊠ *Under church, Tinos town* ☎ *22830/23276.*

Fodor's Choice **Panayia Evangelistria.** The Tiniots, hardly unaware of the icon's poten-
★ tial, immediately built the splendid Panayia Evangelistria, or Church of the Annunciate Virgin, on the site, in 1823. Imposing and beautiful, framed in gleaming yellow and white, it stands atop the town's main hill ("hora"), which is linked to the harbor via Megalochari, a steeply inclined avenue lined with votive shops. Half Venetian, half Cypriot in style, the facade (illuminated at night) has a distinctive two-story arcade and bookend staircases. Lined with the most costly stones from Tinos, Paros, and Delos, the church's **marble courtyards** (note the green-veined Tiniot stone) are paved with pebble mosaics and surrounded by offices, chapels, a health station, and **seven museums.** Inside the **upper three-aisle church** dozens of beeswax candles and precious

tin- and silver-work votives—don't miss the golden orange tree near the door donated by a blind man who was granted sight—dazzle the eye. You must often wait in line to see the little icon, encrusted with jewels, which was donated as thanks for cures. To beseech the icon's aid, a sick person sends a young female relative or a mother brings her sick infant. As the pilgrim descends from the boat, she falls to her knees, with traffic indifferently whizzing about her, and crawls painfully up the faded red padded lane on the main street—1 km (½ mi)—to the church. In the church's courtyards,

> **LOVEY-DOVEY MCMANSIONS**
>
> Tinos is also renowned for its 1,300 dovecotes (*peristeriónes*), which, unlike those on Mykonos or Andros, are mostly well maintained; in fact, new ones are being built. Two stories high, with intricate stonework, carved-dove finials, and thin schist slabs arranged in intricate patterns resembling traditional stitchery, the dovecotes have been much written about—and are much visited by doves.

she and her family camp for several days, praying to the magical icon for a cure, which sometimes comes. This procedure is very similar to the ancient one observed in Tinos's temple of Poseidon. The **lower church,** called the Evresis, celebrates the finding of the icon; in one room a baptismal font is filled with silver and gold votives. The chapel to the left commemorates the torpedoing by the Italians, on Dormition Day, 1940, of the Greek ship *Helle*; in the early stages of the war, the roused Greeks amazingly overpowered the Italians. ⊠ *At end of Megalohari, Tinos town* ☎ *22830/22256* ⊕ *www.tinos.biz/panagia_eng.html* ⊠ *Free* ⊙ *Daily 8:30–3.*

OFF THE BEATEN PATH

Mountain Villages above Chora. At night the lights of the hill villages surrounding Tinos's highest mountain, Mt. Tsiknias—2,200 feet high and the ancient home of Boreas (the wind god)—glitter over Chora like fireworks. By day they are worth visiting. Take the good road that runs through Dio Horia and Monastiri, which ascends and twists around switchbacks while passing fertile fields and a few of Tinos's most fanciful old dovecotes. After 9 km (5½ mi) you reach **Kechrovouni,** or Monastiri, which is a veritable city of nuns, founded in the 10th century. One cell contains the head of St. Pelagia in a wooden chest; another is a small icon museum. Though a nunnery, Kechrovouni is a lively place, since many of the church's pilgrims come here by bus. Out front, a nun sells huge garlic heads and braids to be used as charms against misfortune; the Greeks call these "California garlic." One kilometer (½ mi) farther on, Tinos's telecommunications towers spike the sky, marking the entrance to **Arnados,** a strange village 1,600 feet up, overlooking Chora. Most of the streets here are vaulted, and thus cool and shady, if a bit claustrophobic; no medieval pirate ever penetrated this warren. In one alley is the **Ecclesiastical Museum,** which displays icons from local churches. Another 1½ km (¾ mi) farther on are the **Dio Horia** (Two Villages), with a marble fountain house, unusual in Tinos. The spreading plane tree in front of it, according to the marble plaque, was planted in 1885. Now the road starts winding down again, to reach **Triandaros,** which has a good restaurant. Many of the pretty houses in this misty

Traditional Festivals in the Cyclades

All over Greece, villages, towns, and cities have traditional celebrations that vary from joyous to deeply serious, and the Cyclades are no exception. In Tinos town, the healing icon from Panayia Evangelistria church is paraded with much pomp on Annunciation Day, March 25, and especially Dormition Day, August 15. As it is carried on poles over the heads of the faithful, cures are effected, and religious emotion runs high. On July 23, in honor of St. Pelagia, the icon is paraded from Kechrovouni Nunnery, and afterward the festivities continue long into the night, with music and fireworks. More down to earth is the Tinos International Literary Festival, bringing writers from around the world for three days of readings and performances in locations around the island at the end of July (⊕ www.tinoslitfestival.com).

If you're on Santorini on July 20, you can partake in the celebration of St. Elias's name day, when a traditional pea-and-onion soup is served, followed by walnut and honey desserts and folk dancing.

Naxos has its share of festivals to discover and enjoy. Naxos town celebrates the Dionysia festival during the first week of August, with concerts, costumed folk dancers, and free food and wine in the square. During Carnival, preceding Lent, "bell wearers" take to the streets in Apeiranthos and Filoti, running from house to house making as much noise as possible with strings of bells tied around their waists. They're a disconcerting sight in their hooded cloaks, as they escort a man dressed as a woman from house to house to collect eggs. In Apeiranthos, villagers square off in rhyming-verse contests: on the last Sunday of Lent, the *paliomaskari*, their faces blackened, challenge each other in improvising *kotsakia* (satirical couplets). On July 14, Ayios Nikodemos Day is celebrated in Chora with a procession of the patron saint's icon through town, but the Dormition of the Virgin on August 15 is, after Easter and Christmas, the festival most widely celebrated, especially in Sangri, Filoti (where festivities take place on August 4), and Apeiranthos.

On Paros each year on August 23, eight days after the huge festival in Parikia at the Church of a Hundred Doors, Naousa celebrates the heroic naval battle against the Turks, with children dressed in native costume, great feasts, and traditional dancing. The day ends with 100 boats illuminated by torches converging on the harbor. On June 2 there is much feasting in Lefkes for the Holy Trinity.

place are owned by Germans. Yannis Kyparinis, who made the three-story bell tower in Dio Horia, has his workshop and showroom here.

BEACHES

There is a series of beaches between Chora and Kionia (and beyond, for walkers).

Stavros. Many consider this to be the most romantic of the area beaches.

Ayios Yannis. Long, sandy, and peaceful are the adjectives to describe this sunny strand. ⊠ *Near Porto, Tinos town.*

DID YOU KNOW?

Tinos's spectacular Church of Panayia Evangelistria is considered the Lourdes of Greece, with many pilgrims famously crawling up its steps in hopes of medical cures.

Pachia Ammos. This beach is undeveloped and, therefore, sparkles in some lovely ways. ⊠ *Past Porto, reached by a dirt road, Tinos town.*

WHERE TO EAT

$ ✗ **Metaxi Mas.** On a trellised lane by
GREEK   the harbor, Euripides and Marygo
★   Tatsionas's restaurant, the best in Tinos, turns out to be no more expensive than a taverna. The name means "between us," and a friendly air prevails. The decor is traditional—pale stone walls and high stone arches—and the staff is welcoming. From starters to desserts, the food is homemade, but with an haute-Athenian flair. For a starter, try local artichokes in vinegar sauce or hot eggplant slices wrapped around cheese, mint, and green pepper. Among the main dishes, the spicy lamb cooked in paper is especially succulent; the calimari stuffed with cheese, tomatoes, and peppers is also exceptional. For dessert daughter Argyro's mille feuille is light and rich. With a fireplace in winter and an air-conditioner for summer, this place stays open year-round. ⊠ *Kontogiorgi alley, Tinos town* ☎ *22830/25945.*

CALLING ALL FAITHFUL

Evangelistria, the street parallel to Panayia Evangelistria, the legendary church of Tinos town, is closed to traffic and is a kind of religious flea market, lined with shops hawking immense candles, chunks of incense, tacky souvenirs, tin votives, and sweets. There are several good jewelers' shops on the market street, where, as always on Tinos, the religious note is supreme.

$$ ✗ **Symposion.** Yorgos Vidalis's café and restaurant occupies the prettiest
GREEK   and best-kept neoclassic building on Evangelistria Street, which is closed to traffic. Its second- and third-floor terraces overlook the Turkish fountain and the passing scene, Tinos's liveliest during shop hours. Marble stairs lead to rooms with elegant furnishings in pastel colors. The second-floor café, open all day, serves snacks and drinks. The third floor is an excellent restaurant. You might start with the ambrosia salad and follow it with burger á la crème (with mushrooms and basmati rice). His mixed plates, combining local meats and vegetables, are perfect to accompany an ouzo on the terrace. The wine list is big and Greek. ⊠ *Evangelistrias 13, Tinos town* ☎ *22830/24368* ✎ *info@symposion. gr* ⊕ *www.symposion.gr* ۞ *Closed Nov.–Mar.*

¢   ✗ **Zefki.** It may say Zeyki on the sign out front but no matter the spell-
GREEK   ing, locals—who always know where to find the freshest food—love this place. Andreas Levantis has converted this old wineshop into an attractive room. The local wines and the raki are carefully chosen. He is a specialist with omelets (local eggs, of course). His main dishes include roasted local goat. The desserts are homemade and change with the season. To find Zefki, walk up Evangelistria Street and take the second right. It's open all year. ⊠ *Alex. Lagourou 6, Tinos town* ☎ *22830/22231* ۞ *Closed Nov.–Mar.*

WHERE TO STAY

For expanded reviews, visit Fodors.com.

$ ⊞ **Akti Aegeou.** The family that runs this little resort is lucky to own such a valuable piece of property, as Akti Aegeou, or "Aegean Coast," is right on the uncrowded beach at Porto—a very pretty location. **Pros:** perfect for swimming in pool or beach; a sweet, quiet, and small beach hotel. **Cons:** rather far from town; too bad so many modern villas being built here. ⊠ *Beach of Agios Ioánnis, Porto, Agios Ioánnis, Tinos* ☎ *22830/24248* ✐ *info@aktiaegeou.gr* ⊕ *www.aktiaegeou.gr* ↴ *5 rooms, 6 apartments* ⏃ *In-room: a/c, kitchen. In-hotel: restaurant, bar, pool* ☉ *Closed Nov.–Mar.*

$$ ⊡ **Favie Suzanne Hotel.** Sleek, posh, and convenient, too: if you are willing to give up a sea view, this is the best place to stay in Tinos town, thanks, in good part, to the hotel's lovely decor, which, from fanlights to dovecotes, incorporates many Tiniot details. **Pros:** set right in the heart of the busy town, it has two wings, with the fancier new section added in 2007. **Cons:** Tinos town is a busy place. ⊠ *Antoniou Sochou 22, Tinos town* ☎ *22830/22693* ☎ *22830/25993* ✐ *info@faviesuzanne. gr* ⊕ *www.faviesuzanne.gr* ↴ *49 rooms* ⏃ *In-room: a/c, Wi-Fi. In-hotel: pool* ☉ *Closed Nov.–Feb.*

$$$ ⊡ **Porto Tango.** This ambitiously up-to-date and stylish resort-hotel strives for the best in decor (modular Cycladic architecture is the keynote) and service—little wonder that Greece's late prime minister, Andreas Papandreou, stayed here during his last visit to Tinos. **Pros:** perfect for families. **Cons:** a bit out in the boonies. ⊠ *Follow signed road up hill, Porto, Agios Ioánnis, Tinos* ☎ *22830/24411 through 22830/24415* ✐ *portango@otenet.gr* ⊕ *www.tinosportotangohotel. com* ↴ *55 rooms, 7 suites* ⏃ *In-room: a/c. In-hotel: restaurant, bar, pool* ☉ *Closed Nov.–Mar.*

$$ ⊡ **Vincenzo Family Hotel.** Owner and manager Ioannis Vidalis has given
★ Tinos just what it needs—right in Chora, his hotel is simple, friendly, and attractive, with furnishings in traditional island style. **Pros:** a great budget choice if you want to be in town. **Cons:** town is busy; no breakfast served. ⊠ *15, 25 March street, Chora, Tinos town* ☎ *22830/25888* ✐ *info@pigeon.gr* ⊕ *www.vincenzo.gr* ↴ *14 rooms* ⏃ *In-room: a/c.*

NIGHTLIFE

Tinos has fewer bars and discos than the other big islands, but there is plenty of late-night bar action behind the waterfront between the two boat docks. People go back and forth among the popular clubs **Syvilla,** **Volto,** and **Metropolis,** on the street behind the fish market next to the Archeio Bar.

SHOPPING

FARMERS' AND **square.** Tinos is a rich farming island, and every day but Sunday, farmers
FLEA MARKETS from all the far-flung villages fill the square with vegetables, herbs, and *kritamos* (pickled sea-plant leaves). ⊠ *Between two docks, Tinos town.*

fish market. In a square near town, the local pelican (a rival to Mykonos's Petros) can often be found cadging snacks from the fish market.

Enosis (*Farmers' Cooperative*). Tinos produces a lot of milk. A short way up from the harbor, on the right, is the little store of the Enosis, which sells milk, butter, and cheeses, including sharp kopanistí, perfect with ouzo; local jams and honeys are for sale, too. ⊠ *Megalohari, up from harbor, Tinos town* ☎ *22830/23289.*

7

JEWELRY   **Anna Maria.** By the small park next to the Cultural Center, the entrance
Fodor'sChoice   to this small arts shop is draped by blue morning-glory vines. The bou-
★   tique showcases jewelry by Greek craftsman with ancient and Byzazn-
tine motifs and also marble pieces carved by owner Pavlos Kangas (a
retired mathematics teacher) and other Tinian sculptors. The crowded
shop is a delight. ⊠ *Tinos town* ☎ *22830/23456.*

Ostria. The selection here is especially good; in addition to delicate silver jewelry, it sells silver icon covers, silver plate, and 22-karat gold.
⊠ *Evangelistria 20, Tinos town* ☎ *22830/23893.*

WEAVINGS   **Biotechniki Scholi.** This 100-year-old weaving school sells traditional
weavings—aprons, towels, spreads—made by its students, local girls.
The largest of its three high-ceiling, wooden-floor rooms is filled with
looms and spindles. ⊠ *Evangelistria, three-quarters of way up from sea,
Tinos town* ☎ *22830/22894.*

KIONIA KIONIA

2½ km (1¼ mi) northwest of Tinos town.

Sanctuary of Poseidon. The reason to come to this small community outside Tinos town is to visit the large, untended Sanctuary of Poseidon,
also dedicated to the bearded sea god's sea-nymph consort, Amphitrite.
The present remains are from the 4th century BC and later, though the
sanctuary itself is much older. The sanctuary was a kind of hospital,
where the ailing came to camp and solicit the god's help. The marble
dolphins in the museum were discovered here. According to the Roman
historian Pliny, Tinos was once infested with serpents (goddess symbols) and named Serpenttown (Ophiousa), until supermasculine Poseidon sent storks to clean them out. The sanctuary functioned well into
Roman times. ⊠ *Northwest of Tinos town, Kionia.*

BEACH

The Kiona road ends at a long, sheltered beach, which is unfortunately being worn away by cars heading for the two pretty coves
beyond, including the Gastrion cave, whose entrance bears Byzantine
inscriptions.

WHERE TO EAT AND STAY

$ ✕ **Tsambia.** Abutting the Sanctuary of Poseidon and facing the sea, this
GREEK   multilevel taverna home makes traditional fare. For starters try the
indigenous specialties: *louza* (smoked pork), local Tiniot cheeses rarely
sold in stores (especially fried local goat cheese), and homegrown vegetables. Fresh fish is available, depending on the weather. Tried-and-true
are pork in red wine with lemon, or goat casserole with oregano. To
get here, follow signs for "traditional taverna" before the Sanctuary of
Poseidon. ⊠ *Cement road, Kionia* ☎ *22830/23142.*

$$ 🏨 **Tinos Beach Hotel.** The winning points about this hotel is that it is big,
comfortable, well-appointed, and fronts on Kionia's long beach, and
is considered the best hotel on Tinos for families. **Pros:** very well run.
Cons: not walking distance from town. ⊠ *Kionia, Tinos* ☎ *22830/22626*
✑ *info@tinosbeach.gr* ⊕ *www.tinosbeach.gr* ➳ *160* ⌂ *In-room: a/c. In-*

hotel: restaurant, bar, pool, beach, laundry facilities, business center, parking.

ISTERNIA ΙΣΤΕΡΝΙΑ

24 km (15 mi) northwest of Tinos town.

The village of Isternia (Cisterns) is verdant with lush gardens. Many of the marble plaques hung here over doorways—a specialty of Tinos— indicate the owner's profession, for example, a sailing ship for a fisherman or sea captain. A long, paved road winds down to a little port, **Ayios Nikitas,** with a **beach** and two **fish tavernas**; a small boat ferries people to Chora in good weather.

PIRGOS ΠΥΡΓΟΣ

32 km (20 mi) northwest of Tinos town, 8 km (5 mi) north of Isternia.

★ The village of Pirgos, second in importance to Chora, is inland and up from the little harbor of Panormos. Tinos is famous for its marble carving, and Pirgos, a prosperous town, is noted for its sculpture school (the town's highest building) and marble workshops, where craftsmen make fanlights, fountains, tomb monuments, and small objects for tourists; they also take orders. The village's main square is aptly crafted of all marble; the five cafés, noted for *galaktoboureko* (custard pastry), and one taverna are all shaded by an ancient plane tree. The quarries for the green-vein marble are north of here, reachable by car. The cemetery here is, appropriately, a showplace of marble sculpture.

Museum Iannoulis Chalepas. The marble-working tradition of Tinos survives here from the 19th century and is going strong, as seen in the two adjacent museums Museum Iannoulis Chalepas and Museum of Tenos Artists, which house the work of Pirgos's renowned sculptor, and other works. ⊠ *1 block from bus stop, Pirgos, Tinos* ☎ *22830/31262* ⌨ *€5* ⊙ *Daily 10–2 and 6–8.*

Fodor'sChoice **Museum of Marble Crafts.** The highest building on Pirgos hill, the Museum
★ of Marble Crafts is the latest addition to the Piraeus Bank Cultural Foundation's network of hi-tech museums on the last century's traditional industries. Inside the strikingly modern building exhibits on view show the process of quarrying and carving and they are the best you'll ever see. The master-artists's drawings for altarpieces and tomb sculpture are also on display, as are some of their works. ⊠ *Pirgos, Tinos* ☎ *22830/31290* ⊕ *www.piop.gr.*

PANORMOS BAY ΟΡΜΟΣ ΠΑΝΟΡΜΟΥ

35 km (22 mi) northwest of Tinos town, 3 km (2 mi) north of Pirgos.

Panormos bay, an unpretentious port once used for marble export, has ducks and geese, a row of seafood restaurants, and a good beach with a collapsed sea cave. More coves with secluded swimming are beyond, as is the islet of Panormos. There are many rooms to rent.

BEACHES

The **beaches next to Panormos** are popular in summer.

WHERE TO EAT

$$$ ✕ **The Fishbone.** When any Tinos restaurant features fish from Panormos
GREEK   bay, they tell you; happily, the Fishbone always does (that is, when
weather permits). This small taverna, decorated with lots of blue and
two Tiniot fanlights, is on the quay; boats right out front bring in fresh
fish, which owners Belasarius Lais and Nikos Menardos, brothers-in-
law, serve with flare. Among the appetizers are small fish pies and
mussels in mustard sauce. Fresh fish wrapped in paper to preserve suc-
culence is a specialty; sole with mushrooms is also a top choice. ⊠ *Pa-
normos, Tinos* ☎ *22830/31362* ⊗ *Closed Nov.–Apr.*

NAXOS ΝΑΞΟΣ

190 km (100 nautical mi) southeast of Piraeus harbor in Athens.

"Great sweetness and tranquillity" is how Nikos Kazantzakis, premier
novelist of Greece, described Naxos, and indeed a tour of the island
leaves you with an impression of abundance, prosperity, and serenity.
The greenest, largest, and most fertile of the Cyclades, Naxos, with its
many potato fields, its livestock and its thriving cheese industry, and its
fruit and olive groves framed by the pyramid of Mt. Zas (3,295 feet,
the Cyclades' highest), is practically self-sufficient. Inhabited for 6,000
years, the island has memorable landscapes—abrupt ravines, hidden
valleys, long and sandy beaches—and towns that vary from a Cre-
tan mountain stronghold to the seaside capital that strongly evokes its
Venetian past.

GETTING HERE AND AROUND

AIR TRAVEL   Olympic flies three to five times a day from Athens to Naxos, and back;
it take 35 minutes (in winter connections are much fewer). There are
no other air connections. Summer flights fill up fast, so book well in
advance. Check ⊕ *www.aia.gr.*

BOAT TRAVEL   Boats to Naxos, many of which follow the Paros/Naxos/Santorini route,
take from four to seven hours depending on route, boat, and pelagic
happenstance. In summer there are five a day, in winter fewer. There
are daily connections with Paros and Santorini, and regular connections
with Mykonos, Amorgos, Kythnos, Kea, Ios, and sometimes others.
Book all cars well in advance, and seats for high season. Off-season,
except at Easter, it is not necessary. The town, Venetian castle, and *por-
tara* (ancient temple gate) look especially impressive from an arriving
boat. For boat schedules go to ⊕ *www.openseas.gr.* Also have a look at
⊕ *www.greeka.com.* The Naxos Port Authority (☎ *22850/22300*) also
gives information on boats.

BUS TRAVEL   On Naxos, the bus system is reliable and fairly extensive. Daily buses
(☎ *22850/22440*) go from Naxos town, called Chora (near the boat
dock), to Engares, Melanes, Sangri, Filoti, Apeiranthos, Koronida, and
Apollonas. In summer there is added daily service to the beaches, includ-
ing Ayia Anna, Pyrgaki, Ayiassos, Pachy Ammos, and Abram. Other
villages have bus service but with much less frequency; above destina-
tions usually have three to five runs a day. Schedules are posted; hotel

Naxos's most famous landmark is its "doorway to nowhere." The Portara is the sole remnant of a gigantic ancient Temple to Apollo.

concierges also have this info; fares run from €2.50 to €6. There is a taxi stand near the harbor (☎ *22850/22444*).

Visitor Information and Travel/Tour Agencies **Zas Travel**. This agency runs two good one-day tours of the island sights with different itineraries, each costing about €35, and one-day trips to Delos and Mykonos (about €60). ✉ *Chora, Naxos* ☎ *22850/23330, 22850/23331* ✉ *Ayios Prokopios, Naxos* ☎ *22850/24780* ✆ *zas-travel@nax.forthnet.gr.*

EXPLORING
Naxos is full of history and monuments—classical temples, medieval monasteries, Byzantine churches, Venetian towers—and its huge interior offers endless magnificent hikes, not much pursued by summer tourists, who cling to the lively capital and the developed western beaches, the best in the Cyclades.

NAXOS TOWN ΝΑΞΟΣ (ΧΩΡΑ)

140 km (86 nautical mi) southeast of Piraeus, 33 km (21 mi) southeast of Mykonos, 35 km (22 mi) east of Paros.

As your ferry chugs into the harbor, you see before you the white houses of Naxos town (Chora) on a hill crowned by the one remaining tower of the Venetian castle, a reminder that Naxos was once the proud capital of the Venetian semi-independent Duchy of the Archipelago.

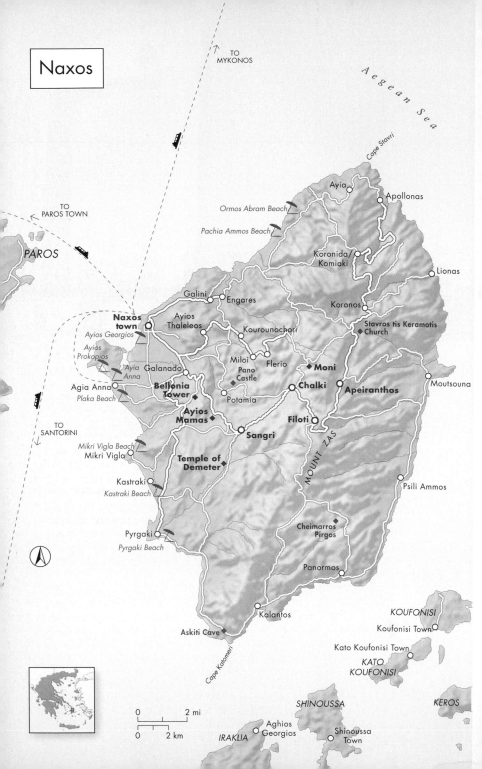

TOP ATTRACTIONS

Ancient Town of Naxos. The most ancient settlements of Naxos were directly on the square in front of the Greek Orthodox cathedral. You'll note that several of the churches set on this square, like the cathedral itself, hint at Naxos's venerable history as they are made of ancient materials. In fact, this square was, in succession, the seat of a flourishing Mycenaean town (1300–1050 BC), a classical agora (when it was a 167-foot by 156-foot square closed on three sides by Doric stoas, so that it looked like the letter "G"; a shorter fourth stoa bordered the east side, leaving room at each end for an entrance), a Roman town, and early Christian church complex. For more of ancient Naxos, explore the nearby precinct of Grotta.

Foundation museum. Although much of the site has been refilled, under the square a museum gives you a well-marked sampling of the foundations. City, cemetery, tumulus, hero shrine: no wonder the early Christians built here. ☎ *22850/24151* 🏷 *Free* ⊘ *Tues.–Sun. 8–2:30*

Domus Venetian Museum. Located in the 800-year-old Dellarocca-Barozzi house, the Domus Venetian Museum lets you, at last, into one of the historic Venetian residences. The house, enclosed within the soaring walls of Chora's castle, adjacent to the "Traini," or Great Gate, was first erected in 1207. Inside, the house is like a Naxian attic filled with fascinating objects ranging from the Cycadic period to Victorian times. One is personally escorted through the house on a tour by the museum's entertaining director, Nikos Karavias, who will tell you all about the French, Greek, and Venetian roots of the Dellarocca and Barozzi clans. The house's idyllic garden, built into the Kastro wall, provides a regular venue in season for a concert series, from classical to jazz to island music. ⊠ *At Kastro north gate, Naxos town* ☎ *22850/22387* ⊕ *www.naxosfestival.com* 🏷 *€4, tour €6* ⊘ *June–Aug., daily 10 am–11 pm.*

★ **Kastro.** You won't miss the gates of the castle. The south gate is called the **Paraporti** (side gate), but it's more interesting to enter through the northern gate, or **Trani** (strong), via Apollonos Street. Note the vertical incision in the gate's marble column—it is the Venetian yard against which drapers measured the bolts of cloth they brought to the noblewomen. Step through the Trani into the citadel and enter another age, where sedate Venetian houses still stand around silent courtyards, their exteriors emblazoned with coats of arms and bedecked with flowers. Half are still owned by the original families; romantic Greeks and foreigners have bought up the rest.

The entire citadel was built in 1207 by Marco Sanudo, a Venetian who, three years after the fall of Constantinople, landed on Naxos as part of the Fourth Crusade. When in 1210 Venice refused to grant him independent status, Sanudo switched allegiance to the Latin emperor in Constantinople, becoming duke of the archipelago. Under the Byzantines, "archipelago" had meant "chief sea," but after Sanudo and his successors, it came to mean "group of islands," that is, the Cyclades. For three centuries Naxos was held by Venetian families, who resisted pirate attacks, introduced Roman Catholicism, and later rebuilt the castle in its present form. In 1564 Naxos came under Turkish rule but, even then, the Venetians still ran the island, while the Turks only collected taxes. The rust-color Glezos tower was home to the last dukes; it displays the coat of arms: a pen and sword crossed under a crown. ⊠ *Kastro, Naxos town.*

★ **Naxos Archaeological Museum.** Today the historic convent and school of the Ursulines houses the Naxos Archaeological Museum, best known for its Cycladic and Mycenaean finds. During the early Cycladic period (3200–2000 BC) there were settlements along Naxos's east coast and outside Naxos town at Grotta. The finds are from these settlements and graveyards scattered around the island. Many of the vessels exhibited are from the early Cycladic I period, hand-built of coarse-grain clay, sometimes decorated with a herringbone pattern. Though the museum has too many items in its glass cases to be appreciated in a short visit, you should try not to miss the white marble Cycladic statuettes, which range from the early "violin" shapes to the more-detailed female forms with their tilted flat heads, folded arms, and legs slightly bent at the knees. The male forms are simpler and often appear to be seated. The most common theory is that the female statuettes were both fertility and grave goddesses, and the males were servant figures. ⊠ *Kastro, Naxos town* ☎ *22850/22725* ⊕ *www.culture.gr* ⊠€3 ☉ *Tues.–Sun. 8:30–3.*

Fodor's Choice **Old Town.** A bewildering maze of twisting cobblestone streets, arched
★ porticoes, and towering doorways, the Old Town plunges you alternatively into cool darkness and then suddenly into pockets of dazzling sunshine. The Old Town is divided into the lower section, **Bourgos,** where the Greeks lived during Venetian times, and the upper part, called **Kastro** (castle), still inhabited by the Venetian Catholic nobility. ⊠ *Along quay, left at first big square, Naxos town.*

Our Lady of Myrtle. This tiny church watches over the local sailors, who built it for divine protection. ⊠ *Perched on sea rock off waterfront, Naxos town.*

★ **Portara.** Although the capital town is primarily beloved for its Venetian elegance and picturesque blind alleys, Naxos's most famous landmark is ancient: the Portara, a massive doorway that leads to nowhere. The Portara stands on the islet of **Palatia,** which was once a hill (since antiquity the Mediterranean has risen quite a bit) and in the 3rd millennium BC was the acropolis for a nearby Cycladic settlement. The Portara, an entrance to an unfinished Temple of Apollo that faces exactly toward Delos, Apollo's birthplace, was begun about 530 BC by the tyrant Lygdamis, who said he would make Naxos's buildings the highest and most glorious in Greece. He was overthrown in 506 BC, and the temple was never completed; by the 5th and 6th centuries AD it had been converted into a church; and under Venetian and Turkish rule it was slowly dismembered, so the marble could be used to build the castle. The gate, built with four blocks of marble, each 16 feet long and weighing 20 tons, was so large it couldn't be demolished, so it remains today, along with the temple floor. Palatia itself has come to be associated with the tragic myth of Ariadne, princess of Crete:

Ariadne, daughter of Crete's King Minos, helped Theseus thread the labyrinth of Knossos and slay the monstrous Minotaur. In exchange, he promised to marry her. Sailing for Athens, the couple stopped in Naxos, where Theseus abandoned her. Jilted Ariadne's curse made Theseus forget to change the ship's sails from black to white, and so his grieving father Aegeus, believing his son dead, plunged into the Aegean. Seeing Ariadne's tears, smitten Dionysus descended in a leopard-drawn chariot to marry her, and set her bridal wreath, the Corona Borealis, in the sky, an eternal token of his love.

The myth inspired one of Titian's best-known paintings, as well as Strauss's opera *Ariadne auf Naxos.*

North of Palatia, **underwater remains of Cycladic buildings** are strewn along an area called **Grotta.** Here are a series of large worked stones, the remains of the waterfront quayside mole, and a few steps that locals say go to a tunnel leading to the islet of Palatia; these remains are Cycladic (before 2000 BC). ⊠ *At harbor's far edge, Naxos town.*

WORTH NOTING

Cathedral. Built by Sanudo in the 13th century, this grand cathedral was restored by Catholic families in the 16th and 17th centuries. The marble floor is paved with tombstones bearing the coats of arms of the noble families. Venetian wealth is evident in the many gold and silver icon frames. The icons reflect a mix of Byzantine and Western influences: the one of the Virgin Mary is unusual because it shows a Byzantine Virgin and Child in the presence of a bishop, a cathedral benefactor. Another 17th-century icon shows the Virgin of the Rosary surrounded by members of the Sommaripa family, whose house is nearby. ⊠ *At Kastro's center, Naxos town.*

Greek Orthodox Cathedral. The Greek Orthodox cathedral was built in 1789 on the site of a church called Zoodochos Pigis (Life-giving Source). The cathedral was built from the materials of ancient temples: the solid granite pillars are said to be from the ruins of Delos. Amid the gold and the carved wood, there is a vividly colored iconostasis painted by a well-known iconographer of the Cretan school, Dimitrios Valvis, and the Gospel Book is believed to be a gift from Catherine the Great of Russia. ⊠ *Bourgos, Naxos town.*

Naxos Folklore Museum. This little museum shows costumes, ceramics, farming implements, and other items from Naxos's far-flung villages. ⊠ *Roubel Sq., Old Market St., Naxos town* ☎ *22850/25531* ⊕ *www. naxosfolkmuseum.com/* ☑ *€3* ☉ *9–8.*

BEACHES

The southwest coast of Naxos, facing Paros and the sunset, offers the Cyclades's longest stretches of sandy beaches. All these have tavernas and rooms. They are listed, in order, heading south.

Ayios Georgios. Now part of town, the Ayios Georgios beach has become very developed.

Ayios Prokopios. With a small leeward harbor, Ayios Prokopios also looks out on lagoons with waterfowl.

Ayia Anna. Very crowded, Ayia Anna has a small harbor with connections to Paros.

Plaka. Ringed by sand dunes and bamboo groves, Plaka is about 8 km (5 mi) south of town.

Mikri Vigla. This beach is sandy and edged by cedar trees.

Kastraki. Semi-nude, this beach is noted for its white marble sand.

Pyrgaki. With its idyllic crystalline waters, this is the island's least-developed beach.

WHERE TO EAT

$$ ╳ **Apolafsis.** Rightly named "Enjoy-
GREEK ment," Lefteris Keramideas's second-floor restaurant offers a balcony with a great view of the harbor and sunset. You'll enjoy live music (always in summer; often in winter), as well as a large assort-

ment of appetizers (try spinach or zucchini tart), local barrel wine, and fresh fish. The sliced pork in wine sauce is good, too. The desserts are homemade. ⊠ *Naxos town waterfront* ☎ *22850/22178* ⊕ *www. naxosrestaurants.com/apolafsi/english/.*

$$ ╳ **Gorgona.** Bearded Dimitris and Koula Kapris's beachfront taverna is
GREEK popular both with sun worshippers on Ayia Anna beach and locals from Chora, who come here winter and summer to get away and sometimes to dance until the late hours, often to live music. The menu is extensive and fresh daily—the fresh fish comes from the caïques that pull up at the dock right in front every morning. Two good appetizers are *kakavia* (fish stew) and shrimp *saganaki* (with cooked cheese), while spaghetti with crab is a fine entrée. The barrel wine is their own (they also bottle it). The small hotel next door is also theirs. ⊠ *Ayia Anna near dock, Naxos town* ☎ *22850/41007* ▭ *No credit cards.*

$$ ╳ **Labyrinth.** Opened in 2006 in the middle of the Old Town, Labyrinth
GREEK was an immediate success with locals. Its more-than-simple food, cozy flagstone garden, and good service are all praiseworthy. A good appe-tizer is sundried tomato and feta tart. Among the best main dishes are salmon fillet with fresh vegetables and orange sauce, and also the chicken fillet with shrimp, potatoes, and herbs. And don't miss out on the light and summery lemon mousse. The wine cellar is Naxos's most extensive. ⊠ *Old Town, Naxos town* ☎ *22850/22253* ▭ *No credit cards* ☉ *Closed Oct.–Apr. No lunch.*

¢ ⛿ **Naxos Café.** Naxos Café is one of a number of cafés in Naxos's Old Town trying for charm and authenticity, and succeeding. *22850/26343.*

$ ╳ **Old Inn.** Berlin-trained chef Dieter von Ranizewski serves German
GERMAN food informed by Naxos. In a courtyard under a chinaberry tree, with
Fodor's Choice rough whitewashed walls and ancient marbles, two of the old church's
★ interior sides open into the wine cellar and gallery; on the fourth side,
Ⓒ with beams and wood paneling, is a fireplace. The menu is extensive. For starters you might try sausages with beer sauce, smoked ham, or

liver pâté—all homemade. For entrées, have the signature steak with tomatoes, olives, Roquefort, and bacon-flecked roast potatoes. For Dieter's famous schnitzel you get to choose one of 48 sauces. For dessert, the apple strudel—it is grandma's recipe—is simply delicious. There is a children's menu and small playground. ⊠ *Naxos town; take car road off waterfront, turn right into 2nd alley* ☎ *22850/27013.*

WHERE TO STAY

For expanded reviews, visit Fodors.com.

$ ⊡ **Abram Village.** If you love island nature and dislike crowds, this is your place—set on Naxos's northern coast (the developers only moved in a few years ago when the road was finally paved), Panyiotis Albertis's rooms and villas recline in a green garden on beautiful Abram beach: the scenery is extraordinary and there are many coves with beaches. **Pros:** right on the sea; in a beautiful area. **Cons:** isolated and far from town. ⊠ *Abram, Naxos town* ✛ *20 km (33 mi) from Chora* ☎ *22850/63244* ⊕ *www.abram.gr* ⟿ *20 rooms, 2 villas* ⚭ *In-room: a/c, kitchen. In-hotel: business center* ⊘ *Closed Oct.–Apr.*

$$ ⊡ **Apollon.** In addition to being comfortable, attractive, and quiet (it's
★ a converted marble workshop), this hotel, set in the Fontana quarter, is convenient to everything in town—even better, it offers parking facilities, a rarity in town. **Pros:** convenient; well done; low prices. **Cons:** small rooms. ⊠ *Behind Orthodox cathedral, car entrance on road out of town Fontana, Chora* ☎ *22850/22468* ⊕ *www.apollonhotel-naxos. gr* ⟿ *13 rooms, 1 suite* ⚭ *In-room: a/c.*

$$ ⊡ **Chateau Zevgoli.** If you stay in Chora, try to settle in to Despina
★ Kitini's fairy-tale pension, which is set in a comfortable Venetian house that offers distinctive guest rooms and a lovingly appointed living room. **Pros:** it is sweetly decorated; set in a fetching neighborhood. **Cons:** it is uphill and you must walk to it. ⊠ *Chora Old Town, follow signs stenciled on walls, Naxos town* ☎ *22850/22993, 22850/26143* ⊕ *www. hotelzevgoli.gr* ⟿ *10 rooms, 1 suite* ⚭ *In-room: a/c. In-hotel: business center.*

$$$$ ⊡ **Galaxy.** All whitewash and stone, this hotel is perfect if you want to be on the beach (and don't mind the crowds at the seaside in summer). **Pros:** a full resort hotel. **Cons:** too far from town to walk. ⊠ *Ayios Georgios beach, Naxos town* ☎ *22850/22422, 22850/22423* ⊕ *www.hotel-galaxy.com* ⟿ *43 studios, 11 rooms* ⚭ *In-room: a/c, kitchen, Internet. In-hotel: restaurant, bar, pool* ⊘ *Closed Nov.–Mar.* ⵏ⊙ⵏ *Breakfast.*

NIGHTLIFE AND THE ARTS

BARS **Ocean Dance.** Nightlife in Naxos is quieter than it is on Santorini or Mykonos, but there are several popular bars at the south end of Chora. Popularity changes fast, so keep your ears open for the latest places. Ocean Dance opens at 11:30 pm, all year round. Locals call it Ocean-Mojo because these two highly popular bars are adjacent to each other. ⊠ *Chora, Naxos town* ☎ *22850/26766.*

ARTS EVENTS **Bazeos tower.** This 17th-century tower is one of the island's most beautiful Venetian-era monuments and is worth a visit in itself (during high season it is open daily 10–5) but also offers a calendar of exhibitions,

Grand Prize winner of Fodor's "Show Us Your Greece" contest, this photo by Timothy Miller gloriously captures Cycladic beauty in all its forms.

concerts, and seminars every summer. ✛ *12 km [18 mi] from Chora toward Chalki* ☎ *22850/31402* ⊕ *www.bazeostower.gr.*

Catholic Cultural Center. Among other things, the Catholic Cultural Center runs art exhibitions; watch for posters. ✉ *Kastro, near church, Naxos town* ☎ *22850/24793.*

Domus Venetian Museum. Set in the 800-year-old Dellarocca-Barozzi house, the Domus Venetian Museum offers a summer concert series in its lovely garden. Check the Web site for the program: ⊕ *www. naxosfestival.com* ✉ *At Kastro north gate, Chora* ☎ *22850/22387* ✎ *venetianmuseum@yahoo.gr.*

Town Hall Exhibition Space. The exhibition hall offers an ambitious program of art exhibitions, concerts, and other events. ✉ *Chora's south end, Naxos town* ☎ *22850/37100.*

SPORTS AND THE OUTDOORS

SAILING AND WATER SPORTS
Naxos-Surf Club. For windsurfing rental and lessons near Chora, contact Naxos-Surf Club. ✉ *Ayios Yorgios beach, Naxos town* ☎ *22850/29170* ⊕ *www.naxos-surf.com/.*

Plaka Watersports. For windsurfing on distant, paradisiacal Plaka beach, contact Plaka Watersports. ✉ *Plaka beach, Naxos town* ☎ *22850/41264* ⊕ *www.plaka-watersports.com.*

SHOPPING

ANTIQUES
Antico Veneziano. Eleni Dellarocca's shop, Antico Veneziano, is in the basement of her Venetian house, built 800 years ago. The columns inside come from Naxos's ancient acropolis. In addition to antiques, she has handmade embroideries, porcelain and glass, mirrors, old

chandeliers, and vintage photographs of Naxos. One room is an art gallery, while the other is devoted to Greece's best CDs. ⊠ *In Kastro, down from museum, Naxos town* ☎ *22850/26206* ⊕ *www.anticoveneziano.com.*

BOOKS **Zoom.** At Eleftherios Primikirios's bookstore, there's an excellent selection of English-language books about Naxos and much more. No other island bookstore is this well stocked. ⊠ *Chora waterfront, Naxos town* ☎ *22850/23675, 22850/23676.*

CLOTHING **Loom.** Vassilis and Kathy Koutelieris sell casual clothes made from organically grown Greek cotton (including the Earth Collection in muted natural colors). ⊠ *Dimitriou Kokkou 8, in old market, off main square, 3rd street on right, Naxos town* ☎ *22850/25531.*

JEWELRY **Nassos Papakonstantinou.** The workshop of Nassos Papakonstantinou sells one-of-a-kind pieces both sculptural and delicate. His father was a wood-carver; Nassos has inherited his talent. The shop has no sign—that is Nassos's style. ⊠ *Ayiou Nikodemou Street, on Old Town's main square, Naxos town* ☎☎ *22850/22607.*

TRADITIONAL CRAFTS, CARPETS, AND JEWELS **Techni.** The embroidery and knitted items made by women in the mountain villages are known throughout Greece. They can be bought at Techni. Techni's two shops, almost facing each other, also sell carpets, jewelry in old designs, linens, and more. ⊠ *Persefonis Street, Old Town, Naxos town* ☎ *22850/24767* ⊕ *www.techni.gr.*

BELLONIA TOWER ΠΥΡΓΟΣ ΤΟΥ ΜΠΕΛΟΝΙΑ

5 km (3 mi) south of Naxos town.

★ **Bellonia Tower.** The graceful Bellonia tower (Pirgos Bellonia) belonged to the area's ruling Venetian family, and like other fortified houses, it was built as a refuge from pirates and as part of the island's alarm system. The towers were located strategically throughout the island; if there was an attack, a large fire would be lighted on the nearest tower's roof, setting off a chain reaction from tower to tower and alerting the islanders. Bellonia's thick stone walls, its Lion of St. Mark emblem, and flat roofs with zigzag chimneys are typical of these pirgi.

"Double Church" of St. John. The unusual 13th-century "double church" of St. John exemplifies Venetian tolerance. On the left side is the Catholic chapel, on the right the Orthodox church, separated only by a double arch. A family lives in the tower, and the church is often open. From here, take a moment to gaze across the peaceful fields to Chora and imagine what the islanders must have felt when they saw pirate ships on the horizon. ⊠ *In front of Bellonia tower, Naxos.*

AYIOS MAMAS ΑΓΙΟΣ ΜΑΜΑΣ

3 km (2 mi) south of Bellonia tower, 8 km (5 mi) south of Naxos town.

Ayios Mamas. A kilometer (½ mi) past a valley with unsurpassed views is one of the island's oldest churches (9th century), Ayios Mamas. St. Mamas is the protector of shepherds and is regarded as a patron saint in Naxos, Cyprus, and Asia Minor. Built in the 8th century, the stone church was the island's cathedral under the Byzantines. Though it was converted into a Catholic church in 1207, it was neglected under the Venetians and is now falling apart. You can also get to it from the Potamia villages.

SANGRI ΣΑΓΚΡΙ

3 km (2 mi) south of Ayios Mamas, 11 km (7 mi) south of Naxos town.

Sangri is the center of an area with so many monuments and ruins spanning the Archaic to the Venetian periods it is sometimes called little Mystras, a reference to the famous abandoned Byzantine city in the Peloponnese.

Timios Stavros (*Holy Cross*). The name Sangri is a corruption of Sainte Croix, which is what the French called the town's 16th-century monastery of Timios Stavros. The town is actually three small villages spread across a plateau. During the Turkish occupation, the monastery served as an illegal school, where children met secretly to learn the Greek language and culture.

Ruins of Kasto Apilarou. Above the town, you can make out the ruins of Kasto Apilarou, the castle Sanudo first attacked. It's a hard climb up. ⊠ *On Mt. Profitis Ilias, Sangri.*

TEMPLE OF DEMETER ΝΑΟΣ ΤΗΣ ΔΗΜΗΤΡΑΣ

5 km (3 mi) south of Sangri.

★ **Temple of Demeter.** Take the asphalt road right (the 25-minute walk is splendid) before the entrance to Sangri to reach the Temple of Demeter, a marble Archaic temple, circa 530 BC, lovingly restored by German archaeologists during the 1990s. Demeter was a grain goddess, and it's not hard to see what she is doing in this beautiful spot. There is also a small museum here (admission is free).

CHALKI ΧΑΛΚΙ

6 km (4 mi) northeast of Sangri, 17 km (10½ mi) southeast of Naxos town.

★ **Main Square.** Katharina Bolesch and Alexander Reichart, husband and wife, have lived in Naxos for decades. They moved to Chalki's old main square in 2006 and started the beautiful town's revival with the restoration of one fine old building. Thanks to them, the square nowadays has a weaving shop, a shop selling olive wood items, a local foods shop, a café, and a tavern, all of high quality. The shop goods have been displayed internationally. As for Ms. Bolesch and Mr. Reichart, their **Fish and Olive** boutique sells Katharina's masterful ceramics and Alexander's sensitive jewlery—all with fish or olive motifs. The back room is an art gallery. The couple also run the Axia music festival in August, which gets grander yearly. ⊠ *Fish and Olive, Central Plateia, Chalki* ☎ *22850/31771* ⊕ *www.fish-olive-creations.com.*

Panayia Protothrone (*First Enthroned Virgin Church*). You are now entering the heart of the lush Tragaia valley, where in spring the air is heavily scented with honeysuckle, roses, and lemon blossoms and many tiny Byzantine churches hide in the dense olive groves. In Chalki is one of the most important of these Byzantine churches: the white, red-roofed Panayia Protothrone. Restoration work has uncovered frescoes from the 6th through the 13th century, and the church has remained alive and functioning for 14 centuries. The oldest layers, in the apse, depict the Apostles. ⊠ *On main road, Chalki* ⊙ *Mornings.*

Frangopoulos tower. Chalki itself is a pretty town, known for its neo-classic houses in shades of pink, yellow, and gray, which are oddly juxtaposed with the plain but stately 17th-century Venetian Frangopoulos tower. ⊠ *Main road, next to Panayia Protothrone, Chalki* ⊡ *Free* ⊙ *Sometimes open in morning.*

MONI MONH

6 km (4 mi) north of Chalki, 23 km (14¼ mi) east of Naxos town.

Panayia Drosiani. Owing to a good asphalt road, Moni ("monastery"), high in the mountains overlooking Naxos's greenest valley, has become a popular place for a meal or coffee on a hot afternoon. Local women make embroideries for Chora's shops. Just below Moni is one of the Balkans' most important churches, Panayia Drosiani, which has faint, rare Byzantine frescoes from the 7th and 8th centuries. Its name means Our Lady of Refreshment, because once during a severe drought, when all the churches took their icons down to the sea to pray for rain, only the icon of this church got results. The fading frescoes are visible in layers: to the right when you enter are the oldest—one shows St. George the Dragon Slayer astride his horse, along with a small boy, an image one usually sees only in Cyprus and Crete. According to legend, the saint saved the child, who had fallen into a well, and there met and slew the giant dragon that had terrorized the town. Opposite him is St. Dimitrios, shown killing barbarians. The church is made up of three chapels—the middle one has a space for the faithful to worship at the altar rather than in the nave, as became common in later centuries. Next to that is a very small opening that housed a secret school during the revolution. It is open mornings and again after siesta; in deserted winter, ring the bell if it is not open. ☎ *22850/31003.*

FILOTI ΦΙΛΟΤΙ

6½ km (4 mi) south of Moni, 20 km (12½ mi) southeast of Naxos town.

Filoti, a peaceful village on the lower slopes of Mt. Zas, is the interior's largest. A three-day festival celebrating the Dormition starts on August 14. In the center of town is another Venetian tower that belonged to the Barozzi and the Church of Filotissa (Filoti's Virgin Mary) with its marble iconostasis and carved bell tower. There are places to eat and rooms to rent.

SPORTS AND THE OUTDOORS

Zas cave. Filoti is the starting place for several walks in the countryside, including the climb up to Zas cave, where obsidian tools and pottery fragments have been found; lots of bats live inside. Mt. Zas, or Zeus, is one of the god's birthplaces; on the path to the summit lies a block of unworked marble that reads *Oros Dios Milosiou*, or "Boundary of the Temple of Zeus Melosios." (Melosios, it is thought, is a word that has to do with sheep.) The islanders say that under the Turks the cave was used as a chapel, and two stalagmites are called the Priest and the Priest's Wife, who are said to have been petrified by God to save them from arrest. ⊠ *Southeast of town on small dirt track, Filoti.*

> **TOWERING VIEWS**
>
> The Cheimarros Pirgos (Tower of the Torrent), a cylindrical Hellenistic tower, can be reached from Filoti by a road that begins from the main road to Apeiranthos, outside town, or by a level, 3½-hour hike with excellent views. The walls, as tall as 45 feet, are intact, with marble blocks perfectly aligned. The tower, which also served as a lookout post for pirates, is often celebrated in the island's poetry: "O, my heart is like a bower/And Cheimarros's lofty tower!"

APEIRANTHOS ΑΠΕΙΡΑΝΘΟΣ

★ *12 km (7½ mi) northeast of Filoti, 32 km (20 mi) southeast of Naxos town.*

Apeiranthos is very picturesque, with views and marble-paved streets running between the Venetian Bardani and Zevgoli towers. As you walk through the arcades and alleys, notice the unusual chimneys—no two are alike. The elders, whose ancestors came from Crete, sit in their doorsteps chatting, while packs of children shout "Hello, hello" at any passerby who looks foreign.

Archaeological Museum. A very small Archaeological Museum, established by a local mathematician, Michael Bardanis, displays Cycladic finds from the east coast. The most important of the artifacts are unique gray marble plaques from the 3rd millennium BC with roughly hammered scenes of daily life: hunters and farmers and sailors going about their business. If it's closed, ask in the square for the guard. ⊠ *Off main square, Apeiranthos* ▦ *Free* ☉ *Daily 8:30–3.*

PAROS AND ANTIPAROS
ΠΑΡΟΣ ΚΑΙ ΑΝΤΙΠΑΡΟΣ

165 km (91 nautical mi) southeast of Piraeus harbor in Athens.

In the classical age, the great sculptor Praxiteles prized the incomparably snowy marble that came from the quarries at Paros; his chief rival was the Parian Scopas. Between them they developed the first true

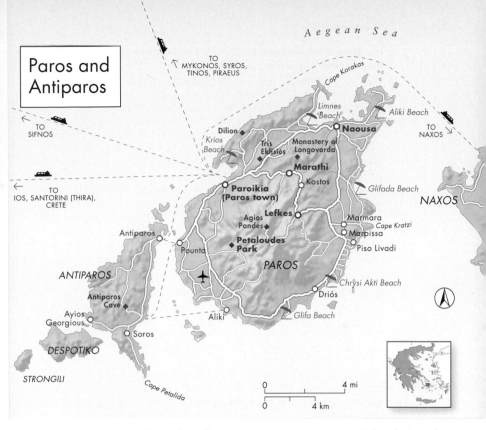

Aegean Sea

TO
MYKONOS, SYROS,
TINOS, PIRAEUS

Cape Korakas

TO
SIFNOS

Limnes
Beach

Aliki Beach

Dilion
Krios
Beach

Naousa

TO
NAXOS

Tris
Eklisiés

Monastery of
Longovarda

TO
IOS, SANTORINI (THIRA),
CRETE

Marathi

Paroikia
(Paros town)

Kostos

Glifada Beach

NAXOS

Lefkes

Agios
Pandes

Marmara

Cape Kratzi

Antiparos

Petaloudes
Park

Marpissa

Pounta

Piso Livadi

ANTIPAROS

PAROS

Chrýsi Akti Beach

Antiparos
Cave

Driós

Ayios
Georgios

Aliki

Glifa Beach

Soros

DESPOTIKO

0   4 mi

STRONGILI

Cape Petalida

0   4 km

female nude, and gentle voluptuousness seems a good description of this historic island. Today, Paros is favored by people for its cafés by the sea, golden sandy beaches, and charming fishing villages. It may lack the chic of Mykonos and have fewer top-class hotels, but at the height of the season it often gets Mykonos's tired and detrending—Madonna (the singer, not Our Lady, who is always here) shows up every summer. The island is large enough to accommodate the traveler in search of peace and quiet, yet the lovely port towns of Paroikía, the capital, and Naousa also have an active nightlife (overactive in August). Paros is a focal point of the Cyclades ferry network, and many people stay here for a night or two while waiting for a connection. Paros town has a good share of bars and discos, though Naousa has a more-chic island atmosphere. And none of the islands has a richer cultural life, with concerts, exhibitions, and readings, than does Paros. For this, check the English monthly, *Paros Life*, available everywhere (⊕ *www.paroslife.gr* and also *www.parosweb.com*).

GETTING HERE AND AROUND

AIR TRAVEL Olympic runs six flights a day to Athens in summer and three in winter. Early reservations are essential. If a dignitary wants a late flight, you may get bumped. The plane flies over Antiparos, and the shallows of the strait flash beautiful colors. How Madonna arrived in 2009 to buy property is not discoverable, but hired helicopters are getting popular. For flights check ⊕ *www.aia.gr.*

BOAT TRAVEL Paros is probably the best served island by boat—there are at least 15 of them—and it is a hub for other destinations. Five boats come daily from Piraeus and two from Rafina. In summer there are daily connections to Tinos, Mykonos, Naxos, and Santorini. There are also regular connections to Milos, Kimolos, Anafi Ios, Iraklia, Donousa, Koufonisi, Schinousa, Crete, Folegandros, Sikinos, Sifnos, Serifos, Kea, Kastelorizo, Kimolos, Astypalea, Kalymnos, Rhodes, Kos, Nisyros, and Astypalea. (It is almost discouraging that all these islands are worth visiting.) There is also a speedboat for hire, much used by lawyers. For boat schedules check ⊕ *www.openseas.gr.*

Polos Tours. The staff here is extremely helpful. ⊠ *Parikia* ☎ *22840/22092* ⊕ *www.polostours.gr.*

The most useful Paros Web site is ⊕ *www.parosweb.com.* The Paros Port Authority (☎ *22840/21240*) doesn't give information, but refers you to an island travel agency.

BUS TRAVEL From the Paros town bus station (☎ *22840/21133*), just west of the dock, there is service every hour to Naousa and less-frequent service to Alyki, Pounta (about 10 a day to this departure point for Antiparos), and the beaches at Piso Livadi, Chrissi Akti, and Drios. Schedules are posted. Buy tickets at the booth; fares run from €1.50 to €6. There is a taxi stand across from the windmill on the harbor (☎ *22840/21500*).

Visitor Information and Travel/Tour Agencies Erkyna Travel ⊠ *On main square, Naousa* ☎ *22840/22654, 22840/22655, 22840/53180* ⊕ *www. erkynatravel.com.* **Polos Tours.** This agency handles all travel arrangments, from boat tickets to car rentals to excursions, with great efficiency. ⊠ *Next to dockside OTE office, Paros town* ☎ *22840/22333.* **Santorineos Travel Services** ⊠ *Quay, Paros town* ☎ *22840/24245* ⊕ *www.parosweb.com/santorineos-travel-services.* Trips by land and sea, such as a tour around Antiparos, are arranged by Polos Tours. Erkyna Travel runs many excursions by boat, bus, and foot. For yacht and other VIP services, check out Nikos Santorineos's office.

EXPLORING

Like all the bigger islands, Paros is developing too fast. In the last 15 years 2,000 new homes have been built on the island, which has a population of 14,000. Another thousand are underway—and this equals the total number of homes ever built here. You'll understand why: you're likely to want to build a little house here yourself. The overflow of visitors is such that it has now washed up on Paros's sister, Antiparos: this island forgetaway still has an off-the-beaten-track vibe, even though the rich and famous—Tom Hanks is most prominent of them—have discovered it.

PAROIKÍA ΠΑΡΟΣ (ΠΑΡΟΙΚΙΑ)

168 km (91 mi) southeast of Piraeus, 35 km (22 mi) west of Naxos.

First impressions of Paroikía (Paros town), pretty as it is, will not necessarily be positive. The port flashes too much concrete, too many boats dock, and the traffic problem, now that Athenian families bring two

Prince Charles (more than once) and many other architecture buffs have visited the great Church of Our Lady of the Hundred Gates, a proto-Byzantine landmark.

cars and local families own two cars, is insoluble. The waterfront is lined with travel agencies, a multitude of car and motorbike rental agencies, and *"fastfood-adika"*—the Greek word means just what you think it does. Then, if you head east on the harbor road, you'll see a lineup of bars, tourist shops, and coffee shops—many, as elsewhere on the more-prosperous islands, rented by Athenians who come to Paros to capitalize on the huge summer influx. Past them are the fishing-boat dock, a partially excavated ancient graveyard, and the post office; then start the beaches (shaded and overpopular), with their hotels and tavernas.

But go the other way straight into town and you'll find it easy to get lost in the maze of narrow, stone-paved lanes that intersect with the streets of the quiet residential areas. The marble plaza at the town's entrance, finished in 2007, is full of strollers and playing children in the evening (during the day, you can fry eggs on this shadeless space). As you check your laptop (Paroikía is Wi-Fi) along the market street chockablock with tourist shops, you'll begin to traverse the centuries: ahead of you looms the seaside Kastro, the ancient acropolis. In 1207 the Venetians conquered Paros, which joined the Duchy of Naxos, and built their huge marble castle wall out of blocks and columns from three temples. At the crest, next to the church of Saints Constantine and Helen (built in 1689), are the visible foundations of a late-Archaic temple to Athena—the area remains Paros's favorite sunset spot.

Anthemion Museum. At the Anthemion Museum, the Kontogiorgos family has lovingly gathered a large, valuable collection of books, manuscripts, prints, coins, jewels, embroideries, weapons, ceramics, and much more, mostly pertaining to Paros, and lovingly displays it in this house-turned-museum. ✉ *Airport road, before Punta split, Paros town* 📞 *22840/91010* ⊕ *www.e-kyklades.gr* 💲*€4* ☉ *Tues.–Sun. 8:30–2:30.*

Archaeological Museum. The Archaeological Museum contains a large chunk of the famed Parian chronicle, which recorded cultural events in Greece from about 1500 BC until 260 BC (another chunk is in Oxford's Ashmolean Museum). It interests scholars that the historian inscribed detailed information about artists, poets, and playwrights, completely ignoring wars and shifts in government. Some primitive pieces from the Aegean's oldest settlement, Saliagos (an islet between Paros and Antiparos), are exhibited in the same room, on the left. A small room contains Archaic finds from the ongoing excavation at Despotiko—and they are finding a lot. In the large room to the right rests a marble slab depicting the poet Archilochus in a banquet scene, lying on a couch, his weapons nearby. The ancients ranked Archilochus, who invented iambic meter and wrote the first signed love lyric, second only to Homer. When he died in battle against the Naxians, his conqueror was cursed by the oracle of Apollo for putting to rest one of the faithful servants of the muse. Also there are a monumental Nike and three superb pieces found in the last decade: a waist-down kouros, a gorgon with intact wings, and a dancing-girl relief. ✉ *Behind Hundred Doors Church, Paros town* 📞 *22840/21231* 💲*€3* ☉ *Tues.–Sun. 8:30–2:30.*

Fodor's Choice
★
Panayia Ekatontapyliani (*Hundred Doors Church*). The square above the port, to the northwest, was built to celebrate the church's 1,700th anniversary. From there note a white wall with two belfries, the front of the former monastic quarters that surround the magnificent Panayia Ekatontapyliani, the earliest remaining proto-Byzantine church in Greece and one of the oldest unaltered churches in the world. As such, it is of inestimable value to architecture buffs (such as Prince Charles, who has been spotted here).

The story began in 326, when St. Helen—the mother of Emperor Constantine the Great—set out on a ship for the Holy Land to find the True Cross. Stopping on Paros, she had a vision of success and vowed to build a church there. Though she died before it was built, her son built the church in 328 as a wooden-roof basilica. Two centuries later, Justinian the Great (who ruled the Byzantine Empire in 527–65) commissioned the splendid dome.

According to legend, 99 doors have been found in the church and the 100th will be discovered only after Constantinople is Greek again—but the name is actually older than the legend. Inside, the subdued light mixes with the dun, reddish, and green tufa (porous volcanic rock). The columns are classical and their capitals Byzantine. At the corners of the dome are two fading Byzantine frescoes depicting six-winged seraphim. The 4th-century iconostasis (with ornate later additions) is divided into five frames by marble columns. One panel contains the 14th-century icon of the Virgin, with a silver covering from 1777. The Virgin is carried in procession on the church's crowded feast day, August 15, the Dormition. During Easter services, thousands of rose petals are dropped from the dome upon the singing celebrant. The adjacent **Baptistery,** nearly unique in Greece, also built from the 4th to the 6th century, has a marble font and bits of mosaic floor. The church **museum,** at the right, contains post-Byzantine icons. ✉ *750 feet east of dock, Paros town* ☎ *22840/21243* ◔ *Daily 8 am–10 pm.*

Scorpios Museum. The Scorpios Museum is set next to a garden full of large models of traditional Parian windmills, dovecotes, churches, and other such things, making for an utterly charming setting. It showcases the creations of fisherman Benetos Skiadas, who loves to make detailed models of ships, including his own, and his scrupulous craftsmanship is on view here; you can also order a model of your own design. ✉ *On road to Aliki, just past airport, Paros town* ☎ *22840/91129* ✉ *€2* ◔ *May–Sept., changeable hrs.*

BEACHES

From Paros town, boats leave throughout the day for beaches across the bay: to sandy Marcellos and **Krios** and the quieter **Kaminia. Livadia,** a five-minute walk, is very developed but has shade. In the other direction, Delfini has a club with live music, and Parasporos has two music bars. Sun-lovers note: Paros is ringed with beaches.

WHERE TO EAT

$ ✕ **The Albatross.** This may be Paros' most popular seafood taverna,

SEAFOOD where traditional dishes are particularly well prepared, and it's little

Fodor's Choice wonder that locals linger here late: for two decades, owner Maria Vou-

★ laraki has never served a bad dish. Properly it is an "ouzeri," where one eats mezedes with wine or ouzo, so you'll find there are many small plates to choose from. Here are a few: shrimp saganaki (with cheese) in tomato sauce, skate salad, calamari salad with sun dried tomatoes, various croquettes (the mushroom ones are very tasty), grilled eggplant with three cheeses, and plates of small fry. Fresh fish is available according to weather. To find this place, head for the waterfront just south of the dock. Although opposite the bus terminal, the Albatross has a sunset view. It is open for lunch and supper April through November. ✉ *Waterfront, Paros town* ☎ *22840/21848.*

¢ ✕ **Gelato Sulla Luna.** Many of the evening strollers on the waterfront

FAST FOOD of Paroikía cannot pass this authentic gelateria; their willpower melts faster than the gelato. Denise Marinucci's father made ice cream in New Jersey, and Denise continues the tradition; some of her recipes come from Venice. She makes everything on the premises. Have another scoop. ✉ *Waterfront, Paros town* ☎ *22840/22868* ⊕ *www.parosweb. com/sullaluna* ▭ *No credit cards* ◔ *Closed Dec.–Mar.*

7

$$ ✕**Levantis.** Owner George Mavridis does his own cooking—always a
GREEK good sign. Though this spot looks like a garden taverna and, amaz-
★ ingly, is almost priced like one, the food is sophisticated and eclectic, as
George often returns from winter travels with exotic new recipes. Two
intriguing starters are marinated octopus in a nest of kataifi with fig
and balsamic sauce; and thinly sliced herb-encrusted beef with greens,
onion marmalade, and wasabi oil. Top entrées include yogurt-encrusted
rabbit ragout with olive and eggplant; and grilled sea bass (*lavraki*) in
chickpea, coriander, and olive oil sauce with green rice. ⊠ *Central mar-
ket street, Paros town* ☎ *22840/23613* ⊕ *www.parosweb.com/levantis*
🕓 *Closed Nov.–Apr.*

WHERE TO STAY

For expanded reviews, visit Fodors.com.

$$ 🛏**Bicycle House.** The name comes from the bicycle (of the noted late
★ dancer Vasilis Iakoumis) mounted to the front of this house, which con-
tains three lovely units in a complex that overlooks the sea and sunset,
is surrounded by greenery, and is scrupulously designed in island style
with the addition of modern comforts. **Pros:** small; attractive; friendly.
Cons: only three rooms; walking distance from nowhere. ⊠ *Paros town*
✛ *8 km (5 mi) from Paroikía on airport road* ☎ *22840/92203* ⊕ *www.
paroshome.com/bicyclehouse* 🛏 *3 apartments* 🛆 *In-room: a/c, kitchen,
Wi-Fi* ▭ *No credit cards.*

$ 🛏**Pandrossos Hotel.** If you want a good night's sleep away from the
pulse of Paros town but you don't want to give up shopping, nightlife, restaurants, and cafés, the Pandrossos—built on a hill with a
splendid view overlooking Paros bay—is the best choice. **Pros:** convenience; great views. **Cons:** some of the rooms are on the small side.
⊠ *On hill at southwest edge of Paros town, Ayia Anna, Paros town*
☎ *22840/22903* ⊕ *www.pandrossoshotel.com* 🛏 *41 rooms, 5 suites*
🛆 *In-room: a/c, Internet. In-hotel: restaurant, bar, pool* 🕓 *Closed Nov.–
Mar.* ❙◉❙ *Breakfast.*

$ 🛏**Parian Village.** This shady, quiet hotel at the far edge of Livadia beach
has small rooms, all with balconies or terraces, most with spectacular
views over Paroikía bay. **Pros:** pretty place near the sea; good vistas.
Cons: 15-minute walk to town past crowds in season. ⊠ *25-min sea
walk from center of Paros town* ☎ *22840/23187* ⊕ *www.parianvillage.
gr* 🛏 *28 rooms* 🛆 *In-room: a/c. In-hotel: pool* 🕓 *Closed Nov.–Apr.*
❙◉❙ *Breakfast.*

$ 🛏**Pension Evangelistria.** Voula Maounis's rooms, all with balconies, are
★ usually full of returnees—archaeologists, painters, and the like—who
enjoy its central location near the Hundred Doors Church, olive trees,
and the gracious welcome and inexpensive rates. **Pros:** the perfect budget choice. **Cons:** this is a straight pension, so make sure that's what
you want. ⊠ *Near dock, Paros town* ☎ *22840/21481* 🛏 *9 rooms* 🛆 *In-
room: a/c, kitchen* ▭ *No credit cards.*

NIGHTLIFE AND THE ARTS

MUSIC AND Turn right along the waterfront from the port in Paros town to find
BARS the town's famous bars; then follow your ears. At the far end of the
Paralia is the laser-light-and-disco section of town, which you may want

to avoid. In the younger bars, cheap alcohol, as everywhere in tourist Greece, is often added to the more-colorful drinks.

Pebbles. For a classier alternative to noisy bars, head for Pebbles, which has live jazz, usually on weekends (Greece's best jazz guitarist, Vasilis Rakopoulos, who summers on Paros, likes to drop by with Parian bassist Petros Varthakouris), and overlooks the sunset. ✉ *On Kastro hill, Paros town* ☎ *22840/22283.*

THE ARTS Of all the islands Paros has the liveliest art scene (check *Paros Life* for openings and events), with dozens of galleries and public spaces presenting exhibitions. Many artists, Greek and foreign, live on the island or visit regularly—painters Jane Pack and Neva Bergmann, sculptor Richard King, photographers Stavros Niflis and Elizabeth Carson, mosaicist Angelika Vaxevanidou, filmmaker Ioannis Tritsibidas, and ceramist Stelios Ghikas are just a few—and the Aegean Center has proved a strong stimulant.

Fodor'sChoice **Aegean Center for the Fine Arts.** A small American arts college, the Aegean
★ Center for the Fine Arts hosts readings, concerts, lectures, and exhibitions in its splendidly restored neoclassic mansion. Director John Pack, an American photographer, lives on the island with his family. Since 1966 the center has offered courses (two three-month semesters) in writing, painting, photography, and classical voice training. ✉ *Main cross street to market street, Paros town* ☎ *22840/23287* ⊕ *www. aegeancenter.org.*

Apothiki. Set on an enchanting alley in the historic Kastro area of Paroikía is this former wine storage space; it's worth a visit just for the beauty of its space. Exhibitions, concerts, and lectures go on all year. ✉ *Near bus stop, Paros town* ☎ *22840/28226* ⊕ *www.apothiki.com.*

Archilochos Cultural Society. This association runs a film club in winter and offers concerts, exhibitions, and lectures throughout the year. ✉ *Between dock and post office, Paros town* ☎ *22840/23595* ⊕ *www. archilochos.gr.*

★ **Environmental and Cultural Park of Paros.** Set on a beautiful peninsula, the new Environmental and Cultural Park of Paros, located at Ai Yiannis Deitis on the Bay of Naous, offers a full summer program of concerts in its outdoor theater. Lectures, ecological talks, marked and labled pathways through the park's peninsula, a café, a beautiful church, and a protected beach for swimming all contribute to the natural preserve's splendor. ⊕ *www.parkoparos.gr.*

Holland Tunnel Gallery. Paulien Lethen's Holland Tunnel Gallery has its main space in Brooklyn. The Paros space, open in summer, is set in a whitewashed town house and has a fine stable of international artists with a Paros connection. Dutch jazz singer and pianist Heleen Schuttevaer, usually performs at openings. ✉ *Market street, Paros town* ☎ *22840/22195* ⊕ *www.hollandtunnelgallery.com.*

SPORTS AND THE OUTDOORS

WATER Many beaches offer water sports, especially windsurfing.
SPORTS
Aegean Diving College. Offering scuba lessons that take you to reefs, shipwrecks, and caves, the Aegean Diving College is headed by director

Peter Nicolaides, who discovered the oldest shipwreck known and is a marine biologist involved in many of Greece's ecological projects. ⊠ *Golden beach, Paros town* ✆ *22840/43347* ⊕ *www.aegeandiving.gr.*

F2 Windsurfing Center. Every summer the F2 Windsurfing Center hosts the International Windsurfing World Cup. ⊠ *New Golden beach, at Philoxenia Hotel, near Marpissa, Paros town* ☎ *22840/41878.*

SHOPPING

CERAMICS **Yria Interiors.** On the market street, look for the house with the beautifully carved Parian marble facade to find Paros's most elegantly designed shop. Here, Stelios Ghikas, Monique Mailloux, and daughter Ramona display their pottery from Studio Yria, as well as a carefully chosen range of stylish household items mostly from France. ⊠ *Start of market street, Paros town* ☎ *22840/24359* ⊕ *www.yriaparos.com.*

JEWELRY **Jewelry Workshop.** Vangelis Skaramagas and Yannis Xenos, uncle and nephew, have been making their own delicate, precious jewelry at Jewelry Workshop for more than 20 years. ⊠ *End of market street, Paros town* ☎ *22840/21008.*

Phaidra. Local Phaidra Apostolopoulou, who studied jewelry in Athens, has a tiny shop, Phaidra, where she shows her sophisticated gold designs, and a line of lighthearted pieces for summer. ⊠ *Near Zoodochos Pyghi church, Paros town* ☎ *22840/23626.*

LOCAL FOODS **Enosis** (*Agricultural Cooperative's shop*). Also known as the Farmers' Cooperative, Enosis sells homemade pasta, honey, cheeses, and especially Paros's renowned wines. The varietal wine Monemvasia (officially rated "Appellation of High Quality Origin Paros") is made from white monemvasia grapes, indigenous to Paros. You can visit the winery for an evocative slide show, a photography exhibition of Paros's agricultural traditions, and a wine tasting. For an appointment call Alexis Gokas (*22840/22235*). ⊠ *Mando Mavrogenous Sq. at front of Paros town under police station, Paros town* ☎ *22820/22181.*

EN ROUTE **Monastery of Longovarda.** Halfway from Paros town to Naousa, on the right, the 17th-century Monastery of Longovarda shines on its mountainside. The monastic community farms the local land and makes honey, wine, and olive oil. Only men, dressed in conservative clothing, are allowed inside, where there are post-Byzantine icons, 17th-century frescoes depicting the Twelve Feasts in the Life of Christ, and a library of rare books; it is usually open mornings. ☎ *22840/21202.*

NAOUSA ΝΑΟΥΣΑ

★ *10 km (6 mi) northeast of Paroikía.*

Naousa, impossibly pretty, long ago discovered the benefits of tourism. Its outskirts are mushrooming with villas and hotels that exploit it further. Along the harbor—which thankfully maintains its beauty and function as a fishing port—red and navy blue boats knock gently against one another as men repair their nets and foreigners relax in the ouzeri—Barbarossa being the traditional favorite—by the water's edge. From here the pirate Hugue Crevelliers operated in the 1570s, and Byron turned him into the corsair. Navies of the ancient Persians, flotillas from medieval Venice, and the imperial Russian fleet have anchored in this harbor. The half-submerged ruins of the Venetian fortifications still remain; they are a pretty sight when lighted up at night. Compared to Paroikía, the scene in Naousa is somewhat more chic, with a more-intimate array of shops, bars, and restaurants, but in winter the town shuts down. Unobtrusive Paros's gay scene is here, if it is anywhere.

Folklore Museum. Naousa's small Folklore Museum, 150 yards from the main town square, is in a traditional house given by Kanstantinos and Marouso Roussos. It exhibits folk costumes from around Greece, but especially Paros. The furniture and implements are also historic. ☏ 22840/52284.

BEACHES

Lageri. A boat goes regularly to Lageri, a long, sandy beach with dunes. ✉ *North of Naousa* .

Santa Maria. The boat that goes to Lageri also travels to Santa Maria, popular with families for its shallows and sand. ✉ *Northeastern shore of Paros* .

Kolimbithres. A boat crosses the bay to Kolimbithres, noted for its anfractuous rock formations, water sports, a choice of tavernas, and two luxury hotels. Head to the top of nearby Koukounaries Hill to view the remains of an ancient site. ✉ *Directly across bay from Naousa.*

Agios Ioánnis. Served by the Kolimbithres boat, Agios Ioánnis is attached to the Eco Park, and kept clean and quiet. ✉ *Across from Naousa.*

WHERE TO EAT

$$$ **✗ Mario.** Good food is enhanced here by the pretty location, a few feet
GREEK from the fishing boats on Naousa's harbor. The taverna specializes in
★ fresh fish (from the fisherman a few feet away), and also fine cuisine. Such starters as tuna carpaccio with aromatic oil and smoked salt, and grilled octopus with bucovo and caper sauce segue to complex entrées like seafood pasta with diced asparagus and saffron, or fresh fish baked in a salt crust (order this in advance). For dessert, try the traditional spoon sweets made by Mario's mother. ✉ *On fishing-boat harbor, Naousa* ☏ 22840/51047 ✉ tsach00@hotmail.com ⊕ www. mario-restaurant.gr ⚲ *Reservations essential.*

$ **✗ Pervolaria.** "An enclosed garden" is the translation of this restaurant's
GREEK Greek name and, indeed, this family tavern is found to be shady and quiet since it resides underneath a lush pergola. A good starter is fava with carmelized onions and capers. As for main dishes, Perivolaria is best known for its pork shank flavored with sage and roasted in a wood oven; another top choice would be the handmade tortellini stuffed with local cheese, spinach, and fresh tomatoes. The homemade *bougatsa* (custard in phyllo) is an exceptional desert. Pervolaria can be entered from the parking riverbed or from a pretty back street. ✉ *Naousa* ☏ 22840/51721 ⊕ www.pervolaria.gr.

$$$$ **✗ Poseidon.** Eat here for elegant dining away from the fray, on a spacious
MEDITERRANEAN terrace with two pools, dozens of palm trees, and the bay of Naousa in front of you. The vegetables are from their own garden, the fish is fresh, and the food has a Mediterranean accent. Top starters? Opt for the agnolotti, forest mushrooms, and prosciutto in a cream sauce, or

Grecian formula: fishing boats, a friendly taverna, great seafood, and a sunset glow add up to wonderful memories.

beef (fresh from France) carpaccio in a crush of herbs and spices with arugula and Parmesan. An excellent main course would be the rack of aromatic lamb with new potatoes and spinach in a merlot-mint sauce. If you can still manage dessert (you will want to sit here a long time), try the chocolate indulgence cake. The lower terrace serves Chinese food. ⊠ *Astir Hotel, Kolimbithres, Naousa* ☎ *22840/51976* ⊕ *www. astirofparos.gr* ☉ *Closed Nov.–Apr.*

WHERE TO STAY
For expanded reviews, visit Fodors.com.

$$$$
Fodor'sChoice
★

Astir of Paros. Across the bay from Naousa twinkle the lights of this deluxe resort hotel, a graceful and expensive retreat (expensive for Paros, not for Mykonos), with green lawns, tall palm trees, extensive subtropical gardens, and an art gallery—and, yes, this luxury hotel fully deserves its superlative reputation. **Pros:** beautiful and elegant. **Cons:** you need a vehicle to get anywhere. ⊠ *Take Kolimbithres road from Naousa* ☎ *22840/51976, 22840/51984* ⊘ *astir@otenet.gr* ⊕ *www.astirofparos. gr* ⇆ *11 rooms, 46 suites* ⚭ *In-room: a/c, Internet. In-hotel: restaurant, bar, pool, tennis court* ☉ *Closed Nov.–Mar.* ⦿| *Breakfast.*

$

Svoronos Bungalows. The best budget choice in Naousa, these bungalow apartments always seem to be fully occupied. **Pros:** convenient; quiet; green. **Cons:** there is no air-conditioning, but it is cool. ⊠ *Behind big church, 1 block in from Santa Maria Rd., Naousa* ☎ *22849/51211, 22840/51409* ⊘ *svoronosbungalows@gmail.com* ⊕ *www.parosweb.gr/ svoronos* ⇆ *19 apartments* ⚭ *In-room: no a/c, kitchen, no TV. In-hotel: bar* ☉ *Closed Nov.–Apr.*

NIGHTLIFE AND THE ARTS

BARS **Agosta.** This occupies one of the town's prettiest spots. ✉ *At fishing harbor, Naousa.*

Linardo's. This is one of those sizzling nightspots that open late and close early. ✉ *At fishing harbo, Naousa.*

DANCE **Music–Dance "Naousa Paros."** The group Music–Dance "Naousa Paros," formed in 1988 to preserve the traditional dances and music of Paros, performs all summer long in Naousa in the costumes of the 16th century and has participated in dance competitions and festivals throughout Europe. Keep an eye out for posters; the schedule is online. ☎ *22840/52284.*

SPORTS AND THE OUTDOORS

Aqua Paros Waterpark. If you're traveling with children, Aqua Paros Waterpark, with its 13 waterslides big and small, will cool a hot afternoon. Admission is €14. ✉ *Kolimbithres, next to Porto Paros Hotel, Naousa* ☎ *22840/53264.*

Santa Maria Surf Club. Popular with sports lovers, thanks to the fine facilities offered for windsurfing, Jet Skiing, waterskiing, and diving. ✉ *Santa Maria beach, about 4 km [2½ mi] north of Naousa* ☎ *22840/52490.*

SHOPPING

ART AND Paros is an art colony and exhibits are everywhere in summer. It is also
JEWELRY home to quite a few creative jewelers.

Nid D'Or. A small shop, Nid D'Or showcases two lines: one is a collection by owner Aliki Meremetis, featuring rough cut semiprecious stones; the second is by other Greek jewelers, such as Katerina Kotsaki. ✉ *On second street from harbor toward main church, Naousa* ☎ *22840/51775.*

FASHION **Tango.** Kostas Mouzedakis's stylish shop has been selling classic sportswear for two decades; its most popular line is its own Tangowear. ✉ *On second street from harbor toward main church, Naousa* ☎ *22840/51014.*

MARATHI ΜΑΡΑΘΙ

10 km (6 mi) east of Paros town.

During the classical period the island of Paros had an estimated 150,000 residents, many of them slaves who worked the ancient marble quarries in Marathi. The island grew rich from the export of this white, granular marble known among ancient architects and sculptors for its ability to absorb light. They called it *lychnites* ("won by lamplight").

Three Caverns. Marked by a sign, three caverns are bored into the hillside, the largest of them 300 feet deep. Here is where the world-famed Parian marble was mined. The most recent quarrying done in these mines was in 1844, when a French company cut marble here for Napoléon's tomb. ✉ *Short walk from main road, Marathi.*

SHOPPING

★ **Studio Yria.** At Studio Yria master potters Stelios Ghikas and Monique Mailloux and other craftspeople can be seen at work. Marble carvers, metalsmiths, painters, and more all make for a true Renaissance workshop. Both the ceramic tableware and the works of art make use of Byzantine and Cycladic motifs in their designs; they have even made ceramic designs for the prince of Wales. Easily accessible by bus, taxi, and rental car, the studio is usually open daily 8–8; call ahead in the off-season. ⊹ *1½ km [¾ mi] east of Marathi, above road to Kostos village* ☎ *22840/53573* ⊕ *www.yriaparos.com.*

LEFKES ΛΕΥΚΕΣ

6 km (4 mi) south of Marathi, 10 km (6 mi) southeast of Paros town.

Rampant piracy in the 17th century forced thousands of people to move inland from the coastal regions; thus for many years the scenic village of Lefkes, built on a hillside in the protective mountains, was the island's capital. It remains the largest village in the interior and has maintained a peaceful, island feeling, with narrow streets fragrant of jasmine and honeysuckle. These days, the old houses are being restored, and in summer the town is full of people. Farming is the major source of income, as you can tell from the well-kept stone walls and olive groves. For one of the best walks on Paros, take the ancient Byzantine road from the main lower square to the lower villages.

Two **17th-century churches** of interest are **Ayia Varvara** (St. Barbara) and **Ayios Sotiris** (Holy Savior).

The big 1830 neo-Renaissance **Ayia Triada** (Holy Trinity) is the pride of the village.

BEACHES

Piso Livadi. The ancient port for the marble quarries, Piso Livadi today is a small resort town convenient to many beaches; the harbor, where boats leave for Naxos and Delos, is being expanded. ✉ *On road past Lefkes, Piso Livadi.*

Lageri. This long stretch of sand has a nicely convenient taverna.

Pounda Beach. Youth-crazed Pounda Beach rocks and rolls; adults beware. ✉ *On road past Piso Livadi, Lefkes.*

WHERE TO EAT AND STAY

For expanded hotel reviews, visit Fodors.com.

$ ✗ **Taverna Klarinos.** You go to Nikos and Anna Ragousis's place for the
GREEK   real thing. Nikos grows the vegetables, raises the meat, makes the cheese (even the feta) from his own goats, and makes the wine from his own vineyards; Anna cooks. Traditional dishes such as fried zucchini or beets with garlic sauce are the best you'll taste, and the grilled meats make the gods envious. ✉ *Main entrance street, opposite square, on 2nd fl., Lefkes* ☎ *22840/41608* ▱ No credit cards ☽ *Closed Oct.–May.*

$ **Lefkes Village.** All the rooms in this elegant hotel are white, and the
★ wooden furniture and fabrics are reproductions of traditional styles;
all have balconies with magnificent views down the olive-tree valley
and over the sea to Naxos. Pros: village style upgraded. Cons: Lefkes
is far from the sea. ⊠ *East of Lefkes on main road* ☎ *22840/41827*
✉ *lefkesvl@otenet.gr* ⊕ *www.lefkesvillage.gr* ⇆ *20 rooms* ⟡ *In-room:*
a/c. In-hotel: restaurant, bar, pool ۞ *Closed Nov.–Mar.* ⟉*Breakfast.*

SHOPPING

WEAVINGS **Anemi.** On the main street at the lower café square, Angela Chanioti's
shop sells particularly fine handwoven bedspreads, towels, and the like
(some of silk). They are colored with natural dyes and use local designs.
Also for sale are iron pieces made by her grandfather, once Lefkes's
blacksmith. ☎ *22840/41182* ⊕ *www.anemi-lefkes.g.*

PETALOUDES PARK ΠΕΤΑΛΟΥΔΕΣ

4 km (2½ mi) south of Paros town.

Petaloudes Park. The Jersey tiger moth returns year after year to mate
in Petaloudes (Butterflies Valley), a lush oasis of greenery in the middle
of this dry island. In May, June, and perhaps July, you can watch them
as they lie dormant during the day, their chocolate-brown wings with
yellow stripes still against the ivy leaves. In the evening they flutter
upward to the cooler air, flashing the coral red undersides of their
wings as they rise. A notice at the entrance asks visitors not to disturb
them by taking photographs or shaking the leaves. ⊠ *Petaloudes* ⊡ *€3*
۞ *Mid-May–mid-Sept., daily 9–8.*

7

NEED A
BREAK? **Kafeneio (*coffeehouse*). Even when the butterflies are not there, it is pleasant to have coffee in the small kafeneio and enjoy the shade of the cypress,
olive, chestnut, mulberry, and lemon trees.** ⊠ *Inside entrance to Petaloudes*
Park.

Venetian Tower. On the summit of a hill beyond the garden reigns a
lopped Venetian tower. Its founder's name, Iakovos Alisafis, and the
date, 1626, are inscribed on it.

WHERE TO EAT

$$$ ✕**Thea.** From the terrace of this fine restaurant you can enjoy the view
GREEK over the Antiparos Strait and the little ferries that ply it. The interior
★ is all of wood and hundreds of bottles of wine shelved from floor to
high ceiling. Owner Nikos Kouroumlis is, in fact, a wine fanatic, and
Thea has the third most extensive wine list in all of Greece; his own
wine is excellent. In winter, a good bottle of the grape and a warm fire
keep Thea popular. Nikos and family hail from northern Greece and
Constantinople and so does their food: Caesaria pie, hot and spicy with
cheeses, salted meat, and tomatoes; Cappodocian lamb, cooked with
dried apricots; or one of their famous T-bone steaks. Save room for
one of the traditional Greek sweets, especially the *ekmek* pastry served
up with mastic ice cream. Reservations are recommended in summer.
⊠ *Pounta* ☎ *22840/91220* ✉ *nikos@theaparos.gr.*

EN ROUTE

Christos sto Dasos (*Christ in the Wood*). A 15-minute walk or 2-minute drive back toward Paros town from the Valley of the Butterflies leads to the convent known as Christos sto Dasos, from where there's a marvelous view of the Aegean. The convent contains the tomb of St. Arsenios (1800–77), who was a schoolteacher, an abbot, and a prophet. He was also a rainmaker whose prayers were believed to have ended a long drought, saving Paros from starvation. The nuns are a bit leery of tourists. If you want to go in, be sure to wear long pants or skirt and a shirt that covers your shoulders, or the sisters will turn you away.

> **BEACHCOMBERS' PARADISE**
>
> Pounta is not even a village, just a few houses, three restaurants (one fine one), and a tiny harbor, whence the ferries leave for Antiparos. The road that turns left just before you get there continues on to many beaches. And beyond— it is a beautiful drive—are the peaceful harbor towns of Aliki and Dryos, both with fine beaches and restaurants, especially Faragas, now overdeveloped. Beyond Dryos toward Naousa are the windsurfers' long beaches, Golden beach and New Golden beach.

ANTIPAROS ΑΝΤΙΠΑΡΟΣ

Fodor's Choice ★ *5 km (2 mi) southwest of Paroikía.*

This smaller, sister isle of Paros may have once been the best little secret of the Cyclades but thanks to such gilt-edged visitors as Brad Pitt, Tom Hanks, and Sean Connery, everybody now knows about this pretty little forgetaway. And let's not forget the fact that this green, inhabited islet belongs to the famously rich Goulandris family, benefactors of the Goulandris Cycladic Museum in Athens (and much else). As a result of all this glamour, Antiparos is developing all too rapidly. A great source of information about Antiparos, with a complete listing of hotels, can be found at ⊕ *www.antiparos-isl.gr.*

Twenty-five years ago you went to the Paros hamlet of Pounta, went to the church, opened its door (as a signal), and waited for a fishing caïque to chug over. Now, 30 car ferries ply the channel all day and a lovely seven-minute ride wafts you from Paros (from Pounta; the ride from Paroikía takes about 20 minutes) to Antiparos. A causeway once crossed the Antiparos Strait, which would be swimmable but for the current, and on one of its still emergent islets, Saliagos, habitations and objects have been found dating back almost to 5000 BC.

Antiparos's one town, also called Antiparos, has a main street and two centers of activity: the quay area and the main square, a block or two in. At both are restaurants and cafés. To the right of the square are houses and the Kastro's 15th-century wall. At the other end of the quay from the ferry dock a road goes to an idyllic sandy beach (it is 10 minutes by foot); you can wade across to the islet opposite, Fira, where sheep and goats graze.

In the 19th century the most famous sight in the Aegean was the **Antiparos cave** (9 km [5½ mi] from town), and it still deservedly attracts hundreds of visitors a year. Four hundred steps descend into huge chambers, pass beneath enormous pipe-organ stalactites, and skirt immense stalagmites. In 1673 the French ambassador famously celebrated Christmas Mass here with 500 guests, who feasted for three days. Look for Lord Byron's autograph. Outside is the church of Agios Ioánnis Spiliótis, built in 1774.

It is pleasant to go around to the other side of Antiparos on the good road to Ayios Georgios, where there are three excellent taverns, perfect after a swim. On request a boat will take you to the nearby islet of **Despotikon,** uninhabited except for seasonal archaeologists excavating a late-Archaic marble temple complex to Apollo. In autumn the hills are fragrant with purple flowering heather.

WHERE TO EAT AND STAY

For expanded hotel reviews, visit Fodors.com.

$$ ✕ **Akrogiali.** Far from the madding crowd, you sit and look across the
GREEK strait to the sacred isle of Despotikon, and, after a swim, eat the fish from right here. The bells you hear belong to the goats of the Pipinos family (yes, they occasionally end up on the table here). Vegetables come from the garden. This is one of three good restaurants by the little dock. ☎ *22840/22107* ▭ *No credit cards* ⊘ *Closed Oct.–Apr.*

$ ⌂ **Kouros Village Hotel.** The hotels on Antiparos tend to be simple, pleasant places to stay near the beach, and this two-story building, which offers a series of rooms, apartments, and suites, most overlooking a pool and beautiful Antiparos bay, nicely fits the bill. **Pros:** attractive, convenient option; has all the usual amenities; balconies and terraces have fine seaviews. **Cons:** you have to want to be in a busy port. ⊠ *Antiparos harbor* ☎ *22840/61084* ⊕ *www.kouros-village.gr* ⌨ *5 rooms, 10 apartments, 5 suites* ⚘ *In-room: a/c, kitchen. In-hotel: restaurant, pool* ⊘ *Closed mid-Oct.–mid-Apr.*

SANTORINI (THIRA) ΣΑΝΤΟΡΙΝΗ (ΘΗΡΑ)

235 km (128 nautical mi) southeast of Piraeus harbor in Athens.

Undoubtedly the most extraordinary island in the Aegean, crescent-shape Santorini remains a mandatory stop on the Cycladic tourist route—even if it's necessary to enjoy the sensational sunsets from Ia, the fascinating excavations, and the dazzling white towns with a million other travelers. Called Kállisti (the "Loveliest") when first settled, the island has now reverted to its subsequent name of Thira, after the 9th-century-BC Dorian colonizer Thiras. The place is better known, however, these days as Santorini, a name derived from its patroness, St. Irene of Thessaloniki, the Byzantine empress who restored icons to Orthodoxy and died in 802.

You can fly conveniently to Santorini, but to enjoy a true Santorini rite of passage, opt instead for the boat trip here, which provides a spectacular introduction. After the boat sails between Sikinos and Ios, your deck-side perch approaches two close islands with a passage between them. The bigger one on the left is Santorini, and the smaller on the right is Thirassia. Passing between them, you see the village of Ia adorning Santorini's northernmost cliff like a white geometric beehive. You are in the caldera (volcanic crater), one of the world's truly breathtaking sights: a demilune of cliffs rising 1,100 feet, with the white clusters of the towns of Fira and Ia perched along the top. The bay, once the high center of the island, is 1,300 feet in some places, so deep that when boats dock in Santorini's shabby little port of Athinios, they do not drop anchor. The encircling cliffs are the ancient rim of a still-active volcano, and you are sailing east across its flooded caldera. On your right are the Burnt isles, the White isle, and other volcanic remnants, all lined up as if some outsize display in a geology museum. Hephaestus's subterranean fires smolder still—the volcano erupted in 198 BC, about 735, and there was an earthquake in 1956.

Indeed, Santorini and its four neighboring islets are the fragmentary remains of a larger landmass that exploded about 1600 BC: the volcano's core blew sky high, and the sea rushed into the abyss to create the great bay, which measures 10 km by 7 km (6 mi by 4½ mi) and is 1,292 feet deep. The other pieces of the rim, which broke off in later eruptions, are Thirassia, where a few hundred people live, and deserted little Aspronissi ("White isle"). In the center of the bay, black and uninhabited, two cones, the Burnt Isles of Palea Kameni and Nea Kameni, appeared between 1573 and 1925.

There has been too much speculation about the identification of Santorini with the mythical Atlantis, mentioned in Egyptian papyri and by Plato (who says it's in the Atlantic), but myths are hard to pin down. *(For the full scoop, see our special photo feature, "Santorini: The Lost Atlantis?" in this chapter.)* This is not true of old arguments about whether tidal waves from Santorini's cataclysmic explosion destroyed Minoan civilization on Crete, 113 km (70 mi) away. The latest carbon-dating evidence, which points to a few years before 1600 BC for the eruption, clearly indicates that the Minoans outlasted the eruption by a couple of hundred years, but most probably in a weakened state. In fact, the island still endures hardships: since antiquity, Santorini has depended on rain collected in cisterns for drinking and irrigating—the well water is often brackish—and the serious shortage is alleviated by the importation of water. However, the volcanic soil also yields riches: small, intense tomatoes with tough skins used for tomato paste (good restaurants here serve them); the famous Santorini fava beans, which have a light, fresh taste; barley; wheat; and white-skin eggplants.

GETTING HERE AND AROUND

AIR TRAVEL   The bay of Santorini is one of the world's great sights, and an incoming flight—45 minutes—gives a unique view of it. There are 12 daily flights, shared by Olympic Airlines, Athens Airways, and Aegean Airlines. There are also flights from Thessaloniki. Reservations, the earlier the better, are essential. Check ⊕ *www.aia.gr.*

BOAT TRAVEL   Six daily boats from Athens's port of Piraeus ply the wine-dark Aegean to Santorini. The trip takes from to four to 10 hours, depending on route, boat, and the weather. Try to make sure your boat enters the harbor before sunset, since this is a spectacular sight, one crucial to savoring Santorini's vibe. There are also daily connections to Paros, Naxos, and Anafi, and there are regular summer connections to Folegandros,

Crete, Ios, Karpathos, Kasos, Amorgos, Kea, Kimolos, Kos, Koufonisi, Kythnos, Milos, Mykonos, and Rhodes. Reservations are needed in summer and at Easter, for cars all year. The port town, Ormos Athinios, is only that, and you must proceed by vehicle to your destination. Buses generally meet the boats, and the drive up the volcano-cut cliff is amazing. For schedules check ⊕ *www.openseas.gr* and for everything else go to ⊕ *www.greeka.com*. The **Santorini Port Authority** (☎ *22860/22239*) sometimes gives detailed information.

BUS TRAVEL Buses leave from the main station in central Fira (✉ *Deorgala* ☎ *22890/ 25404*) just south of the town's main square. In high season, there are hourly buses for Akrotiri and buses on the half-hour for Ia, Monolithos (airport), Kamari, and Perissa. Buses also connect with the main port of Athinios (at least a half-hour ride) as well as the popular Perissa and Kamari beaches. Schedules are posted; hotel concierges should also have this info. Fares run from €1.50 to €4. As might be expected, Santorini's buses can be as crowded as those of rush-hour Athens, so step lively! The main taxi station (☎ *22860/22555*) is near Fira's central square on 25th of March Street. Connecting Fira with the harbor port of Fira Skala is the island's famed cable-car route; there are departures every 20 minutes, 7 am to 10 pm; €4, plus extra charge for luggage. With its spectacular vistas, this is a must-do (a must-don't are the donkey treks up the cliff), even if you're not using the port facilities.

Visitor Information and Travel/Tour Agencies Nomikos Travel. This agency has tours to the main sights along with some off-the-beaten-path attractions, including the island's wineries and the Monastery of Profitis Ilias. ✉ *Fira* ☎ *22860/23660* ⊕ *www.nomikosvillas.gr.*

Pelican Travel. This popular agency runs coach tours, wine tastings, and visits to Ia; it also has daily boat trips to the volcano and Thirassia (half day €20, full day by sailboat €45) and arranges private tours. ✉ *Fira* ☎ *22860/22220* ⊕ *www.pelican.gr.*

EXPLORING

These days, unrestrained tourism has taken a heavy toll on Santorini. Fira, and now Ia, could almost be described as "a street with 40 jewelry shops"; many of the natives are completely burned out by the end of the peak season (the best times to come here are shoulder periods); and, increasingly, business and the loud ringing of cash registers have disrupted the normal flow of Greek life here. For example, if a cruise ship comes in during afternoon siesta, all shops immediately open. And you will have a pushy time walking down Fira's main street in August, so crowded is it. Still and all, if you look beneath the layers of gimcrack tourism, you'll find Greek splendor. No wonder Greece's two Nobel poets, George Seferis and Odysseus Elytis, wrote poems about it. For you, too, will be "watching the rising islands / watching the red islands sink" (Seferis) and consider, "With fire with lava with smoke / You found the great lines of your destiny" (Elytis).

7

Continued on page 368

SANTORINI
The Lost Atlantis?

Did Atlantis, "the island at the center of the earth," ever really exist? And if it did, where? Big-budget Hollywood films have placed it in the middle of the Atlantic Ocean. Several historians think it was located in the Bay of Naples; others that it was a Sumerian island in the Persian Gulf, or a sunken island in the Straits of Gibraltar. Nowadays, more and more experts are making a case for the island of Santorini—and therein lies a tale.

WHOLE LOTTA LAVA

Imagine: A land called Atlantis, with a vast, spectacular city adorned with hanging gardens, gigantic palaces, and marble colossi of Poseidon, ancient god of the sea. One fateful day, more than 3,500 years ago, an enormous earthquake triggers a cataclysmic volcano that destroys the capital. In the space of a few hours, a towering tidal wave washes all traces of this civilization into a fiery cauldron. All, that is, except for a rocky fragment framing a watery caldera. Historical detectives, archaeologists, and volcanologists have long wondered whether Greece's fabled isle of Santorini could be that last remnant of Atlantis. But is this theory more fable than fact?

For those who consider Atlantis merely a symbol or metaphor, the question is not important. Surfacing like a rising island in a deep bay, the notion of a Golden Age is ever-present in the human imagination, and the Atlantis story is among our most durable and poignant ideas of it. Reverberating through Western culture and dazzling the mind, the name "Atlantis" glitters with glamour; it titles hotels, Web sites, towns, submarines, book and film companies, even a pop song by Donovan. But historians today remain divided on whether Atlantis was a funtastic shooting-star of history or just a legend with a moral lesson.

PLATO VERSUS THE VOLCANO

Plato (427–347 BC), the most fearless, and the most substantive writer, of all the ancient Greek philosophers, would have supported the latter option. He liked to end his famous Dialogues with a myth, and Atlantis shows up in both his "Timaeus" and his "Critias," as a parable (and history?) of good and bad government. Plato says that the great 6th-century lawgiver–poet of Athens, Solon (630–560 BC), went to Egypt, and there heard stories of Atlantis. They told him that 9,000 years ago Athens defeated the empire of Atlantis, a huge island in the Atlantic Ocean, in battle.

View of Santorini's caldera

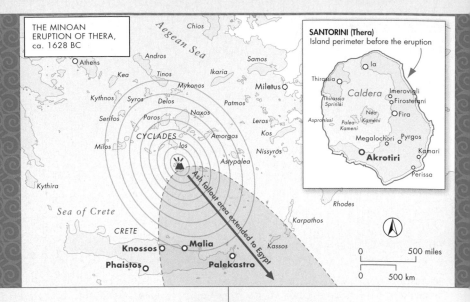

THE MINOAN ERUPTION OF THERA, ca. 1628 BC

Aegean Sea

Chios

Athens
Andros
Samos
Kea
Tinos
Ikaria
Mykonos
Miletus
Kythnos
Syros
Delos
Serifos
Paros
Naxos
Patmos
Leros
CYCLADES
Amorgos
Kos
Milos
Ios
Nissyros
Astypalea

Kythira

Sea of Crete

CRETE

Knossos
Malia
Phaistos
Palekastro
Kassos
Karpathos
Rhodes

Ash fallout area extended to Egypt

SANTORINI (Thera)
Island perimeter before the eruption

Thirassia
Ia
Caldera
Imerovigli
Thirassia Sprintsi
Firostefani
Nea Kameni
Fira
Aspronissi
Palea Kameni
Megalochori
Pyrgos
Akrotiri
Kamari
Perissa

0   500 miles
0   500 km

Then a natural cataclysm destroyed the island in one day, "and Atlantis disappeared in the sea depths." Atlantis was created by and belonged to Poseidon, god of the sea and of earthquakes, and he made it a paradise ruled by his son, King Atlas, with the guidance of wise counselors. When later generations on the island abandoned his prudent ways, catastrophe struck: you mustn't love power more than you love the gods. The Bible had Sodom and Gomorrah; Plato had Atlantis.

Some authors claim the story of Atlantis is history, not fantasy. They believe that Solon misread 9,000 years as 900. If so, Atlantis would have flourished at the same time as Santorini, which, as we know and the classical Greeks suspected, was destroyed by earthquakes followed by a cataclysmic volcanic eruption, probably just before 1600 BC—some historians point to the date of 1628 BC.

THE MINOAN CONNECTION

In the late 1960s, when archaeologist Spyridon Marinatos's excavations of Santorini's caldera revealed the ruin of Akrotiri, preserved under 25 feet of volcanic ash, the island's claim to be Atlantis began to outweigh all others. The buried town had been large, comfortable, and attractive, the art beautiful and gentle, and its high Bronze Age civilization resembled Minoan Crete's, 47 miles south. Since a tsunami from the volcano must have devastated the larger island, it is not surprising that Crete, whose dimensions chime better with Plato's, is also called Atlantis.

Crete and its satellite, Santorini (don't call it this to a Santorini scholar, but it's true), were "feminine" civilizations. They worshipped the goddess of fertility; disliked depictions of war and weapons; kept their towns unwalled; loved magnificent jewelry; and their art eschews the monumental for spontaneous natural forms, such as swallows,

Imaginary view of Santorini's submerged volcano in eruption in 1866; (below) Akrotiri frescoes.

octopi, dolphins, and palm trees. They liked pretty people. The women's elaborate costumes exposed their breasts, and the men, nearly naked, wore gold jewelry and fancy hairstyles. They worshipped not in temples, but in caves, springs, and mountaintops. From our sparse evidence, it seems it was indeed a golden age, when "the earth bore freely all the aromatic substances it bears today, roots, herbs, bushes and gums exuded by flowers or fruit." Perfume was as popular here as in Egypt. A mural preserved in Athens from Akrotiri shows blue monkeys opening doors à la Wizard of Oz. Plato, the stern taskmaster, would probably have disapproved.

. . . ET TU, SANTORINI?

Today, archaeological excavation continues at Akrotiri, situated high—1,300 feet—over the whitecaps of the Aegean Sea. What was Santorini like when the great bay was terra firma, lush with olive trees and abundant harvests? Santorini's own Prehistoric Museum is studying the possibilities, as the writings of historians, poets, and philosophers provide food for thought. The fact remains that the evidence is not all in: there is a possibility that Santorini could, in fact, reawaken from its long slumber and once again erupt, and then subside again. The key to Atlantis's existence may lie in the once and future fury of this fascinating island.

FIRA ΦHPA

76 km (47 mi) southeast of Paros, 10 km (6 mi) west of the Santorini airport, 14 km (8½ mi) southeast of Ia.

To experience life here as it was until only a couple of decades ago, walk down the much-photographed, winding **staircase** that descends from town to the water's edge—walk or take the spectacular **cable car** ride back up, avoiding the drivers who will try to plant you on the sagging back of one of their bedraggled-looking mules. It soon becomes clear what brings the tourists here: with its white, cubical houses clinging to the cliff hundreds of feet above the caldera, Fira is a beautiful place.

Of course, tourism, the island's major industry, adds more than 1 million visitors per year to a population of 7,000. As a result, Fira, the capital, midway along the west coast of the east rim, is no longer only a picturesque village but a major tourist center, overflowing with bars, shops, and restaurants. Many of its employees, East Europeans or young travelers extending their summer vacations, hardly speak Greek. Visually, however, Fira remains an exhilarating Greek extravaganza.

Archaeological Museum. This fascinating squint into the island's millenia of history offers displays of pottery, statues, and grave artifacts found at excavations mostly from ancient Thira and Akrotiri, from the Minoan through the Byzantine periods. ⊠ *Stavrou and Nomikos, Mitropoleos, behind big church, Fira* 🕾 *22860/22217* 🖃 *€2* ☉ *Tues.–Sun. 8:30–3.*

Eikostis Pemptis Martiou (*25th of March street*). Along Eikostis Pemptis Martiou, you'll find inexpensive restaurants and accommodations. ⊠ *East of Panayia Ypapantis, Fira.*

Kato Fira (*Lower Fira*). The blocked-off Ypapantis Street (west of Panayia Ypapantis) leads to Kato Fira, built into the cliff side overlooking the caldera, where prices are higher and the vista wonderful. For centuries the people of the island have been digging themselves rooms-with-a-view right in the cliff face—many bars and hotel rooms now occupy the caves.

★ **Museum of Prehistoric Thera.** This is the treasure house that displays pots and frescoes from the famed excavations at Akrotiri. Note the fresco fragments with the painted swallows (who flocked here because they loved the cliffs) and the women in Minoan dresses. The swallows, which still come in spring, remain the island's favorite design motif. The fossilized olive leaves from 60,000 BC prove the olive to be indigenous. ⊠ *Mitropoleos, behind big church, Fira* 🕾 *22860/23217* ⊕ *www. culture.gr* 🖃 *€3* ☉ *Summer, Tues.–Sun. 8–7:30; winter, 8:30–3.*

Nomikos Conference Center. Upper Fira's new exhibition hall, named for the famous shipowner, hosts many international conferences and also concerts. Its permanent exhibition of fabulous photocopies of the Akrotiri frescoes—the originals from 1600 BC have never been shown—are beautiful and informative. ⊠ *Fira* 🕾 *22860/23016* ⊕ *www. santorini.gr-santorini.com/exhibitions/nomikos.htm* 🖃 *6* ☉ *10–8.*

Panayia Ypapantis. The modern Greek Orthodox cathedral of Panayia Ypapantis is a major landmark; you'll quickly note how the local priests, with somber faces, long beards, and black robes, look strangely

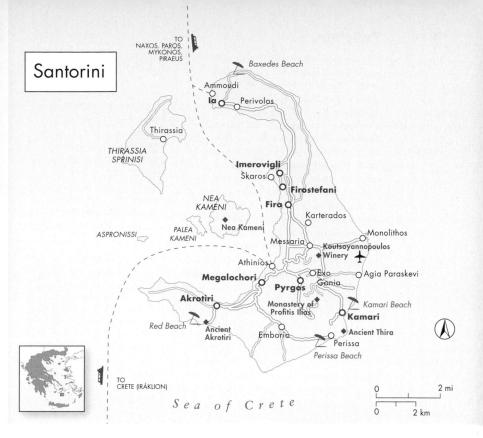

Santorini

TO NAXOS, PAROS, MYKONOS, PIRAEUS

Baxedes Beach

Ammoudi
Ia
Perivolos

Thirassia

THIRASSIA
SPRINISI

Imerovigli
Skaros
Firostefani
NEA
KAMENI
Fira
Karterados
Monolithos
PALEA
KAMENI
Nea Kameni
Koutsoyannopoulos
ASPRONISSI
Winery
Messaria
Athinios
Megalochori
Exo
Gonia
Agia Paraskevi
Pyrgos
Akrotiri
Monastery of
Profitis Ilias
Kamari Beach
Kamari
Red Beach
Ancient
Akrotiri
Emboria
Ancient Thira
Perissa
Perissa Beach

TO
CRETE (IRÁKLION)

Sea of Crete

0   2 mi
0   2 km

out of place in summertime, tourist-jammed Fira. ⊠ *Southern part of town, Fira.*

OFF THE BEATEN PATH **Nea Kameni.** To peer into a live, sometimes smoldering volcano, join one of the popular excursions to Nea Kameni, the larger of the two Burnt isles. After disembarking, you hike 430 feet to the top and walk around the edge of the crater, wondering if the volcano is ready for its fifth eruption during the last hundred years—after all, the last was in 1956. Some tours continue on to Therassia, where there is a village. Tours (about €20) are scheduled regularly by

Nomikos Travel. This agency handles a wide array of tickets. ☎ 22860/23660 🖷 22860/23666 ⊕ *www.nomikosvillas.gr.*

WHERE TO EAT

$$
GREEK
✗**Lithos.** Dimitris Anastopoulos's restaurant deftly proves you can eat well, inexpensively, and have a caldera view. Start with steamed mussels with ouzo and masticha liqueur or pastry flutes with Edam, sun-dried tomatoes, capers, and yogurt. For a main dish try chicken with artichokes and capers in lemon cream sauce, or Lithos pork tenderloin, with mushrooms and *kefalotiri* cheese in red-wine sauce. Desserts are a specialty, and cheesecake with wild blackberries tastes as good as it looks. The oil and wine are from Dimitris's farm in the Peloponnese, and the fish is local. From the high caldera street, walk

down to the lower until you see the sign. This neighborhood jumps at night. ⊠ *Caldera, Fira* ☎ *22860/ 24421* ⊕ *www.lithossantorini.com* ☾ *Closed Nov.–Mar.*

$$$$
GREEK
Fodor's Choice
★

✕ **Selene.** Always a great restaurant, Selene is now probably the best in the Cyclades, with a beautiful location, elegant setting and service, and a deep love of island cuisine with local ingredients. The terrace of the old aristocratic house has two sea views—south and caldera sunset—and overlooks vineyards spreading to the Aegean. Excellent starters include squid with smoked fava and cuttlefish ink flakes, or smoked quail kouskousela on crispy potatoes. Among the subtle entrées are sea bass with stuffed zucchini flowers, and the lamb with spring wild greens and lemon foam. Desserts are not neglected: meringue with lemongrass cream and strawberry sorbet, or the baklava with local pistachios are both supreme. The Greek wine list is extensive. On Selene's lower level there is a café-restaurant where you can sample Selene's dishes or even have a sandwich. Next to it is Selene's agricultural museum in an old winery. Georgia Tsara, the maîtresse d', oversees all with grace, efficiency, and knowledge. In summer, owner George Hatziyianakis gives daylong cooking classes (be sure to check the Web site for details). ⊠ *Pyrgos* ☎ *22860/22249* ⊕ *www.selene.gr* ⚲ *Reservations essential* ☾ *Closed Nov.–Mar.*

$$$$
GREEK
★

✕ **Sphinx.** When Fira locals want more than a taverna, they come to this pretty vaulted room, which glows with spotlighted Cycladic sculptures and peach walls. As lush as this is, however, few can resist an outdoor terrace table, thanks to the striking caldera views in one direction and a vista of the giant cathedral in the other. Owner George Psichas is his own chef, and every dish is evidence of his loving care—even the bread and pasta are homemade. Starters include three fish carpaccio with olive oil, lemon, and arugula, or the eggplant with Santorini tomato sauce and mozzarella. George leans Italian, as the risotto with Santorini tomatoes, zucchini, and marscapone reveals. Fresh fish is usually available—try the fresh grouper steak with shellfish and white wine sauce. The fillet steak with foie gras, wild mushrooms, and Vin Santo sauce is superb. Desserts change day by day, but rich chocolate soufflé is always available. The wine list is long and Greek (and the "cave" is very much worth a look). ⊠ *Cliff-side walkway in front of Panayia Ypapantis, Fira* ☎ *22860/23823* ⊕ *www.sphinx-santorini.com* ⚲ *Reservations essential.*

WHERE TO STAY

For expanded hotel reviews, visit Fodors.com.

$$$$
Fodor's Choice
★

⊞ **Aigialos.** For a taste of old aristocratic Santorini, venture to Aigialos ("seashore"), comprising a cluster of buildings from the 18th and 19th centuries, and discover the most comfortable and discreetly luxurious—as well as the most poetic and serenely quiet—array of one- and two-bedroom villas to stay in Fira. **Pros:** not a phony place set up for tourists; quiet elegance; friendly, discreet service. **Cons:** the usual endless steps; the pool is tiny. ⊠ *South end of cliff-side walkway, Fira* ☎ *22860/25191 through 22860/25195* ⊕ *www.aigialos.gr* ⟿ *17 villas* ☼ *In-room: a/c. In-hotel: bar, pool, business center* ☉ *Closed Nov.–Mar.* ⏋⃝l *Breakfast.*

$$$ ⛭ **Aroma Suites.** For a caldera view, this recent (2006) accommodation is an exceptional value, thanks to its small white cave-rooms with vaulted ceilings—nicely decorated with warm touches of color and sleek marble fixtures—and its common terrace overlooking the caldera, just the place you'll want to sit mornings and evenings, perhaps sipping some excellent wines grown on owner Fanis Kafouros's vineyards. **Pros:** very attractive; small and friendly; perfect for young couples who want a caldera view but aren't high rollers. **Cons:** those stairs; rooms are close together. ⊠ *Caldera walkway, Fira* ☎ *22860/24112* ⊕ *www. aromasuites.gr* ⟿ *4 rooms, suites* ☼ *In-room: a/c.*

$$ ⛭ **Costa Marina Villas.** Set in a tranquil neighborhood, surrounded by a
★ garden, and vaulted and shimmering-white in archetypal Cycladic fashion, this is a nifty option (built in 2002) and one that is open all year. **Pros:** great value for the money. **Cons:** a hike from the caldera. ⊠ *Along road leading to camping grounds, Fira* ☎ *22860/28923* ⊕ *www. costamarina.gr* ⟿ *21 rooms* ☼ *In-room: a/c, kitchen* ⏋⃝l *Breakfast.*

$$$$ ⛭ **Dream Island Hotel.** Opened in 2006, well appointed, and family run, this complex of 20 units rooms is a five-minute walk north from the main (Theotokopoulou) square in Fira—and thus offers no caldera views—and below the main road to Ia. **Pros:** good for families and step haters; you can drive to the door. **Cons:** no caldera view; a walk from the center. ⊠ *Off Martiou Street, Fira* ☎ *22860/24122* ⊕ *www. dreamislandhotel.gr* ⟿ *18 rooms, 2 suites* ☼ *In-room: a/c. In-hotel: business center.*

$$$$ ⛭ **Hotel Aressana.** Though the Aressana lacks a view of the caldera, its own slant of sea view is effulgently wonderful—add in the large freshwater pool, the spacious lobby with Italian design and wood-panel bar, excellent service, gourmet food from the Koukoumavlos restaurant (including breakfast), and location in central Fira, and the sum total makes this a very popular option. **Pros:** drive to the door and avoid steps; stylish design; owner and manager Evangelia Mendrinos keeps it very comfortable and sparkling. **Cons:** no caldera view; few island touches. ⊠ *South end of cliff-side walkway, Fira* ☎ *22860/23900, 22860/23901* ⊕ *www.aressana.gr* ⟿ *42 rooms, 8 suites* ☼ *In-room: a/c, Wi-Fi. In-hotel: bar, pool, gym, spa, business center* ☉ *Closed Nov.– Mar.* ⏋⃝l *Breakfast.*

$ ⛭ **Loizos Apartments.** Lefteris Anapliotis's little hotel, located in a quiet and convenient section of Fira, is the perfect budget choice—the guest rooms, some with sea views, are spacious and the garden is pretty. **Pros:** inexpensive; excellently run; top neighborhood in Fira. **Cons:** no caldera view; not for luxe-lovers. ⊠ *On cobbled road up from main traffic street, near town hall, Fira* ☎ *22860/24046* ⊕ *www.loizos.gr* ⟿ *23*

7

Viewed here from the Nea Kameni anchorage, Santorini's fabled volcanic caldera is near the top of people's must-see-before-I-die list of sights.

rooms ♿ *In-room: a/c, Wi-Fi. In-hotel: pool, business center* ☉ *Closed Nov.–Mar.*

$$ **⛾Pelican Hotel.** Just down from the busy main (Theotokopoulou) square on Danezi Street, this small hotel is in the center of the commercial, non-picturesque part of town but, happily, most rooms are sound-insulated, making for an oasis of quiet. **Pros:** very efficient and inexpensive; good restaurant. **Cons:** in a busy neighborhood away from the caldera. ✉ *On cobbled road up from main traffic street, near town hall, Fira* ☎ *22860/23113* ⊕ *www.pelican.gr* ⬎ *18 rooms* ♿ *In-room: a/c, Wi-Fi. In-hotel: business center.*

$ **⛾Pension Delphini I.** Vassilis Rousseas's pension, on the busy main traffic street, is well run, inexpensive, friendly, and open all year. **Pros:** cheap; friendly; open all year; convenient. **Cons:** front rooms are on the noisy car road; no breakfast served. ✉ *Main traffic street, opposite Piraeus Bank, Fira* ☎ *22860/22780* ⊕ *www.delfini-santorini.gr* ⬎ *10 rooms* ♿ *In-room: a/c, Internet.*

$$$$ **⛾Theoxenia.** Midway along the long scenic caldera walkway and nestled among the jewelry stores on Fira's crowded main street you'll find the narrow door leading up marble steps to this fine hotel. **Pros:** extremely convenient; very well run, open all year. **Cons:** in the thick of the tourist crush. ✉ *Via D'Oro, middle of cliff-side walkway, Fira* ☎ *22860/22740* ⊕ *www.theoxenia.net* ⬎ *9 rooms* ♿ *In-room: a/c, Wi-Fi* ☉ *Open all year.*

NIGHTLIFE AND THE ARTS

DANCING **Casablanca Soul.** Located in the maze to the north, Casablanca Soul offers an ambitious live music program on weekends. ✉ *Fira* ☎ *22860/27188.*

Koo Club. For Fira, this is Disco Central and the township's most popular outdoor club by far. ☒ *North end of cliff-side walkway, Fira* ☏ *22860/22025* ⊕ *www.kooclub.gr.*

FESTIVALS **Bellonias Cultural Center.** Set on the main car crossroads, the Bellonias Cultural Center contains a small auditorium, the latest audiovisual equipment, and a large library. In summer, it presents concerts, readings, and theater festivals; in winter, it becomes an educational center. Its Sound and Image music festival is held at the end of June. ☏ *22860/24960* ⊕ *www.ichosikona.com.*

Santorini Jazz Festival. The music festival fights for funds, but keeps swinging. ☒ *Fira* ☏ *22860/33452* ⊕ *www.jazzfestival.gr.*

Santorini Music Festival. Thank pianist Athena Capodistria for September's Santorini Music Festival, which always includes internationally known musicians. ☒ *Nomikos Conference Center, Fira* ☏ *22860/23166.*

MUSIC **Franco's Bar.** Boasting a caldera view, the popular Franco's Bar plays classical music and serves champagne cocktails. ☒ *Below cliff-side walkway, Fira* ☏ *22860/24428* ⊕ *www.francos.gr.*

SHOPPING

EMBROIDERY **Costas Dimitrokalis.** With purchases that can be mailed anywhere, Costas Dimitrokalis and Matthew Dimitrokalis sell locally made embroideries of Greek linen and Egyptian cotton, rugs, pillowcases in hand-crocheted wool with local designs, and more. ☒ *1 block from cable car, Fira* ☏☏ *22860/22957.*

GALLERIES **Nikola's Art Gallery.** Can you resist an exquisite lapis lazuli box? If you can't, make plans to visit Nikola's Art Gallery, which has been selling stone vases, sculptures, and *objets d'art* for twenty-five years. The highly polished semiprecious stones here glow with color and form. Pantelis and Nikola Kaloteraki can also create jewelry in the stone of your choice. The shop is next to the stairs two streets down from the caldera walkway. ☒ *Fira* ☏ *22860/22283.*

★ **Phenomenon.** Christoforos Asimis studied painting at Athens University, and has had many exhibitions there and abroad. The nearby cathedral's murals are his. His paintings specialize in the light and landscape of his home island. His wife, Eleni, who also studied in Athens, creates some of Santorini's most elegant jewelry. ☒ *Ypapantis walkway, Palia Fabrika, Fira* ☏ *22860/23041* ⊕ *www.santorini.info* .

JEWELRY **Bead Shop.** Marina Tsiagkouri's shop has expanded, but beads are still Fodor'sChoice the main reason to go. Who can resist her unique beads made from San-
★ torini's volcanic rock? ☒ *Opposite entrance to Museum of Prehistoric Thera, Fira* ☏ *22860/25176.*

Kostas Antoniou Jewelry. Many of Kostas's pieces were inspired by ancient Thera. Master jeweler Gerry Kafieris sells his Triton jewelry collection here, including delicate minautre mosaics. ☒ *In Spiliotica shopping*

7

area, near Archaeological Museum, Fira ☎ *22860/22633.*

Sophia's Art Jewelry. Easily above the standard glitter of Santorini, Sophia's Art Jewelry shop sells gold jewelry from several Greek workshops. Letting her work speak for itself, Sophia Koutsogiannopoulou has no Web site or email, nor does she stand at the doorway of her quiet shop (a block in from the cable-car) soliciting customers. ⊠ *Fira* ☎ *22860/23587.*

SPORTS AND THE OUTDOORS

SAILING **Santorini Sailing Center.** This handy outfitter arranges charters and runs weekly two- to three-day sailing trips around the Cyclades for groups of up to 10. ⊠ *Imerovigli* ☎ *22860/23891, 22860/23059.*

FIROSTEFANI ΦΗΡΟΣΤΕΦΑΝΙ

1 km (2/3 mi) northwest of Fira.

Firostefani used to be a separate village, but now it is an elegant suburb north of Fira. The 10-minute walk between them, along the caldera, is one of Santorini's highlights. From Firostefani's single white cliff-side street, walkways descend to traditional vaulted cave houses, which are fast becoming pensions. Though close to the action, Firostefani feels calm and quiet.

WHERE TO EAT AND STAY

$$
GREEK
★
✕**Aktaion.** In his tiny taverna, Vangelis Roussos uses mostly his grandfather's recipes. Outdoor tables overlook the caldera. Inside, the paintings on the walls are Vangelis's own. Salad Santorini, his mother's recipe, has raw cod flakes, caper leaves, and seasonal ingredients. The moussaka, made with white eggplant, is incomparable. ⊠ *Main square, Firostefani* ☎ *22860/22336.*

$$$
GREEK
✕**Vanilia.** Set in a windmill—built in 1872 and preserved by the government after the 1956 earthquake—Vanilia also encompasses pretty terraces, on which to enjoy the good food. You might start with Greek sardines wrapped in vine leaves. Homemade pasta, such as ravioli stuffed with farmer's cheese and tomatoes is a specialty. An intriguing entrée is grilled tuna fish fillet with basil-mint sauce. Yogurt tart with strawberries will make you want to linger at this friendly place. ⊠ *Main square, Firostefani* ☎ *22860/25631* ☉ *Closed Nov.–Apr.*

$
★
⬚**Reverie Traditional Apartments.** Georgios Fytros has converted his family home into an inexpensive and attractive hotel, all cream color with marble insets. **Pros:** friendly and inexpensive; good neighborhood. **Cons:** only suites have caldera views; breakfast is extra. ⊠ *Between Firostefani walkway and main traffic road, Firostefani* ☎ *22860/23322* ⊕ *www.reverie.gr* ⇆ *4 rooms, 11 studios, 2 suites* ⬧ *In-room: a/c, Wi-Fi. In-hotel: pool, business center* ☉ *Closed Nov.–Mar.*

$$$$ ⚏ **Tsitouras Collection.** *Architectural Digest*–worthy decor and earthy
Fodor's Choice Cycladic charm blend here at this complex of six apartments, and the
★ result is true Santorinian splendor—little wonder these apartments have
been homes-away-from-homes for the likes of Nana Mouskouri, Jean-
Paul Gaultier, and other art lovers who adore the unique décor: a fan-
tasia of Chippendale armchairs, ancient amphorae, Byzantine icons,
Corfiot mariner's chests, Picasso ceramics, gilt-framed engravings, and
a picturesque bevy of domes, skylights, and interior windows, most
of which is on show in the striking "House of the Winds," where the
Oscar winner is the grand, double-height, cathedral-roofed living room
ashimmer with elegant antiques and robin's-egg-blue walls. **Pros:** beautiful design; caldera view. **Cons:** all this luxe comes at a very steep price
(€470–€790) with stairs and no pool. ⊠ *Firostefani cliff face, next to
St. Mark's, Firostefani* ☎ *22860/23747* ⊕ *www.tsitouras.gr* ⤴ *6 apartments* ⌂ *In-room: a/c, Wi-Fi. In-hotel: restaurant, pool, business center*
☉ *Closed Nov.–Mar.*

IMEROVIGLI ΗΜΕΡΟΒΙΓΛΙ

3 km (2 mi) northwest of Fira, 2 km (1 mi) northwest of Firostefani.

Set on the highest point of the caldera's rim, Imerovigli (the name means
Watchtower) is what Firostefani was like a decade and a half ago. It is
now being developed, and for good reasons: it is quiet, traditional, and
less expensive. The 25-minute walk from Fira, with incredible views,
should be on everyone's itinerary. The lodgings, some of them traditional cave houses, are mostly down stairways from the cliff-side
walkway. The big rock backing the village was once crowned by Skaros
Castle, whence Venetian overlords reigned after 1207. It collapsed in an
earthquake, leaving only the rock. A trail descending from the church
of Ayios Georgios crosses the isthmus and encircles Skaros; it's only 10
minutes to the castle top. After 1 km (½ mi) it reaches the small chapel
of Theoskepasti with a memorable caldera view.

WHERE TO EAT

$$$ ✕ **Blue Note.** You can't go wrong with the location: a deck extended over
GREEK the cliff, a panoramic caldera view, and a sunset as dessert. For a starter
★ try Gruyère flambé. For a main dish, lamb *klephtiko* (stewed in wine
and herbs in a ceramic dish) is a good choice, as is shrimp Blue Note (a
secret recipe). Part of the lovely Spiliotica Apartments, the Blue Note is
open for lunch and dinner. ⊠ *On main walkway near Maltesa, Spiliotica
Hotel, Imerovigli* ☎ *22860/23771* ☉ *Closed Nov.–Mar.*

$$ ✕ **Skaros Fish Taverna.** This rustic open-air taverna, one of the few restau-
GREEK rants in Imerovigli, has spectacular caldera views. It serves fresh fish and
Santorini specialties, such as octopus in onion sauce, and mussels with
rice and raisins. ⊠ *On cliff-side walkway, Imerovigli* ☎ *22860/23616*
☉ *Closed Nov.–Mar.*

WHERE TO STAY

For expanded hotel reviews, visit Fodors.com.

$$$ ⚏ **Heliades Apartments.** Owner Olympia Sarri knows she has some-
thing special, thanks to her father, who mostly built these apartments,

consisting of four cave houses, white with blue-green accents, on one of the higher cliff ridges, so the verandas here all have really breathtaking (literally) caldera views. **Pros:** terraces with caldera views; few steps; kitchens included. **Cons:** on the simple side. ⊠ *On cliff-side walkway, behind church of Panaghia Maltesa, near parking and bus stop, Imerovigli* ☎ *22860/24102* ⊕ *www.heliades-apts.gr* ⤸ *4 houses* ⌂ *In-room: a/c, kitchen. In-hotel: business center* ☉ *Closed Nov.–Mar.*

$$$$ ⊞ **Spiliotica Apartments and Suites.** With his lively vibe, Tony Spiliotis
★   (a Greek-American) has created an attractive hideaway that attracts everyone from families to celebrities to these accommodations that cascade steeply down the cliff side. **Pros:** caldera view; nice array of conveniences. **Cons:** lots of steep steps. ⊠ *On cliff-side walkway, behind church of Panaghia Maltesa, near parking and bus stop, Imerovigli* ☎ *22860/22637* ⊕ *www.spiliotica.com* ⤸ *21 houses* ⌂ *In-room: a/c, kitchen, Wi-Fi. In-hotel: restaurant, pool, business center* ☉ *Closed Nov.–Mar.*

IA OIA

14 km (8½ mi) northwest of Fira.

Fodor's Choice   At the tip of the northern horn of the island sits Ia (or Oia), Santorini's
★   second-largest town and the Aegean's most-photographed village. Ia is more tasteful than Fira (for one thing, no establishment here is allowed to play music that can be heard on the street), and the town's cubical white houses (some vaulted against earthquakes) stand out against the green-, brown-, and rust-color layers of rock, earth, and solid volcanic ash that rise from the sea. Every summer evening, travelers from all over the world congregate at the caldera's rim—sitting on whitewashed fences, staircases, beneath the town's windmill, on the old **Kastro**—each looking out to sea in anticipation of the performance: the Ia sunset. The three-hour rim-edge walk from Ia to Fira at this hour is unforgettable.

In the middle of the quiet caldera, the volcano smolders away eerily, adding an air of suspense to an already awe-inspiring scene. The 1956 earthquake (7.8 on the Richter scale) left 48 people dead (thankfully, most residents were working outdoors at the time), hundreds injured, and 2,000 houses toppled. Santorini's west side—especially Ia, until then the largest town—was hard hit, and many residents decided to emigrate to Athens, Australia, and America. And although Fira, also damaged, rebuilt rapidly, Ia proceeded slowly, sticking to the traditional architectural style. The perfect example of that style is the restaurant 1800, a renovated ship-captain's villa. In 1900, Ia had nearly 9,000 inhabitants, mostly mariners who owned 164 seafaring vessels and seven shipyards. Now there are about 500 permanent residents, and more than 100 boats. Many of these mariners use the endless flight of stairs from the Kastro to descend down to the water and the small port of **Ammoudi,** where the pebble beach is home to some of the island's nicest fish tavernas. Head east to find the fishing port of **Armeni,** home to all those excursion boats that tour the caldera.

Ia is set up like the other three towns—Fira, Firostefani, and Imerovigli—that adorn the caldera's sinuous rim. There is a car road, which is new, and a cliff-side walkway (Nikolaos Nomikou), which is old. Shops and restaurants are all on the walkway, and hotel entrances mostly descend from it—something to check carefully if you cannot negotiate stairs easily. In Ia there is a lower cliff-side walkway writhing with stone steps, and a long stairway to the tiny blue bay with its dock below. Short streets leading from the car road to the walkway have cheaper eateries and shops. There is a parking lot at either end, and the northern one marks the end of the road and the rim. Nothing is very far from anything else.

The main walkway of Ia can be thought of as a straight river, with a delta at the northern end, where the better shops and restaurants are. The most-luxurious cave-house hotels are at the southern end, and a stroll by them is part of the extended evening promenade. Although it is not as crowded as Fira, where the tour boats deposit their thousands of hasty shoppers, relentless publicity about Ia's beauty and tastefulness, accurate enough, are making it impassable in August. The sunset in Ia may not really be much more spectacular than in Fira, and certainly not better than in higher Imerovigli, but there is something tribally satisfying at the sight of so many people gathering in one spot to celebrate pure beauty. Happily, the night scene isn't as frantic as Fira's—most shop owners are content to sit out front and don't cotton to the few revelers' bars in operation. In winter, Ia feels pretty uninhabited.

Fodor's Choice
★
Naval Museum of Thera. Set in an old neoclassic mansion, once destroyed in the big earthquake, the Naval Museum of Thera has now risen like a phoenix from the ashes. The collection displays ships' figureheads, seamen's chests, maritime equipment, and models—all revealing the extensive nautical history of the island, Santorini's main trade until tourism took over. ⊠ *Near telephone office, Ia* ☎ *22860/71156* ✉ *€4* ☉ *Tues.–Sun. 8:30–3.*

BEACH

Baxedes. There are no beautiful beaches close to Ia, but you can hike down Ia's cliff side or catch a bus to the small sand beach of Baxedes. ⊠ *Port of Armoudhi, Ia.*

WHERE TO EAT

$$$$
GREEK
Fodor's Choice
★
✕**1800.** Clearly, some of Santorini's old sea captains lived graciously, as you'll note when dining at one of the Cyclades's most famous restaurants, 1800 (the name refers to the date when the house was built). Owner, architect, and restaurateur John Zagelidis has lovingly restored this magnificent old captain's house with original colors (white, olive green, and gray) and furnishings, including antique sofas, wooden travel chests, and a hand-painted Venetian bed. To top it all off, a superlative roof terrace was constructed, with a vista framed by Ia's most-spectacular church cupolas—a perfect perch on hot nights for taking in the famous Ia sunset. For starters try octopus and chickpea salad on baby spinach with feta and Florina red peppercorns; or the scallops with an aromatic cauliflower tartare and tandoori cream. Entrées include black angus veal with canelloni stuffed with broccoli and arugula with graviera foam and mushroom sauce; and cod with herb ash, black-eyed beans, beetroot salad, and fish roe with cuttlefish ink. Ivoire

Ia is world-famous for its magnificent sunsets. One evening there was immortalized by Jennifer Duc, Fodors. com member, in this lovely photo.

chocolate with pineapple carpaccio and white chcolate powder is a fine dessert. The wine list is large and nicely tops off a truly fine dining experience. ⊠ *Main St., Ia* ☎ *22860/71485* ⊕ *www.oia-1800.com* ☉ *Closed Nov.–Apr.*

$$$
GREEK
★
✕**Kastro.** Spyros Dimitroulis's restaurant is primarily patronized for its view of the famous Ia sunset, and at the magical hour it is always filled. Happily, the food makes a fitting accompaniment. A good starter is olives stuffed with cream cheese dipped in beer dough and fried, served on arugula with a balsamic sauce. For a main dish try mussels with oil-pepper sauce. Lunch is popular. ⊠ *Near Venetian castle, Ia* ☎ *22860/71045.*

$
GREEK
★
✕ **Meteor.** This café and wine bar on the main street is noted for cocktails, desserts, and stylish decor. The flowery terrace has a seaview. ⊠ *Main St., Ia* ☎ *22860/71015.*

$$$
GREEK
Fodor's Choice
★
✕**Red Bicycle.** Once featured on Giada De Laurentis's Food Network show, this sophisticated café and restaurant is located at the north end of Ia's main walkway, just down the steps; its big terrace offers Ia's finest caldera view. Owner Chara Kourti warmly touts her Santorini puréed fava with onion chutney and kafaifi crust, and also her baked feta in a nacho crust with orange preserves and lemon balm. And no one will complain about the octopus with crabmeat, fresh coriander, potatoes, and truffle foam, or the sea bass cooked in sea salt. Desserts are a specialty; try mastic mousse with carmelized pistachios and rose-petal preserves. This popular spot is open from lunch until late. Note that one level down is Kourti's 39 Steps café. ⊠ *Main Walkway, Ia* ☎ *22860/71918* ✉ *red-bicycle@hotmail.com* ☉ *Closed Nov.–Mar.*

WHERE TO STAY
For expanded hotel reviews, visit Fodors.com.

$$ ★ **Delfini Villas.** If you think a comfortable, convenient room in Ia with a caldera view and terrace has to be expensive, think again: Rena Halari's place is affordable and warmly charming. **Pros:** in the heart of Ia; a great buy for a caldera view. **Cons:** don't expect luxury; stairs. ⊠ *Ia cliff face, Ia* ☎ *22860/71600* ⊕ *www.delfinivillas.com* ↝ *7 rooms, 4 apartments* ⚘ *In-room: a/c, kitchen* ⊘ *Closed Nov.–Mar.*

$$$$ **Katikies.** Sumptuously appointed, this immaculate white cliff-side complex layered on terraces offers ultimate luxury and sleek modern design, including Andy Warhol wall prints, stunning fabrics, and handsome furniture—chic as the surroundings are, the barrel-vaulted ceilings and other architectural details also lend a traditional air to the place. **Pros:** cliff-side infinity pool; all luxuries. **Cons:** many stairs; rather impersonal; superpricey; you have to want white towel-over-the arm service. ⊠ *Ia cliff face, edge of main town, Ia* ☎ *22860/71401* ⊕ *www. katikies.com* ↝ *7 rooms, 20 suites* ⚘ *In-room: a/c, Wi-Fi. In-hotel: restaurant, bar, pool, business center* ⊘ *Closed Nov.–Mar.*

$$$$ **Lampetia Villas.** Eight hundred feet up the cliff from the sea, Lampetia offers charm, comfort, and friendliness, with accommodations—each has private balcony with a view—that are different in size and furnishings. **Pros:** charming decor with caldera view. **Cons:** not as isolated as it could be. ⊠ *Nomikou, Ia cliff face, down from Main Street, Ia* ☎ *22860/71237* ⊕ *www.lampetia.gr* ↝ *8 houses* ⚘ *In-room: a/c, kitchen. In-hotel: pool* ⊘ *Closed Nov.–Mar.*

$$$$ ★ **Perivolas.** Immortalized as one of the most famous infinity pools on Earth (thanks to nearly a dozen magazine covers), the cliff-hanger here seems to make you feel you could easily swim off the edge into the caldera's blue bay 1,000 feet below—this is but one of the highlights here at a luxury resort hotel that even (big compliment) the locals respect. **Pros:** the original infinity pool; attentive but relaxed service; now takes credit cards. **Cons:** lots of steps; a walk to town. ⊠ *Nomikou, Ia cliff face, 8 min by foot from town, Ia* ☎ *22860/71308* ⊕ *www.perivolas. gr* ↝ *20 houses* ⚘ *In-room: a/c, kitchen, no TV, Wi-Fi. In-hotel: restaurant, bar, pool* ⊘ *Closed Nov.–Mar.*

NIGHTLIFE
There are the usual cafés, bars, and pastry shops along the main street but a peaceful note is struck by the fact that establishments are forbidden to play loud music.

★ **1800.** The bar at Santorini's most sophisticated restaurant, 1800, gets lively late, when diners leave. ☎ *22860/71485.*

Skiza. With a balcony overlooking the caldera, Skiza is well known for the excellence of its pastries. ☎ *22860/71569.*

SHOPPING
ACCESSORIES **Silk Shop.** You'll easily recognize the Silk Shop, Judy Neaves and Theodore Xenos's cavernous boutique. Once a bakery, it is now swathed in shimmering silk scarves, shawls, small purses, and sophisticated silk and linen wraps and tunics, many in soft colors. ⊠ *Main shopping street, Ia* ☎ *22860/71923.*

7

ANTIQUES
AND COL-
LECTIBLES

Loulaki. Manolis and Chara Kourtis sell antiques, ceramics, jewelry, and art; exploring the shop is a pleasure. Alexandra Solomos's painted plates are a favorite. ⊠ *Main shopping street, Ia* ☎ *22860/71856.*

BOOKS

Fodor's Choice
★

Atlantis Books. A tiny English bookshop that would be at home in New York's Greenwich Village or London's Bloomsbury, Atlantis Books is an unexpected but wonderful treat—its presence here is a miracle. Only good literature makes it onto the shelves. Writers stop by to chat and give readings. Jeremy Mercer, a writer for *The Guardian*, listed this as one of his ten favorite bookshops anywhere. ⊠ *North end of main shopping street, Ia* ☎ *22869/72346* ⊕ *www.atlantisbooks.org.*

> ### THE REAL DEAL
>
> Ia mostly abjures the jewelry madness of Fira, and instead offers a variety of handcrafted items. Since the shops are not so dependent on cruise ships, a certain sophistication reigns in the quiet streets. Art galleries, "objets" shops, crafts shops, and icon stores set the tone. More open every year.

PYRGOS ΠΥΡΓΟΣ

5½ km (3½ mi) south of Fira.

Fodor's Choice
★

Though today Pyrgos has only 500 inhabitants, until the early 1800s it was the capital of the island. Stop here to see its medieval houses, stacked on top of one another and back to back for protection against pirates. The beautiful neoclassic building on the way up is a luxury hotel. The view from the ruined Venetian castle is panoramic. And reward yourself for the climb up the picturesque streets, which follow the shape of the hill, with a stop at the panoramic terrace of the Café Kastelli, for Greek coffee and homemade sweets. In Pyrgos you are really in old Santorini—hardly anything has changed.

Monastery of Profitis Ilias. Standing on the highest point on Santorini, which spans to 1,856 feet at the summit, the Monastery of Profitis Ilias offers a Cineramic vista: from here you can see the surrounding islands and, on a clear day, the mountains of Crete, more than 100 km (66 mi) away. You may also be able to spot ancient Thira on the peak below Profitis Ilias. Unfortunately, radio towers and a NATO radar installation provide an ugly backdrop for the monastery's wonderful bell tower.

Founded in 1711 by two monks from Pyrgos, Profitis Ilias is cherished by islanders because here, in a secret school, the Greek language and culture were taught during the dark centuries of the Turkish occupation. A **museum** in the monastery contains a model of the secret school in a monk's cell, another model of a traditional carpentry and blacksmith shop, and a display of ecclesiastical items. The monastery's future is in doubt because there are so few monks left. ⊠ *At highest point on Santorini, Pyrgos* ▨ *Free* ⊗ *No visiting hrs; caretaker is sometimes around.*

MEGALOCHORI ΜΕΓΑΛΟΧΩΡΙ

4 km (2½ mi) east of Pyrgos, 9 km (5½ mi) southwest of Fira.

Megalochori is a picturesque, half-abandoned town set. Many of the village's buildings were actually *canavas*, wine-making facilities. The tiny main square is still lively in the evening.

WHERE TO STAY

For expanded hotel reviews, visit Fodors.com.

$$$$
★ **Vedema.** "Angelina Jolie, Oliver Stone, Susan Sarandon, Danny DeVito . . . and now you?" might be the question you'll be asking your mate in trying to win Santorini's hotel sweepstakes but you'll only want to rub elbows with those A-listers if you love isolation: the hotel's black-lava environs keep crowds and paparazzi at bay—but you, too, may truly enjoy the peace of this distant and deluxe outpost. **Pros:** Vedema is not cheap, but you'll get what you're paying for—all the room, food, and service, luxuries. **Cons:** isolated from life, although a handy shuttle service ferries you to other parts of the island. ⊠ *Megalochori* ☎ *22860/81796, 22860/81797* ⊕ *www.vedema.gr* ⌁ *35 rooms, 7 suites* ⚏ *In-room: a/c, kitchen, Wi-Fi. In-hotel: restaurant, pool* ⊗ *Closed Nov.–Mar.* ⊙| *Breakfast.*

VIN BEATS EAU

The locals say that in Santorini there is more wine than water, and it may be true; Santorini produces more wine than any two other Cyclades islands. The volcanic soil, high daytime temperatures, and humidity at night produce 36 varieties of grape, and these unique growing conditions are ideal for the production of distinctive white wine. Farmers twist the vines into a basketlike shape, in which the grapes grow, protected from the wind. A highlight of any Santorini trip is a visit to one of its many wineries—log on to ⊕ *www.santorini.org/wineries* for a helpful intro.

AKROTIRI ΑΚΡΩΤΗΡΙ

7 km (4½ mi) west of Pyrgos, 13 km (8 mi) south of Fira.

★ **Ancient Akrotiri.** If Santorini is known as the "Greek Pompeii" and is claimant to the title of the lost Atlantis, it is because of the archaeological site of ancient Akrotiri, near the tip of the southern horn of the island. The site, long closed for structural repairs, is about to open but, it should be noted, it has long been "about to open." So: please call or check the Web site when you arrive on Santorini.

In the 1860s, in the course of quarrying volcanic ash for use in the Suez Canal, workmen discovered the remains of an ancient town. The town was frozen in time by ash from an eruption 3,600 years ago, long before Pompeii's disaster. In 1967 Spyridon Marinatos of the University of Athens began excavations, which occasionally continue. It is thought that the 40 buildings that have been uncovered are only one-thirtieth of the huge site and that excavating the rest will probably take a century.

Marinatos's team discovered many well-preserved frescoes depicting aspects of Akrotiri life, some now displayed in the National

Archaeological Museum in Athens; Santorini wants them back to join the small selection that are on view in the Museum of Prehistoric Thera in Fira. Meanwhile, postcard-size pictures of them are posted outside the houses where they were found. The antelopes, monkeys, and wildcats they portray suggest trade with Egypt.

Culturally an outpost of Minoan Crete, Akrotiri was settled as early as 3000 BC and reached its peak after 2000 BC, when it developed trade and agriculture and settled the present town. The inhabitants cultivated olive trees and grain, and their advanced architecture—three-story frescoed houses faced with masonry (some with balconies) and public buildings of sophisticated construction—is evidence of an elaborate lifestyle. ✉ *South of modern Akrotiri, near tip of southern horn* ☎ *22860/81366* ⊕ *www.culture.gr* 🎟 *€5* ☉ *Tues.–Sun. 8:30–3.*

BEACH

Red beach. This comes up a winner on several fronts: it is quiet, has a taverna, and is covered with red-hued sands (have your Nikon handy). ✉ *On southwest shore below Akrotiri.*

KAMARI KAMAPI

6½ km (4¼ mi) east of Akrotiri, 6 km (4 mi) south of Fira.

★ **Ancient Thira.** Archaeology buffs will want to visit the site of ancient Thira. There are relics of a Dorian city, with 9th-century BC tombs, an engraved phallus, Hellenistic houses, and traces of Byzantine fortifications and churches. At the Sanctuary of Apollo, graffiti dating to the 8th century BC record the names of some of the boys who danced naked at the god's festival (Satie's famed musical compositions, *Gymnopedies,* reimagine these). To get here, hike up from Perissa or Kamari or take a taxi up **Mesa Vouna.** On the summit are the scattered ruins, excavated by a German archaeology school around the turn of the 20th century; there's a fine view. ✉ *On a switchback up mountain right before Kamari, 2,110 feet high, Kamari* ☎ *22860/31366* ⊕ *www.culture.gr* 🎟 *€5* ☉ *Tues.–Sun. 8:30–3.*

Fodor's Choice **Koutsoyanopoulos Winery.** Founded in 1870, the Koutsoyanopoulos winery offers a tour of its old facility, now a multiroom museum that is ★ picturesque, authentic, and mostly underground. Tools, techniques, and the original business office are from a world long gone—but the wines, as the ensuing tasting proves, are contemporary and refined. The *Wine Spectator* rated their Assyrtiko among the world's top 100 whites. To add your own kudos, note that this admired winery is open year-round. ✉ *On the road to Kamari, Vothonas* ✉ *Greece* ☎ *22860/31322* 📧 *info@volcanwines.gr* ⊕ *www.volcanwines.gr* 🎟 *€7* ☉ *9–6.*

BEACH

The black-sand beach of **Kamari** is a natural treasure of Santorini and crowds head here to rent deck chairs and umbrellas. They also flock to Kamari because tavernas and refreshment stands abound—despite an attractive wooden walkway and lively nightlife, Kamari is the epitome of overdevelopment.

FOLEGANDROS ΦΟΛΕΓΑΝΔΡΟΣ

180 km (96 nautical mi) southeast of Piraeus harbor in Athens, 86 km (53 mi) northwest of Santorini.

If Santorini didn't exist, little, bare Folegandros would be world famous. Its gorgeous Cycladic main town of Chora, built between the walls of a Venetian fort, sits on the edge of a beetling precipice: this hilltop setting represents, with the exception of Santorini, the finest cliff scenery in the Cyclades. Beyond this, the island does not seem to have much to offer on paper—but in person it certainly does. Beautiful and authentic, it has become the secret island of Cyclades lovers, who want a pure dose of the magic essence of the Aegean every year or so. Only 31 square km (12 square mi) in area and 64 km (40 mi) in circumference, it lacks ruins, villages, green valleys, trees, country houses, and graceful cafés at the edge of the sea. But what it does have—one of the most stunning towns, deliberately downplayed touristic development, several good beaches, quiet evenings, traditional local food, and respectful visitors—make it addictive. There are no discos, no bank, but the sea is shining and, in spring, much of the island is redolent of thyme and oregano.

GETTING HERE AND AROUND

BOAT TRAVEL Little islands like Folegandros used to get two or three boats a week. Tourism, however, has changed all that, at least in summer, and Folegandros—an impressive if bare little island whose pretty white rock-outcrop of a village has a cliff-edge setting, nearby beaches, and simple tavernas—is firmly in the loop. No planes, but two boats from Piraeus in summer—fewer in winter—serve it sufficiently. There are also regular connections to Anafi, Ios, Amorgos, Kea, Kimolos, Koufonisi, Kythnos Milos, Naxos, Paros, Serifos, Sifnos, Sikinos, and Santorini. For schedules check ⊕ *www.openseas.gr.* Faster boats are added on weekends but don't run in winter. The trip takes from four to 11 hours, so you better check which boat is going and where it is stopping. For general information on Folegandros check ⊕ *www.greeka.com* and also *www.folegandros.gr.* The **Folegandros Port Authority** (☎ *22860/41530*) sometimes has an English-speaking officer.

BUS TRAVEL Buses (☎ *22860/41425*) go from the little port to Chora every hour or so throughout the day; buses meet the boats. Buses go almost as often to the southern beaches and to Ano Meria (which has a separate Chora bus stop near the Sottovento tourist office). Fares run from €1.50 to €2.50. Taxis (☎ *22890/22400 or 22860/41048*) meet boats and a stand is at the town entrance.

Visitor Information and Travel/Tour Agencies Maraki Travel and Tours. This agency helpfully handles most travel arrangements. ✉ *Chora, Folegandros* ☎ *22860/41273* ✆ *maraki@syr.forth.gr.*

Sottovento. Flavio Facciolo's Sottovento arranges boat trips and general information graciously. ✉ *Main square, Chora, Folegandros* ☎ *22860/41444* ✆ *sottovento@folegandrosisland.com* ⊕ *www.sottovento.eu.*

7

CLOSE UP

A Water Sports Paradise

When it comes to the Cyclades, anyone who invests in a mask, snorkel, and flippers has entry to intense, serene beauty. But even without this underwater gear, this archipelago is a swimmer's paradise.

Most of the Cycladic islands gleam with beaches, from long blond stretches of sand to tiny pebbly coves. The best beaches are probably those on the southwest coast of Naxos, though the ones on Mykonos are trendier. Beaches on Tinos tend to be less crowded than those on other islands in the Cyclades. The strands on Santorini, though strewn with plenty of bathers, are volcanic; you can bask on sands that are strikingly red and black.

As for water sports, there are many options that entice many sunseekers. Waterskiing, parasailing, scuba diving, and especially windsurfing have become ever more popular. Note that many water sports venues change from season to season.

EXPLORING

Visitors to Folegandros—historians are divided on whether the name immortalizes the Cretan explorer Pholegandrus or comes from the Phoenician term for "rock-strewn"—all stay in the main town, and hang around the town's three squares. A walk, a swim at the beach, a visit to the little Folklore Museum at Ano Meria, meeting other people who love the essence of the Greek islands: these require few arrangements. Unless you want to stop on the side of the road to look at views (the island does offer an array of interesting hiking trails), the bus is adequate. There are a number of beaches—Angali and Ayios Nikolaos are especially good. Because Folegandros is so small, it fills up fast in August, and despite the absence of raucous nightlife, it somewhat loses its special flavor.

CHORA ΧΩΡΑ

42 km (27 mi) northwest of Santorini.

As the boat approaches the little port of Karavostasi, bare, sun-scoured cliffs—with a hint of relieving green in wet winter but only gray glare in summer—let you know where you are. Leaving the port immediately, since there is hardly anything here, visitors climb the road 3 km (2 mi) to Chora on buses (which meet all ferries). On the rugged way up, you'll see the spectacular, whitewashed **church of Koímisis tis Theotókou** (or Dormition of the Mother of God) dominating the town on the high cliff where the ancient settlement first stood. On Easter Sunday the chief icon is carried through the town.

After a steep ride, cliff-top Chora comes into view. Its sky-kissing perch is well out of sight of the port, an important consideration in the centuries when the seas here were plagued by pirate raiders. Today, Chora—small, white, old, and preserved lovingly by the islanders—is less hidden and is known as the main reason to visit the island. Its main street, starting at the bus stop (no cars in town) meanders through five

Perched at a nearly angelic height, the Church of the Dormition of the Mother of God lords it over Folegandros's main town.

little squares—the middle three are the main ones—each with a few restaurants and cafés shaded by bougainvillea and hibiscus. Some of the buildings, including a hotel and café, are set into the walls of the Venetian fort, or Kastro, built by the Venetian duke of Naxos in the 13th century. The second street circles the Kastro and the precipice on which the town stands and is strikingly lined with two-story cube houses that form a wall atop the towering cliff. The glory days of Venice came to an end in 1715, when the ruling Turks sacked Folegandros and sold the captives as slaves. The old families go back to 1780, when the island was repopulated. As for dining and lodging, the new fancier places at the edge of town miss the meaning of the island. Opt, instead, for the simple tavernas in Chora, all family-run. Next to one another and competitive, they are all good.

ANO MERIA ΑΝΩ ΜΕΡΙΑ

5 km (3 mi) northwest of Chora.

The paved road connects the port, the capital, and, after a short drive, Ano Meria. On the way there, you can see terraces where barley was coaxed seemingly from stone, though they are hardly farmed now. The tiny town is a smaller version of Chora, and the cafés are perfect places for a drink.

Folklore Museum. Exhibits in the little Folklore Museum reconstruct traditional farming life. The adjacent church of Agios Panteliemon celebrates the feast day of Saint Panteliemon on July 27, and almost

everyone goes. ⊠ *Chora, Folegandros* ☎ *22860/41069* ☜ *Free*
☉ *June–Sept., daily 10–6.*

WHERE TO EAT AND STAY

*For expanded hotel reviews, visit
Fodors.com.*

¢ ✕ **I Piazze.** A middle-square eat-
GREEK ery, this popular option has tables
set out under trees. Specialties
include *kalasouna* cheese pies and
homemade noodles (called *mat-
sata*) with pork or lamb. They also
sell their own aromatic thyme honey. ⊠ *Middle square, Ano Meria*
☎ *22860/41274* ⊟ *No credit cards.*

¢ ✕ **O Kritikos.** Set under a tree and abutting a Byzantine church, Kritikos
GREEK serves exclusively local meats and vegetables. Souroto, a local cheese,
makes a fitting appetizer. *Kontosouli* is usually pork on the spit; here
it is a mixture of lamb and pork, and delicious. ⊠ *Middle square, Ano
Meria* ☎ *22860/41219* ⊟ *No credit cards.*

$$$$ ▦ **Anemomilos Apartments.** Perched on the towering cliff overlooking the
Fodor's Choice sea and set amid a series of small garden terraces (perfect for breakfast
★ and drinks), this complex is the best place to stay in Folegandros—it is
not only the friendly domain of Dimitris and Cornelia Patelis but offers
truly breathtaking vistas of sea and sky. **Pros:** by far the best place to
stay in Chora. **Cons:** some apartments can feel closed in. ⊠ *Chora, Ano
Meria, Folegandros* ☎ *22860/41309* ⊕ *www.anemomilosapartments.
com* ↴ *23 rooms* ☖ *In-room: a/c, Wi-Fi. In-hotel: pool* ☉ *Closed
mid-Oct.–Easter.*

$ ▦ **Meltemi.** If you want a simple, inexpensive, family place to stay, Melt-
emi does the job. **Pros:** pleasant and convenient. **Cons:** no sea view.
⊠ *Chora, Ano Meria* ☎ *22860/41425* ⊕ *www.greekhotel.com* ↴ *11
rooms* ☖ *In-room: a/c.* ⊟ *No credit cards* ☉ *Closed Nov.–Feb.*

SHOPPING

JEWELRY **Jewelry Creations.** Open April through September, this shop features the
jewelry of Apostolos and Eleni, who have been creating their striking
jewels, often with Greek stones, for 20 years. ⊠ *Middle square, Chora*
☎ *22860/41524.*

A TASTE OF ITALY

The island's Italian vibe lingers at
Flavio Facciolo's Café dei Viaggia-
tori. Found on the first bus square,
Flavio and his wife offer a selection of good Italian wines, serve
light Venetian-flavored snacks,
and serve the best espresso on
the isle.

Crete

WORD OF MOUTH

"I visited the Minoan Palace of Knossos, and it is definitely not 'Disneyfied.' If you are interested in history, . . . King Minos's palace at Knossos is a must-see. Our on-site guide, Marinella, a Minoan descendant, spoke excellent English and gave a most informative and relaxing tour of the palace for 10 euros per person."

—Marinos2006

WELCOME TO CRETE

TOP REASONS TO GO

★ **Minoan Magnificence:** At the Palace of Knossos, get up close to the mysteries—and the throne room's dazzling murals—of the 3,500-year-old civilization of the Minoans.

★ **Getting Your Sea Major:** From palm-backed Vai to remote Elafonisi, some of the finest beaches in Greece are lapped by Crete's turquoise waters.

★ **Crete's Venice:** Although it has its bright city lights, Rethymnon is most noted for its time-burnished Venetian/Turkish quarter, threaded with narrow lanes leading to palazzos, fountains, and shady squares.

★ **Walk on the Wild Side:** With its snowcapped peaks and deep gorges, craggy Crete offers lots of escapes for those who want to get away from it all.

★ **Suite Temptation:** New palatial resorts let you live like royalty in a Venetian palace or—at luxurious outposts like the Elounda Mare and Elounda Beach—sun worship the day away in your own private pool.

1 Eastern Crete. Knossos, the most spectacular of the Minoan palaces and Crete's most popular attraction, is here in the east. Just as this sprawling complex was the hub of island civilization 3,500 years ago, nearby Heraklion is Crete's bustling modern capital, and farther east along the coast is the Elounda peninsula, the island's epicenter of luxury, where some of the world's most sumptuous resort getaways are tucked along a stunning shoreline. The east isn't all hustle, bustle, and glitz, though—the beach at Vai is just one example of the natural beauty that abounds here in the east, and in mountain villages like those on the Lasithi plateau, old traditions continue to thrive.

GETTING ORIENTED

Crete is long and narrow, approximately 257 km (159 mi) long and only 60 km (37 mi) at its widest. The most development is present on the north shore; for the most part, the southern coast remains blessedly unspoiled. The island's three major cities, Heraklion, Rethymnon, and Hania, are in the north and are connected by the island's major highway, an east–west route that traverses most of the north coast. Heraklion, Hania, Ayios Nikolaos, and Sitiea are served by ferry from Piraeus, and Heraklion and Hania have international airports. By car or bus, it's easy to reach other parts of the island from these gateways.

CRETE

DIA
Fodhele
Heraklion
Palace of Knossos
Neapolis
Elounda
Gulf of Mirabello
Vai
1
Siteia
DIKTI MOUNTAINS
Kritsa
Ayii Deka
MESARA PLAIN
Ierapetra
CHRISI
KOUFONISI

Libyan Sea

0   15 mi
0   15 km

8

2 **Western Crete.** The scenery gets more rugged as you head west, where the White Mountains pierce the blue sky with snow-capped peaks then plunge into the Libyan Sea along dramatic, rocky shorelines. Mountain scenery and remote seacoast villages—some, like Loutro, accessible only on foot or by boat—attract many visitors to the west. Others come to enjoy the urban pleasures of Rethymnon and Hania, gracious cities that owe their harbors, architectural jewels, and exotic charms to Venetian and Turkish occupiers.

CRETE'S BEST BEACHES

GOOD TO KNOW

All you need on Crete's north shore beaches are a bathing suit and towel—everything else, from beach lounges to umbrellas and snorkeling gear, are available for rent at most.

Beaches at Rethymnon and Malia are even equipped with lifeguards, a rare species in Greece, making these sands especially safe for kids.

On the south coast, equip yourself with a good map to find tucked away coves and remote beaches.

With hundreds of miles of dramatic coastline, Crete serves up an almost endless supply of beaches. Many are soft and powdery, some are action-packed with water sports, and others are blissfully untrammeled. The very best bookend the island: palm-shaded Vai to the east and Elafonisi to the west, where white sands ring an islet just offshore.

Lovers of sand and surf quickly discover that there are really two distinct types of beaches on Crete: the highly developed strands on the north coast and the rugged getaway beaches on the south coast. Northern beaches stretch along the flat, sandy coastal plain between the island's major cities and are easily reached by the east–west national highway, as well as by an extensive bus network. Most are packed with umbrellas and sun beds and backed by hotels, including some of Greece's most luxurious resorts. Beaches on the south coast are tucked into coves and bays, often at the end of poor roads; a rental car is a must to explore the south coast beaches.

MATALA

At this scrappy, low-key resort near the Palace of Phaistos, a place on the sandy beach comes with a remarkable view—a cliff face at one end of the sand is etched with seaside caves that have sheltered everyone from ancient Romans to 1960s hippies.

Sun beds and umbrellas are available for rent, but you're welcome to stretch out on your own towel next to them.

For a more idyllic experience, make the 1-km (½-mi) trek across the adjoining headland to Red beach, named for the clay cliffs that surround this remote cove, where the sound of goat bells from herb-scented hillsides mixes with the sound of the surf.

A couple of buses a day serve Matala from Heraklion.

VAI

A beautiful palm forest and soft sands put this beach at the eastern end of Crete on just about everyone's list of top Greek beaches.

Such assets, of course, don't go unnoticed, and it seems that just about anyone who steps foot on Crete beats the well-worn path to Vai sooner or later (the beach is about 150 km [90 mi] east of Heraklion).

Crystal clear waters are sublime for swimming, snorkeling is rewarding, and concessions provide food and

drink. Best of all, a short hike across a hill at the south end of the beach leads to a delightful strand that is blessedly uncrowded.

ELAFONISI

A Robinson Crusoe–like atmosphere prevails at this expanse of white sands and crystal blue waters, on the southwest coast about 80 km (48 mi) from Hania.

Sand dunes back the beach and a sandy islet just offshore is reached by wading through the warm waters.

Civilization in this remote part of Crete doesn't extend much beyond a small shop selling snacks.

In high season, a public bus makes the trip here from Kastelli Kissamou, about 40 km (25 mi) away (usually one bus a day in the morning, one return bus in the afternoon).

SOUGIA AND PALEOCHORA

The hour-long drive or bus ride across the White Mountains from Hania is breathtaking and spectacular.

Both these nearby, low-key beach towns provide all the right ingredients for a getaway—tavernas, rooms to rent, and long stretches of unspoiled sand washed by the warm surf of the Libyan Sea.

8

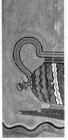

Updated by
Charles Norris

To Greeks, Crete is the Megalonissi (Great Island), a hub of spectacular ancient art and architecture. Fabled as the land of King Minos, it is a unique world where civilization is counted by the millennium. From every point of view travelers discover landscapes of amazing variety. Mountains, split with deep gorges and honeycombed with caves, rise in sheer walls from the sea. Snowcapped peaks loom behind sandy shoreline, vineyards, and olive groves. Miles of beaches, some with a wealth of amenities and others isolated and unspoiled, fringe the coast. Yet despite the attractions of sea and mountains, it is still the mystery surrounding Europe's first civilization and empire that draws the great majority of visitors to Crete and its world-famous Minoan palaces.

Around 1500 BC, while the rest of Europe was still in the grip of primitive barbarity, one of the most brilliant and amazing civilizations the world was ever to know approached its final climax, one that was breathtakingly uncovered through the late 19th-century excavations of Sir Arthur Evans. Paintings of bull-leapers, sculptures of bare-breasted snake charmers, myths of minotaurs, and the oldest throne in Europe were just a few of the wonders that the British archaeologist brought up from the earth to the astonishment of newspapers around the world. They proved telling evidence of the great elegance of King Minos's court (Evans chose the king's name to christen this culture). He determined that the Minoans, prehistoric Cretans, had founded Europe's first urban culture as far back as the 3rd millennium BC, and the island's rich legacy of art and architecture strongly influenced both mainland Greece and the Aegean islands in the Bronze Age. From around 1900 BC the Minoan palaces at Knossos (near present-day Heraklion), Mallia, Phaistos, and elsewhere were centers of political power, religious authority, and economic activity—all concentrated in one sprawling complex of buildings. Their administration seems to have had much in common with contemporary cultures in Egypt and Mesopotamia. What set the Minoans apart from the rest of the Bronze Age world was their art. It was lively and naturalistic, and they excelled in miniature techniques. From the scenes illustrated on their frescoes, stone vases, seal stones, and signet rings, it is possible to build a picture of a productive, well-regulated society. Yet new research suggests that prehistoric Crete was not a peaceful place; there may have been years of warfare before Knossos became the island's dominant power, in around 1600 BC. It is now thought that political upheaval, rather than the devastating volcanic eruption on the island of Santorini, triggered the violent downfall of the palace civilization around 1450 BC.

But there are many memorable places in Crete that belong to a more recent past, one measured in centuries and not millennia. Other invaders and occupiers—Roman colonists, the Byzantines, Arab invaders, Venetian colonists, and Ottoman pashas—have all left their mark on Heraklion, Hania, Rethymnon, and other towns and villages throughout the island. Today Crete welcomes outsiders, who delight in its splendid beaches, charming Old Town quarters, and array of splendid landscapes. Openly inviting to guests who want to experience the real Greece, Cretans remain family oriented and rooted in tradition and you'll find that one of the greatest pleasures on Crete is immersing yourself in the island's lifestyle.

PLANNER

8

WHEN TO GO

The best times for visiting Crete is May, when every outcrop of rock is ablaze with brilliant wildflowers and the sea is warm enough for a brisk dip, or September and October, when the sea is still warm and the light golden but piercingly clear. A spring visit comes with the advantage of long days.

Crete is really only noticeably busy from mid-July through August, when the main Minoan sights and towns on the north coast come close to overflowing with tourists. Take special care at these times to avoid such places as Mallia and Limin Hersonissos, hideously overdeveloped towns where bars and pizzerias fill up with heavy-drinking northern Europeans on summertime package tours.

Even in the height of summer, though, you can enjoy many parts of the west coast without feeling too oppressed by crowds. Crete can also be a pleasure in winter, when you can visit the museums and archaeological sites and enjoy the island's delightful towns without the crush of crowds. Remember, though, that rainfall can be heavy in January and February, and note that many hotels and restaurants, especially resorts, close from late October or November through mid-April or May.

PLANNING YOUR TIME

Enticing as Crete's beaches are, there is much more to the island than sand and surf. Archaeological sites in Crete open at 8 or 8:30 in summer, so get an early start to wander through the ruins before the sun is blazing. You'll also want to visit some of the folklife museums that pay homage to the island's traditional past. One of the finest collections is in Vori, southwest of Heraklion; there are also excellent folk collections at the Historical and Folk Art Museum in Rethymnon and the Historical Museum of Crete in Heraklion. An evening should begin with a stroll around the shady squares that grace every Cretan town and village, or along a waterfront promenade—those in Hania, Ayios Nikolaos, and Siteia are especially picturesque and jammed with locals. Most evenings are spent over a long meal, almost always eaten outdoors in the warm weather. For entertainment, seek out a *kentron* (a taverna that hosts traditional Cretan music and dancing). The star performer is the *lyra* player, who can extract a surprisingly subtle sound from the small pear-shaped instrument, held upright on the thigh and played with a bow. Ask at your hotel where lyra players are performing—the enchanting serenade you wind up hearing could well prove to be a treasured Cretan memory.

EMERGENCIES

Your hotel can help you call an English-speaking doctor. Pharmacies stay open late by turns, and a list of those open late is displayed in their windows.

Ambulance ☎ *166.* **Police (emergency)** ☎ *100.* **Hospitals** ☎ *28410/25221 in Ayios Nikolaos, 28210/27000 in Hania, 2810/392111 in Heraklion, 28310/27814 in Rethymnon.* **Tourist Police** ☎ *171 central operator, 28410/26900 in Ayios Nikolaos, 28210/733331 in Hania, 2810/283190 in Heraklion, 28310/28156 in Rethymnon.*

GETTING HERE AND AROUND

AIR TRAVEL

Olympic Airways connects Athens, and other islands, with Heraklion, Hania, and Siteia.

Aegean Airlines flies between Athens and Heraklion and Hania. Airfares have risen substantially in the past few years, and summertime flights from Athens to Crete are expensive. Expect to pay at least twice as much as (if not much, much more than) you would to make the trip by boat. Fares come down in winter, when special offers are also often available. The principal arrival point on Crete is Heraklion Airport, where up to 16 flights daily arrive from Athens and daily flights arrive from throughout Greece. Heraklion is also serviced directly by charter flights from other European cities. There are several daily flights from Athens to Hania Airport, and several a week from Athens to Siteia, which is also connected to Rhodes with a few weekly flights in summer. In summer, Hania is also served by flights to and from other European cities, mostly charters. A municipal bus just outside Heraklion Airport can take you to Eleftherlou Square in the Heraklion town center. Tickets are sold from a kiosk next to the bus stop; the fare is €1.10. From Hania Airport, Olympic Airlines buses take you to the airline office in the center for €3, but these run infrequently. Cabs line up outside all airports to meet flights; the fare into the respective towns is about €5 for Heraklion, €7 for Hania, and €4 for Siteia.

Airports Hania Airport ⊠ *15 km [9 mi] northeast of Hania, off road to Sterne, Souda Bay* ☎ *28210/83800* ⊕ *www.chania-airport.com.* **Heraklion Airport (Kazantzakis International Airport)** ⊠ *5 km [3 mi] east of town, off road to Gournes, Heraklion* ☎ *2810/397800* ⊕ *www.heraklion-airport.info.* **Siteia Airport** ⊠ *1 km [½ mi] northwest of town, off main coast road, Siteia, Crete* ☎ *28430/24424.*

Carriers Aegean Airlines ☎ *210/6261000 reservations within Greece toll-free, 2810/334324 in Hania, 2810/334330 in Heraklion* ⊕ *www.aegeanairlines. gr.* **Olympic Airways** ☎ *801/8010101 reservations within Greece toll-free, 2810/244802 in Heraklion, 28210/57702 in Hania, 28430/24666 in Siteia* ⊕ *www.olympicairlines.com.*

BIKE AND MOPED TRAVEL

Be cautious: motorbike accidents account for numerous injuries among tourists every year. Reliable rentals can be arranged through Blue Sea Rentals in Heraklion, and you'll find rentals in just about any town on the tourist trail. Expect to pay about €20 a day for a 50cc moped, for which you will need to present only a valid driver's license; law requires a motorcycle license to rent larger bikes. Fees usually cover insurance, but only for repairs to the bike, and usually with a deductible of at least €500. The law mandates that you wear a helmet. Cycling is also increasingly popular in Crete. Six group excursions of varying levels of difficulty, to Minoan sites, mountain monasteries, and remote beaches are offered by Bicycle Sivas, in the south-coast village of the same name; daylong excursions start at about €50, with bike rental included.

Bike and Moped Information Bicycle Sivas ⊠ *Sivas* ☎ *28920/42161.*

Blue Sea Rentals ⊠ *Kosmo Zoutou 5–7, Heraklion* ☎ *2810/241097* ⊕ *www. bluesearentals.com.*

BUS TRAVEL

You can find schedules and book seats in advance at bus stations, and tourist offices are well equipped with schedules and information about service. As efficient as the bus network is, you might have a hard time getting out of Heraklion, what with its confusing multitude of stations. You'll find the bus station for western Crete opposite the port. The station for the south is outside the Hania Gate to the right of the Archaeological Museum. The third station, for transportation heading east, is at the traffic circle at the end of Leoforos D. Bofor, close to the old harbor. Ask someone at the tourist information office to tell you exactly where to find your bus and to show you the spot on a map.

Bus Information KTEL ☎ *28410/22234 in Ayios Nikolaos, 28210/93052 in Hania, 2810/221765 in Heraklion, 28310/22785 in Rethymnon* ⊕ *www.bus-service-crete-ktel.com.*

BOAT AND FERRY TRAVEL

Heraklion and Souda Bay (5 km [3 mi] east of Hania) are the island's main ports, and there is regular service as well to Siteia and once-a-week service to Rethymnon. Service is on overnight crossings from these ports

8

to and from Piraeus, and daytime service from Piraeus to Heraklion and Hania is available in the summer. Ferries also connect Crete with other islands, mostly those in the Cyclades and Dodecanese. Service includes Minoan Lines catamarans between Santorini and Heraklion (cutting travel time to just under two hours) and a ferry linking Siteia with the Dodecanese islands of Kassos, Karpathos, and Rhodes. There is also weekly service from Kalamata and Gythion in the Peloponnese to Kissamos (Kastelli) in the far west of the island. Ships also sail from Heraklion to Limassol, in Cyprus, and to Haifa, Israel. On the overnight runs, you can book either a berth or an airplane-style seat, and there are usually cafeterias, dining rooms, shops, and other services on board. The most economical berth accommodations are in four-berth cabins, which are relatively spacious and comfortable and are equipped with bathrooms.

A one-way fare from Piraeus to Heraklion, Rethymnon, or Hania without accommodation costs about €38, and from about €55 with accommodation. A small discount is given for round-trip tickets. Car fares are about €65 each way, depending on vehicle size. In July and August, a boat service around the Samaria Gorge operates along the southwest coast from Hora Sfakion to Loutro, Ayia Roumeli, Souyia, Lissos, and Paleochora, the main resort on the southwest coast. Ferries also sail from Paleochora to Ghavdos, an island south of Crete, and from Ierapetra to Krissi, an island also to the south. Most travel agencies sell tickets for all ferries and hydrofoils. Make reservations several days in advance during the July to August high season.

Boat Information **Anek (Piraeus to Heraklion, Rethymnon, and Hania)** ✉ *22 Akti Kondili* ☎ *210/4197470* ⊕ *www.anek.gr.* **Anen (Pireaus and Peloponnese to Kissamos)** ✉ *Port, Kissamos* ⊕ *www.anen.gr.* **Hellenic Seaways (Heraklion to Santorini, Paros, and Mykonos via high-speed catamaran)** ✉ *Paleologos Travel, 25 Avgoustou, Heraklion* ☎ *2810/346185* ⊕ *www.hellenicseaways.gr.* **Minoan Lines (Piraeus to Heraklion)** ✉ *Avgoustou 17, Heraklion* ☎ *210/4145700* ⊕ *www.minoan.gr.*

CAR TRAVEL

Roads on Crete are not too congested, yet the accident rate is high compared to other parts of Europe. Driving in the main towns can be nerve-racking, to say the least. Most road signs are in Greek and English, though signage is often nonexistent or inadequate. Be sure to carry a road map at all times, and to stop and ask directions when the need arises—otherwise, you may drive miles out of your way. Gas stations are not plentiful outside the big towns, and gasoline is more expensive in Crete than it is in the United States and on par with prices elsewhere in Europe—expect to pay about €1.70 a liter (about €6.55 a gallon).

Drive defensively wherever you are, as Cretan drivers are aggressive and liable to ignore the rules of the road. Sheep and goats frequently stray onto the roads, with or without their shepherd or sheepdog. In July and August, tourists on motor scooters can be a hazard. Night driving is not advisable.

As for car rentals, you can arrange beforehand with a major agency in the United States or in Athens to pick up a car on arrival in Crete, or work through one of the many local car-rental agencies that have offices in the airports and in the cities, as well as in some resort villages. For the most part, these local agencies are extremely reliable, provide excellent service, and charge very low rates. Many, such as the excellent Crete Car Rental, will meet your ship or plane and drop you off again at no extra charge.

Even without advance reservations, expect to pay about €40 or less a day in high season for a medium-size car with unlimited mileage. Weekly prices are negotiable, but with unlimited mileage rentals start at about €200 in summer. At most agencies, you are responsible for a €500 deductible for any damage, regardless of your insurance coverage.

Avis ⊕ www.avis.com ✉ Hania Airport ☎ 28210/63080 ⊕ www.avis.com ✉ Heraklion Airport ☎ 2810/229402 ⊕ www.avis.com. **Crete Car Rental** ✉ Kallipoleos 11, Heraklion ☎ 2810/213445 ⊕ www.crete-car-rental.com. **Sixt** ✉ Akti Konudourou 28, Ayios Nikolaos, ☎ 28410/82055 ⊕ www.sixt.com ✉ Hania Airport ☎ 28210/20905 ✉ Heraklion Airport ☎ 2810/280915 ✉ Ikariou 93, Heraklion ☎ 2810/284260.

HIKING CRETE

Crete is excellent hiking terrain, and many trails crisscross the mountains and gorges, especially in the southwest. The Greek National Tourism Organization (GNTO or EOT) is a source of information.

Alpine Travel. This outfitter offers one-day, one-week, and two-week hiking tours throughout western Crete and makes transportation and accommodation arrangements for individual trekkers as well. ✉ *Akrotiriou, Pitharia, Hania* ☎ *28210/50939* ⊕ *www.alpine.gr.*

Greek Mountaining Club of Hania. This association operates overnight refuges in the White Mountains and on Mt. Ida and operates expeditions into the mountains of western Crete and other wilderness regions. ✉ *Tzanakaki 90, Hania* ☎ *28210/44647* ⊕ *www.eoshanion.gr.*

RESTAURANTS

Cretans tend to take their meals seriously, and like to sit down in a taverna to a full meal. Family-run tavernas take pride in serving Cretan cooking, and a number of the better restaurants in cities now also stress Cretan produce and traditional dishes. One way to dine casually is to sample the *mezedes* served at some bars and tavernas. These often include such Cretan specialties as *trypopita* (cheese-filled pastry), and a selection of cheeses: Cretan *graviera*, a hard, smooth cheese, is a blend of pasteurized sheep's and goat's milk that resembles Emmentaler in flavor and texture—not too sharp, but with a strong, distinctive flavor—and *mizythra* (a creamy white cheese). As main courses, Cretans enjoy grilled meat, generally lamb and pork, but there is also plenty of fresh fish. Mezedes and main courses are usually shared, from large platters placed in the center of the table.

Cretan olive oil is famous throughout Greece; it's heavier and richer than other varieties. The island's wines are special: look for Boutari Kritikos, a crisp white; and Minos Palace, a smooth red. Make sure you try the *tsikouthia* (also known as *raki*), the Cretan firewater made from fermented grape skins, which is drunk at any hour, often accompanied by a dish of raisins or walnuts drenched in honey, along with a piece

8

of *ravani*, cake made from farina. Many restaurants offer raki free of charge at the end of a meal. Lunch is generally served from 1 to 3 or so. Dinner is an event here, as it is elsewhere in Greece, and is usually served late; in fact, when non-Greeks are finishing up around 10:30 or so, locals usually begin arriving.

DINING AND LODGING PRICES IN EUROS				
	¢	$	$$	$$$	$$$$
Restaurants	under €8	€8–€11	€11–€15	€15–€20	over €20
Hotels	under €60	€60–€90	€90–€120	€120–€160	over €160

Luxury resort prices on Crete are more comparable to the Athens price chart. Restaurant prices are for one main course at dinner, or for two mezedes (small dishes). Hotel prices are for a standard double room in high season, including taxes. Inquire when booking if meal plans (which can entail higher rates) are mandatory.

HOTELS

Some of Greece's finest resorts line the shores of Elounda peninsula, offering sumptuous surroundings and exquisite service. Although the atmosphere at these resorts is more international than Greek, you'll find authentic surroundings in the Venetian palaces and old mansions that are being sensitively restored as small hotels, especially in Hania and Rethymnon. Many of the better hotels on Crete offer special rates and packages through their Web sites, and it's always worthwhile to check out what discounts might be available during your stay—special rates often bring even a luxurious hotel into affordable range, especially outside of high season. For a more rustic yet authentic experience on Crete, opt for simple, whitewashed, tile-floor rooms with rustic pine furniture in the ubiquitous "room to rent" establishments in mountain and seaside villages. Another common term is "studio," which implies the presence of a kitchen or basic cooking facilities. Standards of cleanliness are high in Crete, and service is almost always friendly.

VISITOR INFORMATION

Tourist offices are more plentiful, and more helpful, on Crete than they are in many other parts of Greece. Offices of the Greek National Tourism Organization (GNTO or EOT), in the major towns, are open daily 8–2 and 3–8:30; find their addresses listed under Visitor Information in the Heraklion and Rethymnon pages below. The municipalities of Ayios Nikolaos, Siteia, and Ierapetra operate their own tourist offices, and these provide a wealth of information on the towns and surrounding regions, as well as helping with accommodation and local tours; most keep long summer hours, open daily 8:30 am–9 pm.

Visitor Information Greek National Tourist Organization ⊠ *N. Kazantzakis Airport, Heraklion* ☎ *2810/397305* ⊕ *www.gnto.gr.*

TOUR OPTIONS

Resort hotels and large agents organize guided tours in air-conditioned buses to the main Minoan sites; excursions to spectacular beaches such as Vai in the northeast and Elafonisi in the southwest; and trips to Santorini and to closer islands such as Spinalonga, a former leper colony off Ayios Nikolaos. Diktynna Travel offers small-group tours of the Samaria Gorge, cooking demonstrations, and excursions into the White Mountains, with knowledgeable guides and extras such as traditional meals in mountain tavernas. The Crete Travel Web site is an excellent source for tour information, with insights into many of the island's more worthwhile sights and tours including hiking excursions and visits to out-of-the-way monasteries.

A tour of Knossos and the Archaeological Museum in Heraklion costs about €40; a tour of Phaistos and Gortyna plus a swim at Matala costs about €20; a trip to the Samaria Gorge costs about €25. Travel agents can also arrange for personal guides.

Tour Information Crete Travel ⊠ *Kallipoleos 11, Heraklion* ☎ *2810/213445* ⊕ *www.cretetravel.com.*

EASTERN CRETE ΑΝΑΤΟΛΙΚΗ ΚΡΗΤΗ

Eastern Crete includes the towns and cities of Heraklion, Ayios Nikolaos, Siteia, and Ierapetra, as well as the archaeological sites of Knossos and Gournia. Natural wonders lie amid these man-made places, including the palm-fringed beach at Vai, and the Lasithi plateau and other inland plains and highlands are studded with villages where life goes on untouched by the hedonism of the coastal resorts. You may well make first landfall in Heraklion, the island's major port. You'll want to spend time here to visit the excellent Archaeological Museum and Knossos, but you're likely to have a more relaxing Cretan experience in Ayios Nikolaos, a charming and animated port town; in the resorts on the stunning Elounda peninsula; or on the beautiful and undeveloped eastern end of the island, around Palaikastro.

8

HERAKLION ΗΡΑΚΛΕΙΟ

175 km (109 mi) south of Piraeus harbor in Athens, 69 km (43 mi) west of Ayios Nikolaos, 78 km (49 mi) east of Rethymnon.

In Minoan times, Crete's largest city—the fifth-largest city in Greece— was a harbor for Knossos, the largest palace and effective power center of prehistoric Crete. The Bronze Age remains were built over long ago, and now Heraklion (also known as Iraklion), with more than 120,000 inhabitants, stretches far beyond even the Venetian walls. Heraklion is not immediately appealing: it's a sprawling and untidy collection of apartment blocks and busy roadways. Many travelers looking for Crete's more-rugged pleasures bypass the island's capital altogether, but the city's renowned Archaeological Museum and the nearby Palace of Knossos make Heraklion a mandatory stop for anyone even remotely interested in ancient civilizations.

Besides, at closer look, Heraklion is not without its charms. A walk down Dedalou and the other pedestrians-only streets provides plenty of amusements, and the city has more than its share of outdoor cafés where you can sit and watch life unfold. Seaside promenades and narrow lanes that run off them can be quite animated, thanks to ongoing

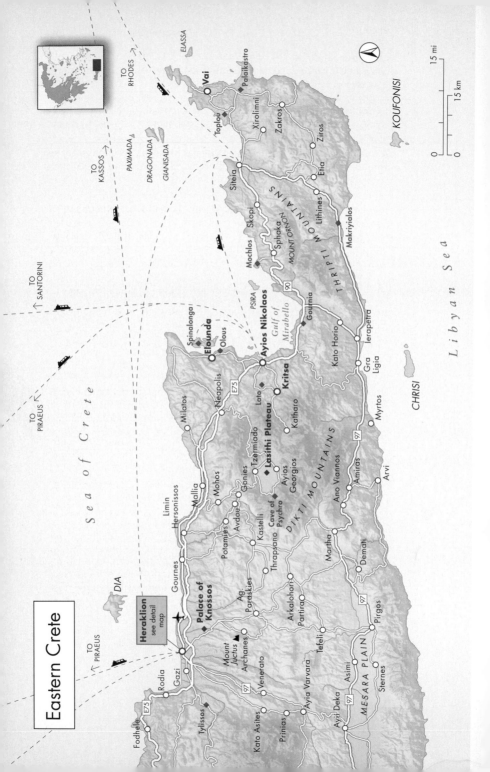

restoration, and the inner harbor dominated by the Koules, a sturdy Venetian fortress, is richly evocative of the island's storied past.

GETTING HERE AND AROUND

AIR TRAVEL Heraklion is Crete's major air hub, and Kazantzakis airport has been greatly expanded in recent years. Flights on Olympic and Aegean airlines arrive almost hourly from Athens, and many charter flights from other European cities use the airport; Aegean also has regularly scheduled flights to Rome and a few other European cities. The airport is only about 5 km (3 mi) east of the city, easy to reach on public bus, €1.10, or taxi, about €10.

BOAT TRAVEL At least five daily sailings, three at night and two during the day, connect Heraklion and Pireaus in the summer, and the trip takes six and half to eight hours, depending on the vessel (daytime crossings are suspended from September through April). Ferries also connect Heraklion with Thessaloniki, with service three times a week in high season and twice a week at other times, usually stopping at Paros, Skiathos, and other island ports during the 22-hour voyage. In high season, daily catamaran service links Heraklion with Santorini, Mykonos, and other popular islands in the Cyclades, and service continues on a much-reduced basis throughout the year. The catamaran crossing to Santorini takes less than two hours. Operators and schedules change frequently; for the latest info, check on your route at ⊕ *www.ferries.gr* or with the travel agencies that operate near all Greek ports.

BUS TRAVEL Heraklion is Crete's bus hub and you can get just about anywhere on the island from of the city's three bus terminals, though finding the right terminal can be as tiring as reaching your destination. Service to the main towns—Ayios Nikolaos, Rethymnon, and Hania—runs hourly. Buses to all these towns arrive at and leave from the two adjacent terminals on the harbor, just east of the city center. Buses to and from points south of Heraklion use the terminal at Hania Gate, in the old city walls off Martyrs Street on the southwest side of the city center.

Visitor Information **Greek National Tourism Organization** ⊠ *Xanthoudidou 1, Heraklion* ☎ *2810/246106* ⊕ *www.gnto.gr.*

EXPLORING

If you have just a day in Heraklion, your time will be tight. Get an early start and spend a couple of hours in the morning doing this walk, stepping into the churches if they're open and poking around the lively market. Save your energy for the Archaeological Museum. Of course, we are not including nearby Knossos, which could easily occupy most of the following day. Either/or, if you're staying overnight in or near Heraklion, take an evening stroll in the busy area around Ta Leontaria and Kornarou Square; half the population seems to converge here.

Heraklion's ever improving road network is making it easier to avoid the all but impassable city center; note that if you're spending any time at all in Heraklion, wait until you are leaving the city to pick up a rental car.

TOP ATTRACTIONS

Fodor's Choice
★
Archaeological Museum. Standing in a class of its own, this museum guards practically all the Minoan treasures uncovered in the legendary excavations of the Palace of Knossos and other monuments of Minoan civilization. These amazing artifacts, many 3,000 years old, were brought to light in 20th-century excavations famed British archaeologist Sir Arthur Evans. A rewarding selection of highlights from the collection is currently well displayed and shown in a one-room annex while the museum undergoes extensive renovation. At press time, the many-times-postponed completion date has been set for mid-2012.

It's best to visit the museum first thing in the morning, before the tour buses arrive, or in late afternoon, once they pull away. Top treasures include the famous seal stones, many inscribed with Linear B script, discovered and deciphered by Evans around the turn of the 20th century. The most stunning and mysterious seal stone is the so-called Phaistos Disk, found at Phaistos Palace in the south, its purpose unknown. (Linear B script is now recognized as an early form of Greek, but the earlier Linear A script that appears on clay tablets and that of the Phaistos Disk have yet to be deciphered.)

But perhaps the most arresting exhibits are the sophisticated frescoes, restored fragments found in Knossos. They depict broad-shouldered, slim-waisted youths, their large eyes fixed with an enigmatic expression on the Prince of the Lilies; ritual processions and scenes from the bullring, with young men and women somersaulting over the back of a charging bull; and groups of court ladies, whose flounced skirts led a French archaeologist to exclaim in surprise, "*Des Parisiennes!*", a name still applied to this striking fresco.

The Minoans' talents at modeling in stone, ivory, and a kind of glass paste known as faience peaked in the later palace period (1700–1450 BC). A famous rhyton, a vase for pouring libations, carved from dark serpentine in the shape of a bull's head, has eyes made of red jasper and clear rock crystal with horns of gilded wood. An ivory acrobat—perhaps a bull-leaper—and two bare-breasted faience goddesses in flounced skirts holding wriggling snakes were among a group of treasures hidden beneath the floor of a storeroom at Knossos. Bull leaping, whether a religious rite or a favorite sport, inspired some of the most memorable images in Minoan art. Note, also, the three vases, probably originally covered in gold leaf, from Ayia Triada that are carved with scenes of Minoan life thought to be rendered by artists from Knossos: boxing matches, a harvest-home ceremony, and a Minoan official taking delivery of a consignment of hides. The most stunning rhyton of all, from Zakro, is made of rock crystal. ✉ *Eleftherias Sq., Heraklion* ☎ *2810/224630* ⊕ *www. culture.gr* ⬚ *€4; combined ticket for museum and Palace of Knossos €10* ☉ *Apr.–mid-Oct., Mon. 12:30–7, Tues.–Sun. 8–7; mid-Oct.–Mar., Mon. 12:30–5, Tues.–Sun. 8–5.*

Fodor's Choice
★
Historical Museum of Crete. An imposing mansion houses a varied collection of early Christian and Byzantine sculptures, Venetian and Ottoman stonework, artifacts of war, and rustic folklife items. The museum provides a wonderful introduction to Cretan culture, and is the only place

The Koules harbor fortress is a mighty reminder of the age when Venetians ruled Crete from their outpost in Heraklion.

in Crete to display the work of famed native son El Greco (Domenikos Theotocopoulos), who left the island—then part of the Venetian Republic—for Italy and, then, Spain around 1567; his *Baptism of Christ* and *View of Mount Sinai and the Monastery of St. Catherine* hang amid frescoes, icons, and other Byzantine pieces. Upstairs, look in on a room arranged as the study of Crete's most famous writer, Nikos Kazantzakis (1883–1957), the author of *Zorba the Greek* and an epic poem, *The Odyssey, a Modern Sequel*; he was born in Heraklion and is buried here, just inside the section of the walls known as the Martinengo. The top floor contains a stunning collection of Cretan textiles, including the brilliant scarlet weavings typical of the island's traditional handwork, and another room arranged as a domestic interior of the early 1900s. ⊠ *Kalokorinou, in a warren of little lanes near seafront, Heraklion* ☎ *2810/283219* ⊕ *www.historical-museum.gr* ☒ *€5* ☉ *Apr.–Oct., Mon.–Sat. 9–5; Nov.–Mar., Mon.–Sat. 9–3:30.*

★ **Koules.** Heraklion's inner harbor, where fishing boats land their catch and yachts are moored, is dominated by the Koules, the massive fortress so named by the Turks but, in fact, built by the Venetians as the Castello del Molo in the 16th century and decorated with three stone lions of St. Mark, symbol of Venetian imperialism. On the east side of the fortress are the vaulted arsenal; here Venetian galleys were repaired and refitted, and timber, cheeses, and sweet Malmsey wine were loaded for the three-week voyage to Venice. The view from the battlements takes in the inner as well as the outer harbor, where freighters and passenger ferries drop anchor, and the sprawling labyrinth of concrete apartment blocks that is modern Heraklion. To the south rises Mt. Iuktas and, to the west, the pointed peak of Mt. Stromboli. ⊠ *North end of 25 Avgoustou, Heraklion* ☎ *2810/288484* 🎟 *€2* ☺ *Apr.–Oct., Tues.–Sun. 8:30–7; Nov.–Mar., daily 8:30–3.*

Loggia. A gathering place for the island's Venetian nobility, this open-air arcade (with a meeting hall above) was built in the early 17th century by Francesco Basilicata, an Italian architect. Now restored to its original Palladian elegance, it adjoins the old Venetian Armory, now the City Hall. ⊠ *25 Avgoustou, Heraklion.*

Kir-Kor. Stop in at Kir-Kor, a venerable old *bougatsa* shop, for an envelope of flaky pastry that's either filled with a sweet, creamy filling and dusted with cinnamon and sugar, or stuffed with soft white cheese. A double portion served warm with Greek coffee is a nice treat. Thick Cretan yogurt and ice cream are other indulgences on offer. Kir-Kor is a popular place to hang out after getting off the night boat from Piraeus and waiting for museums and businesses to open. ⊠ *Eleftheriou Venizelou Sq., Heraklion.*

★ **Martinengo Bastion.** Six bastions shaped like arrowheads jut out from the well-preserved Venetian walls. Martinengo is the largest, designed by Micheli Sanmicheli in the 16th century to keep out Barbary pirates and Turkish invaders. When the Turks overran Crete in 1648, the garrison at Heraklion held out for another 21 years in one of the longest sieges in European history. General Francesco Morosini finally surrendered the city to the Turkish Grand Vizier in September 1669. He was allowed to sail home to Venice with the city's archives and such precious relics as the skull of Ayios Titos—which was not returned until 1966. Literary pilgrims come to the Martinengo to visit the **burial place of writer Nikos Kazantzakis.** The grave is a plain stone slab marked by a weathered wooden cross. The inscription, from his writings, says: "i fear nothing, i hope for nothing, i am free." ⊠ *South of Kyrillou Loukareos on N. G. Mousourou, Heraklion.*

Platia Eleftherias. The city's biggest square is paved in marble and dotted with fountains. The Archaeological Museum is off the north end of the square; at the west side is the beginning of Daidalou, the main thoroughfare, which follows the line of an early fortification wall and is now a pedestrian walkway lined with tavernas, boutiques, jewelers, and souvenir shops. ⊠ *Southeast end of Daidalou, Heraklion.*

Ta Leontaria. "The Lions," a stately marble Renaissance fountain, remains a beloved town landmark. It's the heart of Heraklion's town center—Eleftheriou Venizelou Square, a triangular pedestrian zone filled with cafés and named after the Cretan statesman who united the island with Greece in 1913. The square is known as Ta Leontaria and was the center of the colony founded in the 13th century, when Venice colonized Crete, and Heraklion became an important port of call on the trade routes to the Middle East. The city, and often the whole island (known then as Candia), was ruled by the Duke of Crete, a Venetian administrator. ⊠ *Eleftheriou Venizelou Sq., Heraklion.*

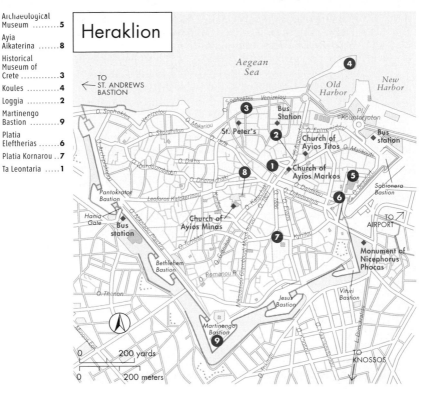

8

WORTH NOTING

★ **Ayia Aikaterina.** Nestled in the shadow of the Ayios Minas cathedral is one of Crete's most attractive small churches, Ayia Aikaterina, built in 1555. The church now houses a museum of icons by Cretan artists, who traveled to Venice to study with Italian Renaissance painters. Look for six icons (Nos. 2, 5, 8, 9, 12, and 15) by Michael Damaskinos, who worked in both Byzantine and Renaissance styles during the 16th century. ⊠ *Kyrillou Loukareos, Heraklion* 📷 *No phone* 💶 *€4* ⏱ *Mon. and Wed. 9:30–1, Thurs. and Sat. 9–1 and 5–7, Fri. 9–1.*

St. Peter's. One of Heraklion's oldest monuments, dating from the 13th century, has been been rebuilt many times over the years and has done duty as a church, monastery, mosque, and cinema. After recent refurbishments, St. Peter's is now an exhibition hall and its 15th-century frescoes, the oldest in the city, have been beautifully restored. ⊠ *West of harbor along seashore road, Heraklion.*

WHERE TO EAT

$ ✕ **Erganos.** One of Heraklion's most traditional restaurants—just out-
GREEK side the old city walls south of Eleftherias Square—takes its name from one of the cities of ancient Crete and serves authentic local fare, including mouthwatering little pies (*pitarakia*) filled with cheese and honey, wild herbs from the mountains, and ground meats. Lunch and dinner

both are often accompanied by Cretan music, sometimes provided by a fellow patron. ⊠ *Georgiadi 5, Heraklion* ☎ *2810/285629.*

$$
SEAFOOD

✕ **Ippokambos.** This seafront institution, always busy, is the most popular spot in town for fish. Service is attentive no matter how busy, and simple preparations of the fresh catch (on display in the kitchen) are accompanied by delicious salads and crisp house wines. ⊠ *Sofokli Venizelou 3, Heraklion* ☎ *2810/280240.*

$
GREEK
★

✕ **Pantheon.** The liveliest restaurant in Heraklion's covered meat market has grilled and spit-roasted meats, as well as hearty tripe soup and other traditional dishes. The surroundings are simple, but that doesn't stop locals from pouring in at all hours for a meal, which is nicely accompanied by salads made from the freshest Cretan produce. ⊠ *Market off Kornarou Sq., Heraklion* ☎ *2810/241652* ▭ *No credit cards.*

WHERE TO STAY

For expanded hotel reviews, visit Fodors.com.

¢

🏨 **El Greco.** At this basic-but-comfortable hotel smack dab in the city center, ask for a garden-facing room for a quieter night, or request a street-side balcony to watch the action around Ta Leontaria fountain, just steps away. **Pros:** central location; excellent value. **Cons:** a little faded; street noise in some rooms. ⊠ *4 Odos 1821, Heraklion* ☎ *2810/281071* 🖷 *2810/281072* ⊕ *www.elgrecohotel.gr* ⇘ *90 rooms* ⌂ *In-room: a/c, Wi-Fi. In-hotel: bar, parking* ⫶❂⫶ *Breakfast.*

$

🏨 **Marin Dream Hotel.** Set on a narrow street, the Marin Dream perches just above the harbor—sleek, contemporary decor and furnishings in the public spaces and guest rooms alike make this small inn on a narrow street just above the harbor especially soothing and restful. **Pros:** central location but on a quiet side street; a welcome oasis in busy Heraklion; nearby parking for €3 a day. **Cons:** somewhat generic furnishings. ⊠ *Doukos Bofor 12, Heraklion* ☎ *2810/300018* ⊕ *www.marinhotel.gr* ⇘ *44 rooms* ⌂ *In-room: a/c, Internet. In-hotel: restaurant, bar* ⫶❂⫶ *Breakfast.*

$$$
★

🏨 **Megaron.** A 1930s office building that for decades stood derelict above the harbor now houses an unusually luxurious and restful hotel, by far the best in town—special Internet rates are often lower than those at other hotels in this class, making the Megaron a relatively affordable indulgence. **Pros:** central location; most rooms with water views; wonderful rooftop pool and restaurant. **Cons:** rather formal surroundings. ⊠ *Doukos Bofor 9, Heraklion* ☎ *2810/305300* ⊕ *www.gdmmegaron.gr* ⇘ *38 rooms, 8 suites* ⌂ *In-room: a/c, Internet. In-hotel: restaurant, bar, pool, gym, laundry facilities, business center, parking* ⫶❂⫶ *Breakfast.*

KNOSSOS ΚΝΩΣΟΥ

5 km (3 mi) south of Heraklion.

GETTING HERE

Municipal buses No. 2 and No. 4 head to the fabled Palace of Knossos every 10 minutes or so from Heraklion, where the main stops include Eleftheriou Venizelous Square and the main bus station serving the eastern sector of the city.

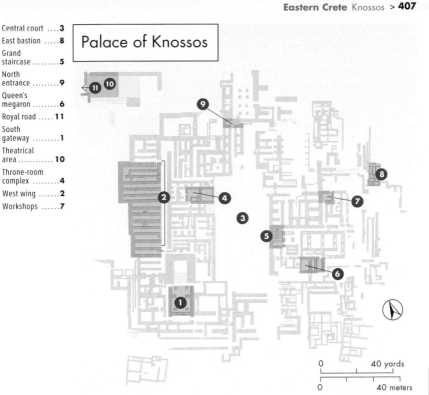

Palace of Knossos

0   40 yards

0   40 meters

8

EXPLORING

Fodor's Choice ★ **Palace of Knossos.** The most amazing of archaeological sites, the Palace of Knossos—in Greek, **Ανάκτορο Κνωσού**—once lay hidden beneath a huge mound hemmed in by low hills. Heinrich Schliemann, father of archaeology and discoverer of Troy, knew it was here, but Turkish obstruction prevented him from exploring his last discovery. Cretan independence from the Ottoman Turks made it possible for Sir Arthur Evans, a British archaeologist, to start excavations in 1899. A forgotten and sublime civilization thus came again to light with the uncovering of the great Palace of Knossos.

The magnificent Minoans flourished on Crete from around 2700 to 1450 BC, and their palaces and cities at Knossos, Phaistos, and Gournia were centers of political power and luxury—they traded in tin, saffron, gold, and spices as far afield as Spain—when the rest of Europe was a place of primitive barbarity. They loved art, farmed bees, and worshipped many goddesses. But what caused their demise? Some say political upheaval, but others point to an eruption on Thera (Santorini), about 100 km (60 mi) north in the Aegean, which caused tsunamis and earthquakes that brought about the end of this sophisticated civilization.

The Palace of Knossos site was occupied from Neolithic times, and the population spread to the surrounding land. Around 1900 BC, the hilltop was leveled and the first palace constructed; around 1700 BC, after an earthquake destroyed the original structure, the later palace was built, surrounded by houses and other buildings. Around 1450 BC, another widespread disaster occurred, perhaps an invasion: palaces and country villas were razed by fire and abandoned, but Knossos remained inhabited even though the palace suffered some damage. But around 1380 BC the palace and its outlying buildings were destroyed by fire, and at the end of the Bronze Age the site was abandoned. Still later, Knossos became a Greek city-state.

You enter the palace from the west, passing a bust of Sir Arthur Evans, who excavated at Knossos on and off for more than 20 years. A path leads you around to the monumental **south gateway.** The **west wing**

MINOS AND THE MINOTAUR

As you tour Knossos, you are stepping into the pages of Greek mythology. As myth has it, Minos coveted the Minoan throne and prayed to Poseidon to send a white bull he would sacrifice in thanksgiving. His wife became smitten and, seducing the animal, gave birth to the Minotaur. Minos ordered the architect Dedalus to build a labyrinthlike prison for the monster, who was half man and half bull. The Minotaur was ultimately killed by Theseus, son of the King of Athens who successfully maneuvered his way through the labyrinth by unwinding a ball of string.

encases lines of long, narrow storerooms where the true wealth of Knossos was kept in tall clay jars: oil, wine, grains, and honey. The **central court** is about 164 feet by 82 feet long. The cool, dark **throne-room complex** has a griffin fresco and a tall, wavy-back gypsum throne, the oldest in Europe. The most spectacular piece of palace architecture is the **grand staircase,** on the east side of the court, leading to the domestic apartments. Four flights of shallow gypsum stairs survive, lighted by a deep light well. Here you get a sense of how noble Minoans lived; rooms were divided by sets of double doors, giving privacy and warmth when closed, coolness and communication when open. The **queen's megaron** (apartment or hall) is decorated with a colorful dolphin fresco and furnished with stone benches. Beside it is a bathroom, complete with a clay tub, and next door a toilet, whose drainage system permitted flushing into a channel flowing into the Kairatos stream far below. The east side of the palace also contained **workshops.** Beside the staircase leading down to the **east bastion** is a stone water channel made up of parabolic curves and settling basins: a Minoan storm drain. Northwest of the east bastion is the **north entrance,** guarded by a relief fresco of a charging bull. Beyond is the **theatrical area,** shaded by pines and overlooking a shallow flight of steps, which lead down to the **royal road.** This, perhaps, was the ceremonial entrance to the palace.

For a complete education in Minoan architecture and civilization, consider touring Knossos and, of course, the Archaeological Museum in Heraklion (where many of the treasures from the palace are on view), then traveling south to the Palace of Phaistos, another great Minoan site, which has not been reconstructed. To reach Knossos by bus, take No. 2 (departing every 15 minutes) from Odos Evans, close to the

Although some critics claim that Sir Arthur Evans's restoration "Disneyfied" the Palace of Knossos, no one can deny the results are spectacular.

market, in Heraklion. ☎ 2810/231940 ⊕ *www.culture.gr* ✉ *€6; combined ticket for Knossos and Archaeological Museum in Heraklion €10* ☉ *Apr.–Oct., daily 8:30–8; Nov.–Mar., daily 8–6.*

LASITHI PLATEAU ΟΡΟΠΕΔΙΟ ΛΑΣΙΘΙΟΥ

47 km (29 mi) southeast of the Palace of Knossos, 52 km (32 mi) southeast of Heraklion.

The Lasithi plateau, 2,800 feet high and the biggest of the upland plains of Crete, lies behind a wall of barren mountains. Windmills still pump water for fields of potatoes and the apple and almond orchards that are a pale haze of blossom in early spring. The plateau is remote and breathtakingly beautiful, and ringed by small villages where shops sell local weaving and embroidery.

Cave of Psychro. The Cave of Psychro is an impressive, stalactite-rich cavern that was once a Minoan sanctuary and has become a popular tourist attraction on the plateau. This is one of a few places in Crete that are claimed to be the birthplace of Zeus, king of the gods, and where he was reared in secret, out of reach of his vengeful father, Kronos. Approach the cave on a short path from the large parking lot on foot or (a rather uncomfortable and expensive experience) by donkey. ⊠ *Near village of Psychro* ☎ No phone ✉ *€5* ☉ *July and Aug., daily 8–7; Sept.–June, daily 8:30–3.*

Cretan Folklore Museum. An old village house in Ayios Georgios contains the delightful Cretan Folklore Museum. The house stands as it was when generations of farmers lived here, and the simple furnishings, embroidery, tools, and combination of living quarters and stables provide a chance to see domestic life as it was, and indeed still is, for many residents. ⊠ *Ayios Georgios* ☎ *28440/31460* 💳 *€3* 🕓 *Mid-Apr.–late Oct., daily 10–4.*

WHERE TO EAT

¢
GREEK

✕**Kronio.** The promise of a meal in this cozy, family-run establishment is alone worth the trip up to the plateau. Delicious meat and vegetable pies as well as homemade casseroles and lamb dishes emerge from the kitchen, to be accompanied by fresh-baked bread and the house wine and followed up with homemade desserts. The charming proprietors, Vassilis and Christine, encourage you to linger over your wine or raki, and are a mine of knowledge about the Lasithi plateau. ⊠ *Tzermiado* ☎ *28440/22375* 🕓 *Closed Nov.–Mar.*

**EN
ROUTE**

A rewarding detour as you travel east toward the Lasithi plateau and Mallia takes you south to Kastelli, about 15 km (9 mi) southeast of Heraklion, where the lovely Byzantine church of Ayios Pandeleimon is decorated with elaborate frescoes. Interspersing the landscape here and there are segments of an aqueduct that served the nearby ancient Greek city of Lyttos, yet to be excavated. Thrapsano, about 7 km (4½ mi) farther southwest, is a famous pottery center, where workshops turn out earthenware jugs, pots, and decorative items for sale in the main square and at shops throughout town.

AYIOS NIKOLAOS ΑΓΙΟΣ ΝΙΚΟΛΑΟΣ

30 km (19 mi) west of the Lasithi Plateau, 69 km (43 mi) east of Heraklion.

★

Ayios Nikolaos is clustered on a peninsula alongside the gulf of Mirabello, a dramatic composition of bare mountains, islets, and deep blue sea. Behind the crowded harbor lies a natural curiosity, tiny lake Voulismeni, linked to the sea by a narrow channel. Hilly, with narrow, steep streets that provide sea views, the town is a welcoming and animated place, far more pleasant than Mallia and the other resort centers in this part of Crete: you can stroll miles of waterside promenades, cafés line the lakeshore, and many streets are open only to pedestrians. Ayios Nikolaos and the nearby Elounda peninsula provide an excellent base for exploring eastern Crete.

GETTING HERE AND AROUND

By ferry, the best option is take it to and from Heraklion, less than an hour way by bus service that runs at least every hour, and often more frequently during the day. A boat also arrives in Ayios Nikolaos from Rhodes once a week. Like other major towns on the north coast, Ayios Nikolaos is on the national highway. Parking in the town center is difficult, though you'll often find spaces along the seafront on Akti Koundourou; look at signs careful to make sure you are not in a space reserved for residents. The bus station is just south of the town center, near the sea on Akti Atlantidos (off Plateia Venizelou at the end of Venizelou street).

Visitor Information Ayios Nikolaos ⊠ *Koundourou 21A, Ayios Nikolaos* ☎ *28410/22357* 🌐 *www.aigosnikolaos.gr* 🕓 *Daily 8:30–9:30.*

Continued on page 419

THE MARCH OF GREEK HISTORY

The 21st-century Greeks are one of the oldest peoples on the face of the earth: they have seen *everything*. While Greeks are now subjected to an annual full-scale invasion by an army of camera-toting legions, their ancestors were conquered by numberless encroachers for the past four millennia. During this epic time span, Greece was forged, torn asunder, and remade into the vital nation it is today.

Paradox is a Greek word and highly applicable to Greek history. Since the rehabilitation of Homer by Hermann Schliemann's excavations, Agamemnon, Great King of Mycenae, and the earliest heroes of ancient Greece have moved from legend into history. Today, the remote 13th century BC sometimes appears more familiar than most Greek events in better documented later periods. Not that subsequent ages were any duller—the one epithet that is utterly unsuitable in Greece—but they lacked the master touch of the great epic poet.

However, while ancient temples still evoke Homer, Sophocles, Plato, and the rest, today's Greeks are not just the watered-down descendants of a noble people living in the ruined halls of their ancestors. From time immemorial the Greeks have been piling the present on top of the past, blithely building, layering, and overlapping their more than 30 centuries of history to create the amazing fabric that is modern Greece.

(top) Gerald Butler as King Leonidas in the 2006 Warner Bros. film *300*

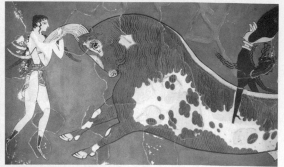

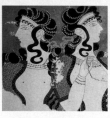

(top) Cycladic female figure; (top right) Bull fresco from Minoan ruins on Crete; (bottom) Fresco of ladies from Minoan ruins on Crete

3000 BC–1900 BC

Cycladic Origins

Greece is far older than the glory days of the Classical age—the 5th century BC—which gave us the Parthenon. It has been inhabited almost continuously for the past 13,000 years. Tools made on the island of Milos around 11,000 BC have been found in a cave in the Peloponnese, suggesting that even in those long-ago reaches of history Greeks were sailing across the sparkling Aegean between islands and mainland shores. Around 3000 BC, about the time cultures were flourishing in Egypt and Mesopotamia, small cities were springing up throughout the Cycladic islands—the first major

Greek settlements, today known as the Keros-Syros culture. These early Cycladic people lived by sea and, as the need for protection from invaders intensified, in fortified towns in the uplands. Objects found in mass graves tell us they made tools, crockery, and jewelry. The most remarkable remnants of Cycladic civilization are flat, two-dimensional female idols, strikingly modern in appearance.

■ Sights to see: Museum of Cycladic Art (Goulandris Foundation), Athens (⇨ Ch. 3).

2000 BC–1150 BC

Minoan Bronze Age

By 2000 BC, a great culture—Europe's oldest state (as opposed to mere tribal groupings)—had taken root on the island of Crete. What these inhabitants of Greece's southernmost island actually called themselves is not known; archaeologist Sir Arthur Evans named the civilization Minoan after Minos, the legendary king of the famous labyrinth who probably ruled from the magnificent palace of Knossos. Their warehouses were filled with spices traded throughout the Mediterranean, and royal chambers were decorated with sophisticated art— statuary, delicate rythons,

(top) Replica of Trojan Horse; (top, right) Lion Gate at Mycenae; (bottom) Mycenean gold funeral mask

and, most evocative of all, alluring frescoes depicting fanciful secular scenes as well as the goddesses who dominated the matriarchal Minoan religion. A system of writing, known as Linear A and Linear B script, appears on seal stones. The cause of the downfall of the Minoans remains a mystery—political unrest, invasions from the mainland, a volcano on nearby Santorini and subsequent earthquakes? Enter the mainland Mycenaeans.

■ Sights to see:
Palace of Knossos, Crete (⇨ Ch. 8).
Archaeological Museum, Heraklion (⇨ Ch. 8).

1600 BC–1100 BC

The Mycenaeans

By the 14th century BC, the Mycenaeans wielded power throughout mainland Greece and much of the rest of the known world, from Sicily to Asia Minor. Their capital, Mycenae (in the Peloponnese), was one of several great cities they built around palaces filled with art and stories of the new Olympian gods and heavily fortified. As civilized as the Mycenaeans were, they were also warlike. Their exploits inspired the *Iliad* and *Odyssey*, and Agamemnon, legendary hero of the 12th-century Trojan Wars—the starting point in the endless ping-pong match between Europe and Asia—is said to have ruled from

Mycenae. For all their might, the Mycenaeans fell into decline sometime around 1100 BC. Soon the Dorians, from northern Greece, moved south, pushing the Mycenaeans into a dark age during which art and writing were lost. But Greeks who sailed across the Aegean to flee the Dorians established Ephesus, Smyrna, and other so-called Ionian cities in Asia Minor, where a rich culture soon flourished.

■ Sights to see:
Lion Gate, Mycenae, the Argolid. Cyclopean Walls, Tiryns. Nestor's Palace, Messinia.

(top) Ancient vase
depicting Olympic
athletes; (left) Bust of
Homer; (right) Statue of
King Leonidas

1000 BC–800 BC

The Age of Homer

By the 8th century BC, Greeks were living in hundreds of *poleis*, city-states that usually comprised a walled city that governed the surrounding country-side. Most poleis were built around a raised acropolis and an agora (a market-place), as well temples and often a gymnasium; limited power lay with a group of elite citizens—the first inklings of democracy. As the need for resources grew, Greeks began to establish colonies in Sicily and Gaul and on the Black Sea, and with this expansion came contact with the written word that laid the foundations of the Greek alphabet.

Two essential elements of Greek culture led the new Greek renaissance that forged a nation's identity: Homeric legends began circulating, recounting the deeds of heroes and gods, and athletes showed off their strength and valor at the Olympic Games, first staged in 776 BC. Participation in these games meant support of Hellenism—the concept of a united Greece.

■ Sights to see:
Greek colonies set up in Asia Minor, Sicily (Agrigento, Syracuse), and southern Italy (Paestum).

499 BC–449 BC

Persian Invasions

The most powerful poleis, Athens and Sparta, would soon become two of history's most famous rivals—but for a brief time in the fifth century, they were allies united against a common foe, the Persians, who, in 490 BC, launched an attack against Athens. Though far outnumbered, the Athenians dealt the Persians a crippling blow on the Marathon plain. Ten years later, the Persians attacked again, this time with a massive army and navy commanded by King Xerxes. The Spartan King Leonidas and his "300"—the men of his royal guard (along with an unknown

(top) Still from Warner Brothers' movie *300*; (top right) Bust of Pericles; (right) Relief sculpture fragment depicting the king of Persia; (bottom) Greek helmet

number of slaves, or Helots)—sacrificed their lives to hold the Persians off at Thermopylae, allowing the Athenians time to muster ships and sink much of the Persian fleet. Xerxes returned the following year, in the summer of 479 BC, to sack Athens, but an army drawn from city-states throughout Greece and under the command of Pausanias, a Spartan general, defeated the Persians and brought the Persian Wars to an end.

■ Sights to see: Marathon Tomb, Marathon, Attica.

460 BC–431 BC Pericles' Golden Age

Athens thrived for much of the fifth century BC under the leadership of Pericles. The city became the center of the Hellenic world—and the cradle of Western civilization. The Parthenon was built; Socrates engaged in the dialogues that, recorded by Plato, became the basis of European philosophy; Aeschylus, Aristophanes, Euripides, and Sophocles wrote dramas; Praxiteles sculpted his masterpieces; and Herodotus became the "father of history."

■ Sights to see: The Parthenon, Athens (⇨ *Ch. 3*). Sanctuary of Apollo, Delphi.

431 BC–404 BC Peloponnesian War

Athens was leader of the Delian League, a confederation of 140 Greek city-states, and Sparta headed the Peloponnesian League, a formidable alliance of city-states of southern and central Greece. From 431 to 404 BC these two powers engaged in battles that plunged much of Greece into bloodshed. Sparta emerged the victor after Athens suffered two devastating defeats: the destruction of a massive force sent to attack Syracuse, a Spartan ally in Sicily, and the sinking of the Athenian fleet.

■ Sights to see: Archaeological Museum, Sparta, Laconia.

8

(top) Alexander the Great listening to his tutor Aristotle; (top right) Byzantine basilica; (bottom) Alexander the Great on horseback

338 BC– AD 323

Alexander the Great

In the years following the Peloponnesian War, Sparta, Athens, and an emerging power, Thebes, battled for control of Greece. Eventually, the victors came from the north: Macedonians led by Philip II defeated Athens in the Battle of Chaeronea in 338 BC. Philip's son, Alexander the Great, who had been tutored by Aristotle, quickly unified Greece and conquered Persia, most of the rest of the Middle East, and Egypt. In the ensuing 11 years of unparalleled triumphs he spread Greek culture from the Nile to the Indus. Alexander died in Babylon of a mysterious illness in 323 BC

and the great empire he amassed soon fell asunder. Roman armies began moving toward Athens, Greece became the Roman province of Achaia in 27 BC, and for the next 300 years of peace Rome readily adapted Greek art, architecture, and thought. This cultural influence during the Pax Romana compensated for the loss of a much-abused independence.

■ Sights to see: Birthplace, Pella, Central Macedonia. Royal Tombs, Vergina, Central Macedonia. Roman Agora, Athens (⇨ Ch. 3). Archaeological Museum, Marathon, Attica.

324–1204

Byzantine Greece

With the division of the Roman Empire into East and West, Greece came under the control of the Eastern Empire, administered from the Greek city of Byzantium (later Constantinople), where Emperor Constantine moved the capital in 324. The empire had embraced Christianity as its official religion, and Byzantium became the seat of the Eastern Orthodox Church, which led to the Great Christian Schism of 1094. Byzantium's Greek culture evolved into a distinct architectural style and religious art forms best represented by mosaics and icon paintings. For centuries Byzantine

IN FOCUS THE MARCH OF GREEK HISTORY

8

(top) Gold-leaf mosaics;
(left) Palace of the
Grand Masters, Rhodes;
(right) Portrait of
Mehmet II

Greece fended off invasions from Visigoths, Vandals, Slavs, Muslims, Bulgars, and Normans. As an ally of the empire, the Republic of Venice developed trading strongholds in Greece in the 11th century. Interested in the control of maritime routes, the Venetians built a network of fortresses and fortified towns along the Ionian coast of Greece. Venice later extended its possessions over several Aegean islands and Crete, which it held until 1669.

■ Sights to see:
Little Mitropolis, Athens
(⇨ Ch. 3). Byzantine
Museum, Rhodes.

1204–1453 Crusaders and Feudal Greece

The Byzantine Empire, and Greece with it, finally succumbed to Crusaders who pillaged Constantinople in 1204. Frankish knights created vassal feudal states in Thessalonica, the Peloponnese, and Rhodes, while other short-lived kingdoms in Epirus and on the shores of the Black Sea became the refuge of Byzantine Greek populations. Soon, however, a new threat loomed as Ottoman Turks under Sultan Mehmet II began marching into Byzantine lands, occupying most of Asia Minor, Macedonia, and Thessaly.

■ Sights to see:
Palace of the Grand Masters,
Rhodes (⇨ Ch. 9).

1453–1821 Ottoman Age

Constantinople fell to the Ottomans in 1453, and by the 16th century Sultan Suleyman the Magnificent had expanded his Empire from Vienna through the Middle East. Greece was the stage of many battles between East and West. In 1687, Athens was besieged and the Parthenon heavily damaged by Venetian bombardments. Only in 1718 all of Greece was conceded to the Ottoman Empire, just in time for a resurgence of Hellenist culture in Europe, Neoclassicism in the arts, and a brand-new interest in Greek archaeology.

■ Sights to see:
Old Town, Rethymnon
(⇨ Ch. 8).

| 1522 Knights of St. John surrender Rhodes to the Attomans | Lord Elgin removes marbles
Greeks drive Turks out | Olympic Games in Athens |

1600   **1800**   **2000**

(top) 2004 Olympic Stadium, Athens; (far left) Portrait of Eleftherios Venizelos; (left) Portrait of Lord Byron

A Greek Nation

1821–1935

Ottoman rulers allowed a degree of autonomy to Greece, yet uprisings became increasingly fierce. In 1821 the bloody War of Independence, which started as a successful rebellion in the Peloponnese, spread across the land. Western Europeans, including the Romantic poet Lord Byron, rushed to the Greek cause. After years of setbacks and civil wars, Britain, France, and Russia mediated with the Ottomans to establish Greece as an autonomous region. Otto of Bavaria, only 17, was named sovereign of Greece in 1831, the first of the often-unpopular monarchs who reigned intermittently until 1974. Public favor soon rested with prime ministers like Eleftherios Venizelos, who colonized Crete in 1908. In 1919 Venizelos, a proponent of a "Greater Greece," sought to conquer ethnic Greek regions of the new Turkish nation, but his forces were defeated and hundreds of thousands, on both sides, were massacred. The subsequent peace decreed the massive population exchange of two million people between the two countries, resulting in the complete expulsion of Greeks from Asia Minor, after 3,000 years of history.

■ Sights to see:
Achilleion Palace, Corfu (⇨ Ch. 6). National Garden, Athens (⇨ Ch. 3).

A New Republic

1936–PRESENT

Greece emerged from the savagery of Axis occupation during World War II in the grip of civil war, with the Communist party battling right-wing forces. The right controlled the Greek government until 1963, when Georgios Papandreou became prime minister and proposed democratic reforms that were soon put down by a repressive colonels' junta led by Georgios Papadopoulos. A new republic was proclaimed in 1973, and a new constitution replaced the monarchy with an elective government—democratic ideals born in Greece more than 2,000 years earlier.

■ Sights to see:
2004 Olympic Stadium, Athens (⇨ Ch. 3).

EXPLORING

Archaeological Museum. The island's second-best showcase for Minoan artifacts (after Heraklion's own archaeological museum), Ayios Nikolaos's museum focuses on those that were unearthed here in eastern Crete. The prize is the *Goddess of Myrtos*, a surprisingly contemporary-looking statue circa 2500 BC (actually, the entire object is a rhyton, or vessel) of a woman cradling a large jug (the spout) in her spindly arms. There are also examples of late Minoan pottery in the naturalist marine style, with lively octopus and shell designs. ⊠ *Odos Palaiologou 74, Ayios Nikolaos* ☎ *28410/24943* ⊠ *€3* ⊗ *Tues.–Sun. 8:30–3.*

Folk Museum. This excellent museum showcases exquisite weavings and embroidered pieces, along with walking sticks, tools, and other artifacts from everyday rural life in Crete. ⊠ *Odos Palaiologou 2, Ayios Nikolaos* ☎ *28410/25093* ⊠ *€3* ⊗ *Sun.–Fri. 9:30–1:30 and 5–9.*

Krista. The mountain village of Kritsa is renowned for its weaving tradition and surrounds a large, shady town square filled with café tables that afford views down the green valleys to the sea. The lovely Byzantine church here, the whitewashed **Panayia Kera,** has an unusual shape, with three naves supported by heavy triangular buttresses. Built in the early years of Venetian occupation, it contains some of the liveliest and best-preserved medieval frescoes on the island, painted in the 13th century. ⊠ *9 km (5½ mi) west of Ayios Nikolaos* ☎ ⊗ *Church, Sat.–Thurs. 9–3.*

BEACHES

You can dip into the clean waters that surround Ayios Nikolaos from several good beaches right in town. **Kitroplatia** and **Ammos** are both only about a five- to 10-minute walk from the center. You can rent lounges and umbrellas at both.

WHERE TO EAT

$$$
MEDITERRANEAN
★

✕ **Migomis.** Dress well (no shorts), ask for a seat by the windows, and partake of an excellent meal accompanied by airy views of the town and the sea. At one of the best restaurants in town, the menu embraces both Greece and Italy, with some excellent pastas and Tuscan steaks and the freshest fish and seafood. Reservations are essential in summer. ⊠ *Plasira near 28th October, Ayios Nikolaos* ☎ *28410/24353* ⊕ *migomis.com* ⌂ *Reservations essential* ⊗ *Nov.–Mar.*

$$
SEAFOOD
★

✕ **Pelagos.** An enchanting garden and the high-ceilinged parlors of an elegant neoclassic mansion are the setting for what many locals consider to be the best seafood tavern in Ayios Nikolaos. Simple is the key word here: fresh catches from the fleet bobbing in the harbor just beyond are grilled and accompanied by local vegetables and Cretan wines. Reservations are recommended. ⊠ *Katehaki 10, Ayios Nikolaos* ☎ *28410/25737.*

¢
GREEK

✕ **Stavrakakis Rakadiko.** Enhance the short trip out to Krista with a stop in the nearby village of Exo Lakonia to enjoy a meal at the homey *kafenion* of Manolis and Katerina Stavrakakis. Dishes are based on family recipes, and most are made from ingredients the couple grow themselves. Dolmades are made with zucchini flowers instead of vine leaves, wild mountain greens are boiled or appear in salads dressed with

8

local olive oil, and even such staples as tzatziki are outstanding. ⊠ *Exo Lakonia, about 8 km (5 mi) west of Ayios Nikolaos* ☎ *28410/22478.*

WHERE TO STAY

For expanded hotel reviews, visit Fodors.com.

¢ ⊡ **Hotel Du Lac.** The handsomely appointed dining room with lakeside terrace serves house specialties such as steaks, other grilled meats, and seafood that's always fresh. **Pros:** studios are especially good value. **Cons:** large differential between rooms and studios. ⊠ *28th October 17, Ayios Nikolaos* ☎ *28410/22711* ⊕ *www.dulachotel.gr* ↯ *18 rooms, 6 studios* ♿ *In-room: a/c. In-hotel: restaurant, bar.*

$$$$ ⊡ **St. Nicolas Bay.** Lovely and luxurious, this seaside resort set in verdant
★ gardens on the edge of Ayios Nikolaos provides a getaway that's within
Fodor's Choice easy reach of the busy town center—but you'll have a hard time get-
★ ting away from this symphony of chic furnishings (indigo batiks, blue-and-white-striped cottons, bouquets of bougainvillea, rough-hewn stone walls, and embroidered butterflies atop a 19th-century chair), all of which make the hotel a delightful Cretan cocoon. **Pros:** convenient yet set apart on a quiet beach; high taste level; personable service; attractive decor and setting. **Cons:** away from the town center; pricey. ⊠ *Thessi Nissi, Ayios Nikolaos* ☎ *28410/25041* 🖷 *28410/24556* ⊕ *www.stnicolasbay. gr* ↯ *102 rooms* ♿ *In-room: a/c, Wi-Fi. In-hotel: restaurant, bar, pool, gym, spa, beach, water sports, business center* ⊗ *Closed Nov.–late Apr.*

SHOPPING

Chez Sonia. An appealing array of beads, quartz and silver jewelry, woven tablecloths and scarves, and carved bowls and other handicrafts fills Chez Sonia. ⊠ *28th October, Ayios Nikolaos* ☎ *28410/28475.*

Elixir. You can get a very nice taste of the island to take home with you at Elixir, which is well stocked with Cretan olive oils and wines and locally harvested honey and spices. The shop also sells a wide variety of sponges, some from Greek waters. ⊠ *Koundourou 15, Ayios Nikolaos* ☎ *28410/82593.*

ELOUNDA ΕΛΟΥΝΤΑ

11 km (7 mi) north of Ayios Nikolaos, 80 km (50 mi) east of Heraklion.

Traversing a steep hillside, a road with spectacular sea views runs north from Ayios Nikolaos around the Gulf of Mirabello to the village of Elounda and the stark peninsula that surrounds it. The beaches tend to be narrow and pebbly, but the water is crystal clear and sheltered from the *meltemi* (the fierce north wind that blows in July and August). Elounda village is a full-scale resort destination: dozens of villas and hotels dot the surrounding hillsides, and the shore of the gulf south of Elounda is crowded with some of the most luxurious hotels in Crete. Don't come here in search of the authentic Greece; expect to meet fellow international travelers.

Olous. Olous is a sunken, ancient city visible beneath the turquoise waters off a causeway that leads to the Spinalonga peninsula (not to be confused with the island of the same name), an undeveloped headland. The combination of warm waters and the promise of seeing the outlines of a Roman settlement on the seabed are alluring to snorkelers and swimmers. A few scant remains, including a mosaic floor, can be seen on dry land (fenced and marked with a sign). ✛ *3 km [2 mi] east of Elounda.*

OFF THE BEATEN PATH

Spinalonga. The Venetians built a huge, forbidding fortress on this small, narrow island in the center of the gulf of Mirabello in the 17th century. In the early 1900s the island became a leper colony, serving this purpose with cruelly primitive conditions for more than 50 years. Travel agents in Ayios Nikolaos and Elounda can arrange boat excursions to the island, some complete with a midday beach barbecue and a swim on a deserted islet; you can also just sign up with any of the many outfitters that leave from the docks in both towns (expect to pay about €10). The real treat is cruising on these azure waters, and as you sail past the islet of Ayioi Pantes, a goat reserve, you're likely to see the *kri-kri* (Cretan wild goat), with its impressive curling horns. 🎫 *Fortress €2 ☉ Daily 8–7.*

WHERE TO EAT

$ GREEK ✕ **Marilena.** In good weather, meals are served in the large rear garden, or you can choose a table in the cavernous dining room or on a sidewalk terrace facing the harbor. The kitchen sends out excellent fresh, grilled fish, and a rich fish soup, as well as grilled steaks and chops; any meal here should begin with a platter of assorted appetizers. ✉ *Harborside, main square, Elounda* ☎ *28410/41322* ⊕ *www.marilenarestaurant.gr* ☉ *Late Oct.–early Mar.*

¢ GREEK ✕ **Pefko.** Despite the presence of an enormous new resort at the edge of town, Plaka remains a delightful fishing village and Pefko (the Pine Tree) a pleasant place to take in village life and sea views. The menu offers a nice assortment of appetizers, salads, and such basics as moussaka and lamb, to be enjoyed on a shady terrace or in a cozy dining room where music is played some evenings. ✉ *Near beach in center of town, Plaka* ☎ *28410/42510* ▭ *No credit cards.*

WHERE TO STAY

$ 🏨 **Akti Olous.** This friendly, unassuming hotel on the edge of the Gulf of Mirabello outside Elounda and near the sunken city of Olous is a step away from a strip of sandy beach and provides sweeping views of the sea and peninsula. **Pros:** seaside location within walking distance of town; beautiful views from rooms. **Cons:** rooms are a bit small; groups can be noisy. ✉ *Waterfront road, Elounda* ☎ *28410/41270* 🖷 *28410/41425* ⊕ *www.greekhotels.net/aktiolous* ⇲ *70 rooms ⚒ In-room: a/c. In-hotel: restaurant, pool, beach, parking ☉ Closed Nov.– mid-Apr.* ⍟ *Breakfast.*

$$$$ Fodor's Choice ★ 🏨 **Elounda Beach Hotel & Villas.** One of Greece's most renowned and luxurious resort hotels, on 40 acres of gardens next to the Gulf of Mirabello, Elounda Beach has inspired dozens of imitators—and little wonder, as the array of delights here are dazzling: five restaurants (including the Kafenion, in a stage-set traditional Greek plaza setting) with cuisines that range from gourmet Continental to casual taverna style; a dramatic Cretan architectural vocabulary of whitewashed walls, shady porches, and cool flagstone floors; and a guest-friendly variety of accommodations, from villas with James Bond–like electronic gadgetry and their own swimming pools to large, gracious doubles in a hotel block. **Pros:**

8

beautiful, comfortable accommodations; lovely gardens; attentive service; one of the world's finest hotels. **Cons:** self-contained resort a distance from town and other services; room rates are €675 and up (but check hotel for deals); too many rooms? ⊠ *3 km (2 mi) south of village, Elounda* 🕾 *28410/41412* ⊕ *www.eloundabeach.gr* 🖙 *215 rooms, 78 suites* ⚬ *In-room: a/c, Wi-Fi. In-hotel: restaurant, bar, pool, tennis court, gym, spa, beach, water sports, children's programs, laundry facilities, business center, parking* ⊗ *Closed Nov.–Mar.* †◯| *Breakfast.*

$$$$
Fodor's Choice
★

🕮 **Elounda Mare.** This extraordinary Relais & Châteaux property on the Gulf of Mirabello is one of the finest hotels in Greece, blending luxury, sophistication, and a comfortably relaxed atmosphere accompanied by attentive service—more than half of the rooms, all bathed in cool marble and stunningly decorated in a soothing blend of traditional Cretan and contemporary furnishings, are in villas set in their own gardens, many with private pools (no matter where you stay you can enjoy the truly beautiful settings of the four restaurants here). *3 km (2 mi) south of village, Elounda* 🕾 *28410/68200* 🖷 *28410/68220* ⊕ *www. eloundamare.gr* 🖙 *24 rooms, 20 suites, 36 bungalows* ⚬ *In-room: a/c, Wi-Fi. In-hotel: restaurant, bar, golf course, pool, tennis court, gym, spa, beach, water sports, children's programs, laundry facilities, business center, parking* ⊗ *Closed Nov.–mid-Apr.* †◯| *Breakfast.*

VAI BAÏ

170 km (104 mi) east of Heraklion.

The appeal of the surrounding, fertile coastal plain was not lost on the ancient Minoans, who left behind some of Crete's most enchanting ruins.

Palaikastro. A sprawling Minoan town currently being excavated by archaeologists, Palaikastro is missing any Knossos-type drama here (for instance, there is no large palace structure), but you get a strong sense of everyday life here amid the stony ruins of streets, squares, and shops. ✛ *9 km (5½ mi) south of Vai, outside modern Palaikastro* 🕾 *28410/22462* ⊕ *www.culture.gr* 🖾 *Free* ⊗ *Daily 8:30–3.*

BEACHES
Unique in Europe, the palm grove of the renowned beach at Vai existed in classical Greek times. The sandy stretch with nearby islets in clear turquoise water is a beaut and everyone knows this, so it gets jammed in the summer.

WHERE TO STAY
For expanded hotel reviews, visit Fodors.com.

¢ 🕮 **Hotel Hellas.** Sparkling clean and comfortable, each of the simple rooms here overlooks Palaikastro and the sea from a balcony. **Pros:** in pleasant town center; near beaches. **Cons:** front rooms can be a bit noisy. ⊠ *Main square, Palaikastro, Vai* 🕾 *28430/61240* ⊕ *www. palaikastro.com/hotelhellas* 🖙 *17 rooms* ⚬ *In-room: a/c. In-hotel: restaurant* 🖃 *No credit cards* †◯| *Breakfast.*

WESTERN CRETE ΔΥΤΙΚΗ ΚΡΗΤΗ

Much of western Crete's landscape—soaring mountains, deep gorges, and rolling green lowlands—remains largely untouched by mass tourism. Only the north coast is developed, leaving many interesting byways to be explored. This region is abundant in Minoan sites—including the palace at Phaistos—as well as Byzantine churches and Venetian monasteries. Two of Greece's more-appealing cities are here: Hania and Rethymnon, both crammed with the houses, narrow lanes, and minarets that hark back to Venetian and Turkish occupation. Friendly villages dot the uplands, and there are some outstanding beaches on the ruggedly beautiful and remote west and south coasts. Immediately southwest of Heraklion lies the traditional agricultural heartland of Crete: long, narrow valleys where olive groves alternate with vineyards of sultana grapes for export.

VORI ΒΟΡΙΟΝ

65 km (40½ mi) southwest of Heraklion, 5 km (3 mi) north of Palace of Phaistos.

Fodor'sChoice
★
Vori, the closest town to Phaistos and Ayia Triada, is a pleasant farming community of whitewashed houses on narrow lanes; you might enjoy stopping here for some refreshment at one of the cafés on the lively main square and to visit the excellent folk museum.

Fodor'sChoice
★
Foundation Museum of Cretan Ethnology. A rich collection of Cretan folk items, this museum showcases exquisite weavings and pottery, basketry, farm implements, household furnishings, and clothing, all beautifully displayed in a well-designed building. ⊠ *Edge of village center, Vori* ☎ *28920/91112* ⊕ *www.cretanethnologymuseum.gr* ☎ *€3* ⊙ *Daily 10–6.*

PALACE OF PHAISTOS ΑΝΑΚΤΟΡΟ ΤΗΣ ΦΑΙΣΤΟΥ

50 km (31 mi) southwest of Heraklion, 11 km (7 mi) south of Vori.

Fodor'sChoice
★
Palace of Phaistos. On a steep hill overlooking olive groves and the sea on one side, and high mountain peaks on the other, Phaistos is the site of the second largest and greatest Minoan palace and the center of Minoan culture in southern Crete. Unlike Knossos, Phaistos has not been reconstructed, though the copious ruins are richly evocative. The palace was built around 1900 BC and rebuilt after a disastrous earthquake around 1650 BC. It was burned and abandoned in the wave of destruction that swept across the island around 1450 BC, though Greeks continued to inhabit the city until the 2nd century BC, when it was eclipsed by Roman Gortyna.

You enter the site by descending a flight of steps leading into the west court, then climb a grand staircase. From here you pass through the **Propylon porch** into a light well and descend a narrow staircase into the **central court.** Much of the southern and eastern sections of the palace have eroded away. But there are large pithoi still in place in the old **storerooms.** On the north side of the court the recesses of an elaborate doorway bear a rare trace: red paint in a diamond pattern on a white

8

ground. A passage from the doorway leads to the **north court** and the **northern domestic apartments,** now roofed and fenced off. The **Phaistos Disk** was found in 1903 in a chest made of mud brick at the northeast edge of the site and is now on display at the Archaeological Museum in Heraklion. East of the central court are the **palace workshops,** with a metalworking furnace fenced off. South of the workshops lie the **southern domestic apartments,** including a clay bath. From there, you have a memorable view across the Messara plain. ⊕ *Follow signs and ascend hill off Ayii Deka–Mires–Timbaki Rd.* ☎ *28920/27100* ⊕ *www.culture.gr* ✉ *€4; combined ticket with Ayia Triada €6* ☉ *Apr.–Oct., daily 8–7:30; Nov.–Mar., daily 8:30–3.*

Ayia Triada. Ayia Triada was destroyed at the same time as Phaistos, which is only a few miles away on the other side of the same hill. It was once thought to have been a summer palace for the rulers of Phaistos but is now believed to have consisted of group of villas for nobility and a warehouse complex. Rooms in the villas were once paneled with gypsum slabs and decorated with frescoes: the two now hanging in the Archaeological Museum in Heraklion show a woman in a garden and a cat hunting a pheasant. Several other lovely pieces, including finely crafted vases, also come from Ayia Triada and are now also on display in Heraklion. Though the complex was at one time just above the seashore, the view now looks across the extensive Messara plain to the Lybian Sea in the distance. ⊕ *Follow signs 3 km (2 mi) west from Phaistos* ☎ *28920/91360* ⊕ *www.culture.gr* ✉ *€4; combined ticket with Phaistos €6* ☉ *May–Sept., daily 8–7:30; Oct.–Apr., daily 8:30–3.*

EN ROUTE The quickest route from Phaistos, Matala, and other places on the Messara plain to the north coast is the Heraklion Road, a small section of which is even four lanes these days. But a very pleasant alternative leads northwest through Ayia Galini (the largest resort on this part of the southern coast) and the mountain town of Spili to Rethymnon. The route shows off the beauty of rural Crete as it traverses deep valleys and gorges and climbs the flanks of the interior mountain ranges. Just beyond Spili, follow signs to Moni Preveli, a stunningly situated monastery perched high above the sea. A monument honors the monks here who sheltered Allied soldiers after the Battle of Crete and helped them escape the Nazi-occupied island via submarine. Below the monastery is lovely Palm beach, where golden sands are shaded by a palm grove watered by a mountain stream. However, avoid this patch of paradise at midday during high season, when it is packed with day-trippers who arrive by tour boat from Ayia Galini.

MATALA ΜΑΤΑΛΑ

10 km (6 mi) southwest of Vori, 70 km (42 mi) southwest of Heraklion.

Renowned in the 1960s as a stopover on the hippie trail across the eastern Mediterranean, Matala today is a small, low-key beach resort. The 2nd-century AD Roman tombs cut in the cliff side attract daytrippers from Heraklion and make an impressive vista from the pleasant town beach.

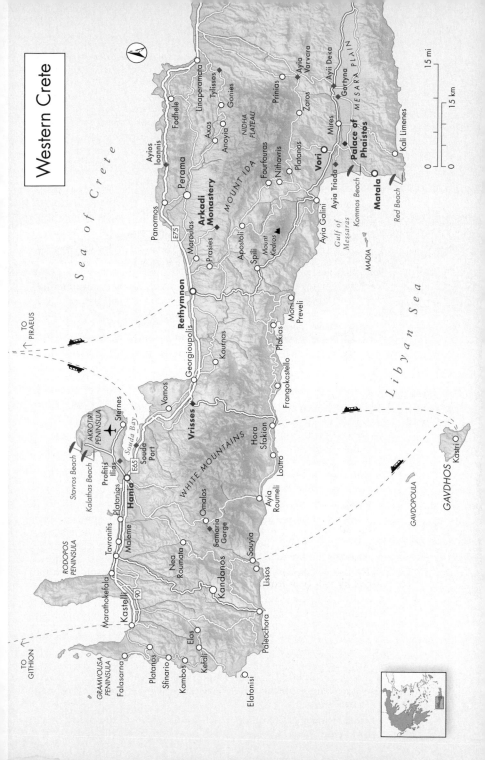

Western Crete

The massive footprint of the Palace of Phaistos proves the might of the Minoan civilization.

Red Beach. Many prefer the more remote Red Beach, a beautiful crescent of sand accessible only by a 20-minute walk across a rocky promontory reached from the path on the south side of town. ⊕ *1 km (½ mi) south of town.*

Kommos Beach. Fabulous, pine-fringed Kommos Beach lies below the Minoan harbor site where excavations are ongoing. At its western end lies the scrappy resort of Kalamaki, but for the most part the beach is an unspoiled stretch of sand. ⊕ *2 km (1 mi) off Mires–Matala Rd., near village of Pitsidia.*

WHERE TO STAY

¢ ⊞ **Taverna and Studios Sigelakis.** Residents from villages for miles around come to the town of Sivas to enjoy a meal of *briam* (baked vegetables), moussaka, and other specialties, along with friendly service and a free glass of raki and a sweet—and if you are a hotel guest here you can join them by sitting out on the front terrace in warm seasons or in the stone-walled, hearth-warmed dining room when the weather's cold. **Pros:** attractive units and terraces; excellent value for the quality. **Cons:** no hotel services or amenities. ⊠ *6 km (4 mi) northeast of Matala, Sivas* ☎ *69748/10905* ⊕ *www.sigelakis-studios.gr* ⊅ *8 apartments* ⌂ *In-room: a/c, kitchen, Wi-Fi.*

ARKADI MONASTERY ΜΟΝΗ ΑΡΚΑΔΙΟΥ

18 km (11 mi) southwest of Fodhele, 30 km (19 mi) southwest of Heraklion.

★ **Arkadi Monastery.** As you approach Arkadi through the rolling lands at the base of Mt. Ida (one of the contenders in the dispute over the alleged Cretan birthplace of Zeus), you'll follow a gorge inland before emerging onto the flat pastureland that is part of the monastery's holdings. Arkadi is a place of pilgrimage for Cretans and one of the most stunning pieces of Venetian Baroque architecture on the island. The ornate facade, decorated with Corinthian columns and an elegant belfry above, was built in the 16th century of a local, honey-color stone. In 1866 the monastery came under siege during a major rebellion against the Turks, and Abbot Gabriel and several hundred rebels, together with their wives and children, refused to surrender. When the Turkish forces broke through the gate, the defenders set the gunpowder store afire, killing themselves together with hundreds of Turks. The monastery was again a center of resistance when Nazis occupied Crete during World War II. ⊠ *South of old Heraklion–Hania Rd.* ☎ *28310/83116* 💳 *€2* ☺ *May–Sept., daily 8–8; Oct.–Apr., daily 9–6.*

WHERE TO STAY

$$$

Fodor's Choice

★

🖼 **Kapsaliana Village Hotel.** A 300-year old hamlet set amid the vast olive groves of the Arkadi Monastery holdings has been converted to one of Crete's most distinctive and relaxing lodgings, with luxurious, stylishly appointed rooms, welcoming lounges, and an excellent dining room, all fashioned out of beautiful old stone houses, and positioned, as if in a painting, in a quintessentially Cretan landscape. **Pros:** a welcome break from anonymous resorts; atmospheric surroundings; extremely attractive accommodations; casual yet attentive service; nicely reasonable rates. **Cons:** remote location makes a rental car a necessity; some distance from beaches. ⊠ *Arkadi, Rethymnon* ☎ *28310/83400* ⊕ *www. kapsalianavillage.gr* 🛏 *11 suites, 6 rooms* ♿ *In-room: a/c. In-hotel: restaurant, bar, pool, laundry facilities, parking.*

8

RETHYMNON ΡΕΘΥΜΝΟ

25 km (15 mi) west of Arkadi Monastery, 78 km (48½ mi) west of Heraklion.

★ Rethymnon is Crete's third-largest town, after Heraklion and Hania. The population (about 30,000) steadily increases as the town expands— a new quarter follows the coast to the east of the Old Town, where the beachfront has been tastelessly developed with large hotels and other resort facilities catering to tourists on package vacations. However, much of Rethymnon's charm perseveres in the old Venetian quarter, which is crowded onto a compact peninsula dominated by the huge, fortified Venetian castle known as the Fortezza. Wandering through the narrow alleyways, you come across handsome carved-stone Renaissance doorways belonging to vanished mansions, fountains, archways, and wooden Turkish houses with latticework screens on the balconies to protect the women of the house from prying eyes.

GETTING HERE AND AROUND

A once-a-week (Sunday) ferry connects Rethymnon with Pireaus, though regular service may be established. A good option is to use the ferry terminal or airport at Hania, about 45 minutes and €55 away by taxi. Rethymon is also served by hourly bus service from Hania and Heraklion, each about an hour away, and the fare to either is about €8 each way. Rethymon's bus terminal is on the west side of town, on the sea near the Venetian fortress, at Atki Kefaloyianithon. Rethymon is on Crete's national highway, which runs along the north coast, and there is public parking on the seaside road around the Venetian fortress, next to the old harbor, and elsewhere around town.

Visitor Information Greek National Tourism Organization ⊠ *Sofokli Venizelou, Rethymnon* 🕾 *28310/29148* ⊕ *www.gnto.gr.*

EXPLORING

Archaeological Museum. Just outside the entrance to the Fortessa, Rethymnon's Archaeological Museum will impress you again with just how long Crete has cradled civilizations: a collection of bone tools is from a Neolithic site at Yerani (west of Rethymnon); Minoan pottery is on display; and an unfinished statue of Aphrodite, the goddess of love, is from the Roman occupation (look for the ancient chisel marks). The museum building used to be a Turkish guardhouse and prison. ⊠ *West end of town, next to entrance of Fortessa, Rethymnon* 🕾 *28310/54668* 💳 *€3* 🕘 *Nov.–Mar., Tues.–Sun. 8:30–3; Apr.–Oct. Tues.–Sun. 8–5.*

Fortessa. The west side of the peninsula is taken up almost entirely with the Fortessa, strategically surrounded by the sea and thick ramparts. Climbing up to the fortress is a bit of a letdown, because the high, well-preserved walls enclose not much more than a vast empty space occupied by a few scattered buildings—and filled with wildflowers in spring. Forced laborers from the town and surrounding villages built the fortress from 1573 to 1583. It didn't fulfill its purpose of keeping out the Turks: Rethymnon surrendered after a three-week siege in 1646. ⊠ *West end of town, Rethymnon* 💳 *€3.10* 🕘 *Daily 8–10.*

★ **Historical and Folk Art Museum.** A restored Venetian palazzo almost in the shadow of the Neratze minaret houses the delightful Historical and Folk Art Museum. Rustic furnishings, tools, and exquisite weavings provide a charming and vivid picture of what life on Crete was like until well into the 20th century. ⊠ *Vernadou 28, Rethymnon* 🕾 *28310/23398* 💳 *€3* 🕘 *Mon.–Fri. 9:30–2:30.*

Neratze. The most visible sign of the Turkish occupation of Rethymnon is the graceful minaret, one of the few to survive in Greece, that rises above the Neratze. This large stone structure looming over the narrow lanes of the city center was a monastery, then church, under the Venetians, and was subsequently converted to a mosque under the Ottomans before being transformed into today's concert hall. ⊠ *Odos Verna and Odos Ethnikis Adistaseos, Rethymnon.*

Venetian Loggia. The carefully restored Venetian loggia was once the clubhouse of the local nobility. It is now enclosed in glass and houses the Archaeological Museum's shop. Just down the street, at the end of Platanos Square, is one of the town's most welcoming sights, the so-called **Rimondi Fountain,** installed by the Venetians and spilling refreshing streams from several lions' heads. You'll come upon several other fountains as you wander through the labyrinth of narrow streets. ⊠ *Arkadiou, near town center, Rethymnon.*

Venetian Harbor. Rethymnon's small Venetian harbor, with its restored 13th-century lighthouse, comes to life in warm weather, when restaurant tables clutter the quayside. Fishing craft and pleasure boats are crammed chockablock into the minute space. ⊠ *Waterfront, Rethymnon.*

WHERE TO EAT

$$$$ ✕**Avli.** This stone, barrel-vaulted dining room and a multitiered garden are part of the gorgeous Avli hotel (*see below*)—the most luxurious accommodations in town—and are attractive settings for creative interpretations of Cretan cuisine: in addition, the grass-fed lamb, fresh-caught fish, and garden vegetables are all organic and natural. Even a simple *horiatiki* (Greek salad) and grilled lamb chop can be transporting here, as is the excellent selection of the island's finest wines. Reservations are a good idea in summer. ⊠ *Paleologou 22, Rethymnon* ☎ *28310/26213* ⊕ *www.avli.gr.*

GREEK

★

$ ✕**Kyria Maria.** At this simple, family-run taverna in the center of the Old Town, good home cooking of the moussaka and pastitsio variety is served from a small menu of traditional Greek specialties. Neighborhood life buzzes around the tables set beneath an arbor in a narrow lane. This place is open from breakfast through late-night dinners daily. ⊠ *Moschovitou 20, Rethymnon* ☎ *28310/29078.*

GREEK

$ ✕**Myrogdies.** The stone-walled garden of this popular *mezedopoleio* (meze restaurant) near the minaret in the Old Town is filled with fruit trees and is the perfect spot to linger on a summer night; an attractive room decorated in a pomegranate theme is a cozy retreat in colder months. The focus is on dozens of tempting small plates that range from homemade dolmades to such local creations as cabbage cooked in red wine. ⊠ *Verndou 32, Rethymnon* ☎ *69726/95170.*

GREEK

¢ ✕**Thalassographia.** The name means "seascape," a poetic notion for this romantic gathering spot that spreads across a series of terraces wedged between the Fortessa and the azure waters below. This is the best place in town for a cocktail, and if you want to stay to enjoy the sunset, you can dine lightly on such delicious mezedes as *hohlioi* (snails fried in rosemary-infused butter) and fresh salads. ⊠ *Kefalogianhidou 33, Rethymnon* ☎ *28310/52569.*

GREEK

WHERE TO STAY

For expanded hotel reviews, visit Fodors.com.

$$$ ⛫**Avli.** One of Crete's finest restaurants also offers the most beautiful accommodations in town—perhaps in all Greece: arranged around the restaurant garden and in an adjacent building are seven suitelike rooms that each could merit the cover of the *World of Interiors*: El Greco-esque baroque gilt frames, rough whitewashed stone walls, glittering chandeliers, Ikat African textiles, Greek antiques, and massive wood beams combine to create a most seductive symphony in Cretan luxury. **Pros:** some of the most fanciful and commodious rooms in the land; pleasant roof terrace; steep discounts for longer stays. **Cons:** stairs to rooms; rooms facing restaurant garden can be noisy at times. ⊠ *Xanthodidou 22, Rethymnon* ☎ *28310/58250* ⊕ *www.avli.gr* ⤚ *7 rooms* ᗜ *In-room: a/c, Internet. In-hotel: restaurant, bar, laundry facilities, pool.*

Fodor's Choice

★

8

$ **Leo Hotel.** Eleni Christonaki oversees this lovely little inn that occupies the 600-year-old house in which she was raised. **Pros:** attractive, comfortable surroundings; friendly service; central location on a quiet street in the Old Town. **Cons:** steep stairs may pose a problem for some guests. ⊠ *Arkadiou 2–4, Rethymnon* ☎ *28310/261967* 🖷 *28310/57197* ⊕ *www.leohotel.gr* ⇆ *8 rooms* ⚫ *In-room: a/c, Wi-Fi. In-hotel: restaurant, bar.*

$$$ **Palazzino di Corina.** Rethymnon has several hotels occupying old
★   palaces; Corina is the most pleasant, with luxurious and stylish surroundings that include a courtyard with wood chaises, topiary planters, and statuary surrounding a small pool. **Pros:** quiet, side-street location yet near the town center and beach. **Cons:** some rooms on upper floors require a bit of a climb. ⊠ *Damvergi and Diakou, Rethymnon* ☎ *28310/21205* ⊕ *www.corina.gr* ⇆ *29 rooms and suites* ⚫ *In-room: a/c, Internet. In-hotel: pool, laundry facilities* ❢⃝ *Breakfast.*

$$$ **Vetera Suites.** A Venetian-Ottoman house evokes the rich ambience
★   of old Rethymnon, with atmospheric and comfortable rooms and two-level suites. **Pros:** distinctive surroundings; quiet location at edge of Old Town. **Cons:** rooms are reached by steep stairs. ⊠ *Kastrinoyannaki 39, Rethymnon* ☎ *28310/23844* ⊕ *www.vetera.gr* ⇆ *4 suites* ⚫ *In-room: a/c, kitchen, Internet* ❢⃝ *Breakfast.*

SPORTS AND THE OUTDOORS

★   **Happy Walker.** This outfitter arranges easy day hikes in the mountains and gorges near Rethymnon, adding a welcome stop for a village lunch to each walk. Each walk costs €30. The outfit also leads multiday treks through the remote regions of Crete and other islands. ⊠ *Tombazi 56, Rethymnon* ☎ *28310/52920* ⊕ *www.happywalker.com* ☉ *Apr.–late Oct.*

SHOPPING

★   **Archaeological Museum Shop.** Handsomely housed in the Venetian Loggia, this store has an excellent selection of books, as well as reproductions of artifacts from its collections and from other sites in Crete and throughout Greece. ⊠ *Paleologou, Rethymnon* ☎ *28310/54668* ☉ *Mon.–Fri. 8–3.*

Kalymnos. For a souvenir that will be light to carry, stop in at Kalymnos, filled to the rafters with sponges harvested off the eponymous island and in other Greek waters. ⊠ *Arampatzouglou 26, Rethymnon* ☎ *28310/50802.*

Omodamos Clayart. Omodamos Clayart sells charming ceramic pieces from artisans throughout Greece, whose creations range from hand-thrown pots to whimsical figurines. ⊠ *5 Souliou, Rethymnon* ☎ *28310/58763* ⊕ *www.rethymnoguide.com/omodamos.*

VRISSES ΒΡΥΣΕΣ

26 km (14 mi) west of Rethymnon, 105 km (65 mi) west of Heraklion.

This appealing old village is famous throughout Crete for its thick, creamy yogurt—best eaten with a large spoonful of honey on top—that is served in the cafés beneath the plane trees at the center of town. Georgioupolis, on the coast about 7 km (4½ mi) due west, is another shady, lovely old town, where the Almiros river flows into the sea. The coast here is being rather unattractively developed, but inland walks—including one through a eucalyptus-scented valley that links Vrisses and Georgioupolis—make it easy to get away from the fray.

HANIA XANIA

52 km (33 mi) west of Vrisses, 78 km (48 mi) west of Rethymnon.

Fodor's Choice

★

Hania surrendered its role of capital of Crete to Heraklion in 1971, but this elegant city of eucalyptus-lined avenues, miles of waterfront promenades, and shady, cobbled alleyways lined with Venetian and Ottoman houses is still close to the heart of all Cretans. It was here that the Greek flag was raised in 1913 to mark Crete's unification with Greece, and the place is simply one of the most beautiful of all Greek cities.

GETTING HERE AND AROUND

Daily ferry service connects Hania with Pireaus, arriving at the harbor on Souda Bay every morning at about 6 am and departing around 8 pm. The crossing takes about eight hours. During summer, ferries also provide daytime service between Pireaus and Hania, and crossings take about six hours. Souda is about a 20-minute taxi ride from the town center, about €15, and municipal buses also run from Souda to Hania, €1.10. Hania's airport, also on Souda Bay, handles daily several flights to and from Athens on Olympic and two on Aegean airways, as well as flights from many European cities, mostly charters, during high season. Buses run from the airport infrequently, so plan on taking a taxi or picking up your rental car at the airport. Hourly buses connect Hania with Rethymnon, about €8, and Heraklion, about €13. Less frequent bus service connects Hania with Kissamos, Paleohora, and many other places in western Crete. The bus station is at 25 Kidonias street, just off Halidon. The city center is well marked from the national road. For parking, drive to the center and make your way, following well posted parking signs, to the west side of the Old City, where you'll find free parking near the sea. Be careful where you park, as some places are open only to residents, and violators are fined.

Visitor Information Greek National Tourism Organization ✉ *Odos Kriari 40, Hania* ☎ *28210/92943* ⊕ *www.gnto.gr.* **Dyktynna Travel** ✉ *Archontaki 6, Hania* ☎ *28210/41458* ⊕ *www.dyktynna-travel.gr.*

EXPLORING

The sizable Old Town is strung along the harbor (divided by a centuries-old seawall into outer and inner harbors), where tall Venetian houses face a pedestrians-only, taverna-lined waterside walkway, and fishing boats moor beside a long stretch of Venetian arsenals and warehouses. Well-preserved Venetian and Turkish quarters surround the harbors and a covered food and spice market, a remnant of Venetian trade and Turkish bazaars, is set amid a maze of narrow streets.

TOP ATTRACTIONS

Archaeological Museum. Two of the city's museums are at the edge of the old city, amid a busy shopping district in the shadow of the Venetian walls. Artifacts on display at the Archaeological Museum come from all over western Crete, and bear witness to the presence of Minoans,

8

ancient Greeks, Romans, Venetians, and Ottomans. The painted Minoan clay coffins and elegant late Minoan pottery indicate that the region was as wealthy as the center of the island in the Bronze Age, though no palace has yet been located. The museum occupies the former Venetian church of St. Francis and surrounds a lovely garden. ⊠ *Chalidron, Hania* ☎ *28210/90334* ⬛ *€2; combined admission with Byzantine and Post-Byzantine Collection €3* ⊗ *Mon. 12:30–7, Tues.– Sat. 8–7, Sun. 8–2:30.*

★ **Ayia Triada.** Lands at the northeast corner of the Akrotiri peninsula, which extends into the sea from the east side of Hania, are the holdings of several monasteries. The olive groves that surround and finance the monasteries yield excellent oils, and the shop at Ayia Triada is stocked with some of the island's finest olive oils. Ayia Triada is a delightful place, where you can visit the flower-filled cloisters and the ornately decorated chapel, which dates from the monastery's founding in 1611 (by two brothers of a Venetian-Cretan family). ✚ *16 km (10 mi) north of Hania, follow road from Chordaki* ☎ *28210/63572* ⊕ *www.agiatriada-chania.gr* ⊗ *Daily 9–3.*

★ **Byzantine and Post-Byzantine Collection.** You'll get some insight into the Venetian occupation *and* the Christian centuries that preceded it at the Byzantine and Post-Byzantine Collection, housed in the charming 15th-century church of San Salvadore alongside the city walls just behind the Firka. Mosaics, icons, coins, and other artifacts bring to life Cretan civilization as it was after the Roman Empire colonized the island and Christianity took root as early as the 1st century. ⊠ *Theotokopoulou 82, Hania* ☎ *28210/96046* ⊕ *odysseus.culture.gr* ⬛ *€2; combined ticket with Archaeological Museum €3* ⊗ *Tues.–Sun. 8:30–3.*

Fodor's Choice
★ **Firka.** Just across the narrow channel from the lighthouse and marking the west entrance to the harbor is the Firka, the old Turkish prison, which is now the naval museum. Exhibits, more riveting than might be expected, trace the island's seafaring history from the time of the Minoans, with a reproduction of an Athenian *trireme*, amphora from Roman shipwrecks, Ottoman weaponry, and other relics. Look for the photos and mementos from the World War II Battle of Crete, when Allied forces moved across the island and, with the help of Cretans, ousted the German occupiers. Much of the fighting centered on Hania, and great swaths of the city were destroyed during the war. Almost worth the price of admission alone is the opportunity to walk along the Firka's ramparts for bracing views of the city, sea, and mountains. ⊠ *Waterfront at far west end of port, Hania* ☎ *28210/91875* ⬛ *€2.50* ⊗ *Apr.–Oct., daily 9–4; Nov.–Mar., daily 9–2.*

★ **Gouvernetou.** The 16th-century, Venetian-era monastery at Gouvernetou, on the north end of the Akrotiri peninsula, is said to be one of the oldest and largest remaining religious communities on Crete. Delightful frescoes cover the wall of the courtyard chapel. A path leads down the flanks of a seaside ravine past several caves used as hermitages and churches to the remote, 11th-century Katholiko, the monastery of St. John the Hermit, who persued his solitary life in a nearby cave. Follow the path along a riverbank for another mile or so to a secluded cove that is the perfect place for a refreshing dip. The return walk requires a steep uphill climb. ✛ *19 km (12 mi) north of Hania, follow road north from Chordaki* ☎ *28430/63319* ✉ *Free* ⊙ *Mon., Tues., Thurs. 9–noon and 5–7, Sat.–Sun. 5–11 and 5–8.*

★ **Venetian Arsenali.** As you follow the harbor front east from the mosque, you come to a long line of Venetian *arsenali* (warehouses) from the 16th and 17th centuries, used to store wares and repair craft. The seawalls swing around to enclose the harbor and end at the **old lighthouse** that stands at the east side of the harbor entrance; from here you get a magnificent view of the town, with the imposing White Mountains looming beyond and the animated harbor below.

WORTH NOTING

Cretan House. A folklife museum, the Cretan House is bursting at the seams with farm equipment, tools, household items, wedding garb, and a wealth of other material reflecting the island's traditional heritage. Packed to the rafters as the stuffy house is, the collection is not nearly as extensive or of the same high quality as those in folk and history museums in Heraklion, Vori, and Rethymnon. ✉ *Off courtyard at Chalidron 46, near Archaeological Museum, Hania* ☎ *28210/90816* ✉ *€2* ⊙ *Mon.–Sat. 9:30–3 and 6–9.*

Janissaries Mosque. Kastelli Hill creates a backdrop to the Janissaries Mosque, built at the water's edge when Turks captured the town in 1645 after a two-month siege. You can enter the building only when the town uses it to host temporary art and trade exhibitions, but the presence of the domed structure at the edge of the shimmering sea lends Hania an exotic air. Hours vary from show to show; the place is most often closed. ✉ *East side of inner harbor, Hania.*

Kastelli Hill. The hill where the Venetians first settled rises above the east end of the harbor. It became the quarter of the local nobility, and their palaces, partially in ruin from neglect and World War II bombings, still line the ridge above the harbor. Kastelli had been occupied much earlier: parts of what may be a Minoan palace have been excavated at the base of the hill. ✉ *Above harbor, Hania.*

OFF THE BEATEN PATH

Samaria Gorge. South of Hania a deep, verdant crevice extends 10 km (6 mi) from near the village of Xyloskalo to the Libyan Sea. The landscape—of forest, sheer rock faces, and running streams and inhabited by the elusive and endangered *kri-kri* (wild goat)—is magnificent. The Samaria, protected as a national park, is the most traveled of the dozens of gorges that cut through Crete's mountains and emerge at the sea, but the walk through the canyon—in places only a few feet wide and almost 2,000 feet deep—is thrilling nonetheless. Buses depart the central bus station in Hania at 7:30 and 8:30 am for Xyloskalo. Boats leave in the afternoon from the mouth of the gorge (most people don't hike back up) at Ayia Roumeli for Hora Sfakion, from where buses return to Hania. Travel agents also arrange day trips to the gorge. ✉ *25 km (15 mi) south of Hania, Omalos* ☎ *28210/45570* ⊕ *www.samariagorge.eu* ✉ *€5.*

8

DID YOU KNOW?

Hiking the Samaria Gorge—
Europe's longest—you'll
encounter wildflowers,
streams (which can close
the gorge in early spring),
vultures, and maybe even the
kri-kri, the Cretan wild goat.

BEACHES

A string of beaches extend west from the city center, and you can easily reach them on foot by following the sea past the old olive-oil factory just west of the walls and the Byzantine Museum. They are not idyllic, but the water is clean. Locals who want to spend a day at the beach often head out to the end of the Akrotiri peninsula, which extends north from the city's eastern suburbs, where **Kalathas** and **Stavros,** both about 15 km (9 mi) north of Hania, have excellent sand beaches. Part of *Zorba the Greek* was filmed at Stavros.

★ **Western Beaches.** Drive west from Hania to the magnificent beaches on the far coast, such as **Falasarna,** near Crete's northwestern tip, and **Elafonisi,** on the southwestern tip of the island. These are rarely crowded even in summer, perhaps because they are a bit off the beaten path. Elafonisi islet has white-sand beaches and black rocks in a turquoise sea (to get there you wade across a narrow channel). You can also head south from Hania across the craggy White Mountains to explore the isolated Libyan Sea villages of **Paleochora,** the main resort of the southwest coast, and **Souyia,** a pleasant collection of whitewashed houses facing a long beach. Much of this section of the coast, including the village of **Loutro,** is accessible only by boat or by a seaside path.

WHERE TO EAT

$$ ✕**Apostolis.** What is reputed to be the freshest and best-prepared fish in town is served on a lively terrace toward the east end of the old harbor, near the Venetian arsenals. Choose your fish from the bed of ice and decide how you would like it prepared, or opt for the calamari stuffed with feta, rich fish soup, or even one of the expertly grilled and seasoned chops. ⊠ *Akti Enoseos, 10, Hania* ☏ *28210/43470.*

SEAFOOD

$$ ✕**Karnagio.** Hania's favorite outpost for traditional Cretan cuisine is tucked away amid the Venetian warehouses in the old-harbor district. Meals, served in a rustic room and a terrace overlooking the sea, are a feast of locally grown ingredients, which appear in such creations as a salad of fresh mountain greens, *graviera* cheese, and smoked pork and a house version of souvlaki—here, pork fillet served with *stika,* a cow's milk custard. ⊠ *Katechaki 8, Hania* ☏ *28210/53366.*

GREEK

$$ ✕**Portes.** Irish-born Susanna Koutoulaki shows a great flare for hospitality as well as a knack for traditional Greek cooking, while an out-of-the-way corner of the Old Town next to the city walls adds a dash of romantic atmosphere to a meal. Eggplant simmered with walnuts, fennel pies, and onion fitters are great preludes to such main courses as oven-baked lamb and a memorable moussaka. ⊠ *Portou 48, Hania* ☏ *28210/76261.*

GREEK

$ ✕**Tamam.** An ancient Turkish bath has been converted to one of the most atmospheric restaurants in Hania's Old Town. Specialties served up in the tiled dining room, and on the narrow lane outside, include peppers with grilled feta cheese and eggplant stuffed with chicken. ⊠ *Zambeliou 49, Hania* ☏ *28210/96080* ⊕ *www.tamamrestaurant.com.*

MEDITERRANEAN
★

$ ✕**Well of the Turk.** It's an adventure just finding this restaurant: ask passersby for help, because everyone in the neighborhood knows the place. Behind the Venetian warehouses on the harbor, it stands in a narrow alley near the minaret in the old Arab quarter. The food ranges

MEDITERRANEAN

8

from simple Greek fare (a prerequisite is the wonderful, large appetizer platter) to some Continental dishes, such as sautéed chicken in a wine sauce. ⊠ *Kalinikou Sarpaki 1–3, Splantiza, Hania* ☎ *28210/54547* ▤ *No credit cards* ☾ *No dinner Tues.*

WHERE TO STAY
For expanded hotel reviews, visit Fodors.com.

$$$$ 🏨 **Casa Delfino.** In the 1880s this Venetian Renaissance palace was the
★ home of Pedro Delfino, an Italian merchant; today it belongs to two of his descendants. **Pros:** character-filled surroundings; large, handsomely appointed rooms. **Cons:** can only be reached on foot from streets at the edge of the Old Town. ⊠ *Theofanous 9, Palio Limani, Hania,* ☎ *28210/87400* ⊕ *www.casadelfino.com* ⤳ *24 suites* ⚷ *In-room: a/c, Wi-Fi. In-hotel: bar, spa, laundry facilities, parking* ⵏⵐ *Breakfast.*

$ 🏨 **Doma.** A 19th-century seaside mansion on the eastern edge of town,
★ about a 20-minute walk along the water from the Venetian harbor, Doma is an outpost of Old World taste. **Pros:** lovely atmosphere; garden; gracious service. **Cons:** front, sea-facing rooms can be noisy when the windows are open. ⊠ *Eleftheriou Venizelou St. 124, Hania* ☎ *28210/51772,* *28210/41578* ⊕ *www.hotel-doma.gr* ⤳ *20 rooms, 4 suites* ⚷ *In-room: a/c, Wi-Fi. In-hotel: bar, parking* ☾ *Closed Nov.–Mar.* ⵏⵐ *Breakfast.*

$$ 🏨 **Hotel Amphora.** Relax on the rooftop terrace and gaze out at views of the harbor, town, and mountains. **Pros:** wonderful harbor views from the rooftop terrace and many rooms; distinctly Cretan surroundings. **Cons:** some rooms can be noisy from crowds at surrounding bars; can only be reached on foot from streets at the edge of the Old Town. ⊠ *Parodos Theotokopoulou, Hania* ☎ *28210/93224* ⊕ *www.amphora. gr* ⤳ *20 rooms* ⚷ *In-room: a/c, kitchen. In-hotel: restaurant.*

$$ 🏨 **Porto Veneziano.** Bright, airy accommodations in a modern building are perched over the harbor at the edge of the Old Town, providing stylish comfort within an easy walk of the city's sights and attractions. **Pros:** excellent location; sea views come with most rooms (and can be enjoyed on balconies); lovely rear garden. **Cons:** guest rooms are extremely comfortable but lack character. ⊠ *Old Venetian Harbor, Hania* ☎ *28210/27100* 🖷 *28210/27105* ⊕ *www.portoveneziano-crete. com* ⤳ *51 rooms, 6 suites* ⚷ *In-room: a/c. In-hotel: bar, laundry facilities, parking.*

SHOPPING
One or two souvenir stores on the waterfront sell English-language books and newspapers. The most exotic shopping experience in town is a stroll through Hania's covered market to see local merchants selling rounds of Cretan cheese, jars of golden honey, lengths of salami, salt fish, lentils, and herbs.

★ **Carmela.** The silver jewelry and ceramics at Carmela are striking. The store represents contemporary jewelers and other craftspeople from Crete and throughout Greece, as well as the work of owner Carmela Iatropoulou. ⊠ *Odos Anghelou 7, Hania* ☎ *28210/90487.*

★ **Cretan Rugs and Blankets.** Head here to find a good selection of antique blankets and rugs, most of them made for dowries from homespun wool and natural dyes. ⊠ *Odos Anghelou 3, Hania* ☎ *28210/98571.*

Rhodes and the Dodecanese

WORD OF MOUTH

"We spent a perfectly pleasant week on Rhodes with plenty to explore, good beaches to relax on, and good food. Kos town was well worth a visit—for anyone who enjoys wandering around ruins, there were plenty, from 2,000-year-old Greek and Roman remains to a huge Crusader castle."

—Maria_H

WELCOME TO RHODES AND THE DODECANESE

TOP REASONS TO GO

★ **Medieval Magic:** As much as sun and sand, the monuments built by the Knights of St. John some 700 years ago are what draw visitors to Rhodes—no more so than its walled-in Old Town, a remarkably well-preserved and photogenic testimony to the Crusader past.

★ **Healing Hippocrates:** Kos's site of ancient healing, the Asklepieion, was the renowned medical school founded by Hippocrates, father of Western medicine.

★ **Natural Wonders:** The terrain yields butterflies (Rhodes), hot sea springs (Kos), countless coves (Patmos), and mountain paths (Symi).

★ **St John's Patmos:** Called the "Jerusalem of the Aegean," Patmos is as peaceful as it was when the Apostle John glimpsed the Apocalypse in his cave here—the spiritual mystique of this little island is still strong.

1 Rhodes. Start, like the crusading Knights of St. John did, with the walled city of Rhodes's Old Town with its monuments, shops, and restaurants. Heading south around the island, discover the moth-mecca of the Valley of the Butterflies in Petaloudes, then take the island's mountainous western road to ancient Kameiros city and medieval Monolithos fortress. The eastern road leads to lovely, car-free Lindos and many, many beaches.

2 Symi. "Picturesque" is the word for both Yialos harbor, with its restaurants and shops, and Chorio located just above it. The inner island is littered with small churches. The impressive and popular Panormitis Monastery is serviced by boats.

3 Kos. The port town is a funny yet appealing blend of ancient stones and northern European partying teens. A short drive out of town, Asklepieion was once the greatest healing site of the ancient era. Large swaths of coast are perfect for swimming.

4 Patmos. Make your pilgrimage to Chora to see the cave and the surrounding Monastery of the Apocalypse, hallowed by the presence of St. John. Towering over Chora's skyline is the imposing, fortified Monastery of St. John the Theologian, and far below is Skala, Patmos's pleasant main town and harbor.

GETTING ORIENTED

The Dodecanese (Twelve Islands) are the easternmost holdings of Greece and are set around the shores of Turkey and Asia Minor. Here, classic, Byzantine, and Ottoman architectures blend and multiculturalism is an old idea. Romans, Crusaders, Turks, and Venetians have all left their marks on Rhodes, in the south of the archipelago and the busiest, most populated, and most visited of the 12 islands. Just to the north is tiny, craggy Symi, sparsely inhabited and ringed by enticing coves. Kos, with its lush fields and sandy beaches, lies between Symi and Patmos, the northernmost island of the group, where arid hillsides are occasionally clad in great stands of cypress.

9

RHODES AND THE DODECANESE'S BEST BEACHES

The "Twelve Islands" have lured visitors since ancients from around the world came to be healed at the Asklepieion on Kos and medieval crusaders took shelter in Rhodes. Today sun worshippers, drawn every year by miles of golden strands, enjoy a sandtastic choice of islands and beach experiences.

A pick-your-pleasure principle applies here. If you want a beach experience enhanced with water sports, head to Kos or Rhodes. Both islands are fringed with soft sands that are the launching pads for Jet Skiers, water-skiers, and snorkelers. On Rhodes, Elia and Falakari fill this bill; on Kos, Tingaki and Kardamena are action-packed, and just plain packed as well. Symi's and Patmos's low-key beaches suit the islands' peaceful moods. Symi's beaches are pebbly, but most are wonderfully secluded, and many are reached only by boat; the 24 sand-and-pebble beaches on Patmos are accessible by boat, car, or on foot, but they are no less pristine.

RHODES AND THE DODECANESE'S BEST BEACHES

KOS: BAY OF KEFALOS

At beaches along this beautiful bay on the southeastern end of Kos, you can have it both ways. Ayios Stefanos and nearby Paradise beach are action-packed, loaded with beach bars and water sports outlets.

A short walk along the broad, golden sands brings you to the relative seclusion of long stretches of empty beach backed only by pines and dunes.

Paradise beach, easily reached by bus from Kos town (about 40 km [25 mi] north) is the jumping-off point for these Bay of Kefalos beauties.

SYMI: NIBORIOS

Beaches on this rocky little island are pebbly, tucked into coves along the rugged coastline.

Most can only easily be reached by boat from Yialos harbor, easily reached on foot or in the island's one bus.

An easier alternative is to walk out to the pebble beach in the little fishing community of Nimborios, about 2 km (1 mi) northwest of Yialos.

Just follow the dirt road past the lighthouse. Nimborios beach has a simple taverna with tables that are practically lapped by the waves—a perfect spot for lunch.

PATMOS: PSILI AMOS

Most of the beaches on lovely little Patmos are a mix of sands and pebbles, and a few, such as those at Mellio and Kambos, offer umbrellas and sun beds. Beachgoers who can do without these amenities should head to the sandy strand at Psili Amos, out of the way near the southern tip of the island. You can reach the beach by caïque from Skala or on foot along a 2 km (1 mi) long path from Diakofti. Pines back the sands, and a basic taverna provides some simple creature comforts.

RHODES: AYIOS GIORGIOS

If you're on a quest for the perfect strand and are armed with four-wheel-drive and a good map, aim for the pristine, cedar-lined beach at Ayios Georgios—though it will take some doing. If you dare, drive about 4 km (2½ mi) west of Plimiri on the Genadi–Katavia road until you see the abandoned Italian monastery of Ayios Pavlos. Just before the monastery, turn left down the cypress-lined dirt road. Follow the route about 8 km (5 mi) to the little church of Ayios Georgios, where the road forks. Keep going straight to reach the sandy beach, one of Rhodes's loveliest secret spots.

9

Updated by
Charles Norris

Wrapped enticingly around the shores of Turkey and Asia Minor, the southernmost group of Greek islands called the Dodecanese (Twelve Islands) lies at the eastern edge of the Aegean Sea. The Dodekánissa archipelago first grabbed the spotlight when Rhodes was colonized by the crusading Knights of the Order of St. John in the 14th century. Today, of course, the Visa-wielding Order of the Holy Camcorder now besieges its famed capital, Ródos town, but happily Kos's native Hippocrates—father of Western medicine— seems to have immunized many of the inland landscapes of blissfully peaceful Symi and Patmos against tourists.

Of the 12 islands, 4 are highlighted here and they have long shared a common history: Romans, Crusaders, Turks, and Venetians all left their mark with picturesque temples, castles, and fortresses in exotic towns of shady lanes and tall houses. Strategically located Rhodes has by far the most important place in history thanks to its starring role during the Crusades. Kos comes in second in popularity and has vestiges of antiquity; the Sanctuary of Asklepios, a center of healing, drew people from all over the ancient world. Today, parts of Kos town and the coast have been malled (or mauled) into an endless line of shops and restaurants. Retreat inland, however, to find hundreds of hillsides crowded only with bleating goats.

Symi is a virtual museum of 19th-century neoclassic architecture almost untouched by modern development, while Patmos, where St. John wrote his *Revelation,* became a renowned monastic center during the Byzantine period. Sometimes called the Jerusalem of the Aegean, this little island is as peaceful as it must have been when St. John lived here. It continues as a significant focal point of the Greek Orthodox faith, and today has become a favorite getaway for both Greeks and an elite international crowd (a 2011 issue of *Vogue* profiled several homesteads recently settled by an array of artists and designers). Symi and Patmos both offer a sense of peace and quiet that in large part has been lost on overdeveloped Rhodes and Kos. But despite the invasion of sun seekers, there are still delightful pockets of local color on these islands, too.

PLANNER

WHEN TO GO

To avoid crowds, just before and after peak seasons (May–June and September) are good seasons to visit. August is the busiest season on all these islands, when hotel reservations and even spots on interisland ferries can be hard to come by. Patmos is packed at Easter. From October to May, most archaeological places remain open, but many hotels, restaurants, and shops are closed and boat travel is limited by the weather's whims.

These islands offer a rich and packed calendar of special events and festivals—you may wish to time your visit to coincide with one or more of these. Easter is celebrated with traditional flare on the island, especially in Rhodes town, where festivities begin with candlelight processions and fireworks late Saturday around midnight; island bakeries serve *tsoureki*, sweet braided bread. You can get a glimpse at medieval life on Rhodes during the Medieval Rose Festival (⊕ *www.medievalfestival.gr*) in late May, when jugglers, fire-eaters, and jesters parade through the cobblestone streets of Old Town. A rich schedule of concerts and dance and theatrical performances, including a dramatic presentation of the Hippocratic Oath, is featured at Kos's Ippokratia Festival (⊕ *www.kosinfo. gr*) in August. The Symi Festival (⊕ *www.symi.gr*), June–September, is jam-packed with events, including dance and musical performances, as well as film screenings; venues include some of the island's most historic landmarks, such as the Chatziagapitos Mansion and the monastery of Taxiarchis Michael Panormitis. Patmos's high-profile Festival of Sacred Music (⊕ *www.patmos-island.com*) in September brings Byzantine and classical music to the amphitheater outside the Apocalypse Monastery (⊕ *www.patmos-island.com*).

PLANNING YOUR TIME

Rhodes and Kos are two of Greece's most popular resort islands, and for good reason: they offer not only some real historical dazzlers but also some rich, off-the-beach experiences. On Rhodes, cultural must-dos include visits to the Palace of the Grand Master and other sights in Rhodes's Old Town, as well as the Acropolis of Lindos; Kos's great archaeological treasure is the Asklepieion, the great healing center of antiquity. All open as early as 8 am in the summer and stay open well into the evening, and on an early or late visit you will avoid the heat and crowds.

On these busy islands it's also easy to wander off the beaten path to enjoy mountainous hinterlands carpeted in pine forests, vineyards, and groves of olives and oranges. A visit to either island should include a country drive (or bus excursion) and lunch in a village taverna; good stops would be Siana in Rhodes and Kefalos or Zia on Kos. Symi

9

and Patmos are geared to travelers looking for low-key retreats and a glimpse of authentic island life. It's easy to slip away to uncrowded beaches and coves on either, but also join islanders for their time-honored ritual of an evening stroll—chances are you might meet one of the artists, writers, or designers who are making Patmos into one of the newest international getaways, as you'll see on the main waterfront promenade and also the narrow lanes of Skala, which come alive in the evening. On Symi, you can amble around the harbor in Yialos then walk up the Kali Strata (Good Steps) to Chorio.

EMERGENCIES

Rhodes attracts so many thousands of tourists that some precautions are necessary. Confirm prices (especially taxis, boats, and sports-equipment rental) in advance, and have the tourist police number handy (☎ *22410/27423*). Your hotel can help you to call an English-speaking doctor. Pharmacies stay open late by turns, and a list of those open late is displayed in their windows.

Emergency Contacts Ambulance ☎ *166.* **Police (emergency)** ☎ *100.*

GETTING HERE AND AROUND

Though you can get to the hubs of Rhodes or Kos in under-10 hours nowadays on the faster boats, if there is limited time it's best to fly to the airports on these two islands. Symi is only an hour from Rhodes by frequent (in season) ferry service, and Patmos can be reached by ferry from Piraeus (about 12 hours) or by ferry or hydrofoil from Kos, served by frequent flights from Athens. In August, for good rates and an assured spot, it is essential that you book as far as possible (at least two weeks) in advance. Boats at this time can be uncomfortably crowded, with deck class passengers claiming key spots on the floor, in the lounge areas, and even—in peak season—on the metal deck under the stars. If you're taking an overnight boat in August, book a berth so you'll be assured a comfortable place to lay your head.

Renting a car (for €30–€40 a day) is useful for exploring Rhodes or Kos, or to hop between Patmos's many beaches. (Make sure the rental includes unlimited mileage, and that the engine has the power for hills!) In Symi, with its few roads, a car is of little use and you should opt for the vans that serve as the island bus, make use of the island taxis, or walk along the paths that connect most places on the island. Rhodes, Kos, and Patmos have regular (usually morning-oriented) bus service to sites and beaches. All islands have taxi service, and it's possible to travel to some spots by boat on Symi and Patmos (check prices in advance). If you island hop through the Dodecanese islands for the day, confirm the return boat schedule, as service is fairly limited outside the summer season.

AIR TRAVEL

There are more than eight flights per day to Rhodes from Athens on Olympic Airlines or Aegean Airlines. Extra flights are added during high season. The 45-minute flight costs about €115 one-way. Olympic and Sky Express fly to Rhodes from Heraklion (1 hour, €100) at least three times per day and Olympic flies several times a week from Thessaloniki (1¼ hours, €117). It is possible to fly directly to Rhodes from a number of European capitals, especially on charters. To Kos, Olympic Airlines runs three daily flights from Athens, and three flights a week from Rhodes. Schedules are reduced in winter. Neither Patmos nor Symi have airports.

Airline Contacts Aegean Airlines ⊠ *Rhodes Airport, Rhodes town* ☎ *22410/88700, 80111/20000 toll-free within Greece, 210/626-2000 Athens booking line* ⊕ *www.aegeanair.gr.* **Olympic Airlines** ☎ *22410/24571, 210/3550500 in Athens* ☏ *80180/10101 toll-free within Greece* ⊕ *www.olympicairlines.com* ☎ *22420/28331 airport* ⊕ *www.olympicair.com.* **Sky Express** ☎ *2810/223500* ⊕ *www.skyexpress.gr.*

AIRPORTS   Rhodes Airport is about 20 minutes from Rhodes town, and it's best to take a taxi (about €15) or a public bus (€3). Though private vehicles must have permits to enter the Old Town, a taxi may enter if carrying luggage, no matter what a reluctant driver tells you.

Kos airport is located 26 km (16 mi) southwest of Kos town. There is bus and taxi service from there to Kos town; expect to pay about €20 for the taxi fare, €3 for the bus.

Airport Contacts Kos Airport ⊠ *Near Antimahia* ☎ *22420/56000* ⊕ *www.kos-airport.com.* **Rhodes Airport** ☎ *22410/88700* ⊕ *www.rhodes-airport.info.*

BUS TRAVEL

There is a decent bus network on all the islands, though there are more-infrequent routes on smaller islands. Buses from Rhodes town leave from two different points on Averoff Street for the island's east and west sides. Symi's and Patmos's bus stations are located on the harbor. Kos has a city bus and KTEL island buses; locations of both stations are expected to change by 2012, so call if you can't find the relevant stop.

Bus Contacts Kos KTEL bus station ⊠ *Cleopatras, Kos town* ☎ *22420/22292.* **Kos town bus station** ⊠ *Akti Koundouriotou [main harbor], Kos town* ☎ *22420/26276.* **Rhodes east-side buses** ⊠ *Averoff near end of Rimini Sq., Rhodes town, Rhodes* ☎ *22410/27706.* **Rhodes west-side buses** ⊠ *Averoff next to market, Rhodes town, Rhodes* ☎ *22410/26300.*

BOAT AND FERRY TRAVEL

When traveling from Piraeus to Rhodes by ferry (12–18 hours, €35–€90), you first make several stops, including at Patmos (6–10 hours, €25–€81) and Kos (10–16 hours, €30–€80). Bringing a car aboard can quadruple costs. Of the several ferry lines serving the Dodecanese and Blue Star Ferries have the largest boats and the most frequent service, both sailing several times a week out of Piraeus. The Athens–Dodecanese ferry schedule changes seasonally, and ferries to Patmos do not run daily out of season, so contact ferry lines, the Greek National Tourism Organization (GNTO or EOT) in Athens, or a travel agency for details. An excellent source for ferry schedules is the Web-based tourist site, the Greek Travel Pages (GTP). The easiest way to travel among the Dodecanese islands is by hydrofoil or catamaran. ANES has hydrofoils and catamarans running in summer between Symi and Rhodes and other islands, as does Dodekanisos Seaways. Times and fares: Rhodes to/from Symi takes 50 minutes (€14); Rhodes to/from Kos takes 2¼ hours (€28); Rhodes to/from Patmos takes 5 hours (€43).

9

Boat and Ferry Contacts ANES ✉ *Harbor front, Yialos, Symi* ☎ *22460/71444* ⊕ *www.anes.gr.*GTP (Greek Travel Pages—Boat/Ferry Schedules) ✉ *Yialos, Symi* ☎ ⊕ *www.gtp.gr.* **Rhodes Port Authority** ☎ *22410/22220.*

CAR TRAVEL

You may take a car to the Dodecanese on one of the large ferries that sail daily from Piraeus to Rhodes and less frequently to the smaller islands. The bad news is that there are not many roads on Rhodes while the good news is that they are all in fine condition and, even better, detailed maps are available. It is possible to tour the island in one day if you rent a car. Traffic is likely to be heavy only from Rhodes town to Lindos. In Kos, a car is advisable only if you are interested in seeing points outside Kos town, and even then it's not necessary. A car, though, makes it easy to skirt the coast and make stops at the many sandy beaches. In Patmos, a car or motorbike makes it easy to tour the island, though most other sights and outlying restaurants are easily reached by bus or taxi, and a few beaches can be reached by either bus or boat. Symi, which has only one road suitable for cars, is best explored on foot or by boat.

TAXI TRAVEL

Taxis are available throughout most of Rhodes. All taxi stands have a sign listing set fares to destinations around the island. Expect a delay when calling radio taxis in high season. Patmos taxi drivers move at breakneck speed on twisty roads.

Taxi Contacts Taxi ✉ *Kos* ☎ *22420/23333.* **Taxis** ✉ *Plateia Rimini, Rhodes town, Rhodes* ☎ *22410/27666.* **Taxis** ✉ *Skala, Patmos* ☎ *22470/31225.*

RESTAURANTS

Throughout the Dodecanese, you can find sophisticated restaurants, as well as simple tavernas serving excellent food. On Rhodes and Kos, beware of many completely mediocre eateries catering to tourists with fast food. It is sometimes best to wait until after 9 pm to see where the Greeks are eating. Because Rhodes and Kos produce most of their own foodstuffs, you can count on fresh fruit and vegetables. Fish, of course, is readily available on all islands. Large fish goes by the kilo, so confirm the exact amount you'd like when ordering. Tiny, tender Symi shrimp, found only in the waters around this island, have such soft shells they can be easily popped in the mouth whole. They are used in dozens of local dishes. Wherever you dine, ask about the specialty of the day, and check the food on display in the kitchen of tavernas. Rhodes produces some excellent wines that appear on tables throughout the Dodecanese, and vintages from throughout Greece also show up on wine lists. With the exception of a few very high-end spots, dress on all the islands is casual; reservations are not necessary unless specified.

DINING AND LODGING PRICES IN EUROS					
	¢	$	$$	$$$	$$$$
Restaurants	under €8	€8–€11	€12–€15	€16–€20	over €20
Hotels	under €60	€60–€90	€91–€120	€121–€160	over €160

Luxury resort prices on Crete are more comparable to the Athens price chart. Restaurant prices are for one main course at dinner, or for two mezedes (small dishes). Hotel prices are for a standard double room in high season, including taxes. Inquire when booking if meal plans (which can entail higher rates) are mandatory.

HOTELS

Rhodes has more hotels per capita than anywhere else in Greece (except for Athens). Most of them are resort or tourist hotels, with sea views and easy access to beaches. Many old houses in Rhodes's Old Town have been converted to hotels, some modest and others quite luxurious. Mass tourist accommodations are also plentiful on Kos but, as in Rhodes, most lodging isn't especially Greek in style. Hotels on Symi are small and usually charming, since the island never encouraged the development of mammoth caravansaries. Similarly, Patmos has attractive, high-quality lodgings that tend to be both more elegant and traditional than its resort-magnet neighbors. High season can prove extremely crowded and you may have difficulty finding a room on any of these islands if you don't book well in advance. Many hotels throughout the Dodecanese are closed from November through April. Lodgings in water-poor Symi and Patmos may remind you to limit water use.

VISITOR INFORMATION

In Rhodes, the Greek National Tourism Organization (GNTO or EOT), close to the medieval walls in the New Town, has brochures and schedules for buses and boats. It's open June–September, weekdays 9–9 (8–3 the rest of the year).

Visitor Contacts Greek National Tourism Organization (GNTO or EOT)
✉ *Archbishop Makarios and Papagou, Rhodes town, Rhodes* ☎ *22410/44333* ⊕ *www.ando.gr/eot.*

TOUR OPTIONS

From April to October, local island boat tours take you to area sights and may include a picnic on a remote beach or even a visit to the shores of Turkey. For example, Triton Holidays of Rhodes organizes a visit to Lindos by boat; a caïque leaves Mandraki harbor in Rhodes town in the morning, deposits you in Lindos for a day of sightseeing and beachgoing, and returns you in the evening for €25. On Symi, Kalodoukas Tours runs boat trips to the Monastery of Panormitis, as well as to secluded beaches and islets, which include swimming and a barbecue lunch. A1 Yacht Trade Consortium organizes sailing tours around the Greek islands near the Turkish coast. If you're not renting a car on Rhodes, it can be worth it to take a bus tour to its southern points and interior. Triton Holidays has, among other trips, a guided bus tour to Thermes Kallitheas, Epta Piges, and Lindos (€30); a bus tour to Kameiros, Filerimos, and Petaloudes (€30); and a full-day trip through several points in the interior and south (€35). Astoria Travel provides day bus trips

9

to Patmos's St. John the Theologian Monastery and the Monastery of the Apocalypse (€20). On Symi, George Kalodoukas of Kalodoukas Tours leads wonderful guided hiking tours around the island and does an excursion to his Marathoudas beach–area organic farm. The company sells a short book by Frances Noble (€7) that outlines 25 walks around the island. On Rhodes, you can pick up a book with 18 walks from the Rhodes town EOT office.

Tour Contacts A1 Yacht Trade Consortium ✉ *Rhodes–Kallithea Rd., Rhodes town, Rhodes* ☎ *22410/01000* ⊕ *www.a1yachting.com.* **Astoria Travel** ✉ *Skala harbor, Patmos* ☎ *22470/31205* ⊕ *www.astoriatravel.com.* **Kalodoukas Tours** ✉ *Behind Trawler's taverna, Yialos, Symi* ☎ *22460/71077* ⊕ *www.symi-greece. com.* **Symi Tours** ✉ *Symi harbor, Yialos, Symi* ☎ *22460/71307* ⊕ *www.symitours. com.* **Triton Holidays** ✉ *Plastira 9, Rhodes town, Rhodes* ☎ *22410/21690* ⊕ *www.tritondmc.gr.*

RHODES ΡΟΔΟΣ

Rhodes (1,400 square km [540 square mi]) is the fourth-largest Greek island and, along with Sicily and Cyprus, is one of the great islands of the Mediterranean. It lies almost exactly halfway between Piraeus and Cyprus, 18 km (11 mi) off the coast of Asia Minor, and it was long considered a bridge between Europe and the East. Geologically similar to the Turkish mainland, it was probably once a part of Asia Minor, separated by one of the frequent volcanic upheavals this volatile region has experienced.

Today Rhodes retains its role as the center of Dodecanese trade, politics, and culture. Its diversity ensures it remains a polestar of tourism as well: Rhodes town brings together fascinating artifacts, medieval architecture, an active nightlife, and is reputedly the sunniest spot in all Europe. Like a gigantic historical pop-up book, Rhodes offers layers upon layers of sights: Romans, Crusaders, Turks, and Venetians left their mark through a remarkable array of temples, castles, and fortresses in exotic quarters of shady lanes and tall houses. But if you head out to the island's east coast you'll find it blessed with white-sand beaches and dotted with copses of trees, interspersed with fertile valleys full of figs and olives. And though some of the shore is beset by vast resort hotels and holiday villages, there are still some wonderfully unsullied sections of beach to be found all around the island; if you look for it, you'll even find a taste of rural life.

GETTING HERE AND AROUND

BY AIR Rhodes is well served by flights, with several a day throughout the year on Olympic and Aegean airlines to and from Athens as well as Thessaloniki. SkyWest flies between Heraklion, Crete, and Rhodes, and during the summer also serves Rhodes from Santorini and Heraklion. Rhodes is also well served by scheduled and charter flights from London, Rome, and other major European cities. Diogoras Airport is in Paradissi, 15 km (12 mi) southwest of Rhodes town and well connected by public bus (running from 6 am to 11 pm, €3) and taxi, about €15 for the half-hour drive.

The Colossus of Rhodes may be long gone, but the Palace of the Grand Masters remains a colossal landmark of the Old Town quarter.

BY BOAT Rhodes is connected to Piraeus by two ferries a day, and the overnight trip takes about 15 hours. You will find schedules and booking information for ferry service to and from Rhodes and other islands in the Dodecanese at ⊕ *www.ferries.gr or www.gtp.gr*. Rhodes is also a hub for boat service, often via fast-moving catamaran, to other islands in the Dodecanese, with at least two boats a day in high season to and from Kos and about four to and from nearby Symi. Smaller boats, including those to other islands in the Dodecanese, dock at Rhodes town's 2,500-year-old Mandraki harbor; the larger overnight ferries use the adjacent new harbor.

BY BUS Rhodes town's two bus terminals are hubs for service throughout the island—points on the western side of the island are served by buses from the West Side Station, near the shopping district of the New Town on Averof; most places on the eastern side are served from the East Side Station on Plateia Rimini, next to the market on Mandraki harbor. Bus service is excellent, with, for example, buses to and from Lindos running almost hourly from the East Side Station; €3.70 each way, €25 by taxi.

VISITOR INFORMATION

The central Rhodes Municipal Tourism Office, near the bus station, is open May–October, daily 7:30 am–11 pm. The city of Rhodes maintains a helpful English Web site. Also see the Greek National Tourism Organization office located at Archbishop Makarios and Papagou (*see Visitor Information in the Planner section, above*).

Rhodes Municipal Tourism Office ✉ *Averoff 3, Rhodes town* ☎ *22410/35945* ⊕ *www.rhodes.gr*.

EXPLORING

The island's history unfolds as an especially rich pageant. Rhodes saw successive waves of settlement, including the arrival of the Dorian Greeks from Argos and Laconia early in the 1st millennium BC. From the 8th to the 6th century BC, Rhodian cities established settlements in Italy, France, Spain, and Egypt and actively traded with mainland Greece, exporting pottery, oil, wine, and figs. Independence and expansion came to a halt when the Persians took over the island at the end of the 6th century BC and forced Rhodians to provide ships and men for King Xerxes's failed attack on the mainland (480 BC). A league of city-states rose under Athenian leadership. In 408 BC the united city of Rhodes was created on the site of the modern town; much of the populace moved there, and the history of the island and the town became synonymous. As the new city grew and flourished, its political organization became the model for the city of Alexandria in Egypt.

In 42 BC, Rhodes came under the hegemony of Rome, and through the years of the empire it was fabled as a beautiful city where straight roads were lined with porticoes, houses, and gardens. According to Pliny, who described the city in the 1st century AD, the town possessed some 2,000 statues, at least 100 of them of colossal scale. One of the most famous examples of the island's sculptural school is the world-famous *Laocöon*—probably executed in the 1st century BC—which showed the priest who warned the Trojans to beware of Greeks bearing gifts (it stands in the Vatican today). Sadly, the ancient glory of Rhodes has few visible remnants. The city was ravaged by Arab invaders in AD 654 and 807, and only with the expulsion of the Arabs and the reconquest of Rhodes by the Byzantine emperors, did the city begin to revive—gloriously. Rhodes was a crucial stop on the road to the Holy Land during the Crusades. It came briefly under Venetian influence, then Byzantine, then Genoese. In 1309, when the Knights of St. John took the city from its Genoese masters, the island's most important modern era began.

The Knights of St. John, an order of Hospitalers, organized to protect and care for Christian pilgrims. By the beginning of the 12th century the order had become military in nature, and after the fall of Acre in 1291, the Knights fled from Palestine, withdrawing first to Cyprus and then to Rhodes. In 1312 the Knights inherited the immense wealth of the Templars (another religious military order, which had just been outlawed by the pope) and used it to fortify Rhodes. But for all their power and the strength of their walls, moats, and artillery, the Knights could not hold back the Turks. In 1522 the Ottomans, with 300 ships and 100,000 men under Süleyman the Magnificent, began what was to be the final siege, taking the city after six months.

During the Turkish occupation, Rhodes became a possession of the Grand Admiral, who collected taxes but left the Rhodians to pursue a generally peaceful and prosperous existence. They continued to build ships and trade with Greece, Constantinople (later Istanbul), Syria, and Egypt. The Greek mainland was liberated by the War of Independence in 1821, but Rhodes and the Dodecanese remained part of the Ottoman Empire until 1912, when the Italians took over. After World War II, the Dodecanese were formally united with Greece in 1947.

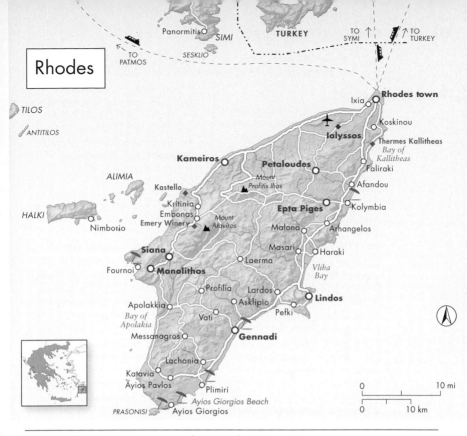

Rhodes

TO PATMOS

Panormitis○ SIMI

TURKEY

SESKLIO

TO SYMI ↑

↑ TO TURKEY

TILOS

ANTITILOS

Rhodes town

Ixia○

Koskinou

Ialyssos

Thermes Kallitheas
Bay of
Kallitheas

Kameiros○

Petaloudes

Faliraki

ALIMIA

Mount
Profitis Ilias

Afandou

Kastello○

Kritinia○

Kolymbia

HALKI

Embonas
Emery Winery

Mount
Ataviros

Epta Piges

Nimborio

Malona○

Arhangelos

Siana

Masari○

Haraki

Laerma○

Vliha
Bay

Fournoi○ ○Monolithos

Profilia○

Lardos○

Lindos

Apolakkia○

Asklipio○

Pefki○

Bay of
Apolakia

Vati○

Messanagros○

Gennadi

Lachania○

Katavia○
Ayios Pavlos○

Plimiri○

Ayios Giorgios Beach

PRASONISI

Ayios Giorgios

0 _____ 10 mi

0 _____ 10 km

RHODES TOWN ΡΟΔΟΣ (ΠΟΛΗ)

463 km (287 mi) east of Piraeus harbor at Athens.

Fodor'sChoice
★

Early travelers described Rhodes as a town of two parts: a castle or high town (Collachium) and a lower city. Today Rhodes town—sometimes referred to as Ródos town—is still a city of two parts: the Old Town, a UNESCO World Heritage site that incorporates the high town and lower city, and the modern metropolis, or New Town, spreading away from the walls that encircle the Old Town. The narrow streets of the Old Town are for the most part closed to cars and are lined with Orthodox and Catholic churches, Turkish houses (some of which follow the ancient orthogonal plan), and medieval public buildings with exterior staircases and facades elegantly constructed of well-cut limestone from Lindos. Careful reconstruction in recent years has enhanced the harmonious effect.

TOP ATTRACTIONS

Archaeological Museum. The Hospital of the Knights, completed in 1489, houses the town's Archaeological Museum. In the courtyard just beyond the imposing facade are cannonballs from the Ottoman siege of 1522, and, in surrounding halls, are two well-known representations of Aphrodite: the *Aphrodite of Rhodes,* who, while bathing, pushes aside her hair as if she's listening; and a standing figure, known as *Aphrodite Thalassia,* or "of the sea," as she was discovered in the water off the northern city beach. Other important works include two 6th-century BC *kouros* (statues of idealized male youth) found in the nearby ancient city of Kameiros, and the beautiful 5th-century BC

funerary stela of Timarista bidding farewell to her mother, Crito. ✉ *Mouseou Square, Rhodes town* ☎ *22410/75674* 🎟 *€6* 🕐 *Apr.–Oct., Tues.–Sun. 8:30–8; Nov.–Mar., Tues.–Sun. 8:30–3.*

Inn of France. About halfway down the Street of the Knights from the Loggia is the Inn of France, the most elaborate of the striking inns on this famously historic street; today it houses a French language institute (appropriately enough). The facade is ornately carved with the fleur-de-lis and heraldic patterns and bears an inscription that dates the building between 1492 and 1509. ✉ *About halfway down street of Knights from Loggia of St. John, Rhodes town.*

Loggia of St. John. Before the court of the Palace of the Grand Masters is the Loggia of St. John. This 19th-century neo-Gothic structure stands on the site of the 14th-century church of St. John, patron of the Knights of St. John and the final resting place of many members of the order. Used as an ammunition storehouse during Turkish occupation, the church was reduced to rubble in an explosion sparked by lightning in 1856.

Fodor's Choice
★
Palace of the Grand Masters. In the castle area, a city within a city, the Knights built most of their monuments. This great palace, at the highest spot of the medieval city, is the best place to begin a tour of Rhodes; here you can get orientated before wandering through the labyrinthine old town. In that district, the Knights of St. John built most of their monuments along the **Street of the Knights** (Ippoton), which links the commercial port to the Palace of the Grand Masters. This cobbled lane is a little more than a third of a mile long and follows the route that once connected the ancient acropolis to the harbor. This medieval assemblage is bordered on both sides by the **Inns of the Tongues,** where the Knights supped and held their meetings. **The Palace of the Grand Masters of the Knights of Rhodes** (to use its official name) is a massive affair with fairy-tale towers, crenellated ramparts, and more than 150 rooms. Situated at the top of the Street of the Knights, it is the place to begin a tour. Unscathed during the Turkish siege of Rhodes in 1522, the palace was destroyed in 1856 by an explosion of ammunition stored nearby in the cellars of the Church of St. John; the present structure—a Mussolini-era Italian reconstruction—was rebuilt in a storybook, pseudo-medieval style then all the rage in the early 20th century and was later used as a holiday abode for King Vittorio Emmanuele III of Italy. Today, the palace's collection of antiques and antiquities includes Hellenistic and Roman mosaic floors from Italian excavations in Kos, and in the

Continued on page 456

NECTAR OF THE GODS

The roots of Greek wine run deep: Naughty Dionysus partied his way through mythology as the God of Wine and became a symbol for celebration in Greece. During the ancient festivities called Dionysia, husbands and wives alike let loose and drank themselves into a heady joy. Now that you're in the land of the god, be sure to enjoy some liquid Dionysian delights. Greece's wine is flavorful and original, so much so that some of the wines here you won't find anywhere else.

This is one reason why few can resist taking some bottles home (a bottle of excellent Greek wine will cost at least €15 to €20, but good varieties can be found for around €10). Remember to ask the clerk to pad them with bubble wrap so they won't break in your suitcase on the journey back. Following are some tips about vintners who are leading the Greek winemaking renaissance, along with a rundown of the grape varietals that Greek wineries specialize in.

Hillside vineyard, Samos Island

THE GREEK WINES TO LOOK FOR

REDS

Agiorgitiko. The name means St. George and it's mainly found in the Nemea region of the Peloponnese. Richly colored and scented, with aromas of sour cherries and pomegranate, it goes well with red meat and yellow soft cheeses.

Kotsifali. Grown mainly in Crete, it is rich and aromatic, with hints of raisins, prunes, and sage. Pair with red meat, light red sauces, and yellow cheeses.

Mandilaria. Mainly cultivated in Rhodes and Crete, it is rich and intense, with hints of pomegranate. Pair with grilled and stewed meats with spicy sauces and mild cheeses.

Mavrodaphne. Found in the Peloponnese regions of Achaia and Ilia and the Ionian Islands, it is a lovely dessert wine. Drink alone or with a light dessert.

Xinomavro. Found in Macedonia, it is rich, acidic, and bursting with aromas such as gooseberry with hints of olives and spices. Pair with grilled meats, casseroles, and yellow spicy cheeses.

WHITES

Assyrtiko. One of Greece's finest white wines and found mainly in Santorini, Attica, and Macedonia, it is rich and dry with honeysuckle and citrus aromas and an earthy aftertaste. Pair with grilled fish, poultry, or pork and feta.

Athiri. An ancient variety found mainly in Santorini, Macedonia, Attica, and Rhodes, it is vibrant and fruity with tropical fruit and honey tones. Pair with poultry or pork, pasta, grilled fish, or white cheeses.

Moschofilero. Originating in the Peloponnese, it is vivid and has rich fruity and floral aromas. Pair with poultry, pasta, and seafood.

Roditis. Popular in Attica, Macedonia, Thessaly, and Peloponnese, it is light and has vibrant scents of pine apple, pear, melon, and jasmine. Pair with poultry, fish, and mild cheeses.

Rombola. Grown in the Ionian island of Cephalonia, it is scented with citrus and peach and has a lemony aftertaste. Pair with fish or poultry.

Savatiano. Grown in Attica, it is full-bodied with fruity tones of apple, pear, and peach. Pair with poultry, pork, or fish as well as soft white cheeses.

White Muscat. Cultivated on the Aegean island of Samos and in the northern Peloponnese city of Patras, it is sweet and intense. Pair with desserts and ice cream.

PICK OF THE VINE

(left) Dionysos Kantharos, God of wine; (right) a toast with Santorini wine.

Wherever you head in Greece, wine-makers are perfecting the millennia-old traditions of Greek wine, with high-class estates such as Gaia, Boutari, and Porto Carras leading the way. These wineries can all be visited by appointment. A good introductory Web site is ⊕ *www.allaboutgreekwine.com*.

Crete, Nikolaos Douloufakis. He is gaining attention with his bottlings of Vilana, an obscure grape with spicy aromas and notes of banana and clementine, and also is known for his Sauvignon Blancs and Syrahs. Douloufakis comes from an established, nearly 80-years-old winemaking family in Dafnes (⊕ *www.cretanwines.gr*), near the major city of Heraklion in Crete.

Cyclades, Haridimos Hatzidakis. On Santorini, his winery (⊕ *www.hatzidakiswines.gr*) near Pyrgos Kallistis comprises a celebrated set of organic vineyards. One of his top organic wines is the Aidani Assyritiko, a dry, fruity white.

Macedonia, Yiannis Boutaris. Up north, in Naoussa, Imathia wine lovers make a beeline to Yiannis's Ktima Kir-Yianni winery (⊕ *www.kiryianni.gr*). He split from his family's estate ten years ago to concentrate on producing standout dry reds.

WHEN IN RHODES . . .

Today, Rhodes has become a vibrant wine culture center. While its viticultural history goes back to the ancient Phoenicians, its vintages have become newly popular, thanks to two delicious grape varieties, the Mandilaria and the aromatic Athiri, and the good showing of the native sweet Muscats. The Cair cooperative produces most of the island's wine, including first-rate Mandilaria and Athiri, as well as reds such as Xinomavro, Cabernet, Grenache, and Syrah. The most prominent winemaking force on the island is the Triantafyllou family, who opened the groundbreaking boutique Emery winery in the village of Embonas (⊕ *www.emery.gr*; near Siana). The family has received notice for its Granrose made from Dimitina, a type of Mandilaria. Other top Emery wines include Athiri Vounouplagias, Rodofili, and Zacosta.

permanent exhibition downstairs, extensive displays, maps, and plans showing the layout of the city will help you get oriented before wandering through the labyrinthine Old Town. ⊠ *Ippoton, Old Town, Rhodes town* ☎ *22410/23359* ☑ *€6* ⊙ *May–Oct., Mon. 12:30–7, Tues.–Sun. 8–7:30; Nov.–Apr., Tues.–Sun. 8–3.*

★ **Turkish Library.** The Turkish Library dates to the late 18th century and houses a rare collection of Turkish, Persian, and Arab manuscripts, including many rare Korans. Striking reminders of the Ottoman presence, the library and the Mosque of Suleyman are still used by those members of Rhodes's Turkish community who stayed in Rhodes after the 1923 population exchange, a mass repatriation of Greek and Turkish migrants. ⊠ *Sokratous, opposite Mosque of Süleyman, Rhodes town* ☎ *22410/74090* ☑ *Free* ⊙ *Mon.–Sat. 9:30–4.*

Walls of Rhodes. One of the great medieval monuments in the Mediterranean, the walls of Rhodes are wonderfully restored and illustrate the engineering capabilities as well as the financial and human resources available to the Knights of St. John. For 200 years the Knights strengthened the walls by thickening them, up to 40 feet in places, and curving them so as to deflect cannonballs. The moat between the inner and outer walls never contained water; it was a device to prevent invaders from constructing siege towers. You can also get a sense of the enclosed city's massive scale by walking inside the moat.

Wall Tours. Parts of the road that runs the 4 km (2½ mi) along the top of the walls is sometimes accessible for an extra fee to visitors to the Archaeological Museum and to the Palace of the Grand Masters; access is through the Palace of the Grand Masters. ⊠ *Tours depart from Palace of the Grand Masters entrance in Ippoton, Old Town, Rhodes town* ☎ *22410/75674* ☑ *€3* ⊙ *Tues. and Sat. at 8 am; moat free.*

WORTH NOTING

★ **Acropolis.** Atop Mt. Smith are the freely accessible ruins of the Acropolis, a fine example of the stately sanctuaries that the ancient Greeks situated atop many of their cities. The complex includes a **theater** that the Italians restored in the early 20th century; a **stadium;** the three restored columns of the **Temple of Apollo Pythios,** and the scrappy remains of the **Temple of Athena Polias;** a **Nymphaia;** and an **Odeon.** ⊠ *Mt. Smith, Rhodes town* ☎ *22410/25500* ⊕ *www.culture.gr* ☑ *Free.*

Byzantine Museum. Icons and frescos from churches throughout Rhodes town (most of them long since destroyed) are displayed within the 11th-century Lady of the Castle church, once the Byzantine cathedral and, under the Turks, a mosque. ⊠ *Off Mouseou Sq., Rhodes town* ☎ *22410/25500* ☑ *€3* ⊙ *Apr.–Oct., Tues.–Sun. 8:30–7; Nov.–Mar., Tues.–Sun. 8:30–3.*

Commercial Harbor. Set at the "mouth" of the Old Town, the commercial harbor is Rhodes's port for traffic to and from Pireaus and most boats to other islands in the Dodecanese. The port authority and customs offices are found here.

Evangelismos Church. The town's cathedral, Evangelismos Church, is a 1920s Italian-built replica of the Knights Church of St. John in the

Mighty fortifications, like this Castle of the Knights of St. John, remind us that the Crusaders dominated Rhodes until the Ottoman era.

Old Town and rises next to the harbor. ⊠ *New Town, Rhodes town* ☎ *22410/77916* ☉ *Daily 7–noon and 5–7:30.*

Fort Ayios Nikolas. Circular Fort Ayios Nikolas, a fortress built by the Knights in the 15th century, guards the entrance to Mandraki harbor, near a row of picturesque but disused windmills. ⊠ *North of Old Town walls, bordering Mandraki harbor, Rhodes town.*

Mandraki Harbor. Once the main harbor and in use since the 5th century BC, Mandraki harbor adjoins the commercial harbor and is home to the city's municipal buildings and an open-air bazaar.

Mosque of Süleyman. The Mosque of Süleyman was built circa 1522 to commemorate Sultan Süleyman's conquest of Rhodes and rebuilt in 1808, with a graceful minaret and distinctive pink and white stripes. ⊠ *At top of Sokratous, Rhodes town* ☎ *22410/24918* ✉ *Closed for renovation.*

Mt. Smith. Mt. Smith rises about 2 km (1 mi) to the west of Rhodes's town center. Villas and gardens dot its slopes, but many have been torn down to make way for modern apartment buildings. For a dramatic view, make your way to the westernmost edge of the summit, which drops via a sharp and almost inaccessible cliff to the shore below, now lined with enormous hotels. A road climbs to the top of the mountain, and a "train" from Mandraki harbor plies the route during the summer (May–Sept., daily every hour, 9–2 pm, sometimes later, €7 round-trip).

New Town. Spreading out in all directions from the original city walls, the New Town is "new" only in relative terms—islanders began settling outside the walls of the Old Town with the arrival of the Turks

CLOSE UP

The Great Colussus

At the end of the 4th century BC the Rhodians commissioned the sculptor Chares, from Lindos, to create the famous Colossus, a huge bronze statue of the sun god, Helios, and one of the Seven Wonders of the Ancient World. Two bronze deer statues mark the spot where legend says the Colossus once straddled the Mandraki harbor entrance, and plans are afoot to erect an enormous light sculpture on the spot. The 110-foot-high statue only stood for half a century. In 227 BC, when an earthquake razed the city and toppled the Colossus, help poured in from all quarters of the eastern Mediterranean. After the calamity the Delphic oracle advised the Rhodians to let the great Colossus remain where it had fallen. So there it rested for some eight centuries, until AD 654 when it was sold as scrap metal and carted off to Syria allegedly by a caravan of 900 camels. After that, nothing is known of its fate.

in 1522. Italians added a great deal of flair in the first part of the 20th century, adding the art deco administrative buildings clustered near the harbor. Later growth has also been relatively kind to New Town, and the streets of low-rise modern apartment blocks are tree-lined and many commercial streets are attractive pedestrian walkways.

NEED A BREAK?

Rhodes's Hammam. Partake in an Ottoman-era ritual by visiting Rhodes's Hammam, built in 1515 and open all year long for steam therapy. Locals visit the traditional Turkish-style public baths (with separate male and female facilities) to soothe arthritis, circulation problems, and muscle aches. Bathers start in a warm room, then pass into a hotter room, where they can "steam" for hours before cooling off with a shower and a massage (€15 for steam and massage; €5 for steam only). A wood-stoked fire heats the stone building, which is very stark apart from the carved stars in the domed shower area. ⚠ Check with your doctor before visiting, as the temperatures get very high. ✉ *Arionos Square, Rhodes town* ☎ *22410/27739* 💶 *€1.50* ⏱ *Weekdays 10–5, Sat. 8–5.*

Fodor's Choice
★

Thermes Kallitheas. As you travel south along the east coast, a strange sight meets you: the buildings of the Thermes Kallitheas look as if they have been transplanted from Morocco. In fact, this spectacular mosaic-tile bath complex was built in 1929 by the Italians. As far back as the early 2nd century BC, area mineral springs were prized; the great physician Hippocrates of Kos extolled these springs for alleviating liver, kidney, and rheumatic ailments. Though the baths are no longer in use, the ornate **Rotunda** has been restored (art exhibitions are often on view), as have peristyles and pergolas, and you can wander through the beautifully landscaped grounds—note the pebble mosaics, an ancient folk tradition come alive again, with mosaics of fish, deer, and other images—and have a drink or snack in the attractive café. Nearby coves are ringed with beaches. ✉ *10 km [6 mi] south* *of Rhodes town* ☎ *22410/65691* ⊕ *www.kallitheasprings.gr* ✉ *€2.50* ⊙ *Apr.–Oct., daily 8–8; Nov.–Mar., daily 8–3.*

BEACHES

Elli. The beach at Elli has fine sand; an easy slope; chairs, umbrellas, and pedal boats for rent; showers; and plenty of sunbathing tourists. All of the coast around Rhodes town is developed; though all beaches are open to the public, you can reach some of the best only through the hotels that occupy them. ✉ *North of Old Town, near Rhodes Yacht Club, Rhodes town.*

WHERE TO EAT

$$$$
SEAFOOD
Fodor's Choice
★

✕ **Alexis.** Continuing the tradition begun by his father in 1957, Yiannis Katsimprakis serves the very best seafood on Rhodes and speaks passionately of eating fish as though it's a lost art. Don't bother with the menu; just ask for suggestions, throw pecuniary cautions to the winds, and savor every bite, whether you choose caviar, mussels in wine, smoked eel, or sea urchins. He even cooks up *porphyra,* the mollusk yielding the famous purple dye of the Byzantine emperors. A side dish might be sautéed squash with wild *glistrida* (purslane), grown in the restaurant's own gardens. **Alexis 4 Seasons.** If you visit during the off-season, try Katsimprakis's other restaurant, Alexis 4 Seasons, which is open year-round. ✉ *Aristotelous 33, Rhodes town* ☎ *22410/70522, 22410/70523* ✉ *Sokratous 18, Rhodes town* ☎ *22410/29347* ⊙ *Closed Nov.–Apr. No lunch.*

$$$$
SEAFOOD
★

✕ **Dinoris.** The great hall that holds Dinoris was built in AD 310 as a hospital and then converted into a stable for the Knights in 1530. The fish specialties and the spacious, classy setting lure appreciative and demanding clients, from visiting celebs to Middle Eastern sheikhs. For appetizers, try the variety platter, which includes *psarokeftedakia* (fish balls made from a secret recipe) as well as mussels, shrimp, and lobster. Other special dishes are sea urchin salad and grilled calamari stuffed with cheese. In warm months, cool sea air drifts through the outdoor garden area enclosed by part of the city's walls. ✉ *Mouseou Sq. 14a, Rhodes town* ☎ *22410/25824* ⚐ *Reservations essential* ⊙ *Closed Jan.*

$$$
GREEK

✕ **Palia Istoria.** The name means "Old Story" and the setting is an old house with high ceilings and genteel murals, but a sense of exuberance prevails, largely due to the innovative cooking of Chef Mihalis Boukouris. The menu is devoted to *mezedes* (starters) and a meal made up of several should include shrimp ouzo with orange juice, pork tenderloin in garlic-and-wine sauce (the house specialty), marinated anchovies (which Boukouris calls "Greek sushi"), and spearmint-spiced *keftedes* (meatballs). Cleopatra's Salad, with arugula and dried fig, reigns over the extensive salad choices. With 100 Greek wines, a drink may be harder to select. Luckily the flambéed banana dessert wrapped in phyllo and topped with a portlike Komantaria liqueur means you never have to choose between dessert and digestif. Palia Istoria is a bit out of the way, in the New Town—about €3 by taxi from the Old Town. ✉ *Odos Mitropoleos 108, Ayios Dimitrios, Rhodes town* ☎ *22410/32421* ⚐ *Reservations essential* ⊙ *Closed Dec.–Apr. No lunch.*

¢
GREEK

✕ **To Steno.** When Rhodians want a traditional meal, they head to this simple little taverna on a residential street in the New Town. Dining is

9

in a plain room and on a sparkling white terrace in warmer months, where you can compose a meal of such delicious mezedes as *baccala* (salted cod) in garlic sauce, pumpkin fritters, and zucchini flowers filled with feta cheese. ⊠ *Agion Anargiron 29, Rhodes town* ☎ *22410/35914* ⊘ *No lunch.*

WHERE TO STAY
For expanded hotel reviews, visit Fodors.com.

$$
★
Marco Polo Mansion. Entering this renovated 15th-century Ottoman mansion in the maze of the Old Town's colorful Turkish section is like stepping into another world: individually styled guest rooms are painted in deep-hue, warm colors, with Oriental rugs and rare Eastern antiques (including large beds draped with translucent canopies) adorning the pitch-pine floors and embroidered cushions beckoning from low sofas. **Pros:** exotic ambience; warm hospitality. **Cons:** rooms are beginning to fray; rooms are reached via several sets of stairs; hotel can only be reached on foot. ⊠ *Aghiou Fanouriou 40–42, Rhodes town* ☎ *22410/25562* ⊕ *www.marcopolomansion.gr* ⌿ *17 rooms* ⌂ *In-room: no a/c, no TV, Wi-Fi. In-hotel: restaurant* ⊘ *Closed Nov.–Feb.* ⦿ *Breakfast.*

¢
Pink Elephant Pension. Set in a corner of the Old Town, these simple, whitewashed lodgings on a quiet street are sparkling clean and surround a flowery courtyard. **Pros:** excellent location; very clean and comfortable; friendly service; bargain priced. **Cons:** basic comforts; some bathrooms, while private, are outside the room; can only be reached on foot. ⊠ *Timakida 9, Rhodes town* ☎ *22410/22469* ⊕ *www. pinkelephantpension.com* ⌿ *10 rooms* ⌂ *In-room: no a/c.*

$$
Fodor's Choice
★
S. Nikolis Hotel. All the atmospheric magic of Rhodes's medieval Old Town is captured here at this charmingly restored house: guest rooms all individually decorated and enlivened by centuries-old arches, mosaic floors, and adorable *objets d'art* (think vases of roses, romantic busts, old books), with many giving onto an enchanting garden, shaded by plants and dotted with "antique" statues. **Pros:** atmospheric rooms and surroundings; beautiful garden; warm hospitality. **Cons:** some rooms are small. ⊠ *Odos Ippodamou 61, Rhodes town* ☎ *22410/34561* ⊕ *www.s-nikolis.gr* ⌿ *10 rooms, 8 suites* ⌂ *In-room: a/c, kitchen. In-hotel: bar* ⦿ *Breakfast.*

$$$$
Fodor's Choice
★
Spirit of the Knights. A restored Ottoman house on the quiet back lanes of the Old Town is one of Rhodes's most distinctive getaways, stylish, exotic, and extremely comfortable—fountains splash in a shady courtyard surrounded by commodious rooms and suites exquisitely decorated with a mix of antiques and contemporary furnishings (the beds are supremely comfortable). **Pros:** beautiful and exotic surroundings; lovely courtyard with plunge pool; quiet location; excellent service; free bicycles for guest use. **Cons:** can only be reached on foot; no elevator. ⊠ *Alexandridou 14, Rhodes town* ☎ *22410/39765* ⊕ *www. rhodesluxuryhotel.com* ⌿ *1 room, 5 suites* ⌂ *In-room: a/c, Wi-Fi. In-hotel: bar, pool, business center* ⦿ *Breakfast.*

NIGHTLIFE AND THE ARTS

BARS AND DISCOS A stylish nightlife has sprung up amid the medieval buildings and flower-filled courtyards of the Old Town. Some bars and cafés here are open all day for drinks, and many—often those with beautiful medieval interiors—stay open most of the year. Nighttime-only spots in the Old Town open up around 10 pm and close around 3 or 4 am. The action centers on narrow, pebble-paved Miltiadou Street, where seats spill out from trendy bars set in stone buildings. Another hot spot is Arionos Square. Those wanting to venture to the New Town's throbbing discos should head to Orfanidou Street, where bronzed, scantily clad tourists gyrate 'til dawn at massive clubs.

Baduz. Bar-café Baduz plays a range of international music and, in keeping with its location on "Bath Square," is decorated with old marble basins. ⊠ *Arionos Sq., Rhodes town* ☎ *69476/92069.*

Colorado. The biggest disco on the island is the three-stage complex Colorado with live rock, as well as dance hits and R&B. ⊠ *Orfanidou and Akti Miaouli, New Town, Rhodes town* ☎ *22410/75120.*

Hammam. Located in a 14th-century bathhouse, Hammam occasionally hosts live Greek bands and is an atmospheric stop for a drink at any time. ⊠ *Aischylou 26, Rhodes town* ☎ *22410/33242.*

ENTERTAIN-MENT **Casino of Rhodes.** Housed in a 1920s, Italian-built faux-palace of Byzantine and Arabesque design, Rhodes's municipal casino is open 24 hours a day, every day. The entry fee is €15 but drinks are free. To enter, you must be at least 23 years old and present a passport. ⊠ *Hotel Grande Albergo Delle Rose, Papanikolaou 4, New Town, Rhodes town* ☎ *22410/97500* ⊕ *www.casinorodos.gr.*

PERFOR-MANCES **Nelly Dimoglou Folk Dance Theatre.** This company is often on tour, but when in Rhodes during the summer it performs at its atmospheric Old Town theater. Its performances have kept alive the tradition of Greek dance since 1971, with strict adherence to authentic detail in costume and performance. ⊠ *Andronikou 7, behind Turkish baths, Old Town, Rhodes town* ☎ *22410/20157.*

SPORTS AND THE OUTDOORS

Dive Med College. For €52.50 Dive Med takes you by boat to Thermes Kallitheas and, after a 30-minute theory lesson and practice in shallow water, you descend for a 20-minute dive. They also have dives at Ladiko, 15 km (9 mi) south of Rhodes town. ⊠ *Lissavonas 33, Rodini, Rhodes town* ☎ *22410/61115* ⊕ *www.divemedcollege.com.*

SHOPPING

In Rhodes town you can buy good copies of Lindos ware, a delicate pottery decorated with green and red floral motifs. The Old Town's shopping area, on Sokratous, is lined with boutiques selling furs, jewelry, and other high-ticket items.

Astero Antiques. Mahalis Hatziz, owner of Astero Antiques, travels throughout Greece each winter to fill his shop with some of the most enticing goods on offer on the island. ⊠ *Ayiou Fanouriou 4, off Sokratous, Rhodes town* ☎ *22410/34753.*

9

EPTA PIGES ΕΠΤΑ ΠΗΓΕΣ

30 km (19 mi) south of Rhodes town.

Epta Piges. Seven Springs, or Epta Piges, is a deeply shaded glen watered by mountain springs. They are made all the more photogenic thanks to the imported peacocks that flaunt their plumage in the woods around the springs. The waters are channeled through a 164-yard-long tunnel, which you

EASY AS 1-2-3

Most of Lindos's mazelike streets don't have conventional names or addresses; instead, buildings are numbered, from 1 through about 500. Lower numbers are on the north side of town, higher numbers on the south.

can walk through, emerging at the edge of a cascading dam and a small man-made lake where you can swim. Here an enterprising local shepherd began serving simple fare in 1945, and his sideline turned into the busy waterside taverna ($) and tourist site of today. Despite its many visitors, Seven Springs' beauty remains unspoiled. To get here, turn right on the inland road near Kolymbia and follow signs. ☏ *22410/56259* ⊕ *eptapiges.com.*

LINDOS ΛΙΝΔΟΣ

19 km (12 mi) southwest of Epta Piges, 48 km (30 mi) southwest of Rhodes town.

Lindos, cradled between two harbors, had a particular importance in antiquity. Before the existence of Rhodes town, it was the island's principal maritime center. Lindos possessed a revered sanctuary, consecrated to Athena, whose cult probably succeeded that of a pre-Hellenic divinity named Lindia; the sanctuary was dedicated to Athena Lindia. By the 6th century BC, an impressive temple dominated the settlement, and after the foundation of Rhodes, the Lindians set up a *propylaia* (monumental entrance gate) on the model of that in Athens. In the mid-4th century BC, the temple was destroyed by fire and almost immediately rebuilt, with a new wooden statue of the goddess covered by gold leaf, and with arms, head, and legs of marble or ivory. Lindos prospered into Roman times, during the Middle Ages, and under the Knights of St. John. Only at the beginning of the 19th century did the age-old shipping activity cease.

Lindos is remarkably well preserved, and many 15th-century houses are still in use. Everywhere are examples of the Crusader architecture you see in Rhodes town: substantial houses of finely cut Lindos limestone, with windows crowned by elaborate arches. Many floors are paved with black-and-white pebble mosaics. Intermixed with these Crusader-era buildings are whitewashed Cycladic-style houses with square, blue-shuttered windows.

Like Rhodes town, Lindos is enchanting off-season but can get unbearably crowded when summertime pilgrims make the trek from Rhodes town daily and passage through narrow streets lined with shops selling clothes and trinkets slows to a snail's pace. At these times, an overnight

One of the most magnificent examples of Crusader Era architecture is the great fortress at Lindos.

visit allows you to enjoy the town's beauties after the day-trippers leave. Only pedestrians and donkeys are allowed in Lindos because the town's narrow alleys are not wide enough for vehicles. If you're arriving by car, park in the lot above town and walk the 10 minutes down (about 1,200 feet) to town.

🕙 **Acropolis of Lindos.** For about €5, you can hire a donkey for the **Fodor's Choice** 15-minute climb from the modern town up to the Acropolis of Lindos. ★ The winding path leads past a gauntlet of Lindian women who spread out their lace and embroidery like fresh laundry over the rocks. The final approach ascends a steep flight of stairs, past a marvelous 2nd-century BC **relief of the prow of a Lindian ship,** carved into the rock.

The entrance to the Acropolis takes you through the **Medieval Castle** built by the Knights of St. John, then to the Byzantine **Chapel of St. John** on the next level. The Romans, too, left their mark on the acropolis, with a temple dedicated to Diocletian. On the **upper terraces,** begun by classical Greeks around 300 BC, are the remains of elaborate **porticoes** and **stoas,** commanding an immense sweep of sea and making a powerful statement on behalf of Athena and the Lydians (who dedicated the monuments on the Acropolis to her); the lofty white columns of the temple and stoa on the summit must have presented a magnificent picture. The main portico of the stoa had 42 Doric columns, at the center of which an opening led to the staircase up to the **Propylaia** (or sanctuary). The **Temple of Athena Lindia** at the very top is surprisingly modest, given the drama of the approach. As was common in the 4th century BC, both the front and the rear are flanked by four Doric columns. Numerous inscribed statue bases were found all over the summit, attesting in many cases to the work of Lindian sculptors, who were clearly second to none. ⊠ *Above New Town, Lindos* ☎ *22440/31258* ⊕ *www.culture.gr* 🖾 *€6* ⊗ *May–Oct., Tues.–Sun. 8–7:40, Mon. 12:30– 7:40; Nov.–Apr., Tues.–Sun. 8–2:40.*

Church of the Panayia. A graceful building with a beautiful bell tower, the Church of the Panayia probably antedates the Knights, though the bell tower bears the arms of Grand Master d'Aubusson with the dates 1484–90. Frescoes in the elaborate interior were painted in 1779 by Gregory of Symi, and the black-and-white pebble floor is a popular Byzantine design. ⊠ *Off main square, Lindos* ☎ *No phone* ⊗ *May–Oct., daily 9–2 and 5–9; Nov.–Apr., call number posted on church to have door unlocked.*

WHERE TO EAT AND STAY

For expanded hotel reviews, visit Fodors.com.

$$$
GREEK
Fodor's Choice
★

✕ **Mavrikos.** The secret of this longtime favorite, one of the finest and most fashionable restaurants in all Greece, is an elegant, perfect simplicity. That ranges from the white-on-white Crusader arches that form the décor—sitting under these bangled-with-grape-vines vaults, on a soft summer night, is one of the great joys of a Greek vacation—to the seemingly straightforward dishes, such as sea-urchin salad, fried *manouri* cheese with basil and pine nuts, swordfish in caper sauce, steak in pomegranate sauce, and lobster risotto. These dishes become transcendent with the magic touch of third-generation chef Dimitris Mavrikos, who now owns this 75-year-old family-run institution with his brother, Michalis. He combines the freshest ingredients with classical training and an abiding love for the best of Greek village cuisine. The meat dishes, including oven-baked lamb, are also sublime. ⊠ *Main square, Lindos* ☎ *22440/31232* ⊗ *Closed Nov.–Mar.*

$$$$
★

🏠 **Melenos Hotel.** Michalis Melenos worked for years to make this stone villa set into gardens overlooking Lindos bay into a truly special retreat, filling rooms with traditional Lindian village beds, hand-carved woodwork, Turkish tiles, and antique furnishings brought from throughout Greece and Turkey. **Pros:** atmospheric surrounds; beautiful garden; terraces with sea views; exquisite service. **Cons:** quite expensive (though high-season discounts are available on the hotel Web site). ⊠ *At edge of Lindos, on path to Acropolis, Lindos* ☎ *22440/32222* ⊕ *www. melenoslindos.com* ↪ *12 suites* ⚏ *In-room: a/c, Wi-Fi. In-hotel: restaurant, bar, laundry facilities* ⊗ *Closed Nov.–Mar.* ⊗*Breakfast.*

¢

🏠 **Pension Electra.** Linger on the spacious terrace, with views of the town and sea, or down in the blossoming garden of this simple decades-old pension, where many of the high-ceiling rooms have sea views. **Pros:** sea views; pleasant atmosphere; friendly staff; nice location on pedestrian lanes of Old Town. **Cons:** comforts are basic; a bit of a trek from bus or parking with luggage. ⊠ *No. 66, Lindos* ☎ *22440/31266* ↪ *7 rooms, 1 with bath in hall* ⚏ *In-room: a/c, no TV* ▭ *No credit cards* ⊗ *Closed Nov.–May.*

MONOLITHOS TO KAMEIROS ΜΟΝΟΛΙΘΟΣ ΠΡΟΣ ΚΑΜΕΙΡΟΣ

28 km (17 mi) northwest of Gennadi, 74 km (46 mi) southwest of Rhodes town.

Rhodes's west coast is more forested, with fewer good beaches than its east coast—but if you're looking to get away from the hordes, you'll find peace and quiet among the sylvan scenery, august ruins, and vineyards.

Kameiros. Classical Kameiros is one of the three ancient cities of Rhodes. The ruins, excavated by the Italians in 1929, lie on three levels on a slope above the sea. Most of the city, apparently never fortified, that is visible today dates to the classical period and later, and include an acropolis, a large reservoir, a gridlike pattern of streets lined with houses and shops, and several temples. The hill hides many more ruins, yet to be excavated. ⊠ *Off main Rhodes road, 23 km (14 mi) northeast of Siana; turn at sign for Ancient Kameiros* ☎ *22410/25550* ⊕ *www. culture.gr* 🖾 *€4* ☉ *Tues.–Sun. 8:30–3.*

Kastello. The ruined-yet-still impressive Kastello, a fortress built by the Knights in the late 15th century, rises high above the sea on the coast just north of Mt. Avrios, with good views in every direction. ⊠ *13 km (8 mi) northeast of Siana* ☎ *No phone* 🖾 *Free.*

Fodor's Choice **Monolithos.** The medieval fortress of Monolithos—so named for the ★ jutting, 750-foot monolith on which it is built—rises above a fairy-tale landscape of deep green forests and sharp cliffs plunging into the sea. Inside the Venetian stronghold (accessible only by a steep path and series of stone steps) there is a chapel, and the ramparts provide magnificent views of Rhodes's emerald inland and the island of Halki. The small pebble beach of Fourni beneath the castle is a delightful place for a swim. ⊠ *Take western road from middle of Monolithos village; near hairpin turn there's a path up to fortress* ☎ *No phone* 🖾 *Free.*

Siana. Siana perches on the wooded slopes of Mt. Acramitis above a vast, fertile valley. The small town, a popular stop on the tourist trail, is known for its fragrant honey and for Souma (a very strong, sweet wine that resembles a grape-flavor schnapps); look for stands (Manos, past the town church, on the main road, is famed for its honey) selling both. ⊠ *5 km [3 mi] northeast of Monolithos.*

EN ROUTE Beyond Siana, the road continues on a high ridge through thick pine forests, which carpet the precipitous slopes dropping toward the sea. To the east looms the bare, stony massif of Mt. Ataviros, Rhodes's highest peak, at 3,986 feet. If you follow the road inland rather than continue north along the coast toward Kritinia, you'll climb the flanks of the mountains to the traditional, arbor-filled village of Embonas in Rhodes's richest wine country *(see "Nectar of the Gods" in this chapter).*

PETALOUDES AND IALYSSOS ΠΕΤΑΛΟΥΔΕΣ ΚΑΙ ΙΑΛΥΣΟΣ

22 km (14 mi) east of Kameiros, 25 km (16 mi) southwest of Rhodes town.

★ **Petaloudes.** The "Valley of the Butterflies," Petaloudes, lives up to its name, especially in July and August. In summer the *callimorpha* *quadripunctaria,* actually a moth species, cluster by the thousands around the low bushes of the pungent storax plant, which grows all over the area. Through the years the numbers have diminished, partly owing to busloads of tourists clapping hands to see them fly up in dense clouds, revealing their red underbellies—an antic that causes the moths to deplete their scant energy reserves and is strongly discouraged. Access to the valley involves an easy walk up an idyllic yet crowded trail through a too pretty "woodlands." ⊠ *Turn off coastal road south and follow signs leading to the site with its own parking lot* ☎ *22410/81801* ☜ *€4* ⏲ *Late Apr.–Oct., daily 8–7.*

SYMI ΣΥΜΗ

The island of Symi, 45 km (27 mi) north of Rhodes, is an enchanting place, with Chorio, a 19th-century town of neoclassic mansions, crowning a hillside above the harbor. The island has few beaches and almost no flat land, so it is not attractive to developers. As a result, quiet Symi provides a peaceful retreat for travelers, who tend to fall in love with the island on their first visit and return year after year.

GETTING HERE AND AROUND

BY BOAT Little Symi is well served by boats, either on one-day excursion trips from Mandraki harbor in Rhodes town (check with any travel agent like Triton Holidays [⊕ *www.tritondmc.gr*] or one of the shills on the harbor; €32 round-trip) or by commercial boat. These include catamarans that arrive about four times a day (€16, 50 minutes) in high season as well as a daily car ferry (€6 one-way, 50 minutes). All boats arrive in Yialos, Symi's main harbor, and catamarans also make a stop in Panormitis or Pedi, though these remote places are of most interest to day-trippers who just want a day at a remote beach.

BY BUS A sturdy bus makes the hourly trip from Yialos harbor up to Chorio and on to Pedi Bay, €0.80. But once on Symi, you'll learn that the easiest way to get around is by foot, as roads are few and many of those are quite rough. If you are staying in Nimborios or another outlying place, make arrangements in advance for your hotel to pick you up, as taxis refuse to make the trip on unimproved roads.

VISITOR INFORMATION

The region's only English-language newspaper is found on Symi. The *Symi Visitor,* available at tourist spots, is full of information on events, news, and activities, plus has an overview of the sites, and bus and ferry schedules. The Web site (⊕ *www.symivisitor.com*) also has weather updates and information on finding accommodations on Symi.

EXPLORING

Nireus, the ancient king of Symi noted for his looks, sailed with three vessels to assist the Greeks at Troy, as mentioned in Homer. Symi was later part of the Dorian Hexapolis dominated by Rhodes, and it remained under Rhodian dominance throughout the Roman and Byzantine periods. The island has good natural harbors, and the nearby coast of Asia Minor provided plentiful timber for the Symiotes, who were shipbuilders, fearless seafarers and sponge divers, and rich and

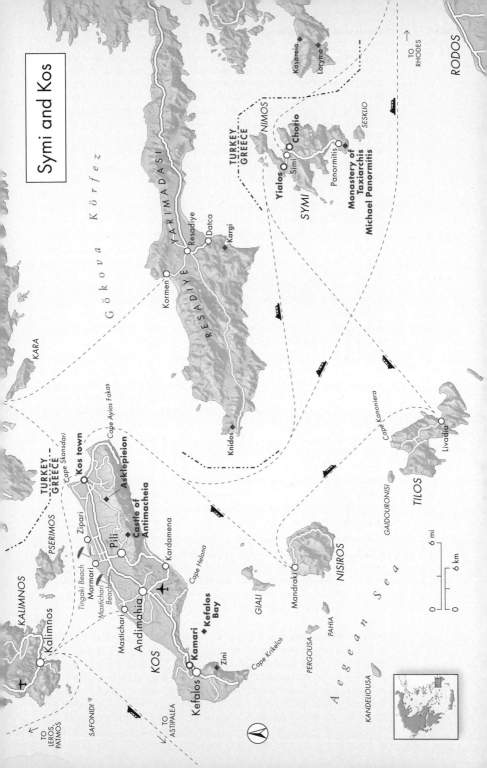

Symi and Kos

RODOS

TO
RHODES →

RODOS

Kasareia

Loryma

TURKEY
GREECE

NIMOS

Chorio

SESKLIO

Yialos
Simi

Panormitis

SYMI

Monastery of
Taxiarchis
Michael Panormitis

Resadiye
Datca

Kargi

YARIMADASI

Kormen

RESADIYE

G ö k o v a   K ö r f e z

KARA

Knidos

Cape Kanoniera

TILOS

Livadia

TURKEY –
GREECE

Cape Skansdari

Cape Ayios Fokas

Kos town
Asklepieion

Zipari

Castle of
Antimacheia

Pili

Kardamena

Cape Helona

Tingaki Beach
Marmari
Mastichari Beach

Mastichari

Andimahia

Kefalos
Bay

Kefalos

Kamari

Zini

Cape Krikelos

KOS

KALIMNOS

Kalimnos

PSERIMOS

TO
LEROS,
PATMOS

SAFONIDI

TO
ASTIPALEA

GIALI

Mandraki

NISIROS

PERGOUSA

PAHIA

GAIDOURONISI

KANDELIOUSA

A e g e a n   S e a

6 mi

6 km

0

0

successful merchants. Under the Ottomans their harbor was proclaimed a free port and attracted the trade of the entire region. The Symiotes' continuous travel and trade and their frequent contact with Europe led them to incorporate foreign elements in their furnishings, clothes, and cultural life. At first they lived in Chorio, high on the hillside above the port, and in the second half of the 19th century spread down to the seaside at Yialos.

Witness to their prosperity are the neoclassic mansions that line the narrow streets of Chorio and the main harbor in Yialos. There were some 20,000 inhabitants at this acme, but under the Italian occupation at the end of the Italo-Turkish war in 1912, the island declined; the Symiotes lost their holdings in Asia Minor and were unable to convert their fleets to steam. Many emigrated to work elsewhere, and now there are just a few thousand inhabitants in Chorio and Yialos.

YIALOS ΓΙΑΛΟΣ

45 km (27 mi) north of Rhodes.

As the boat from Rhodes to Symi rounds the last of many rocky barren spurs, the port of Yialos, at the back of a deep, narrow harbor, comes into view. The shore is lined with mansions whose ground floors have been converted to cafés with waterside terraces perfect for whiling away lazy hours.

Church of Ayhios Ioannis. Built in 1838, the Church of Ayhios Ioannis incorporates in its walls fragments of ancient blocks from a temple that apparently stood on this site and is surrounded by a plaza paved in an intricate mosaic, fashioned from inlaid pebbles. ⊠ *Near center of Yialos village.*

Symi Naval Museum. Sponge-diving tools, model ships, antique navigation tools, and vintage anchors fill the small Symi Naval Museum and give a good taste of life in Symi in the 19th and early 20th centuries. It's hard to miss the ornamental blue-and-yellow building—a landmark on Yialos Harbor, which was once one of the world's great sponge-diving centers. ⊠ *Yialos waterfront* 🖾 *€2* ☉ *Tues.–Sun. 10–2.*

WHERE TO EAT AND STAY

For expanded hotel reviews, visit Fodors.com.

$$$$
CONTEMPORARY
Fodor's Choice
★

✕**Mylopetra.** A delightfully converted old flour mill, Mylopetra is a feast for the eyes, with rich stone work accented with island antiques, rich fabrics, and an ancient tomb embedded in glass beneath the floor. German couple Hans and Eva Sworoski painstakingly oversee this extraordinary restaurant, ensuring gracious service and a daily menu that always includes inventive sauces made with wild herbs gathered on the island, homemade pasta married with anything from spinach to rabbit to salmon, and abundant seafood and meat (often game) options. ⊠ *Behind church on backstreet, Yialos* 🕾 *22460/72333* ⊕ *www.mylopetra. com* 🍴 *Reservations essential* ☉ *Closed late-Oct.–Apr. No lunch.*

$$$
GREEK

✕**Tholos.** A seaside perch at the end of Yialos harbor is the picturesque setting for an excellent meal, which often begins with such traditional appetizers as stuffed zucchini or boiled greens and includes fresh grilled fish and other daily offerings. You may want to arrive early enough to enjoy sunset views of the harbor. ⊠ *Waterfront, Yialos* ☎ *22460/72033* ⟨ *Reservations essential* ⊙ *Closed mid-Oct.–Apr.*

$$$
★
🖬 **Aliki Hotel.** At this three-story, 1895 mansion on the waterfront, guest rooms are furnished with a tasteful mix of antiques and newer pieces—the best, of course, are those that face the water. **Pros:** lovely old house with plenty of atmosphere; waterfront location. **Cons:** rooms are reached by a climb up steep stairs. ⊠ *Waterfront, Yialos* ☎ *22460/71665* ⊕ *www.hotelaliki.gr* ⇆ *12 rooms, 3 suites* ⟨ *In-room: a/c, no TV, Wi-Fi. In-hotel: restaurant, bar* ⦿ *Breakfast.*

$
★
🖬 **Niriides.** The little fishing village of Nimborios, about a mile from Yialos, is the setting for a get-away-from-it-all retreat in these pleasant apartments overlooking the sea and the coast of Turkey. **Pros:** wonderful relaxing atmosphere; great hospitality; spacious, attractive accommodations; beautiful rural location. **Cons:** remote location. ⊠ *Nimborios, Yialos* ☎ *22460/71784* 🖷 *22460/71892* ⊕ *www.niriideshotel.com* ⇆ *11 rooms* ⟨ *In-room: kitchen. In-hotel: bar, parking* ⊙ *Closed Nov.–Apr.* ⦿ *Breakfast.*

$$$$
Fodor's Choice
★
🖬 **The Old Markets.** Symi's historic sponge trading halls—one of many landmarks that surround the old harbor—have been restored as an intimate and atmospheric inn where centuries-old surroundings are accented by stone walls, painted ceilings, exquisite antiques, and such 21st century touches as high-tech lighting and supremely comfortable beds. **Pros:** extremely comfortable accommodations, including a lavish suite. **Cons:** harbor location puts you amidst the one busy spot on the island. ⊠ *Kali Strata, Yialos* ☎ *22460/71440* ⊕ *theoldmarkets.com* ⇆ *5* ⟨ *In-room: a/c. In-hotel: laundry facilities* ⊙ *Nov.–Apr.*

BEACHES

One reason Symi's beaches are so pristine is that almost none are reachable by car. From the main harbor at Yialos, boats leave every half hour between 10:30 am and 12:30 pm to the beautiful beaches of **Aghia Marina, Aghios Nikolas, Aghios Giorgos,** and **Nanou** bay. Return trips run 4–6 pm. The round-trips cost €5–€10. In summer, there are also small boats for hire from the clock tower.

For a swim near Yialos, you can go to the little strip of beach beyond the **Yialos** harbor—follow the road past the bell tower and the Aliki Hotel and you come to a seaside taverna that rents umbrellas and beach chairs for €5 a day. If you continue walking on the same road for about 2 km (1 mi), you come to the pine-shaded beach at **Nimborios** bay, where there is another taverna.

FESTIVAL

Symi Festival. The Symi Festival brings free dance, music, theater performances, and cinema screenings to the island every year from June through September. Most events take place in the main harbor square in Yialos, but some are scheduled in the Chatziagapitos villa, the Monastery of Taxiarchis Michael Panormitis, and other historic places around the island. A schedule of events is posted at the square, and programs can be found at local shops, travel agents, and the town hall. ⊠ *Municipality of Symi* ⊕ *www.symi.gr.*

9

CHORIO ΧΩΡΙΟ

1 km (½ mi) east of Yialos.

It's a 10-minute walk from the main harbor of Yialos up to the hilltop town of Chorio, along a staircase of some 400 steps, known as Kali Strata (Good Steps). There is also a road that can be traveled in one of the island's few taxis or by bus, which makes a circuit with stops at the harbor in Yialos, Chorio, and the seaside community of Pedi. The Kali Strata is flanked by elegant neoclassic houses with elaborate stonework, lavish pediments, and intricate wrought-iron balconies. Just before the top of the stairs (and the welcome little Kali Strata bar), a line of windmills crowns the hill of **Noulia.** Most of Chorio's many churches date to the 18th and 19th centuries, and many are ornamented with richly decorated iconostases and ornate bell towers. Donkeys are often used to carry materials through the narrow streets for the town's steady construction and renovation work.

Archaeological Museum. The collection at the Archaeological Museum, housed in a neoclassic dwelling amid the maze of Chorio's lanes, displays Hellenistic and Roman sculptures and inscriptions as well as more-recent carvings, icons, costumes, and handicrafts; the re-creation of a simple Symi dwelling is especially charming. ⊠ *Follow signs from central square to Lieni neighborhood, Chorio* ☎ *22460/71114* ✉ *€2* ☉ *Tues.–Sun. 8–2:30.*

Chatziagapitos Mansion. The restored home of a wealthy 18th-century merchant/seafaring family provides a look at life in Symi as it once was under Ottoman rule, when the island was a major port. ⊠ *Chorio* ✉ *€1.50* ☉ *Tues.–Sun. 8–2:30; hours vary considerably.*

Kastro *(castle).* Incorporating fragments of an ancient acropolis within its walls, the kastro is also landmarked by a church and several chapels which dot the sparse hillside around the remnants of its walls, first built by the Knights of St. John in a short-lived attempt to expand their holdings in Rhodes. The hilltop view takes in both sides of the narrow peninsula that Chorio crowns, with the villages of Yialos and Pedi (and their sparkling harbors) far below. ⊠ *At top of town, in ancient acropolis, Chorio.*

WHERE TO EAT AND STAY

For expanded hotel reviews, visit Fodors.com.

$
GREEK

✕ **Georgio and Maria's Taverna.** Meals at this simple Chorio taverna, which is as popular with locals as it is with tourists, are served in a high-ceilinged, whitewashed dining room or on a terrace that is partially shaded by a grape arbor and affords wonderful views over the sea and surrounding hills. Fish is a specialty, and simply prepared *mezedes* (small dishes), such as roasted peppers topped with feta cheese and fried zucchini, can constitute a delicious meal in themselves. If you're lucky, one of the neighbors will stroll in with instrument in hand to provide an impromptu serenade. ⊠ *Off main square at top of the Kali Strata, Chorio* ☎ *22460/71984.*

¢
★

☷ **Hotel Fiona.** At this bright, cheerful hotel perched on the hillside in Chorio, just about all of the large, white-tile-floored rooms have a sea-facing balcony—blue-painted furnishings are basic but comfortable, and the breezy decor is accented throughout with pastel fabrics and perhaps a copy of the very helpful *Symi Visitor*, an English-language newspaper about Symi that this hotel management publishes. **Pros:** friendly service; excellent views over the harbor far below. **Cons:** on foot, the nearby Yialos waterfront and beaches are reached by an atmospheric yet strenuous climb down and back up 400 steps. ✉ *Near main square, Chorio* ☎ *22460/72088* 🌐 *www.symivisitor.com* *14 rooms, 3 studios* *In-room: a/c, kitchen, no TV, Wi-Fi. In-hotel: bar* *No credit cards* ⏲ *Closed Nov.–Apr.* *Breakfast.*

MONASTERY OF TAXIARCHIS MICHAEL PANORMITIS
ΜΟΝΗ ΤΑΞΙΑΡΧΗ ΜΙΧΑΗΛ ΠΑΝΟΡΜΙΤΗ

7 km (4½ mi) south of Chorio.

Fodor's Choice ★ **Monastery of Taxiarchis Michael Panormitis.** The main reason to venture to the atypically green, pine-covered hills surrounding the little Gulf of Panormitis is to visit the Monastery of Taxiarchis Michael Panormitis, dedicated to Symi's patron saint, the protector of sailors. The site's entrance is surmounted by an elaborate **bell tower,** of the multilevel wedding-cake variety on display in Yialos and Chorio. A black-and-white pebble mosaic adorns the floor of the **courtyard,** which is surrounded by a vaulted stoa. The interior of the **church,** entirely frescoed in the 18th century, contains a marvelously ornate wooden iconostasis, which is flanked by a heroic-size 18th-century representation of Michael, all but his face covered with silver. There are two small **museums** devoted to Byzantine and folk art. The Byzantine includes a collection of votive offerings, including an enchanting collection of wooden ship models and bottles with notes containing wishes and money in them, which, according to local lore, travel to Symi on their own after having been thrown into the sea. A trip to the monastery can be accompanied by a refreshing swim at the designated edges of the deep-blue harbor. There's bus service twice a day from Yialos, which passes through Chorio, and boats from Yialos and Rhodes daily. Several tour companies organize day trips to the monastery, with time for a swim and a hike in the surrounding countryside, for about €15, including lunch.

If a day trip isn't enough for you, the monastery, which no longer houses monks but is staffed by two clergy people, rents 60 spartan rooms (*22460/72414*) with kitchens and private baths for about €20. Though the price doesn't include a towel or air-conditioning and there are insects (some rather large), the spiritual aspect makes for an enriching experience. A market, bakery, and a few other businesses make up the rest of the settlement. The monastery is at its busiest for the week leading up to November 8, Michael's feast day, an event that draws the faithful from throughout the Dodecanese and beyond. ✉ *Symi's south side, at harbor* ☎ *22460/71581* *Monastery free; museums €1.50* ⏲ *Monastery: daily 7–8; museums: Apr.–Oct. 8:30–1 and 3–4; Nov.–Apr. by appointment.*

KOS ΚΩΣ

Glow with flowering oleanders and hibiscus, the island of Kos is the third largest in the Dodecanese. It certainly remains one of the most verdant in the otherwise arid archipelago, with lush fields and tree-clad mountains, surrounded by miles of sandy beach. Its highest peak, part of a small mountain range in the northeast, is a respectable 2,800 feet. All this beauty has not gone unnoticed, of course, and Kos undeniably suffers from the effects of mass tourism: its beaches are often crowded, most of its seaside towns have been recklessly overdeveloped, and the main town is noisy and busy between June and September.

GETTING HERE AND AROUND

BY AIR Kos is a major air hub, with regular service from Athens on Olympic and Aegean airlines, several flights a day on each in high season, in and out of Hippocrates Airport. During high season, charter flights also fly into Kos from many other European cities. The airport is about 25 km (15 mi) outside of Kos town, about an hour by bus (€5) and half an hour by taxi (€20), so keep the time and cost factor in mind when booking an early morning outgoing flight.

BY BOAT Kos is well served by boat, with at least two ferries arriving from Pireaus daily in high season (10 hours) and at least two high-speed catamarans arriving from Rhodes (about 2½ hours). Boats also arrive from Mykonos, Paros, and other islands in the Cyclades about twice a week. Schedules change all the time, so check with ⊕ *www.ferries.gr, www. gtp.gr,* or with any of the many travel agencies along the waterfront in Kos town for the latest info on boat service. Kos harbor is adjacent to the city center, so convenient to services and bus connections.

BY BUS An excellent bus network serves most of the island, putting most resort towns around the island within easy reach of Kos town by public transportation; as many as six buses a day connect Kos town in the north and Kefalos in the south, for example, and the trip takes about an hour and costs €3.

Visitor Information Kos Municipal Tourism Office ⊠ *Vasileos Georgiou 1, Kos town* ☎ *22420/28724* ⊕ *www.kos.gr.*

EXPLORING

In Mycenaean times and during the Archaic period, the island prospered. In the 6th century BC it was conquered by the Persians but later joined the Delian League, supporting Athens against Sparta in the Peloponnesian War. Kos was invaded and destroyed by the Spartan fleet, ruled by Alexander and his various successors, and has twice been devastated by earthquakes. Nevertheless, the city and the economy flourished, as did the arts and sciences. The painter Apelles, the Michelangelo of his time, came from Kos, as did Hippocrates, father of modern medicine. Under the Roman Empire, the island's Asklepieion and its renowned healing center drew emperors and ordinary citizens alike. The Knights of St. John arrived in 1315 and ruled for the next two centuries, until they were replaced by the Ottomans. In 1912 the Italians took over, and in 1947 the island was united with Greece.

9

KOS TOWN ΚΩΣ ΠΟΛΗ

92 km (57 mi) north of Rhodes.

The modern town lies on a flat plain encircling spacious Mandraki harbor and is a pleasant assemblage of low-lying buildings and shady lanes, with a skyline pierced by minarets and palm trees. The fortress, which crowns the west side of town, is a good place to begin your exploration of Kos town. Hippocrates is supposed to have taught near here, in the shade of a plane tree that is said to have grown on one side of little Platanou Square—but this is merely legend, as the Koan capital, called Astypalaia, was at the far, western end of the island and Thucydides recounts its destruction by an earthquake. A loggia, actually a mosque built in 1786, now graces the square.

Agora and Harbor Ruins. Excavations by Italian and Greek archaeologists have revealed ancient Agora and harbor ruins that date from the 4th century BC through Roman times. Remnants include parts of the walls of the old city, of a Hellenistic stoa, and of temples dedicated to Aphrodite and Hercules. The ruins are not fenced and, laced with pine-shaded paths, are a pleasant retreat in the modern city. In spring the site is covered with brightly colored flowers, which nicely frame the ancient gray-and-white marble blocks tumbled in every direction. ⊠ *Over bridge from Platanou Sq., behind Castle of the Knights, Kos town.*

★ **Archaeological Museum.** The island's archaeological museum houses Hellenistic and Roman sculpture by Koan artists, much of it unearthed by Italians during their tenure on the island in the early 20th century. Among the treasures are a renowned statue of Hippocrates—the great physician who practiced on Kos—and Asclepius, god of healing; a group of sculptures from various Roman phases, all discovered in the House of the Europa Mosaic; and a remarkable series of Hellenistic draped female statues mainly from the Sanctuary of Demeter at Kyparissi and the Odeon. ⊠ *Eleftherias Sq., west of agora through gate leading to Platanou Sq., Kos town* ☎ *22420/28326* ⊕ *www.culture.gr* ✉ *€3* ☉ *Nov.–May, Tues.–Sun. 8:30–3; June–Oct., Tues.–Sun. 8.*

☾ **Casa Romana** (*Roman House*). The Casa Romana (Roman House) is a lavish restoration of a 3rd-century Roman mansion, with 36 rooms grouped around three atriums. The house provides a look at what everyday life of the well-to-do residents of the Roman town might have been like, and also houses some beautiful frescoes and mosaics. However, the Greek and Roman ruins that surround the house are freely accessible and are just as evocative. ⊠ *Pavlou and Grigoriou, Kos town* ☎ *22420/23234* ✉ *€3* ☉ *Tues.–Sun. 8:30–3.*

Castle of the Knights. Built by the Knights of St. John in the 15th century and taken by the Turks in 1522 (with the rest of the knights' Dodecanese holdings), the Castle of the Knights is an imposing presence on the harbor. It's best to let that remain the impression you have of this massive structure: Little remains inside the walls but a field littered with fragments of ancient funerary monuments and other sculptural material from the island's Greek and Roman inhabitants. ⊠ *Over bridge from Platanou Sq., Kos town* ☎ *22420/27927* ✉ *€4* ☉ *Tues.–Sun. 8:30–2:30.*

West Excavations. These excavations have uncovered a portion of one of the main Roman streets with many houses, including the **House of the Europa Mosaic,** and part of the **Roman baths** (near main Roman street) that was later converted into a basilica. The **gymnasium** is distinguished by its partly reconstructed colonnade, and the so-called **Nymphaion** is a lavish public latrine that has been restored. In the **Odeon,** 18 rows of stone seats remain intact. The West Excavations are always open, with free access, and significant finds are labeled. ⊠ *Southwest of agora and harbor ruins, Kos town.*

BEACHES

If you must get wet but can't leave Kos town, try the narrow pebble strip of beach immediately south of the main harbor.

Tingaki. Tingaki has a pretty, sandy beach that stretches for miles; though resorts and other attractions line the sands, much of this part of the coast remains rural, with fields and salts marshes spreading out across the plain just beyond the beach strip. ⊠ *On north coast, 13 km [8 mi] west of Kos town.*

Mastichari. At the resort and fishing port of Mastichari, you'll find a wide sand beach backed by shade-providing pines, tavernas, rooms for rent, and a pier where boats set sail on day trips to the uncrowded islet of Pserimos. ⊠ *On north coast, 32 km [20 mi] west of Kos town.*

WHERE TO EAT AND STAY

For expanded hotel reviews, visit Fodors.com.

$$ ✕**Petrino.** Greek-Canadian brothers Mike and George Gerovasilis have
EUROPEAN created a calm oasis a few streets in from the hustle and bustle of Kos harbor. A 150-year-old stone house provides cozy dining in cool months, and in summer, tables pepper a garden full of private nooks, fountains, and gentle music. The enormous menu lists Greek recipes, like zucchini pancakes and liver with oregano, side-by-side with much-heralded house creations that include figs wrapped in prosciutto and stuffed with blue cheese, or the shrimp sautéed with mushrooms in ouzo. Servings are generous, and the service tends to be informal yet gracious. ⊠ *Ioannou Theologou Sq., Kos town* ☎ *22420/27251* ⊕ *www. petrino-kos.gr.*

$$$ ✕**Platanos.** Not only is the setting, on the shady square where Hip-
GREEK pocrates once taught, the most romantic in Kos, but this island institution maintains its high standards. Occupying an early-20th-century Italian club, the surroundings may be elaborate (with dining in arched, elaborately tiled rooms or on a candlelit balcony) but the cuisine here is simply prepared and delicious—try the beautifully spiced grilled lamb chops or chicken stuffed with dates. Live music accompanies meals as the evenings wear on. ⊠ *Plateia Platanos, Kos town* ☎ *22420/28991* ⌂ *Reservations essential* ⊗ *Closed Nov.–Mar.*

$$$$ ⌂**Grecotel Kos Imperial.** The grounds of this resort, covering a gentle
★ slope next to the Aegean, comprise a water world, laced with seawater and freshwater pools, artificial rivers and lagoons, glimmering glass-tile hydrotherapy pools, and dozens of spa treatment basins—and set amid them are airy and beautifully designed guest rooms, with sitting areas, terraces, and in many, private hot tubs and plunge pools. **Pros:** finest

9

of the big resorts on Kos; excellent facilities; attractive and comfortable guest rooms; beautiful grounds; idyllic beach. **Cons:** big resort feel; a distance from Kos town (but easily accessible by bus or taxi). ⊠ *4 km (2½ mi) east of Kos town, Psalidi* ☎ *22420/58000* ⊕ *www.grecotel.com* ⤳ *330 rooms, 55 suites* ⚐ *In-room: a/c, Wi-Fi. In-hotel: restaurant, bar, pool, spa, beach, water sports, children's programs, business center, parking* ❐| *Breakfast.*

¢ ⊞ **Hotel Afendoulis.** At this simple and friendly in-town guesthouse, the plain, whitewashed rooms with dark-wood furniture are spotless and of far better quality than most in this price range; the best open to little balconies with sea views. **Pros:** pleasant, quiet surroundings; in-town location; excellent hospitality includes laundry service. **Cons:** no pool or other resort amenities. ⊠ *Evripilou 1, Kos town* ☎ *22420/25321* ⊕ *www.afendoulishotel.com* ⤳ *23 rooms* ⚐ *In-room: a/c. In-hotel: bar, laundry facilities.*

NIGHTLIFE

Things start cooking before 7 pm and in many cases roar on past 7 am on Akti Koundourioti and in the nearby Exarhia area, which includes rowdy Nafklirou and Plessa streets. Competing bars try to lure in bar-hoppers with ads for cheap beer and neon-colored drinks.

Fashion. A massive club off Delphinia Square, Fashion has an outdoor bar, happy hour, a throbbing indoor dance floor, and guest DJs, who seek to provide young, international travelers the kind of club music they'd hear back home. ⊠ *Odos Kanari 2, Kos town* ☎ *22420/22592.*

H20. The loungey seaside club H20 has a small, sleek interior as well as outdoor seating, and superb meals are served in the adjoining restaurant of the same name. ⊠ *Aktis Art Hotel, beachfront, Vasileos Georgiou 7, Kos town* ☎ *22420/47207.*

FESTIVAL

Hippocrates Festival. Every summer from July through mid-September Kos hosts the Hippocrates Festival. Music, dance, movie screenings, and theater performances enliven venues such as the Castle of the Knights and the Odeon. The festival also includes exhibits around town and activities for children. ☎ *22420/48222* ✎ *www.kosinfo.gr.*

THE OUTDOORS

Kos, particularly the area around the town, is good for bicycle riding. Ride to the Asklepieion for a picnic, or visit the Castle of Antimacheia. Note: be aware of hazards such as cistern openings, for very few have security fences around them. You can rent bicycles everywhere—in Kos town and at the more-popular resorts. Try the many shops along Eleftheriou Venizelou Street in town. Renting a bike costs about €6 per day.

ASKLEPIEION ΑΣΚΛΗΠΙΕΙΟΝ

4 km (2½ mi) west of Kos town.

Fodor's Choice **Asklepieion.** One of the great healing centers of antiquity, the ruins of
★ the Asklepieion still impress and fire the imagination, framed by a thick grove of cypress trees and laid out on several **broad terraces** connected

by a monumental staircase. Hippocrates began to teach the art of healing here in the 5th century BC and, until the decline of the Roman Empire, the Asklepieion was the most renowned medical facility in the Western world. The lower terrace probably held the Asklepieion Festivals, famed drama and dance contests held in honor of the god of healing. On the middle terrace is an **Ionic temple,** once decorated with works by the legendary 4th-century BC painter Apelles, including his renowned depiction of Aphrodite (much celebrated in antiquity, it was said the artist used a mistress of Alexander the Great as a model). On the uppermost terrace is the **Doric Temple of Asklepios,** once surrounded by colonnaded porticoes. ⊠ *Asklepieion* ✢ *Take the local bus from Kos town to the hamlet of Platani and walk to the ruins from there* ☎ *22420/28763* ⊠ *€4* ☉ *Apr.–Oct., Tues.–Sun. 8–6; Nov.–Mar., Tues.–Sun. 8–3.*

OFF THE BEATEN PATH

Mountain villages. Leaving the main road southwest of the Asklepieion (turnoff is at Zipari, 9 km [5½ mi] southwest of Kos town), you can explore an enchanting landscape of cypress and pine trees on a route that climbs to a handful of lovely, whitewashed rural villages that cling to the craggy slopes of the island's central mountains, including Asfendiou, Zia, and Lagoudi. The busiest of them is Zia, with an appealing smattering of churches; crafts shops selling local honey, weavings, and handmade soaps; and open-air tavernas where you can enjoy the views over the surrounding forests and fields toward the sea.

WHERE TO EAT

¢

GREEK

Fodor's Choice

★

✕ **Taverna Ampavris.** The surroundings and the food are both delightful at this charming, rustic taverna, outside Kos town on a lane leading to the village of Platani. Meals are served in the courtyard of an old farmhouse, and the kitchen's emphasis is on local country food—including wonderful stews and grilled meats, accompanied by vegetables from nearby gardens. The owners wait on you, steering you toward tasty meals (you can't go wrong with the zucchini blossoms stuffed with rice), or offering detailed advice on sightseeing. ⊠ *On the way from Kos town to Platani, Ampavris* ☎ *22420/25696* ⊕ *www.ampavris.gr* ▭ *No credit cards* ☉ *No lunch.*

CASTLE OF ANTIMACHEIA ΚΑΣΤΡΟ ΑΝΤΙΜΑΧΕΙΑΣ

21 km (13 mi) southwest of Asklepieion, 25 km (15 mi) southwest of Kos town.

Castle of Antimacheia. The thick, well-preserved walls of this 14th-century fortress look out over the sweeping Aegean and Kos's green interior. Antimacheia was another stronghold of the Knights of St. John, whose coat of arms hangs above the entrance gate. Within the walls, little of the original complex remains, with the exception of two stark churches; in one of them, Ayios Nikolaos, you can make out a primitive fresco of St. Christopher carrying the infant Jesus. ⊠ *On main road from Kos, turn left 3 km (2 mi) before village of Antimacheia, following signs to castle.*

Love sand castles? Head to the gorgeous Ayios Stefanos beach, located near Kamari.

KAMARI ΚΑΜΑΡΙ

10 km (6 mi) south of the Castle of Antimacheia, 35 km (22 mi) south-west of Kos town.

On Kefalos bay, the little beach community of Kamari is pleasant and less frantic than the island's other seaside resorts. On a summit above is the lovely **Old Town of Kefalos,** a pleasant place to wander for its views and quintessential Greekness. Close offshore is a little rock formation holding a chapel to St. Nicholas. Opposite are the ruins of a magnificent 5th-century Christian basilica.

BEACH

Paradise. Nearby Paradise beach has plenty of parking, and thus crowds, but the broad, sandy beach is magnificent and the long stretch of sand curves around the enchanting Gulf of Kefalos; its northern end is undeveloped, almost deserted, and consequently popular with nude bathers. ⊠ *3 km [2 mi] north of Kamari.*

WHERE TO STAY

For expanded hotel reviews, visit Fodors.com.

¢   ⊞ **Hotel Kokalakis Beach.** Many guests return annually to enjoy the peaceful proximity to pebble and sand beaches and the hospitality of the Kokalakis family; guest rooms are squeaky clean and whitewashed, with ceramic tile floors and balconies, and six include cooking facilities. **Pros:** close to beach; nice pool area; extremely welcoming hosts. **Cons:** fairly basic accommodations. ⊠ *Waterfront, Kamari* ☎ *22420/71466* ⤴ *32 rooms* ⚬ *In-room: a/c. In-hotel: bar, pool, business center* ▭ *No credit cards* ☉ *Closed Oct–Apr.*

$$$$ ⊞ **Palazzo del Mare.** Should you wish to bask in big-resort luxury, look no further than this pleasure palace where the many amenities include the pleasure of jumping into a massive, riverlike, acre-plus pool directly from your room—many of the deluxe accommodations also have sea views. **Pros:** attractive rooms and grounds, first-rate service, remarkable swimming pools; full board available. **Cons:** anonymous, big-resort feel; expensive extras. ⊠ *Marmari* ☎ *22420/42320* ⊕ *www.palazzodelmare. gr* ⤳ *178 rooms* ♿ *In- room: a/c. In-hotel: restaurant, bar, pool, gym, spa, beach, water sports, children's programs, laundry facilities, business center, parking* ⊘ *Nov.–Mar.* ⦿*Multiple meal plans.*

PATMOS ΠΑΤΜΟΣ

For better or worse, it can be difficult to reach Patmos—for many travelers, this lack of access is definitely for the better, since the island retains the air of an unspoiled retreat. Rocky and barren, the small, 34-square-km (21-square-mi) island lies beyond the islands of Kalymnos and Leros, northwest of Kos. Here on a hillside is the Monastery of the Apocalypse, which enshrines the cave where St. John received the Revelation in AD 95. Scattered evidence of Mycenaean presence remains on Patmos, and walls of the classical period indicate the existence of a town near Skala. Most of the island's approximately 2,800 people live in three villages: Skala, medieval Chora, and the small rural settlement of Kambos. The island is popular among the faithful making pilgrimages to the monastery as well as with vacationing Athenians and a newly growing community of international trendsetters—designers, artists, poets, and "taste gurus" (to quote *Vogue*'s July 2011 write-up of the island)—who have bought homes in Chora. These stylemeisters followed in the footsteps of Alexandrian John Stefanidis and the English artist Teddy Millington-Drake who, in the early '60s, set about creating what eventually became hailed as one of the most gorgeous island homes in the world. The word soon spread thanks to their many guests (who included Jacqueline Kennedy Onassis) but, happily, administrators have carefully contained development, and as a result, Patmos retains its charm and natural beauty—even in the busy month of August.

GETTING HERE AND AROUND

BY BOAT   Patmos has no airport, and outside of July and August, ferries wending through the Dodecanese from Athens call only every other day or so, with daily service in high season; the trip from Athens takes only seven hours, but boats arrive at the ungodly hour of 2 am. The most popular alternative to the ferry is to fly to Kos and board one of the approximately four daily catamarans for the two-hour trip up to Patmos. On days when ferries do not call at Patmos, the boat to Kos and catamaran to Patmos is also an option. A convenient way to reach beaches around the island is to board a water taxi from Skala harbor.

BY BUS   The island's limited bus route provides regular service from Skala to Chora, Kambos, and other popular spots. Once on the island, it is easy to move around by taxi—and fairly inexpensive since distances are short.

9

Visitor Information **Patmos Municipal Tourism Office** ✉ *Near ferry dock, Skala* ☎ *22470/31235* ⊕ *www.patmosweb.gr.*

SKALA ΣΚΑΛΑ

161 km (100 mi) north of Kos.

Skala, the island's small but sophisticated main town, is where almost all the hotels and restaurants are located. It's a popular port of call for cruise ships, and in summer the huge liners often loom over the shops and restaurants. There's not much to see in the town, but it is lively and very attractive. Most of the town center is closed to cars and, since strict building codes have been enforced, even new buildings have traditional architectural detail. The medieval town of Chora and the island's legendary monasteries loom above Skala on a nearby hill. Take a 20-minute hike up to **Kastelli**, on a hill overlooking Skala, to see the stone remains of the city's 6th- to 4th-century BC town and acropolis.

BEACHES

The small island is endowed with at least 24 beaches. Although most of them, which tend to be coarse shingle, are accessible by land, sun worshippers can sail to a few (as well as to the nearby islet cluster of **Arkoi**) on the caïques that make regular runs from Skala, leaving in the morning. Prices vary with the number of people making the trip (or with the boat); transport to and from a beach for a family for a day may cost around €35.

Melloi. The beach at Melloi, a 2-km (1-mi) taxi ride north of Skala or a quick caïque ride, is a sand-and-pebble strip with a taverna nearby.

Kambos. The beach at Kambos Bay is the most popular on the island. It has mostly fine pebbles and sand, nearby tavernas, windsurfing, water-skiing, and pedal boats for rent. ✉ *6 km [4 mi] from Skala.*

OFF THE
BEATEN
PATH

Psili Amos. Psili Amos, a sand beach shaded by pines some 15 km (9 mi) south of Skala, is worth the extra effort to reach: it is arguably the most beautiful beach on the island. Getting there requires a 45-minute caïque ride (€10) from Skala or a 20-minute walk on a footpath from Diakofti (the narrowest point on the island), where visitors can park their cars by the taverna. Nude bathers sometimes line the edges of the beach.

WHERE TO EAT

$$$

MEDITERRANEAN

Fodor's Choice

★

✗ **Benetos.** A native Patmian, Benetos Matthaiou, and his American wife, Susan, operate this lovely restaurant abutting a seaside garden that supplies the kitchen with fresh herbs and vegetables. These homegrown ingredients find their way into a selection of Mediterranean-style dishes that are influenced by the couple's travels and include phyllo parcels stuffed with spinach and cheese, the island's freshest Greek salad, and a juicy grilled swordfish in citrus sauce. Accompany your meal with a selection from the eclectic Greek wine list. Service is gracious and friendly, and an evening on the terrace here is one of the island's nicest experiences. ✉ *On harborside road between Skala and Grikos, Sapsila* ☎ *22470/33089* ⊕ *www.benetosrestaurant.com* ⊙ *Closed Mon. and mid-Oct.–May.*

¢ ✕**Tzivaeri.** The excellent island cooking here is spiced up by the sea
GREEK views, which you can savor from a seaside balcony table or right on
the beach below. The mezedes menu includes such traditional favorites
as leek pie, fried eggplant, and smoked pork, and grilled lamb chops
and other main courses are served as well. Live music (*Tzivaeri*, which
roughly translates as "my beloved," is also the name of a popular Greek
folk song) is performed many nights, usually not earlier than around
midnight. ⊠ *Harborside road, Skala* ☎ *22470/31170* ▬ *No credit cards*
☉ *No lunch.*

$$$$ ✕**Vegghera.** A handsome mansion overlooking the harbor is the setting
GREEK for an exquisite meal that combines traditional Greek and international
influences. Fresh seafood tops the menu, but pastas, herb-flavored chops,
and the lavish creations fashioned by vegetables chef George Grillis from
his own garden are a delight as well. Summertime dining is on a terrace overlooking the marina. ⊠ *Facing marina, Skala* ☎ *22470/32988*
⌂ *Reservations essential* ☉ *Closed Nov.–Easter. No lunch.*

WHERE TO STAY
For expanded hotel reviews, visit Fodors.com.

$$$$ ⌘**Hotel Petra.** One of Greece's truly special retreats sits high above
Fodor'sChoice Girkos Bay south of Skala and provides a luxurious yet informal get-
★ away, with large and sumptuous guest quarters, delightful outdoor
lounges, a welcoming pool, and soothing sea views. **Pros:** attractive and
comfortable surroundings; wonderful outdoor spaces; superb service
and hospitality; beach is just steps away. **Cons:** the hotel climbs a series
of terraces reached only by steps. ⊠ *Girkos, Skala* ☎ *22470/34020*
⊕ *www.petrahotel-patmos.com* ⇡ *13 rooms* ⌂ *In-room: a/c, Wi-Fi.
In-hotel: restaurant, bar, pool, laundry facilities* ☉ *Closed Nov.–mid-
Apr.* ⏀*Breakfast.*

$$$ ⌘**Hotel Skala.** Skala's best in-town lodgings place you in the center of
the action, steps from the municipal beach yet removed from the harbor
noise and offering simple but comfortable guest rooms that surround
a bougainvillea-filled garden. **Pros:** top location; attractive terrace and
pool. **Cons:** the hotel occasionally hosts large groups; high-season rates
are high, given quality of accommodation. ⊠ *Skala* ☎ *22470/31343*
⊕ *www.skalahotel.gr* ⇡ *78 rooms* ⌂ *In-room: a/c, Wi-Fi. In-hotel: bar,
pool* ☉ *Closed Nov.–Mar.* ⏀*Breakfast.*

$$$ ⌘**Porto Scoutari.** It seems only fitting that Patmos should have a hotel
Fodor'sChoice that reflects the architectural beauty of the island while providing luxu-
★ rious accommodations, and these enormous, suitelike guest rooms and
verdant garden (with a swimming pool) fit the bill. **Pros:** large, very
attractive rooms with sleeping and sitting areas; beautiful grounds; near
beach; excellent service; extremely attractive rates available for longer
stays. **Cons:** only ground-floor rooms would be suitable for travelers
with mobility issues. ⊠ *1 km (½ mi) northeast of Skala center, Skala*
☎ *22470/33123* ⊕ *www.portoscoutari.com* ⇡ *30 rooms, 4 suites* ⌂ *In-
room: a/c, kitchen, Internet. In-hotel: restaurant, bar, pool, gym, spa*
☉ *Closed Nov.–Apr.* ⏀*Breakfast.*

9

SHOPPING

Patmos has some elegant boutiques selling jewelry and crafts, including antiques, mainly from the island.

Katoi. Head here to explore a wide selection of ceramics, icons, and silver jewelry of traditional design. ✉ *Skala–Chora Rd., Skala* ☎ *22470/31487.*

Parousia. This is a top place to purchase Byzantine-style icons, wooden children's toys, and small religious items. ✉ *Past square at beginning of road to Chora, Skala* ☎ *22470/32549.*

> **MMMMM...**
>
> The best goods on the island might be of the sweet variety. Be sure to sample specialties like *poogies* (confectioners' sugar-coated cookies stuffed with almond and walnut chunks) and soufflé-like cheese pies.
>
> **Desantis.** This shop dispenses gelato that many fans claim could hold its own in Italy. ✉ *Off central square in Skala* ☎ *22470/31791.*

★ **Selene.** Whether made of ceramic, glass, silver, or wood, each work here—by one of 40 different Greek artists—is unique. ✉ *Skala harbor, Skala* ☎ *22470/31742.*

CHORA ΧΩΡΑ

5 km (3 mi) south, above Skala.

Atop a hill due south of Skala, the village of Chora, clustered around the walls of the Monastery of St. John the Theologian, has become a preserve of international wealth. Though the short distance from Skala may make walking seem attractive, a steep incline can make this challenging. A taxi ride is not expensive, about €6, and there is frequent bus service (€1) from Skala and other points on the island.

★ **Monastery of the Apocalypse.** In AD 95, during the emperor Domitian's persecution of Christians, St. John the Theologian was banished to Patmos, where he lived until his reprieve two years later. He writes that it was on Patmos that he "heard . . . a great voice, as of a trumpet," commanding him to write a book and "send it unto the seven churches." According to tradition, St. John wrote the text of *Revelation* in the little cave, the Sacred Grotto, now built into the Monastery of the Apocalypse. The voice of God spoke through a threefold crack in the rock, and the saint dictated to his follower Prochorus. A slope in the wall is pointed to as the desk where Prochorus wrote, and a silver halo is set on the stone that was the apostle's pillow. The grotto is decorated with wall paintings from the 12th century and icons from the 16th. The monastery, which is accessible via several flights of outdoor stairs, was constructed in the 17th century from architectural fragments of earlier buildings, and further embellished in later years; the complex also contains chapels to St. Artemios and St. Nicholas. In late August or early September, the monastery hosts the **Festival of Sacred Music of Patmos**, with world-class Byzantine and ecclesiastical music performances in an outdoor performance space. ✉ *2 km (1 mi) south of Chora on Skala–Chora Rd.* ☎ *22470/31284 monastery, 22470/29363*

The luckiest monks on Patmos—famed for its vibrant community of monks—get to call the Monastery of St. John the Theologian home.

festival 🖾 Free ⊙ *May–Aug., daily 8–1:30 (also 2–6 on Sun., Tues., and Thurs.); Sept.–Apr., hours vary.*

Fodor's Choice

★ **Monastery of St. John the Theologian.** On its high perch at the top of Chora, the Monastery of St. John the Theologian is one of the world's best-preserved fortified medieval monastic complexes, a center of learning since the 11th century, and today recognized as a UNESCO World Heritage Site. Hosios Christodoulos, a man of education, energy, devotion, and vision, established the monastery in 1088 and the complex soon became an intellectual center, with a rich library and a tradition of teaching. Monks of education and social standing ornamented the monastery with the best sculpture, carvings, and paintings and, by the end of the 12th century, the community owned land on Leros, Limnos, Crete, and Asia Minor, as well as ships, which carried on trade exempt from taxes.

A broad staircase leads to the entrance, which is fortified by towers and buttresses.

The complex consists of buildings from a number of periods: in front of the entrance is the 17th-century **Chapel of the Holy Apostles**; the **main church** dates from the 11th century, the time of Christodoulos (whose skull, along with that of Apostle Thomas, is encased in a silver sarcophagus here); the **Chapel of the Virgin** is 12th century.

The **treasury** contains relics, icons, silver, and vestments, most dating from 1600 to 1800. An 11th-century icon of St. Nicholas is executed in fine mosaic work and encased in a silver frame. Another icon is allegedly the work of El Greco. On display, too, are some of the library's oldest codices, dating to the late 5th and the 8th centuries, such as pages from the Gospel of St. Mark and the Book of Job. For the most part, however, the **library** is not open to the public and special permission is required to research its extensive treasures: illuminated manuscripts, approximately 1,000 codices, and more than 3,000 printed volumes. The collection was first cataloged in 1200; of the 267 works of that time, the library still has 111. The archives preserve a near-continuous record, down to the present, of the history of the monastery as well as the political and economic history of the region. ⊠ *Chora, 3 km (2 mi) south of Monastery of the Apocalypse, Chora* ☎ *22470/20800* ⊕ *whc. unesco.org* ✉ *Church and chapels free, treasury €6* ☉ *Daily 8–1:30 (also 2–6 on Sun., Tues., and Thurs.); Dec.–Mar., call to arrange a treasury visit, as hrs are irregular.*

WHERE TO EAT

⚹   ✕ **Vangelis.** Choose between a table on the main square (perfect for
GREEK   people-watching) or in the Paradise Garden out back, where a raised
Fodor's Choice   terrace has stunning views of the sea. Fresh grilled fish and lemon-
★   and-oregano-flavor goat are the specialties, and simple dishes such as mint-flavored *dolmades* (stuffed grape leaves) and *tzatziki* (yogurt and cucumber dip) are excellent. Want traditional lodging to go with that meal? The management is happy to help find rooms in private homes in Chora. ⊠ *Main square, Chora* ☎ *22470/31967* ▬ *No credit cards.*

The Northern Aegean Islands

LESBOS, CHIOS, AND SAMOS

WORD OF MOUTH

"If you are looking for someplace a little off the beaten path, and don't care about trendy nightlife, you might want to look at Lesbos and Chios. Both are gorgeous, have incredibly beautiful beaches, and are very relaxing places. The food in this region of Greece, particularly the seafood, is wonderful."

—eleni

10

WELCOME TO THE NORTHERN AEGEAN ISLANDS

TOP REASONS TO GO

★ **Samos Block Party:** Math genius Pythagoras, freedom-loving Epicurus, and the fabled Aesop were just a few of this island's brightest stars, and their spirits probably still haunt the ancient Heraion temple.

★ **Mesmerizing Mastic Villages:** Pirgi in Chios is known for the resin it produces, but with its Genoese houses patterned in black and white, it's the Escher-like landscape that's likely to draw you in.

★ **Sappho's Island:** If it's poetic truth you seek, head to one of Lesbos's oldest towns, Molyvos—a haven for artists and an aesthete's dream.

★ **Sailing to Byzantium:** Colorful Byzantine mosaics make Chios's 11th-century Nea Moni monastery an important piece of history—and a marvel to behold.

★ **Dizzyingly Good Ouzo:** Though you can get this potent potable anywhere in Greece, Lesbos's is reputedly the best—enjoy it with famed salt-baked Kalloni sardines.

1 Samos. This famously fertile island, in classical antiquity a center of Ionian culture and luxury, is still renowned for its fruitful land and the delectable Muscat wines it produces. The island attracts active archaeology fanatics and lazy beach lovers alike, leaving visitors spoiled for choice among a plethora of ancient sights (such as the Temple at Heraion—once four times larger than the Parthenon) and long sandy beaches with crystal waters.

2 Lesbos. Often called Mytilini after its historic (but today somewhat boisterous) capital, Lesbos is the third-largest island in Greece. Known as the "sweet home" of lesbians from around the world, this was the land of origin of the ancient poetess Sappho, whose dramatic lyrical poetry was said to be addressed to women. Sapphic followers who flock to the island mostly stay in Skala Eressou, but Lesbos has something for everyone: exquisite cuisine and ouzo, beautiful beaches, monasteries with miraculous icons, and lush landscapes.

3 Chios. The island relies on the sea and its mastic production more than on tourism, so you'll find something of the authentic Greece here. But do look beyond the architecturally unappealing main town to explore the isle's allurements, including a lush countryside and quaint village squares. Chios is the "mastic island," producing the highly beneficial resin that is used in chewing gum and cosmetic products; the most noted mastic village is Pirgi, famed for the geometric patterns on its house facades. In addition, the 11th-century monastery of Nea Moni is celebrated for its Byzantine art.

GETTING ORIENTED

About the only thing the islands of Samos, Chios, and Lesbos share is their proximity to Turkey: from their shores, reaching from Macedonia down to the Dodecanese along the coast of Asia Minor, you can see the very fields of Greece's age-old rival. No matter that these three islands may be a long haul from Athens: few parts of the Aegean have greater variety and beauty of landscape—a stunning blend of pristine shores and craggy (Homer's word) mountains.

10

TURKEY / GREECE

Molyvos

Mandamados

Sigri

2 **LESBOS** 36

Skala Eressou Vasilika Mytilini

Skala Mount Olympus ▲ Kratigos

Plomari

PSARA

Marmaro INOUSSES UZUN

Volissos **3** CHIOS

Nea Moni ◆ Chios Ilair

75 Çesme Q32

Pasa-Limani

Pirgi

Aegean Sea

Karlovassi Kokkari

TURKEY / GREECE

SAMOS **1** 62 Samos

Heraion Temple Pythagorio

IKARIA

Fourni

Agios FOURNI

0 ——— 20 mi

0 ——— 20 km

THE NORTHERN AEGEAN'S BEST BEACHES

Have beach, will travel? If sun and fun are at the top of your agenda, this region is blessed with a surfeit of beaches. And not just any beaches. The sun-savvy set likes to think these are Greece's best, and they may well be right.

With their beautiful shores and endless strands, the beaches of the Northern Aegean are Grecian wet dreams. The skinny on taking a dip? These are some of the cleanest waters in Greece, period.

And swimmers find themselves in a water world framed by verdant hills and rocky landscapes.

For complete immersion, there's lots of waterskiing, windsurfing, and canoeing—and the winds of the Northern Aegean are considered tops for sailing.

Nature lovers can have the chance to hand-feed terrapins or visit the unique Petrified Forest, one of the world's best natural landmarks, while those keen on archaeology can seek out some ruins—"sand castles" of a different sort.

LICENSE TO CHILL

Most beaches have handy facilities, with sun beds and umbrellas for hire, while beach bars and tavernas cater to swimmers who need fuel during those hot summer days. Road conditions are generally good, although access to some remotely located beaches may present some difficulties.

LESBOS: SKALA ERESSOS

With its 3 km (2 mi) of unspoilt sands, Skala Eressos is a marvelous beach with crystal clear waters and a motor-free promenade.

Apart from swimming, sunbathing, and sea sports, a grand highlight is the freshwater river that runs into a natural pool halfway along the beach, becoming home to hundreds of terrapins, which can be hand-fed by swimmers; needless to say, this is a major attraction for the kids.

Must-sees: the idyllic sunset, the ancient acropolis ruins close to the beach, and the unique Petrified Forest—one of the world's most important natural landmarks, also located in the vicinity. Too bad there's no handy parking available.

CHIOS: ELINA BEACH

Located 27 km (16 mi) west from Chios town, Elinda (or Elinta), near the village of Anavatos, is a nicely sheltered cove with thick sand, pretty pebbles, and deep, cool, crystalline waters.

The secluded beach is ideal for nature lovers who enjoy spending the entire day quietly swimming, snorkeling, and sunbathing; and the trees that line it offer shady respite from the sun during the hottest hours.

There is a wreck of a Roman ship not far from the shore, where children often gather to play.

The name Elinda or Alinda derives from the ancient Greek word "alios" meaning marine.

Bring some packed lunch and water along if you intend to spend the day as there is not even a canteen here.

LESBOS: EFTALOU BEACH

Around 20 minutes walk (around 3 km [2 mi]) from Molyvos town, Eftalou beach is so peaceful it is called a "healing spot" by locals.

Arriving you'll find a municipal building housing Ottoman-era baths—why not enjoy a soak under the impressive domed roof?

As the sunlight streams to reflect upon the steaming water, the very accommodating staff offers towels and bottled water.

They also instruct visitors about the careful "ritual" required to enjoy the bath (for a bargain price of €3), which can be a scorcher at 100-plus degrees.

Half an hour of healing can be followed by a massage or a stroll along the full length of the sand and pebble beach, whose clear, clean waters attract a go-with-the-flow crowd.

You can also have a spot of lunch at the Eftalou restaurant, set on a raised veranda.

10

Updated by
Adrian Vrettos
and Alexia
Amvrazi

Quirky, seductive, fertile, sensual, faded, sunny, worldly, ravishing, long-suffering, hedonistic, luscious, mysterious, legendary—these adjectives only begin to describe the islands of the northeastern Aegean. This startling and rather arbitrary archipelago includes a sizeable number of islands, such as Ikaria, Samothraki, and Thassos, but in this chapter we focus only on the three largest—Lesbos, Chios, and Samos. Closer to Turkey's coast than to Greece's, and quite separate from one another, these islands are hilly, sometimes mountainous, with dramatic coastlines and uncrowded beaches, brilliant architecture, and unforgettable historic sites.

Lesbos, Greece's third-largest island and birthplace of legendary artists and writers, is dense with gnarled olive groves and dappled with mineral springs. Chios, though ravaged by fire, retains an eerie beauty and has fortified villages, old mansions, Byzantine monasteries, and stenciled-wall houses. Samos, the lush, mountainous land of wine and honey, whispers of the classical wonders of antiquity.

Despite the northern islands' proximity to Asia Minor, the Northern Aegean islands are the essence of Greece, the result of 4,000 years of Hellenic influence. Lesbos, Chios, and Samos prospered gloriously in the ancient world as important commercial and religious centers, though their significance waned under the Ottoman Empire. They also were cultural hothouses, producing such geniuses as Pythagoras, Sappho, and probably Homer.

These are not strictly sun-and-fun islands with the extent of tourist infrastructure of, say, the Cyclades. Many young backpackers and party seekers seem to bypass the northern Aegean. You can still carve out plenty of beach time by day and wander into lively restaurants and bars at night, but these islands reveal a deeper character, tracing histories that date back to ancient, Byzantine, and post-Byzantine times, and offering landscapes that are both serene and unspoiled. Visitors to the Northern Islands should expect to find history, culture, beauty, and hospitality. These islands offer commodities that are valued ever more highly by travelers—a sense of discovery and the chance to interact with rich, enduring cultures.

PLANNER

WHEN TO GO

Like everywhere else in the world, Greece is affected by the climate change phenomenon, which guarantees unpredictable weather; sometimes periods that are expected to be sizzling hot will be classified by rainfall and wind and vice versa.

However, as changes are not yet completely drastic, one can basically rely on the knowledge that from early May to early June, the weather is sunny and warm and the sea is still a bit chilly for swimming in. From mid-June until the end of August, the weather goes through quite a sweeping change and can become very hot, although the waters of the Aegean can prove sufficiently refreshing. In September the weather begins to mellow considerably, and by mid-October is usually at its warmth limit for swimming, although sunshine can continue throughout the year on and off. Between November and March these islands can make for an enjoyable trip, and although unlike the smaller islands there are enough restaurants, museums, and sites open to visitors, the cold weather can make ferries unreliable.

PLANNING YOUR TIME

If you have time to visit two islands over a 5–14 day period, start by exploring Mytilini, the capital of Lesbos, a bustling center of commerce and learning, with its grand old mansions overlooking the harbor. From there, head to the countryside to the northern destinations: Molyvos, a medieval town sprawling under the impressive Molyvos castle; Skala Eressou with its fine beach and bars; and the hilltop Agiassos, immersed in verdant forests. For your second stop, take a ferry to Chios, where you can enjoy the nightlife in the main town, and don't miss the old quarter. Travel via Lithi—derived from *Alithis limin*, meaning "true haven," which is rather apt for this beautiful fishing village—to enjoy a good fish lunch. Next, go to Pirgi (famous for its unique mosaics) and Mesta, part of the "masticohoria" or mastic villages, world renowned for their cultivation of mastic trees, which preserve a Greece of centuries past. Alternatively, take the ferry from Piraeus directly to Samos, a fine scenario if you can visit only one island. Circle the island, stopping at its lovely beaches and at Pythagorio, the ancient capital, or the temple at Heraion, one of the Wonders of the Ancient World. Consider visiting the popular traditional fishing village of Kokkari, which has managed to keep its architectural authenticity, then to the beaches Tsamadou and Lemonaki, where the green pine slopes meet the cobalt blue waters

10

of the Mediterranean. If you're drawn to the shores of Turkey, Samos makes a convenient stopover, as there's a daily ferry service.

EMERGENCIES

Contacts **Ambulance** ☎ *166.* **Police (emergency)** ☎ *100.*

GETTING HERE AND AROUND

AIR TRAVEL

Even if they have the time, many people avoid the 8- to 10-hour ferry ride from Athens and start their island-hopping trip by taking air flights to all three islands; they take less than an hour. Olympic Air has at least a dozen flights a week (3-4 flights per day) from Athens to Lesbos and Chios in summer and at least four daily flights to Samos. Aegean Airlines flies once per day from Athens to Chios. There are several Olympic Air flights a week from Chios to Lesbos, Limnos, Rhodes, and Thessaloniki; and several a week from Lesbos to Chios, Limnos, and Thessaloniki. From Samos there are several weekly Olympic flights to Limnos, Rhodes, and Thessaloniki; there are few flights (usually only one per week) between Samos and the other Northern Islands. Be aware that overbooking happens; if you have a reservation, you should be entitled to a free flight if you get bumped.

Carrier Information **Aegean Airlines** ✉ *Odysseas Elitis airport, Mytilini, Lesbos* ☎ *22510/61120, 22510/61059, 22510/61889, 22710/81051 through 22710/81052; Chios airport, 22730/62790; Samos airport* ⊕ *www.aegeanair. gr.* **Olympic Airlines** ☎ *80180/10101, 210/3550500 in Athens* ⊕ *www. olympicairlines.com* ✉ *Chios National Airport, Chios* ☎ *22710/23998* ✉ *Odysseas Elitis airport, Mytilini, Lesbos* ☎ *22510/61590* ✉ *Samos International Airport, Samos town, Samos* ☎ *22730/27237, 22730/61219.*

AIRPORTS   Lesbos Airport is 7 km (4½ mi) south of Mytilini. Chios Airport is 4½ km (3 mi) south of Chios town. The busiest airport in the region is on Samos, 17 km (10½ mi) southwest of Samos town. More than 40 international charters arrive every week in midsummer.

Airport Information **Chios Airport** ☎ *22710/81400.* **Lesbos Airport** ☎ *22510/38700.* **Samos Airport** ☎ *22730/87800.*

BUS TRAVEL

The public (KTEL) bus system on the Northern Aegean islands is reliable, cheap (a few euros one way), and obliging. Buses run from Chios town to other villages to the north, west, northwest, and south, from three to six times per day (usually from 7 am to 4:30 pm, depending on the part of the island). Buses depart from Mytilini town chiefly to Petra and Molyvos, and schedules depend largely on the time of year and day of the week, usually leaving at 11 am and 1:15 pm and taking around two hours each way. Buses on Samos are, as in Chios, more numbered and regular throughout the summer months, heading to the majority of towns and villages around the island. Particularly in the case of Lesbos, where bus services leave something to be desired, but also on Chios and Samos, it is worth renting a car or motorbike to really explore the island.

Bus Information **Kos KTEL bus station** ✉ *Cleopatras, Kos town, Kos* ☎ *22420/22292.*

BOAT AND FERRY TRAVEL

Expect ferries between any of the Northern Islands and Piraeus, Athens's port, to take 8 to 10 hours (Piraeus–Samos, approximately €49). There are at least four boats per week from Piraeus and three per week from Thessaloniki to Lesbos. Boats arrive daily to Chios from Piraeus (€30–€35). Ferries arrive on Samos at ports in Samos town and Karlovassi (28 km [17 mi] northwest of Samos town) four to nine times per week from Piraeus, stopping at Paros and Naxos and Evdilos/Ikaria; and most of the year two or three ferries weekly serve Pythagorio from Kos and Patmos. Ferries and hydrofoils to Kusadası, on the Turkish coast, leave from Samos town. Owing to sudden changes, no advance ferry schedule can be trusted. Port Authority offices have the most recent ferry schedule information and the Greek Travel Pages Web site is helpful. As for service between the various Northern Aegean islands, there is daily service between Lesbos and Chios. The regular ferry takes 3½ hours; the fast ferry 1½ hours. There can be as many as three ferries per week between Lesbos or Chios and Samos (both three-hour trips). Another way to reach Samos from Lesbos or Chios is to fly via Athens (an expensive alternative) on Olympic Air.

Boat Information Chios Port Authority ☎ *22710/44433, 22710/44434 in Chios town.* **Greek Travel Pages** ⊕ *www.gtp.gr.* **Lesbos Port Authority** ☎ *22510/40827 in Mytilini, 22510/37447.* **Piraeus Port Authority** ☎ *14944.* **Samos Port Authority** ☎ *22730/27318 in Samos town, 22730/30888 in Karlovassi, 22730/61225 in Pythagorio.*

CAR TRAVEL

Lesbos and Chios are large, so a car is useful. You might also want to rent a car on Samos, where mountain roads are steep; motorbikes are a popular mode of transport along the coast. Expect to spend about €35–€80 per day for a compact car with insurance and unlimited mileage. Note that you must have an international driver's license to rent a car on Chios. Though a national license may be sufficient to rent a car at some agencies on other islands, if you are stopped by the police or get into an accident and cannot produce an international or EU license, you may find the rental companies' stance isn't an official one. Budget, at Lesbos Airport, has newer cars and is cheaper than other agencies. Vassilakis on Chios has reliable, well-priced vehicles. Aramis Rent-a-Car, part of Sixt, has fair rates and reliable service on Samos.

10

Rental Agencies Aramis Rent-A-Car ✉ *Directly across from port, Samos town, Samos* ☎ *22730/23253* 🖷 *22730/23620* ✉ *Near port, Karlovasis, Samos* ☎ *22730/30360, 22730/37177* ✉ *Town center, opposite Commercial Bank, Kokkari, Samos* ☎ *22730/92385.* **Budget** ✉ *Airport, Mytilini, Lesbos* ☎ *22510/61665, 22510/29600 at the port* ⊕ *www.budget.com.* **Vassilakis** ✉ *Chandris 3, Chios town, Chios* ☎ *22710/29300* 🖷 *22710/23205* ⊕ *www.rentacar-chios.com.*

TAXI TRAVEL

In some places there are taxi phones at the port or main bus stops. Due to the small number of cabs, prices are high: expect to shell out around double what you'd pay in Athens, but always check the rates in advance.

If you do spring for a ride, it's a good idea to ask for a card with the driver's number in case you need a lift later in your trip.

Taxis ⊠ *Plateia Rimini, Rhodes town, Rhodes* ☏ *22410/27666.*</R>**Taxis** ⊠ *Skala, Patmos* ☏ *22470/31225.*

RESTAURANTS

Although waterfront restaurants in the touristed areas can be mediocre, you can most often find delightful meals, especially in the villages. Unless noted, reservations are unnecessary, and casual dress is always acceptable. Go to the kitchen and point to what you want (the Greek names for fish can be tricky to decipher), or be adventurous and let the waiter choose for you (although you may wind up with enough food to feed a village). Remember, however, that fresh fish is very expensive across the islands, €50 and up per kilo, with a typical individual portion measured at about half a kilo. The price for fish is not factored into the price categories below (and lobster is even more expensive). Many restaurants close from October to May.

Over on Lesbos, sardines—the tastiest in the Mediterranean, traditionally left in sea salt for a few hours and eaten at a sushi-like consistency—from the Gulf of Kalloni are famous nationwide, as is the island's impressive ouzo variety. Apart from classic salads and vegetable dishes like seasonal *briam* (a kind of ratatouille), and oven-baked or stewed Greek-Turkish dishes, meat can also be cooked in ways atypical in other Greek destinations because of the Turkish influence—try *soutzoukakia* meatballs spiced with cumin and cinnamon, or *keskek*, a special meat mixed with wheat, served most often at festivals. Local figs, almonds, and sun-ripened raisins are delicious; a Lesbos dessert incorporating one of those native treats is *baleze* (almond pudding). Besides being recognized for its mastic products, Chios is also known for mandarines—try the "mandarini" ice cream or juice in the main town. Thyme-scented honey, *yiorti* (the local version of keskek), and *revithokeftedes* (chickpea patties), are Samos's edible claims to fame. In Chios you'll also find a great variety of mastic-flavor sweets as well as savory foods.

DINING AND LODGING PRICES IN EUROS				
	¢	$	$$	$$$	$$$$
Restaurants	under €8	€8–€11	€12–€15	€16–€20	over €20
Hotels	under €60	€60–€90	€91–€120	€121–€160	over €160

Restaurant prices are for one main course at dinner, or for two mezedes (small dishes). Hotel prices are for a standard double room in high season, including taxes. Inquire when booking if meal plans (which can entail higher rates) are mandatory.

HOTELS

Restored mansions, village houses, sophisticated hotels, and budget accommodations are all options. Reserve early in high season for better-category hotels, especially in Pythagorio on Samos and Molyvos on Lesbos. Off-season you can usually bargain down the official prices and you may be able to avoid paying for a compulsory breakfast. Lodging in general remains less costly here than elsewhere in Greece. Many hotel rooms are basic, with simple pine furniture and sparse furnishings often created by local craftspeople. Happily, islanders are extremely friendly hosts, and although they may become more standoffish when the multitudes descend in August, they treat you as a guest rather than a billfold. On Lesbos, stay in Mytilini if you like a busy, citylike ambience, on Molyvos for its dramatic medieval beauty, or on Skala Eressou for its laid-back beach style. On Chios avoid staying in the main town unless you're just stopping over briefly, as it lacks in beauty and style, and opt to stay in the picturesque mastic village of Mesta instead. Vathi (Samos town), the main town, is a good central option in Samos, but even more ideal is the atmospheric Pythagorio.

VISITOR INFORMATION
Please see the Visitor Information listing in the pages devoted to each island: Lesbos, Chios, and Samos.

TOUR OPTIONS
Aeolic Cruises on Lesbos runs several island tours. In Molyvos, Panatella Holidays has two tours that take in villages, monasteries, and other sights. Petra Tours, located in Petra, just south of Molyvos, plans birdwatching, botanical, walking, and scuba-diving excursions. Masticulture in Chios orients visitors to a hearty perspective of local traditional life; organizing everything from walking tours, cooking classes, tending mastic trees, grape pressing, and offering original accommodations to suit every taste, they are happy to provide plugged-in tips on what to see and do locally, and stand out among other travel agencies for nicely providing what eclectic travelers are looking for today.

Tour Information **Chios Tours** ⊠ *Aigeou, waterfront, Kokkali 4, Chios town, Chios* ☎ 22710/29444, 22710/29555 ⊕ www.chiostours.gr. **Panatella Holidays** ⊠ *Possidonion, at town entrance, Molyvos, Lesbos* ☎ 22530/71520, 22530/71643, 22530/71644 ⊕ www.panatella-holidays.com. **Petra Tours** ⊠ *Petra, Lesbos* ☎ 22530/41390, 22530/42011 ⊕ www.petratours-lesvos.com.

★ **Pure Samos.** "Don't just visit—experience!" And that's what this travel agency, created by locals, lets visitors to Samos do, thanks to their wide array of experiential vacations: from yoga workshops to wine tours, from horseback-riding to spear-fishing and scuba diving, visitors can experience a memorable tailor-made holiday (which can include unique accommodations such as country cottages). ⊠ *Iras, 2, Pythagorio, Samos* ☎ *22730/62760* ☎ *30/6938744978* ⊕ *www.puresamos.gr.*

10

LESBOS ΛΕΣΒΟΣ

The Turks called Lesbos the "garden of the empire" for its fertility: in the east and center of the island, about 12 million olive trees line the hills in seemingly endless undulating groves. The western landscape is filled with oak trees, sheep pastures, rocky outcrops, and mountains. Wildflowers and grain cover the valleys, and the higher peaks are wreathed in dark green pines. This third-largest island in Greece is filled with beauty, but its real treasures are the creative artists and thinkers it has produced and inspired through the ages.

Lesbos was once a major cultural center known for its Philosophical Academy, where Epicurus and Aristotle taught. It was also the birthplace of the philosopher Theophrastus, who presided over the Academy in Athens; of the great lyric poet Sappho; of Terpander, the "father of Greek music"; and of Arion, who influenced the later playwrights Sophocles and Alcaeus, inventors of the dithyramb (a short poem with an erratic strain). Even in modernity, artists have emerged from Lesbos: Theophilos, a poor villager who earned his ouzo by painting some of the finest naive modern art Greece has produced; novelists Stratis Myrivilis and Argyris Eftaliotis; and the 1979 Nobel Prize–winning poet Odysseus Elytis.

The island's history stretches back to the 6th century BC, when its two mightiest cities, Mytilini and Mythimna (now Molyvos), settled their squabbles under the tyrant Pittacus, considered one of Greece's Seven Sages. Thus began the creative era, but later times brought forth the same pillaging and conquest that overturned other Greek islands. In 527 BC the Persians conquered Lesbos, and the Athenians, Romans, Byzantines, Venetians, Genoese, and Turks took their turns adding their influences. After the Turkish conquest, from 1462 to 1912, much of the population was sent to Turkey, and traces of past civilizations that weren't already destroyed by earthquakes were wiped out by the conquerors. Greece gained sovereignty over the island in 1923. This led to the breaking of trade ties with Asia Minor, diminishing the island's wealth, and limiting the economy to agriculture, making this one of the greener islands of Greece.

GETTING HERE AND AROUND

BY AIR   From Athens there are three direct flights every day, which take 50 minutes and cost between €90 and €150 one-way.

BY BOAT   There are one or two ferryboats that leave from Piraeus daily and take between 9 and 12 hours and cost €35–€37. These pass Chios on the way there and on the way back so there are regular links to this neighboring island (€12–€19.50 and a three-hour trip). Once a week there is a ferry from Thessaloniki to Lesbos, similarly priced as from Piraeus and taking up to 12 hours.

BY BUS   Lesbos's buses are infrequent, though there are several a day from Mytilini to Molyvos via Kalloni. The main bus station (☎ 22510/28873) is located on Aghias Eirinis 2 in central Mytilini.

Visitor Information Greek National Tourism Organization (*GNTO or EOT*). ⊕ *www.visitgreece.gr.* **Lesbos Municipal Tourist Office** ⊠ *Harbor front, James Aristarchou 6, Mytilini* ☎ *22510/42511, 22510/42512* ⊕ *www.lesvos.gr.* **Tourist Police** ⊠ *Harbor front, Megaro telwneiou, Mytilini* ☎ *22510/22776.*

EXPLORING

Lesbos has more inhabitants than either Corfu or Rhodes with only a fraction of the tourists, so here you can get a good idea of real island life in Greece. Many Byzantine and post-Byzantine sites dot the island's landscape, including castles and archaeological monuments, churches, and monasteries. The traditional architecture of stone and wood, inspired by Asia Minor, adorns the mansions, tower houses, and other homes of the villages. Beach composition varies throughout the island

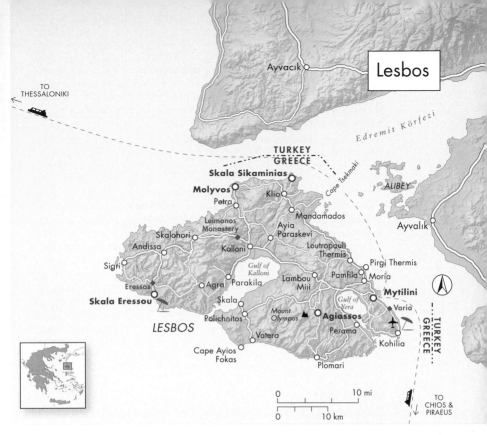

from pebble to sand. Some of the most spectacular sandy beaches and coves are in the southwest.

MYTILINI ΜΥΤΙΛΗΝΗ

350 km (217 mi) northeast of Piraeus, 218 km (135 mi) southeast of Thessaloniki.

Set on the ruins of an ancient city, Mytilini (so important through history that many call Lesbos by the port's name alone) is, like Lesbos, sculpted by two bays, making its coast resemble a jigsaw-puzzle piece. This busy main town and port, with stretches of grand waterfront mansions and a busy old bazaar area, were once the scene of a dramatic moment in Greek history. Early in the Peloponnesian War, Mytilini revolted against Athens but surrendered in 428 BC. As punishment, the Athens assembly decided to kill all men in Lesbos and enslave all women and children, and a boat was dispatched to carry out the order. The next day a less vengeful mood prevailed; the assembly repealed its decision and sent a second ship after the first. The second ship pulled into the harbor just as the commander of the first finished reading the death sentence. Just in time, Mytilini was saved. The bustling waterfront just south of the headland between the town's two bays is where most of the town's sights are clustered.

Ancient Theater. The only vestige of ancient Mytilini is the freely accessible ruin of an ancient theater, one of the largest in ancient Greece, from the Hellenistic period. Pompey admired it so much that he copied it for his theater in Rome. Though the marbles are gone, the shape, carved out of the mountain, remains beautifully intact. ⊠ *In pine forest northeast of town, Mytilini.*

Archaeological Museum of Mytilene. Set in a 1912 neoclassic mansion, this archaeological museum displays finds from the Neolithic through the Roman eras, a period of 5,000 years. A garden in the back displays the famous 6th-century Aeolian capitals from the columns of Klopedi's temples. The museum's modern wing, in a separate building, contains finds from prehistoric Thermi, mosaics from Hellenistic houses, reliefs of comic scenes from the 3rd-century Roman house of Menander, and temporary exhibits. ⊠ *Mansion:, Argiri Eftaliotis 7, behind ferry dock; modern wing: corner of Noemvriou and Melinas Merkouri, Mytilini* ☎ *22510/28032* ⊕ *www.culture.gr* ☜ *€3 for both* ☉ *Mansion, Tues.– Sun. 8:30–3; modern wing, Tues.–Sun. 8:30–3.*

Ayios Therapon. The enormous post-baroque church of Ayios Therapon, built in the 19th century, is reminiscent of some styles in Italy. It has an ornate interior, a frescoed dome, and, in its courtyard, a **Vizantino Mouseio**, or Byzantine Museum, filled with icons. ⊠ *Southern waterfront, Mytilini* ☎ *22510/22561* ⊕ *odysseus.culture.gr* ☜ *Church and museum €2 (free on 1st Sun.of month)* ☉ *Mon.–Sat. 9–1.*

Ermou. Stroll the main bazaar street, Ermou, which goes from port to port. Walk past the fish market on the southern end, where men haul in their sardines, mullet, and octopus. Narrow lanes are filled with antiques shops and grand old mansions. Head toward the sea to find the elegant suburb of Varia, home to the modern "naive" artist Theophilos; Tériade, famous publisher of modern art journals; and the poet Odysseus Elytis.

Kastro. The pine-covered headland between the bays—a nice spot for a picnic—supports a kastro, a stone fortress with intact walls that seem to protect the town even today. Built by the Byzantines on a 600 BC temple of Apollo, it was repaired with available material (note the ancient pillars crammed between the stones) by Francesco Gateluzzi of the famous Genoese family. Look above the gates for the two-headed eagle of the Palaiologos emperors, the horseshoe arms of the Gateluzzi family, and inscriptions made by Turks, who enlarged it; today it is a **military bastion.** Inside the castle there's only a crumbling prison and a Roman cistern, but you should make the visit for the fine view. ⊠ *On pine-covered hill, Mytilini* ☎ ⊕ *odysseus.culture.gr* ☜ *€2* ☉ *Tues.–Sun. 8–2:30.*

Musée–Bibliothèque Tériade. The Musée–Bibliothèque Tériade was the home of Stratis Eleftheriadis, better known by his French name, Tériade. His Paris publications *Minotaure* and *Verve* helped promote modern art. Among the works on display are lithographs done for him by Picasso, Matisse, Chagall, Rouault, Giacometti, and Miró. The museum is set among the olive trees of Varia, near the Museum of Theophilos. ⊠ *4 km (2½ mi) southeast of Mytilini, Varia* ☎ *22510/23372* ⊕ *www. museumteriade.gr* ☜ *€2* ☉ *Tues.–Sun. 9–2 and 5–8.*

★ **Museum of Theophilos.** Crammed to the ceiling in this museum are 86 of the eponymous artist's "naive," precise works detailing the everyday life of local folk such as fishermen and farmers, and fantasies of another age. Theophilos lived in poverty but painted airplanes and cities he had never seen. He painted in bakeries for bread, and in cafés for ouzo, and walked around in ancient dress. ✉ *4 km (2½ mi) southeast of Mytilini, Varia* ☎ *22510/41644* 💶 *€3* ⏰ *Mon.–Fri. 9–3.*

WHERE TO EAT

¢ ✕ **Ermis Ouzeri.** Lesbos is famed for its ouzo, so visitors must go to an *ouzeri* (ouzo bar) at least once—if not thrice—and there are few better than this centuries-old landmark located on the main thoroughfare between the old and new harbors. This old-school ouzeri has a selection of 15 types of ouzo, whose distinctive island tastes are nicely accompanied by some delicious "aperitif" mezedes such as stuffed courgette flowers and *tsoutsoukakia* (spiced meatballs in tomato sauce). Marble tables, hand-carved mirrors, and leather seats deck out this establishment, which has been serving locals and visitors since Ottoman times. ✉ *Toward the end of the street, Ermou 2, Mytilini* ☎ *22510/26232* 🚫 *No credit cards.*

GREEK

★

¢ ✕ **Hermes.** Founded in 1790 in a building 100 years older, this ouzeri (ouzo bar, though the sign calls it a *kafeneio*, or coffeehouse) is where local and visiting artists, poets, and politicians prefer to sip their ouzo on a vine-shaded terrace, with marble-top tables. You might try octopus in wine sauce, long-cooked chickpeas, or homemade sausages. The interior, a popular gathering spot in winter, provides a glimpse of traditional Lesbos design with old wood and mirrors. The long-standing hangout has similarly long hours: from 6 in the morning until the last person leaves at night. ✉ *Kornarou 2, near end of Ermou, Mytilini* ☎ *22510/26232* 🚫 *No credit cards.*

GREEK

¢ ✕ **Polytechnos.** Locals and visiting Athenians pack the outdoor tables— a solid indication this restaurant has earned its reputation. Some folks choose from the impressive fish selection; others order simple, traditional, Greek dishes like souvlaki or succulent pork medallions, and get a small salad of tomatoes and cucumbers to go with it. This casual restaurant lies across from the municipal building on the waterfront, and is the first along the quay. ✉ *Fanari quay, Mytilini* ☎ *22510/44128* 🚫 *No credit cards.*

GREEK

WHERE TO STAY
For expanded hotel reviews, visit Fodors.com.

10

$$$ 🖭 **Loriet Hotel.** The most exclusive digs in the area may be in the Loriet's
★ 1880 stone mansion, where high frescoed ceilings, friezes, and antique
furniture set the mood—little wonder you'll sometimes find visiting
dignitaries booking the fancy "suites" here (these start at €550 in high
season). **Pros:** beautifully restored mansion transports you to wealthy
mercantile era of the 19th century. **Cons:** the long stretch of beach
in front is distinctly average. ✉ *2 km (1 mi) south of Mytilini, Varia*
☎ *22510/43111* ⊕ *www.loriet-hotel.com* ↩ *35 rooms* ⚷ *In-room: no*
a/c, kitchen. In-hotel: restaurant, bar, pool, business center.

$ 🖭 **Porto Lesvos I.** If you want to stay in the center of Mytilini, this old,
carefully renovated building a block inland from the harbor is a solid
moderately priced choice—the guest rooms all have exposed stonework
and some have sea views; the breakfast room is nicely done in wood and
stone. **Pros:** you can feel the Papadakis family touch in the furnishings
and service. **Cons:** some rooms do not face the harbor. ✉ *Komninaki*
21, Mytilini ☎ *22510/41771* ⊕ *www.portolesvos.gr* ↩ *12 rooms* ⚷ *In-*
room: a/c, Wi-Fi. In-hotel: bar ⏸ *Breakfast.*

$$ 🖭 **Pyrgos of Mytilene.** A restored 1916 mansion in the ornate Second Empire style, replete with amazing white-and-Grecian-blue tile
work, fuses modern-day amenities and 19th-century nostalgia, with
the emphasis on the latter in the frilly guest rooms, thanks to their
period furniture, chandeliers, and stucco moldings, each room coming with its own style and color scheme (pistachio green to Venetian
red). **Pros:** adorable exterior; spacious reception rooms; variety of guest
rooms. **Cons:** few hotel facilities; room decor verges on kitsch, with
too much Trump-y gilt and gold. ✉ *Eleftherios Venizelou 49, Mytilini*
☎ *22510/27977, 22510/25069* ⊕ *www.pyrgoshotel.gr* ↩ *12 rooms*
⚷ *In-room: a/c, Wi-Fi. In-hotel: bar, parking* ⏸ *Breakfast.*

NIGHTLIFE

The cafés along the harbor turn into bars after sunset, generally closing at 3 am.

Hacienda. For a relaxed Caribbean-style start to your night, start with
a cocktail at Hacienda. ✉ *East end of port, Mytilini* ☎ *22510/46850.*

Kohilia. You need transportation to reach this outdoor beach bar with
an upscale, artistic vibe. ✉ *7 km [4½ mi] south of Mytilini, on beach*
opposite airport, Mytilini ☎ *6955586412.*

SHOPPING

Much of the best shopping is along the Ermou Street bazaar. Here you
can buy a little of everything, from food (especially olive oil and ouzo)
to pottery, wood carvings, and embroidery.

Veto. Lesbos produces 50 brands of ouzo, and George Spentzas's shop,
Veto, right on the main harbor, has made its own varieties on the
premises since 1948. It also sells local foods. ✉ *J. Arisarchi 1, Mytilini*
☎ *22510/24660.*

DID YOU KNOW?

Other than the breathtaking views from its stone terrace, the Byzantine-Genoese kastro fortress atop Molyvos is also known for its full calendar of summer concerts.

SKALA SIKAMINIAS ΣΚΑΛΑ ΣΥΚΑΜΙΝΙΑΣ

35 km (22 mi) northwest of Mytilini.

★ At the northernmost point of Lesbos, past Pelopi, is the exceptionally lovely fishing port of Skala Sikaminias, a miniature gem—serene and real, with several good fish tavernas on the edge of the dock. The novelist Stratis Myrivilis used the village as the setting for his *Mermaid Madonna*. Those who have read the book will recognize the tiny chapel at the base of the jetty. The author's birthplace and childhood home are in Sikaminia, the village overlooking Skala Sikaminias—and the Turkish coast—from its perch high above the sea.

WHERE TO EAT

$ ✕ **Skamnia.** Sit at a table of Skala Sikaminias's oldest taverna, under
GREEK   the same spreading mulberry tree where Myrivilis wrote, to sip a glass of ouzo and watch the fishing boats bob. Stuffed zucchini blossoms or cucumbers and tomatoes tossed with local olive oil are food for thought: light, tasty, and ideal for picking at. Other tempting dishes on the creative menu include fresh shrimp with garlic and parsley, and chicken in grape leaves. ✉ *On waterfront, Skala Sikaminias* ☎ *22530/55319.*

MOLYVOS ΜΟΛΥΒΟΣ

17 km (10½ mi) southwest of Skala Sikaminias, 61 km (38 mi) west of Mytilini.

Fodor's Choice   Molyvos, also known by its ancient name, Mythimna, is a place that
★ has attracted people since antiquity. Legend says that Achilles besieged the town until the king's daughter fell for him and opened the gates; then Achilles killed her. Before 1923 the Turks made up about a third of the population, living in many of the best stone houses. Today these balconied buildings with center staircases are weighed down by roses and geraniums; the red-tile roofs and cobblestone streets are required by law. Attracted by the town's charms, many artists live here. Don't miss a walk down to the picture-perfect harbor front.

Fodor's Choice   **Kastro.** Come before high season and walk or drive up to the kastro, a
★ Byzantine-Genoese fortified castle, for a hypnotic view down the tiers of red-tile roofs to the glittering sea. At dawn the sky begins to light up from behind the mountains of Asia Minor, casting silver streaks through the placid water as weary night fishermen come in. Purple wisteria vines shelter the lanes that descend from the castle and pass numerous Turkish fountains, some still in use. ✉ *Above town, Molyvos* ☎ *22530/71803* 💶 *€2* ☉ *Tues.–Sun. 8–3.*

Fodor's Choice   **Leimonos Monastery.** The stunning 16th-century Leimonos Monastery
★ houses 40 chapels and an impressive collection of precious objects. Founded by St. Ignatios Agalianos on the ruins of an older Byzantine monastery, it earned its name from the "flowering meadow of souls"

surrounding it. The intimate St. Ignatios church is filled with colorful frescoes and is patrolled by peacocks. A **folk-art museum** with historic and religious works is accompanied by a **treasury** of 450 Byzantine manuscripts. Women are not allowed inside the main church. ⊠ *Up a marked road 5 km (3 mi) northwest of Kalloni, 15 km (9 mi) southwest of Molyvos* ☎ *22530/22289* ⊕ *http://84.205.233.134* ⊠ *Museum and treasury €2* ⊗ *Daily 7–12, 3–sunset.*

WHERE TO EAT

$ ✕ **Captain's Table.** At the end of a quay, this wonderful taverna serves mouth-watering seafood caught on its own trawler, moored opposite. Try the special of the day or mix-and-match a series of small *mezede* dishes; best bets include *aujuka* (spicy eggplant slices) or the smoked mackerel with olives. Fresh fish may include red snapper, sea bream, lobster, and gilt, or spring for the Captain's Platter of assorted fish—it is easily satisfying for two. Owners Melinda and Theo (wonderful resources for visitors) also rent upscale houses a short walk away. Grab a seat early, as the Table gets busy quickly. ⊠ *Molyvos harbor across from Ayios Nikolaos chapel, Molyvos* ☎ *22530/71241* ⊗ *Mid-Oct.–mid-Apr. No lunch.*

SEAFOOD
Fodor's Choice
★

$ ✕ **Gatos.** Gaze over the island and harbor from the veranda of this yellow-and-green-dressed charmer, or sit inside and watch the cooks chop and grind in the open kitchen: Gatos is known for its grilled meats. The beef fillet is tender, the lamb chops nicely spiced, and the salads fresh. You might also consider ordering the *kokkinisto* (beef in tomato sauce) with garlic and savory onion. ⊠ *Center of old market, Molyvos* ☎ *22530/71661* ⊕ *www.gatos-restaurant.gr.*

GREEK

$ ✕ **Panorama.** High over the town, this terraced restaurant cooks terrific Greek food and, as the name suggests, it has a spectacular view. It's worth coming here just for a sunset drink, to see the sun illuminate the red roofs of Molyvos and the sea beyond. Good appetizers include spicy cheese salad, and fried stuffed peppers; among the main courses are moussaka and other home-style dishes, meat on the grill, and fresh fish. It is also open for breakfast. ⊠ *Under kastro, Molyvos* ☎ *22530/71848* ⊟ *No credit cards.*

GREEK

WHERE TO STAY

For expanded hotel reviews, visit Fodors.com.

$ ⊞ **Belvedere Hotel.** A little away from the buzz of Molyvos, this cluster of traditional red-roof buildings offers ample chance to relax, thanks to deep-seated sofas, an airy lounge, and a swimming pool—hard to find in Molyvos proper—not to mention the poolside jacuzzi. **Pros:** hotel shuttle service runs up to town, as does the local bus. **Cons:** nearby beach is rather mediocre; unexceptional hotel decor. ⊠ *On road to Eftalou, Molyvos* ☎ *22530/71772* ⊕ *www.aeolishotel.gr* ⥲ *71 rooms* △ *In-room: a/c, kitchen. In-hotel: restaurant, bar, pool* ⊗ *Closed Nov.–Mar.* ⊙|*Breakfast.*

$$$ ⊞ **Clara.** Laid out in "village style," the Clara weaves its way down an amphitheatrical hill, allowing its red-roofed bungalows to share in grand bayside views of Petra and Molyvos—you'll be drinking in this vista from your own veranda but you'll also love just chilling out

10

in the guest rooms, many of which are symphonies of lovely Greek accents, such as the blue-on-blue palettes (each room has its own color scheme), the cathedral ceilings, and the traditional wood wainscotting. **Pros:** plush, great facilities; aesthetically pleasing, some would say gorgeous, room decor. **Cons:** beach nearest to hotel clean but has seaweed. ⊠ *South of Petrazz, Avlaki* ☎ *22530/41532 through 22530/41534* ⊕ *www.clarahotel.gr* ⟳ *51 rooms* ⚲ *In-room: a/c, Wi-Fi. In-hotel: restaurant, bar, pool, tennis court, business center* ☉ *Closed Nov.–Mar.* ⁏◯⁍ *Breakfast.*

$ ★ ⚏ **Sea Horse Hotel.** This delightful stone-front hotel on Molyvos harbor overlooks the eateries on the photogenic quay; the lobby even extends into a waterfront café. **Pros:** port setting gives you real Greek fishing village experience; enchanting bay views. **Cons:** even though small, hotel attracts group bookings. ⊠ *Molyvos quay, Molyvos* ☎ *22530/71320, 22530/71630* ⊕ *www.seahorse-hotel.com* ⟳ *16 rooms* ⚲ *In-room: a/c. In-hotel: restaurant, bar, business center* ☉ *Mid-Oct.–mid-Apr.* ⁏◯⁍ *Breakfast.*

NIGHTLIFE AND THE ARTS

Molly's Bar. Two-story Molly's Bar plays music to unwind to in a friendly environment graced with waterside views (Molly's is open from 6 pm until the early hours). ⊠ *On street above harbor, Molyvos* ☎.

Molyvos Theater Festival. The best-known celebration on the islands is the Molyvos Theater Festival in July and August. With the castle as backdrop, artists from Greece and elsewhere in Europe stage entertainments that range from a Dario Fo play to contemporary music concerts. ☎ *22530/71323 tickets.*

Music Cafe Del Mar. This popular spot hosts live acoustic bouzouki music and has a cocktail terrace with a fetching sea view. ⊠ *Harbor front, Molyvos* ☎ *22530/71588.*

SHOPPING

Earth Collection. Go "green" by shopping here for organic clothes made exclusively of natural products. ⊠ *Molyvos quay, Molyvos* ☎ *22530/72094.*

Evelyn. A wide variety of local goods is available here, including ceramics, pastas, olive oil, wines, ouzo, sauces, and marmalades. ⊠ *Kyriakou Sq., Molyvos* ☎ *22530/72197.*

SKALA ERESSOU ΣΚΑΛΑ ΕΡΕΣΟΥ

40 km (25 mi) southwest of Molyvos, 89 km (55 mi) west of Mytilini.

★ The poet Sappho, according to unreliable late biographies, was born here circa 612 BC. Dubbed the Tenth Muse by Plato because of her skill and sensitivity, she perhaps presided over a finishing school for marriageable young women. She was married herself and had a daughter. Some of her songs erotically praise these girls and celebrate their marriages. Sappho's works, proper and popular in their time, were burned by Christians, so that mostly fragments survive; one is "and I yearn, and I desire." Sapphic meter was in great favor in Roman and medieval times; both Catullus and Gregory the Great used it, and in the

19th century, so did Tennyson. Since the 1970s and until today, many gay women have come to Skala Eressou to celebrate Sappho (the word "lesbian" derives from Lesbos), although the welcoming town is also filled with plenty of heterosexual couples.

Acropolis. On the acropolis of ancient Eressos overlooking the coastal area and beach are **remains of pre-Hellenistic walls, castle ruins,** and the AD 5th-century church, **Ayios Andreas.** The church has a mosaic floor and a tiny adjacent **museum** housing local finds from tombs in the ancient cemetery. ⊠ *1 km (½ mi) north of Skala Eressou* ☏ *22530/53332* 🖥 *Free* ⊙ *Tues.–Sun. 7:30–3:30.*

Eressos. The old village of Eressos, separated from the coast by a large plain, was developed to protect its inhabitants from pirate raids. Along the mulberry tree–lined road leading from the beach you might encounter a villager wearing a traditional head scarf (*mandila*), plodding by on her donkey. This village of two-story, 19th-century stone and shingle houses is filled with superb architectural details. Note the huge wooden doors decorated with nails and elaborate door knockers, loophole windows in thick stone walls, elegant pediments topping imposing mansions, and fountains spilling under Gothic arches. ⊠ *11 km [7 mi] inland, north of Skala Eressou.*

BEACH

Some of the island's best beaches are in this area, which has been built up rapidly—and not always tastefully.

Skala Eressou. Especially popular is the 4-km-long (2½-mi-long) town beach at Skala Eressou, where the wide stretch of dark sand is lined with tamarisk trees. A small island is within swimming distance, and northerly winds lure windsurfers as well as swimmers and sunbathers. There are many rooms to rent within walking distance of the beach.

WHERE TO EAT

¢
CAFÉ

✕ **Parasol.** Totem poles, colored coconut lamps, and other knickknacks from exotic travels make this beach bar endearing. The owner and his wife serve omelets, fruits, yogurt, and sweet Greek coffee for breakfast, and simple dishes like pizzas, veggie spring rolls, and cheese platters the rest of the day. But the most obvious reason to come here is to relax after sundown with one of the bar's creative drinks, such as the signature green cocktail, the Wooloomooloo Wonder, made with vodka and fresh melon. The music might be characterized as sophisticated lounge; the owner calls it "intellectual." ⊠ *Beachfront, Skala Eressou* ☏ *No phone* 🖃 *No credit cards* ⊙ *Closed Nov.–Apr.*

$$
SEAFOOD

✕ **Soulatso.** The enormous anchor outside is a sign that you're in for some seriously good seafood. On a wooden deck, tables are set just a skipping-stone's throw from the break of the waves. Owner Sarandos Tzinieris serves, and his mother cooks. Fresh grilled squid is mellifluous, and the fish are carefully chosen every morning. ⊠ *At beach center, Skala Eressou* ☏ *22530/52078* 🖃 *No credit cards.*

WHERE TO STAY

For expanded hotel reviews, visit Fodors.com.

10

$ 🏠**Heliotopos.** Less than 10 minutes drive away from the beachfront
★   "action," this lovely option is set in a delightfully peaceful and lovingly maintained large garden, cared for by delightful hosts Patrick
and Debbie. **Pros:** peacefulness; lush garden; delightful hominess.
Cons: no breakfast served. ⊠ *Skala Eressos* 🕾 *30/6977146229* ⊕ *www.
heliotoposeressos.com* ⇆ *5 studios, 3 apartments* ⚭ *In-room: a/c,
kitchen, Wi-Fi. In-hotel: laundry facilities* ☉ *Closed mid-Nov.–Feb.*
🍴*Breakfast.*

AGIASSOS ΑΓΙΑΣΟΣ

*87 km (53 mi) northwest of Skala Eressou, 28 km (17½ mi) southwest
of Mytilini.*

★   *Agiassos village, the prettiest hill town on Lesbos, sits in an isolated
valley amid thousands of olive trees, near the foot of Mt. Olympus, the
highest peak. (In case you're confused, 19 mountains in the Mediterranean are named Olympus, almost all of them peaks sacred to the local
sky god, who eventually became associated with Zeus.) Exempted from
taxes by the Turks, the town thrived. The age-old charm of Agiassos
can be seen in its gray stone houses, cobblestone lanes, medieval castle,
and local handicrafts, particularly pottery and woodwork.*

Panayia Vrefokratousa (*Madonna Holding the Infant*). The church of
Panayia Vrefokratousa was founded in the 12th century to house an
icon of the Virgin Mary, believed to be the work of St. Luke, and
remains a popular place of pilgrimage. Built into its foundation are
shops whose revenues support the church, as they have through the
ages. The **church museum** has a little Bible from AD 500, with legible,
elegant calligraphy. 🖼*€0.80* ☉ *Daily 8–1 and 5:30–8:30.*

WHERE TO EAT

¢   ✗**Dagielles.** Stop here for a coffee made by owner Stavritsa and served
GREEK   by her no-nonsense staff. You might also try the *kolokitholouloudo*
(stuffed squash blossoms) and the dishes that entice throughout winter: *kritharaki* (orzo pasta) and *varkoules* ("little boats" of eggplant
slices with minced meat). For a few short weeks in spring the air is
laden with the scent of overhanging wisteria. ⊠ *Near bus stop, Agiassos* 🕾 *22520/22241* ▭ *No credit cards.*

BEACHES

Gera Bay. The sandy beach has clean waters and is located southeast in
Gera Bay. ⊠ *Just south of Skala Polihnitos, Vatera.*

Vatera. The Vatera town beach, with its curving, southern exposure,
is idyllic.

CHIOS ΧΙΟΣ

"Craggy Chios" is what local boy Homer, its first publicist, so to speak,
called this starkly beautiful island, which almost touches Turkey's coast
and shares its topography. The island may not appear overly charming when you first see its principal city and capital, Chios town, but
consider its misfortunes: the bloody Turkish massacre of 1822 during

the fight for Greek independence; major earthquakes, including one in 1881 that killed almost 6,000 Chiotes; severe fires, which in the 1980s burned two-thirds of its pine trees; and, through the ages, the steady stripping of forests to ax-wielding boat builders. Yet despite these disadvantages, the island remains a wonderful destination, with friendly inhabitants, and villages so rare and captivating that even having just one of them on this island would make it a gem.

GETTING HERE AND AROUND

BY AIR From Athens, Olympic Air usually offers three 50-minute flights daily to Chios (around €60–€80 one-way); Aegean Air flies daily from Athens to Chios. There are several Olympic Airlines flights a week from Chios to Lesbos, Limnos, Rhodes, and Thessaloniki; and several a week from Lesbos to Chios. Chios Airport (☎ 22710/81400) is 4½ km (3 mi) south of Chios town; a taxi ride runs around €18-20.

BY BOAT There are one to two ferryboats that leave from Piraeus daily; they take 6–8 hours and cost €34–€37. These go on to Lesvos (€13-€20 and a three-hour trip if taken from Chios). Several times a week there is a ferry from Thessaloniki similarly priced as from Piraeus and that similarly takes up to 12 hours. For schedule information, see ⊕ *www.gtp.gr*.

BY BUS Blue and Green Bus System buses leave the town of Chios several times per day for Mesta and Pirgi. The main bus station (☎ 22710/23086) is at Vlatarias 13 in central Chios town, to the north of the park by Plateia Plastira. A second bus station, which services the long-distance Green KTEL buses, is found to the south of the park adjacent to the main taxi stand on the central square. Bus fares run €2–€6.

Visitor Information Chios Municipal Tourist Office ✉ *Kanari 18, Chios town* ☎ *22710/24442* ⊕ *www.chios.gr.* **Greek National Tourism Organization** (*GNTO or EOT*). ⊕ *www.visitgreece.gr.* **Tourist Police** ✉ *Kountouriotou 32, Chios town* ☎ *22710/81539.*

EXPLORING

The name Chios comes from the Phoenician word for "mastic," the resin of the *Pistacia lentisca*, evergreen shrubs that with few exceptions thrive only here, in the southern part of the island. Every August, incisions are made in the bark of the shrubs; the sap leaks out, permeating the air with a sweet fragrance, and in September it is harvested. This aromatic resin, which brought huge revenues until the introduction of petroleum products, is still used in cosmetics and chewing gum sold on the island today. Pirgi, Mesta, and other villages where the mastic is grown and processed are quite enchanting. In these towns you can wind your way through narrow, labyrinthine Byzantine streets protected by medieval gates and lined with homes that date back half a millennium.

Chios is also home to the elite families that control Greece's private shipping empires: Livanos, Karas, Chandris; even Onassis came here from Smyrna. The island has never seemed to need tourists, nor to draw them. Yet Chios intrigues, with its deep valleys, uncrowded sand and black-pebble beaches, fields of wild tulips, Byzantine monasteries, and haunting villages—all remnants of a poignant history.

10

CHIOS TOWN ΧΙΟΣ ΠΟΛΗ

285 km (177 mi) northeast of Piraeus, 55 km (34 mi) south of Mytilini.
The main port and capital, Chios town, or Chora (which means "town"), is a busy commercial settlement on the east coast, across from Turkey. This is the best base from which to explore the island, and you don't need to venture far from the port to discover the beautiful mansions of Kambos or the captivating orange groves just south of town. The daytime charm of the port area is limited, in part because no buildings predate the 1881 earthquake, in part because it badly needs a face-lift. But in the evening when the lights twinkle on the water and the scene is softened by a mingling of blue hues, the cafés begin to overflow with ouzo and good cheer and locals proudly promenade along the bayside.

Bazaar District. The capital is crowded with half the island's population, but its fascinating heart is the sprawling bazaar district. Merchants hawk everything from local mastic gum and fresh dark bread to kitchen utensils in the morning but typically it closes in the afternoon. ⊠ *South and east of Vounakiou Sq. (the main square), Chios town.*

Byzantine Museum. The only intact mosque in this part of the Aegean, complete with a slender minaret, houses the Byzantine Museum, which has been under renovation for years. It holds a *tugra* (the swirling monogram of the sultan that indicated royal possession), rarely seen outside Istanbul; its presence indicated the favor Chios once enjoyed under the sultan. Housed inside are the Jewish, Turkish, and Armenian gravestones leaning with age in the courtyard. ⊠ *Vounakiou Sq., Chios town* ☎ 22710/26866 ☜ €2 ☉ *Tues.–Sun 8:30–2:30.*

Chios Archaeological Museum. A collection that ranges from proto-Helladic pottery dug up in Emborio to a letter, on stone, from Alexander the Great addressed to the Chiotes and dated 332 BC, this museum also displays beautiful Ionian sculptures crafted by Chiotes. ⊠ *Michalon 10, Chios town* ☎ 22710/44239 ☜ €2 ☉ *Tues.–Sun. 8:30–2:45.*

Chios Maritime Museum. Livanos, Karas, Chandris, Onassis: many of the world-famous shipping families were based or born on Chios. In celebration of the sea-based heritage of the island, this museum showcases exquisite ship models and portraits of vessels that have belonged to Chios owners over time. One exhibit highlights the Liberty ships and others constructed during World War II that contributed to the beginning of Greece's postwar shipping industry. ⊠ *Stefanou Tsouri 20, Chios town* ☎ 22710/44139 ⊕ *www.chiosnauticalmuseum.gr* ☜ *Free (with donation box)* ☉ *Mon.–Sat. 9–2.*

★ **Chios Prison.** In 1822, in the tiny prison, 75 leading Chiotes were jailed as hostages before they were hanged by the Turks, part of the worst massacre committed during the War of Independence. The Turks drove out the Genoese in 1566, and Chios, spurred by Samians who had fled to the island, joined the rest of Greece in rebellion in the early 19th century. The revolt failed, and the sultan retaliated: the Turks killed 30,000 Chiotes and enslaved 45,000, an event written about by Victor Hugo and depicted by Eugène Delacroix in *The Massacre of Chios*. The

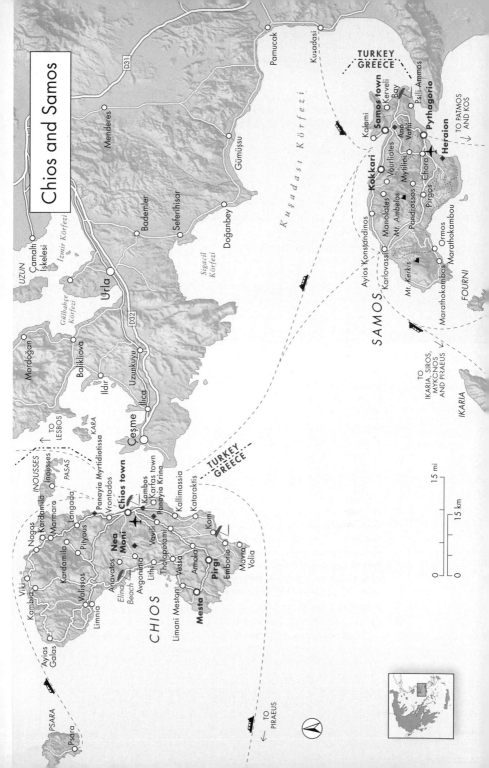

Chios and Samos

Many of the churches on the Northern Aegean islands are picture-perfect, thanks to their beautiful frescoes.

painting, now in the Louvre, shocked western Europe and increased support for Greek independence. Copies of *The Massacre of Chios* hang in many places on Chios. ⊠ *Inside main gate of castle, near Giustiniani Museum, Chios town.*

Citrus Museum. The Kambos district is famed as one of the most superlatively fertile orchard regions of Greece—orange and lemon groves here are given the status of museums and landmarks, so it is only fitting that the owners of the Perleas Mansion hotel have now opened this beautifully fragrant estate, known officially as the Citrus Museum, to showcase the history of citrus products on the island, and, oh yes, also entice visitors with a shop and café selling citrus-inspired sweets. Happily, the estate buildings are gorgeous, centered on a terra-cotta-hue farm, set with hunter-green window shutters and replete with folkloric-painted watermill. Nearby is an exceedingly picturesque arbor. In Greek, they call this museum "the aroma of memories" and this title may be more fitting. ⊠ *Artzenti St., Kambos, Chios town* ☎ *22710/31513* ⊕ *www. citrus-chios.gr* ☉ *Tues.–Sun. 10–10.*

Frouriou Square. In Frouriou Square, look for the **Turkish cemetery** and the large **marble tomb** (with the fringed hat) of Kara Ali, chief of the Turkish flagship in 1822. ⊠ *At fort, old quarter, Chios town.*

Giustiniani Museum. Housed inside a 15th-century building that may have acted as the headquarters of the Genoese, the Giustiniani Museum exhibits Byzantine murals and sculptures, post-Byzantine icons, and other small Genoese and Byzantine works of art. ⊠ *Just inside old quarter, Chios town* ☎ *22710/22819* ⊠ *€2* ☉ *Tues.–Sun. 8–7.*

Kambos District. Mastodon bones were found in the Kambos district, a fertile plain of tangerine, lemon, and orange groves just south of Chios town. In medieval times and later, wealthy Genoese and Greek merchants built ornate, earth-color, three-story mansions here. Behind forbidding stone walls adorned with coats of arms, each is a world of its own, with multicolor sandstone patterns, arched doorways, and pebble-mosaic courtyards. Some houses have crumbled and some still stand, reminders of the wealth, power, and eventual downfall of an earlier time. These suburbs of Chios town are exceptional, but the unmarked lanes can be confusing, so leave time to get lost and to peek behind the walls into another world. ⊠ *4 km (2½ mi) south of Chios town.*

> **BEDROCK OF EDUCATION**
>
> **Daskalopetra** (*Teacher's Rock*). Daskalopetra, where Homer is said to have taught his pupils, stands just above the port of Vrontados, 4 km (2½ mi) north of Chios town. Archaeologists think this rocky outcrop above the sea is part of an ancient altar to Cybele; you can sit on it and muse about how the blind storyteller might have spoken here of the fall of Troy in *The Iliad*. .

Kronos Ice Cream Parlor. This spot has been making the best-selling Kronos praline ice cream since 1930. ⊠ *Philipos Argenti 2, Chios town* ☎ *22710/22311.*

Main Street. Along the Main Street are the elegant **Ayios Georgios** church (closed most of the time), which has icons from Asia Minor; houses from the Genoese period; and the **remains of Turkish baths** (north corner of fort).

Fodor's Choice ★ **Old Quarter.** The Old Quarter is inside the **kastro** (castle) fortifications, built in the 10th century by the Byzantines and enlarged in the 14th century by the Genoese Giustiniani family. Under Turkish rule, the Greeks lived outside the wall; the gate was closed daily at sundown. A deep dry moat remains on the western side. Note the old wood-and-plaster houses on the narrow backstreets, typically decorated with latticework and jutting balconies. An air of mystery pervades this old Muslim and Jewish neighborhood, full of decaying monuments, fountains, baths, and mosques. ⊠ *Chios town.*

Philip Argenti Museum. This historic and folkloric collection sits on the second floor above the **Korais Library**, Greece's third largest. The museum displays meticulously designed costumes, embroidery, pastoral wood carvings, and furniture of a village home. ⊠ *Korais 2, near cathedral, Chios town* ☎ *22710/44246* ⊕ *www.koraeslibrary.gr* ⊠ *€1.50* ☉ *Weekdays 8–2.*

BEACHES

Karfas Beach. This beach fronts a shallow sandy bay. Tavernas are in the area, and in summer there is transportation to town. Farther south, Komi has a fine, sandy beach. ⊠ *8 km [5 mi] south of Chios town.*

10

WHERE TO EAT

¢ **✕O Hotzas.** Family portraits and brass implements hang below a wood-beam ceiling at this spacious taverna with a medieval interior. In addition to deep-fried dishes, there's also succulent lamb with lemon sauce and several vegetable choices. The squid is always reli-able, and it's delicious with the homemade retsina or ouzo. For des-sert order homemade yogurt with cherry or quince preserves. ⊠ *Yiory-iou Kondili 3, Chios town* ☎ *22710/42787* ⊘ *Closed Sun. No lunch.*

GREEK

$$ **✕Pyrgos.** Attentive service, fine food, and pretty surroundings charac-terize a meal at the poolside garden restaurant of the Grecian Castle hotel. Beef carpaccio and spinach salad are excellent starters, followed by beef *pagiar,* a fillet stuffed with *mastello* (the local goat cheese), sun-dried tomatoes, and pesto-olive sauce. Or try the pork with prunes, mushrooms, and *Vin Santo* (a sweet wine) sauce. The extensive menu also includes crepes, pastas, and seafood. Mastic ice cream with rose syrup closes a meal on a richly local note. ⊠ *Chios harbor, Chios town* ☎ *22710/44740.*

MEDITERRANEAN

¢ **✕Taverna tou Tassou.** Dependably delicious traditional food is why so many locals eat here in a garden courtyard beneath a canopy of trees. Fresh fish and seafood, lamb chops and other meats, stuffed peppers and cooked greens—you can't go wrong. Expect Greek owner Dimi-trius Doulos and his son, the chef, to warmly welcome you. The tav-erna is at the south edge of town toward the airport, and there's a playground nearby for kids. ⊠ *Livanou 8, south toward airport, Chios town* ☎ *22710/27542* ⊘ *Closed Nov.*

GREEK
★
☺

WHERE TO STAY

For expanded hotel reviews, visit Fodors.com.

¢ **Chios Rooms.** A budget option, the Chios Rooms are sweetly set in a 19th-century neoclassical building located on the southern corner of Chios's harbor, with casual rooms inside that quickly make guests feel welcome. **Pros:** very friendly management makes you feel right at home. **Cons:** noisy at night due to street traffic out front; not a cen-tral location. ⊠ *Leoforos Aigaiou 110, Chios town* ☎ *22710/20198* ⊕ *www.chiosrooms.gr* ⟿ *10* ☺ *In-room: no a/c, no TV, Wi-Fi* ▭ *No credit cards.*

$$$ **Grecian Castle Hotel.** With spacious guest rooms, a pretty pool, and carefully landscaped grounds this sophisticated hotel sets a high stan-dard for Chios, as you'll see once you pass the impressive stone gateway and head up a regal avenue to arrive at the main building—a grandly proportioned building whose stone facade is echoic of Chios's medieval castle. **Pros:** urbane ambience; gorgeous stone building; lovely grounds and pool. **Cons:** a few not-so-spacious rooms. ⊠ *Leoforos Enosseos, 1 km (½ mi) south toward airport, Chios town* ☎ *22710/44740* ⊕ *www. greciancastle.gr* ⟿ *51 rooms, 4 suites* ☺ *In-room: a/c. In-hotel: restau-rant, bar, pool.*

Fodor's Choice
★

$ ☷**Kyma Hotel.** Begun in 1917 for a shipping magnate, this neoclassic villa on the waterfront was completed in 1922, when it served as Colonel Plastiras's headquarters after the Greek defeat in Asia Minor (Plastiras went on to become a general and prime minister of Greece). **Pros:** friendliest staff; sea views from balconies. **Cons:** needs some sprucing up. ✉ *Chandris 1, Chios town* ☎ *22710/44500* ✉ *kyma@chi.forthnet. gr* ✎ *59 rooms* ⚬ *In-room: a/c, Wi-Fi* ▭ *No credit cards* ⏣ *Breakfast.*

$$ ☷**Perleas Mansion.** With its start back as an estate constructed by rich
Fodor'sChoice Genoese merchants in the 16th century, this house is a tough cousin
★   to a "mansion," but today it is a striking blend of rough hewn stone, dramatic steel beams, and lovely medieval touches—including a Gothic-style stone water cistern—all surrounded by lovely gardens fragrant with orange blossom. **Pros:** simple exclusive beauty with wonderful homegrown food; the real deal. **Cons:** 10-minute drive from nearest beach. ✉ *Vitiadou, Kambos district, 4 km (2½ mi) south of center, Chios town* ☎ *22710/32217, 22710/32962* ⊕ *www.perleas.gr* ✎ *7 rooms* ⚬ *In-room: a/c, no TV* ⏣ *Breakfast.*

NIGHTLIFE

Design-centered nightspots along the harbor are trendier than those on most of the other Northern Aegean islands, and many of the clubs are filled with well-off young tourists and locals. You can just walk along, listen to the music, and size up the crowd; most clubs are open to the harbor and dramatically lighted.

Cosmo. This spot stands out as an inviting cocktail lounge playing international and Greek music. ✉ *Aigeou 100, Chios town* ☎ *22710/81695.*

SHOPPING

The resinous gum made from the sap of the mastic tree is a best buy in Chios. It makes a fun and notoriously healthy souvenir and conversation piece; the brand is Elma. You can also find mastic (digestif) liquor called *mastíha*, and *gliko koutaliou*, sugar-preserved fruit served with a spoon in small portions. Stores are typically closed Sunday, and open mornings only Monday through Wednesday.

Mastic Spa. At the elegant shop of Mastic Spa, all the beauty and health products contain the local balm. ✉ *Aigeou 74, on waterfront close to the dock, Chios town* ☎ *22710/40223.*

Moutafis. Try this place for its fine array of mastíha, fruit preserves, and other sweets and spirits. ✉ *Venizelou 7, Chios town* ☎ *22710/25330.*

Zaharoplasteion Avgoustakis. A traditional candy store, this spot specializes in *masourakia* (crispy rolled pastries dripping in syrup and nuts) and *rodinia* (melt-in-your-mouth cookies stuffed with almond cream). ✉ *Psychari 4, Chios town* ☎ *22710/44480.*

10

NEA MONI NEA MONH

17 km (10½ mi) west of Chios town.

Fodor'sChoice **Nea Moni.** Almost hidden among the olive groves, the island's most
★   important monastery—with one of the finest examples of mosaic art anywhere—is the 11th-century Nea Moni. Emperor Constantine IX

On Chios, you'll often find imposing medieval structures side by side with charming villages. Here is a view of Nea Moni Monastery.

Monomachos ("the Dueler") ordered the monastery built where three monks found an icon of the Virgin in a myrtle bush. The octagonal *katholikon* (medieval church) is the only surviving example of 11th-century court art—none survives in Constantinople. The church has been renovated a number of times: the dome was completely rebuilt following an earthquake in 1881, and a great deal of effort has gone into the restoration and preservation of the mosaics over the years. The distinctive three-part vaulted sanctuary has a double narthex, with no buttresses supporting the dome. This design, a single square space covered by a dome, is rarely seen in Greece. Blazing with color, the church's interior gleams with marble slabs and mosaics of Christ's life, austere yet sumptuous, with azure blue, ruby red, velvet green, and skillful applications of gold. The saints' expressiveness comes from their vigorous poses and severe gazes, with heavy shadows under the eyes. On the iconostasis hangs the icon—a small Virgin and Child facing left. Also inside the grounds are an **ancient refectory, a vaulted cistern, a chapel** filled with victims' bones from the massacre at Chios, and a large **clock** still keeping Byzantine time, with the sunrise reckoned as 12 o'clock. ⊠ *In mountains west of Chios town* ☎ 22710/79391 ⌨ *Donations accepted* ☉ *Tues.–Sun. 8–1 and 4–8.*

PIRGI ΠΥΡΓΙ

25 km (15½ mi) south of Nea Moni, 20 km (12½ mi) south of Chios town.

★ Beginning in the 14th century, the Genoese founded 20 or so fortified inland villages in southern Chios. These villages shared a defensive design with double-thick walls, a maze of narrow streets, and a square tower, or *pyrgos*, in the middle—a last resort to hold the residents in case of pirate attack. The villages prospered on the sales of mastic gum and were spared by the Turks because of the industry. Today they depend on mastic production, unique to the island—and tourists.

Pirgi is the largest of these mastic villages, and aesthetically, the most wondrous. It could be a graphic designer's model, a set of a mad moviemaker, or a still town from another planet. Many of the buildings along the tiny arched streets are adorned with *xysta* (like Italian sgraffito); they are coated with a mix of cement and volcanic sand from nearby beaches, then whitewashed and stenciled, often top to bottom, in patterns of animals, flowers, and geometric designs. The effect is both delicate and dazzling. This exuberant village has more than 50 churches.

Armolia. In the small mastic village of Armolia, 5 km (3 mi) north of Pirgi, pottery is a specialty. In fact, the Greek word *armolousis* ("man from Armola") is synonymous with potter.

Ayioi Apostoli (*Holy Apostles*). Check out the fresco-embellished 12th-century church Ayioi Apostoli, a very small replica of the katholikon at the Nea Moni Monastery. The 17th-century frescoes that completely cover the interior, the work of a Cretan artist, have a distinct folk-art leaning. ✉ *Northwest of main square, Pirgi* ⊙ *Tues.–Sun. 8:30–3.*

Kimisis tis Theotokou church (*Dormition of the Virgin church*). Look for especially lavish xysta on buildings near the main square, including the Kimisis tis Theotokou church, built in 1694. ✉ *Off main square, Pirgi* ⊙ *Daily 9–1 and 4–8.*

WHERE TO STAY

$ ★ ⊞ **Votsala Hotel.** Brightly attempting to break out of the hotel mold, Votsala bravely rejects the provision of usual hotel "comforts" (such as a cheesy disco, contrived Greek "taverna", or in-room TV—although it does offer free Wi-Fi) and instead prides itself in offering a gracefully refined, familylike ambience headed by gracious nature-loving owners Yiannis and wife Daphne. ✉ *Pirgi Thermis* ☎ *22510/71231* ⊕ *www. votsalahotel.com* ⌁ *45* ⌂ *In-room: a/c, no TV, Wi-Fi. In-hotel: restaurant, beach* ⊙ *Nov.–Mar.*

BEACH

Mavra Volia (*Black Pebbles*). From Pirgi it's 8 km (5 mi) southeast to the glittering black volcanic beach near Emborio, known by locals as Mavra Volia. The cove is backed by jutting volcanic cliffs, the calm water's dark-blue color created by the deeply tinted seabed. Here perhaps was an inspiration for the "wine-dark sea" that Homer wrote about.

10

SHOPPING

Earthal Art. Hand-painted pottery and handicrafts, as well as quality, inexpensive oil paintings of the Greek islands, are available for sale at Earthal Art. ⊠ *Pirgi–Armolia Rd., Pirgi* ☎ *22710/72693.*

MESTA ΜΕΣΤΑ

11 km (7 mi) west of Pirgi, 30 km (18½ mi) southwest of Chios town.

Fodor's Choice
★
Pirgi may be the most unusual of the mastic villages, but Mesta is the island's best preserved: a labyrinth of twisting vaulted streets link two-story stone-and-mortar houses that are supported by buttresses against earthquakes. The enchanted village sits inside a system of 3-foot-thick walls, and the outer row of houses also doubles as protection. In fact, the village homes were built next to each other to form a castle, reinforced with towers. Most of the narrow streets, free of cars and motorbikes, lead to blind alleys; the rest lead to the six gates. The one in the northeast retains an iron grate. Artists and craftspeople are attracted to this ancient area, so you'll unearth art galleries and craft boutiques with a little hunting here.

Megas Taxiarchis (*Great Archangel*). One of the largest and wealthiest churches in Greece, the 18th-century church of Megas Taxiarchis commands the main square; its vernacular baroque is combined with the late-folk-art style of Chios. The church was built on the ruins of the central refuge tower. Ask at the main square for Elias, the gentle old man in the village who is the keeper of the keys.

BEACHES

Escape to the string of secluded coves, between Elatas and Trahiliou bays, for good swimming.

Nudist beach. This beach is noted for its fine white pebbles. ⊠ *2 km [1 mi] north of Lithi, Mesta.*

WHERE TO EAT

¢
GREEK
★
✕ **Restaurant Café Mesconas.** A traditional Greek kitchen turns out the delicious food served on outdoor tables in the small village square, adjacent to Megas Taxiarchis. You dine surrounded by medieval homes and magical lights at night, but the setting is lovely even for a daytime coffee and relaxed conversation. The best dishes include rabbit *stifado* (stew), made with shallots, tomatoes, and olive oil; and *pastitsio,* a meat pie with macaroni and béchamel sauce. All the recipes use local ingredients, with herbs and spices gathered from the region. *Soyma* is the local equivalent of ouzo but made from figs—it can be blindingly strong, up to 70% alcohol. ⊠ *Main square, Mesta* ☎ *22710/76050.*

NIGHTLIFE

Karnayio. This is one of the island's most popular spots for dancing. ⊠ *Leoforos Stenoseos, outside town on road to airport, Mesta* ☎ *No phone.*

THE OUTDOORS

☁ **Masticulture.** The ecotourist specialists on Chios, Masticulture leads
Fodor's Choice all kinds of tours throughout the week. Trek through the mastic tree
★ groves, where local farmers show you how they gather mastic through
grooves carved into the trees' bark. Learn how wine, *Souma* (a type of
ouzo made from distilled figs), and olive oil are produced, and go on
fascinating custom-designed walks discovering the unique flora and
fauna of Chios. Greek cooking courses are also available, which focus
on seasonal foods in accordance with the Mediterranean diet. Check
the Web site for dates, times, and prices. The nature of the mastic villages is such that finding lodgings is a bit of a lottery so the best option,
if you wish to stay in these mesmerizing medieval communities, is to
book through Masticulture. ⊠ *Main square, Mesta* ☎ *22710/76084*
⊕ *www.masticulture.com.*

SAMOS ΣΑΜΟΣ

The southernmost of this group of three North Aegean islands, Samos
lies the closest to Turkey of any Greek island, separated by only 3 km
(2 mi). It was, in fact, a part of Asia Minor until it split off during the
Ice Age. Samos means "high" in Phoenician, and its abrupt volcanic
mountains soaring dramatically like huge hunched shoulders from the
rock surface of the island are among the tallest in the Aegean, geologically part of the great spur that runs across western Turkey. As you
approach from the west, Mt. Kerkis seems to spin out of the sea, and
in the distance Mt. Ambelos guards the terraced vineyards that produce
the famous Samian wine. The felicitous landscape has surprising twists,
with lacy coasts and mountain villages perched on ravines carpeted in
pink oleander, red poppy, and purple sage.

When Athens was young, in the 7th century BC, Samos was already
a political, economic, and naval power. In the next century, during
Polycrates's reign, it was noted for its arts and sciences and was the
expanded site of the vast Temple of Hera, one of the Seven Wonders of
the Ancient World. The Persian Wars led to the decline of Samos, however, which fell first under Persian rule, and then became subordinate
to the expanding power of Athens. Samos was defeated by Pericles in
439 BC and forced to pay tribute to Athens.

Pirates controlled this deserted island after the fall of the Byzantine
Empire, but in 1562 an Ottoman admiral repopulated Samos with
expatriates and Orthodox believers. It languished under the sun for
hundreds of years until tobacco and shipping revived the economy in
the 19th century.

Small though it may be, Samos has a formidable list of great Samians
stretching through the ages. The fabled Aesop, the philosopher Epicurus, and Aristarchos (first in history to place the sun at the center of the
solar system) all lived on Samos. The mathematician Pythagoras was
born in Samos's ancient capital in 580 BC; in his honor, it was renamed
Pythagorio in AD 1955 (it only took a couple of millennia). Plutarch
wrote that in Roman times Anthony and Cleopatra took a long holiday

10

on Samos, "giving themselves over to the feasting," and that artists came from afar to entertain them.

GETTING HERE AND AROUND

BY AIR   There are plenty of direct flights from Athens every day, which take 55 minutes and cost around €80–€90 one-way; Olympic has three flights daily to Samos. Two Samos flights a week connect with Thessaloniki. The Samos airport is 3 km (1 mi) from Pithagorio; taxis from the airport cost €15 to Vathi or €9 to Pithagorio.

BY BOAT   The main port of Samos is Vathi, also known as Samos. Ferries from the Piraeus and Cyclades usually stop at both Vathi and Karlovassi (Samos' second port) and take 10–13 hours and cost €35–€49. During high season, there are usually two ferries to Pireaus, three to Chios, five to Naxos and Paxos (with transfers available to Mykonos and Santorini). There is usually two ferries a week to Patmos and one to Rhodes. For hydrofoils, there are three sailings a week to Mykonos, and three to Patmos, Naxos, and Paros. Fares range from €20 to €60. For full schedule information, see ⊕ *www.gtp.gr*.

BY BUS   Samos has reliable bus service, with frequent trips (as many as eight daily) between Pythagorio, Samos town (Vathi), and Kokkari. Samos town is home to the island's main bus station (☎ 22730/27262), located at Ioannou Lekati and Kanari in central Samos town. Fares range from €1.5 to €3. Taxis can be hailed on Plateia Pithagora.

Visitor Information Greek National Tourism Organization (*GNTO or EOT*). ⊕ *www.visitgreece.gr*. **Tourist Police** ✉ *Harbor front, Samos town* ☎ *22730/87344.*

EXPLORING

In the last decade Samos has become popular with European charter tourists, particularly in July and August. Thankfully the curving terrain allows you to escape the crowds easily and feel as if you are still in an undiscovered Eden.

SAMOS TOWN ΣΑΜΟΣ ΠΟΛΗ

278 km (174 mi) east of Piraeus, 111 km (69 mi) southeast of Mytilini.

On the northeast coast at the head of a sharply deep bay is the capital, Samos town, also known as Vathi (which actually refers to the old settlement just above the port). Red-tile roofs sweep around the arc of the bay and reach toward the top of red-earth hills. In the morning at the sheltered port, fishermen still grapple with their nets, spreading them to dry in the sun, and in the early afternoon everything shuts down. Slow summer sunsets over the sparkling harbor match the relaxed pace of locals.

Ano Vathi. In the quaint 17th-century enclave of Ano Vathi, wood-and-plaster houses with pastel facades and red-tile roofs are clustered together, their balconies protruding over cobbled paths so narrow that the street's water channel takes up most of the space. From here savor a beautiful view of the gulf. ✉ *Southern edge of Samos town, beyond museum, to right.*

★ **Archaeological Museum.** The stepped streets ascend from the shopping thoroughfare, which meanders from the port to the city park next to the Archaeological Museum, the town's most important sight. Samian sculptures from past millennia were considered among the best in Greece, and examples here show why. The newest wing holds the impressive **kouros from Heraion,** a colossal statue of a male youth, built as an offering to the goddess Hera and the largest freestanding sculpture surviving from ancient Greece, dating from 580 BC. The work of a Samian artist, this statue was made of the typical Samian gray-and-white-band marble. Pieces of the kouros were discovered in various peculiar locations: its thigh was being used as part of a Hellenistic house wall, and its left forearm was being used as a step for a Roman cistern. The statue is so large (16½ feet tall) that the wing had to be rebuilt specifically to house it. The museum's older section has a collection of pottery and cast-bronze griffin heads (the symbol of Samos). An exceptional collection of tributary gifts from ancient cities far and wide, including bronzes and ivory miniatures, affirms the importance of the shrine to Hera. ⊠ *Dimarhiou Sq., Samos town* ☎ *22730/27469* ⬚ *€4* ⊙ *Tues.–Sun. 8:30–3.*

Museum of Samos Wines. Samos is famous for its (internationally awarded) wines, particularly its delectable *Vin Doux* liqueur wine or other sweet wines such as Nectar and Anthemis, and more recently its dry whites such as Phyllas, made with organic Muscat grapes. All wines produced on Samos are by law made by the Union of Vinicultural Cooperatives, who in 2005 created this museum on the winery's grounds in tribute to the island's winemaking past—and present. Start by looking at the photo exhibition of local winemaking over the last century and proceed to see the large and small tools used in production, as well as early 20th-century casks, and finally the French oak barrels used today, before proceeding to the main hall to indulge in a wine tasting of the union's wines, which are also sold at the museum shop (in some cases at a higher price than you will find in other local shops). ⊠ *Samos town* ☎ *22730/87551.*

OFF THE BEATEN PATH

Turkey. From Samos town (and from Pythagorio and from Ormos Marathokambos), you can easily ferry to Turkey. Once you're there, it's a 13-km (8-mi) drive from the Kuṭadasˊ Kud on the Turkish coast, where the boats dock, to Ephesus, one of the great archaeological sites and a major city of the ancient world. (Note that the Temple of Artemis in Ephesus is a copy of the Temple of Hera in Heraion, which now lies in ruins.) Many travel agencies have guided round-trip full-day tours to the site (€100), although you can take an unguided ferry trip for €35 with same-day return. You leave your passport with the agency, and it is returned when you come back from Turkey.

10

BEACHES

Kerveli Bay. The beach at Kerveli Bay has an enticing pebble-to-sand beach with calm, turquoise waters, and shade from pine trees. ⊠ *On coast east of Samos town.*

Psili Ammos. One of the island's most popular beaches is Psili Ammos—a pristine, sandy beach protected from the wind by cliffs. There are

The Byzantine era enriched Samos with many magnificent churches.

two tavernas here, and it can get extremely busy during high season. ⊠ *Southeast of Samos town, near Mesokambos.*

WHERE TO EAT AND STAY

$ ✕ **Ta Kotopoula.** Chicken is the star on the menu of this affordable grill
GREEK restaurant, which serves simple yet delicious, seasonal dishes throughout the day in a laid-back ambiance. ⊠ *Samos town* ☎ *22730/28415* ⊟ *No credit cards.*

¢ ✕ **Zen.** Vathy (Samos town) is sadly not known for its good restaurants
SEAFOOD and Zen is yet one more unremarkable dining option; however it is good enough for a pleasant, affordable meal. Open at lunch and dinner, the restaurant's focus is on fresh fish, while it also serves home-style dishes based on local recipes, grilled meat, and seasonal salads. ⊠ *Kefalopoulou, 6, Samos town* ☎ *22730/80983.*

WHERE TO STAY
For expanded hotel reviews, visit Fodors.com.

$ 🛏 **Hotel Samos.** Sleek modern rooms come equipped with amenities uncommon in this price range, like soundproof windows (the hotel faces the sometimes noisy harbor front), hair dryers, and wireless Internet. **Pros:** more luxurious than it may seem at first sight; given a rooftop pool, hot tub, and garden, the prices are relatively low. **Cons:** no parking. ⊠ *Them. Soufouli 11, Samos town* ☎ *22730/28377* ⊕ *www.samoshotel.gr* 🛏 *98 rooms, 2 suites* ⌂ *In-room: a/c, Internet, Wi-Fi. In-hotel: restaurant, bar, pool.*

$ 🛏 **Ino Village Hotel.** Set in a tranquil setting that makes you feel you're
Fodor'sChoice in the more peaceful outskirts of Vathy, the Ino Village is ideal for
★ friends or families that enjoy lounging around the pool or enjoying a

satisfying meal on the refreshing terrace (plugged into Wi-Fi)—drink in the vista here or request guest rooms in the 800 block for a spectacular view of Samos Bay and the mountains beyond. **Pros:** friendly, clued-in staff; great quality for the price; fine kitchen. **Cons:** you have to walk 15 minutes uphill from the town center, but you can call the hotel to arrange for transport back up (a car is best here). ✉ *1 km (½ mi) north of Samos town center, Kalami* ☏ *22730/23241* 🖷 *22730/23245* ⊕ *www. inovillagehotel.com* ↻ *65 rooms* ♿ *In-room: a/c. In-hotel: restaurant, bar, pool, parking.*

NIGHTLIFE
Bars generally are open May to September from about 8 or 10 pm to 3 am.

Selini. A stylish beachfront cocktail bar designed in Cycladic white, Selini attracts a trendy Greek and international crowd eager to mingle and dance as the club's blue lights reflect off the sea below. ✉ *Kefalopoulou 3–5, Samos town.*

PYTHAGORIO ΠΥΘΑΓΟΡΕΙΟ

14 km (8½ mi) southwest of Samos town.

Samos was a democratic state until 535 BC, when the town now called Pythagorio (formerly Tigani, or "frying pan") fell to the tyrant Polycrates (540–22 BC). Polycrates used his fleet of 100 ships to make profitable raids around the Aegean, until he was caught by the Persians and crucified in 522 BC. His rule produced what Herodotus described as "three of the greatest building and engineering feats in the Greek world." One is the Heraion, west of Pythagorio, the largest temple ever built in Greece and one of the Seven Wonders of the Ancient World. Another is the ancient mole protecting the harbor on the southeast coast, on which the present 1,400-foot jetty rests. The third is the Efpalinio tunnel, built to guarantee that water flowing from mountain streams would be available even to besieged Samians. Pythagorio remains a picturesque little port, with red-tile-roof houses and a curving harbor filled with fishing boats, but it is popular with tourists. There are more busy restaurants and cafés here than elsewhere on the island.

Archaia Polis *(ancient city).* Among acres of excavations, little remains from the Archaia Polis, or Ancient City, except a few pieces of the **Polycrates wall** and the **ancient theater** a few hundred yards above the tunnel. ✉ *Bordering small harbor and hill, Pythagorio.*

Kastro *(castle, or fortress).* At the east corner of Pythagorio lie the crumbling ruins of the Kastro, probably built on top of the ruins of the Acropolis. Revolutionary hero Lykourgou Logotheti built this 19th-century edifice; his statue is next door, in the **courtyard** of the church built to honor the victory. He held back the Turks on Transfiguration Day, and a sign on the church announces in Greek: "Christ saved Samos 6 August 1824." On some nights the villagers light votive candles in the church cemetery, a moving sight with the ghostly silhouette of the fortress and the moonlit sea in the background.

10

Panayia Spiliani Church. Enter this spacious cave and descend sharply downward to the tiny church of Panayia Spiliani (Virgin of the Grotto). Half-church, half-cavern, this most unique landmark, located northwest of Pythagorio, is also called *Kaliarmenissa* ("for good travels"), and features an antique icon of the Virgin Mary as well as a pool of what is considered to be holy water.

Samos Pythagorio Museum. This tiny but impressive museum contains local finds, including headless statues, grave markers with epigrams to the dead, human and animal figurines, in addition to some notably beautiful portrait busts of the Roman emperors Claudius, Caesar, and Augustus. ✉ *Pythagora Sq., in municipal bldg., Pythagorio* ☎ *22730/61400* 🎟 *Free* 🕓 *Tues.–Sun. 8:30–3.*

Fodor's Choice
★

To Efpalinio Hydragogeio. Considered by Herodotus as the world's Eighth Wonder, this famed underground aqueduct, the To Efpalinio Hydragogeio (or Efpalinio tunnel), was completed in 524 BC with primitive tools and without measuring instruments. Polycrates, not a man who liked to leave himself vulnerable, ordered the construction of the tunnel to ensure that Samos's water supply could never be cut off during an attack. Efpalinos of Megara, a hydraulics engineer, set perhaps 1,000 slaves into two teams, one digging on each side of Mt. Kastri. Fifteen years later, they met in the middle with just a tiny difference in the elevation between the two halves. The tunnel is about 3,340 feet long, and it remained in use as an aqueduct for almost 1,000 years. More than a mile of (long-gone) ceramic water pipe once filled the space, which was also used as a hiding place during pirate raids in the 7th century. Today the tunnel is exclusively a tourist attraction, and though some spaces are tight and slippery, you can walk the first 1,000 feet—also a wonderful way to enjoy natural coolness on swelteringly hot days. ✉ *Just north of town, Pythagorio* ☎ 🎟 *€4* 🕓 *Tues.–Sun. 8:45–2:45.*

WHERE TO EAT AND STAY
For expanded hotel reviews, visit Fodors.com.

$$
MODERN GREEK

✕ **Elia.** If you'd tired of the usual views and culinary suspects found along the harbor front, stroll past its row of cafés, bars, and tavernas to this place for a nice change in ambience and style. The chef here is Swedish and so his menu offers a refreshingly eclectic take on Greek cuisine. Pawns sautééd in ouzo, a Summer Salad with prosciutto, baby spinach, rocket, and peaches, and the pork cooked with Samos wine all tempt with their engaging flavors. Results are not always spectacular—considering very few local restaurants use the magnificent local wine in their cooking, one hoped the pork would have been better—but meals here are usually worthwhile. ✉ *Far end of the harbor front, Pythagorio* ☎ *22730/61436.*

$
GREEK

✕ **Maritsa.** A regular Pythagorio clientele frequents Maritsa, a simple fish taverna in a garden courtyard on a quiet, tree-lined side street. You might try shrimp souvlaki, red mullet, octopus, or squid garnished with garlicky *skordalia* (a thick lemony sauce with pureed potatoes, vinegar, and parsley). The usual appetizers include a sharp *tzatziki* (tangy garlic-yogurt dip with cucumber) and a large *horiatiki* ("village" or "country" salad) piled high with tomatoes, olives, onion, and feta cheese.

Additional recommendations include lamb on the spit, the mixed grill, and stuffed tomatoes. ⊠ *Off Lykourgou Logotheti, 1 block from waterfront, Pythagorio* ☎ *22730/61957.*

$$$$
★ 🍽 **Doryssa Bay Hotel-Village.** The hotel's Web site announces this place as "A true village!" and it is true: this lovely hotel is a painstakingly created "village," complete with winding cobblestone streets, colorful town-house facades, boutiques, and rustic main square—all in all, a delightful "stage-set" of traditional Samian architecture. **Pros:** hotel is a world within a world; lots of delightful amenities; enchanting "village" stage-set. **Cons:** lots of tour groups in summer. ⊠ *Pythagorio beach, near road to airport, Pythagorio* ☎ *22730/88300, 22730/88400* ⊕ *www.doryssa-bay.gr* ⇆ *172 rooms, 125 bungalows, 5 suites* ♿ *In-room: a/c, Wi-Fi. In-hotel: restaurant, bar, pool, spa, business center, some pets allowed* ⊗ *Closed Nov.–Mar.*

$
★ 🍽 **Fito Bay Bungalows.** A complex of individual white bungalows all aglisten with terra-cotta roofs set neatly around a sparkling long pool and next to winding paths lined with roses and lavender: the first impression here can be a little generic and cold but everything quickly warms up thanks to the welcome of the friendly staff who do their best to make you feel at ease at this economical and family-friendly place just steps from Pythagorio beach. **Pros:** close to beach and town; nice view over the lovely garden; beautifully kept grounds. **Cons:** bare corridors; no sea view. ⊠ *Pythagorio beach, on road to airport, Pythagorio* ☎ *22730/61314* ⊕ *www.fitobay.gr* ⇆ *87 rooms, 1 suite* ♿ *In-room: a/c, no TV. In-hotel: restaurant, bar, pool, business center* ⊗ *Closed Oct.–Apr.*

$$$$
☺
★ 🍽 **Proteas Blu Resort.** With a villagelike layout, this resort hotel is designed in a fresh, contemporary style with large, airy spaces, gardens planted with local flowers, an Olympic-size pool, a beautiful secluded-cove beach, and guest rooms that offer balconies that open out to a sparkling sea view: the blue sea and sky and mountains of Turkey rising up from the water. **Pros:** great place for quiet and pampered stay; disability-friendly. **Cons:** some of the rooms are boxy. ⊠ *Pythagorio Rd., Pythagorio* ☎ *22730/62144, 22730/62146* ⊕ *www.proteasbluresort.gr* ⇆ *20 rooms, 72 suites* ♿ *In-room: a/c, Internet, Wi-Fi. In-hotel: restaurant, bar, pool, tennis court, spa, laundry facilities, business center* ⊗ *Closed Oct.–May.*

10

NIGHTLIFE

Beyond. Run by Michael, the Beyond Martini Lounge is a showcase for his cultivated taste in bar decor, superb skill in cocktails, and elegant finger food, refined delights mostly exported from Boston back to his local Samos. Try his tantalizing Beyond Basil Bliss—a play on mohito that replaces mint with basil and rum with tequila—as you sit at the space-age white and neon bar or perch over the waterfront on the second-floor terrace. ⊠ *Pythagorio* ☎ *30/699–416–3663* ⊕ *http://beyondsamos.com.*

SPORTS AND THE OUTDOORS

Sun Yachting. Based in Athens, this outfitter specializes in charter rentals to Samos; you can pick up the boat in Piraeus or Pythagorio for one- and two-week rentals. ⊠ *Poseidonos 21, Kalamaki* ☎ *210/9837312, 210/9837313* ⊕ *www.sunyachting.gr.*

HERAION ΗΡΑΙΟΝ

6 km (4 mi) southwest of Pythagorio, 20 km (12½ southwest of Samos town.

★   **Heraion.** The early Samians worshipped the goddess Hera, believing she was born here beneath a bush near the stream Imbrassos and that there she also lay with Zeus. Several temples were subsequently built on the site in her honor, the earliest dating back to the 8th century BC. Polycrates rebuilt the **To Hraio,** or Temple of Hera, around 540 BC, making it four times larger than the Parthenon and the largest Greek temple ever conceived, with two rows of columns (155 in all). The temple was damaged by fire in 525 BC and never completed, owing to Polycrates's untimely death. In the intervening years, masons recycled the stones to create other buildings, including a basilica (foundations remain at the site) to the Virgin Mary. Today you can only imagine the To Hraio's massive glory; of its forest of columns only one remains standing, slightly askew and only half its original height, amid acres of marble remnants in marshy ground thick with poppies.

At the ancient celebrations to honor Hera, the faithful approached from the sea along the **Sacred Road,** which is still visible at the site's northeast corner. Nearby are replicas of a 6th-century BC sculpture depicting an aristocratic family; its chiseled signature reads "Genelaos made me." The kouros from Heraion was found here, and now is in the Archaeological Museum in Samos town. Hours may be shortened in winter. ⊠ *Near the Imvisos river* ☏ ⊕ *www.culture.gr* 🎫 *€4* ⊘ *Apr.– Oct., daily 8:30–3.*

GREEK VOCABULARY

THE GREEK ABC'S

The proper names in this book are transliterated versions of the Greek name, so when you come upon signs written in the Greek alphabet, use this list to decipher them.

GREEK	ROMAN	GREEK	ROMAN
A, α	a	N, ν	n
B, β	v	Ξ, ξ	x or ks
Γ, γ	g or y	O, o	o
Δ, δ	th, dh, or d	Π, π	p
E, ε	e	P, ρ	r
Z, ζ	z	Σ, σ, ς	s
H, η	i	T, τ	t
Θ, θ	th	Y, υ	i
I, ι	i	Φ, φ	f
K, κ	k	X, χ	h or ch
Λ, λ	l	Ψ, ψ	ps
M, μ	m	Ω, ω	o

The phonetic spelling used in English differs somewhat from the internationalized form of Greek place names. There are no long and short vowels in Greek; the pronunciation never changes. Note, also, that the accent is a stress mark, showing where the stress is placed in pronunciation.

BASICS

Do you speak English?	Miláte angliká?
"Yes, no"	"Málista or Né, óchi"
Impossible	Adínato
"Good morning, Good day"	Kaliméra
"Good evening, Good night"	"Kalispéra, Kaliníchta"
Good-bye	Yá sas
"Mister, Madam, Miss"	"Kírie, kiría, despiní"
Please	Parakaló
Excuse me	Me sinchórite or signómi
How are you?	Ti kánete or pós íste
How do you do (Pleased to meet you)	Chéro polí

I don't understand.	Dén katalavéno.
To your health!	Giá sas!
Thank you	Efcharistó

NUMBERS

one	éna
two	dío
three	tría
four	téssera
five	pénde
six	éxi
seven	eptá
eight	októ
nine	enéa
ten	déka
twenty	íkossi
thirty	triánda
forty	saránda
fifty	penínda
sixty	exínda
seventy	evdomínda
eighty	ogdónda
ninety	enenínda
one hundred	ekató
two hundred	diakóssia
three hundred	triakóssia
one thousand	hília
two thousand	dió hiliádes
three thousand	trís hiliádes

DAYS OF THE WEEK

Monday	Deftéra
Tuesday	Tríti

Wednesday	Tetárti
Thursday	Pémpti
Friday	Paraskeví
Saturday	Sávato
Sunday	Kyriakí

MONTHS

January	Ianouários
February	Fevrouários
March	Mártios
April	Aprílios
May	Maíos
June	Ióunios
July	Ióulios
August	Ávgoustos
September	Septémvrios
October	Októvrios
November	Noémvrios
December	Dekémvrios

TRAVELING

I am traveling by car . . .	Taxidévo mé aftokínito . . . me
train . . . plane . . . boat.	tréno . . . me aeropláno . . . me vapóri.
"Taxi, to the station . . ."	"Taxí, stó stathmó . . ."
harbor . . . airport	limáni . . . aerodrómio
"Porter, take the luggage."	"Akthofóre, pare aftá tá" prámata.
Where is the filling station?	Pou íne tó vensinádiko?
When does the train leave for . . . ?	Tí óra thá fíyi to tréno ya . . . ?
Which is the train for . . . ?	Pío íne to tréno gía . . . ?
Which is the road to . . . ?	Piós íne o drómos giá . . . ?
A first-class ticket	Éna isitírio prótis táxis

Smoking is forbidden.	Apagorévete to kápnisma.
Where is the toilet?	Póu íne í toaléta?
"Ladies, men"	"Ginekón, andrón"
Where? When?	Póu? Póte?
"Sleeping car, dining car"	"Wagonlí, wagonrestorán"
Compartment	Vagóni
"Entrance, exit"	"Íssodos, éxodos"
Nothing to declare	Den écho típota na dilósso
I am coming for my vacation.	Érchome giá tis diakopés mou.
Nothing	Típota
Personal use	Prossopikí chríssi
How much?	Pósso?
"I want to eat, to drink, to sleep."	"Thélo na fáo, na pió, na kimithó."
"Sunrise, sunset"	"Anatolí, díssi"
"Sun, moon"	"Ílios, fengári"
"Day, night"	"Méra, níchta"
"Morning, afternoon"	"Proí, mesiméri, or apóyevma"
"The weather is good, bad."	"Ó kerós íne kalós, kakós."

ON THE ROAD

Straight ahead	Kat efthían
"To the right, to the left"	"Dexiá, aristerá"
Show me the way to . . .	Díxte mou to drómo . . .
Please.	Parakaló.
Where is . . . ?	Pou íne . . . ?
Crossroad	Diastávrosi
Danger	Kíndinos

IN TOWN

Will you lead me? take me?	Thélete na me odigíste? Me pérnete mazí sas?
"Street, square"	"Drómos, platía"

Where is the bank?	Pou íne i trápeza?
Far	Makriá
Police station	Astinomikó tmíma
"Consulate (American, British)"	"Proxenío (Amerikániko, Anglikó)"
"Theater, cinema"	"Théatro, cinemá"
At what time does the film start?	Tí óra archízi ee tenía?
Where is the travel office?	Pou íne to touristikó grafío?
Where are the tourist police?	Pou íne i touristikí astinomía?

SHOPPING

I would like to buy	Tha íthela na agorásso
"Show me, please."	"Díxte mou, parakaló."
May I look around?	Boró na ríxo miá matyá?
How much is it?	Pósso káni? (or kostízi)
It is too expensive.	Íne polí akrivó.
Have you any sandals?	Échete pédila?
Have you foreign newspapers?	Échete xénes efimerídes?
"Show me that blouse, please."	Díxte mou aftí tí blouza.
Show me that suitcase.	Díxte mou aftí tí valítza.
"Envelopes, writing paper"	"Fakélous, hartí íli"
Roll of film	Film
Map of the city	Hárti tis póleos
Something handmade	Hiropíito
"Wrap it up, please."	"Tilixteto, parakaló."
"Cigarettes, matches, please."	"Tsigára, spírta, parakaló."
Ham	Zambón
"Sausage, salami"	"Loukániko, salámi"
"Sugar, salt, pepper"	"Záchari, aláti, pipéri"
"Grapes, cherries"	"Stafília, kerássia"
"Apple, pear, orange"	"Mílo, achládi, portokáli"
"Bread, butter"	"Psomí, voútiro"

"Peach, figs"	"Rodákino, síka"

AT THE HOTEL

A good hotel	Éna kaló xenodochío
Have you a room?	Échete domátio?
Where can I find a furnished room?	Pou boró na vró epiploméno domátio?
"A single room, double room"	"Éna monóklino, éna díklino"
With bathroom	Me bánio
How much is it per day?	Pósso kostízi tin iméra?
A room overlooking the sea	Éna domátio prós ti thálassa
"For one day, for two days"	"Giá miá méra, giá dió méres"
For a week	Giá miá evdomáda
My name is . . .	Onomázome . . .
My passport	Tó diavatirió mou
What is the number of my room?	Piós íne o arithmós tou domatíou mou?
"The key, please."	"To klidí, parakaló."
"Breakfast, lunch, supper"	"Proinó, messimergianó," vradinó
"The bill, please."	"To logariasmó, parakaló."
I am leaving tomorrow.	Févgo ávrio.

AT THE RESTAURANT

Waiter	Garsón
Where is the restaurant?	Pou íne to estiatório?
I would like to eat.	Tha íthela na fáo.
"The menu, please."	"To katálogo, parakaló."
Fixed-price menu	Menú
Soup	Soúpa
Bread	Psomí
Hors d'oeuvre	"Mezédes, orektiká"
Ham omelet	Omelétta zambón
Chicken	Kotópoulo

Roast pork	Psitó hirinó
Beef	Moschári
Potatoes (fried)	Patátes (tiganités)
Tomato salad	Domatosaláta
Vegetables	Lachaniká
"Watermelon, melon"	"Karpoúzi, pepóni"
"Desserts, pastry"	Gliká or pástes
"Fruit, cheese, ice cream"	"Fróuta, tirí, pagotó"
"Fish, eggs"	"Psári, avgá"
Serve me on the terrace.	Na mou servírete sti tarátza.
Where can I wash my hands?	Pou boró na plíno ta héria mou?
"Red wine, white wine"	"Kokivó krasí, áspro krasí"
Unresinated wine	Krasí aretsínato
"Beer, soda water, water, milk"	"Bíra, sóda, neró, gála"
Greek coffee	Ellenikó kafé
"Coffee with milk, without"	"Kafé gallikó me, gála skéto,"
"sugar, medium, sweet"	"métrio, glikó"

AT THE BANK, AT THE POST OFFICE

Where is the bank? . . . post office?	Pou íne i trápeza? . . . to tachidromío?
I would like to cash a check.	Thélo ná xargiróso mía epitagí.
Stamps	Grammatóssima
By airmail	Aëroporikós
"Postcard, letter"	"Kárta, grámma"
Letterbox	Tachidromikó koutí
I would like to telephone.	Thélo na tilephonísso.

AT THE GARAGE

"Garage, gas (petrol)"	"Garáz, venzíni"
Oil	Ládi
Change the oil.	Aláksete to ládi.
Look at the tires.	Rixte mia matiá sta lástika.

Wash the car.	Plínete to aftokínito.
Breakdown	Vlávi
Tow the car.	Rimúlkiste tó aftokínito.
Spark plugs	Buzí
Brakes	Fréna
Gearbox	Kivótio tachitíton
Carburetor	Karbiratér
Headlight	Provoléfs
Starter	Míza
Axle	Áksonas
Shock absorber	Amortisér
Spare part	Antalaktikó

Travel Smart
Greek Islands

WORD OF MOUTH

"Keep in mind there are no hydrofoils going to Santorini, only catamarans, which are an entirely different type of ship. The big Hellenic Seaways car carrying, high-speed catamarans that travel from Athens's harbor of Piraeus to Santorini and get you to the island in just over four hours, as opposed to eight hours on Blue Star, the fastest conventional ferry. There is also another smaller class of catamaran, e.g. Superjet and Hellenic Seaways 'flying cats,' which are passenger-only and not as stable as the larger ships. One plus for ferries: if you have the time, and want to enjoy your ferry experience, they offer the freedom to walk on the outside deck, taking in the views."
—heimdall

GETTING HERE AND AROUND

▌ AIR TRAVEL

Flying time to Athens is 3½ hours from London, 9½ hours from New York, 12 hours from Chicago, 16½ hours from Los Angeles, and 19 hours from Sydney.

Always find out your carrier's check-in policy. Plan to arrive at the airport about 2 hours before your scheduled departure time for flights within the United States and 2½ to 3 hours before international flights from the United States. You may need to arrive earlier if you're flying from one of the busier airports or during peak air-traffic times. Any sharp objects, such as nail files or scissors, may be removed if you take them through airport security. Pack such items in luggage you plan to check.

In Greece, you need to show identification for both domestic and international flights. For domestic flights in Greece, arrive no later than 1 hour before departure time; for flights to the rest of Europe, 1½ hours; and for other international flights, 2 hours. If you get bumped because of overbooking, international carriers try to find an alternative route on another airline, but Olympic Airlines and Aegean Airlines usually put you on their next available flight, which might not be until the next day. (Under European Union law, you are entitled to receive up to €250 compensation for overbooking on flights of 1,500 km [930 mi] or shorter, €400 on flights between 1,500 km and 3,500 km [2,170 mi], and up to €600 for longer flights.) In the past, Olympic Airlines staff and Greek air traffic controllers have gone on strike for several hours a day; keep attuned to the local news. Check-in is straightforward and easy at Greece's larger airports, but on small islands, it sometimes gets confusing, since several airlines may use the same check-in counter, indicated by garbled announcements. Watch for movement en masse by the crowd.

If you have been wait-listed on an Olympic or Aegean flight in Greece, remember that this list does not apply on the day of departure. A new waiting list goes into effect at the airport two hours prior to takeoff for domestic flights and three hours before international flights; you must be there to get a place.

You do not need to reconfirm flights within Greece. Athens International Airport (Eleftherios Venizelos) posts real-time flight information on its Web site (⊕ *www. aia.gr*). It also has customer information desks throughout the airport that operate on a 24-hour basis, as well as more than a dozen courtesy phones that put you through to the customer call center. You can contact the Hellenic Civil Aviation Authority at the main Athens airport if you have complaints or concerns.

Airline Security Issues Transportation Security Administration. This agency has answers for almost every question that might come up. ⊕ *www.tsa.gov*.

Air Travel Resources in Greece Hellenic Civil Aviation Authority at Athens International Airport–Eleftherios Venizelos ✉ *Level 3, Room 607, main terminal bldg., Spata* ☎ *210/353–4157 weekdays 9–5* ⊕ *www.hcaa.gr*.

AIRPORTS

Athens International Airport at Spata, 33 km (20 mi) southeast of the city center, opened in 2001 as the country's main airport. Officially named Eleftherios Venizelos, after Greece's first prime minister, the airport is user-friendly and high-tech. The main terminal building has two levels: upper for departures, ground level for arrivals. Unless you plan to avoid Athens altogether or to fly via charter directly to the islands, the Athens airport is the most convenient because you can easily switch from international to domestic flights or get to Greece's main harbor, Piraeus, about a one-hour train ride south of the airport. Greece's second largest city has the Thessaloniki Makedonia airport, which handles international flights. The airport on Rhodes (in the Dodecanese islands) is being expanded.

Five major airports in Greece, listed below, service international flights. Airports on many smaller islands (Santorini, Syros, Mykonos, Karpathos, Kos, and Paros among them) take international charter flights during the busier summer months. Locals will sometimes refer to the airports with their secondary names, so these names—along with the three-letter airport codes—are also given. Information about airports other than Athens is given on the Olympic Airlines Web site (⊕ *www.olympicair.com*) and on the Civil Aviation Authority Web site (⊕ *www. hcaa.gr*).

Airport Information Athens International Airport–Eleftherios Venizelos (ATH) ⊠ *Spata* 🕾 *210/353–0000 flight information and customer service, 210/353–1335 visitor services, 210/353–0515 lost and found* ⊕ *www.aia.gr*. Heraklion International Airport–Nikos Kazantzakis (HER) ⊠ *Heraklion, Crete* 🕾 *2810/397800.* Kerkyra (Corfu) Airport–Ioannis Kapodistrias (CFU) ⊠ *Corfu Town* 🕾 *26610/89600.* Rhodes International Airport Diagoras (RHO) ⊠ *Rhodes town* 🕾 *22410/88700.* Thessaloniki International Airport–Makedonia (SKG) ⊠ *Kalamaria* 🕾 *2310/985000* ⊕ *www.thessalonikiairport.gr.*

GROUND TRANSPORTATION
See Athens Getting Around in Chapter 3 for information on transfers between the airport and Athens and Piraeus. In Thessaloniki, municipal Bus 078 (€0.50) picks up travelers about every 30 minutes until 11 pm for the 45-minute ride (up to 90 minutes if there is traffic) into town; its final stop is the train station. There is also night bus 78N running every half hour, from 11:30 to 5:30 in the morning (check ⊕ *www.oasth.gr*). The EOT (GNTO, or Greek National Tourism Office) desk in the airport arrivals terminal has information. At other airports throughout Greece, especially on the islands, public transportation is infrequent or nonexistent; ask your hotel to make arrangements or take a taxi; rates are usually set to fixed destinations.

FLIGHTS
When flying internationally, you must usually choose between a domestic carrier, the national carriers of the country you are visiting, and a foreign carrier from a third country. You may, for example, choose to fly Olympic Air or Aegean Airlines to Greece. National carriers have the greatest number of nonstops. Domestic carriers may have better connections to your home town and serve a greater number of gateway cities. Third-party carriers may have a price advantage.

In Greece, when faced with a boat journey of six hours or more, consider flying. Olympic Air (previously known as Olympic Airlines) in the past dominated the domestic market, with flights to more than 30 cities and islands. In past years it has faced stiff competition from rapidly growing Aegean Airlines, which offers at times cheaper fares and a younger aircraft fleet. Olympic Air, the recently privatized Greek carrier, has incurred criticism over the years for its on-time record, indifferent service, and aging aircraft, and the new investors hope to provide a better standard of services and some brand-new aircraft. The airline has a fleet of more than 44 aircraft, including A340-300 airbuses. Improved service and fewer cancellations, especially since the opening of Athens International Airport, have left more passengers pleasantly surprised. Olympic is rated among the top three carriers worldwide for safety, while Aegean was awarded Best European Regional Airline for 2011. Many European national airlines fly to Athens from the United States and Canada via their home country's major cities. Remember that these are often connecting flights that include at least one stop and may require a change of planes. Air France, British Airways, Delta, KLM, and Lufthansa all now operate code-share flights within

Greece; British Airways has some direct flights to Thessaloniki and Crete. During the summer months, EasyJet also flies directly from various London airports to various Greek destinations, such as Crete (Heraklion and Chania), Corfu, Kos, Mykonos, Athens, Thessaloniki, Rhodes, Santorini, and Zante (Zakynthos). Check the carrier's Web site for changes in the winter schedule. Ryanair has also introduced flights to Corfu, Crete (Chania), Kos, Rhodes, Thessaloniki, and Volos, flying out mainly from Brussels, Frankfurt, Milan, and London. Check the Web site for details.

FLIGHTS WITHIN GREECE

The frequency of flights varies according to the time of year (with an increase between Greek Easter and November), and it is essential to book well in advance for summer or for festivals and holidays, especially on three-day weekends. Domestic flights are a good deal for many destinations. In summer 2011 the one-way economy Athens–Rhodes fare offered by Olympic Air was €60; to Corfu, €118; to Santorini (Thira), €60; and to Chania, €118. Unless the flight is part of an international journey, the baggage allowance is 44 pounds (20 kilograms) per passenger.

Scheduled (i.e., nonchartered) domestic air travel in Greece is provided by Olympic Air and Aegean Airlines, both of which operate out of Athens International Airport in Spata. **Olympic Air** offers service from Athens to and from Alexandroupolis, Ioannina, and Thessaloniki, all on the mainland; the Aegean islands: Astypalaia, Karpathos, Kassos, Kythira, Crete (Chania, Heraklion, and Siteia), Chios, Ikaria, Kos, Lesbos (listed as Mytilini in Greek), Limnos, Leros, Milos, Mykonos, Naxos, Paros, Rhodes, Samos, Skiathos, Syros, Kalymnos, Kastellorizo (only via Rhodes), and Santorini (Thira); Corfu (called Kerkyra in Greek), Kefalonia, and Zakynthos in the Ionian sea. Flights also connect Thessaloniki with Hania, Heraklion, Mykonos, and Rhodes. Inter-island flights, depending on the season, include

the following: from Karpathos to Kassos; from Santorini to Rhodes and Heraklion; from Rhodes to Karpathos, Kassos, Kastellorizo, and Mykonos, as well as Kos (summer only); between Kefalonia and Zakynthos (winter); and from Lesbos to Chios, Limnos, and Samos (winter). **Aegean Airlines** has regular scheduled flights and sometimes even cheaper prices than Olympic. It also has flights that connect Athens with Alexandroupolis, Chios, Corfu, Chania, Heraklion, Kalamata, Kos, Lesbos, Mykonos, Rhodes, Santorini (Thira), Samos, Sitia, and Thessaloniki. Planes connect Thessaloniki with Chania, Heraklion, Kos, Lesbos (Mytilene), Limnos, Mykonos, Rhodes, Samos, and Santorini (Thira).

To and from Greece **Air Canada**
☏ 1–888/247–2262 ⊕ www.aircanada.com. **Air France** ☏ 1–800/992–3932 ⊕ www.airfrance. us. **Alitalia** ☏ 800/223–5730 ⊕ www.alitalia. com. **British Airways** ☏ 1–800/247–9297 ⊕ www.britishairways.com. **Continental Airlines** ☏ 1–800/523–3273 for U.S. and Mexico reservations, 1–800/231–0856 for international reservations, 00800/441–43592 for Greece travel ⊕ www.continental.com. **Delta Airlines** ☏ 1–800/221–1212 for U.S. reservations, 210/998–0444 Greek office, 210/353–0116 Athens airport ⊕ www.delta.com. **easyJet** ☏ 0870/600–0000 in UK, 210/353–0300 Athens airport ⊕ www.easyjet.com. **Iberia Airlines** ☏ 1–800/772–4642, 210/353–7600 in Athens ⊕ www.iberia.com. **KLM Royal Dutch Airlines** ☏ 1–800/618–0104 Reservations, 210/353–3436 Athens airport ⊕ www.klm. com. **Lufthansa** ☏ 1–800/645–3880 Reservations, 210/617–5200 Athens airport ⊕ www. lufthansa.com. **Olympic Air** ☏ 210/355–0500 Athens airport, 801/80110101 toll-free within Greece, 855/359–6200 US Sales ⊕ www. olympicair.com .**Ryanair** ☏ 0044/871 2460002 ⊕ www.ryanair.com.

Swiss International Airlines ☏ 877/359–7947, 210/617–5320 in Athens, 210/353–0382 in Athens airport ⊕ www.swiss.com.

Within Greece **Aegean Airlines** ⊠ Viltanioti 31, Kifissia, Athens ☏ 801/112–0000

toll-free in Greece, 210/353-0101 in Athens airport, 210/626-1000 from abroad/mobile phones ⊕ www.aegeanair.com. **Air France** ✆ *210/998-0000 Greek office, 210/353-0380 Athens airport, 1-800/237-2747 U.S. reservations.*

British Airways ✆ *801/115-6000, 210/353-1170 Athens airport ⊕ www.britishairways.gr.* **KLM Royal Dutch Airlines** ✆ *210/998-0000, 210/353-3436.* **Lufthansa** ✆ *210/617-5200.* **Olympic Air** ✉ *Main Athens ticket office, 1st km Leof. Varis-Koropiou, Koropi, Athens* ✆ *801/8010101, 210/355-0500 airport arrival and departure information ⊕ www.olympicair.com.*

▌ BOAT TRAVEL

Ferries, catamarans, and hydrofoils make up an essential part of the national transport system of Greece. With so many private companies operating, so many islands to choose from, and complicated timetables, with departures changing not just by season but also by day of the week, the most sensible way to arrange island hopping is to select the islands you would like to see, then visit a travel agent to ask how your journey can be put together.

Greece's largest and busiest port is Piraeus, which lies 10 km (6 mi) south of downtown Athens. Every day dozens of vessels depart for the Saronic Gulf islands, the Cyclades, the Dodecanese, and Crete. In fact, the only island groups that are not served by Piraeus are the Ionian Islands and the Sporades. Athens's second port is Rafina, with regular daily ferry crossings to Evia (Euboea) and the Cycladic islands Andros, Tinos, and Mykonos. The smaller port of Lavrion, close to Sounion, serves the less-visited Cyclades Kea (Tzia) and Kythnos, and there are also (less-regular) crossings to Syros, Mykonos, Paros, Naxos, Ios, Sikinos, Folegandros, Kimolos, Milos, Tinos, Andros, Ag. Efstratios, Limnos, and Alexandroupolis.

Patras, on the Peloponnese, is the main port for ferries to Italy and the Ionian Islands and Corfu, Ithaca, and Kefalonia.

A short distance south of Patras, Killini has ferries to Kefalonia and Zakynthos, also in the Ionian chain. Igoumenitsa, on Greece's northwest coast, has ships to Italy, plus a local ferry to Corfu, which runs several times daily in each direction.

Boats for the Sporades islands depart from Agios Konstantinos and Volos on the central mainland, from Thessaloniki in northern Greece, and from Kimi on the east coast of Evia. The island of Skyros is only served by ferries from Kimi.

In the northeast Aegean, the islands of Limnos, Samothrace (Samothraki), and Thassos are more easily reached from the northern mainland towns of Kavala and Alexandroupolis.

When choosing a ferry, take into account the number of stops and the estimated arrival time. Sometimes a ferry that leaves an hour later gets you there faster. High-speed ferries are more expensive, with airplanelike seating, including fare classes and numbered seats. They'll get you where you're going more quickly but lack the flavor of the older ferries with the open decks. Note that really fast ferries can pitch like crazy (and often don't travel in high seas)—if you're prone to seasickness, chose a boat with an open deck as the breeze keeps queasiness in check.

From Piraeus port, the quickest way to get into Athens, if you are traveling light, is to walk to the metro station and take a 25-minute ride on the electric train to Monastiraki, Thisseion, Omonia, or Syntagma (the last one involves a train change at Monastiraki). Alternatively, you can take a taxi, though this will undoubtedly take longer because of traffic and will cost around €20, plus baggage and port surcharges. Often, drivers wait until they fill their taxi with debarking passengers headed in roughly the same direction, which leads to a longer, more circuitous route to accommodate everyone's destination. It's faster to walk to the main street and hail a passing cab.

Be aware that Piraeus port is so vast that you may need to walk some distance to your gate (quay) of departure. So be sure to arrive with plenty of time to spare. Confusingly, the gates of departure are occasionally changed at the last moment. Just confirm at an information kiosk.

Usually, the gates serve the following destinations:

E1 the Dodecanese

E2 Crete, Chios, Mytiline (Lesbos), Ikaria, Samos

E3 Crete, Kithira

E4 Kithira

E5 Main pedestrian entrance

E6 Cyclades, Rethimno (Crete)

E7 Cyclades, Rethimno (Crete)

E8 Saronic Islands,

E9 Cyckades, Samos, Ikaria

E10 Cyclades, Samos, Ikaria

Gates E1 and E2 are a fair distance away from the main pedestrian entrance, but you can take the port minibus (gratis), which starts at gate E5 and finishes at E1.

To get to Attica's second port, Rafina, take a KTEL bus, which leaves at approximately every half hour (or every 15 minutes during rush hours; inquire about their schedule before your departure). Usually KTEL buses run from 5:30 am to 9:30 pm from Aigyptou Square near Pedion Areos park in Athens (close to Viktoria electrical train station). The KTEL bus (€2.40) takes about an hour to get to Rafina; the port is slightly downhill from the bus station.

Boat timetables change in winter and summer, and special sailings are often added around holiday weekends in summer when demand is high. For the Cycladic, Dodecanese, and Ionian islands, small ferry companies operate local routes that are not published nationally; passage can be booked through travel agents on the islands served. Boats may be delayed by weather conditions, especially when the northern winds called *meltemia* hit

in August, so stay flexible—one advantage of not buying a ticket in advance. You usually can get on a boat at the last minute. However, it is better to buy your ticket at least two or three days ahead if you are traveling between July 15 and August 30, when most Greeks vacation, if you need a cabin (good for long trips), or if you are taking a car. If possible, don't travel by boat around August 15, when most ferries are so crowded, the situation becomes comically desperate—although things have improved since strict enforcement of capacity limits. First-class tickets are almost as expensive as flying.

If the boat journey will be more than a couple of hours, it's a good idea to take along water and snacks. Greek fast-food franchises operate on most ferries, charging higher prices, and on longer trips boats have both cafeteria-style and full-service restaurants.

If your ship's departure is delayed for any reason (with the exception of force majeure), you have the right to stay on board in the class indicated on your ticket or, in case of prolonged delay, to cancel your ticket for a full refund. If you miss your ship, you forfeit your ticket; if you cancel in advance, you receive a partial or full refund, depending on how far in advance you cancel.

You can buy tickets from a travel agency representing the shipping line you need, from the local shipping agency office, online through travel Web sites (a popular one is ⊕ *www.greekferries.gr*), or direct from ferry companies. Generally you can pay by either credit card or cash, though the latter is often preferred. For schedules, any travel agent can call the port to check information for you, although they may not be as helpful about a shipping line for which they don't sell tickets. On islands the local office of each shipping line posts a board with departure times, or you can contact the port authority *(limenarchio)*, where some English is usually spoken. Schedules are also posted online by the Merchant Marine Ministry (⊕ *www.yen.*

gr). The weekly newspaper *Athens News* and the English edition of *Kathimerini,* published as an insert to the *International Herald Tribune,* lists daily departures from the capital. Or you can call the port authorities for a recording, in Greek, of the day's domestic departures from major ports. At 1 pm, a new recording lists boats leaving the following morning.

Information Agios Konstantinos Port Authority ☎ 22350/31759. Ferry departures ☎ 1440. Igoumenitsa Port Authority ☎ 26650/99400. Kimi Port Authority ☎ 22220/22606. KTEL bus to Rafina ☎ 210/808–8082 Athens to Rafina, 210/808–0800 General information, 22940/23440 Rafina to Athens ⊕ www.ktelattikis.gr. Lavrion Port Authority ☎ 22920/25249, 22920/26859. Liner Schedules (recorded in Greek) ☎ 14944. Patras Port Authority ☎ 2610/341002, 2610/341024. Piraeus Port Authority ☎ 210/4147800, 210/422–6000. Rafina Port Authority ☎ 22940/22300, 22940/28888. Thessaloniki Port Authority ☎ 2310/531505, 2310/531645. Volos Port Authority ☎ 24210/28888, 2410/38888.

CATAMARANS AND HYDROFOILS

Catamarans and hydrofoils, known as *iptamena delphinia* (flying dolphins), carry passengers from Piraeus to the Saronic islands (Aegina, Hydra, Poros, Angistri, and Spetses) and the eastern Peloponnesian ports of Hermioni and Porto Heli. Separate services run from Piraeus to the Cycladic islands (Amorgos, Folegandros, Ios, Milos, Mykonos, Naxos, Paros, Santorini, Serifos, Sifnos, Syros, and Tinos) and to the Dodecanese islands (Samos, Ikaria, Mytilene, and Chios), and from Rafina to the Cycladic islands (Mykonos, Paros, Tinos, and Andros). You can also take hydrofoils from Agios Konstantinos, Volos, or Thessaloniki to the Sporades islands of Alonissos, Skiathos, and Skopelos). Through summer only, there is a service from Heraklion (on Crete) to the Cycladic islands Mykonos, Paros, and Santorini.

These boats are somewhat pricey, and the limited number of seats means that you should reserve (especially in summer), but they cut travel time in half. The catamarans are larger, with more space to move around, although on both boats passengers are not allowed outside when the boat is not docked. If the sea is choppy, these boats often cannot travel, and cancellations are common. Tickets can be purchased through authorized agents or at the port (if available just before departure). Book your return upon arrival if you are pressed for time.

Information Hellenic Seaways ✉ Astigos 6, Plateia Karaiskaki, Piraeus, Greece ☎ 210/419–9000 Ticket information, 210/419–9100 Administration ⊕ www.hellenicseaways.gr. Seajets ✉ Dim. Gounari 2, 2nd floor, Piraeus, Greece ☎ 210/412–0001, 210/412–1901 ⊕ www.seajets.gr.

INTERNATIONAL FERRIES

You can cross to Turkey from the northeast Aegean islands. The Aegean Shipping Company sails between Rhodes and Marmaris, while Miniotis Lines sails between Chios and Çeşme. In addition, other routes have included Lesbos to Dikeli with Nel Lines and from Samos to Kuşadası. Note that British passport holders must have £10 with them to purchase a visa on landing in Turkey, Australian citizens need $20 (American dollars) or €14 and U.S. citizens need $20 or €14; New Zealanders don't need a visa. Canadian citizens need $60 or €42. You can also opt to purchase the visa beforehand, paying euros, at the Turkish Consulate in Athens (visa hours are weekdays 9 to 1).

There are also frequent sails between Italy and Greece, with stops at Ancona, Bari, Brindisi, and Venice. The shipping lines covering these routes are Agoudimos Lines (Bari to Corfu, Igoumenitsa; Bari to Igoumenitsa, Kefalonia, and Patras; Zakynthos/Zante to Igoumenitsa, Corfu, and Brindisi; Brindisi to Aulona), Anek-Superfast Lines (Ancona to Igoumenitsa and Patras; and Venice to Patras), Minoan

Lines (Venice to Patras; and Ancona to Igoumenitsa and Patras), and Ventouris Ferries (Bari to Corfu and Igoumenitsa; Brindisi to Corfu and Igoumenitsa).

The most respected and competitively priced is Minoan Lines. Its modern, well-maintained vessels are outfitted with bars, a self-service restaurant, a pool, a spa, a gym, an Internet café, a casino, shops, and even a conference center. The trip from Patras to Ancona takes 21 hours (which includes a stop at Igoumenitsa en route); from Patras to Bari, 15 hours; and from Igoumenitsa to Bari, 9 hours.

Prices range widely, depending on the season and the way you choose to travel (deck, air seat, or cabin). Traveling on Minoan Lines from Patras to Ancona during high season 2011 costs €90 for a one-way ticket on deck; €114 for a one-way ticket with seating; €194 for a one-way ticket with overnight accommodation in an inside cabin with four beds; and €334 for a one-way ticket with overnight accommodation in a deluxe outside cabin with two beds. Taking a car aboard from Patras to Ancona during high season on the same line costs €150. High season runs from late July to late August; prices drop considerably in low and middle season. Some companies offer special family or group discounts, while others charge extra for pets or offer deep discounts on return tickets, so comparing rates does pay off. When booking, also consider when you will be traveling; an overnight trip can be offset against hotel costs, and you will spend more on incidentals like food and drink when traveling during the day.

Contacts Sea Dreams - Aegean Shipping Company ⊠ *Grigoriou Lampraki 46, Rhodes* ☎ *22410/76535* ⊕ *www.seadreams.gr.* **Agoudimos Lines** ⊠ *Kapodistriou 2, Piraeus* ☎ *210/414–1301* ⊕ *www.agoudimos-lines. com.* **Anek Lines** ⊠ *Akti Kondyli 22, Piraeus* ☎ *210/419–7400 ticket info, 210/419–7470 customer service, 210/419–7420 reservations* ⊕ *www.anek.gr.* **Anes Ferries** ⊠ *Gounari 2, Piraeus* ☎ *210/422–5625* ⊕ *www.anes.gr.* **Blue Star Ferries** ⊠ *123-125 Syngrou Ave & Torva 3, Athens* ☎ *210/891–9800, 18130 Reservation/Call within Greece, 210/891–9810 Customer Service* ⊕ *www.bluestarferries. gr.* **Miniotis Lines** ⊠ *Neoreion 23, Chios* ☎ *22710/41073, 22710/41423* ⊕ *www. miniotis.gr.* **Minoan Lines** ⊠ *Panepimistimiou [(Eleftheriou Venizelou)] 59 and Em. Benaki, Athens* ☎ *210/337–6910 Athens office, 210/414–5700 Call center* ⊕ *www.minoan. gr.* **NEL Lines.** Boats from Mytilene (Lesbos) to Dikeli and to Ayvalik in Turkey. ⊠ *Astiggos 2, Piraeus* ☎ *210/412–5888, 210/411–5015* ⊕ *www.nel.gr.*

Superfast Ferries ⊠ *123-125 Syngrou Ave & 30 Torva street, Athens* ☎ *210/891–9130* ⊕ *www.superfast.com.* **Ventouris Ferries** ⊠ *Grigoriou Lampraki 17, Piraeus* ☎ *210/482–8001 through 210/482–8004* ⊕ *www.ventouris.gr.*

Information Turkish Consulate in Athens ⊠ *Vassileos Pavlou 22, Paleo Psyhiko, Athens* ☎ *210/671–4828, 210/672–1153.*

CRUISES

For full information about the top cruiss lines sailing Greek waters and their best itineraries, see Chapter 2, Cruising the Greek Islands.

▮ BUS TRAVEL

Organized bus tours can be booked together with hotel reservations by your travel agent. Many tour operators have offices in and around Syntagma and Omonia squares in Athens. Bus tours often depart from Syntagma or adjacent streets. *Most chapters in this guide have information about guided tours.*

It is easy to get around Greece on buses, which travel to even the most far-flung villages. The price of public transportation in Greece has risen in recent years, but it is still much cheaper than in other western European cities. Greece has an extensive, inexpensive, and fairly reliable regional bus system (KTEL) made up of local operators. Each city has connections to towns and villages in its vicinity; visit the local KTEL office to check routes or use the fairly comprehensive Web site (⊕ *www.ktel.org*, which, as of this writing, was in Greek only) to plan your trip in advance. Buses from Athens, however, travel throughout the country. The buses, which are punctual, span the range from slightly dilapidated to luxurious and air-conditioned with upholstered seats. There is just one class of ticket. Board early, because Greeks have a loose attitude about assigned seating, and ownership is nine-tenth's possession. Taking the bus from Athens to Corinth costs €7.50 and takes about 1 hour; to Nafplion, €11.80, 2½ hours; to Patras, €17, 2½–3 hours; and to Thessaloniki, €42, 6½ hours. For KTEL buses travelling within Attica and from Athens to Thessaloniki, check their Web site (⊕ *www.ktelattikis.org*).

Although smoking is forbidden on KTEL buses, the driver stops every two hours or so at a roadside establishment; smokers can light up then.

In Athens, KTEL's Terminal A is the arrival and departure point for bus lines to northern Greece, including Thessaloniki, and to the Peloponnese destinations of Epidauros, Mycenae, Nafplion, and Corinth. Terminal B serves Evia, most of Thrace, and central Greece, including Delphi. To get into the city center, take Bus 051 from Terminal A (terminus at Zinonos and Menandrou off Omonia Square) or Bus 024 from Terminal B (downtown stop in front of the National Gardens on Amalias Avenue). Most KTEL buses to the east Attica coast—including those for Sounion, Marathon, and the ports of Lavrion and Rafina—leave from the downtown KTEL terminal near Pedion Areos park.

In Athens and Thessaloniki avoid riding city buses during rush hour. Buses and trolleys do not automatically stop at every station; on the street you must hold out your hand to summon the vehicle you want (just be careful of the other traffic). Upon boarding, validate your ticket in the canceling machines at the front and back of buses (this goes for the trolleys and the subway train platforms, too). If you're too far from the machine and the bus is crowded, don't be shy: pass your ticket forward with the appropriate ingratiating gestures, and it will eventually return, properly punched. Keep your ticket until you reach your destination, as inspectors who occasionally board are strict about fining offenders; a fine may cost you up to 60 times the fare. On intracity buses, an inspector also boards to check your ticket, so keep it handy.

The KTEL buses provide a comprehensive network of coverage within the country. That said, the buses are fairly basic in remoter villages and on some of the islands—no toilets or refreshments. However, main intercity lines have preassigned seating and a better standard of vehicle.

See our Athens chapter Getting Around section for information on the city's convenient multiday transportation passes (good for buses, trolleys, and the metro). In large cities, you can buy individual tickets for urban buses at terminal booths, convenience stores, or at selected *periptera* (street kiosks). KTEL tickets must be purchased at the KTEL station or on the bus. On islands, in smaller towns, and on the KTEL buses that leave from Aigyptou Square in Athens, you buy tickets from the driver's assistant once seated; try not to pay with anything more than a €10 bill to avoid commotion. Athens bus stops have signs diagramming each route. It still helps if you can read some Greek, since most stops are only labeled in Greek. Or ask the driver's assistant to warn you for the correct stop well in advance.

The Organization for Urban Public Transportation (OASA), based just north of the National Archaeological Museum, gives Athens route information and distributes maps (weekdays 7:30–2), but the best source for non-Greek speakers is the EOT (GNTO) regional offices or information kiosks, which distribute information on Athens and KTEL bus schedules, including prices for each destination and the essential phone numbers for the regional ticket desks.

Throughout Greece, you must pay cash for local and regional bus tickets, although for the KTEL journey from Athens to Thessaloniki you can now also pay by credit card through their Web site (⊕ *www.ktelattikis.org*). For bus tours, a travel agency usually lets you pay by credit card or traveler's checks.

For KTEL, you can make reservations for many destinations free by phone; each destination has a different phone number. Reservations are unnecessary on most routes, especially those with several round-trips a day. Book your seat a few days in advance, however, if you are traveling on holiday weekends, especially if you are headed out of Athens. Because reservations sometimes get jumbled in the holiday exodus, it's best to go to the station and buy your ticket beforehand. If you plan to travel on a Greek bank holiday, call the station in advance to find out if all outward journeys are taking place as planned.

Athens Public Transportation Organization for Urban Public Transportation ✉ *Metsovou 15, Athens* ☎ *185 Travel info, 210/820–0999 Central office* ⊕ *www.oasa.gr.*

Regional Bus Service Downtown Athens KTEL terminal ✉ *Aigyptou Sq., Mavromateon and Leoforos Alexandras, near Pedion Areos park, Athens* ☎ *210/880–8080, 210/818–0221* ⊕ *www.ktel.org, www.ktelattikis.gr.* **Terminal A - KTEL Kifissou** ✉ *Kifissou 100, Kolonos, Athens* ☎ *210/512–4910, 210/512–4911.* **Terminal B - KTEL Liossion** ✉ *Liossion 260, Kato Patissia, Athens* ☎ *210/831–7186 Morning hrs., 210/831–7173.*

▌ CAR TRAVEL

Road conditions in Greece have improved in the last decade, yet driving in Greece still presents certain challenges. In Athens, traffic is mind-boggling most of the time and parking is scarce, although the situation has improved somewhat; public transportation or taxis are a much better choice than a rented car. If you are traveling quite a bit by boat, taking along a car increases ticket costs substantially and limits your ease in hopping on any ferry. On islands, you can always rent a taxi or a car for the day if you want to see something distant, and domestic flights are fairly cheap, especially if you book well in advance. The only real reason to drive is if it's your passion, you are a large party with many suitcases and many out-of-the-way places to see, or you need the freedom to change routes and make unexpected stops not permitted on public transportation. Remember to always buckle your seat belt when driving in Greece, as fines are very costly. Children 10 years old or younger are required to sit in the backseat. You have to be at least 18 to be able to drive in Greece.

International driving permits (IDPs), required for drivers who are not citizens of an EU country, are available from the American, Australian, Canadian, and New Zealand automobile associations. These international permits, valid only in conjunction with your regular driver's license, are universally recognized; having one may save you a problem with local authorities. Getting one is not the hassle it used to be in the past.

Regular registration papers and insurance contracted in any EU country or a green card are required, in addition to a driver's license (EU or international). EU members can travel freely without paying any additional taxes. Cars with foreign plates and rental cars are exempt from the rule that allows only alternate-day driving in Athens's center depending on whether the license plate is odd or even. The zone restriction is usually lifted during the month of August, following an announcement annually made by the Greek Ministry of Transport (⊕ *www.yme.gr*).

The expansion and upgrading of Greece's two main highways, the Athens–Corinth and Athens–Thessaloniki highways (Ethniki Odos), and construction of an Athens beltway, the Attiki Odos, has made leaving Athens much easier. Avoid using them during periods of mass exodus, such as Friday afternoon or Sunday evenings! These highways (and the new Egnatia Odos, which goes east to west across northern Greece), along with the secondary roads, cover most of the mainland, but on islands, some areas (beaches, for example) are accessible via dirt or gravel paths. With the exception of main highways and a few flat areas like the Thessalian plain, you will average about 60 km (37 mi) an hour: expect some badly paved or disintegrating roads; stray flocks of goats; slowpoke farm vehicles; detours; curves; and, near Athens and Thessaloniki, traffic jams. At the Athens city limits, signs in English mark the way to Syntagma and Omonia squares in the center. When you exit Athens, signs are well marked for the National Road, usually naming Lamia and Thessaloniki for the north and Corinth or Patras for the southwest.

AUTO CLUB

The Automobile Touring Club of Greece, known as ELPA, operates a special phone line for tourist information that works throughout the country; the club also has several branch offices. If you don't belong to an auto club at home, you can join ELPA for €145, which gives you free emergency road service, though you must pay for spare parts. Membership lasts for a year and is good on discounts for emergency calls throughout the EU. Visit your local auto association before you leave for Greece; they can help you plan your trip and provide you with maps. They also can issue you an international driver's permit good for one year. Your local membership may qualify you for cheaper emergency service in Greece and abroad.

In Greece **Automobile Touring Club of Greece - ELPA** (*ELPA*). ✉ *Mesogeion 395, Agia Paraskevi, Athens* ☎ *210/606-8800, 10400 for road assistance* ⊕ *www.elpa.gr* ✉ *Ethniki Odos Patras-Athinas 18, Patras* ☎☎ *2610/426416, 2610/425411* ✉ *Papanastasiou 66, Heraklion,*

Crete ☎ *2810/210581, 2810/210654* ✉ *Vas. Olgas 230 and Aegeou, Thessaloniki* ☎ *2310/426319, 2310/426320.* **Tourist Information Line** ☎ *171.*

GASOLINE

Gas pumps and service stations are everywhere, and lead-free gas is widely available. However, away from the main towns, especially at night, open gas stations can be very far apart (⇨ *Hours of Operation, below*). Don't let your gas supply drop to less than a quarter tank when driving through rural areas. Gas costs about €1.7 a liter for unleaded ("ah-*mo*-lee-vdee"), €1.3 a liter for diesel ("*dee*-zel"). Prices may vary by as much as €0.30 per liter from one region to another, but a price ceiling has been imposed on gas prices during the busy summer months in popular tourist destinations. You aren't usually allowed to pump your own gas, though you can do everything else yourself. If you ask the attendant to give you extra service (check oil, air, and water or clean the windows), leave a small tip. Gas stations are now required by law to issue receipts, so make sure you pick up yours from the attendant. The word is *apodiksi*. Credit cards are usually accepted in big gas (fuel) stations (BP, Shell, Elinoil, EKO, Avin, Aegean, Revoil, etc.), less so at stations found in remote areas.

Customs Stamps **Directorate for the Supervision and Control of Cars** (*DIPEAK*). ✉ *Akti Kondili 32, 1st fl., Piraeus* ☎ *210/462-7325, 210/462-6325.*

INSURANCE

In general, auto insurance is not as expensive as in other countries. You must have third-party car insurance to drive in Greece. If possible, get an insurance "green card" valid for Greece from your insurance company before arriving. You can also buy a policy with local companies; keep the papers in a plastic pocket on the inside right front windshield. To get more information, or to locate a local representative for your insurance company, call the Hellenic Union of Insurance Firms/Motor Insurance Bureau.

Insurance Bureau Hellenic Union of Insurance Firms/Motor Insurance Bureau ✉ *Xenofontos 10, Athens* ☎ *210/333–41000* ⊕ *www.eaee.gr.*

PARKING

The scarcity of parking spaces in Athens is one good reason not to drive in the city. Although a number of car parks operate in the city center and near suburban metro stations, these aren't enough to accommodate demand. They can also be quite expensive, with prices starting at €10 for an hour. Pedestrians are often frustrated by cars parked on pavements, although police have become stricter about ticketing. "Controlled parking" zones in some downtown districts like Kolonaki have introduced some order to the chaotic system; a one-hour card costs €1.5, with a maximum of three hours permitted (for a total cost of €6). Buy a parking card from the kiosk or meter and display it inside your windshield. Be careful not to park in the spots reserved for residents, even if you have a parking card, as you may find your license plates mischievously gone when you return!

Outside Athens, the situation is slightly better. Many villages, towns and islands have designated free parking areas just outside the center where you can leave your car.

ROAD CONDITIONS

Driving defensively is the key to safety in Greece, one of the most hazardous European countries for motorists. In the cities and on the highways, the streets can be riddled with potholes; motorcyclists seem to come out of nowhere, often passing on the right; and cars may even go the wrong way down a one-way street. In the countryside and on islands, you must watch for livestock crossing the road, as well as for tourists shakily learning to use rented motorcycles.

The many motorcycles and scooters weaving through traffic and the aggressive attitude of fellow motorists can make driving in Greece's large cities unpleasant—and the life of a pedestrian dangerous. Greeks often run red lights or ignore stop signs on side streets, or round corners fast without stopping. It's a good idea at night at city intersections and at any time on curvy country lanes to beep your horn to warn errant drivers.

In cities, you will find pedestrians have no qualms about standing in the middle of a busy boulevard, waiting to dart between cars. Make eye contact so you can both determine who's going to slow. Rush hour in the cities runs from 7 to 10 am and 1:30 to 3:30 pm on weekdays, plus 8 to 10 pm on Tuesday, Thursday, and Friday. Saturday mornings bring bumper-to-bumper traffic in shopping districts, and weekend nights guarantee crowding around nightlife hubs. In Athens, the only time you won't find traffic is very early morning and most of Sunday (unless you're foolish enough to stay at a local beach until evening in summer, which means heavy end-of-weekend traffic when you return). Finally, perhaps because they are untrained, drivers seldom pull over for wailing ambulances; the most they'll do is slow down and slightly move over in different directions.

Highways are color-coded: green for the new, toll roads and blue for old, National Roads. Tolls are usually €2.50–€3. The older routes are slower and somewhat longer, but they follow more-scenic routes, so driving is more enjoyable. The National Roads can be very slick in places when wet—avoid driving in rain and on the days preceding or following major holidays, when traffic is at its worst as urban dwellers leave for villages. As this guide went to press, extended road works still taking place on the National Roads from Athens to Thessaloniki and Athens to Patras made driving on them even more demanding.

ROADSIDE EMERGENCIES

You must put out a triangular danger sign if you have a breakdown. Roving repair trucks, owned by the major road assistance companies, such as ELPA, patrol the major highways, except the Attiki Odos, which has its own contracted road assistance company. They assist tourists with breakdowns for free if they belong to an auto club, such as AAA or ELPA; otherwise, there is a charge. The Greek National Tourism Organization, in cooperation with ELPA, the tourist police, and Greek scouts, provides an emergency telephone line for those who spot a dead or wounded animal on the National Road.

Emergency Services Automobile Touring Club of Greece - ELPA (*ELPA*). ☎ *10400 for breakdowns, 171 for a dead or hurt animal, 210/606–8800 Head office.*

RULES OF THE ROAD

International road signs are in use throughout Greece. You drive on the right, pass on the left, and yield right-of-way to all vehicles approaching from the right (except on posted main highways). Cars may not make a right turn on a red light. The speed limits are 120 "kph" (74 "mph") on a National Road, 90 "kph" (56 "mph") outside urban areas, and 50 "kph" (31 "mph") in cities, unless lower limits are posted. The presence of traffic police on the highways has increased, and they are now much more diligent in enforcing speed limits or any other rules. However, limits are often not posted, and signs indicating a lower limit may not always be visible, so if you see Greek drivers slowing down, take the cue to avoid speed traps in rural areas.

In central Athens there is an odd-even rule to avoid traffic congestion. This rule is strictly adhered to and applies weekdays; license plates ending in odd or even numbers can drive into central Athens according to whether the date is odd or even. (The *daktylios,* as this inner ring is called, is marked by signs with a large yellow triangle.) This rule does not apply to rental cars, provided the renter and driver has a foreign passport. If you are renting a car, ask the rental agency about any special parking or circulation regulations in force. Although sidewalk parking is illegal, it is common. And although it's tempting as a visitor to ignore parking tickets, keep in mind that if you've surrendered your ID to the rental agency, you won't get it back until you clear up the matter. You can pay your ticket at the rental agency or local police station. Under a driving code aimed at cracking down on violations, fines start at €50 (for illegal parking in places reserved for the disabled) and can go as high as €1,200, if you fail an alcohol test; fines for running a red light or speeding are now €700, plus you have your license revoked for 60 days and your plates revoked for 20 days. If fines are paid in cash within ten days, there is a 50% discount in the amount that you actually pay.

If you are involved in an accident, don't drive away. Accidents must be reported (something Greek motorists often fail to do) before the insurance companies consider claims. Try to get the other driver's details as soon as possible; hit-and-run is all too common in Greece. If the police take you in (they can hold you for 24 hours if there is a fatality, regardless of fault), you have the right to call your local embassy or consulate for help getting a lawyer.

The use of seat belts and motorcycle helmets is compulsory, though Greeks tend to ignore these rules, or comply with them by "wearing" the helmet strapped to their arms.

CAR RENTAL

When you reserve a car, ask about cancellation penalties, taxes, drop-off charges (if you're planning to pick up the car in one city and leave it in another), and surcharges (for being under or over a certain age, for additional drivers, or for driving across state or country borders or beyond a specific distance from your point of rental). Don't forget to check if the rental price includes unlimited mileage. All these things can add substantially to your costs. Request car seats and extras such as GPS when you book.

Rates are sometimes—but not always—better if you book in advance or reserve through a rental agency's or an airline's Web site. There are other reasons to book ahead, though: for popular destinations, during busy times of the year, or to ensure that you get certain types of cars (vans, SUVs, exotic sports cars).

■TIP➜ Make sure that a confirmed reservation guarantees you a car. Agencies sometimes overbook, particularly for busy weekends and holiday periods.

Because driving in Greece can be harrowing, car rental prices can be higher than in the United States, and transporting a car by ferry hikes up the fare substantially, think twice before deciding on a car rental. It's much easier to take public transportation or taxis, which are among the cheapest in Europe. The exception is on large islands where the distance between towns is greater and taxi fares are higher; you may want to rent a car or a moped for the day for concentrated bouts of sightseeing.

In summer, renting a small car with standard transmission will cost you about €250 to €350 for a week's rental (including tax, insurance, and unlimited mileage). Four-wheel-drives can cost you anywhere from €80 to €160 a day, depending on availability and the season. Luxury cars are available at some agencies, such as Europcar, but renting a BMW or a Mercedes can fetch a hefty price—anywhere from €100 per day in low season to €500 a day in high season. This does not include the 23% V.A.T. Convertibles ("open" cars) and minibuses are also available. Probably the most difficult car to rent, unless you reserve from abroad, is an automatic. Note that car rental fees really follow laws of supply/demand so there can be huge fluctuations and, in low season, lots of room for bargaining. Off-

season, rental agencies are often closed on islands and in less-populated areas.

If you're considering moped or motorcycle rental, which is cheaper than a car, especially for getting around on the islands, try Motorent or Easy Moto Rent, both in Athens. On the islands, independent moped rentals are available through local agents.

You can usually reduce prices by reserving a car through a major rental agency before you leave. Or opt for a midsize Greek agency and bargain for a price; you should discuss when kilometers become free. These agencies provide good service, and prices are at the owner's discretion. It helps if you have shopped around and can mention another agency's offer. If you're visiting several islands or destinations, larger agencies may be able to negotiate a better total package through their local offices or franchises. Some hotels or airlines may also have partner agencies that offer discounts to guests.

Official rates in Greece during high season (July–September) are much cheaper if you rent through local agents rather than the large international companies. For example, a small car, such as the Hyundai i10, will cost you about €235 for a week's rental (including tax, insurance, and unlimited mileage) as opposed to at least €370 if you go through an international chain. Outside high season you can get some good deals with local agents; a car may cost you about €35 per day, all-inclusive. Rates are cheaper if you book for three or more days. On the islands, you can often get a lower price by renting for a half day—between the time when a client drops off a car and the next booked rental.

In Greece your own driver's license is not acceptable unless you are a citizen of the European Union. For non-EU citizens an international driver's permit (IDP) is necessary (⇨ *Car Travel, above*). To rent, you must have had your driver's license for one year and be at least 21 years old if you use a credit card (sometimes you must be

23 if you pay cash); for some car categories and for some agencies, you must be 25. You need the agency's permission to ferry the car or cross the border (Europcar does not allow across-the-border rentals). A valid driver's license is usually acceptable for renting a moped, but you will need a motorcycle driver's license if you want to rent a larger bike.

▌ TAXI TRAVEL

In Greece, as everywhere, unscrupulous taxi drivers sometimes try to take advantage of out-of-towners, using such tricks as rigging meters or tacking on a few zeros to the metered price. All taxis must display the rate card; it's usually on the dashboard, though taxis outside the big cities don't bother. Ask your hotel concierge or owner before engaging a taxi what the fare to your destination ought to be. It should cost between €35 and €50 from the airport (depending on whether you are travelling with Rate 1 or Rate 2 taxi charges) to the Athens city center (this includes tolls) and about €15 from Piraeus port to the center. It does not matter how many are in your party (the driver isn't supposed to squeeze in more than four); the metered price remains the same. Taxis must give passengers a receipt (*apodiksi*) if requested.

Make sure that the driver turns on the meter to Rate (Tarifa) 1 (€0.68), unless it's between midnight and 5 am, when Rate (Tarifa) 2 (€1.19) applies. Remember that the meter starts at €1.19 and the minimum is €3.16 in Athens and Thessaloniki (€3.39 for the rest of the country). A surcharge applies when taking a taxi to and from the airport (€3.84) and from (but not to) ports, bus and train stations (€1.07). There is also a surcharge charge of €0.40 for each item of baggage that's over 10 kilograms (22 pounds). If you suspect a driver is overcharging, demand to be taken to the police station; this usually brings them around. Complaints about service or overcharging should be directed

to the tourist police; at the Athens airport, contact the Taxi Syndicate information desk. When calling to complain, be sure to report the driver's license number.

Taxi rates are inexpensive compared to fares in most other European countries, mainly because they operate on the jitney system, indicating willingness to pick up others by blinking their headlights or slowing down. Would-be passengers shout their destination as the driver cruises past. Don't be alarmed if your driver picks up other passengers (although he should ask your permission first). Drivers rarely pick up additional passengers if you are a woman traveling alone at night. Each new party pays full fare for the distance he or she has traveled.

A taxi is available when a white-and-red sign ("elefthero") is up or the light is on at night. Once the driver indicates he is free, he cannot refuse your destination, so get in the taxi before you give an address. He also must wait for you up to 15 minutes, if requested, although most drivers would be unhappy with such a demand. Drivers are familiar with the major hotels, but it's good to know a landmark near your hotel and to have the address and phone number written in Greek. If all else fails, the driver can call the hotel from his mobile phone or a kiosk (many taxis in Athens now have GPS displays).

On islands and in the countryside, the meter may often be on Rate (Tarifa) 2 (outside city limits). Do not assume taxis will be waiting at smaller island airports when your flight lands; often, they have all been booked by arriving locals. If you get stuck, try to join a passenger going in your direction, or call your hotel to arrange transportation.

When you're taking an early-morning flight, it's a good idea to reserve a radio taxi the night before, for an additional charge of €3.39 to €5.65 (depending on whether it is daytime or night tariff). These taxis are usually quite reliable and punctual; if you're not staying in a hotel, the local tourist police can give you some phone numbers for companies. Taxis charge €10.85 per hour of waiting.

Complaints in Athens Taxi Syndicate ☎ 210/523–6904 *for Greece, 210/523–9524 for Attica.* **Tourist police** ☎ *171.*

▌ TRAIN TRAVEL

ARRIVING AND DEPARTING

The main line running north from Athens divides into three lines at Thessaloniki, continuing on to Skopje and Belgrade; the Turkish border and Istanbul; and Sofia, Bucharest, and Budapest. The Peloponnese in the south is served by a narrow-gauge line dividing at Corinth into the Tripoli–Kalamata and Patras–Kalamata routes. Two sample fares: Athens–Corinth, €9 (on the Proastiakos train, which is now part of the Greek National Railway network TrainOSE), and Athens–Thessaloniki, €29 (on TrainOSE, B class).

The Greek Railway Organization (TrainOSE) currently has one train terminal in operation, Stathmos Larissis, off Diliyianni street west of Omonia Square (⇨ *Athens Getting Around in Chapter 3 for more information*). The *Proastiakos* light-rail line (⊕ *www.trainoses.gr*) linking the airport to Stathmos Larissis in Athens has been extended past Corinth to Kiato; fares are €9 from Athens to Corinth and €12 from the airport to Corinth.

InterCity Express service from Athens to Thessaloniki is fast and reliable. At the time of writing, the IC train costs €39 (A class, versus €29 for B class) and the journey lasts about 4½ hours. The Athens to Patras railway line is no longer in operation, but is made up of two different legs, one the Athens–Kiato on the Proastiakos and the second leg is from Kiato to Patras with a local bus. If you book your IC tickets online at least two days in advance, you can get a 15% discount on the total price (20% if it is a round-trip ticket).

At the moment, the Greek Railway Organization is at a stage of complete reshuffling as it tries to curb its steep debts, so expect to see changes and—hopefully improvements— on the schedule of operations. One first change was the change in name, from OSE to TrainOSE (although most Greeks still use them both interchangeably). On the whole, train fares are reasonable, and the railways offer a good, though slower, alternative to long drives, bus rides, or even flights. One of the most impressive stretches is the rack-and-pinion line between Kalavrita and Diakofto, which travels up a pine-crested gorge in the Peloponnese Mountains. It is one of the oldest rail lines in Greece, assigned by PM Harilaos Trikoupis in 1889. Its renovation was completed in late 2008. In fact, this leisurely Peloponnesian train is one of the more pleasant ways to see southern Greece, together with the new scenic route from Katakolo to ancient Olympia, which has recently been introduced. In central and northern Greece, the Pelion route crosses breathtaking landscapes.

RULES OF THE GAME

Trains are generally on time. At smaller stations, allow about 15–20 minutes for changing trains; on some routes, connecting routes are coordinated with the main line.

All trains have both first- and second-class seating. On any train, it is best during high season, around holidays, or for long distances to travel first-class, with a reserved seat, as the difference between the first- and second-class coaches can be significant: the cars are cleaner, the seats are wider and plusher, and, most important, the cars are emptier. The assigned seating of first class *(proti thesi)* is a good idea in July and August, for example, when many trains are packed with tourists. First class costs about 30% more than second class *(thefteri thesi)*.

Many travelers assume that rail passes guarantee them seats on the trains they wish to ride. Not so. You need to book seats ahead even if you are using a rail pass *(for information on Eurail passes, see Rail Passes below)*; seat reservations are required on some European trains, particularly high-speed trains, and are a good idea on trains that may be crowded—particularly in summer on popular routes. You also need a reservation if you purchase sleeping accommodations. On high-speed (IC) trains, you pay a surcharge.

You can pay for all train tickets purchased in Greece with cash (euros) or with credit cards (Visa and MasterCard only). Note that any ticket issued on the train costs 50% more. The best, most efficient contact is TrainOSE's general-information switchboard (☏ 1110) for timetables and prices. You can get train schedules and fares from EOT (GNTO) and from TrainOSE offices. The Thomas Cook European Timetable, published monthly, is useful, too.

RAIL PASSES

Greece is one of 25 countries in which you can use Eurail passes, which provide unlimited first-class rail travel, in all of the participating countries, for the duration of the pass. Please note that the Greek National Organization has suspended circulation of international trains indefinitely (i.e., trains connecting Greece to Bulgaria, Fyrom, or Turkey), though you will still be able to use your pass within the country, or to travel from Italy to Greece. If you plan to rack up the miles in several countries, get a standard Eurail Global Pass. These are available for 15 days of travel ($798), 21 days ($1,031), one month ($1,269), two months ($1,793), and three months ($2,210).

In addition to standard Eurail passes, ask about special rail-pass plans. Among these are the Eurail Pass Youth (for those under age 26), the Eurail Saver Pass (which gives a discount for two or more people traveling together), and the Eurail Flexi Pass (which allows a certain number of travel days within a set period). Among those passes you might want to consider: the Greece Pass allows first-class rail travel throughout Greece; the standard three

days' unlimited travel in a month costs $158, and the rate rises per day of travel added. The Greece–Italy Pass gives you four days' travel time over a span of two months; the cost is $395 for first class, $314 for second. Youths (18–25 years of age) pay about 50% less, and there are special rates for groups and families.

Passes can be shipped to anywhere you are in Europe, as well as worldwide, but can't be shipped to a particular train station. Shipping is by registered mail. Residents of Canada must purchase their tickets from the Rail Europe's Canadian site at ⊕ *www.raileurope.ca*. You can access this link by clicking on Canada under the Non-U.S. residents section at ⊕ *www.raileurope.com*.

Train Information Greek Railway Organization - OSE *(OSE)*. ✉ *Karolou 1, Omonia Sq., Athens* ☏ *210/529–7006 Central Office, 210/529–7007* ⊕ *www.ose.gr* ✉ *Sina 6, Athens* ☏ *210/362–4402, 210/362–4405.*

OSE Customer Service. This service is operational daily 7 am–10 pm. ☏ *1110 Customer Service.* **Proastiakos Railway - TrainOSE** ✉ *Karolou 1-3, Omonia Sq., Athens* ☏ *210/522–3478, 1110 customer service (7 am–10 pm).*

Train Timetables Thomas Cook, Timetable Publishing Office. Europe Rail Timetable is published monthly and has more than 500 pages of rail and ferry travel all over Europe and beyond. ✉ *Unit 9, Coningsby Rd., Peterborough, England* ☏ *44/01733–416477* ⊕ *www. thomascookpublishing.com.*

Rail Passes Rail Europe ✉ *44 S. Broadway, White Plains, New York, USA* ☏ *1800/622–8600, 1800/361–7245 in Canada* ⊕ *www. raileurope.com.*

ESSENTIALS

▪ ADDRESS ABC'S

To make finding your way around as easy as possible, it's wise to learn to recognize letters in the Greek alphabet. Most areas have few road signs in English, and even those that *are* in English don't necessarily follow the official standardized transliteration code (⊕ *www.elot.gr*), resulting in odd spellings of foreign names. Sometimes there are several spelling variations in English for the same place: Agios, Aghios, or Ayios; Georgios or Yiorgos. Also, the English version may be quite different from the Greek, or even what locals use informally: Corfu is known as Kerkyra; island capitals are often just called Chora (town), no matter what their formal title; and Panepistimiou, a main Athens boulevard, is officially named Eleftheriou Venizelou, but if you ask for that name, no one will know what you're talking about. A long street may change names several times, and a city may have more than one street by the same name, so know the district you're headed for, or a major landmark nearby, especially if you're taking a taxi. In this guide, street numbers appear after the street name. Finally, there are odd- and even-numbered sides of the streets, but No. 124 could be several blocks away from No. 125.

▪ ACCOMMODATIONS

Unless you're visiting Athens or a resort at the height of the tourist season, you'll probably not have a hard time finding a room in Greece. The issue is finding a place you'll enjoy. Chances are you won't want to stay in one of the banal hotels geared to package tourism that have marred many a Greek shoreline, and you will want certain amenities—not necessarily luxuries, mind you, but a terrace, a view of the sea or the mountains, a fridge to keep water and snacks cool.

When it comes to making reservations, it is probably wise to book one month in advance for the months of June, July, and September, and ideally even two to three months in advance for the high season, from late July to the end of August, especially when booking top-end hotels in high-profile destinations like Santorini and Hydra. Sometimes during off-season you can bargain down the official prices (rumor has it to as much as a quarter of the officially quoted price). The most advisable method is to politely propose a price that's preferable to you, and persevere. The response you get will depend largely on the length of your stay, the hotel's policy, and on the season in question. When booking, it's worth asking whether the hotel provides transportation from the airport/port as part of their services. If you're not certain about directions, ask a travel agent at the port/airport for detailed directions.

Many hotels in Athens underwent massive renovations before the 2004 Olympics; a number of new hotels were built in the city, and prices of accommodation have risen in recent years, although some hotels have reduced their prices in the past year to remain competitive in the times of financial crisis. Often you can reduce the price by eliminating breakfast, by bargaining when it's off-season, or by going through a local travel agency for the larger hotels on major islands and in Athens and Thessaloniki. If you stay longer, the manager or owner will usually give you a better daily rate. A 6.5% government value-added tax and 0.5% municipality tax are added to all hotel bills, though usually the rate quoted includes the tax; be sure to ask. If your room rate covers meals, another 23% tax is added on the meals price quote. Accommodations may be hard to find in smaller summer resort towns in winter (when many hotels close for repairs) and at the beginning of spring.

Remember that the plumbing in rooms and most low-end hotels (and restaurants, shops, and other public places) is delicate enough to require that toilet paper and other detritus be put in the wastebasket and not flushed.

The lodgings we list are the cream of the crop in each price category. We always list the facilities that are available—but we don't generally specify whether they cost extra. When pricing accommodations, always ask what's included and what's not. Common items that may add to your basic room rate are breakfast, parking facilities, use of certain facilities, Wi-Fi, etc.

Note that some resort hotels also offer half- and full-board arrangements for part of the year. And all-inclusive resorts are mushrooming. Inquire about your options when booking.

For price charts detailing our array of hotel price categories, see the Planner section in every regional chapter.

HOTELS

The EOT (GNTO) authorizes the construction and classification of hotels throughout Greece. It classifies them into five categories: A–E, which govern the rates that can be charged, though don't expect hotels to have the same amenities as their U.S. and northern European counterparts. Ratings are based on considerations such as room size, hotel services, and amenities including the furnishing of the room. Within each category, quality varies greatly, but prices don't. Still, you may come across an A-category hotel that charges less than a B-class, depending on facilities. The classifications can be misleading—a hotel rated C in one town might qualify as a B in another. For category A expect the equivalent of a 5-star hotel in the United States, although the room will probably be somewhat smaller. A room in a C class hotel can be perfectly acceptable; with a D the bathroom may or may not be shared. Ask to see the room before checking in. You can sometimes

find a bargain if a hotel has just renovated but has not yet been reclassified. A great hotel may never move up to a better category just because its lobby isn't the required size.

Official prices are posted in each room, usually on the back of the door or inside the wardrobe. The room charge varies over the course of the year, peaking in the high season when breakfast or half-board (at hotel complexes) may also be obligatory.

A hotel may ask you for a deposit of the first night's stay or up to 25% of the room rate. If you cancel your reservations at least 21 days in advance, you are entitled to a full refund of your deposit.

Unless otherwise noted, in this guide, hotels have air-conditioning (*climatismo*), room TVs, and private bathrooms (*banio*). Bathrooms mostly contain showers, though some older or more luxurious hotels may have tubs. Beds are usually twins (*diklina*). If you want a double bed, ask for a *diplo krevati*. In upper-end hotels, the mattresses are full- or queen-size. This guide lists amenities that are available but doesn't always specify if there is a surcharge. When pricing accommodations, always ask what costs extra (air-conditioning, private bathroom, Internet connectivity).

Use the following as a guide to making accommodation inquiries: to reserve a double room, *thelo na kleiso ena diklino*; with a bath, *me banio*; without a bath, *horis banio*; or a room with a view, *domatio me thea*. If you need a quiet room (*isiho domatio*), get one with double-glazed windows (*dipla parathyra*) and air-conditioning, away from the elevator and public areas, as high up (*psila*) as possible, and off the street.

Information Hellenic Chamber of Hotels. This office is open weekdays 9–3. ⊠ *Stadiou 24, Athens* 🕾 *213/216–9900* ⊕ *www.grhotels.gr.*

RENTAL ROOMS

For low-cost accommodations, consider Greece's ubiquitous "rooms to rent," bed-and-breakfasts without the breakfast. You can count on a clean room, often with such amenities as a terrace, air-conditioning, and a private bath, at a very reasonable price, in the range of €40–€50 for two. Look for signs in any Greek town or village; or, let the proprietors find you—they have a knack for spotting strangers who look like they might need a bed for the night. When renting a room, take a good look first and be sure to check the bathroom before you commit. If there are extra beds in the room, clarify in advance that the amount agreed on is for the entire room—owners occasionally try to put another person in the same room.

When approached by one of the touts who meet the island ferries, make sure he or she tells you the location of the rooms being pushed, and look before you commit. Avoid places on main roads or near all-night discos. Around August 15 (an important religious holiday of the Greek Orthodox Church, commemorating the Assumption of the Virgin Mary), when it seems all Greeks go on vacation, even the most-basic rooms are almost impossible to locate, although you can query the tourist police or the municipal tourist office. On some islands, the local rental room owners' association sets up an information booth. Room touts may show up at the dock when boats arrive; sometimes, they're a good way to find accommodations, but ask to view the rooms before agreeing to a booking.

■ COMMUNICATIONS

INTERNET

Greece may lag behind other European countries in Internet home penetration, but the country is wired. Major hotels have high-speed Internet connections in rooms and most smaller ones have at least a terminal in the lounge for guests' use. Telecom privatization has helped Greece close the Internet gap with other European countries and, especially on touristed islands, you'll find at least one Internet café with high-speed connections. On the mainland, several villages have created public wireless networks—a trend that seems to be growing.

Although major companies such as Toshiba, Canon, and Hewlett-Packard have representatives in Greece, computer parts, batteries, and adaptors are expensive in Greece and may not be in stock when you need them, so carry spares for your laptop. Your best bets are the national Plaisio, Multirama, and Germanos chains, although some camera shops carry computer equipment, too. Also note that many upscale hotels will rent you a laptop.

If you want to access your e-mail, you can visit one of the Internet cafés that have sprung up throughout Greece. Athens has more than 60, several of which are open 24 hours, and you're sure to find at least one on most islands. Besides coffee and soft drinks, they offer a range of computer services and charge about €2 per hour; most do not accept credit cards. A few establishments, including Athens Airport, Flocafe coffee shops, and Starbucks, have Wi-Fi service. The City of Athens offers free wireless access in Syntagma Square, Thiseion, Gazi, and Plateia Kotzia (Kotzia Square) and a number of rural towns also have free wireless in public areas. If your cell phone works in Greece and you have a connection kit for your laptop, then you can buy a mobile connect card to get online.

Contacts City of Athens Wi-Fi Spots. This Web site has a list of Wi-Fi hook-up spots and cafés in Athens. ⊕ *www.athenswifi.gr.*

Cybercafes. The Web site lists more than 4,200 Internet cafés in 141 countries around the world. ⊕ *www.cybercafes.com.*

Free Wi-Fi in Greece. This Web site lists free Wi-Fi Internet hotspots in Greece, according to region. ⊕ *www.free-wifi.gr.*

CUSTOMS OF THE COUNTRY

Greeks are friendly and openly affectionate. It is not uncommon, for example, to see women strolling arm in arm, or men kissing and hugging each other. Displays of anger are also quite common. To the person who doesn't understand Greek, the loud, intense conversations may all sound angry—but they're not. But there's a negative side to Greeks' outgoing nature. Eager to engage in conversation over any topic, they won't shy away from launching into political discussions about the state of the economy or foreign policy (best politely avoided) or asking personal questions like how much money you earn. The latter isn't considered rude in Greece, but don't feel like you need to respond. Visitors are sometimes taken aback by Greeks' gestures or the ease in which they touch the person they're speaking with—take it all in stride. If a pat on the hand becomes a bit too intimate, just shift politely and the other person will take a hint. On the other hand, kissing someone you've just met good-bye on the cheek is quite acceptable—even between men.

GREETINGS AND GESTURES

When you meet someone for the first time, it is customary to shake hands, but with acquaintances the usual is a two-cheek kiss hello and good-bye. One thing that may disconcert foreigners is that when they run into a Greek with another person, he or she usually doesn't introduce the other party, even if there is a long verbal exchange. If you can't stand it anymore, just introduce yourself. Greeks tend to stand closer to people than North Americans and northern Europeans, and they rely more on gestures when communicating. One gesture you should never use is the open palm, fingers slightly spread, shoved toward someone's face. The *moutza* is a serious insult. Another gesture you should remember, especially if trying to catch a taxi, is the Greek "no," which looks like "yes": a slight or exaggerated (depending on the sentiment) tipping back of the head, sometimes with the eyes closed and eyebrows raised. When you wave with your palm toward people, they may interpret it as "come here" instead of "good-bye"; and Greeks often wave good-bye with the palm facing them, which looks like "come here" to English speakers.

OUT ON THE TOWN

Greeks often eat out of communal serving plates, so it's considered normal in informal settings to spear your tomato out of the salad bowl rather than securing an individual portion. Sometimes in tavernas you don't even get your own plate. Note that it is considered *tsigounia*, stinginess, to run separate tabs, especially because much of the meal is Chinese-style (to share). Greeks either divide the bill equally among the party, no matter who ate what, or one person magnanimously treats. A good host insists that you eat or drink more, and only when you have refused a number of times will you get a reprieve; be charmingly persistent in your "No." Always keep in mind that Greeks have a loose sense of time! They may be punctual if meeting you to go to a movie, but if they say they'll come round your hotel at 7 pm, they may show up at 8 pm. Don't take it personally unless it's a romantic date!

PHONES

Greece's phone system has improved markedly. You can direct dial in most better hotels, but there is usually a huge surcharge, so use your calling card or a card telephone in the lobby or on the street. You can make calls from most large establishments, kiosks, card phones (which are everywhere), and from the local office of Greece's major telephone company, known as OTE ("oh-*teh*").

Establishments may have several phone numbers rather than a central switchboard. Also, many now use mobile phones, indicated by an area code that begins with 69.

Doing business over the phone in Greece can be frustrating—the lines always seem to be busy, and English-speaking operators and clerks are few. You may also find people too busy to address your problem—the independent-minded Greeks are *not* service-conscious. It is far better to develop a relationship with someone, for example a travel agent, to get information about ferry schedules and the like, or to go in person and ask for information face-to-face. Though OTE has updated its phone system in recent years, it may still take you several attempts to get through when calling from an island or the countryside.

The country code for Greece is 30. When dialing Greece from the United States, Canada, or Australia, you would first dial 011, then 30, the country code, before punching in the area code and local number. From continental Europe, the United Kingdom, or New Zealand, start with 0030.

CALLING WITHIN GREECE

For Greek directory information, dial 11888; many operators speak English. In most cases you must give the surname of the shop or restaurant proprietor to be able to get the phone number of the establishment; tourist police are more helpful for tracking down the numbers of such establishments. For operator-assisted calls and international directory information in English, dial the International Exchange at ☎ 161. In most cases, there is a three-minute minimum charge for operator-assisted station-to-station and person-to-person connections.

Pronunciations for the numbers in Greek are: one ("*eh*-na"); two ("*dthee*-oh"); three ("*tree*-a"); four ("*tess*-ehr-a"); five ("*pen*-de"); six ("*eh*-ksee"); seven ("ef-*ta*"); eight ("och-*toh*"); nine ("eh-*nay*-ah"); ten ("*dtheh*-ka").

All telephone numbers in Greece have 10 digits. Area codes now have to be dialed even when you are dialing locally. For cell phones, dial both the cell prefix (a four-digit number beginning with 69) and the telephone number from anywhere in Greece.

You can make local calls from the public OTE phones using phone cards, not coins, or from kiosks, which have metered telephones and allow you to make local or international calls. The dial ring will be familiar to English speakers: two beats, the second much longer than the first.

OTE has card phones virtually everywhere, though some may not be in working order. If you want more privacy—the card phones tend to be on busy street corners and other people waiting to make calls may try to hurry you—use a card phone in a hotel lobby or OTE offices, though these tend to have limited hours. You can also use a kiosk phone. If you don't get a dial tone at first, you should ask the kiosk owner to set the meter to zero. (*Boreéte na to meetheneésete?*)

CALLING OUTSIDE GREECE

To place an international call from Greece, dial 00 to connect to an international network, then dial the country code (for the United States and Canada, it's 1), and then the area code and number. If you need assistance, call 134 to be connected to an international operator. You can use AT&T, Sprint, and MCI services from public phones as well as from hotels.

Long-Distance Carriers AT&T ☏ *1–800/225–5288.* **MCI-Verizon** ☏ *1–800/888–8000, 1–800/444–3333.* **Sprint** ☏ *1–800/877–7746.*

Access Codes AT&T Direct ☏ *00/800–1311 for Greece, 1–800/225–5288 in U.S.* **MCI-Verizon WorldPhone** ☏ *00/800–1211 for Greece, 1-800/888–8000 in U.S.* **Sprint International Access** ☏ *00/800–1411 for Greece, 1–800/877–4646 in U.S.*

CALLING CARDS

Phone cards worth €4 or €10 can be purchased at kiosks, convenience stores, or the local OTE office and are the easiest way to make calls from anywhere in Greece. These phone cards can be used for domestic and international calls (the Chronocarta phone card especially costs €6 and allows one to talk for up to 290 minutes to U.S. and Canadian land lines and mobile phones). Once you insert the phone card, the number of units on the card will appear; as you begin talking, the units will go down. Once all the units have been used, the card does not get recharged—you must purchase another. The Smile + Web card is another popular OTE product that enables one to place international and local calls from any phone as well as providing Internet access.

MOBILE PHONES

If you have a multiband phone (some countries use different frequencies from what's used in the United States) and your service provider uses the world-standard GSM network (as do T-Mobile, Cingular, and Verizon), you can probably use your phone abroad. Roaming fees can be steep, however: 99¢ a minute is considered reasonable. And overseas you normally pay the toll charges for incoming calls. It's almost always cheaper to send a text message than to make a call, since text messages have a very low set fee (often less than 5¢). In Greek mobile phone contracts, only the caller and not the person receiving the call can be charged for local phone calls (both are charged for international calls, however).

If you just want to make local calls, consider buying a new SIM card (note that your provider may have to unlock your phone for you to use a different SIM card) and a prepaid service plan in the destination. You'll then have a local number and can make local calls at local rates. If your trip is extensive, you could also simply buy a new cell phone in your destination, as the initial cost will be offset over time.

■**TIP→** If you travel internationally frequently, save one of your old mobile phones or buy a cheap one on the Internet; ask your cell phone company to unlock it for you, and take it with you as a travel phone, buying a new SIM card with pay-as-you-go service in each destination.

If you take your cell phone with you, call your provider in advance and ask if it has a connection agreement with a Greek mobile carrier. If so, manually switch your phone to that network's settings as soon as you arrive. To do this, go to the Settings menu, then look for the Network settings and follow the prompts.

If you're traveling with a companion or group of friends and plan to use your cell phones to communicate with each other, buying a local prepaid connection kit is far cheaper for voice calls or sending text messages than using your regular provider. The most popular local prepaid connection kits are Cosmote's What's Up, Vodafone's Unlimited and CU, or Wind's F2G or Card To All—these carriers all have branded stores, but you can also buy cell phones and cell phone packages from the Germanos and Plaisio chain stores as well as large supermarkets like Carrefour.

Contacts Cellular Abroad. This company rents and sells cell phones and sells SIM cards that work in many countries. ☏ *1–800/287–5072, 1–310/862–7100* ⊕ *www.cellularabroad.com.* **Mobal.** This company rents mobiles and sells GSM cell phones (starting at $29) that will operate in more than 170 countries. Per-call rates are charged per minute, there are no monthly or annual service charges and vary throughout the world. ☏ *888/888–9162*

⊕ *www.mobal.com.* **Planet Fone.** This company rents cell phones, but the per-minute rates are expensive. ☎ *1–888/988–4777* ⊕ *www.planetfone.com.*

■ CUSTOMS AND DUTIES

You may bring into Greece duty-free: food and beverages up to 22 pounds (10 kilos); 200 cigarettes, 100 cigarillos, or 50 cigars; 1 liter of alcoholic spirits or 2 liters of wine; and gift articles up to a total of €430. For non-EU citizens, foreign banknotes amounting to more than $2,500 must be declared for re-export, but there are no restrictions on traveler's checks.

Only one per person of such expensive portable items as cameras, camcorders, computers, and the like is permitted into Greece. You should register these with Greek Customs upon arrival to avoid any problems when taking them out of the country again. Sports equipment, such as bicycles and skis, is also limited to one (or one pair) per person. One windsurf board per person may be imported/exported duty-free.

To bring in a dog or a cat, they must have a pet passport and be identified by the electronic identification system (microchip) according to ISO standard 11794 or 11785. They must also have been vaccinated against rabies. Travelling pets must also be accompanied by a health certificate for noncommercial movement of pets (regulation EC No. 998/2003) endorsed by a USDA state veterinarian.

For more information on Greek Customs, check with your local Greek Consulate or the Greek Ministry of Finance in Athens, which has more-detailed information on customs and import/export regulations.

Information in Greece Ministry of Finance - Customs Office ✉ *'El. Venizelos' Athens Airport Customs Office, Spata, Athens* ☎ *210/354–2138 Foreign exchange declaration, 210/354–2122 Information* ⊕ *www.gsis.gr.*

U.S. Information U.S. Customs and Border Protection ⊕ *www.cbp.gov.*

■ EATING OUT

MEALS AND MEALTIMES

Greeks don't really eat breakfast and with the exception of hotel dining rooms, few places serve that meal. You can pick up a cheese pie, a baguette sandwich, and rolls at a bakery or a sesame-coated bread ring called a *koulouri* sold by city vendors; order a *tost* ("toast"), a sort of dry grilled sandwich, usually with cheese or paper-thin ham slices, at a café; or dig into a plate of yogurt with honey. Local bakeries may offer fresh doughnuts in the morning. On the islands in summer, cafés serve breakfast, from Continental to combinations that might include Spanish omelets and French coffee. Caffeine junkies can get a cup of coffee practically anywhere.

Greeks eat their main meal at either lunch or dinner, so the offerings are the same. For lunch, heavyweight meat-and-potato dishes can be had, but you might prefer a real Greek salad (no lettuce, a slice of feta with a pinch of oregano, and ripe tomatoes, cucumber, onions, and green peppers) or souvlaki or grilled chicken from a taverna. For a light bite you can also try one of the popular Greek chain eateries such as Everest or Grigori's, found fairly easily throughout the country, for grilled sandwiches or spanakopita and *tiropita* (cheese pie); or Goody's, the local equivalent of McDonald's, where you'll find good-quality burgers, pasta dishes, and salads.

Coffee and pastries are eaten in the afternoon, usually at a café or *zaharoplastio* (pastry shop). The hour or so before restaurants open for dinner—around 7—is a pleasant time to have an ouzo or glass of wine and try Greek hors d'oeuvres, called *mezedes,* in a bar, ouzeri, or *mezedopoleio* (Greek tapas place). Dinner is often the main meal of the day, and there's plenty of food. Starters include dips such as *taramosalata* (made from fish roe), *melitzanosalata* (made from smoked eggplant, lemon, oil, and garlic), and the well-known yogurt, cucumber, and garlic *tzatziki*. A typical dinner for a couple might be two to three appetizers, an entrée, a salad, and wine. Diners can order as little or as much as they like, except at very expensive establishments. If a Greek eats dessert at all, it will be fruit or a modest wedge of a syrup-drenched cake like *ravani* or semolina halvah, often shared between two or three diners. Only in fancier restaurants might diners order a tiramisu or crème brûleé with an espresso. One option for those who want a lighter, shared meal is the mezedopoleio.

In most places, the menu is broken down into appetizers (*orektika*) and entrées (*kiria piata*), with additional headings for salads (Greek salad or *horta*, boiled wild greens; this also includes dips like tzatziki) and vegetable side plates. However, this doesn't mean there is any sense of a first or second "course," as in France. Often the food arrives all at the same time, or as it becomes ready.

Breakfast is usually available until 10:30 or 11 at many hotels and until early afternoon in beach cafés. Lunch is between 1:00 and 6 (especially during summer months), and dinner is served from about 8:00 to midnight, or even later in the big cities and resort islands. Most Greeks dine very late, around 10 or 11 pm. Unless otherwise noted, the restaurants listed in this guide are open daily for lunch and dinner.

PAYING

For price charts, detailing our array of restaurant price categories, see the Planner section in every regional chapter. For guidelines on tipping see Tipping, below.

RESERVATIONS AND DRESS

Regardless of where you are, it's a good idea to make a reservation if you can. In some places (especially the more upmarket restaurants), it's expected. We only mention them specifically when reservations are essential (there's no other way you'll ever get a table) or when they are

> ## WORD OF MOUTH
>
> Was the service stellar or not up to snuff? Did the food give you shivers of delight or leave you cold? Did the prices and portions make you happy or sad? Rate restaurants and write your own reviews in Travel Ratings or start a discussion about your favorite places in Travel Talk on ⊕ *www.fodors.com.* Your comments might even appear in our books. Yes, you, too, can be a correspondent!

not accepted. For popular restaurants, book as far ahead as you can and reconfirm on the day of your reservation. (Large parties should always call ahead to check the reservations policy.) We mention dress only when men are required to wear a jacket or a jacket and tie.

▌ ELECTRICITY

The electrical current in Greece is 220 volts, 50 cycles AC. Wall outlets take Continental-type plugs with two round oversize prongs. If your appliances are dual-voltage, you'll need only an adapter; if not, you'll also need a step-down converter/transformer (United States and Canada).

Consider making a small investment in a universal adapter, which has several types of plugs in one lightweight, compact unit. Most laptops and mobile phone chargers are dual voltage (i.e., they operate equally well on 110 and 220 volts) so require only an adapter. These days the same is true of small appliances such as hair dryers. Always check labels and manufacturer instructions to be sure. Don't use 110-volt outlets marked "for shavers only" for high-wattage appliances such as hair dryers.

Contacts Steve Kropla's Help for World Travelers. This Web site has information on electrical and telephone plugs around the world. ⊕ *www.kropla.com.* **Walkabout Travel Gear.** This Web site has a good coverage of electricity under "adapters." ⊕ *www.walkabouttravelgear.com.*

▌ EMERGENCIES

Regrettably, vacations are sometimes marred by emergencies, so it's good to know where you should turn for help. In Athens and other cities, hospitals treat emergencies on a rotating basis; an ambulance driver will know where to take you. Or, since waving down a taxi can be faster than waiting for an ambulance, ask a cab driver to take you to the closest *"e-phee-me-re-von"* (duty) hospital. Large islands and rural towns have small medical centers (*iatreio*) that can treat minor illnesses or arrange for transport to another facility.

Medications are only sold at pharmacies, which are by law staffed by licensed pharmacists who can treat minor cuts, take blood pressure, and recommend cold medication. Pharmacies are marked with a green-and-white cross and there's one every few city blocks. Outside standard trading hours, there are duty pharmacies offering 24-hour coverage. These are posted in the window of every pharmacy. The *Athens News,* and *Kathimerini* (the latter is inserted in the *International Herald Tribune*) have listings for pharmacies that are open late on a particular day. And if you speak Greek, you can call for a recorded message listing the off-hours pharmacies. In cases of emergencies, locals are fairly helpful and will come to your aid. The tourist police throughout Greece *(numbers are given in each chapter)* can provide general information and help in emergencies and can mediate in disputes.

Foreign Embassy United States ✉ *Vasilissis Sofias 91, Mavili Sq., Athens* ☏ *210/721–2951 Switchboard* ⊕ *http://athens.usembassy.gov.*

General Emergency Contacts Coast Guard ☏ *108.* **Doctors at Home** ☏ *1151.*

Duty hospitals and pharmacies ☏ *1434, 14944.* **Fire** ☏ *199.* **Forest Service** ☏ *191 in case of fire.* **National Ambulance Service (EKAV)** ☏ *166.* **Off-hours pharmacies** ☏ *1434, 14944.* **Police** ☏ *100.* **Road assistance - ELPA**

☏ *10400.* **S.O.S. Doctors.** This is a 24-hour private medical service. ☏ *1016.* **Tourist Police** ✉ *Veikou 43-45, Athens* ☏ *171 For complaints and reports, valid throughout Greece, 210/920–0730 central office.*

▌ HEALTH

Greece's strong summer sun and low humidity can lead to sunburn or sunstroke if you're not careful. A hat, a light-color long-sleeve shirt, and long pants or a sarong are advised for spending a day at the beach or visiting archaeological sites. Sunglasses, a hat, and sunblock are necessities, and be sure to drink plenty of water. Most beaches present few dangers, but keep a lookout for the occasional jellyfish and, on rocky coves, sea urchins. Should you step on one, don't break off the embedded spines, which may lead to infection, but instead remove them with heated olive oil and a needle. Food is seldom a problem, but the liberal amounts of olive oil used in Greek cooking may be indigestible for some. Tap water in Greece is fine in most urban areas, and bottled spring water is readily available. Avoid drinking tap water in many rural areas. For minor ailments, go to a local pharmacy first, where the licensed staff can make recommendations for over-the-counter drugs. Most pharmacies are closed in the evenings and on weekends, but each posts the name of the nearest pharmacy open off-hours (⇨ *Emergencies, above*). Most state hospitals and rural clinics won't charge you for tending to minor ailments, even if you're not an EU citizen; at most, you'll pay a minimal fee. Hotels will usually call a doctor for you, though in Athens, you can locate a doctor by calling S.O.S. Doctors (⇨ *Emergencies, above*). For a dentist, check with your hotel, embassy, or the tourist police. Do not fly within 24 hours of scuba diving. In greener, wetter areas, mosquitoes may be a problem. In addition to wearing insect repellent, you can burn coils ("spee-rahl") or buy plug-in devices that burn medicated tabs ("pah-*steel*-ya"). Hotels usually provide these. Citronella candles are usually an effective and a more natural way to keep insects away. The only poisonous snakes in Greece are the adder and the sand viper, which are brown or red, with dark zigzags. The adder has a V or X behind its head, and the sand viper sports a small horn on its nose. When hiking, wear high tops and hiking socks and don't put your feet or hands in crevices without looking first. If bitten, try to slow the spread of the venom until a doctor comes. Lie still with the affected limb lower than the rest of your body. Apply a tourniquet, releasing it every few minutes, and cut the wound a bit in case the venom can bleed out. Do NOT suck on the bite. Whereas snakes like to lie in the sun, the scorpion (rare) likes cool, wet places, in woodpiles, and under stones. Apply Benadryl or Phenergan to minor stings, but if you have nausea or fever, see a doctor at once.

▌HOURS OF OPERATION

A new law passed in 2005 set uniform business hours (weekdays 6 am–9 pm, Saturday 6 am–8 pm) for retailers across Greece, leaving each establishment the discretion of establishing its own particular timetable within those limits). Today establishments in tourist resorts may remain open longer, even after midnight. For certain categories such as pharmacies, banks, and government offices, hours have always been standardized, but again there are some establishments in tourist resorts which follow extended hours. Many small businesses and shops in main urban hubs close for at least a week around mid-August, and most tourist establishments, including hotels, shut down on the islands and northern Greece from November until mid-spring. Restaurants, especially tavernas, often stay open on holidays; some close in summer or move to cooler locations. Christmas, New Year's, Orthodox Easter, and August 15 are the days everything shuts down, although, for example, bars work full

force on Christmas Eve, since it's a social occasion and not particularly family-oriented. Orthodox Easter changes dates every year, so check your calendar. On Orthodox Easter Week, most shops follow a different schedule while on Good Friday, shops open after church services, around 1 pm.

Banks are normally open Monday–Thursday 8–2:30, Friday 8–2, but a few branches of Alpha and Eurobank are open until 7 pm weekdays and on Saturday mornings. Hotels also cash traveler's checks on weekends, and the banks at the Athens airport have longer hours.

Government offices are open weekdays from 8 to 2. For commercial offices, the hours depend on the business, although most private companies have by now adopted the 9–5 schedule. The days and hours for public museums and archaeological sites are set by the Ministry of Culture; they are usually open Tuesday–Sunday 8:30 to 3, and as late as 7:30 in summer. (Summer hours are generally published on the ministry's Web site, ⊕ *www.culture.gr*, in April or May.) Throughout the year arrive at least 30 minutes before closing time to ensure a ticket. Archaeological sites and museums close on January 1, March 25, the morning of Orthodox Good Friday, Orthodox Easter, May 1, and December 25–26. Sunday visiting hours apply to museums on Epiphany, Ash Monday, Good Saturday, Easter Monday, and Whitsunday (Orthodox dates, which change every year), August 15, and October 28. Museums close early (around 12:30) on January 2, the last Saturday of Carnival, Orthodox Good Thursday, Christmas Eve, and New Year's Eve. Throughout the guide, the hours of sights and attractions are denoted by the clock icon, ☻.

All gas stations are open daily 6–9 (some close Sunday). These hours are extended during the high season (usually from May 1 to September 30) from 6 am to 10:30 pm and some stations pump all night in the major cities and along the National

Road and Attica Highway. They do not close for lunch.

Department stores, shops, and supermarkets may stay open until 9 pm on weekdays and 8 pm on Saturday, but some merchants are sticking to the old business hours and continue to close on Monday, Wednesday, and Saturday afternoons. There are no Sunday trading hours, except for the last Sunday of the year and in tourist areas like Plaka in Athens and island or mainland resorts.

Pharmacies are open Monday, Wednesday, and Friday from about 8 to 2:30 and Tuesday, Thursday, and Friday from 8 to 2 and 5:30 until 8:30 at night. The pharmacy at Athens International Airport operates 24 hours. According to a rotation system, there is always at least one pharmacy open in any area (⇨ *Emergencies, above)*.

If it's late in the evening and you need an aspirin, a soft drink, cigarettes, a newspaper, or a pen, look for the nearest open kiosk, called a *periptero*; these kiosks on street corners everywhere brim with all kinds of necessities. Owners stagger their hours, and many towns have at least one kiosk that stays open late, occasionally through the night. Neighborhood minimarkets also stay open late.

HOLIDAYS FOR CALENDAR YEAR 2012

January 1 (New Year's Day); January 6 (Epiphany); Clean Monday (first day of Lent); March 25 (Feast of the Annunciation and Independence Day); Good Friday; Greek Easter Sunday; Greek Easter Monday; May 1 (Labor Day); Pentecost; August 15 (Assumption of the Holy Virgin); October 28 (Ochi Day); December 25–26 (Christmas Day and Boxing Day).

Only on Orthodox Easter and August 15 do you find that just about *everything* shuts down. It's harder getting a room at the last minute on Easter and August 15 (especially the latter), and traveling requires stamina, if you want to survive on the ferries and the highways. On the other hand, the local rituals and rites associated with these two celebrations are interesting and occasionally moving (like the Epitaphios procession on Good Friday).

▌ MAIL

Letters and postcards take about five days to reach the United States. That's airmail. It takes even longer in August, when postal staff is reduced; and during Christmas and Easter holidays. If what you're mailing is important, send it registered, which costs about €3.25 in Greece. For about €2.20 for a 20-gram envelope or postcard (with the cost increasing depending on the weight), you can send your letter "express"; this earns you a red sticker and faster local delivery. The ELTA post office also operates a courier service, EMS Express (otherwise known as ELTA courier). Delivery to the continental United States takes about two to four days, and costs €40. Packages take three to five days and cost depends on the weight. If you're planning on writing several letters, prepaid envelopes are convenient and cost €0.95 each.

Post offices are open weekdays 7:30–2, although in city centers they may stay open in the evenings and on weekends. The main post offices in Athens and Piraeus are open weekdays 7:30 am–8 pm, Saturday 7:30–2, and Sunday 9–1:30. The post offices at Athens International Airport and the Acropolis are open weekends, too. Throughout the country, mailboxes are yellow and sometimes divided into domestic and international containers; express boxes are red.

At this writing, airmail letters and postcards to destinations other than Europe and weighing up to 20 grams cost €0.75, and €1.30 for 50 grams (€0.75 and €1.15, respectively, to other European countries, including the United Kingdom).

Contacts ELTA Courier ☎ *800/118–3000* ⊕ *www.elta-courier.gr.* **Hellenic Post (ELTA)** ☎ *800/118–2000 Toll-free, 210/335–3777* ⊕ *www.elta.gr.*

∎ MONEY

Although costs have risen astronomically since Greece switched to the euro currency in 2002, the country will seem reasonably priced to travelers from the United States and Great Britain. Popular tourist resorts (including some of the islands) and the larger cities are markedly more expensive than the countryside. Though the price of eating in a restaurant has increased, you can still get a bargain. Hotels are generally moderately priced outside the major cities, and the extra cost of accommodations in a luxury hotel, compared to in an average hotel, often seems unwarranted.

ITEM	AVERAGE COST
Cup of Coffee	€2.50–€5 (in a central-city café; Greek coffee is a bit cheaper)
Glass of Wine	€5–€8
Glass of Beer	€3.5; €5–€9 in a bar
Sandwich	€2.80–€4
1-mile (½-km) Taxi Ride in Capital City	€3.50
Archaeo-logical Site Admission	€2–€6

Other typical costs: soft drink (can) €1.50, in a café €2.5; spinach pie, €2.20; souvlaki, €2.50; local bus, €1.20; foreign newspaper, €3–€5.30.

Prices throughout this guide are given for adults. Reduced fees are almost always available for children, students, and senior citizens.

∎TIP➔ Banks never have every foreign currency on hand, and it may take as long as a week to order. If you're planning to exchange funds before leaving home, don't wait until the last minute.

ATMS AND BANKS

Your own bank will probably charge a fee for using ATMs abroad; the foreign bank you use may also charge a fee. Nevertheless, you'll usually get a better rate of exchange at an ATM than you will at a currency-exchange office or even when changing money in a bank. And extracting funds as you need them is a safer option than carrying around a large amount of cash.

∎TIP➔ PIN numbers with more than four digits are not recognized at ATMs in many countries. If yours has five or more, remember to change it before you leave.

ATMs are widely available throughout the country. Virtually all banks, including the National Bank of Greece (known as Ethniki), have machines that dispense money to Cirrus or Plus cardholders. You may find bank-sponsored ATMs at harbors and in airports as well. Other systems accepted include Visa, MasterCard, American Express, Diners Club, and Eurocard, but exchange and withdrawal rates vary, so shop around and check fees with your bank before leaving home. For use in Greece, your PIN must be four digits long. The word for PIN is pronounced "peen," and ATMs are called *alpha taf mi*, after the letters, or just *to mihanima*, "the machine." Machines usually let you complete the transaction in English, French, or German and seldom create problems, except Sunday night, when they sometimes run out of cash. For most machines, the minimum amount dispensed is €20. Sometimes an ATM may refuse to "read" your card. Don't panic; it's probably the machine. Try another bank.

∎TIP➔ At some ATMs in Greece you may not have a choice of drawing from a specific account. If you have linked savings and checking accounts, make sure there's money in both before you depart.

CREDIT CARDS

It's a good idea to inform your credit-card company before you travel, especially if you're going abroad and don't travel internationally very often. Otherwise, the credit-card company might put a hold on your card owing to unusual activity—not a good thing halfway through your trip. Record all your credit-card numbers—as well as the phone numbers to call if your cards are lost or stolen—in a safe place, so you're prepared should something go wrong. Both MasterCard and Visa have general numbers you can call (collect if you're abroad) if your card is lost, but you're better off calling the number of your issuing bank, since MasterCard and Visa usually just transfer you to your bank; your bank's number is usually printed on your card.

If you plan to use your credit card for cash advances, you'll need to apply for a PIN at least two weeks before your trip. Although it's usually cheaper (and safer) to use a credit card abroad for large purchases (so you can cancel payments or be reimbursed if there's a problem), note that some credit-card companies *and* the banks that issue them add substantial percentages to all foreign transactions, whether they're in a foreign currency or not. Check on these fees before leaving home, so there won't be any surprises when you get the bill.

■TIP➔ Before you charge something, ask the merchant whether or not he or she plans to do a dynamic currency conversion (DCC). In such a transaction the credit-card *processor* (shop, restaurant, or hotel, not Visa or MasterCard) converts the currency and charges you in dollars. In most cases you'll pay the merchant a 3% fee for this service in addition to any credit-card company and issuing-bank foreign-transaction surcharges.

Dynamic currency conversion programs are becoming increasingly widespread. Merchants who participate in them are supposed to ask whether you want to be charged in dollars or the local currency, but they don't always do so. And even if they do offer you a choice, they may well avoid mentioning the additional surcharges. The good news is that you *do* have a choice. And if this practice really gets your goat, you can avoid it entirely thanks to American Express; with its cards, DCC simply isn't an option.

Should you use a credit card or a debit card when traveling? Both have benefits. A credit card allows you to delay payment and gives you certain rights as a consumer. A debit card, also known as a check card, deducts funds directly from your checking account and helps you stay within your budget. When you want to rent a car, though, you may still need an old-fashioned credit card.

Both types of plastic get you cash advances at ATMs worldwide if your card is properly programmed with your personal identification number (PIN). Both offer excellent, wholesale exchange rates. And both protect you against unauthorized use if the card is lost or stolen. Your liability is limited to $50, as long as you report the card missing. However, shop owners often give you a lower price if you pay with cash rather than credit, because they want to avoid the credit-card bank fees. Note that the Discover card is not widely accepted in Greece.

Reporting Lost Cards American Express ☏ *1-800/528-4800 in U.S., 715/343-7977 collect from abroad* ⊕ *www.americanexpress. com.* **Diners Club** ☏ *800/234-6377 in U.S., 1-303/799-1504 collect from abroad* ⊕ *www. dinersclub.com.* **Discover** ☏ *1-800/347-2683 in U.S., 1-801/902-3100 collect from abroad* ⊕ *www.discovercard.com.* **MasterCard** ☏ *1-800/627-8372 in U.S., 1-636/722-7111 collect from abroad, 800-11/887-0303 in Greece, toll free* ⊕ *www.mastercard.com.* **Visa** ☏ *800/847-2911 in U.S., 1-303/967-1096 collect from abroad, 800-11/638-0304 toll-free in Greece* ⊕ *www.visa.com.*

CURRENCY AND EXCHANGE

Greece's former national currency, the drachma, was replaced by the currency of the European Union, the euro (€), on the first of January 2001. Under the euro system, there are eight coins: 1 and 2 euros, plus 1, 2, 5, 10, 20, and 50 euro cents. Euros are pronounced "evros" in Greek; cents are known as "lepta." All coins have the euro value on one side; the other side has each country's unique national symbol. Greece's range from images of triremes to a depiction of the mythological Europa being abducted by Zeus transformed as a bull. Bills (banknotes) come in seven denominations: 5, 10, 20, 50, 100, 200, and 500 euros. Bills are the same for all EU countries.

Off Syntagma Square in Athens, the National Bank of Greece, Alpha Bank, Commercial Bank, Eurobank, and Pireos Bank have automated machines that change your foreign currency into euros. When you shop, remember that it's always easier to bargain on prices when paying in cash instead of by credit card.

If you do use an exchange service, good options are American Express and Eurochange. Watch daily fluctuations and shop around. Daily exchange rates are prominently displayed in banks and listed in the *International Herald Tribune*. In Athens, around Syntagma Square is the best place to look. In some tourist resorts you might be able to change money at the post office, where commissions may be lower than at banks. To avoid lines at airport exchange booths, get a bit of local currency before you leave home. At this writing the average exchange rate for the euro was €0.69 to the U.S. dollar, €0.99 to the Canadian dollar, €0.62 to the pound sterling, €0.95 to the Australian dollar, and €1.20 to the New Zealand dollar.

■TIP➜ Even if a currency-exchange booth has a sign promising no commission, rest assured that there's some kind of substantial, hidden fee. (Oh . . . that's right. The sign didn't say no fee.) And as for rates, you're almost always better off getting foreign currency at an ATM or exchanging money at a bank.

Eurochange ✉ *Karageorgi Servias 2, Syntagma Sq., Athens* ☎ *210/331-2462* ⊕ *www.eurochange.gr* ⊙ *Sun.-Fri. 9-9, Sat. 9-4* ✉ *Marikas Kotopouli 10, Omonia Sq., Athens* ☎ *210/522-0314* ⊙ *Daily 9-9.* **Kapa Change** ✉ *Filellinon 1, Syntagma, Athens* ☎ *210/331-3830* ⊕ *www.kapachange.gr* ⊙ *Mon.-Sat. 8:30-8:30, Sun. 8:30-5.* **Bank of**

Greece. Greece's Central Bank offers foreign exchange at competitive rates. ✉ *21 Panepistimiou (El. Venizelou) Ave., Syntagma, Athens* ☎ *210/320-1111* ⊕ *www.bankofgreece. gr* ⊙ *Mon.-Thurs. 8-2:30, Fri. 8-2.* **National Bank of Greece.** This offers extended foreign exchange. ✉ *Karageorgi Servias 2, Syntagma, Athens* ☎ *210/334-8015* ⊙ *Mon.-Thurs. 8-2:30, Fri. 8-2.*

■ PASSPORTS AND VISAS

All citizens (even infants) of the United States, Canada, Australia, and New Zealand need only a valid passport to enter Greece for stays of up to 90 days. Your passport should be valid for at least three months beyond the period of your stay. If you leave after 90 days and don't have a visa extension, you will be fined anywhere from €600 to €1,300 (depending on how long you overstay) by Greek airport officials, who are not flexible on this issue. Even worse perhaps, you must provide *hartosima* (revenue stamps) for the documents, which you don't want to have to run around and find as your flight is boarding. If you want to extend your stay beyond 90 days, there is heavy bureaucracy involved but eventually you will be able to do it for a cost of about €150. Enquire at your local police station for details.

If you are going to visit Greece, you can enroll to the Smart Traveler Enrollment Program of the U.S. Embassy in Greece. Then, you can be kept up to date with important safety and security announcements. Enrolling also will help your friends and family get in touch with you in an emergency.

PASSPORTS

U.S. passports are valid for 10 years. You must apply in person if you're getting a passport for the first time; if your previous passport was lost, stolen, or damaged; or if your previous passport has expired and was issued more than 15 years ago or when you were under 16. All children under 18 must appear in person to apply for or renew a passport. Both parents must accompany any child under 16 (or send a notarized statement with their permission) and provide proof of their relationship to the child.

■**TIP→** Before your trip, make two copies of your passport's data page (one for someone at home and another for you to carry separately). Or scan the page and e-mail it to someone at home and/or yourself.

There are 24 regional passport agencies, as well as 9,000 passport acceptance facilities in post offices, public libraries, and other governmental offices. If you're renewing a passport, you can do so by mail. Forms are available at passport acceptance facilities and online. If you are in a hurry, the regional passport agencies are the places to go to, as the procedure can take less than 2 weeks.

The cost to apply in-person for a new passport is $135 for adults, $105 for children under 16; renewals are $110 (note: it's cheaper by mail). Allow four to six weeks for processing, both for first-time passports and renewals. For an expediting fee of $60 plus overnight delivery costs you can reduce this time to about two to three weeks. If your trip is less than two weeks away, you can get a passport even more rapidly by going to a passport office with the necessary documentation. Private expediters can get things done in as little as 48 hours but charge hefty fees for their services.

VISAS

On the U.S. Visa for Greece front, there is important news. On April 5, 2010, Greece was finally admitted into the U.S. Visa Waiver Program, which enables nationals of 36 participating countries to travel to the United States for tourism or business (visitor [B] visa purposes only) for stays of 90 days or less without obtaining a visa. The program was established to eliminate unnecessary barriers to travel, stimulating the tourism industry, and permitting the Department of State to focus consular resources in other areas.

This means that U.S. citizens travelling to Greece no longer need to have a visa either. Greece is a party to the Schengen Agreement. As such, U.S. citizens may enter Greece for up to 90 days for tourist or business purposes without a visa. Your passport should be valid for at least three months beyond the period of your stay. You may also need to demonstrate at the port of entry (or during the visa interview if you are applying for a visa) that you have sufficient funds for your trip and that you have a return airline ticket.

There are 25 European countries that are party to the Schengen Agreement. Once you enter one Schengen country you may travel continuously for up to 90 days within the member countries. Within the Schengen area, you do not show your passport when crossing country borders.

If you are traveling for business or tourism you don't need a visa for the initial entry into the Schengen area, but you must have a passport valid three months beyond the proposed stay. For example, for a two-week business trip, the passport must be valid for four months; for a two-month holiday the passport must be valid for five months.

Travelers for business or tourism are permitted to stay in the Schengen area for 90 days within a six-month period. Once the 90-day maximum is reached, leaving for a brief period and reentering the area does not entitle a traveler to 90 more days within the Schengen states. The traveler would have to remain outside the Schengen zone for 90 days before reentering without a visa. Immigration officers at the port of entry have the right to determine whether your planned activities are consistent with business or tourism. You should check with the embassy or consulate of the country to which you are traveling if you have questions about whether your proposed trip qualifies for visa-free travel. U.S. embassies cannot intervene on behalf of U.S. citizens who are denied entry into a foreign country.

For other entry requirements to Greece, U.S travelers should contact the **Embassy of Greece** (✉ 2221 Massachusetts Avenue NW, Washington, DC 20008 ☎ 202/939–1300), or the Greek Consulate in Atlanta, Boston, Chicago, Houston, Los Angeles, Tampa, New York, or San Francisco.

Although European Union regulations require that non-EU visitors obtain a stamp in their passports upon initial entry to a Schengen country, many borders are not staffed with officers carrying out this function. If you want to be sure your entry is properly documented, you must ask for a stamp at an official point of entry. Without the stamp, you may be questioned and asked to prove how long you have been staying in Schengen countries when you leave.

U.S. Passport Information U.S. Department of State ☎ *1–877/487–2778* ⊕ *travel.state. gov/passport.*

U.S. Passport and Visa Expediters A. Briggs Passport and Visa Expediters ☎ *1–800/806–0581, 1–202/338–0111* ⊕ *www.abriggs.com.* **American Passport** ☎ *1–800/455–5166* ⊕ *http://americanpassport.com.* **Travel Document Systems** ☎ *1–888/874–5100 San Francisco office, 202/638–3800 Washington, 1–877/874–5104 New York* ⊕ *www.traveldocs. com.* **Travel the World Visas** ☎ *1–866/886–8472, 202/223–8822* ⊕ *www.world-visa.com.*

▌TAXES

Taxes are always included in the stated price, unless otherwise noted. The Greek airport tax (€12 for travel within the EU and €22 outside the EU) is included in your ticket (as are a further €29 terminal facility charge and a €5 passenger security charge), and the 6.5% hotel tax rate is usually included in the quoted price (note that tax is a high 23% for meals in the hotels).

Value-added tax, 6.5% for books and 23% (VAT is 30% less on some remote Aegean islands, i.e., 15%) for almost everything else, called FPA (pronounced "fee-pee-ah") by Greeks, is included in the cost of most consumer goods and services, including most groceries. If you are a citizen of a non-EU country, you may get a V.A.T. refund on products (except alcohol, cigarettes, or toiletries) worth €120 or more bought in Greece in one shopping spree from licensed stores that usually display a Tax-Free Shopping sticker in their window. Ask the shop to complete a refund form called a Tax-Free Check receipt for you, which you show at Greek customs.

Have the form stamped like any customs form by customs officials when you leave the country or, if you're visiting several European Union countries, when you leave the EU. Be ready to show customs officials what you've bought (pack purchases together, in your carry-on luggage); budget extra time for this. After you're through passport control, take the form to a refund-service counter for an on-the-spot refund, or mail it back in the pre-addressed envelope given to you at the store. You receive the total refund stated on the form, but the processing time can be long, especially if you request a credit-card adjustment. Note that there are no cash refunds issued in the United States anymore.

If you are leaving from the El. Venizelos airport for a country outside the EU, after your Tax-Free Check form has been stamped, you can go directly to the Euro-change bureau de change (extra-Schengen area, Gates 1–4) and get your refund cash.

A refund service can save you some hassle, for a fee. Global Blue is a Europe-wide service with 300,000 affiliated stores and more than 200 international tax refund offices at major airports and border crossings. The service issues refunds in the form of cash, check, or credit-card adjustment, minus a processing fee. If you don't have time to wait at the refund counter, you can mail in the form instead.

V.A.T. Refunds Global Blue ☎ *+421/232–111111* ⊕ *www.global-blue.com.*

▊ TIME

Greek time is Greenwich Mean Time (GMT) plus two hours. To estimate the time back home, subtract 7 hours from the local time for New York and Washington, 8 hours for Chicago, 9 for Denver, and 10 for Los Angeles. Londoners subtract two hours. Those living in Sydney or Melbourne, add eight hours. Greek Daylight Saving Time starts on the last Sunday in March and ends the last Sunday in October. Stay alert—newspapers barely publicize the change.

▊ TIPPING

How much to tip in Greece, especially at restaurants, is confusing and is usually up to the discretion of the individual.

▊ TOURS

In Greece, there are a variety of guided tours and special-interest or cultural programs organized throughout the country. Top of the list is reserved for True Greece, a dazzling outfitter run by Christos Stergiou, a Brandeis and Stamford grad who is one of the most personable guys around. He has put together a crack team of guides who blend local knowledge with a chic, international spin, and wrapped everything up in deftly designed tours to the most idyllic islands, best city finds, and luxury hangouts. Yes, his array of pricey tours is aimed at high rollers but every penny has been intelligently allotted and with the finest taste, culture, and chill-out ratios going, you get your money's worth and then some. Stergiou has been called one of the world's Top Travel Specialists by *Condé Nast Traveler,* so if you want to enjoy a superbly stylish way to tour and get acquainted with the best Greece has to offer, check out his enticingly informative Web site for all the details. Although headquartered in the Cayman Islands, True Greece has an office in Greenbrae, California, and Marousi, Greece.

TIPPING GUIDELINES FOR GREECE	
Bartender	10% maximum
Bellhop	€1 per bag
Hotel Concierge	€3–€5, if he or she performs a service for you
Hotel Maid	Up to €10 per stay
Hotel Room-Service Waiter	€2–€3 per delivery, even if a service charge has been added
Porter at Airport or Train Station	€1 per bag
WSW Skycap Services at Airport	€1–€3 per bag checked
Taxi Driver	Round up the fare to the nearest €0.50 or €1
Tour Guide	10% of fee
Waiter	By law a 13% service charge is figured into the price of a meal. However, it is customary to round up the bill if the service was satisfactory. During the Christmas and Greek Easter holiday periods, restaurants tack on an obligatory 18% holiday bonus to your bill for the waiters.
Others	For restroom attendants €1–2 is appropriate. People dispensing programs at theaters get about €2.

Skyros Holidays on the isle of Skyros run the Skyros Center and the Atsitsa Retreat, which organize local island tours as part of a broader program of yoga, writing, and other life-enhancing activities. Culinary Sanctuaries is based in Crete and run by Nikki Rose, who puts together fascinating customized tours with an emphasis on traditional Mediterranean cuisine. In addition, the Spirit of Life Centre offers holistic workshops near the southern Peloponnese city of Kalamata, visiting several ancient sites nearby such us Corinth and Epidauros. In Athens, Greek Fork's team of dedicated foodies (Helena

Iatrou, Maria Paravantes, and Karitas Mitragogos) organizes culinary tours of Athens' lively street markets and arranges cooking classes that give insight into the preparation of authentic Greek cuisine.

Contacts Crete's Culinary Sanctuaries ⊕ *www.cookingincrete.com.* **The Greek Fork.** Culinary tours of Athens, and cooking classes dedicated to authentic Greek cuisine. ⊠ *P.O. Box 17131, Athens* ☎ *6986-957862, 6986-957863* ⊕ *www.thegreekfork.com.* **Skyros Centre** ⊠ *9 Eastcliff Rd., Shanklin, Isle of Wight,England* ☎ *0044 (0)1983/865566* ⊕ *www.skyros.com.* **Spirit of Life Centre** ⊠ *Agios Nikolaos, Messinia, Peloponnese* ☎ *27210/78240* ⊕ *www.thespiritoflife.co.uk.* **True Greece** ⊠ *Box 309GT, Ugland House, South Church St., Georgetown, Grand Cayman, Cayman Islands* ☎ *1-800/817-7098, 210/612-0656 in Greece* ⊕ *www.truegreece.com.*

▌ VISITOR INFORMATION

Tourist police, stationed near the most-popular tourist sites, can answer questions in English about transportation, steer you to an open pharmacy or doctor, and locate phone numbers of hotels, rooms, and restaurants. Also helpful are the municipal tourism offices. You can contact the Greek National Tourism Organization (GNTO; EOT in Greece), as well, which has offices throughout the world.

The complete *Greek Travel Pages,* a monthly publication available at the international bookstore Eleftheroudakis (its main branch is located in the center of Athens), lists travel agencies; yacht brokers; bus, boat, and airplane schedules; and museum hours.

In Greece EOT ⊠ *Tsocha 7, Ambelokipi, Athens* ☎ *210/870-7000* ⊕ *www.visitgreece.gr* ☾ *8-3* ⊠ *El. Venizelos' Athens International Airport, Spata* ☎ *210/354-5101* ⊠ *Tsimiski 136, Thessaloniki* ☎ *2310/2211000* ⊠ *"Makedonia," Thessaloniki International Airport, Thessaloniki* ☎ *2310/471170* ⊠ *Filopimenos 26, Patras* ☎ *2610/620353.*

In the United States Greek National Tourism Organization - GNTO ⊠ *305 East 47th St., New York, New York* ☎ *212/421-5777* ⊕ *www.greektourism.com.*

Guide Eleftheroudakis International Book Store ⊠ *Panepistimiou 11, Athens* ☎ *210/325-8440* ⊕ *www.books.gr.* **Greek Travel Pages** ⊠ *International Publications Ltd., Psylla 6, Athens* ☎ *210/324-7511* ⊕ *www. gtp.gr.*

ONLINE TRAVEL TOOLS

Although the brunt of the Web sites listed in this book have English translations (look for the American or British flag), there are a few that don't, or that aren't fully translated. If you hit upon a site that's Greek to you, try Yahoo's's Babel Fish Translation site (⊕ *babelfish. yahoo.com*), which converts Greek text and some Web sites to English: just paste in a block of text or the site's URL, select "Greek to English" and hit "Translate." The translations can be amusingly literal but are often sufficient for finding out information like opening hours and prices. Google also has a similar translation facility.

ALL ABOUT GREECE

The Web site of the Greek National Tourism Organization (GNTO, or EOT in Greek) is a good starting point for travelers: ⊕ *www.gnto.gr* (or, equivalently, its mirror site ⊕ *www.visitgreece.com*). You can also research the official Web site of Athens (⊕ *www.cityofathens.gr*); the site of the Hellenic Ministry of Culture (⊕ *www.culture.gr*) has basic information about museums, monuments, and archaeological sites. Packed with info about traveling by ferry are ⊕ *www. greekferries.gr* and *www.ferries.gr*, which let you book online. Another source for ferry schedules is ⊕ *www.gtp.gr.* And you can check the Greek weather forecast on ⊕ *www.meteo.gr.*

SPECIAL INTEREST

The Athens Festival site, ⊕ *www. greekfestival.gr*, lists summer programs for the Athens Festival and the Festival

WORD OF MOUTH

After your trip, be sure to rate the places you visited and share your experiences and travel tips with us and other Fodorites in Travel Ratings and Talk on ⊕ *www.fodors. com.*

of Epidauros. The site of the Athens Concert Hall, ⊕ *www.megaron.gr,* describes all the activities at this venue, while the recently inaugurated Onassis Cultural Center also has a Web site (⊕ *www.sgt. gr*). A good resource guide to ancient Greece is ⊕ *www.ancientgreece.com.* A noted Web site about all Greek coasts is ⊕ *www.archipelago.gr* which includes maps and information about water quality at beaches, sailing, and sea life. The Foundation for Environmental Education awards the Blue Flag designation to beaches, including those in Greece, that are clean, safe, and environmentally aware; ⊕ *www.blueflag.org* has details.

Currency Conversion Google ⊕ *www. google.com.* **Oanda.com** ⊕ *www.oanda.com.* **XE.com** ⊕ *www.xe.com.*

INDEX

PHOTO CREDITS

1, Barry Fishman, Fodors.com member. 3, Alfred Rijnders/iStockphoto. **Chapter 1: Experience Greece:** 6-7, SUETONE Emilio/age fotostock. 8, aggsPanorama, Fodors.com member. 9 (left), Evy73, Fodors.com member. 9 (right), Pascal Arseneau, Fodors.com member. 10, Pierdelune/Shutterstock. 11 (left), Natalia Pavlova/iStockphoto. 11 (right), Georgios Alexandris/Shutterstock. 12, Greek National Tourism Organization. 13 (left), Meredith, Fodors.com member. 13 (right), Saso Novoselic/iStockphoto. 18, David Kriegman, Fodors.com member. 19 (left), Fred Goldstein/Shutterstock. 19 (right), Tim Harper, Fodors.com member. 20 (left), Marc C. Johnson/Shutterstock. 20 (top center), byrdiegyrl/Flickr. 20 (bottom center), Betsy Bobo, Fodors.com member. 20 (right), Karel Gallas/Shutterstock. 21 (left), Blue-Orange Studio/Shutterstock. 21 (top center), PixAchi/Shutterstock. 21 (bottom center), baldovina/Shutterstock. 21 (right), Karel Gallas/iStockphoto. 22, terry harris just greece photo library/Alamy. 23, Tommaso di Girolamo/age fotostock. 24, Graham McLellan/Flickr. 25 (left), Cheryl Jenkins, fodors.com member. 25 (right), Tim Arbaev/Shutterstock. 28, Wolfgang Staudt/Flickr. 30, Kreder Katja/age fotostock. 32 (top), Andreas G. Karelias/Shutterstock. 32 (bottom), Wolfgang Staudt/Flickr. 33 (top), Juergen Richter/age fotostock. 33 (bottom), Netfalls/Shutterstock. 34 (left), Milos Jokic/iStockphoto. 34 (top right), Anders Ljungberg/Flickr. 34 (bottom right), Alfred Rijnders/iStockphoto. 35, Vandelizer/Flickr. 36, Johanna Huber/SIME/eStock Photo. **Chapter 2: Cruising the Greek Islands:** 37, Danny Lehman/Princess Cruises. 38, Sidell Chase/iStockphoto. 48, Marco Simoni/age fotostock. 58, Khirman Vladimir/Shutterstock. **Chapter 3: Athens:** 67, SuperStock/age fotostock. 70, Andreas Trepte/wikipedia.org. 84-85, SIME s.a.s/eStock Photo. 86, Vidler/age fotostock. 87, Kord.com/age fotostock. 90, Juha-Pekka Kervinen/Shutterstock. 91, Green Bear/Shutterstock. 92 and 93 (left and right), Nikos Daniilidis. 94 (top left), Javier Larrea/age fotostock. 94 (bottom left and bottom right), Visual Arts Library (London)/Alamy. 94 (top right), wikipedia.org. 95 (top left), Mary Evans Picture Library/Alamy. 95 (top right), Picture History. 95 (bottom), POPPERFOTO/Alamy. 102, George Kavallierakis/age fotostock. 115, P. Narayan/age fotostock. 118, bobthenavigator, Fodors.com member. 123, Stefan Obermeier/age fotostock. 130, rj lerich/Shutterstock. 131 (top), Adam Przezak/Shutterstock. 131 (bottom), kozcank/Shutterstock. 138, Ingolf Pompe 24/Alamy. 151, Alvaro Leiva/age fotostock. 155 (top), Hotel Grande Bretagne/Starwood Hotels & Resorts. 155 (bottom), Baby Grand Hotel/leonardo.com. 161, Fvie Fylaktou. 167, vittorio sciosia/age fotostock. 168 (top left), Elpis Ioannidis/Shutterstock. 168 (bottom left), Bridget McGill/iStockphoto. 168 (right), Charles Stirling (Travel)/Alamy. 169 (left), Amal Sajdak/iStockphoto. 169 (top right), Inger Anne Hulbækdal/Shutterstock. 169 (bottom right), Rene Mattes/age fotostock. 170, Greece/Alamy. **Chapter 4: The Saronic Gulf Islands:** 173, TTL Images/Alamy. 174, byrdiegyrl/Flickr. 175 (top), Jeje42/wikipedia.org. 175 (bottom), Evy73, Fodors.com member. 176, byrdiegyrl/Flickr. 186, SGM/age fotostock. 189, Natalia Pavlova/iStockphoto. 195, vlas2000/Shutterstock. 196 (top), LOOK Die Bildagentur der Fotografen GmbH/Alamy. 196 (bottom), franco pizzochero/age fotostock. 197 (top), Alvaro Leiva/age fotostock. 197 (bottom), Ingolf Pompe/Aurora Photos. 198 (top), foodfolio/Alamy. 198 (2nd from top), Liv friis-larsen/Shutterstock. 198 (3rd from top), imagebroker/Alamy. 198 (4th from top), Colin Dutton/SIME s.a.s/eStock Photo. 198 (bottom), IML Image Group Ltd/Alamy. 199 (left), Roberto Meazza/IML Image Group/Aurora Photos. 199 (top right), Christopher Leggett/age fotostock. 199 (center right), IML Image Group Ltd/Alamy. 199 (bottom right), Ingolf Pompe/Aurora Photos. 203, IML Image Group Ltd/Alamy. 207, vaggelis Vlahos/wikipedia.org. 209, IML Image Group Ltd/Alamy. **Chapter 5: The Sporades:** 211, SIME s.a.s/eStock Photo. 212, Milos Jokic/iStockphoto. 213 (top), iStockphoto. 213 (bottom left), David Newton/iStockphoto. 213 (bottom right), Paul Phillips/iStockphoto. 214, David Newton/iStockphoto. 215 (top), Eleni Sagia/wikipedia.org. 215 (bottom), Dimitrios Rizopoulos/Shutterstock. 216, philos from Athens/Flickr. 226, nevio doz/age fotostock. 232, mediacolor's/Alamy. 236, 238, and 242, Robert Harding Produc/age fotostock. 246 and 250, Genetzakis/IML/age fotostock. **Chapter 6: Corfu:** 253, PCL/Alamy. 254 (top), sanderovski & linda/Flickr. 254 (bottom), Philippe Teuwen/wikipedia.org. 255 (top), Ljupco Smokovski/Shutterstock. 255 (bottom), Netfalls/Shutterstock. 256, bbobo, Fodors.com member. 267, Ellen Rooney/age fotostock. 274, Werner Otto/age fotostock. 278, Giovanni Simeone/SIME/eStock Photo. 281, Ljupco Smokovski/Shutterstock. **Chapter 7: The Cyclades:** 283, Barry Fishman, Fodors.com member. 284, Petros Tsonis/Shutterstock. 285, byrdiegyrl/Flickr. 286, Moustafellou/IML/age fotostock. 287 (top), hassan abdel-rahman/Flickr. 287 (bottom), Gina Halkias-Seugling, Fodors.com member. 288, Barry Fishman, Fodors.com member. 296, Kord.com/age fotostock. 297, stefg74/Flickr. 298, Ingolf Pompe 3/Alamy. 299, LOOK Die Bildagentur der Fotografen GmbH/Alamy. 309, San Rostro/age fotostock. 313, Willine Thoe, Fodors.com member. 318, Marco Simoni/age fotostock. 319, volk65/Shutterstock. 322, Anthro/Shutterstock. 324, Danilo Ascione/Shutterstock. 329, Hemis /Alamy. 335, Cheryl Jenkins, Fodors.com member. 342, Timothy Miller, Fodors.com member. 349, Spyropoulos/IML/age fotostock. 356, Dennis Cox/age fotostock. 364, Apollofoto/Shutterstock. 366, Wolfgang Amri/Shut-

ABOUT OUR WRITERS

Alexia Amvrazi was born and raised in Rome, and then enjoyed an international education in Italy, Egypt, Greece, and her university years in the U.K. She has been based in Greece since the mid 1990s. While working as a journalist in English-language newspapers, magazines, TV, and radio media in Athens, her main energies have gone into producing and hosting a live interview radio show on the City of Athens's 16-language station. In addition, she has hosted on-air poetry and book readings, music performances, and cultural debates and loves to offer her listeners fascinating information on lifestyle, food and wine, travel, news, and survival tips for life in Greece. Alexia has recently relocated to Laconia, where she works and lives with her husband on the Eumelia organic farm, organizing workshops on permaculture, yoga, and holistic living. For this edition, she updated our Sporades chapter.

Jeffrey and Elizabeth Carson, native New Yorkers, have lived on Paros since 1970; they teach at the Aegean Center for the Fine Arts. Jeffrey, a poet, translator, and critic, has published many articles and books. Elizabeth is a photographer who has been published widely, including the book *The Church of 100 Doors*. For this edition, they updated our Cyclades chapter, along with its photo features on mythology, Atlantis, and (with Liam Storms, Edward Prendergast, and novelist Jeffrey Siger) Mykonos.

Linda Coffman, Fodor's resident Cruise Diva and author of this edition's "Cruising the Greek Islands" chapter, is a freelance travel writer for many magazines. For Fodor's, her most recent books are *The Complete Guide to Caribbean Cruises* and *The Complete Guide to European Cruises*.

Angelike Contis is living in New York after a decade spent in Greece and is on the staff of the National Herald weekly newspaper. She makes independent documentaries, including films about the 2004 Olympic Games and on Athens's stray dogs. For this edition, she cowrote the What's New/Greece Today sections of our Experience Greece chapter.

Natasha Giannousi-Varney is a lifestyle journalist, amateur marathoner, and ardent traveler, currently dividing her time between Athens and Oxford, U.K. Over the past 14 years, she has covered a wide range of topics ranging from ecology and economy to fashion and design. Just a few Greek publications she has worked for: *Ethnos* (one of Greece's biggest daily newspapers), *Athens News* (English-language weekly newspaper), *Harper's Bazaar* (Greek edition), *Ideal Home* (Greek edition), *Bravacasa*, *To Vima* daily newspaper, *Eikones* weekly newspaper, and *Runner*. Born and raised in Athens, she loves spending time at her summer home in Nea Makri and enjoying some of the best windsurfing spots in northeast Attica. But her main sports endeavor has been competitive running: her first attempt at completing the Berlin Marathon was captured by fellow Fodorian and filmmaker Angelike Contis in the 2004 sports documentary *Run Natasha Run*. A mum-to-be at the time, she missed the starting line of the 2011 Athens Classic Marathon but is looking forward to the 2012 race. For this edition, Natasha updated our entire Athens chapter, along with updating our Experience Greece, the Saronic Gulf Islands, and Travel Smart chapters; she also cowrote the What's New/Greece Today sections of Experience Greece together with Angelike Contis.

Charles Norris is a New York-based writer and editor for many publications. While he also writes about such northern locales as England and Venice, he especially cherishes his experiences climbing hairpin bends on the roads between Knossos and Phaestos. For this edition, he updated two regional chapters in this book: Crete, and Rhodes and the Dodecanese, along with writing much of our Experience Greece chapter, plus authoring our special photo features on Greek beaches, design, history, Rhodian wine, and seafood.

Hilary Whitton Paipeti is an English-born publisher, journalist, author, and hiking guru who lives in the beautiful depths of rural Corfu, the most famed of the Ionian Islands. She shares her large garden with two rescued dogs, who accompany her everywhere on her many mountain walks, either by herself or with hiking groups she leads during weekends. Hiking prompted Hilary to research and publish *The Corfu Book of Walks* (which went to four editions over a decade) and she has now produced (to date) nine hiking and non-hiking guides to Corfu, originally published by Pedestrian Publications and now available through www.corfuwalks.com. Along the way, her treks prompted her to create "The Corfu Trail," a now-celebrated island-long trekking route, which every year attracts hundreds of outdoor enthusiasts to Corfu (www.thecorfutrail.com). Away from hiking,

for 20 years she published and edited *The Corfiot*, an English-language news and lifestyle magazine aimed at resident foreigners and summer visitors. She has also written a definitive guide to the Durrell brothers' stay on Corfu, *In the Footsteps of Lawrence Durrell and Gerald Durrell in Corfu (1935–1939)*, which, when published in 1998, was reviewed in London's *Sunday Times* newspaper as "Travel Book of the Week." Hilary updated our Corfu chapter.

Adrian Vrettos first traveled to Greece from London over a decade ago to work as a field archaeologist on classical excavations. All he managed to uncover, however, was the ancient inscription, "The laptop is mightier than the trowel" (loosely translated from Linear B). Thus he set to work decoding modern Greek life instead, and is now a freelance journalist and editor in Athens. Adrian updated, together with Alexia Amvrazi, our Northern Aegean Islands chapter.